William

December

T5-ADW-895

RIDGE STUDIO PHOTO

ARRANGED BY MRS. ALFRED R. WALPOLE

Pink peonies in a Japanese stoneware usabata placed on two mahogany scroll stands

PEONIES, OUTDOORS AND IN

BY ARNO NEHRLING AND IRENE NEHRLING

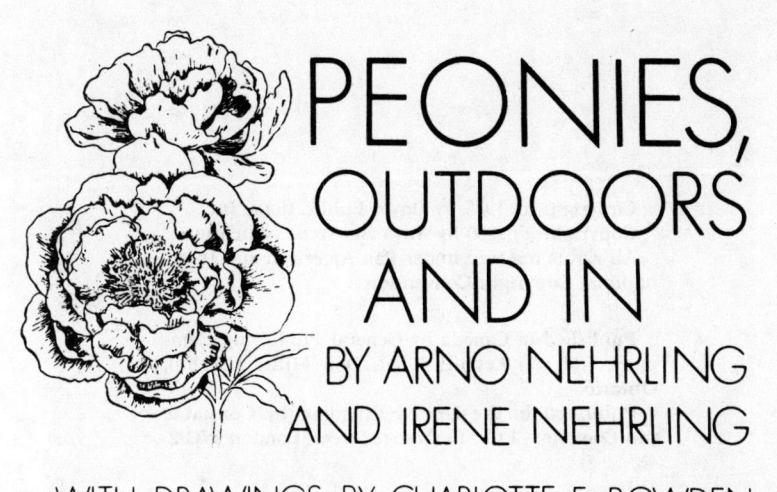

WITH DRAWINGS BY CHARLOTTE E BOWDEN

DOVER PUBLICATIONS, INC., NEW YORK

Copyright © 1975 by Dover Publications, Inc.
Copyright © 1960 by Arno and Irene Nehrling.
All rights reserved under Pan American and International Copyright Conventions.

Published in Canada by General Publishing Company, Ltd., 30 Lesmill Road, Don Mills, Toronto, Ontario.
Published in the United Kingdom by Constable and Company, Ltd., 10 Orange Street, London WC 2.

This Dover edition, first published in 1975, is a republication of the work originally published in 1960. It is reprinted by special arrangement with the original publisher, Hearthside Press, Inc., 445 Northern Boulevard, Great Neck, New York 11021. The color plate section that appeared in the original edition has been omitted, but four of the ten original color plates are reproduced on the covers of this edition. For further bibliographical details see the Publisher's Note, prepared especially for this edition.

International Standard Book Number: 0-486-23229-8
Library of Congress Catalog Card Number: 7517125

Manufactured in the United States of America
Dover Publications, Inc.
180 Varick Street
New York, N.Y. 10014

Dedicated to Amy Irene

PUBLISHER'S NOTE TO THE DOVER EDITION

The lists of public and private plantings and retail sources have been deleted from this reprint edition because they were no longer valid. Up-to-date information may be obtained by writing to the Secretary of the American Peony Society, 250 Interlachen Road, Hopkins, Minnesota 55343.

The names of the Japanese peonies have been left as they appeared in the original edition since these are the forms you may find in dealers' catalogs. For the sake of accuracy we should like to point out the following corrections:

	should read
ANYO-NO-HIKARE	ANYA-NO-HIDARI
GODAISHU (Large Globe-like)	GODAISHU (Giant Symmetrical)
HANA-DAIGIN	HANA-DAIJIN
HATSU-GARASHU	HATSU-GARASU
KINTAJIO	KINUTAJO
NISHIKI-NO-TSUYA (Beauty of Brocade)	NISHIKI-NO-TSUYA (Shimmer of Brocade)
NISSHO (Sunbeam)	NISSHO (Sun Flag)
SHIN-MOMO-ZOMA (New Bloom of the Peach Flower Garden)	SHIN-MOMO-ZOMA (New Bloom of the Peach Grove)
SHOGYOMON	SHOGYOMON (Shogyo Gate)
SHUCHIUKA (Flower in Wine)	SHUCHIUKA (Shower of Wine)
SUMA-NO-ICHI	SUMI-NO-ICHI
UBA-TAMA (Beautiful Black King)	UBA-TAMA (Pitch Black)
YACHIYO-TSUBAKI (Long Hedge of Camellias)	YACHIYO-TSUBAKI (Eternity of Camellias)

Contents

List of Color Illustrations, 12
Foreword, 13
In Appreciation, 15
Why Grow Them, 17

PART I — THE QUEEN OF FLOWERS, 19-47

1. A Fascinating History, 21
   Old-Fashioned Peony Recipes, 25
2. Peonies Classified, 27
   Botanical Classification, 27
   Flower Parts, 29
   Plant Parts, 30
   Five Flower Types, 31
   How the Tree Differs From the Herbaceous Peony, 37
   Where They Will Grow, 38
   May Starts the Peony Parade, 40
3. Calendar of Things To Do, 43

PART II — THE HERBACEOUS PEONY, 49-124

4. In Garden Design, 50
   Landscape Ideas, 50
   Space Required In Border, 54
   Border Ideas, 55
   Good Companion Plants, 60
   See Varieties In Flower, 65
5. Selecting Varieties, 67
   25 Tested Plants for the Beginner, 69

25 Rare Peonies for the Connoisseur, 70
  Vote Winners, 71
    Forty Most Popular — All Types, 71
    The "One" Best — All Types, 73
    Ten Most Popular In Each Color — Each Type, 73
  According To Purpose, 77
    Good Garden Border Varieties, 77
    For Emphasis or Spectacular Effects, 79
    For Outstanding Foliage, 81
    For Fragrance, 81
  By Color and Season, 82
  Recommended for the South, 85
    For Beginners, 86
    For General Garden Use, 86
  Recommended for Canada, 86
  Some Peyton Notes on Varieties, 89
  Herbaceous Species, 90

6. **Hybrids, 93**
  American Hybridizers, 94
  Popular Hybrid Varieties According to Color, 97
  Myron D. Bigger Herbaceous Hybrid Selections, 98
  Hybrids Bloom for a Month or More, 99

7. **Making New Plantings, 103**
  Buying Peony Roots, 103
  Choosing the Site, 105
  Plant in September and October, 106
  Plan Ample Space for Roots, 106
  Prepare Beds and Soil Carefully, 107
  How to Set Out the Roots, 108

8. **Caring for Established Plants, 110**
  Food and Water, 110
  Cultivation to Keep Down Weeds, 111
  Disbudding for Larger Flowers, 111
  Supports, 112
  Burn Foliage After Frost, 113

To Divide Old Clumps, 113
Spray to Prevent Disease, 115

9. Diseases and Insects, 116
Botrytis Blight, 116
Root Knot or Lemoine's Disease, 117
Root Rot, 117
Nemas and Nematodes, 117
Ants, 118
Thrips, 118
Rose Chafers, 118
Moles — Rabbits, 118

10. Propagation, Forcing, 119
Propagation, 119
Forcing Blooms Ahead of Schedule, 120

11. Peony Questions and Answers, 122
Why Do Peonies Fail to Bloom?, 122
Why Are the Flowers Poor?, 123
Where Will They Grow?, 123

PART III — THE TREE PEONY, 125-163

12. General Types and Hybrids, 126
Hybrids, 127

13. Tree Peonies In The Landscape, 131
Where to Plant, 132
Japanese Influence, 136
Companion Plants, 138

14. Making New Plantings, 142
Buying the Plants, 142
Choosing the Location, 143
Prepare Beds and Soil Carefully, 143
When and How to Plant, 144

15. Caring for Established Plants, 147
Food and Water, 147
Cultivation to Keep Down Weeds, 147
Pruning and Staking, 148
Mulching, 148

Diseases and Pests, 149
Forcing, 149
16. Propagating the Tree Peony, 151
    Grafting, 151
    From Seed, 153
17. Selecting Varieties, 155
    Early and Late Varieties, 155
    According to Color Groupings, 157
    European-Chinese, Japanese and Hybrids, 158
    Most Popular Tree Peony Varieties, 161

PART IV — PEONIES INDOORS, 165-216

18. An Ancient and Modern Favorite for the Home, 166
19. Peonies In Floral Design, 169
    Alone With Own Foliage, 169
    With Spring Branches, 172
    With Other Plant Material, 174
    For Larger Scale Decorations, 177
        Visibility, 178
        Church, 178
        Weddings, 179
    Historical or Period Designs, 181
20. How to Cut, Condition and Dry, 182
    How To Cut, 182
    Conditioning, 183
    Storage, 184
    Dry for Winter Bouquets, 185
        Buds and Blossoms, 185
        Foliage, 189
        Seed Pods, 189
        Dried Petals, 190
        Wax White Peonies, 190
        Storage, 190
    Tips For the Novice, 190
    Mechanics Required, 191

CONTENTS 11

21. Varieties Best For Cutting, 193
    Herbaceous, Regular, 194
      Single, 194
      Japanese, 195
      Anemone, 196
      Semi-Double, 196
      Double, 197
    Herbaceous, Hybrids, 198
    Tree Peonies, 199

22. Flower Shows, 200
    Dates, 200
    Management, 200
    Schedule, 202
    Rules, 203
    Classes, 203
      Horticultural Classes, 203
        Displays, 204
        Collections, 204
        Specimen, 205
        New Hybrids and Seedlings, 206
        Tree Peonies, 206
        Arrangement, 206
      Gardens, 206
      Arrangement Classes, 206
      Junior Classes and Awards, 208
      Educational Exhibits, 208
    Entries, 208
    Staging, 209
    Point Scales For Judging, 210
    Judging, 214
    Awards, 215

    PART V — SUPPLEMENT, 217

    Descriptive List of Registered Varieties, 219
    Index, 259

COLOR PLATES

Front Cover:
Tree peony Virginia Irving Pierce, in the garden of Mrs. Irving C. Wright, Chestnut Hill, Mass. *Paul Genereux photo*

Inside Front Cover:
Japanese and double peonies from Cherry Hill Nurseries, West Newbury, Mass. Top: Frances Willard (double). Second row: Two blooms of Matilda Lewis (double). Third row, center, Hari-ai-nin (Japanese), left and right, Hakodate (Japanese). Bottom: Jeannot (double). *Ralph Sanborn photo*

Inside Back Cover:
Ten varieties for the home garden. Back row: Festiva Maxima, Currant Red, Annisquam, King of England. Center row: Therese, Le Jour, Thomas C. Thurlow. Bottom row: Amberglow, Hari-ai-nin, Walter Faxon. *Paul Genereux photo*

Fifteen doubles in pinks and reds from Gilbert H. Wild and Son, Sarcoxi, Mo. Varieties included are Mrs. Harry F. Little, May Morn, Blanche King, Sarah Bernhardt, Mons. Jules Elie, Lady Kate, Felix Crousse, The Mighty Mo, Prairie King, Queen of Hamburg, Ozark Beauty, Karl Rosenfield, Andy, Dixie, Pierre Dessert. *Courtesy A. B. Morse Co., St. Joseph, Mich.*

FOREWORD

During the past quarter century miracles in plant breeding have brought to the modern garden plants of hitherto undreamed utility and beauty. Many of these plants have been praised in books and plant catalogs. For instance, scarcely a year goes by without one or more excellent books on roses. One great nursery advertises it has to grow nine million Rose plants a year, so great is the demand from amateur gardeners.

The production of new types, new forms, and new colors of Peonies has been no less spectacular than that of the Rose, Daffodil, Iris, Chrysanthemum and other flowers so widely seen in our gardens. Curiously enough no Peony book designed for the home gardener has been written for 25 years, and it, as well as the larger one 42 years old, is out of print.

The splendid publications of the American Peony Society have been of untold value to a comparatively small group of Peony specialists. These publications, however, are not often seen by the hundreds of thousands or possibly millions of those persons who now comprise our gardening public, and who should be growing and enjoying at least a few of the newer Peonies.

It is, therefore, very gratifying to all who love gardens that Arno and Irene Nehrling have prepared this present book. Mr. Nehrling has unusual qualifications for presenting practical advice for the amateur. He is, and long has been, secretary of the Massachusetts Horticultural Society, the largest and most active horticultural society in the country. In that position he is in daily contact with amateur gardeners and their problems. He is responsible for the magazine "Horticulture," the official organ of the society, which has a nationwide distribution. Year after year he has staged the Boston Peony Shows, as well as similar shows of Daffodils, Tulips, Dahlias and Chrysanthemums, and the much larger spring show which has consistently been one of the greatest shows of the country.

Mrs. Nehrling, in addition to being a good gardener, has been particularly interested in arrangement of flowers for the home, and has written much on this subject in the past.

From beginning to end the book abounds in plain, practical advice that the home gardener needs in order to take advantage of the great development of Peonies during this past quarter century. While much of the information is aimed at beginners, the advanced gardener and even the Peony specialist have not been neglected.

The authors, in addition, have done a great service to the American Peony Society and its many experts by assembling and publishing, for the first time, a complete list of varieties registered by that society during the more than half century of its existence.

I hope the present book will have a wide distribution. I am sure that it will greatly increase the number of gardeners growing Peonies.

John C. Wister

Swarthmore College
Swarthmore, Pennsylvania
September 1, 1959

IN APPRECIATION

First of all we want to thank George W. Peyton, secretary of the American Peony Society, for his splendid cooperation and assistance, certainly far beyond the call of duty. His wonderful spirit and genuine interest were an inspiration. He writes a fine letter, too, and we'll miss them, now the book is completed.

Our sincere thanks to Miss Silvia Saunders of Clinton, New York, for reading the material on herbaceous hybrids and tree peonies,. and for her good advice and suggestions.

We are grateful to four landscape friends: John Brimer, Suffern, New York; Allen C. Haskell, New Bedford; Ruth D. Leiby, Weston and Harold D. Stevenson of Marshfield, the latter three from Massachusetts, who took time out from their busy spring schedules to draw garden plans featuring peonies.

Our thanks to Myron D. Bigger of Topeka, Kansas, President of the American Peony Society, for his comments on herbaceous hybrids; to Miss Dorothy Manks and her fine staff at the Massachusetts Horticultural Library for research and for the compilation of a list of all peonies registered with the American Peony Society as published in its bulletins through 1958; to John C. Wister and Miss Gertrude Smith for lending us the "Scott Foundation" tree peony pictures and answering many questions; to Winthrop Thurlow for his cooperation and assistance; and to the accomplished arrangers who supplied us with excellent photographs of their fine work.

We are particularly appreciative of all those who answered our questionnaire; they are listed in the supplement. We thank those who added extra interesting information about their peonies or personal good wishes and wonder if writers in other fields receive the same generous, enthusiastic response!

We are grateful to Horticulture and Paul Genereux for the use of photographs; to Mrs. Charlotte Bowden for her lovely sketches and to Miss Ann White who was helpful in so many ways.

Finally our deep appreciation to Nedda Anders of Hearthside Press for her encouragement and assistance in helping us plan, organize and edit the book.

Arno and Irene Nehrling

Needham Heights
Massachusetts
July, 1959

WHY GROW THEM?

The modern peony now surpasses all other garden flowers for sheer majesty and splendor. Its natural beauty has been enhanced by peony experts and hybridizers who for a century or more have worked devotedly in developing and improving this favorite perennial. Their efforts have produced improved types of exquisite distinction and magnificence. Here are eight reasons why peonies are called the "Queen of Flowers":

1. Superior blooms of breathtaking loveliness are available in a wide variety of forms and colors. Starting with the lovely singles, some like huge, beautiful anemones, and the semi-doubles resembling water lilies, to the gorgeous double forms, there is great variety. The glossy, satiny petals come in hundreds of shades, tints and combinations of white, pink, red and yellow. Some of the flowers, which are outstandingly beautiful, also have a delightful fragrance.

2. Its wide diversity of foliage and habit of growth. The leaves of some are much divided and fern-like while others are strong and broad, usually lustrous and frequently with leather-like qualities in a range of greens, often tinged with copper or red. Some sorts are dwarf and bushy, some medium in height and spreading, yet others tall and bold in silhouette.

3. Excellent for use in the landscape, it is the glory of the spring and early summer garden. For the home grounds its substantial size and beauty make it valuable. Magnificent in mass, yet its individual size and perfection of detail make it an

excellent specimen or accent plant as well. And after the blooming season it still has landscape value since the shining foliage remains attractive throughout the growing season and takes on interesting coloring in the autumn.

4. The peony provides excellent cut flowers. The exquisite beauty and infinite variety in both flower and foliage, plus lasting qualities, make it an ideal cut flower.

5. It is extremely hardy and dependable, thriving in severe climates, enduring temperatures fatal to many other perennials. All have a sturdy quality and self-reliance.

6. Of easy culture, once planted it requires a minimum of care and expense.

7. The peony is practically free of disease and pests if a few simple rules are observed.

8. It is a permanent investment and will bloom for years if it is not disturbed.

PART I — THE QUEEN OF FLOWERS

1
A Fascinating History

Copy of woodcut in herbal published
by Peter Schoeffer at Mainz in 1485

The peony, according to legend and Greek mythology, was named for Paeon, a physician of antiquity. Zeus and Leto were the parents of Apollo, god of healing and the father of Aesculapius, god of medicine. Paeon was his pupil and the physician who attended the Greek gods. Paeon was first given the potent peony by Leto on Mount Olympus. With it he is said to have cured Pluto of a wound inflicted by Hercules during the Trojan war, the first to have used the peony as a medicine. He is also credited with healing Mars of a wound with this powerful herb. These successes so aroused the jealousy and envy of his teacher, Aesculapius, that he secretly plotted Paeon's death. Pluto, grateful to Paeon for saving his life, when he heard of the plot, saved the physician from the fate of mortals by changing him into the plant that had been used in the cure, and the plant has ever since borne Paeon's name.

In prehistoric Greece many magical attributes, myths and legends centered around the peony. A familiar flower that glowed in the dark when the moon was full surely must possess great and supernatural powers. Thought to drive away devils and evil spirits where it was growing in the ground, a piece of the plant worn on one's person might be equally potent as a protection, not only against evil spirits but as a magic for healing. Its medical history is by far the most interesting of any flower and the most consistent in ancient folk medicine based on magic.

Pliny in his Natural History (about 77 A.D.) gives the first detailed description of a peony plant and seeds. He sets out twenty ills which it will cure. Another early herbal, the work of the Greek author and medical man, Dioscorides, was written in the first century, A.D. and includes about five hundred medicinal plants. This treatise was accepted as an almost infallible authority throughout the entire Middle Ages. In it Dioscorides describes as the medical peony what is apparently P. officinalis and growing wild in Europe. These writings take the peony back to a folk medicine of undeterminable antiquity.

According to Banckes' Herbal, the peony is "good for women for diverse sickness. Peony seed when it is black, it maketh deliverance ... of the child in her womb, and at every time when she shall use to drink it, she must drink fifteen seeds at one time. ... Also, for a man or woman that has the falling evil (epilepsy), eat it and drink it with wine, also hang the root about his neck and it will save him without doubt within fifteen days." As late as the nineteenth century, faith in the value of the peony for epilepsy still hung on here and there, its magic power still potent in the minds of simple people.

The peony also served a career in the kitchen; P. edulis, a deep crimson peony, was so named because its roots were eaten in soups in Siberia.

In China in 536 A.D. the peony was fairly well distributed over the country and used for both medicinal and kitchen purposes, as was the custom with herbs in early days. (The scholar Alcuin is said to have inquired of his pupil, Charlemagne, "What is an herb?" "The friend of physicians and the praise of cooks" was his reply.)

The peony seeds were used as a seasoning in food and drinks. Along with pepper, salt, garlic and other spices, they added flavor to soups.

The rich in England during the medieval fourteenth and fifteenth centuries used its roots (P. officinalis) as a fine accompaniment with roast pork. The poor could only afford it as a seasoning. Much was written about herbs for the medieval household, for cooking, healing virtues and divers uses. The Alewife in Piers Plowman (1362) says "I have pepper and peony seed and a pound of garlic and a farthingsworth of fennel seed for fasting days."

Practically the national flower of China, the peony figures often in its poetry, linking it by legend, history and romance to the golden age of Chinese poetry and to the most famous of Chinese love stories. In China its name "Sho Yo" means most beautiful and it is considered the aristocrat of all the flowers.

P. lactiflora, which was a pure white, has been in cultivation since time immemorial and the tree peony (P. suffruticosa), a native of China, has been domesticated since the seventh century, during the Tang dynasty (619-906 A.D.), when it appeared first in the imperial garden. The gardeners of those days, realizing the ornamental possibilities of the peony, "with the use of strong fertilizers and great diligence in cultivation", began to produce flowers of larger size.

The fields where the peony was grown were consecrated by inscriptions of a religious enthusiasm. Its culture was the favorite amusement of the nobility, the literary and the rich. Some varieties were held in such high esteem, far above the ordinary rates of barter, they were exchanged for gold. Some were considered heirlooms and willed to descendants. Frequently a prize plant was offered as a portion of the marriage dowry.

The tree peony of ancient lineage has been known as the "King of Flowers" since time immemorial in its native China, and as a symbol of royalty, wealth and rank, and one of the main motifs in their art. The herbaceous peony "Prime Minister Of All Flowers" is second in grandeur only to the tree peony. The lofty position of the peacock among birds is just like that of the peony among flowers. Both are a symbol of splendor. Peacocks and peonies are frequently associated in pictorial and decorative arts and found together in paintings on silk, screens, woodblock prints, porcelains and tapestries of the past, from the twelfth century down to the eighteenth.

Introduced into Japan by Buddhist monks, the peony is one of its most highly prized flowering plants and held in high esteem by the flower-loving Japanese. It is known in Japan as the flower of prosperity, an age-old association and symbolism, which came about because the difficulties encountered in its early cultivation caused it to be confined to the gardens of the wealthy.

The history of the peony in England is largely the story of its cultivation in gardens from early times. In 1157 an English writer gives a description of what a noble garden should contain and includes the peony, perhaps P. officinalis. From early poems it would appear that by 1375 the use of peonies in the hardy border had begun. The first printed picture, in England, a woodcut, appeared in 1484. In Tudor times the peony is described as "coming into fashion, widely grown and regarded with affection." Shakespeare, in "The Taming of The Shrew" (1603) refers to the peony in his line "Thy banks with peonied and lilied brims."

During the nineteenth century French hybridizers became very

A FASCINATING HISTORY

much interested in the peony and their efforts produced many fine new varieties. An early and still well beloved variety is the large double white with crimson flecked center, Festiva Maxima, originated by Miellez of France in 1851. Beginning around 1898 Victor Lemoine of Nancy, France. became recognized as one of the world's greatest peony hybridizers; his introductions were notable for their distinction of form and coloring in addition to their rare beauty. He produced some very fine varieties crossing P. lactiflora with P. wittmanniana. A very remarkable race of hybrids was produced by crossing the tree peony, P. suffruticosa with the yellow P. lutea. Breeders also crossed an improved type of the Chinese lactiflora with the European officinalis to obtain new varieties.

In America, as in France, peony experts, collectors and commercial growers became interested in producing new improved plants, not quite like any others yet on the market. Although there have been many discards, many wonderful and unique varieties of startling beauty have been produced.

From Thomas Jefferson's Garden Book, we know peonies were grown in Virginia as early as 1771. This knowledge gives those in authority in Virginia at Mount Vernon and eighteenth century Williamsburg the privilege to grow peonies in their restored present day gardens.

The introduction of a number of varieties of the species of P. lactiflora from China around 1850 caused an increase in the popularity of the peony. The fragrance, hardiness and erect habit of growth, variability as to color and form of flowers combined to create a demand for this new Chinese peony. The tree peony also arrived in America at about this same time.

OLD-FASHIONED PEONY RECIPES

Liber Cure Cocorum

Liber Cure Cocorum, a copy of the Sloane manuscript by Richard Morris, published by Asher and Co., Berlin, 1862 has a recipe for "Peions istued" (stewed peonies) that goes as follows:

"Take peions and hew him in morselle smalle,
Put hom (them) in a erpyn (earthen) pot, pou (thou) shalle;
Take pilled garlek and herbys anon,
Hack (cut) hom smalle er pou more don (when this is done)
Put hom in po pot, and per (then) to take
Gode (good) brothe with wyte (white) greece, pou nost forsake; (do not forget)
Do (to) powder them to and gode verius (to powder them very well)
Coloure hit with saffron and salt inow (enough);
Pou (then) put in pote pese pyngs alle, (all these things)
And stue py peions pus pou schalle.
(And stew thy peonies thus you shall)

The Complete Confectioner

The Complete Confectioner, by Hannah Glasse, published by J. Cooke, 1782, has the following recipe.

COMPOUND PIONY WATER: Take eighteen *piony roots* fresh gathered, six ounces of bitter almonds, the leaves of rosemary, rue, wild thyme, and flowers of lavender dried, of each three ounces; of cinnamon, cubebs, seeds of angelica, coriander seed, carraway and anniseeds, each half an ounce, one gallon of rectified spirits of wine, with five gallons of soft water, and draw of three gallons by distillation. This is good in all nervous disorders.

THE USE OF THIS WATER: It is strong and powerful that it cannot be taken without the assistance of some other thing; but when dropt on crumbs of bread and sugar, you must take it the first thing in the morning, at four in the afternoon, and the last thing at night; you must not eat for an hour either before or after you take it; it is exceeding efficacious in all swoonings, weakness of heart, decayed spirits, palsies, appoplexies, and both to help and prevent a fit, it will also destroy all heaviness and coldness in the liver, restores lost appetite, and fortifies and surprisingly strengthens the stomach.

2
Peonies Classified

BOTANICAL CLASSIFICATION

Family — Ranunculaceae

A plant family is made up of a group of related plants (genera, plural for genus) sufficiently alike in general characteristics to show relationship and to justify being classed together into a family group. This relationship is based on similarities in structure in relation to their evolution or descent from common ancestors. The grouping of plants into families is essential for purposes of systematic classification.

The peony is a member of the Ranunculaceae, also called the buttercup or crowfoot family. This hardy group is mainly herbaceous but it also includes some shrubby and woody climbing plants. The family is widely distributed over the Temperate and Arctic regions.

Genus — Paeonia

A genus is a subdivision of a plant family, designed to simplify identification of plants and indicate relationship. It includes a group of species more or less closely related, having certain obviously structural characteristics in common. Members of a genus resemble each other more than they do members of other genera. The first part of a plant's Latin or botanical name is that of the genus to which it belongs. The Latin or botanical name is universal and precise and means the same thing to botanists in all countries, while common names are frequently

27

colloquialisms and a single plant may have a dozen different names in different parts of the country.

Paeonia is by far the most important garden genus of the Ranunculaceae family although the delphinium, anemone, aquilegia (columbine), clematis, pulsatilla and aconitum (monkshood) are also extremely popular garden plants in this same family.

Species

A number of species, there may be many or few, make up a genus. This group of plants is so nearly alike in their more stable characteristics they differ no more than offsprings from the same parent and represent a collection of closely related subjects. The plants may differ among themselves within a species to some degree by minor and less stable variations. The second part of a plant's botanical name is that of the species to which it belongs. To illustrate: Paeonia lactiflora is the Latin or botanical name of the common Chinese peony. Paeonia is the genus, lactiflora the species. If a third word is added, as P. lactiflora var. festiva, it refers to the variety, a variation derived from P. lactiflora.

The species of the genus Paeonia are composed of both woody and herbaceous perennial plants, an interesting, attractive and valuable garden genus.

Three Groups Under Paeonia

Paeon, suffruticosa and onaepia are the three divisions that make up the genus, Paeonia, which supplies the spring and early summer garden with beautiful, showy flowers in a wide assortment of color and form. At the height of its blooming season one is held spellbound in admiration.

1. *Paeon* includes all the herbaceous species native to Europe, Asia and Africa. This hardy group of perennials forms bushy plants 2′ to 4½′ high that die down to the ground in the autumn and now includes hundreds of named varieties. In a large measure this group is indebted to P. lactiflora (native of Siberia, Manchuria, Mongolia, China and Tibet) as the progeny of the modern herbaceous peony, familiar and popular with garden enthusiasts today. While this parentage is responsible for the

larger group, P. officinalis from southern Europe has also contributed its share to the present day race. Since its flowers usually begin to bloom about ten days before the "Chinese" or P. lactiflora peony descendants, they make a welcome extension to the blooming season.

The botanical names lactiflora or albiflora denote and refer to the same species and are synonyms. It has been found recently that lactiflora is probably the more correct name for the species. Botanists have adopted this term so we too are using lactiflora to denote that species in this book, but albiflora, through usage, will long remain in the trade and in common usage.

2. Moutan, suffruticosa, arborea, or the tree peony, native of China and Tibet, is a much branched shrubby or woody type plant (a shrub, not a tree) which grows from 3 to 6 feet in height. Its woody stems do not die down to the ground in the fall but it does lose its leaves. Truly the aristocrat of the flower kingdom, prized for its bushy habit and wide range of jewel-like flowers, it is a beautiful sight to behold when in flower.

3. *Onaepia* is composed of two low, fleshy species native to California and Washington, the only peony species found on this continent. This group has no importance in commerce.

FLOWER PARTS

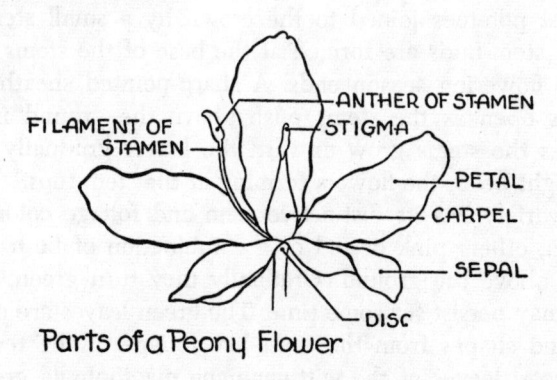

Parts of a Peony Flower

1. SEPALS—which make up the calyx, the outer green covering of the bud.

2. PETALS—which make up the corolla. There are five or more depending upon the flower type.
3. STAMENS—the male, pollen bearing organs composed of the:
   Anther—which develops and contains the pollen, usually yellow.
   Filament—a thread-like stalk which supports the anther, may be yellow or some other color, as pink or crimson.
4. CARPELS—the female organs, which when impregnated form the seed pods, usually some shade of green; may turn to other colors with age.
   Stigma—the sticky tip or end of the carpel which receives the pollen, of many different colors varying with each variety.
5. DISC—the base to which petals, etc. are attached on which often appear around the base of the carpels seed-like bodies of many colors. In some hybrids and tree peonies, it takes the form of a sheath surrounding the carpels.

PLANT PARTS

The peony plant consists of a crown underground from which all growth originates. The roots grow downward and outward. In some species they taper to a point while in others they grow like sweet potatoes joined to the crown by a small stem. The "eyes" or stem-buds are formed at the base of the stems shortly after the flowering season ends. A sharp-pointed sheath covering splits open as the stems push above the ground in early spring. As the stems grow upward the leaves gradually unfold from a tight head, the flowers forming at the stem tops.

Each variety has its distinctive stem and foliage color. Some are green, others pink or red or a combination of both as they push up above the ground. Gradually they turn green, though the red may persist for some time. The green leaves are of many shades and shapes from the grass-like foliage of the tenuifolia to the broad leaves of the wittmanniana macrophylla group.

The plants vary in height from low or dwarf forms 6" to 2½'

or in other varieties, form rings among the petals. They are always a prominent and interesting feature of the flower, which includes some of the most artistic of peony blooms. The carpels may be normal or transformed either in whole or in part. The center may be made up of a greater or lesser number of broad petals.

Although the flowers of some are flamboyant they are never heavy and will not overwhelm a small planting or an indoor arrangement. Excellent for the suburban garden and for cutting they are long lasting and with the doubles are the most widely grown of all the peony varieties.

Dependable semi-double whites include such favorites as Miss America, Minnie Shaylor, Mildred May and Margaret Lough. White Rose is one of the most exquisite of all. In the pink group Lady Alexandra Duff, Silvia Saunders, Phyllis Kelway and Auguste Dessert are popular. Red Goddess, The Mighty Mo, Rosalie and Chippewa are lovely and popular reds.

5. DOUBLE—This type has five or more outer or guard petals with a center of stamens and carpels, more or less fully transformed into petals, which make up the main body of the flower. Often no trace is left of these parts. Sometimes the carpels appear with the stigmas either normal or partially transformed into petalodes or petals. When the outer or guard petals are shorter than the transformed petals the flower takes on a globular shape. When the transformed petals are shorter a so-called bomb shape is formed. Sometimes hidden stamens may appear imbedded in the flower.

The magnificent double kinds with their solid mass of petals, some looking like huge roses, are the most familiar, most grown and most loved of all and include many old favorites. Besides the white and blush kinds, many shades of pink and red are available in early, mid-season and late varieties. Some of the doubles owe their beauty to informality but almost all of the great exhibition varieties are prized for their symmetrically arranged petals. One of the earliest to open is the old favorite

Bomb-shaped double   Globular-shaped double

the lovely white, Festiva Maxima, with flecks of crimson in the center. In spite of its weak stems requiring support it heads the list of popular early, double whites along with varieties like Kelway's Glorious and Le Cygne. Elsa Sass which blooms late, is a fully double, creamy white, veiled pink, with a true rose form, nice fragrance and unusually strong stems. Solange, Moonstone, Alice Harding and La Lorraine are good representatives and favorites in the "blush" colored group.

Therese flowers early, is satiny pink changing to lilac-white in the center, with heavy foliage and strong stems. Mrs. Franklin D. Roosevelt also comes early to mid-season with exquisite rose-shaped, light pink flowers. Reine Hortense, a delicate pink with occasional crimson flecks has a crisp look, is wonderful for both cut flowers and garden display and blooms in mid-season. Hansina Brand's flowers are flesh pink with salmon tints. They have splendid substance and good stems, are late to flower. Nick Shaylor and Myrtle Gentry are also dependable in the light pink group and late season bloomers.

Monsieur Jules Elie blooms early and is a joy to grow with its huge, fragrant rose-pink flowers. Sarah Bernhardt and Walter Faxon are two other reliable dark pinks which flower mid-season to late. Blanche King, immense and fragrant with never failing blooms of sparkling deep pink, is late to flower. Never disbud it except for exhibition purposes.

Louis Joliet is an early dark, lustrous, non-fading red. Felix Crousse and Karl Rosenfield are both fine, mid-season reds;

Felix has weaker stems but is a better cut flower. Philippe Rivoire and Mary Brand are also popular in the dark red group.

HOW THE TREE DIFFERS FROM THE HERBACEOUS PEONY

Although the tree and herbaceous peonies have much in common, they also have distinct differences. The tree peony develops rough-barked, woody stems that do not die down to the ground in the fall, continuing to grow year after year so a bush is formed. Their leaves are dissimilar in outline and the tree peony foliage is usually of a paler shade of green. Its buds are larger and flatter and are raised to a sharp point in the center. Its flowers, like the herbaceous, have both single and double forms; however, they usually attain a larger size, eight to twelve inches

A TREE PEONY
Its woody stems do not die down to the ground in the fall. Leaves are dissimilar in outline and usually of paler shade than herbaceous. Buds are larger, flatter and raised to sharp point in the center

A HERBACEOUS PEONY
Stems die down to the ground in autumn. Both tree and herbaceous peonies have single and double flowers. Tree peony flowers usually attain larger size

across, and flower about two weeks earlier than the common herbaceous peony. In the Orient the tree peony has had a more extended history and wider cultivation than the herbaceous, the reverse being the case in Europe and the United States.

The tree peony's requirements are more exacting than those of the herbaceous type, yet it is not fragile or as difficult to grow as many less rewarding plants that require greater care and attention. Although the original cost for tree peonies may seem high both type peonies are notably long-lived and improve with age, so considered as a longtime investment, peonies are not expensive but a real bargain, giving much in return for the minimum attention they require.

WHERE THEY WILL GROW

Peonies are easy to grow and do well in all sections of the country except Florida, southern California and the deep south where lack of winter cold prevents dormancy. In dry areas like northern Arizona and California plenty of water must be supplied every few days.

The South

As a rule easy opening varieties of loose petalage and the earlier blooming kinds of the single and Japanese types are best for the south or any locality where extreme heat comes quickly. Very late sorts with tight buds and full flowers need cool, somewhat moist weather to make them open best. Two year plants will give better results than smaller ones and the "eyes" in the south should be planted not more than one inch below the surface.

George W. Peyton, secretary of The American Peony Society, writes, "We run into some curious facts. A great many of the full doubles do as well in the South as the others but the extra late ones are almost always so badly damaged by either heat or thrips that they will not open. Yet some almost never fail, like Nick Shaylor, Mattie Lafuze and others. We also find that the kinds that do best in the further north sections like Duluth, Minnesota and the Peace River Country of Canada are exactly the same that do best in the South and the lates fail for one of the same reasons, excessive heat which almost always comes at the end of the peony season. And again we find a rather strange thing that the variety Mrs. A. M. Brand, a late white double, which almost never opens anywhere, is one of the best bloomers in the state of Georgia.

"Better results will be obtained in the South by always spraying the later doubles for thrips as they are primarily responsible for many failures of these to open."

Further south where the winter climate is very mild tree peonies do not flower as well as in the north since they may start into growth during warm January and February spells and then get nipped by later frosts. If they are nipped, protect them from the strong morning sun after the night of the frost so they will thaw gradually. We know of some tree peonies growing satisfactorily as far south as Northern Florida.

To force dormancy in the warmer climates, withhold water from around September 1 until October 15, and cut herbaceous varieties back to the ground.

California

Secretary Peyton writes: "There are successful plantings in California as far south as San Diego in the higher altitudes. South of Sacramento tree peonies seem to do better than the herbaceous at the lower levels, often blooming over a six months period from Christmas until June, though the bloom is sparse except in March and April. This is especially true where there is little frost. The late full doubles should be avoided." If you live in California and want advice on varieties that do best contact some successful, reliable peony grower in the state.

The Far North

Peonies are hardy and do well in Canada where they are at their best in late June and early July. Where winter temperatures range 20° below zero or lower for any length of time, especially if there is little snow covering, winter protection is recommended. In severe climates protect the tree peony if you want to preserve the growth above ground. If not protected and the above ground growth dies, cut it off at ground level like an herbaceous peony. With this treatment it will perhaps not live to as ripe an age, but should do well for several years.

In parts of the north with low temperatures and no or little snow covering, a winter mulch or covering for the herbaceous hybrids and tree peonies is imperative to prevent losses. The lactiflora varieties can take such conditions as a general rule, but the hybrids need protection.

MAY STARTS THE PEONY PARADE

Peonies dominate the garden when in bloom and with care in selection of species and varieties it is now possible to have flowers in blossom for at least eight weeks. Plant breeders, with their many new fine hybrids and by their methods of selection, are constantly increasing the flowering season.

Our daughter attended Swarthmore College and we frequently made trips from Boston to Philadelphia during those four years. In comparing vegetation it seemed to us that Boston was always about two weeks later than Philadelphia. Of course, in the very early spring during forsythia time Boston is perhaps a month behind Philadelphia but as the season progresses by about June, Boston catches up to within a couple of weeks of the more southerly city. Mrs. Arthur Hoyt Scott told us she read somewhere that the season progresses north 17 miles a day and according to her observations she thought that this was quite true. It is helpful information in approximating blooming dates in other sections of the country by comparison with your own location. Of course, the season and local conditions, whether protected, in the open, etc. must be considered, too.

1. Of the garden peonies *P. tenuifolia* is the earliest to bloom. Peony lovers can extend the season two or three weeks by planting this old time favorite. The little plant grows to only 16″ or 18″ in height, has fragrant, bright blood-red flowers, both single and double, which make up in brightness for their smaller size. Its distinctive, lacy, finely cut, fern-like foliage dies down to the ground a few weeks after blooming, differing in this respect from the other species whose foliage remains lovely and decorative all through the growing season. Their space in the garden may be filled in with annuals. These peonies make fine accents in the rock garden or in city gardens where space is at

a premium. P. tenuifolia latifolia, sometimes sold as P. officinalis tenuifolia, has fine grassy, emerald-green foliage to set off its open blossoms of rosy-red. The variety flore pleno has deep-red double, 3" blossoms.

2. P. WITTMANNIANA and the beautiful wittmanniana hybrids (crossed with lactiflora) closely follow P. tenuifolia, blooming early in May, a month ahead of the Chinese varieties. They are frequently referred to as the May-flowering peonies. The flowers are single with large firm petals, the first yellow peony to be discovered, although not a strong yellow. Its seeds are bright coral red. Crossed with the Chinese varieties valuable early-flowering hybrids have been devoloped. They have large, fragrant, single flowers of great beauty in delicate tints of white, yellow, rose and salmon. Their thick leaves are of vigorous and luxuriant growth. Excellent for cutting.

3. P. OFFICINALIS, in the North, blooms around Decoration Day, near the end of May. It grows to three feet in height, has coarsely cut foliage and wide-open single flowers varying from white to crimson, set off by recurving stigmas forming crimson centers. The double variety rubra plena is the familiar "piney" so common in our grandmothers' gardens, and characterized by its vivid ruby-red blossoms, large size and persistent growth. The variety rosea superba plena is a double variety of almost watermelon pink. The tuberous roots of these species are more delicate than the lactiflora varieties so plant them carefully. Up until about 1850 P. officinalis was the only peony grown to any extent in America. It has become one of the parents of some of the beautiful peonies in today's garden: alba plena has pink buds but the flower is a double white; and rosea plena has full, bright rose double flowers.

4. THE LOVELY TREE PEONIES, Japanese and European, come into bloom in the North around the middle of May. Remarkable for their beauty, the flowers are large, some measuring 8" to 12" across. P. suffruticosa varieties come in a wide range of colors from purest white and pale pink through rose-pinks, vermillion, scarlet, crimson and purple.

5. THE RESULTANT TREE PEONY HYBRIDS from interbreeding P. delavayi and P. lutea with P. suffruticosa, bloom about ten days to two weeks later along with many of the herbaceous hybrids. P. delavayi, the first maroon species discovered, probably enters into the parentage of most of the darker hybrid varieties. P. lutea, a wonderful golden yellow, is the parent of the yellow and orange colored blooms. These excellent strains are responsible for wonderful new colors, shapely and attractive plants with great vigor which transport and handle easily and extend the blooming period by at least two weeks. One may now have tree peonies in bloom over a period of a month. P. lutea will occasionally have a bloom or two in the early autumn, but there are no fall blooming peonies.

6. P. LACTIFLORA, (syns.— albiflora, chinensis, edulis, sinensis) the so-called Chinese peony, flowers in June and is the last to bloom, and one of the finest. One of its most famous varieties, Festiva Maxima, has large, white, double flowers flecked in the center with carmine. There are several thousand named double varieties of lactiflora on the market today. It has been crossed with other species. While originally white, pink or crimson, these crossings have produced a wide range of color and form. The newer introductions include clear tints and intermediate tones of shell pink, bright rose and deep velvety red. Other exciting colors are deep black-reds, brilliant orange-scarlets and pastel salmon. The inter-specific hybrids are well known for their precocity and beauty. These hybrids make possible a sequence of bloom which is remarkable.

3

Calendar of Things To Do

Peonies will do surprisingly well with little attention but special care will bring rewarding results.

January
1. This is the month for armchair reading and browsing. Study the catalogs and look over your peony notes taken the previous year, so you won't make the same mistakes twice. Figure out ways to improve on your previous methods.
2. Look over any new literature on the peony and reread some of the old.
3. This is a good time for garden clubs to sponsor a talk on peonies with colored slides showing gardens, varieties, care, culture, etc.

February
1. In the event of a mild winter make the rounds of the garden, pressing back into place any newly planted roots that may have heaved or been raised due to intermittent frosts.

March and April
1. Remove any mulch or hilled soil from around new plants early to avoid breaking the new young, tender shoots as they come up.
2. Cut out any dead tree peony wood on the older plants, keeping the plant vigorous, neat and trim in appearance.
3. If you want large flowers, thin out the clumps leaving fewer

stems, cutting away the weaker shoots soon after they appear above the ground.
4. To prevent botrytis, burn or destroy any material removed, including the mulch, and soon after the young shoots appear spray or dust with bordeaux mixture, fermate or any good modern fungicide at ten day to two week intervals; repeat at least two or three times.
5. As early as the ground can be worked, cultivate but be careful not to cut into the crown or new shoots when hoeing. Go no deeper than 2" up near the plant, farther from the plant you can cultivate deeper.
6. If the peony has been planted three or four years, a handful of well rotted sheep manure to a plant, worked into the soil, will improve the bloom. Liquid manure may also be used. Some say manure should never be used. It must be well rotted and great care must be taken to keep it from getting over the crowns of the peony plants.
7. Tiny seedlings may come up around established plants. You may want to mark, later transplant, and coddle them to see what results you can get if you have the patience to grow peonies from seed (see page 119). It takes 4 to 10 years.

May and June

1. Continue to keep plants cultivated to cut down the weeds and keep the soil well aerated. Cultivate after each hard rain to prevent soil from hardening on top.
2. If the spring season is very dry, and the plants begin to wilt from lack of moisture, give them a good watering, a thorough soaking, once a week, enough to wet the ground down to the bottom of the roots. Repeat when the soil becomes dry.
3. If you want fewer and larger herbaceous flowers rather than a quantity of smaller ones, pick off the side buds while they are small, leaving only the terminal bud on each stalk.
4. Heavy double flowered peonies or varieties with weak stems should be staked before the plant becomes very large. An inconspicuous support that will encircle the whole plant loosely is best (see sketch, page 112).

5. If ants become annoying treat the soil around the plants with a strong solution of nicotine sulfate or chlordane to get rid of them.
6. Cut flowers and foliage for fresh arrangements and also to dry for dried arrangements for the winter. See page 187 for instructions.
7. Always cut flowers left on the plants as soon as they fade to keep the garden looking tidy and to keep the flowers from forming seed pods, except for the few you want for arrangements or for seeds. *Never* cut herbaceous plants to the ground until they are killed by frost.
8. While enthusiasm is high, at the height of the peony season, visit other peony gardens, see peonies in bloom in nurseries, and make out your peony order for September delivery. See variety lists pages 67 and 155.
9. Visit and participate in peony flower shows.

July
1. If you wish to grow peonies from seed, watch the seed pods from late July on. Collect as soon as the seeds can readily be removed from the pods, before they spill out. Only hard seed is good. Soft seed will not germinate.
2. Remove any seed pods you let form on the plants to use in fresh arrangements or later in dried arrangements.
3. Continue to cultivate as long as weeds grow.

August
1. If the summer is very dry, water thoroughly once a week to insure good blooms the following year. If you haven't already done so, order peonies for September planting.
2. Cut some of the lovely autumn peony foliage to dry for winter bouquets and to use fresh with fall flower arrangements.

September and October
1. Plant a peony for posterity. This is the best time to plant new peonies and to divide old clumps that must be divided so they will become established before hard frost, September in the north and October in the south. In sections in the

north where hard frosts come in late September, plant and divide old clumps earlier.
2. When the herbaceous foliage turns brown in the fall, cut stems to the ground. Brush away any partially rotted leaves, weeds, stems, or any material that has collected at the base of the plant and burn or destroy along with the foliage and stems as this material may harbor trouble, especially botrytis fungus for next year.
3. If the peony has been planted for three or four years, use about half a handful of commercial fertilizer like a 20% superphosphate or one handful of bonemeal to a plant, carefully working it into the soil, to build up the plant so it will flower well next season.

November
1. Peonies may be planted or transplanted until the ground freezes.
2. If you haven't already made a dried arrangement using flowers, buds, foliage and seed pods of the peony, now is the time.
3. Herbaceous hybrids and tree peonies in those below zero climates must be protected to prevent severe damage or loss from lack of snow covering.

December
1. Winter protection for herbaceous peonies is only necessary the first winter to help prevent heaving by frost. Mound the soil over the new planting for several inches, or after the ground freezes hard, mulch with evergreen boughs or straw, anything that will not mat down as leaves do. In extremely cold climates, 10°-20° below zero, protection is necessary for hybrids and tree peonies.
2. Why not join the American Peony Society! A membership will entitle you to the quarterly bulletin, which will keep you up to date on latest developments, give you information on peony culture, relate experiences in growing peonies in various sections of the country and give reports on local and national shows. While primarily an organization for amateurs,

all the prominent peony growers belong since the Society is open to both professionals and amateurs. Getting together for fellowship and discussion of mutual problems at the annual meetings and shows of this organization is no small part of its value. The American peony world revolves around this Society.

At present (1975) the membership fee for a calendar year (January 1 to January 1) is $7.50, and the secretary's address is: Ms. Greta M. Kessenich, 250 Interlachen Road, Hopkins, Minnesota 55343.

Festiva Maxima, an old favorite, softens the harsh lines of a picket fence

J. HORACE MCFARLAND PHOTO

GENEREUX PHOTO

Above, shading flowers from the hot sun keeps them from fading quickly

Below, Peonies form a pleasant pathway in this handsome garden

ROCHE PHOTO

A. B. MORSE PHOTO

Iris and holly in the background and double peonies in the foreground are planted in an informal design in the garden of a rustic house

GENEREUX PHOTOS

Tulips, boxwood, alyssum and peonies for accent
in the garden of Mrs. Irving C. Wright

Left, Magnolia, a Japanese type peony, has bright rose-pink flowers with
yellow stamens. An outstanding deep pink variety, Mons. Jules Elie,
is on the right

GENEREUX PHOTOS

Queen Rose and Constance Spry, semi-double to double, above. Below is the lutea hybrid peony Age of Gold

GENEREUX PHOTOS

Two views of the tree peony are shown, one in closeup and below a plant in full bloom

ARRANGED BY MRS. JAMES C. RALEIGH   A. L. DEAN PHOTO

Three varieties of peony, mostly Sarah Bernhardt, an apple blossom shell-pink, two blooms of Walter Faxon, a true pink, and rosy-white buds of Myrtle Gentry are arranged in an alabaster compote

ARRANGED BY MRS. L. V. JACOBS   WAYNE L. ADAMS, SR. PHOTO

Opposite An arrangement in an antique chafing dish features three rose-colored peonies and one white and one green caladium leaf. Golden ninebark is the foliage used for the back line

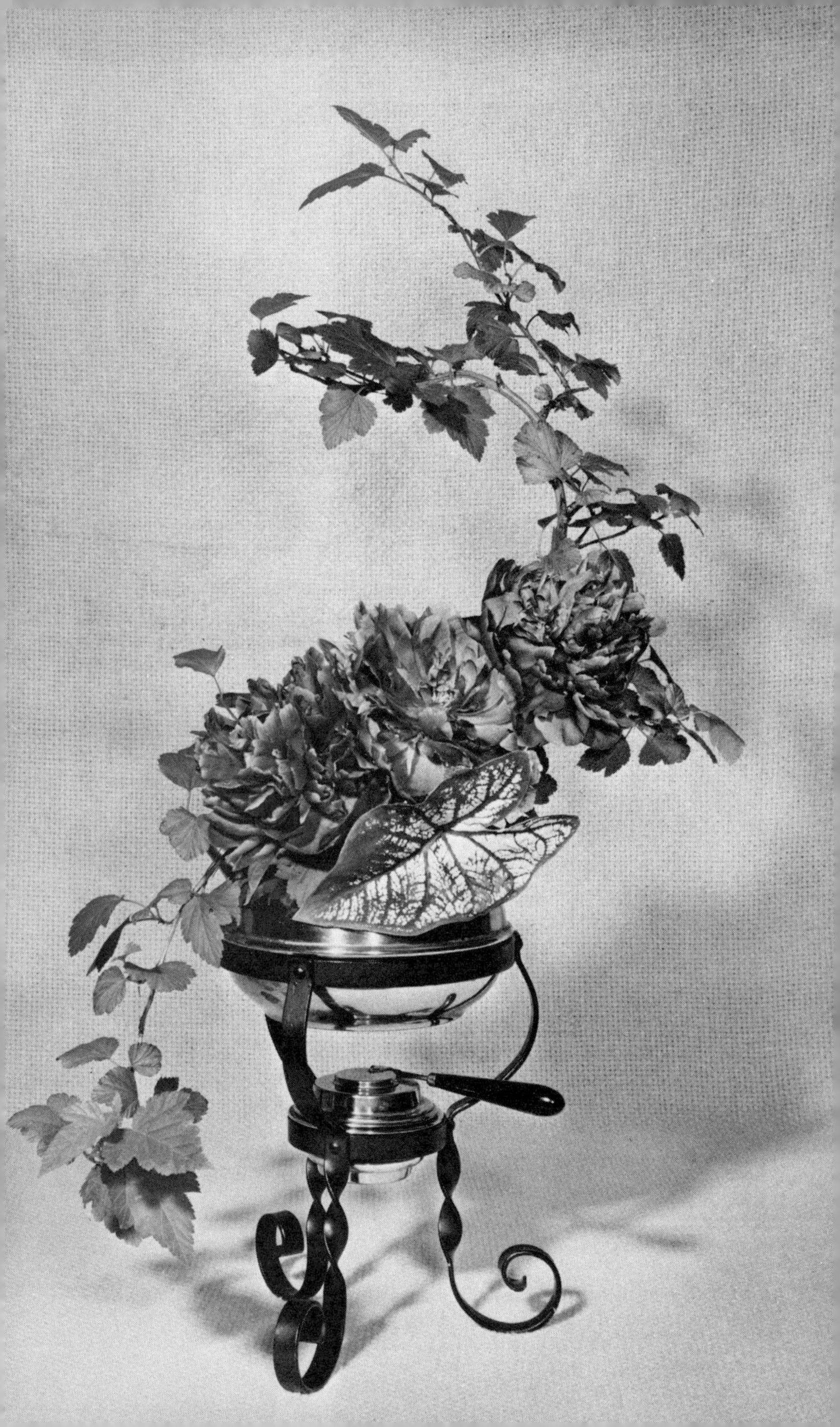

ARRANGED BY MRS. WILLIAM G. WHEELER BOUTRELLE PHOTO

Branches of flowering crab and flowers of the single pale pink Japanese peony Akashigata against a gold background, with a Chinese figurine and a bronze bird to complete the design

ARRANGED BY MRS. GEORGE GOLDSON BOUTRELLE PHOTO

Framing an Oriental jade figurine are branches of pine and white peonies with their own foliage

ARRANGED BY MRS. FRED TROXLER

Dried flowers can be lovely! This design includes pale pink to deep rose-red peonies, pink larkspur for line, pale blue salvia, pink to deep red roses and pressed beach leaves

Opposite, This Kakubana arrangement conforms to the strict rules which govern traditional Japanese designs. The Heaven line is $2\frac{1}{2}$ times the height of the container, the Man line is $\frac{2}{3}$ of Heaven, Earth is $\frac{2}{3}$ of Man. The material is first arranged in the hand, and subordinating branches added and cut to desired lengths. A fork-shaped branch wedged firmly into the wide mouth of the container holds the material

ARRANGED BY MRS. SEIHO ARAKAWA

Left, pink peonies are combined with coralbells and fleece flower in an ivory cherub compote. Below, White Japanese type peony Isani Gidui with blossoms of sweet rocket in a round porcelain container

ARRANGED BY
MRS. ALFRED R. WALPOLE

RIDGE STUDIO PHOTO

ARRANGED AND
PHOTOGRAPHED BY
JEANNETTE GROSSMAN

GENEREUX PHOTOS

Tree peony gardens staged by Marinus Vander Pol and designed by Allen C. Haskell are popular at the New England Spring Flower Show. The authentic Japanese garden above features exotic tree peonies (ranging in color from pearly white through pinks to deep garnet), dainty cut-leaved maples, low pine and larch, lavender-pink wisteria and late flowering cherries. Rock, water and moss, basic to any Japanese garden, are featured

In the photo which follows, an informal contemporary garden uses tree peonies, a yew hedge, flowering dogwoods, shad, birch, and pine. The sitting area is bluestone slate. A pixie, a piece of driftwood, ferns and epimedium complete the picture

Described on the preceding page

PART II — THE HERBACEOUS PEONY

4 LUPINUS
polyphyllus
mixed June

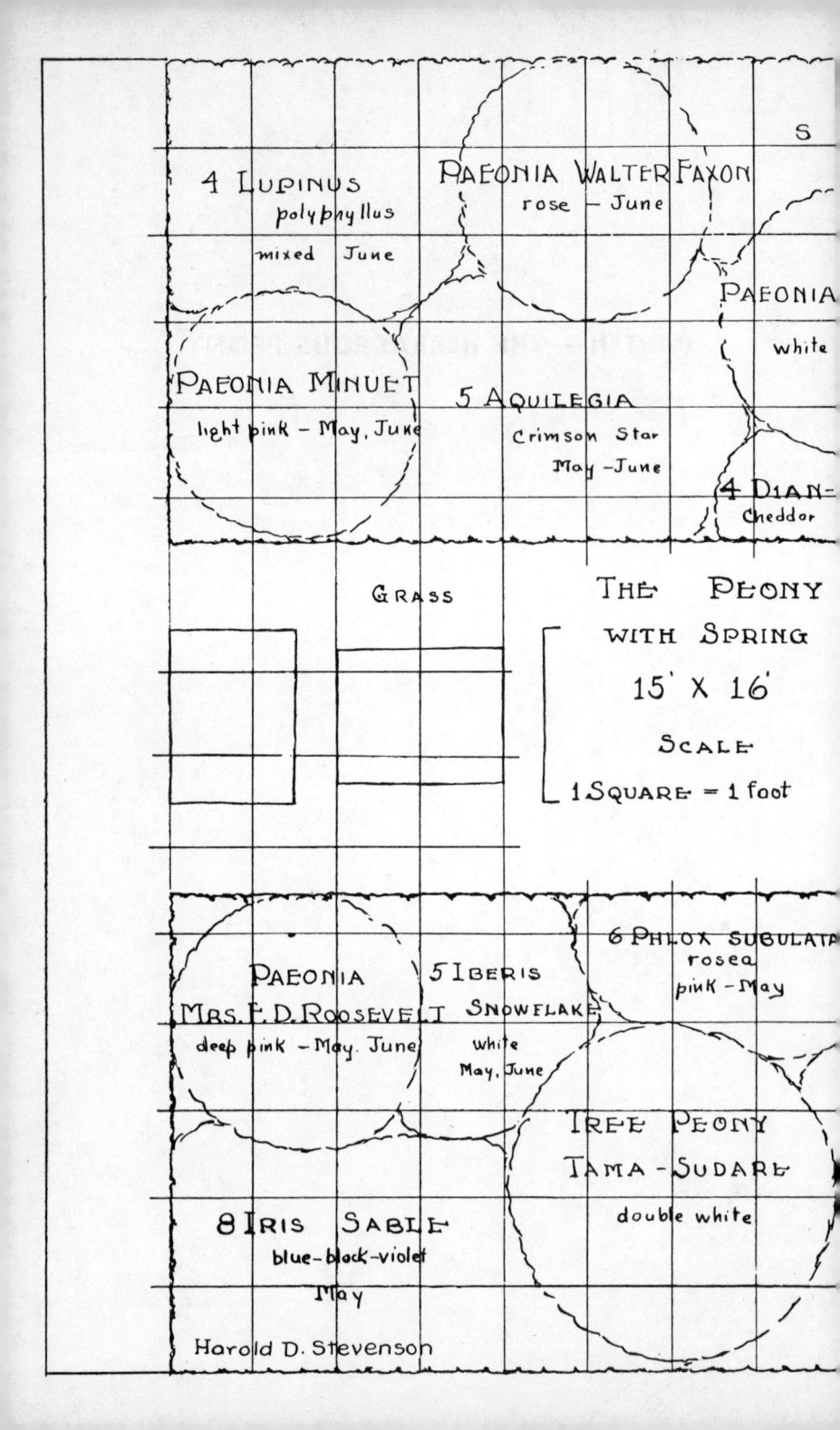

PAEONIA WALTER FAXON
rose – June

PAEONIA
white

PAEONIA MINUET
light pink – May, June

5 AQUILEGIA
Crimson Star
May – June

4 DIAN-
Cheddar

GRASS

THE PEONY
WITH SPRING
15' X 16'
SCALE
1 SQUARE = 1 foot

PAEONIA
MRS. F. D. ROOSEVELT
deep pink – May, June

5 IBERIS
SNOWFLAKE
white
May, June

6 PHLOX SUBULATA
rosea
pink – May

TREE PEONY
TAMA-SUDARE
double white

8 IRIS SABLE
blue-black-violet
May

Harold D. Stevenson

IRIS GREAT LAKES

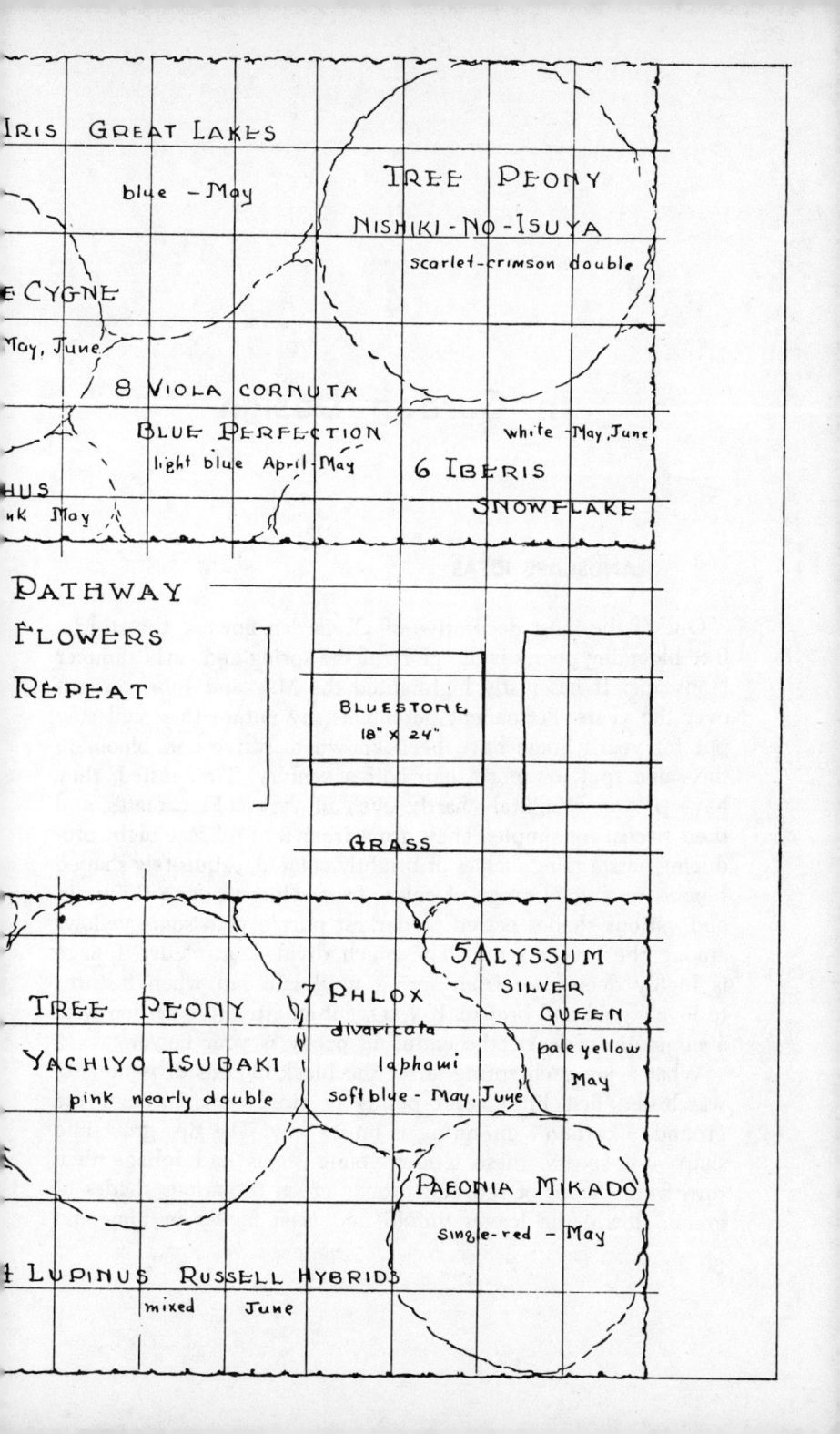

blue — May

TREE PEONY
NISHIKI-NO-ISUYA
scarlet-crimson double

E CYGNE

May, June

8 VIOLA CORNUTA
BLUE PERFECTION
light blue April-May

white — May, June
6 IBERIS
SNOWFLAKE

HUS
nk May

PATHWAY
FLOWERS
REPEAT

BLUESTONE
18" x 24"

GRASS

TREE PEONY
YACHIYO TSUBAKI
pink nearly double

7 PHLOX
divaricata
laphami
soft blue — May, June

5 ALYSSUM
SILVER
QUEEN
pale yellow
May

PAEONIA MIKADO
single-red — May

4 LUPINUS RUSSELL HYBRIDS
mixed   June

4

In Garden Design

LANDSCAPE IDEAS

One of the most decorative of all garden flowers, the sturdy, free-blooming peony is the glory of the spring and early summer landscape. It has justly highlighted the May and June gardens over the years. Permanent perennials, by nature they will stay put for years. Some have been known to thrive and bloom in the same spot for more than half a century. Time-tested, they have proven absolutely hardy even in very cold climates and their needs are simple. They grow from 2 to 4½ feet high, producing outstanding masses of brightly colored, exquisitely shaped blooms in a wide range of colors from white through the pinks and various shades of red to darkest purple with some yellows among the newer types. The much divided, attractive foliage is highly decorative from spring until late fall when it turns to lovely gold and bronze. If you want an attractive garden with a minimum of work, the enduring peony is your flower.

What a joy each spring, after the bleak months of winter, to watch the first little coral points or tips break through the ground, a certain sign spring is on its way. The tips grow into sharp red spears, these tender young stems and foliage then turn from shades of red and bronzy green to various shades of green, slowly the leaves unfold and then finally in May and

IN GARDEN DESIGN
51

Peonies In The Landscape

Grouping types

Edging brick walk

As foundation planting (under window)

With other perennials and annuals

Along low fence or garden wall

4'6" WA[LL]

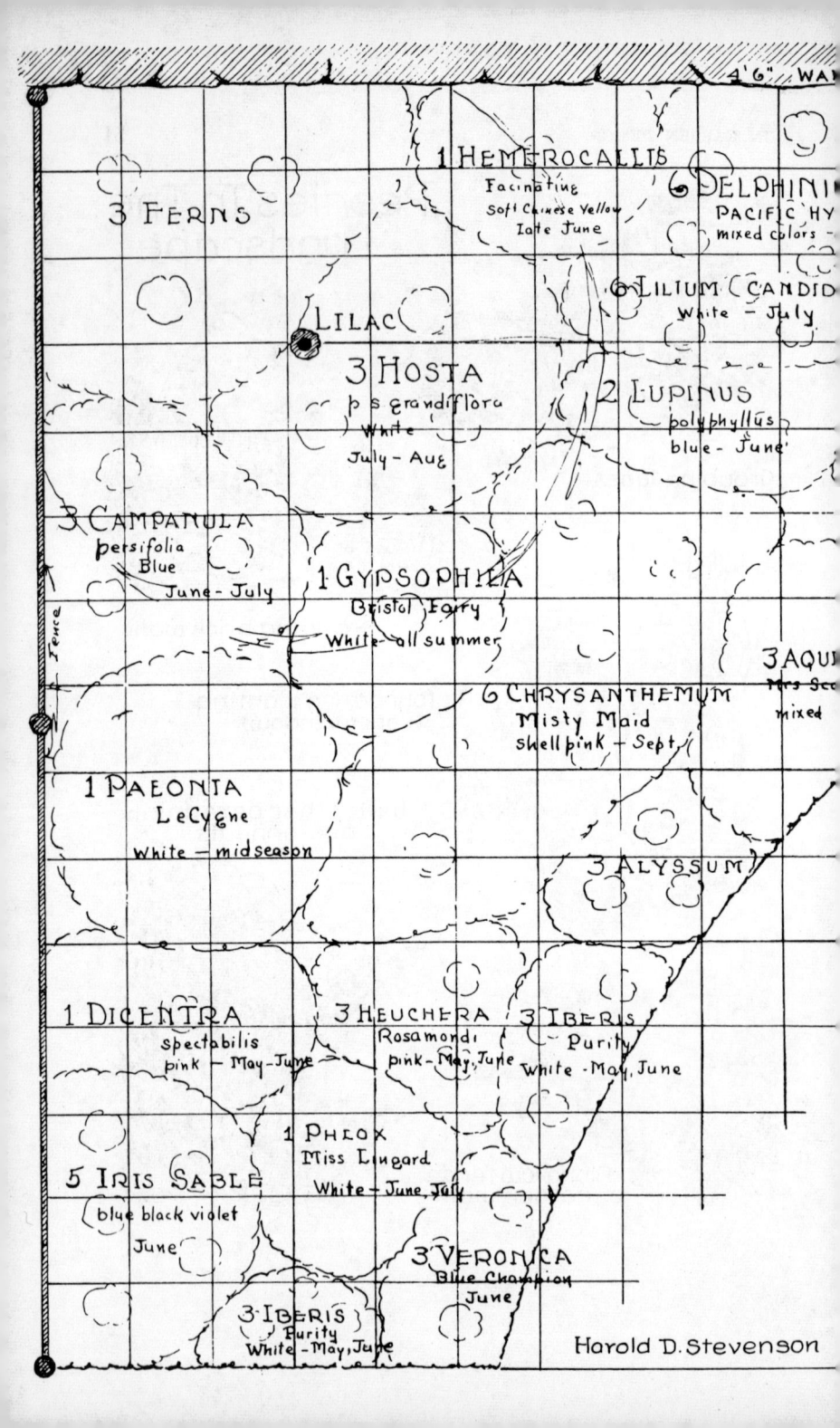

1 HEMEROCALLIS
Facinating
Soft Chinese Yellow
late June

3 FERNS

6 DELPHINI[UM]
PACIFIC HY[BRIDS]
mixed colors

LILAC

6 LILIUM CANDID[UM]
White - July

3 HOSTA
p s grandiflora
White
July - Aug

2 LUPINUS
polyphyllus
blue - June

3 CAMPANULA
persifolia
Blue
June - July

1 GYPSOPHILA
Bristol Fairy
White - all summer

3 AQU[ILEGIA]
Mrs Sco[tt]
mixed

6 CHRYSANTHEMUM
Misty Maid
shell pink - Sept

1 PAEONIA
LeCygne
White - midseason

3 ALYSSUM

1 DICENTRA
spectabilis
pink - May-June

3 HEUCHERA
Rosamondi
pink - May, June

3 IBERIS
Purity
White - May, June

5 IRIS SABLE
blue black violet
June

1 PHLOX
Miss Lingard
White - June, July

3 VERONICA
Blue Champion
June

3 IBERIS
Purity
White - May, June

Harold D. Stevenson

Existing Euonymus vegetus

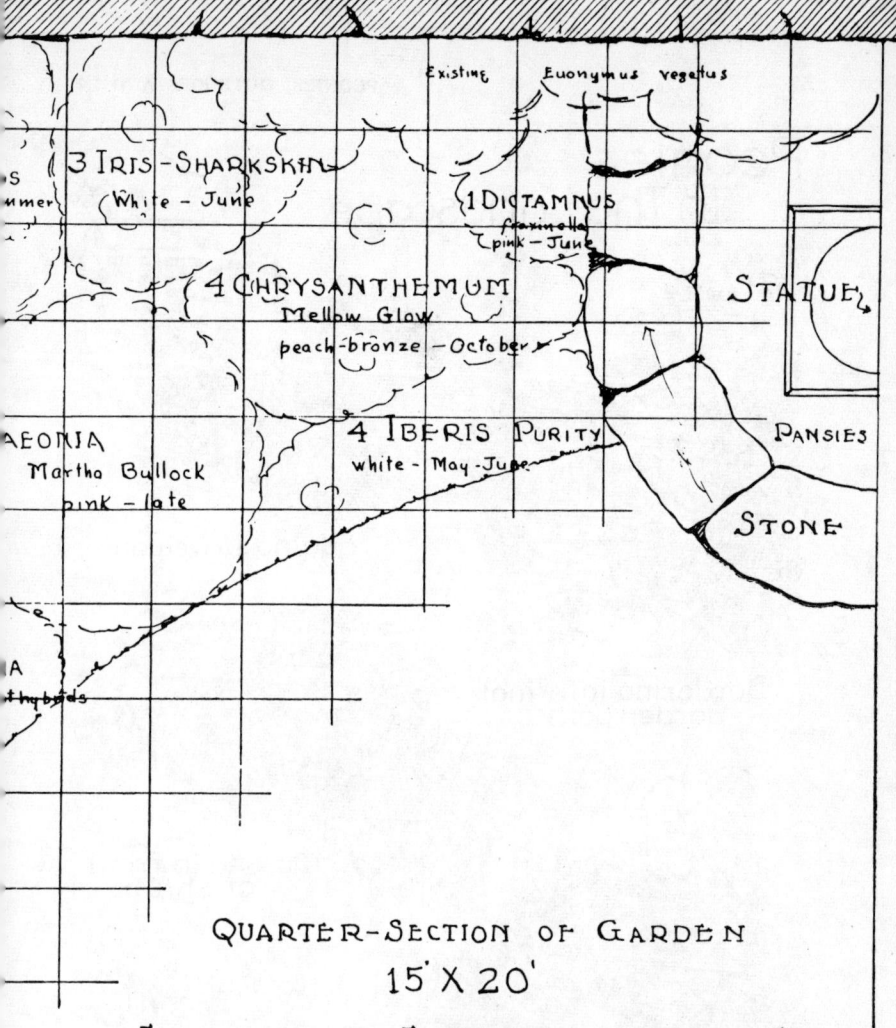

3 IRIS-SHARKSKIN
White - June

1 DICTAMNUS
fraxinella
pink - June

4 CHRYSANTHEMUM
Mellow Glow
peach-bronze - October

STATUE

PAEONIA
Martha Bullock
pink - late

4 IBERIS PURITY
white - May - June

PANSIES

STONE

QUARTER-SECTION OF GARDEN
15' X 20'

EMPHASIS ON FLOWERS — SPRING & FALL

Background TULIPS NIPHETOS — D. lemon yellow
                    ZWANENBURG — D. white
                    QUEEN OF THE NIGHT — D. maroon purple

Middle   NARCISSUS SPRING GLORY — white-yellow
                       BEERSHEBA   — white
                       SCARLET GEM — yellow, orange scarlet

Foreground SCILLA campanulata — white, blue, pink.
                    siberica   — blue

SCALE 1 SQUARE = 1 foot.

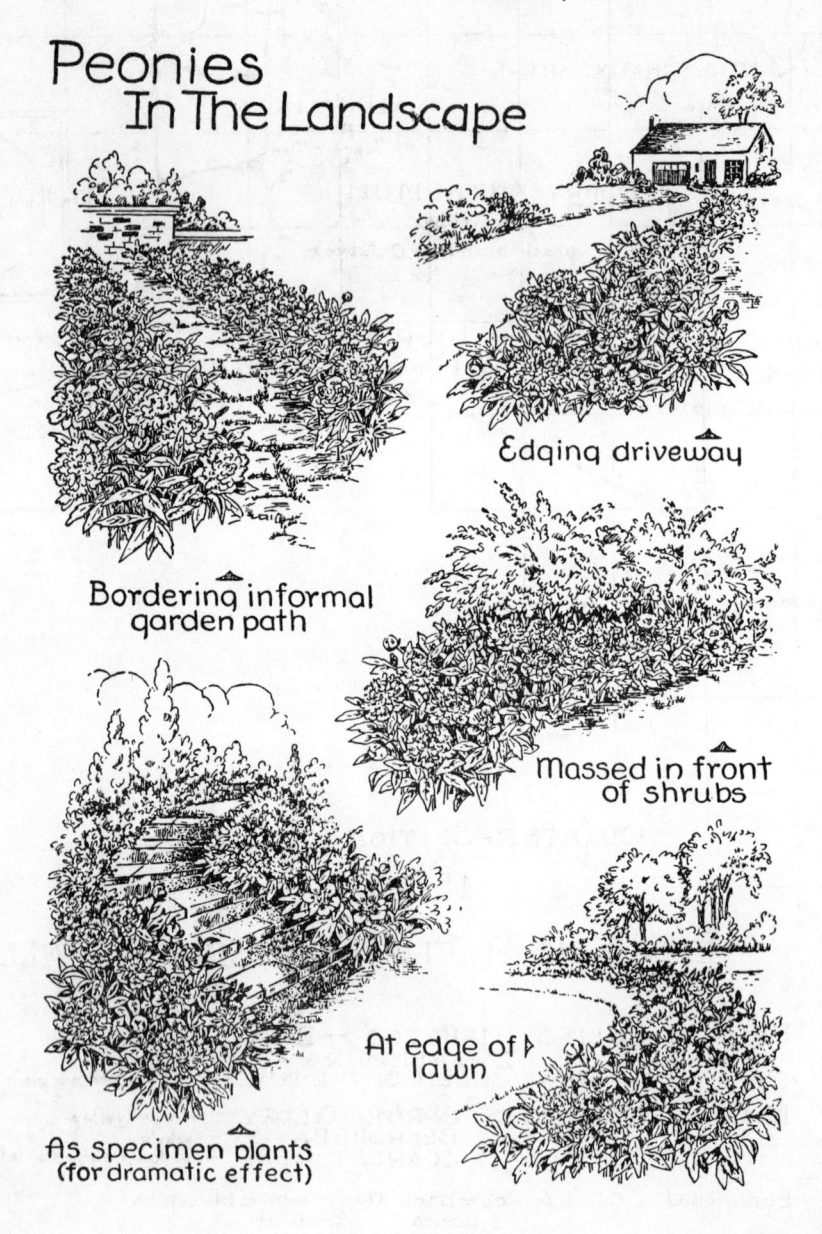

Peonies In The Landscape

Bordering informal garden path

Edging driveway

Massed in front of shrubs

As specimen plants (for dramatic effect)

At edge of lawn

June comes the burst of glory of the beautiful flowers. An appealing subject all through the growing season, the gold and bronze autumn foliage is highly decorative. Truly "the old reliable" of the garden, the peony just goes on growing, blooming and surviving winters, year after year. Plant a peony for posterity. Some old clumps may have 50 or more blossoms open at once, a really spectacular sight.

Everybody loves the peony and anybody can grow it. It is fortunate that the peony can be utilized in so many ways in the landscape.

A flower for everyone, it is found growing at the back steps of many farm houses, as well as in the gardens of the most elaborate estates. The peony fits nicely into many situations. Where space is adequate landscape architects like to use it in strategic well placed areas for masses of color. It is also useful for small-scale landscaping. The very smallest garden may have a peony. Used instead of a small shrub one can find many places for it even in a small area.

Peonies may be planted in broad masses at the lawns edge, grouped in front of evergreen, deciduous and flowering shrubs are used as accent plants. Interplanted with other perennials or annuals in the border or grouped in special beds of their own, peonies make an elaborate show when at their peak.

Perhaps the choicest perennial from the standpoint of both flowers and foliage, its nicely cut, dark green leaves remain crisp and attractive all through the growing season. Planted as a hedge along a garden path, driveway, low wall or fence the massed border of peony foliage is as bright with the reds and golds of autumn as the nearby oaks and maples.

An old timer, the peony has long been a dooryard plant in New England and is still enjoyed as a specimen plant near the doorway or some other prominent place where its lovely blossoms may be appreciated to the fullest. As a foundation planting under a picture window, the peony may be enjoyed from both indoors and out providing there is ample root space, good soil, good drainage and sun to make it thrive.

Peonies are at home in the old fashioned garden, informal and unstudied in appearance with an abundance of bloom and color from early spring until late in the season. The newer and better varieties of such old-time favorites as peonies, hollyhocks, roses, phlox and lilies in no way spoil the character of the garden but rather improve the general effect. Used together harmoniously the large masses of plants give a delightful feeling of luxury and opulence. Once established in good fertile soil, these hardy favorites, if given sufficient moisture, do not require coddling.

For an attractive color effect in a long peony border, commence at either end with the whites and paler shades, working gradually from blush through the pinks to the center using a grouping of brilliant and dark reds in the middle. The reds and pinks make wonderful splashes of color.

Many fine color effects are possible or an all white garden is always effective, relaxing and cool looking in the summer. Spring and early summer white blooms may be had from azaleas, rhododendrons, dogwood, daphne, deutzia, kalmia, lilacs, spirea, viburnum, buddleia, climbing roses, peonies, iris and clematis, to mention only a few.

SPACE REQUIRED IN BORDER

In the smaller gardens with limited space which many of us cultivate today, we usually use peonies in combination with other perennials so we are of necessity limited in the number of peonies we can plant. Care must be taken not to overcrowd or dwarf a small suburban planting.

As to the space required for peonies, Secretary Peyton writes, "It will depend a great deal on the situation and the other material used in the border. While peonies vary in height, they rarely increase in number of stems or spread at the base after they put out 20 to 30 stems. They rarely grow over 18 or 20 inches in diameter at the base and 30 to 40 inches at the top or widest part. When almost any peony plant is full grown if the clumps were planted 4 feet apart, they will touch and there is little room for anything else. If grown with other material, however, they will not increase much after 5 or 6 years, especially if somewhat crowded. Tree peonies will expand more, if given a chance, than the herbaceous kinds. Some tree peonies will make a spread of 4 to 5 feet in diameter or even more if kept growing in good conditions".

Mr. Peyton also writes, "The peony rows in my garden are only 30" apart and the plants not more than 18" (not ideal), but I took notes for you on two plants planted ten years ago. Mildred May has 15 stems with a spread at the base of 12" and it is 36" tall, the widest part measures 30". It is a good grower and makes a nice garden plant. Lady Aroostock, put out by Cherry Hill Nurseries, has 20 stems and a 14" spread at the base, measures 40" at its widest part and is 40" tall. It makes one of the finest plants I have. Though its bloom is good and of large size it is not one of the top ten in beauty but it surely makes a beautiful garden plant. An old friend, Festiva Maxima, planted in 1907 and still growing vigorously makes blooms often 8" in diameter. This variety frequently grows 4 feet in height with a spread of 40", yet with only 10 to 20 stems".

Secretary Peyton advises, "Plant any herbaceous variety you like if height does not matter. Expect a base spread of from 12" to 18" as a maximum and a spread at the top of from 30" to 40". If height is a factor, choose lower growers".

He further states, "Hybrid herbaceous peonies will vary from small plants 6" to 10" in height to some that may reach 5 feet, their ultimate behavior depending largely on the cross and the individual variety".

BORDER IDEAS

Most borders are backed by a fence, garage, wall or a hedge of evergreens or semi-evergreens, interspersed now and then by groups of tall flowering shrubs. The tallest plants are placed at the back in front of the hedge, the other plants arranged to

Peony and Perennial Border
OF SOFT TONES

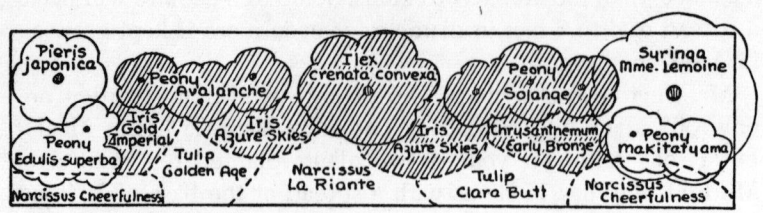

Early Season

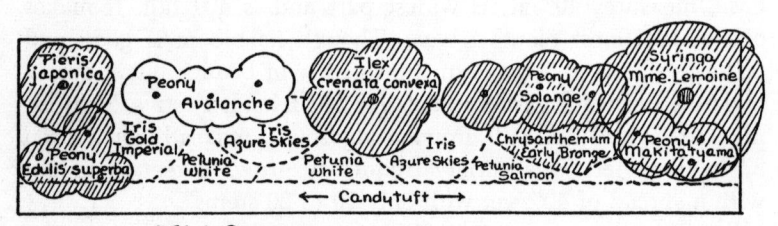

Mid-Season

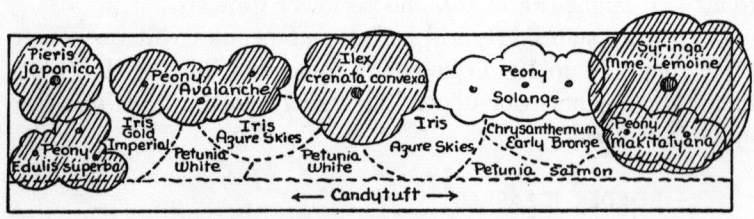

Late Season

Ruth D. Leiby, Designer

Plants Not in Bloom
Scale ½" = 1'-0"

IN GARDEN DESIGN　　　　　　　　　　　　　　　　　　　　57

Peony Border of Bright Colors
(Using early, mid-season and late peony varieties)

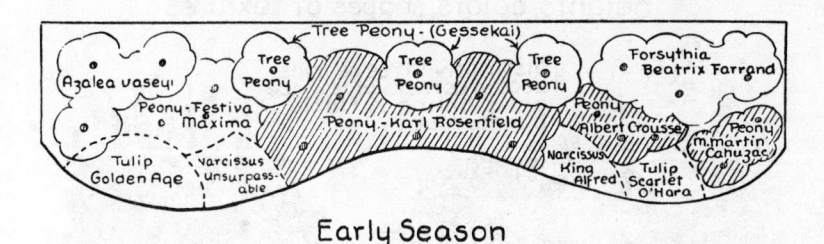

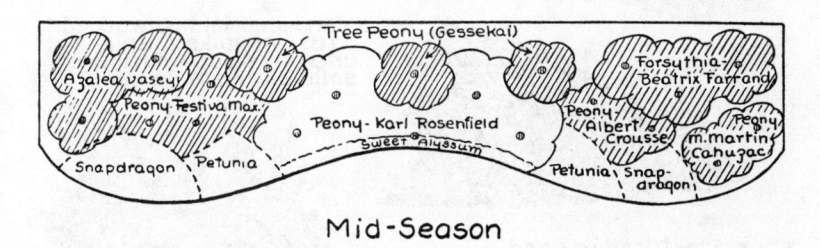

Early Season

Mid-Season

Late Season

Ruth D. Leiby, Designer

Plants Not in Bloom ▨
Scale ½"=1'-0"

Accent Borders or Garden Enclosures
To Create Interest
using distinctive plants, contrasting heights, colors, shapes or textures

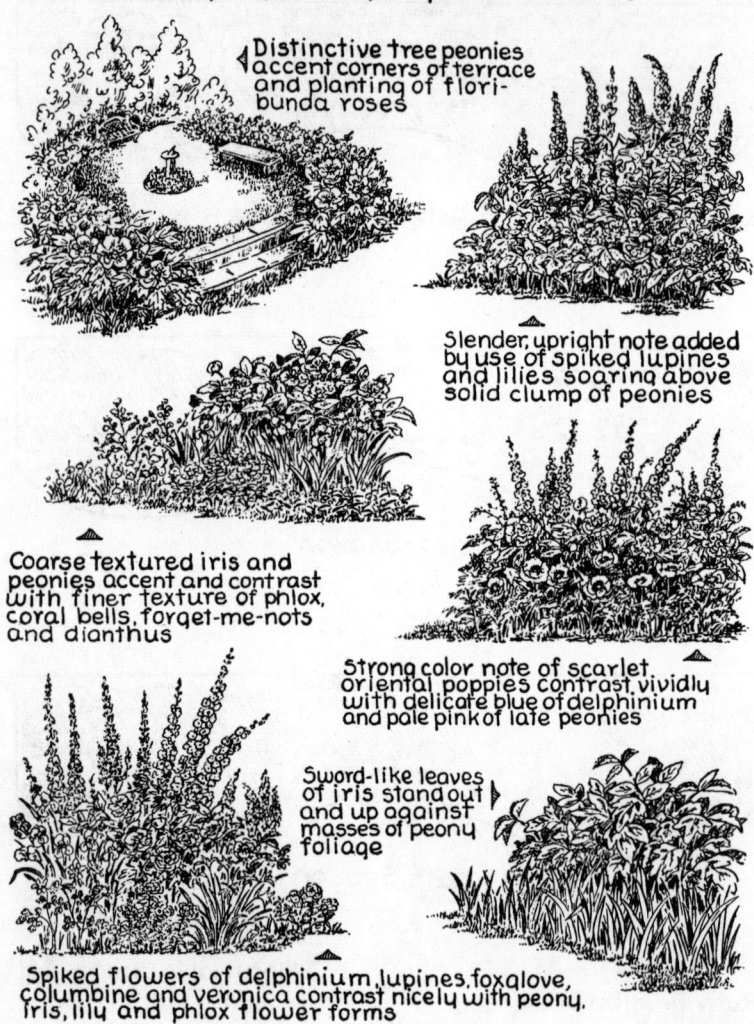

Distinctive tree peonies accent corners of terrace and planting of floribunda roses

Slender, upright note added by use of spiked lupines and lilies soaring above solid clump of peonies

Coarse textured iris and peonies accent and contrast with finer texture of phlox, coral bells, forget-me-nots and dianthus

Strong color note of scarlet oriental poppies contrast vividly with delicate blue of delphinium and pale pink of late peonies

Sword-like leaves of iris stand out and up against masses of peony foliage

Spiked flowers of delphinium, lupines, foxglove, columbine and veronica contrast nicely with peony, iris, lily and phlox flower forms

grade down to the lowest ones which are at the front. Occasionally a tall plant like hollyhock, peony, boltonia, lily or Iris kaempferi is brought forward to break the monotony and serve as an accent.

Along the walk or grass use edging plants 6" to 18" tall like dianthus, Iberis sempervirens, Nepeta mussini, Veronica latifolia, viola, sea-pink (Armeria) or white rock-cress (Arabis). Gradually fill in behind with taller plants 1' to 1½' to 2' to 2½' in height, plants tall and sturdy in growth, using color masses which form a continuity and add special interest.

At the back tall, heavy foliage plants fit in well. Use material of special interest as some of the newer and unusual peony varieties that will attract attention. When the garden is new, in the bare spaces between these important plants use filler material or plants which you do not mind sacrificing later as they are crowded out by the growth of more important neighbors. Some good filler plants are the false dragonhead (Physostegia virginiana), globe thistle (Echinops ritro), goatsbeard (Aruncus sylvester), monkshood (Aconitum fisheri) and white snakeroot (Eupatorium rugosum).

Special interest plants should be used for variety and to draw emphasis to the good elements or features of the garden design or to special plant combinations. Accent long borders by using contrasting heights, colors, textures and shapes. Lilies soaring high above a grouping of peonies complement them and will draw attention to the peonies. Bright roses on a climber backing a clump of white peonies add interest and by contrast emphasize the peonies; both show off to better advantage. A strong color note among paler shades can be very effective. The heavier, coarser textured foliage of the peony contrasts interestingly with finely dissected, almost fernlike leaves of the garden heliotrope (Valeriana officinalis). Although the leaf of the iris is also of a heavy texture, its spear-like form contrasts nicely in shape with the large, compound foliage of the peony.

Peonies, iris, chrysanthemums, phlox and a few other hardy

perennials are excellent stand-by plants in the border throughout the season.

GOOD COMPANION PLANTS

(see plans by landscape architects, which appear in this chapter)

While peonies are attractive alone, their fine qualities show off to best advantage when judiciously combined with other plant material. Backed by lilacs, deutzia or mockorange flowering at the same time, peonies are in harmony with the old-fashioned character of the plants. The common white flowering lilac (Syringa vulgaris alba) forms a bold, tall growing plant that blooms in May. The Persian lilac grows 5 to 6 feet tall and has fragrant pale lilac flowers on gracefully arching branches in May. There is also a white flowering form. Philadelphus coronarius (sweet mockorange) grows 10 to 12 feet high and produces fragrant white flowers in May and June.

Sir Thomas Lipton is a fine Rosa rugosa hybrid, a semi-double fragrant shrub rose; it has pure white flowers and is one of the earliest to bloom, in late May on through the season. Plants reach a height of 4 to 5 feet. R. rugosa alba and the cherry-red Grootendorst, another rugosa hybrid, are also good shrub roses to plant with peonies. The creamy white flowers of the fragrant viburnum (V. carlesi) are at their best in April and May and it is one of the most fragrant of the deciduous flowering shrubs. It forms a compact plant 5 to 6 feet in height. Often overlooked and delightful backing up peonies is Neilla sinensis closely allied to spirea, a small dense graceful shrub not over 6 feet high with showy dainty pink terminal clusters. There are many, many fine shrubs that bloom with the peony and combine beautifully with it in the landscape. Weigela, white, pink or red, with its foxglove-like flowers blooms in May and June as do some of the interesting honeysuckles. Both make excellent companion plants in the landscape and in arrangements.

In the spring when peonies thrust up their soft red shoots they are especially pretty with the green leaves of white and yellow daffodils. The leaf buds unfold remarkable form and color with red stems and sea-green leaflets varying in hue from one plant to the next. As the peony leaves expand, they in turn hide the drying daffodil foliage. As the new shoots of the peony come up in the spring, before the foliage is fully developed, the extra space may be utilized by some of the other very early spring flowering bulbs; like the crocus, snowdrop, scilla, chionodoxa, and extra early flowering tulips. These blooms may be enjoyed while the peonies are making their new growth. The foliage of most die down naturally and the luxuriant peony foliage as it develops will do them no harm. Hardy lilies do well interplanted with peonies. Summer flowering bulbs such as the ismene (Peruvian daffodil), lycoris (Wonder Lily) and summer hyacinth add color and interest when the peonies are through blooming.

Grouped together in a border, peonies contrast massively with the spiked, more slender vertical flower forms. A fine mixer, many delightful and exciting color combinations are possible when peonies are interplanted with late iris, early phlox and the triumphant poppies or clumps of spire-like lupines in deep pink and rose, spikes of blue delphinium or the tall stately foxglove.

Some of the early flowering hybrid hemerocallis or daylilies make excellent companion plants. The Madonna and regal lilies can be used effectively between peonies. Other tall growing perennials which give picturesque effects are the spikes of yellow thermopsis (T. caroliniana) with pea-like foliage or the wild false indigo (Baptisis australs) with its blue-green foliage. Also the long-spurred columbine, coreopsis or pyrethrum (both single and double), and the early-flowering spireas all make charming peony companions as do feverfew, garden heliotrope and filipendula.

Late peonies are good with plants like gladiolus which, when set out in the spring, flower shortly after the peonies have finished. Since gladiolus corms must be taken up each fall and

May: Introducing the Peony Display

Lilacs bloom. Viburnums just beginning and Althaeas in small leaf stage. Tree Peonies in bloom with early and midseason in full to opening stage, midseason lates and lates in bud. Border plants in bloom. Others in various stages of shoots, small to medium in height, filling in between peonies, small iris in front of tree peonies partly in bloom, many in bud

Lilacs gone by. Viburnums in full tilt. Althaeas in full leaf. Tree peonies gone by, earlies, also. Midseason and lates in full bloom. Delphiniums in just opening to full open stage. Siberian iris in full bloom. Good clump in center. Border plants in bloom. Those gone by now mounds of leaves, others in bloom but tapering off as in case of edging plants

June: "The Queen of Flowers" in all its glory

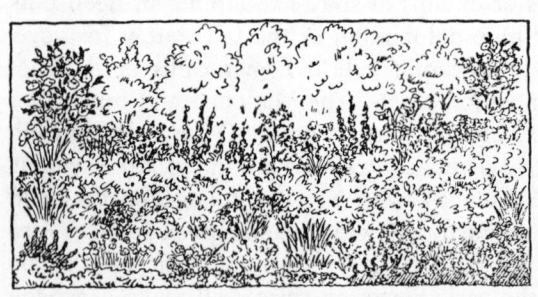

Only Althaeas now in bloom. Delphiniums in second blooming with verbascums, lilies, Jap. iris, daylilies and other lilies carrying on, chrysanthemums and tall asters making nice mounds but not yet in bloom, while dianthus carries on and chrysanthemum arcticum is now in bloom. All peonies in leafy stage making fine mounds

July: Other flowering plants supply the color

(plan by John Brimer)

IN GARDEN DESIGN

Peony Garden
(Plan by John Brimer)

E - Early, M - Midseason, L - Late

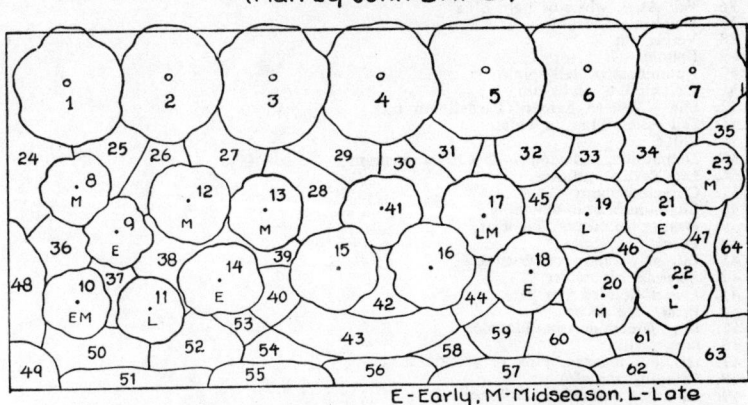

The above plan is for an area 12' x 25' which includes the space devoted to the shrubs backing up the peonies and other perennials. The shrubs give some auxiliary bloom with a couple for late summer. The peonies give a range of bloom, form and timing as well as utilizing all colors.

The border is one which might extend across the back yard at the rear of a lawn patch with the shrubbery masking a vegetable garden or maybe up against a garage or other building or maybe just a property line fence. The herbaceous plants mixed in among the peonies were chosen for size, for blooming time and to give some kind of color all season long with the main emphasis on the peony-time bloom. However all will be good looking most of the season (not ragged or unkempt in appearance) with a minimum of care.

1. Althaea, Snowdrift
2. Viburnum tomentosum
3. Hybrid French Lilac, Firament
4. Hybrid French Lilac, Miss Ellen Willmott
5. Hybrid French Lilac, Ami Schott
6. Viburnum tomentosum plicatum grandiflorum
7. Althaea, rubis or Celestial Blue

PEONIES: E-Early M-Midseason L-Late

8. Irwin Altman — M. Rd
9. Pico — E. Single white
10. Hargrove Hudson — EM Pink
11. June Brilliant — L. Red
12. Lottie Dawson Rea — M. Pink
13. Rashoomon — M. Jap. Red
14. Festiva Maxima — E. White
15. *Tree Peony* Reine Elizabeth — Salmon Rose
16. *Tree Peony* Comtesse de Tudor — Salmon tipped white
17. Better Times — LM Rose
18. Mrs. F. D. Roosevelt — E. Pink
19. Roberta — L. Jap. white
20. M. Martin Cahuzac — M. Dark red
21. Kansas — E. Red
22. Solange — L. Ivory White
23. Mandaleen — M. Light Pink
40. and 44. Fern leaved single and double peonies.

List continued on page 64

PERENNIALS (see plan on page 63)
24. Jap. Iris
25. Phlox
26. Fall Aster, white or light blue
27. Delphinium, white
28. Verbascum
29. Boltonia
30. Autumn aster, tall, pink
31. Delphinium, light blue
32. Lily—Western Sunset (Pardalinum hyb.)
33. Fall Aster, blue or white
34. Phlox
35. Delphinium belladonna or Chrysanthemum
36. Late daylily, yellow
37. Chrysanthemum
38. Lily—midseason blooming
39. Daylily, midseason bloomer
40. Peony, see above
41. Lilium auratum or Eremurus
42. Siberian iris, white
43. Dwarf bearded iris
44. Peony, see above
45. Lily, late midseason bloomer
46. Late daylily
47. Iris, tall breaded. Pink or salmon shades
48. Creeping veronica
49. Dianthus deltoides, "Brilliant"
50. Armeria
51. Arabis
52. Iberis
53. Heuchera, red
54. Dianthus heddewigi
55. Aubrietia or Arenaria
56. Cerastium
57. Creeping Veronica
58. Heuchera, pink
59. Dwarf fall aster, pink
60. Artemisia, Silver Mound
61. Dianthus, Old Spice
62. Chrysanthemum arcticum
63. Armeria
64. Viola cornuta, Catherine Sharp

replanted in the spring (3″ deep and 6″ apart) they may be properly spaced each spring in relation to the growth of the peony plant. The upright spikes require very little lateral room and are able to take care of themselves.

While the peony maintains its attractive massive foliage throughout the season, to cover spaces left empty by flowering bulbs and such flowers as bleeding-heart (Dicentra spectabilis), Virginia-bluebell (Mertensia virginica), and poppies, annuals may be used to augment and harmonize with the permanent plants in the border. Where space permits annuals such as mallow or gypsophila will branch out and grow right over any flowers past their best and completely hide them.

Edging or border plants which flower with peonies and combine well include coral-bells (Heuchera sanguinea), varying in color from white to deep red with compact tufts of attractive foliage. Snow-in-summer (Cerastium tomentosum) a hardy creeping perennial, has grayish, downy foliage and abundant white flowers. The low evergreen white candytuft (Iberis sempervirens), Gold-Dust, the yellow Alyssum saxatile compactum, the English daisy (Bellis perennis) a dwarf compact perennial with profusion of flowers in all colors except yellow and pansies, make attractive edgings. The various hardy border pinks planted in drifts make mats of blue-green foliage covered with white or pink, sweetly-scented flowers. Cut them back after flowering to encourage new growth. What could be more delightful than the early blooming peony Festiva Maxima's large white flowers, flecked with crimson, displayed above a bed of May blooming Maiden Pink (Dianthus deltoides). The edging adds much and gives a finish to the peony planting.

SEE VARIETIES IN FLOWER

In order to choose wisely one must know what is available. Catalogs are interesting to leaf through and study but one should see varieties in bloom to know them and compare their habits of growth, form and color. As you see the varieties growing, select those with special appeal for you and those suited to your conditions and needs.

If you are really interested in learning about varieties, visit nearby peony gardens open to you when they are in bloom. At that time make notes for fall buying and planting. Visit nearby commercial nurseries when at their height of bloom and public plantings of peonies, if you are fortunate enough to have such a planting nearby. Take advantage of private collections where visitors are welcome and visit peony shows or exhibitions. If you are sincerely interested, most private growers will welcome you as a visitor to their private collections.

Most peony shows have all flowers well labeled and usually feature the newer varieties as well as the old favorites so attend shows to acquaint yourself with the latest introductions. But keep in mind that most show blooms entered for competition have been pampered and given extra special care to attain the perfection of culture they represent.

5

Selecting Varieties

Although new varieties are constantly being offered to the trade, by comparison with some flowers, varieties change slowly and do not vary noticeably from season to season or become quickly out of date. Many still favored, and deservedly so, were introduced years ago. The problem of keeping up with new varieties is simple compared with the iris or rose where many varieties introduced are soon lost in the struggle for survival.

No two people will agree on the same favorites or best varieties since individual tastes differ widely. Some people find it interesting to experiment with novelties and new varieties, others prefer old reliables. In beauty and reliability many of the old kinds are hard to beat and not so expensive but it is also fun and exciting to try some of the new types. By variation and hybridization the garden forms are now fabulous with many hundreds from which to choose.

In regard to lists, our good friend Winthrop Thurlow of Cherry Hill Nurseries writes, "I object to making out a list of the best twelve as I could not make a list of the twelve people whom I like best or which of my children I like best. There are too many variables".

George W. Peyton of the American Peony Society writes, "Many requests are received by the Secretary for lists of vari-

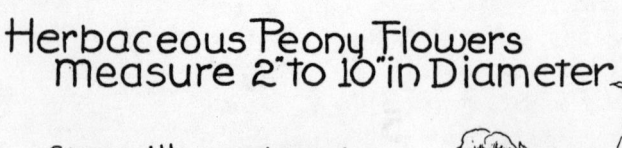

Herbaceous Peony Flowers Measure 2" to 10" in Diameter

Sizes will vary depending upon conditions. Among the smallest are the Saunder's hybrids, about 2" across. (Early and Late Windflower) Fairy Princess, a dark red single is also about 2" across

Fairy Princess, originated by the late Lymon D. Glasscock of Ill. has yellow stamens. The nicely rounded plant grows about 6" high

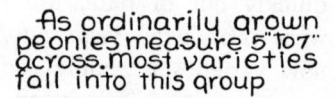

As ordinarily grown peonies measure 5" to 7" across. most varieties fall into this group

Nippon Beauty, Japanese type, rich deep red, center petaloids edged yellow

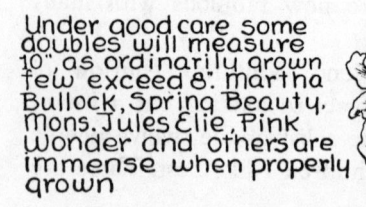

Under good care some doubles will measure 10", as ordinarily grown few exceed 8". Martha Bullock, Spring Beauty, Mons. Jules Elie, Pink Wonder and others are immense when properly grown

Mrs. Franklin D. Roosevelt a pink double will reach 10" with proper care

SELECTING VARIETIES

eties to plant, especially from those who are more or less confused by the glowing descriptions given, not only in catalogs but in articles published in magazines and even in our Bulletin, your Secretary sometimes being the guilty party. The beautiful blooms seen in our shows occasionally add fuel to the fire.

"In answering such requests, it must be remembered that every individual has his own idea of what he wants in his garden and so for another to make the selection is rather dangerous as the varieties chosen may be far from those that will please. For this reason it is always wise to call the attention of the inquirer to this fact. He is also advised that the Society publishes lists of the ones that have been chosen by the members as those most popular.

"If the inquirer still insists that a specific list be recommended, it is done. Then if the ones listed do not please the inquirer, the Secretary's skirts are clear.

"Picking varieties at an exhibition is often not a satisfactory way of doing the job. Flowers shown in exhibitions are there to win prizes and are not shown for garden effect and use. Every lawful device, such as bagging to prevent injury and preserve color, and disbudding and fertilizing to produce size is employed—and it is proper for the exhibitor to do so. For this reason varieties for garden use should be picked, if possible, in a garden, where they are grown as they would be by the ordinary gardener. Then, if a 'lemon' is chosen, the buyer did it with his eyes open".

Variety lists can be helpful, especially for the beginner, to indicate what is available, so we are including several. The fact you do not find a variety on the list in no way condemns it. It may be equally good.

25 TESTED PLANTS FOR THE BEGINNER

Singles
Arcturus, red
Krinkled White, blush
Le Jour, white

Seashell, pink

Japanese
Ama-no-sode, pink

Charm, dark red
Shaylor's Sunburst, blush to white

Anemone
Primevere, white and yellow

Semi-Doubles
Silvia Saunders, light pink

Doubles, white or blush
Alice Harding, white tinted pink
Elsa Sass, white tinted pink
Festiva Maxima, white red spots
James Kelway, blush
Kelway's Glorious, white,. fragrant
La Lorraine, blush

Doubles, light pink
Mrs. F. D. Roosevelt
Nick Shaylor
Reine Hortense
Therese

Doubles, dark pink
Loren Franklin
Mons. Jules Elie
Sarah Bernhardt
Walter Faxon

Doubles, red
Mary Brand, bright red
Philippe Rivoire, dark red, fragrant

25 RARE PEONIES FOR THE CONNOISSEUR

Also see growers' lists for many more fine varieties.

Hybrids
Archangel, white, single
Claire de Lune, yellow, single
Red Charm, red double, best

Singles
Champlain, blush
Dawn Pink, bright pink
Pico, white

Japanese
Isani Gidui, white
Mount Palomar, red
Westerner, pink

Semi-Doubles
Mildred May, pure white
White Rose, exquisite

Doubles
Alma Hansen, white tinted pink
Bonanza, red
Dolorodell, light pink
Doris Cooper, light pink
Florence Ellis, light pink
Frances Mains, light pink
Mary E. Nicholls, white
Mattie Lafuze, blush
Moonstone, pale pink
Mother's Choice, white faintly tinted pink
Mrs. Livingston Farrand, purest pink, temperamental
Oriental Gold, yellow. Syns. Yokihi and Golden Dream
Victory, white tinted pink
Yosemite, white tinted yellow

VOTE WINNERS

The following four somewhat shortened lists tabulate results from a poll of the members of the American Peony Society for 1958. It must be kept in mind that not all members voted. One hundred and eight questionnaires were returned to the Secretary.

Forty Most Popular—All Types
(in order of popularity)
Mons. Jules Elie, double, dark pink
Nick Shaylor, double, light pink
  the above two tied
Mrs. Franklin D. Roosevelt, double, light pink
Kansas, double, red
Kelway's Glorious, double white
  the above two tied
Philippe Rivoire, double red

Myrtle Gentry, double, light pink
Elsa Sass, double, white
Festiva Maxima, double, white
Red Charm, hybrid, double, red
  the above two tied
Le Cygne, double, white
Blanche King, double, dark pink
Therese, double, light pink
  the above two tied
Hansina Brand, double, light pink
Victory, double, white
  the above two tied
Solange, double, blush
Karl Rosenfield, double, red
Seashell, single, pink
  the above two tied
Krinkled White, single, blush
Minuet, double, light pink
  the above two tied
Martha Bulloch, double, dark pink
Mary Brand, double, red
Moonstone, double, light pink
Walter Faxon, double, medium pink
  the above three tied
Isani Gidui, Japanese, white
Mrs. Livingston Farrand, double, light pink
Alice Harding, double blush
Mrs. J. V. Edlund, double, white
Tempest, double, red
  the above two tied
Alesia, double, white
Nancy Nicholls, double, blush
Pico, single, white
  the above three tied
Chocolate Soldier, hybrid, semi-double, red
Ella Christiansen, double, light pink

Felix Crousse, double, red
Longfellow, double, red
  the above four tied
La Lorraine, double, blush
Nippon Brilliant, Japanese, red
Ruth Elizabeth, double, red
Sarah Bernhardt, double, dark pink
  the above four tied

You will notice that the doubles won most of the votes. First honors went to two full doubles; Mons. Jules Elie with an immense dark pink flower which looks like a big chrysanthemum and is an excellent keeper, and Nick Shaylor a top-notch variety with light delicate pink petals shaped like a rose.

Mrs. Franklin D. Roosevelt, another double, fragrant, light pink, was voted second place. It has good substance and keeps well cut. In third place the light red Kansas tied with the white Kelway's Glorious which received the most votes in the 1958 poll as the "One Best" peony. It is a fine mid-season, lacy white, rose type, with strong stems and fully deserves its high rating.

The "One" Best
(in order of popularity)
Kelway's Glorious, double, white
Elsa Sass, double, white
Kansas, double, red
Hansina Brand, double, light pink
Le Cygne, double, white
Mons. Jules Elie, double, dark pink
Mrs. F. D. Roosevelt, double, light pink
Red Charm, hybrid, double, red
  the above four tied
Festiva Maxima, double, white
Nick Shaylor, double, light pink
  the above two tied

Ten Most Popular in Each Color and Type
(1-2-3 indicate top three in popularity)

SINGLES

White or Blush	Pink	Red
Albiflora, The Bride	Angelus	Arcturus (1)
Dancing Nymph	Dawn Pink	Flander's Fields
Dunlora	Elfin Pink	Fortune Teller
Exquisite	Helen (2)	Imperial Red (3)
Krinkled White (1)	Josette	Kaskaskia
Le Jour (3)	L'Etincelante	Kewanee
Pico (2)	Mischief (3)	Kickapoo
Rebecca	Pride of Langport	Man O' War
Virginia Dare	Seashell (1)	President Lincoln (2)
Watchman	Sparkling Star	Vera

The singles, if not disbudded, will bloom for almost the entire peony season.

JAPANESE

White or Blush	Pink	Red
Bu-te	Akashigata	Break o' Day
Carrara	Ama-no-sode (3)	Charm
Isani Gidui (1)	Doreen	Dignity
Lotus Queen (2)	Goddess	Hari-ai-nin (3)
Midway Island	Largo	Midnight Sun
Moon of Nippon	Sky Pilot	Mikado
Plainsman	Tamate Boku (2)	Mrs. Wilder Bancroft
Shaylor's Sunburst	Vanity	Nippon Beauty (2)
Toro-no-maki (3)	Westerner (1)	Nippon Brilliant (1)
	Yellow King	Rashoomon

ANEMONE—(Listed in catalogs as either Japanese or Doubles)

Aureolin (Japanese)—Pink guard peteals, yellow center fading to white.

SELECTING VARIETIES

Cathedral (Japanese)—Pink guard petals, yellow center fading to white.
Fancy Nancy (Japanese)—Cerise pink.
Gay Paree (Japanese)—Pink guard petals, white center. (3)
J. C. Legg (Double)—White guard petals, yellow center.
Laura Dessert (Double)—White guard petals, yellow center.
Madame Butterfly (Japanese)—Pink.
Nippon Gold (Japanese)—Pink guard petals, yellow center. (1)
Philomele (Japanese)—Pink guard petals, yellow center.
Prairie Afire (Japanese)—Pink guard petals, red center. (3)
Primevere (Double)—White guard petals, yellow center. (2)
Torpilleur (Japanese)—Red.
Ada Priscilla (Double)—White guard petals and yellow center, mid-season. One of the finest of all but did not appear on any list.

SEMI-DOUBLES

White or Blush	Pink	Red
A. G. Perry	Aerie	Albuquerque
Margaret Lough (3)	Auguste Dessert	Blazing Star
Marie Jacquin	Ave Maria	Chippewa (3)
Mildred May (3)	Banner Bright	Maestro
Minnie Shaylor (2)	Lady Alexandra	Mr. L. Van Leeuwen
Miss America (1)	Duff (1)	Red Goddess (1)
Nanette	Mrs. Deane Funk	Rosalie (3)
Rare China	Prairie Belle	Sinbad
Susan B. White	Phyllis Kelway (3)	The Mighty Mo (2)
White Rose	Silvia Saunders (2)	William F. Turner
	Spring Beauty	

DOUBLES

White
Alesia, late
Dr. J. H. Neeley, mid-season
Elsa Sass, late (2)

Blush
A. B. Franklin, late
Alice Harding, mid-season to late (3)

DOUBLES (continued)

White
Festiva Maxima, early (2)
Frances Willard, mid-season
Kelway's Glorious, early (1)
Le Cygne, early (3)
Mary E. Nicholls, mid-season to late
Mrs. J. V. Edlund, late
Victory, late

Blush
Baroness Schroeder, mid-season
Florence Nicholls, mid-season
Gardenia, mid-season
George W. Peyton, mid-season to late*
La Lorraine, mid-season to late
Mattie Lafuze, late
Moonstone, mid-season (2)
Nancy Nicholls, mid-season to late
Solange, late (1)
Tourangelle, mid season to late

*George W. Peyton sometimes does not open well and stem is not of the best but it is one of the most exquisitely colored of all peonies and its informality gives it added beauty. Loved by artists.

Light Pink
Auten's Pride, mid-season to late
Doris Cooper, late
Ella Christiansen, mid-season
Hansina Brand, late
Minuet, mid-season to late
Mrs. F. D. Roosevelt, early to mid-season (2)
Myrtle Gentry, late (3)
Nick Shaylor, late (1)
Reine Hortense, mid-season
Therese, early

Dark Pink
Blanche King, late (3)
Edulis Superba, early, fragrant
Helen Hayes, late
Loren Franklin, mid-season to late
Martha Bulloch, mid-season to late
Mons. Jules Elie, early (1)
Mrs. Livingston Farrand, mid-season to late
Sarah Bernhardt, mid-season to late (2)
Souv. de Louis Bigot, mid-season
Walter Faxon, mid-season to late

SELECTING VARIETIES

DOUBLES (continued)

Red
Felix Crousse, mid-season to late
Kansas, mid-season (1)
Karl Rosenfield, mid-season (2)
Longfellow, mid-season
Mary Brand, mid-season (3)
Mons. Martin Cahusac, mid-season
Philippe Rivoire, late, fragrant (1)
Richard Carvel, early
Ruth Elizabeth, late
Tempest, mid-season

Yellow
Oriental Gold, mid-season

ACCORDING TO PURPOSE

1. Good Garden Border Varieties

Suitable garden varieties depend on the individual border. This is a general list of some good garden varieties according to *height* and *time of blooming*. Select those that best fit your situation.

TALL

Extra Early
Any hybrid.
Angelo Cobb Freeborn—strong stems, distinctive red color, sometimes fails.
Garden Peace—good stems, beautiful white single, good bloomer.
Illini Warrior—extra tall, strong plant, red single.
White Innocence—distinctive white flower, single.

Early
Any single tall enough.
Big Ben—strong stems, rather loose globular flower, good red double, dependable.

Festiva Maxima—white double, dependable. If many blooms, stems may bend.

Mons. Jules Elie—stems not so strong, immense globular double flower, pink double.

Mid-season

Kansas—good in every way, light red double.

Sanctuary—similar to Titania (below), but often petals edged with red.

Titania—good stems, outstanding flowers, white semi-double.

Late

Mattie Lafuze—stems, foliage and flowers outstanding, blush double.

Mrs. W. L. Gumm—light pink double, strong stems, good bloomer, large well formed flowers.

MEDIUM HEIGHT—innumerable ones.

Extra Early

Any good hybrid.

Alexander Woollcott—brilliant crimson semi-double. Extra good color. Plant good.

Cardinal's Robe—Scarlet single. Plant good.

Carina—one of the best and most outstanding in color, bright red.

Chocolate Soldier—outstanding almost black, semi-double with brilliant yellow markings. Often Japanese type, single type or almost full double.

Claire de Lune—foliage and flower out of the ordinary, pale yellow. Single.

Flame—glowing color. Plant good. Single.

Helen Matthews—brilliant red, semi-double. Expensive. Stems good.

Sophie—brilliant pink. Plant good. Single.

Many others equally as good.

Early

Any single not tall. Any early Japanese type.

Aerie—pale pink to white semi-double, fine plant. Floriferous.

Kelway's Glorious—white fragrant double. Fair stems. Floriferous.

Mons. Jules Elie—immense globular flower. Should be supported. Pink double.

Mid-season—Hundreds of all types except singles.
Adolphe Rousseau—tallest of medium height, showy crimson flowers sometimes almost single, often semi-double and double.
James Kelway, blush double, good plant, floriferous.
Lady Alexandra Duff—light pink, strong stemmed, semi-double.
Miss America—large flower, blush to white, semi-double. Good stems slightly bending at times.

Late

Elsa Sass—grand in every way.
Mary E. Nicholls—fine plant and foliage, large, white double.
Nick Shaylor—also one of the ten best in every way.
Philippe Rivoire—fragrant red. Fair plant, dark-red double. Fair stems.

DWARF

Extra Early

Tenuifolia and macrophylla hybrids.

Early

Mme. de Verneville—fragrant, white double, stems not so good. Floriferous. Red markings.
Octavie Demay—light pink double, fine stems, floriferous.

Mid-season

Not many outstanding.

Late

Joseph Christie. Grand white double, yellow shaded.

2. For Emphasis or Spectacular Effects
There are also many fine varieties not listed .

Extra Early

Any extra brilliant hybrid.

Early

Champlain, tall strong stems, makes large plant with extra large smooth light green foliage. Opens slightly blush.
Dawn Pink, brilliant pink single. Good plant, also floriferous.

Krinkled White, abundance of medium sized flowers on medium tall upstanding stems.

Pico, white single, large flowers, immense foliage, tall.

Silvia Saunders, rather dwarf grower, compact plant, usually hidden by its charming almost single medium sized flowers of light pink.

Sparkling Star, same effects as Dawn Pink. See above.

Mid-season

The brilliant red and pink Japanese types are excellent.

Break o'Day, Jap.;, contrasting shades of unusual reds. Good plant.

Doreen, brilliant pink guards, bright yellow staminodes. Tall. Fair stems. Japanese.

Dragon's Nest, distinctive coloring and placement of petals and staminodes. Good plant. Strongly contrasting red and yellow.

Garden Princess, splendid plant habit, medium height, beautiful light pink semi-double.

John Howard Wigell, dark brilliant pink of distinctive shade. Rather dwarf and spreading habit.

June Rose, extra bright pink, double, with some stamens showing. Medium height and medium sized flowers.

Largo, large flowers, strong medium tall plants. Good stems. Dark pink.

Mabel L. Gore, brilliant dark pink double. Fine plant.

Nippon Brilliant, extra bright red and brilliant yellow staminodes. Medium sized flowers usually. Tall good stems. Japanese.

Sword Dance, darker red, not so tall. Japanese.

Late

Mattie Lafuze, often immense flowers of blush pink, strong tall stems. Dark green foliage heavily ribbed and large.

Mildred May, may be late midseason. Extra fine plant, covered with medium sized pure white flowers often born in triangular clusters. Circles of stamens intermingled with petals. Tall and upstanding. Foliage medium to large, extra good.

SELECTING VARIETIES 81

Yosemite, medium tall plant, fine foliage and stem. Exquisitely tinted white, double yellow tints.

The most spectacular of all are the many brilliantly colored hybrids, followed by the brilliant Japanese types. For both foliage and flowers, Laddie, an extra early dwarf hybrid with finely cut foliage and brilliant scarlet single flowers is outstanding.

Annisquam, Champlain, Florence Ellis, Garden Princess, Largo, Mildred May, Minuet and Pico make grand plants and flowers.

3. For Outstanding Foliage

Look over varieties listed under "Spectacular Effects". Many have outstanding foliage. Others with outstanding foliage include:

Amberglow, double, amber tinted white.

Flamingo, early semi-double, light pink.

Lady Aristook, white flowers with some red markings, not so outstanding but has tall, fine, strong stems and showy foliage.

Lowell Thomas, red double with rounded, thickly set foliage, quite distinctive.

Macrophylla, a low spreading plant has extra large uncut foliage. Its hybrids have the same characteristics.

Mlokosewitschi, often hard to grow, has small yellow single flowers with red stems which contrast with its distinctive foliage.

Tenuifolia, dwarf plants with brilliant red flowers, both single and double forms, and cosmos like foliage.

4. For Fragrance

Some people like the strong pollen odor of the singles and semi-doubles, others do not. The following peonies have a pleasing fragrance.

Edulis Superba, double, dark pink, early.

Kelway's Glorious, double, white, early mid-season.

Mandaleen, double, light pink, medium late.

Mrs. R. M. Bacheller, double, white with some stamens, mid-season.

Myrtle Gentry, double, light pink, late.
Philippe Rivoire, double, red, mid-season.
Sistie, double pink that fades to white, late mid-season to late.

BY COLOR AND SEASON

It must be noted that color and season of bloom vary with the climate and situation.

White or Blush

EXTRA EARLY
Camellia, SD.
Chalice, S.
Early Windflower, S.
Garden Peace. S.
White Innocence, S.

EARLY
Festiva Maxima, D.
Isani Gidui, J.
James Kelway, D.
Kelway's Glorious, D.
Le Cygne, D.
Le Jour, S.
Minnie Shaylor, SD.
Mrs. Edward Harding, D.
Pico, S.
Shaylor's Sunburst, J.

MID-SEASON
Alice Harding, D.
Baroness Schroeder, D.
Dr. J. H. Neeley, D.
Florence Nicholls, D.
Gardenia, D.
Krinkled White, S.
Lotus Queen, J.
Margaret Lough, SD.
Moon of Nippon, J.
White Gold, J.

LATE MID-SEASON OR LATE
Alesia, D.
Alma Hansen, D.
Dorothy J., D.
Elsa Sass, D.
Mary E. Nicholls, D.
Mattie Lafuze, D.
Mildred May, SD
Nancy Nicholls Blush, D.
Solange, Blush, D.
Victory, D.
White Rose, SD.

SELECTING VARIETIES

Yellow
Claire de Lune, S.—Extra Early
Moonrise, S.—Extra Early
Oriental Gold, D.—Mid-Season

White with Yellow Centers (Yellow fades to white with age)

EARLY	MID-SEASON	LATE
Carolina Moon, D.	Ada Priscilla, D.	Couronne d'Or, D.
Duchesse de Nemours, D.	Gleam of Gold, D.	Joseph Christie, D.
Laura Dessert, D.	Golden Bracelet, D.	Moonglow, D.
	Golden Dawn, D.	Yosemite, D.
	Matchless Beauty, D.	
	Primevere, D.	

Light Pink

EXTRA EARLY	MID-SEASON	LATE MID-SEASON OR LATE
Arbutus Pink, S.	Auten's Pride, D.	Annisquam, D.
Birthday, S.	Ella Christiansen, D.	Dolorodell, D.
Lovely Rose, SD.	Mischief, S.	Doris Cooper, D.
Madrigal, S.	Moonstone, D.	Mandaleen, D.
Shell Pink, S.	Prairie Belle, SD.	Minuet, D.
	Reine Hortense, D.	Myrtle Gentry, D.
	Seashell, S.	Nick Shaylor, D.
	Vanity, J.	Tourangelle, D.
	Victory Chateau Thierry, D.	Virginia Lee, D.
	Westerner, J.	

EARLY
Aerie, SD.
Josette, S.
Lady Alexandra Duff, SD.
Madame Calot, D.
Mrs. F. D. Roosevelt, D.

Light Pink, Early (continued)
Pride of Langport, S.
Silvia Saunders, SD.
Therese, D.
Westhill, D.
Yellow King, J.

Dark Pink

EXTRA EARLY	MID-SEASON	LATE MID-SEASON OR LATE
Flame, S.	Ama-no-sode, J.	Anne Bigger, D.
Laura Magnuson, SD.	Auguste Dessert, SD.	Blanche King, D.
Ludovica, SD.	Hermione, D.	Ensign Moriarty, D.
Salmon Beauty, D.	June Rose, D.	Helen Hayes, D.
Salmon Glow, S.	Largo, J.	Loren Franklin, D.
	Martha Bulloch, D.	Pres. F. D. Roosevelt, D.
	Mrs. Livingston Farrand, D.	Sky Pilot, J.
	Nippon Gold, A.J.	Tamate Boku, J.
	Pink Wonder, D.	Tondeleyo, D.
	Sarah Bernhardt, D.	Walter Faxon, D.

EARLY
Dawn Pink, S.
Edulis Superba, D.
Harriet Olney, S.
Helen, S.
L'Etincelante, S.
Mons. Jules Elie, D.
Off. rosea superba, D.
Prairie Rose, S.

NOTE: Some of the above are sometimes found in light pink lists.

Red

EXTRA EARLY	MID-SEASON	LATE MID-SEASON OR LATE
Alexander Woollcott, SD.	Adolphe Rousseau, D-SD.	Bonanza, D.

SELECTING VARIETIES

Red (continued)

EXTRA EARLY
Chocolate Soldier, SD.
Golden Glow, S.
Laddie, S.
Red Charm, D.

MID-SEASON
Chippewa, SD.
Dignity, J.
Hari-ai-nin, J.
Kansas, D.
Karl Rosenfield, D.
Longfellow, D.
Mary Brand, D.
Nippon Beauty, J.
Red Goddess, SD.
Sword Dance, J.
Tempest, D.

LATE MID-SEASON OR LATE
Charm, J.
Felix Crousse, D.
King Midas, D.
Lowell Thomas, D.
Philippe Rivoire, D.
Ruth Clay, D.
Ruth Elizabeth, D.

EARLY
Arcturus, S.
Big Ben, D.
Cherry Hill, D.
Flander's Fields, S.
Imperial Red, S.
Man O' War, S.
Nippon Brilliant, J.
Officinalis rubra plena, D.
Richard Carvel, D.
President Lincoln, S.
Note: This list could be expanded many times.

Other Colors

EXTRA EARLY
Ballerina, SD, greenish yellow.
Carina, SD, scarlet.
Green Ivory, S, light green.
Lavender, SD, lilac.

RECOMMENDED FOR THE SOUTH

George W. Peyton of Rapidan, Virginia, recommends the following herbaceous varieties for southern gardeners:

For Beginners

Kelway's Glorious	White	Double	Early
Mons. Jules Elie	Pink	Double	Early
Sea Shell	Pink	Single	Mid-season
Karl Rosenfield	Red	Double	Mid-season
Shaylor's Sunburst	Blush	Japanese	Mid-season

For General Garden Use

Elsa Sass	White to Pink	Double	Late
Florence Nicholls	Blush	Double	Mid-season
Therese	Light Pink	Double	Early
Philippe Rivoire	Dark Red	Double	
Minnie Shaylor	Blush	Semi-Double	Late Mid-season
Le Jour	White	Single	Early
Imperial Red	Light Red	Single	Early
Ama-no-sode	Pink	Japanese	Mid-season
Isani Gidui	White	Japanese	Mid-season
Sword Dance	Red	Japanese	Mid-season

RECOMMENDED FOR CANADA

We received the following letter from R. W. Oliver, Horticulturist—Ornamentals, Plant Research Institute, Ottawa, Canada.

"Herbaceous peonies are among the most successful perennials in Canadian gardens because of their hardiness. One of the finest collections in the country was maintained by the late Mr. C. M. Clarke near Beaverlodge, Alberta which is over four hundred miles north of the U. S. border. The deep rich clay loam of that area suited their taste in spite of the −50°F temperatures in winter.

"Likewise in the light sandy garden at the Central Experimental Farm at Ottawa, peonies have been grown with success for the last seventy years. While space limits us to approximately two hundred varieties at one time, something over six hundred different varieties have been tried. Replacements are made whenever a variety is discarded because of disease or inferiority. As the collection is moved from one location to another every ten or twelve years, this operation gives an opportunity for more numerous replacements of varieties.

"So long as we stick to herbaceous varieties, winter does very little damage, as we usually have sufficient snow to provide good insulation. The open winter of 1938, when the collection was covered by a sheet of ice which resulted from mild weather, was the only one to cause much damage in the last twenty-five years. We do not use mulch except over new varieties planted in early September to make sure that they are well established before the ground freezes in early November.

"Our chief battles have been with diseases. Botrytis which seems ever on the alert in cool damp summers, requires constant watching and the removal of affected stems as soon as symptoms are observed. Modern fungicides applied just as foliage is opening and again just after bloom have reduced the damage from this pest. More baffling is a sort of "stunt" that causes the plant to put out numerous thin dwarfed stems with no flower buds. For years we referred to it as Lemoine's disease, which no one seemed clear about. Now being more fashionable, we are inclined to blame it on a virus, but so far have not isolated the culprit. It is quite distinct from the Ring Spot and Leaf Curl viruses that also affect peonies. So far we have no adequate defence but to rogue out and burn affected plants and to sterilize the soil where they have grown before replanting.

"Insects do little damage to peonies directly but aphids and ants may spread the above virus, so we wage war on them with Lindane.

"Unfortunately we cannot devote funds necessary to keep our collection abreast of the newest varieties and have tried very few of the new "hybrids". We hope to make arrangements to obtain "guests" from some of the more generous originators, so that the best of these seedlings can be seen by the three thousand people that go through our display garden each week during the summer months. Peonies are usually one of the chief attractions from June 15-30 though the dates vary from year to year as much as five days on either side.

"Under our conditions many of the older varieties have proven of more value for garden purposes than some recent introductions we have had. The following varieties are recommended most highly for our section of the country."

DOUBLE	SEMI-DOUBLE	SINGLE & JAPANESE
	White	
Festiva Maxima	Couronne d'Or	Isani Gidui, Japanese
Kelway's Glorious	Rare China*	Krinkled White, Single
Le Cygne		
Mrs. Edward Harding		
	Blush	
Baroness Schroeder	Lady Alexandra Duff	Josette, Single*
Blush	Marie Jacquin	Toro-no-maki, Japanese
Solange		
Tourangelle		
	Light Pink	
Georgiana Shaylor	Silvia Saunders	Helen, Single*
Hansina Brand		Kukenijishi, Japanese
Milton Hill		
Myrtle Gentry		
	Medium Pink	
Edulis Superba	Phyllis Kelway	Largo, Japanese*
La France		Tokio, Japanese
Martha Bulloch		
Sarah Bernhardt		
Walter Faxon		
	Dark Pink	
Blanche King	Auguste Dessert	L'Etincelante, Single
	Reine Baronet	Tamate-Boku, Japanese

*Newer expensive varieties

SELECTING VARIETIES

Red

Adolphe Rousseau
Cherry Hill
Felix Crousse
Karl Rosenfield
Mons. Martin
   Cahuzac
Mary Brand
Philippe Rivoire

Instituteur Doriat
Anemone (J.)
Mikado, red,
Japanese

SOME PEYTON NOTES ON VARIETIES

The oldest named variety in cultivation: Officinalis rubra plena, about 2,000 years.

The oldest named varieties imported into Europe from China: Fragrans (1805); Whitleyi (Queen Victoria) 1808. Peonies may have been imported into Holland from China, early in the 17th century.

The most beloved and most famous: Festiva Maxima, double white flecked carmine.

The most fragrant: Edulis Superba, double, dark pink.

The "One Best": Kelway's Glorious, beautiful double white flower, good stems, dependable bloomer and fragrant to an unusual degree. So voted by people from New Zealand to the Peace River country of Canada.

The most popular: Mons. Jules Elie, double dark pink and Nick Shaylor, double light pink.

The most perfect flower: Le Cygne, double white.

The most beautifully colored: Mrs. Livingston Farrand, double light pink. Solange, 2nd, double blush. Others: Walter Faxon, double pink; Ramona Lins, double blush pink; Geo. W. Peyton, double blush.

The "loveliest": Japanese type, Isani Gidui and White Rose, a semi-double.

The most charming: Elsa Sass, double white, and Mrs. F. D. Roosevelt, double light pink.

The purest white: Mildred May, semi-double, and Amalia Olson (new double).

The purest pink: Mrs. Livingston Farrand, double light pink, and Walter Faxon, double pink.

The only true yellow double: Oriental Gold also known as Aurea, Golden Dream, Yokihi (Japanese name). Native of Japan.

The blackest: Sable (hybrid.). The bluest: Lavender (hybrid). and Blue Rose (Lins), a double.

HERBACEOUS SPECIES

The species are of extreme importance to the botanist since it is from this source they make their classifications. Many gardeners also find the species of particular interest since a knowledge of species forms a good background for understanding the inter-specific hybrids being developed today. Many catalogs list species for sale and they are sought by both collectors and hybridizers. We are listing some of the more prominent. All the species listed have only one flower to a stem except emodi, lactiflora and veitchi and their varieties. The flowers are always single, however officinalis and tenuifolia both have double forms.

The average American gardener will not be interested in growing the species. You must be a real fan to want to grow anomala. Cambessedesi and wittmanniana are very hard to grow. Many others will be deeply disappointing and equally difficult, so keep this in mind.

ANOMALA—Early, bright scarlet-crimson. Cut leaves. Native of Russia and Central Asia.

ARIETINA—Flowers red, but vary to a soft rose-pink. Native to Italy, Greece and Asia Minor.

BROTERI—Cup-shaped rose flowers with yellow center. Charming shiny-leaved plant. Native to Spain and Portugal.

CAMBESSEDESI—Deep rose, blossoms medium sized. Native to Western Mediterranean Islands.

CLUSI—Cup-shaped white flowers with golden stamens, fine green leaves. Native to Crete.

CORIACEA—Rose red. Used by hybridizers to produce lavender,

SELECTING VARIETIES

violet and light purple hybrids. Its hybrids are the nearest to blue we have. Native to Spain, Morocco and Algeria.

DAURICA—Deep rose-red with yellow center, oval leaves. Native to Crimea, Asia Minor and Caucasus.

EMODI—Handsome fern-like foliage with nodding white flowers. Tallest of all. Native to India.

HUMILIS—Deep red flowers. Native to Spain and France.

JAPONICA—White flowers. Native to Japan.

LACTIFLORA (syns. albiflora, chinensis, edulis and sinensis)— White. Chief source of the Chinese or common peony. Native to Siberia, Manchuria, Mongolia, China and Tibet.

MASCULA—Red-rose, purplish shadings. Native from England to Russia and south to Asia Minor.

MLOKOSEWITSCHI—Lemon sherbet, transparent yellow flowers, light grey-green foliage. Not reliable, often just fades away after a year or two but where it does grow it makes a beautiful plant. Native to region between the Black and Caspian Seas.

MOLLIS—Fine red, also white. Gardens only.

OBOVATA—White to rose-purple. Native to Siberia, Manchuria, China and Japan. Oval leaves.

OBOVATA WILLMOTTIAE—Gorgeous white with immense round leaves. Native to China.

OFFICINALIS—Red. Native to southern Europe.

PEREGRINA—Glistening red. Native to the Balkans.

PEREGRINA LOBATA—A dwarf plant with brilliant vermilion flowers. Blooms early in June in North. Native to the Balkans.

RUSSI—Lovely rose color. Native to the Western Mediterranean Islands.

TENUIFOLIA—Fern-leaved peony. Most finely cut of all peony foliage. Small, gay, deep crimson flowers. Var. rosea is a single pink. Native to Bulgaria, Caucasus. Early.

TENUIFOLIA LATIFOLIA—Very early, rosy-red single, bright and free flowering, very vigorous.

VEITCHI—Magenta blush-pink. Native to China.

VEITCHI WOODWARDI—Magenta blush-pink. Native to Western China.

WITTMANNIANA—The first yellow peony to be discovered. Creamy yellow flowers, pale green carpels. Native to region between the Black and Caspian Seas. Charming species. Blooms early with tall May tulips.

WITTMANNIANA MACROPHYLLA—Vies with P. tenuifolia for the honor of opening the peony season. Flowers around May 12 in the north. Has creamy-white goblet flowers, largest of all peony leaves, highly glossy with odor of boxwood.

6

Hybrids

The hybrid peony has won a place for itself in the average garden, as well as in the fanciers' collection. Every garden should have a few hybrids to supplement lactiflora and officinalis, in this way lengthening the season of bloom and adding new colors and flower forms.

A hybrid peony is produced by crossing a variety of one species with one of another. The scientific breeder or hybridizer makes crosses of known parentage in an effort to work toward a definite goal or objective.

Early in the nineteenth century lactiflora was brought from China to England in three varieties: Fragrans, pink (1805); Whitleyi, white (1808) and Humei, dark pink (1810). One or more of these three varieties were found in nearly all old gardens. These varieties were known for their vigorous constitution and resistance to disease. Most of our peonies are of lactiflora origin. In reading about the peony remember that the words albiflora, chinensis, edulis and sinensis denote the same species as lactiflora, they are synonymous. Early crossings were with lactiflora and officinalis. The majority of officinalis hybrids are notable for a brilliance and purity of color. The early red double found in our grandmother's garden was officinalis rubra plena. Alba plena and rosea plena, with a variation rosea superba, are two other varieties commonly grown.

The great French hybridizer, Victor Lemoine, at the beginning of the century crossed lactiflora with the species wittmanniana, producing for us four new hybrids: Avant Garde, a single pink and Le Printemps, Mai Fleuri and Messagere, three white singles with yellow and green tints.

AMERICAN HYBRIDIZERS

Since 1924 the number of American hybrids have increased by leaps and bounds and now they make a very long list and this undoubtedly is only a beginning in the peony hybridizing field. However, hybridizing is a slow process requiring infinite patience. It takes one year for germination, another three for new hybrids to reach blooming size, and another three to obtain mature performance. In about 1917 in the United States Lyman D. Glassock of Elwood, Illinois, and Prof. A. P. Saunders of Clinton, New York, independently, and a thousand miles apart, started working toward a similar goal, crossing species to prolong the season of bloom, widen and vary the color range, height, form and size and produce better plants. Edward Auten, Jr. of Princeville, Illinois, must havve started planting hybrid seed shortly after that time Mr. Glassock's Legionaire at Des Moines, Iowa, in 1924 was the first showing of a hybrid in this country. Col. Benjamin M. Guppy of Melrose, Massachusetts, began to hybridize about the same time and exhibited some of his hybrids at the Massachusetts Horticultural Society in Boston. He celebrated his ninetieth birthday last May and is still very much interested in the peony, doing some hybridizing in his back yard.

Enthused by the success of these men, others were encouraged to join the group: Mrs. Mary E. G. Freeborn of Proctor, Vermont, W. S. Bockstoce of Pittsburgh, Pennsylvania and Walter Mains of Belle Center, Ohio.

In the beginning these hybridizers used mainly the species lactiflora and officinalis and their varieties, which produced in general shades of pink and red. Prof. Saunders became adventuresome and used almost every available species. Dr. Earle B.

White, formerly of Maryland and now of Florida, followed Prof. Saunders' pattern and made the first known cross between the yellow species, mlokosewitschi, and lactiflora. A pale yellow single, Claire de Lune, was the result after making 4000 crosses.

The extraordinary results already obtained with the hybrid peonies give great promise and hope for the future. Many of the originations of these hybridizers are now on the market. They are scarce, so should be ordered in ample time. They vary in price from $5.00 to $50.00 a root. The wide color range includes every color except a true blue.

With the discovery of the creamy yellow wittmanniana and the light yellow mlokosewitschi hopes mounted that a yellow double would soon be on its way. The greatest success along this line was achieved by Dr. White in his origination of the pale yellow single, Claire de Lune, a variety of charm and distinction. Now with the discovery of the new yellow double "Oriental Gold" we have the only double yellow and the deepest yellow in a herbaceous peony. It was first listed as "Aurea". Certainly the correct name is Yokihi after the most noted of Japanese Geisha girls but since it was sent to this country under a number of different names it was registered as Oriental Gold. It is listed in one catalog as "Golden Dream". No one knows the origin or species from which it came, it is probably a hybrid, perhaps of a species still unknown except in its native habitat.

The pink hybrids embrace all shades including salmons and corals. There are crimsons of all intensities, black-reds, purples, lilacs and lavenders. The coriacea hybrids are a lovely clear pale lilac. Green Ivory is a white with greenish tints. The hybrid "Sable" is the nearest approach to black.

Among the hybrids one finds the earliest to flower, the shortest and tallest, the sturdiest and most graceful of all herbaceous peonies. Mostly singles, many are semi-doubles and some full doubles, with a few of the Japanese type.

Some of the herbaceous hybrids in some locations will die to the ground naturally, often in late July or August, much sooner than the lactifloras which wait for frost. When this happens many think they have lost the plant but it is just its nature. Of course, this does spoil the foliage effect of these hybrids in late season.

Herbaceous hybrids in those 10° to 20° below zero climates (for extended periods) must be protected to prevent severe damage or loss from lack of snow covering.

We are describing just a few of our many favorite hybrids.

We saw Red Charm, a Glasscock introduction, in the Stedman' Buttrick garden (Concord, Mass.) this spring. It blooms a week earlier than the regulars, is a bright, rich ruby-red with tall strong stems, a very fine plant and surely one of the finest red doubles in existence.

Chocolate Soldier, an Auten introduction, is early, an exceptionally fine flower with rich black-red petals (almost black) and contrasting yellow dots on the center petals.

Claire de Lune (parentage Mons. Jules Elie x mlokosewitschi) was originated by Dr. White and introduced by Wild and Son in 1954. It is an equisite pale ivory yellow with crinkled petals, yellow filaments and orange anthers forming an attractive orange center. Its stems are thin but very stiff, a really elegant early single peony.

Five fine semi-double hybrids in the Saunders group of "lobatas" (lactiflora x lobata) which bloom through the first half of June include Lovely Rose, a "creamy" rose pink and all that its name implies. Ludovica, a very large clear rose pink with prettily rounded petals and Nathalie with intense clear rose petals and a magnificent flat bloom, semi-double or more. Alexander Woollcott, a brilliant red and Carina, a shining scarlet, vie for honors in the group of reds.

POPULAR HYBRID VARIETIES ACCORDING TO COLOR

(as voted by members of the American Peony Society—1958)

White
Archangel, single
Campagna, single
Chalice, single
Requiem, single
Starlight, ivory, single
White Innocence, single

Yellow
Claire de Lune, ivory, single
Daystar, single
Mlokosewitschi, single (species)
Moonrise, single
Rushlight, single
Sunlight, single

Pink
Dainty Lass, Japanese
Elizabeth Foster, single
Eros, single
Eventide, single
Janice, single
Laura Magnuson, semi-double
Lotus Bloom, semi-double
Lovely Rose, semi-double
Ludovica, semi-double
May Dawn, single
Nathalie, semi-double
Queen Rose, semi-double
   to double
Roselette, single
Salmon Beauty, double
Salmon Glow, single
Sophie, single
Victoria Lincoln, double

Red
Alexander Woollcott, semi-
   double
Freeborn
Angelo Cobb Freeborn, double
Bright Knight, single
Carina, semi-double
Chocolate Soldier, semi-double
Crusader, double
Flame, single
Gay Cavalier, single
Golden Glow, single
Helen Matthews, semi-double
Illini Belle, semi-double
John Harvard, single
Laddie, single
Mahogany, single
Red Charm, double
Red Red Rose, semi-double
Robert W. Auten, double
Rose Marie, double
Veritas, semi-double
Walter Mains, Japanese

MYRON D. BIGGER HERBACEOUS HYBRID SELECTIONS

Myron D. Bigger of Topeka, Kansas, President of the American Peony Society, lists his choice of herbaceous hybrids and makes some personal comments.

"The time has arrived when every peony lover should plant a few herbaceous hybrid peonies. To my knowledge there is no other group of peonies that contain the wonderful bright reds and pinks the hybrids do. [Ed. Note: Tree peony enthusiasts may disagree.] Most hybrids I have grown are good growers and have been very free from disease.

"A large percentage of the named hybrids are single or semi-double but some are full double and are very lovely indeed. Your peony collection is not complete without some of these new up-to-date peonies.

"As the single hybrid varieties open, most of them are like immense goblets and the colors will dazzle your eyes. Many of them are as bright as the Oriental poppies.

"Because the hybrids are predominantly red, I shall begin with that color. I shall not try to list them as to my preference because I like one variety best this year and liked another one best last year. I shall list only varieties I have grown and shall take them alphabetically. I have omitted some fine ones and I know it. Not because they are not good, but because I have never grown them or have not grown them long enough to risk an opinion.

"Some hybrids are a little difficult to divide while others are very prolific. Only experience will tell you which is which. Like all plants, some varieties will do well in one location, or one soil, and others will do better some place else.

Red

"Alexander Woollcott, semi-double, crimson.
Avelyn, red, bomb.
Cardinal's Robe, very bright single.
Carina, very bright, semi-double to double.
Chocolate Soldier, very dark, bomb type.

Diana Parks, very bright double.
Golden Glow, single, orange-scarlet, large flower.
Jean E. Bockstoce, double.
Marta, double.
Old Main, red, bomb.
Orange Glory, very tall, semi-double with a little orange.
Rosedale, semi-double.
Rose Marie, double.
Red Charm, large, fully double bomb type.
Red Monarch, double with some purple.
Red Signal, small cups, make fine corsages.
Sophie, very bright. On the borderline but really a deep cherry pink.
Tecumseh, very bright single.
Topeka, double.
Veritas, dark semi-double.

Pink

"Angelo Cobb Freeborn, fully double and an extremely pretty plant.
Ceceilia, enormous single.
Janice, single.
Laura Magnuson, semi-double.
Queen of the Dawn, pink single.
Victoria Lincoln, double on established plants.

White, Cream or Yellow

"Chalice, white single.
Claire de Lune, light yellow, ten petaled single.
Daystar, cream, single.
Moonrise, light yellow, single.
Oriental Gold, yellow double. I believe this is a hybrid."

HYBRIDS BLOOM FOR A MONTH OR MORE

In general, the hybrid herbaceous and tree peonies flower at about the same time, continuing over a period of about a month starting, in the north, around May 5th to 15th and blooming for three to four weeks, with the proper selection. The following list will show you how, if you choose carefully, selecting the right parentage, starting with the tenuifolias and ending with the lobatas, you are able to have a sequence of constantly blooming hybrid plants for a period of a month. The lobatas are the last hybrids to bloom and they come with the lactifloras or Chinese peonies in the first two weeks of June in the north.

EARLYBIRD (woodwardi x tenuifolia)—One of the first peonies to bloom. Handsome little plant with finely cut foliage and an abundance of bright crimson flowers.

PLAYMATE (mlokosewitschi x tenuifolia)—Small bright rosy flowers held high above fern-like foliage.

DAYSTAR (tenuifolia x mlokosewitschi)—Third generation. Single goblets of clear pale yellow, about 3 feet tall with red stems and handsomely pointed leaves.

ROSELETTE (lactiflora x second generation tenuifolia x mlokosewitschi)—Prettily-formed large flowers of light rose pink. Blooms just after middle of May.

EARLY WINDFLOWER (veitchi x emodi)—Blooms about May 20. Graceful and unusual plants. Flowers like white anemones, slightly nodding, borne on tall stems. Foliage fern-like and handsome. Sets no seeds.

CHALICE (lactiflora x macrophylla)—Large, pure shimmering white flowers, long silky stamens on good stems, about 3 feet tall. Immense dark glossy leaves. Blooms mid-May in the north.

LATE WINDFLOWER (beresowskyi x emodi)—Almost exactly like Early Windflower but blooms one week later.

FIRELIGHT—Pink, combines four species; lactiflora, officinalis,

HYBRIDS

macrophylla and mlokosewitschi. Deep rose pink with deeper flares and crimson stigmas. Gold center.

STARLIGHT—Ivory-yellow, 5"-6" wide, sometimes faintly blushed. Small creamy center. Fine. Combines 4 species as does Firelight.

EMBLEM (lactiflora x officinalis)—Single deep lusterless red of fine substance. Late May or early June in north.

REWARD (lactiflora x decora)—Good and very early red, dark maroon single, blooms last week in May.

PAGEANT (lactiflora x coriacea)—Fine tall, light rose pink, before the lobata pinks begin. Immense splash of long gold stamens. The heart alone is 4" across.

GARDEN PEACE (lactiflora x macrophylla)—Great single white flowers, several on a stem, with gold and crimson centers. Its side blooms give it a long season. The dark red stems are so tall they may need a stake. Early June in the north.

REQUIEM (lactiflora x macrophylla)—Another lovely waxy-white single about one week later than Garden Peace. Fine substance and foliage.

JANICE (lactiflora x lobata)—The first of the lobata hybrids to bloom and one of the best, perhaps *the* best. Pale salmon, very vigorous. Tall and erect.

CLAUDIA (lactiflora x lobata)—Semi-double, opens light cherry, becoming pale salmon pink, golden heart. Blooms first half of June in the north.

For bloom during the first two weeks in June there is a long list of wonderful hybrids from which to choose. Following are just a few of the many choice ones on the market today:

ALEXANDER WOOLLCOTT—Brilliant red, semi-double.

BRIGHT KNIGHT—Cherry-red, large semi-double; tall, stiff stems.

CAMELLIA—Large semi-double white with silky luster and flushed peach-pink.

CHOCOLATE SOLDIER—Large semi to full double, maroon almost black with yellow dots on center petals.

CLAIRE DE LUNE—Pale ivory-yellow, single.

CRUSADER—Semi-double bright red with yellow center of golden stamens.

DAINTY LASS—Japanese type, cup-shaped soft coral-pink flowers.

GOLDEN GLOW—Cup-shaped, brilliant orange-scarlet flowers with golden stamens. Single to semi-double. Tall, sturdy stems. Foliage coarse, but an attractive green.

HORIZON—Tall. Very large flesh colored single with enormous center of golden stamens.

JOHN HARVARD—Georgeous ruby-red single that often blooms almost double with attractive golden center.

MONTEZUMA—Bright crimson goblets with shining rounded petals. Tall heavy stems.

NADIA—Deep bright cherry, wide-open blooms.

RED CHARM—Brilliant ruby double.

7

Making New Plantings

BUYING PEONY ROOTS

For the average gardener a standard division is the best root to buy. It is a piece cut from a plant with at least three good roots branching from the crown and 3 to 5 eyes or buds for next year's growth. The roots should be around ½" to 1" in diameter, not too large, and 4" to 6" long. With roots too long

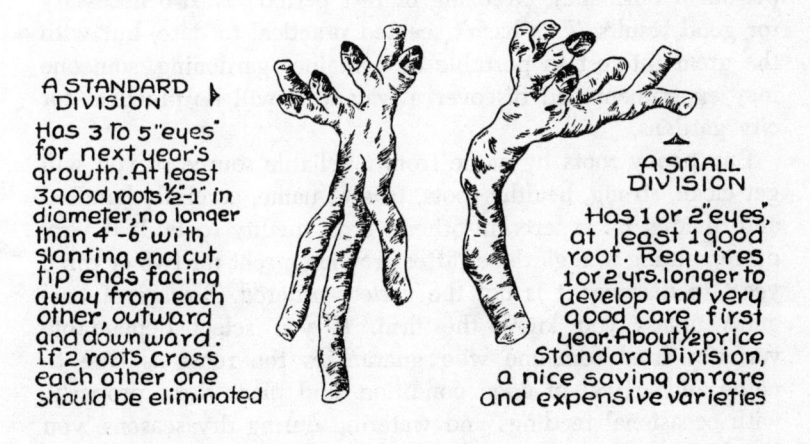

A STANDARD DIVISION ▶
Has 3 to 5 "eyes" for next year's growth. At least 3 good roots ½-1" in diameter, no longer than 4"-6" with slanting end cut. tip ends facing away from each other, outward and downward. If 2 roots cross each other one should be eliminated

A SMALL DIVISION
Has 1 or 2 "eyes", at least 1 good root. Requires 1 or 2 yrs. longer to develop and very good care first year. About ½ price Standard Division, a nice saving on rare and expensive varieties

and too numerous, little growth will be made for several years. The end cuts should be sloping with the tip ends facing away from each other and outward and downward. If two roots cross each other, one should be eliminated. A one year plant is usually considered equivalent to a standard division.

A small division with 1 or 2 eyes and one good root is sold for about half the price of the standard division. They will do as well, but will require a year or two longer to develop and need very good care the first year, especially during a long, hot dry summer. When buying expensive varieties, this can be a means of quite a saving however.

In southern states a 2 or 3 year old plant gives best results, although carefully cared for small divisions will give good results too. Any plant over 3 years should be divided before planting and then the divisions given a year or two to recover and come back.

Specimen plants can be obtained as tub or pot-grown plants for display on the terrace or planting out but are more costly and require more care. If not to be replanted in the garden in the fall, they should be given large enough containers so they can grow undisturbed for many years. A sixty day or more period of dormancy (freezing or rest period) is also necessary for good results. This hasn't seemed practical to date, but with the great interest in portable or container gardening, someone may experiment and discover a way so it will be practical for city gardens.

Buy peony roots by name from a reliable source so you will get clean, strong, healthy roots, true to name, carefully handled and divided by experts, in other words, quality roots. It is very disappointing to a gardener after growing a root for two or three years to discover it is not the variety ordered. Beware of bargains unless you know the firm. If you select dependable varieties from someone who guarantees the roots as true to name and arrival in good condition, and plant them properly, with occasional feedings and watering during dry seasons, you should have lovely peonies. Small, shrivelled roots, which have been drying out in open baskets in stores, will not make as good a showing as husky, freshly dug roots obtained from peony growers.

It makes absolutely no difference whether a root is grown in the north, east, south or west, if it is from a reliable grower. They all will do equally well for you when properly planted. Customers in Canada have had good success with roots grown in Virginia. Peony roots do not need to be grown nearby.

Place your order early enough so you will have the roots in time for September and October planting. Nurseries that specialize in peonies start shipping freshly dug roots late in August.

CHOOSING THE SITE

You cannot be too careful in deciding the best location for your peonies. Choosing the varieties to plant and the place to plant them are the two most important decisions. They live easily and graciously in an environment suited to their taste and since they represent a lifetime investment, give plenty of consideration to the best location. Once planted a peony will thrive in the same place for twenty-five to fifty years or more.

1. Peonies do require more space than most perennials and do not like to be disturbed, so if possible give 3 feet of space to each plant to allow room for it to grow for years without being moved.
2. Peony roots should not be crowded and resent the intrusion of roots from large trees, shrubs or hedge plants in their ground area, since the roots will rob them of the food and water they need for healthy growth. The strong stems, heavy foliage and masses of large flowers require plenty of food and drink.
3. Peonies need full sun. They can take some shade but should have at least one-half day of sun to do well. A light protection from direct sunlight after the flowers open will save them from fading too rapidly.
4. It is an advantage to have them sheltered from severe winds.

5. Good drainage is essential. This is a point that cannot be too strongly stressed.
6. Never plant where a peony has been planted before unless all soil has been removed to a depth of at least three feet and the same in width.
7. Never plant near a black walnut tree or the plant will, invariably, be killed.

PLANT IN SEPTEMBER AND OCTOBER

Peony tubers or roots are often wrapped in polyethylene for shipment. They should arrive in good condition at the proper planting time. When they arrive look them over carefully and report any damage to the shipper and the transportation company. If very dry, soak them in water several hours. Either heel them in or plant them at once, with as little delay as possible.

The fall planting and transplanting season starts in early September in the north, early October in the south, and continues until the ground freezes. Don't wait too long as it is better to get them in the ground in September in the North, so root growth can start while the soil is still warm and they will have time to become established before the ground freezes. Pot-grown plants may be planted spring or fall, anytime. The only reason peonies should not be planted too early in the south is that a hot, dry, September is not good for newly planted roots.

Roots kept in storage for spring planting, while they will not do as well as fall planted roots the first year, do well planted in the north but not in the south. Never plant them south of Philadelphia in the spring unless they are given extra good care, and even then they often die.

PLAN AMPLE SPACE FOR ROOTS

If peonies are to be planted in beds or borders, the ideal situation would be a space 3 feet wide and a depth of at least 24 inches. Allow an area 2 feet in diameter and 2 feet deep for each peony root, if possible. Some varieties like even more space. For specimen plants dig holes 3 feet in diameter and 3 feet deep. See page 108. Crowded roots or those encroached upon by roots of nearby trees or shrubs will weaken the plant and it may fail to bloom.

PREPARE BEDS AND SOIL CAREFULLY

Preparation of a good, friable garden soil with good drainage is important. Lighten heavy clay with sand or coal ashes and add humus to improve drainage and supply organic matter. To improve a sandy soil, add plenty of humus or organic matter using leafmold (rotted leaves), compost or peat moss. One-fourth humus by volume is a good proportion to good top soil.

To this good top soil with humus added, also use a good garden fertilizer such as 20% superphosphate, bonemeal or one low in nitrogen. Too much nitrogen causes the plants to make tall spindly growth and poor flowers. Bonemeal is slow acting so there is little danger of it burning plants. Use a pound to a plant. With other stronger fertilizers only use one-half pound or follow directions on the package. Mix the fertilizer with the soil thoroughly. Some people use well rotted manure. It should never come in contact with the newly planted roots, as it is thought to bring in disease.

Peonies like a slightly acid soil up to pH 6. If the soil tests higher, and is too acid, mix a generous supply of finely ground limestone into the soil, using 5 lbs. per 100 sq. ft. or 1 qt. for each bushel of soil.

When the beds or holes have been dug, discard the subsoil. Use a few handfuls of pebbles at the bottom of the hole to help drainage. Refill with good garden soil well mixed and enriched with fertilizer, up to 8" or 10" from the surface of the ground. Then fill to the top and mound up a few inches with good garden soil *without* any fertilizer added. Prepare the beds at least two weeks or more before planting time so the soil will have sufficient time to settle properly, then the roots will not sink after planting. If you must plant immediately, pack the soil with your feet to prevent roots from settling too deeply.

How To Plant A Peony Root

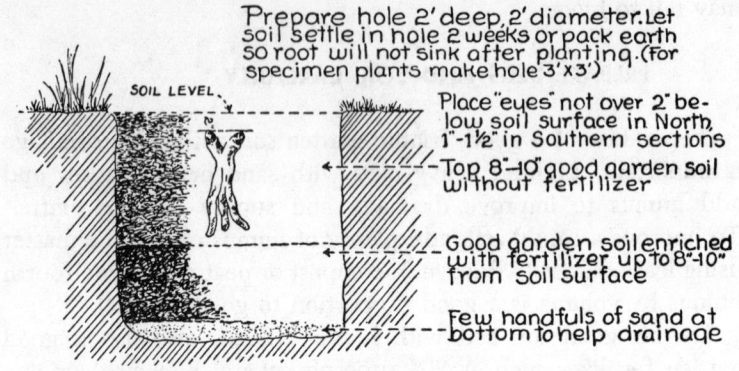

Prepare hole 2' deep, 2' diameter. Let soil settle in hole 2 weeks or pack earth so root will not sink after planting. (For specimen plants make hole 3'x3')

SOIL LEVEL

Place "eyes" not over 2" below soil surface in North, 1"-1½" in Southern sections

Top 8"-10" good garden soil without fertilizer

Good garden soil enriched with fertilizer up to 8"-10" from soil surface

Few handfuls of sand at bottom to help drainage

To topsoil add ¼ humus by volume. Use 1 lb. of bonemeal for each plant. With other quick acting fertilizers use only ½ lb. Mix soil thoroughly. Water thoroughly and label each plant

HOW TO SET OUT THE ROOTS

Place or set the crown, from which all growth springs and from which the buds, "eyes", or sprouts arise, not more than 2" below the ground or soil surface, shallower (1") in southern sections of the country.

Care should be taken not to plant the roots upside down. It is truly amazing how many good gardeners do just that and then wonder why the peony did not come up. Please see sketch above.

Firm the soil well around the root, working it in with your fingers until there are no open spaces left. When the root is completely covered, use your feet if necessary to firm properly but be careful not to break the root or "eyes" in so doing. Water each root generously after planting and when the water has soaked in poke your finger down gently into the soil to make sure the soil did not settle and pull the root down with it. Peony specialists are agreed that too deep planting may be the cause of lack of flowers. Roots of all peonies are fleshy, brittle and fragile so handle carefully.

If peony roots are planted late, and do not have time to become anchored before winter, light mulching for the first winter is recommended to prevent heaving. Hill the soil at the time of planting and then after there is frost in the ground apply any loose material like evergreen boughs or straw. Remove the mulch and hilled soil carefully early in the spring, to avoid breaking the new shoots.

Label each plant with a long-lasting label which can be stuck into the soil, or if you have a sketch or blueprint of the garden, mark on it where and what was planted.

8

Caring for Established Plants

FOOD AND WATER

Peonies like fertile loam as they are gross feeders and need plenty of food and moisture to keep them healthy and in full vigor. However, if the soil was properly prepared and enriched at planting time, further fertilization will not be necessary for several years. In good soil little fertilizer will be needed. Porous or sandy soils will, of course, need additional fertilizer oftener than others, as the rains wash it away.

Keep all fertilizers away from the crown of the plants. Spread it over the area where the roots grow, 6" to 18" from the crown, thoroughly working it into the soil around the plants.

About the third or fourth year after planting peonies, assuming you started with good fertile loam, use half a handful of bonemeal to a plant each spring and fall. A good garden fertilizer not too rich in nitrogen as 20% superphosphate or rock phosphate is good. Wood ashes containing lime and potash have proven satisfactory. Some peony growers like to use well aged manure in the spring to improve the flowers, others will not use it claiming it brings disease. If you do use manure, do so with discretion, never letting it get over the crown of the plant. Do not overfeed as it encourages soft growth and poor blooms.

CARING FOR ESTABLISHED PLANTS 111

Although plants need a great deal of water, nature usually supplies enough. However, watering in a very dry season is necessary. If the spring season is dry, the plants should be given a good watering once a week, and if August and September are dry, it is wise to give the peony plants a good watering weekly. Give them a thorough soaking, enough to wet the ground down to the bottom of the roots. Then repeat again when the soil becomes dry.

CULTIVATION TO KEEP DOWN WEEDS

The first warm days, when the ground is no longer frozen, remove any mulch that may have been used, and when the soil is sufficiently dry, loosen or cultivate it sparingly, being careful not to touch or injure the crown or new growth. If you are not certain where the new growth will appear, do not work around the plant until it comes up. From then on weed and loosen the soil as weeds appear, still not cultivating over 2" near the crown. Some people prefer a mulch to cut down on weed growth and the labor of cultivating, using ground corn cobs, sawdust or a similar mulch. If mulches are used, since mulches use up all the available nitrogen, a good dressing of nitrogen must be supplied. Apply a spoonful or two to a plant.

DISBUDDING FOR LARGER FLOWERS

For maximum show in the garden, do not disbud plants but let all side flowers develop to form a generous display. If you want large flowers for exhibition purposes, pinch off the lateral or side buds as soon as they form, leaving only the terminal or top buds. Another way to get larger flowers is to cut off several of the weaker shoots soon after they appear above the ground, sending more strength into the remaining stems.

For Larger Flowers

1. Disbud
Leave terminal bud.
Pinch off lateral buds ▶

--TERMINAL BUD
--LATERAL BUD

2. Cut away several of the weaker shoots soon after they appear

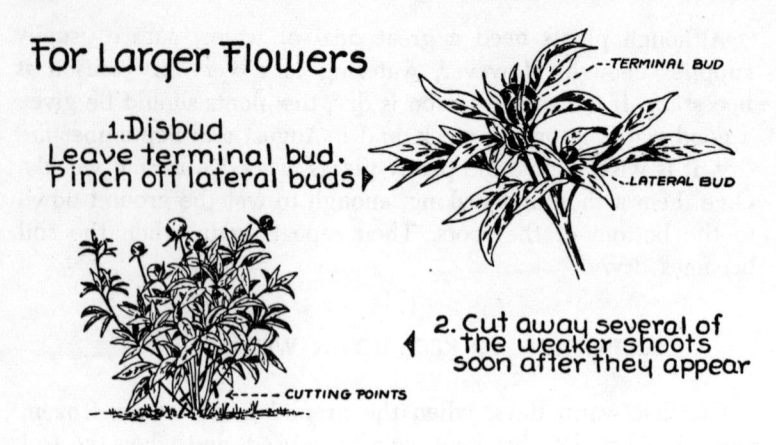

◀---- CUTTING POINTS

SUPPORTS

Some of the fully petaled peony flowers become top heavy and their stems must be supported to bear the weight of the large double flowers, otherwise they will bend to the ground after heavy rains and strong winds. The commonly used circular wire rings are excellent, as they permit plants to maintain their natural and graceful shapes. Stake when plants are about half grown to facilitate the job.

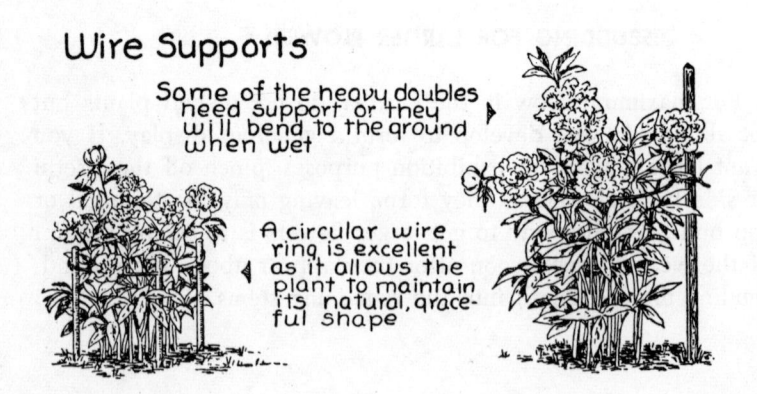

Wire Supports

Some of the heavy doubles need support or they will bend to the ground when wet ▶

A circular wire ring is excellent as it allows the plant to maintain its natural, graceful shape

BURN FOLIAGE AFTER FROST

Some gardeners allow the foliage on an old clump to remain over winter to hold snow and act as a mulch but disease may winter over on the old leaves. It is much safer to cut off the old leaf stalks at ground level, after frost browns the foliage, and then burn them along with hollyhock, iris and other pest-ridden leaves. Never place cut peony foliage and stems on a compost pile because they are susceptible to botrytis disease. As an added precaution, brush away any partially rotted leaves, weed stems, etc., that have collected at the base of the plant and burn or destroy.

TO DIVIDE OLD CLUMPS

If you must divide a clump because of space, or because it is not flowering, dig it up anytime after mid-September. This will allow time for the roots to get well established, after replanting, by the time growth starts in the spring. Cut off all the foliage and stems, then carefully pry up the clump.

Wash away all soil from the roots with a hose and allow them to lie in a shady spot for a few hours to lose their brittleness and avoid root breakage. Cut away any damaged parts and with sharp, heavy shears, lappers or pruning knife cut the clump apart in such a way that each piece will have 3 or 5 dormant "eyes" (never over 8) and several, or a generous proportion, of strong roots. Treat any wound with dusting sulphur. Keep all divisions properly labeled as to varieties.

Shorten the heavy roots back to a maximum of 6", 4" stubs are even better. Divisions from the outer edges of the clump are preferred. If possible, replant each division in a spot where peonies were not formerly grown, never in ground occupied by one that was diseased.

Place the root so that the visible buds or "eyes" are not over 2" below the surface of the soil, 1" in the south. Surround the

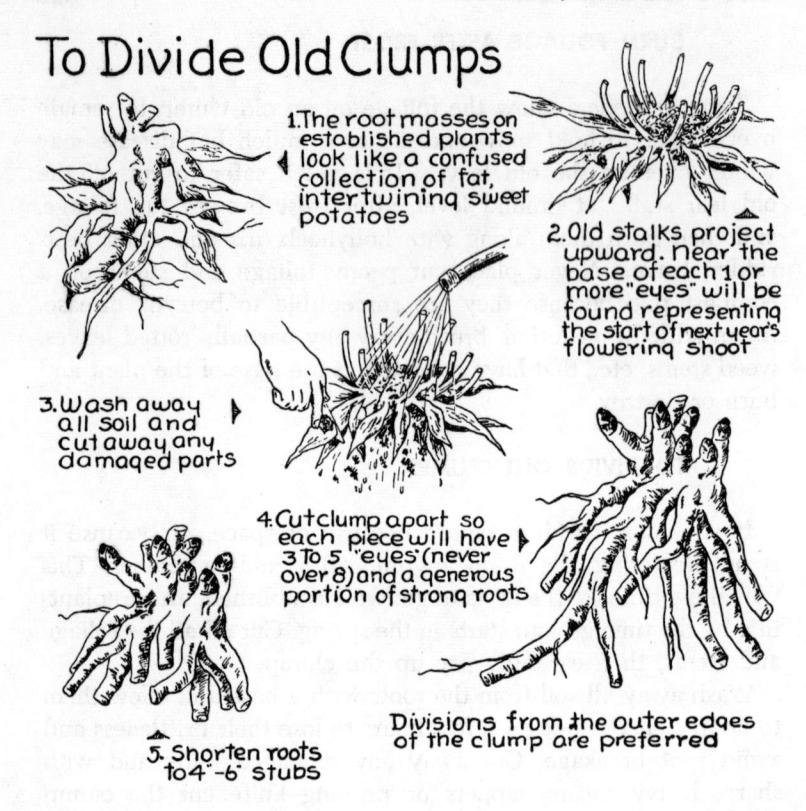

To Divide Old Clumps

1. The root masses on established plants look like a confused collection of fat, intertwining sweet potatoes

2. Old stalks project upward. Near the base of each 1 or more "eyes" will be found representing the start of next year's flowering shoot

3. Wash away all soil and cut away any damaged parts

4. Cut clump apart so each piece will have 3 to 5 "eyes" (never over 8) and a generous portion of strong roots

5. Shorten roots to 4"-6" stubs

Divisions from the outer edges of the clump are preferred

root with pure top soil. Never apply any fertilizer or summer mulches over the crown of the plant.

Frequently no blooms are produced the first year after planting and the plant may be somewhat dwarfed. By the third year, however, the plant should produce abundant blooms.

Professional growers who sell peony roots propagate by division usually using three year old stock, since young roots cut up easily, saving time and producing plants which flower freely.

Home gardeners should never divide old clumps which are blooming well, unless there is a special reason or need for it.

SPRAY TO PREVENT DISEASE

Spray or dust with a good fungicide just as the peony plants break through the ground to prevent disease. Repeat again when half grown and a third time just before flowering.

Spraying with fermate or bordeaux mixture, or some similar fungicide, will also prevent leaf spot, so spray several times after the blooming season as well.

9

Diseases and Insects

BOTRYTIS BLIGHT

Fungus diseases are more detrimental to peonies than are insects. Botrytis fungus or blight is the most common and troublesome disease of the peony and may appear during a wet spring, causing the rotting of the stems, buds and leaves in that order. The effects are easily recognized. The young stems rot, there is browning of the buds and discoloration of the flowers and foliage.

Control of botrytis begins with preventive measures, good

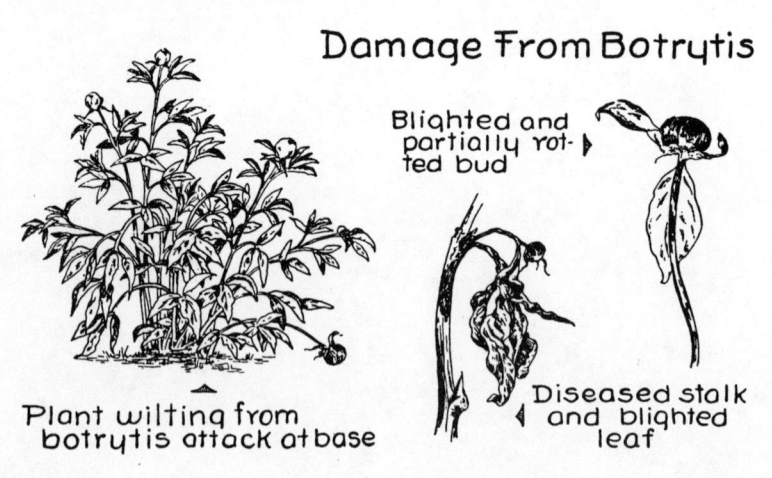

Damage From Botrytis

Plant wilting from botrytis attack at base

Blighted and partially rotted bud

Diseased stalk and blighted leaf

sanitation and good air circulation. Remove all infected parts and burn or destroy them. In the fall, just before frost, cut down the stalks close to the ground and burn or destroy. Dig up and destroy any badly infected plants. As soon as growth starts in the spring, spray or dust with fermate, bordeaux mixture or any good fungicide according to directions on the package, directing the material at the base of the plants and the surface of the soil, repeating at two week intervals until August.

ROOT KNOT OR LEMOINE'S DISEASE

Many varieties bloom in spite of it, others stop blooming. A beadlike swelling appears in infected roots, probably caused by a virus which is difficult to kill. There is evidence it does spread, though slowly. There seems to be no cure so either destroy the plant or replant it in an area by itself.

ROOT ROT

This may be indicated by part of the plant dying down prematurely. Examine the root and if rot is present, dig it up, cut away all diseased parts and then soak the root in a solution of arasan, formaldehyde, semesan or some such chemical for 45 minutes. Replant in soil which has not been exposed to the infection.

NEMAS AND NEMATODES

Occasionally plants are attacked by nemas, microscopic eel-like worms which burrow into the fine roots causing irregular swellings or nodules called nematodes which look like a lot of peas on the ends of the roots. Infested plants are generally stunted, weak in growth and pale green. The roots are unable to take up sufficient nourishment for the plant. Before suspecting nematodes, check other factors for poor growth. If infested, discard the entire plant and do not replant newly purchased plants in the same area.

Several nemacides are now being offered for which the claim is made that they may be used around growing plants and will not harm them. One at least is extremely poisonous to humans and all must be used with the greatest of caution for this reason.

ANTS

Ants crawling over the buds as they begin to open do not eat the buds but feed on the sweet syrup the buds give off. Since they may spread botrytis or aphis, it's best to get rid of them. Treat the soil around the plant with a strong solution of nicotine sulfate or chlordane to take care of them.

THRIPS

Thrips, which are tiny insects, may infest the buds and opening flowers particularly of the late varieties causing failure of buds to open, or a browning of the petals. They are especially bothersome in the south. Lindane or DDT and several sprays on the market may be used to control them. Make three applications ten days apart.

ROSE CHAFERS

Rose chafers or beetles chew the petals. DDT, lindane or chlordane help to control them, if the ground under the plant and surrounding lawn area is treated.

MOLES — RABBITS

If moles are destructive, spray flower beds and adjacent lawn with chlordane. This kills the insects in the soil, the moles' chief food. There are several advertised remedies you can try. If rabbits start to nibble terminal buds as they form protect the plants with some type of wire enclosure.

10
Propagation, Forcing

PROPAGATION

Only species peonies may be propagated, true to name, from seed and only if carefully protected from cross pollination. Seedlings from all other peonies are never true to name but are always new varieties.

Professional peony growers who sell peony roots propagate by root division (see page 103) usually using three year old stock. Root division is the only way to propagate peonies true to name.

The offsprings grown from seed never come true to either parent. It's a fascinating and sometimes heartbreaking pursuit, since one never knows what the seedling will be like and it takes from four to ten years from pollination to get the first flowers.

If peony seeds are allowed to dry out after ripening, they will not germinate under two years so the seeds are gathered and planted immediately, before they dry out, just as they are turning brown. Watch the seed pods from the middle of July on and gather just before the seeds fall from the pod, just as they harden. Seeds may be stratified in peat moss or vermiculite until they sprout, if you wish, for planting. Plant in the open or in boxes set in cold frames, about 2" deep, in good, friable loam. Care must be taken that the seedlings in the cold frames receive sufficient air and moisture and partial shade to prevent drying out. Transplant the seedlings at least 18" apart in a permanent bed and be sure they are properly labeled. After four years the hybridizer may expect to see his much anticipated blooms.

Pollination by bees and insects may produce inferior results so hand pollination, careful cross-breeding, is employed. The two parent flowers are carefully selected, breeding two varieties which have most nearly the characteristics wanted to strengthen certain features.

A covering, as an oiled paper bag, or polyethylene is placed over the two parent flowers. The anthers on the flower to be pollinated are removed to prevent self-pollination. The stigmas are closely watched to see when they are ready to receive the pollen. When they present a waxy, granulated surface they are ready and the pollen is then taken from the ripe anthers of the pollen parent flower and applied to the receptive stigmas of the carpel, the ovule parent flower. The paper bag protection is removed, a label with the parent varieties is fastened to the stem, and from the seeds of the ovule parent flower, young seedlings are grown. The singles and semi-doubles produce seeds freely, the full double varieties seldom bear seeds. If the seedling is not more beautiful, with better form or color and stronger stems ,or a freer bloomer, or more fragrant, or a better yellow or having less blue in its pink, unless it is superior to existing varieties and tests show it will do well in most sections of the country, better discard it.

FORCING BLOOMS AHEAD OF SCHEDULE

Mr. Edward Auten, Jr., of Princeville, Illinois, relates in the second edition of the *Handbook of the Peony* his experience in forcing herbaceous peonies into flower ahead of their normal time, as early as February or March.

"Three or four year old clumps should be dug early in the fall and potted immediately, using a ten-quart pail or larger. Take care to remove as little dirt from the clump as possible. Punch a number of drainage holes in the bottom of the pail. Put an inch or two of gravel or other coarse material over the holes. Shorten the roots no more than necessary to get the clump into the container. Pack new soil around, between the roots, and under the plant, being sure no voids are left unfilled. Water thoroughly to wash the soil down among the roots to be sure this has been done. The eyes should be one inch below the surface.

"Stand the plant outdoors in a cool place until early winter. Freezing is beneficial provided the container has been sunk in the ground. If it freezes while standing above ground, the roots may be damaged.

"After December 20th, bring the plant indoors, first into a cool temperature, later into heat. 60 to 65 degrees F. is best, but 70 is not too high. It is important to water carefully. The time of blooming can be regulated by the time the plant is brought into heat, by temperature, and probably also by amount of light given. This may be done either in home or greenhouse, which will take from six to ten weeks.

"Hybrids can be forced and should bloom earlier than the albiflora (lactiflora) varieties.

Singles, Japanese, semi-doubles and the early, loose doubles will force easier than the full doubles. Some difficulty may be experienced with these, especially the full petaled hybrid doubles which may not respond satisfactorily."

The flowers will not be as large nor the colors quite the same as for normal outdoor blooming but it is possible to have peonies with flowers in February or in March for the large spring flower shows and very special occasions. Forcing peonies in greenhouses for commercial purposes is too costly to be profitable.

11

Peony Questions and Answers

WHY DO PEONIES FAIL TO BLOOM?

1. Plant may be too young. By the third year a plant should bloom freely.
2. Planted too deep. In the north plant "eyes" no more than 2" below soil level, 1" in the south.
3. Moved too often. Peonies do not like to be disturbed. It sets them back.
4. Poor location, too shady or too near voracious shrubs or trees. Peonies need plenty of sun. Their roots should not be crowded or robbed of the food and water they require.
5. Poor drainage, can't tolerate prolonged wet feet. Peony roots will rot or develop a blight or fungus if its roots are kept wet.
6. Soil too acid. Soil should be just slightly acid. If it tests over pH 6 add limestone (see page 107).
7. Failure to divide an old clump when moving it. An old clump must be divided into pieces with only 3 to 5 eyes when moved. If too many eyes are left it will not bloom (see page 114).
8. Too much foliage removed in cutting long stemmed flowers. Some foliage is essential for the health of the plant and to develop a good root system (see page 183).

9. Lack of food. The peony has large leaves and flowers and requires plenty of food, good soil.
10. Not enough moisture. Moisture is necessary for good growth and development.
11. Lack of disease control. Spraying or dusting is a must to keep plants free from disease and vigorous and healthy.

WHY ARE THE FLOWERS POOR?

1. Insufficient nutrients. Flowers will not develop properly or take on their best color unless properly nourished.
2. Overfed with high nitrogen fertilizer. This causes soft growth and poor blooms.
3. Dry weather or a sudden hot spell. A thorough soaking or watering may help. Hope for a better season next year!
4. Wet weather may cause buds to "ball" or fail to open. There isn't too much you can do about this but really good drainage is your salvation.
5. Late frost may kill buds. This is disappointing but gardeners are optimistic and it can't happen twice in succession!

WHERE WILL THEY GROW?

Peonies grow well in all sections of the country except Florida, southern California and the deep south. In dry areas, like northern Arizona and California, there are successful plantings but plenty of water must be supplied every two or three days. In the south two year plants give better results than the smaller ones, unless carefully nursed. Plant the "eyes" only 1" below the surface of the soil; and use a mulch to keep ground cool. To force dormancy in warm sections, withhold water from September through the first half of October and cut the herbaceous varieties back to the ground.

Some peonies bloom better in one part of the country than in others. As a rule easy-opening varieties of loose petalage and the earlier blooming kinds of the single and Japanese types are best for the south or any locality where extreme heat comes quickly. Very late sorts with tight buds and full flowers need cool, somewhat moist weather to make them open best (see page 38). Peonies are hardy and do well in Canada where they are at their best in late June and early July.

Where temperatures get down to 10°-20° below zero for a week at a time, with little snow covering, winter protection as evergreen boughs or straw or soil around the base of the plants to a depth of about 6" is recommended. Herbaceous hybrids must be protected in such a climate to prevent severe losses.

PART III — THE TREE PEONY

12

General Types and Hybrids

The tree peony, which is a shrub and not a tree, has been cultivated and appreciated in China and Japan for many centuries. It was first exported to England in 1787 where it received much attention and later it was introduced into France and the United States.

Accorded the highest honor in its native China, the tree peony has been known in that country as the "King of Flowers" since time immemorial. It has been the subject of painting and poetry for over 1500 years and is one of the four flowers associated with their four seasons. The white blossomed plum of winter, the peony of springtime, the lotus of summer and the chrysanthemum of fall are well recognized symbols in the Orient.

For several centuries it was decreed by the Chinese rulers that such regal flowers could only be grown in the imperial palaces where they were grown in their natural shape as a bush and also espaliered in many designs. The tree peony was symbolic of high position and wealth as well as being an omen of good fortune.

Introduced into Japan by Buddhist monks sometime between the fifth and eighth centuries, the tree peony became a great favorite, second only to the chrysanthemum and classed with the cherry and lotus as flowers of royal rank. The tree peony and chrysanthemum are generally not used in the landscape proper, their special display being restricted to flower beds arranged in long sheltered areas, usually near the apartments for ladies. In the grounds of the palaces, peonies adorn the open spaces facing the ladies' chambers from which the beauty of the flowers can be readily viewed and enjoyed.

In Japanese art the tree peony is inseparably connected with the peafowl or peacock and they form the constant decoration of temple and palace walls. The affection of the Japanese people for the peony is shown in their legends and folklore, all marked by a charming symbolism. The beauty of texture, color and form of the tree peony through the centuries has made an irresistible appeal and enjoyed great esteem.

There are two general types of tree peonies, the European varieties brought here from China by way of England and favored in the nineteenth century, and the Japanese varieties from Japan, originally from China and Tibet. These later arrivals from Japan, where the tree peony has reached its highest degree of development, are generally more attractive.

The Chinese or European tree peonies are easily recognized for their shaggy, double flowers, usually so heavy they cause the stems to droop. The Japanese varieties have straight stems. The Japanese have selected the more informal single and semi-double flowers from among their seedlings. The plants are graceful, of attractive form, the foliage is beautiful and the usually single to semi-double flowers are generally borne well above the foliage. Not nearly so susceptible to frost damage, they are more reliable in bloom than the European type. They do not need protection from early frost, necessary with the European varieties, and are better suited to our climate.

HYBRIDS

In catalogs you will find three major types of tree peonies to choose from; the Chinese, Japanese and the hybrids. Sir Frederick C. Stern in his "A Study of the Genus Paeonia", published by the Royal Horticultural Society in London in 1946, calls all three tree peonies P. moutan and he groups the garden forms that come from China and Japan as P. suffruticosa. The species delavayi, lutea and potanini he calls the delavayi group, but in catalogs this group is offered to the trade under lutea hybrids. The Chinese and Japanese tree peonies flower first and the lutea and delavayi hybrids follow them about two weeks later. On Long Island, New York, Dr. David Gurin says the flowering time for him lasts from around May 5 to June 5. Around Boston it is about a week or more later. The dates will vary several days according to the season.

P. suffruticosa (syn. P. arborea—P. moutan) has an ancient and interesting history. It has large white flowers with magenta-purple blotches at the base of the petals. The group now includes many varieties of delicate tints and surprising brilliance with a range of colors from purest white and palest pink through rose-pink, vermillion, blazing scarlets, crimson and rich purples, mauves, lilac and a wisteria blue. Some have feathered white petals striped with crimson, others open pale salmon, fading white with age. Since records show only this one species of the tree peony in the Orient before comparatively recent times, it is probable that early varieties resulted from seedling variation or natural mutations.

Of comparatively recent discovery (brought to Paris from China in 1883 and 1884) are P. lutea and P. delavayi, the first known yellow and maroon species.

P. delavayi, the first maroon tree peony to be discovered, is believed to be the oldest and most primitive species of the group. It has single flowers 2″ to 4″ across, dark mahogany in color and is commonly called the maroon or Delavay tree peony. This species probably enters into the parentage of most of all the darker hybrid varieties. Potanini is another deep maroon-red, a native of China and Tibet.

P. lutea has thick, deeply lobed, dark-green leaves and fragrant, single, cup-shaped flowers about 2″ to 3½″ across with waxy, fleshy petals of a wonderful golden yellow, strong and pure. In some blooms the lower half of the filament is red giving the effect of a red ring in the center of the flower. This little peony has great beauty and in addition has a pleasant fragrance. Crossed with P. suffruticosa it has become one of the parents of a long list of hybrids, the origin of the yellow and orange colored flowers. The wide color range in single, semi-double and fully double blossoms starts with a silvery-cream through all the yellows to the color of golden ripe grain.

Interbred with P. suffruticosa, using the pollen of the moutan varieties on the maroon and yellow species, the resultant hybrids have supplied us with a totally new range of impressive colors from white and ivory, pale and golden yellow, blush to dusky rose-pink, to scarlet, crimson and maroon, to almost black. Many varieties are fragrant and they may be had in single, semi-double and double forms. Some varieties are compact, others spreading and some upright in form. There is also a low type. The outstanding hybrids have more vigor, grow better, are more shapely and attractive and easier to handle and transport than the P. suffruticosa varieties. They also bloom about 10 days later extending the peony season by at least 2 weeks.

The tree peony hybrids resulted from the work of Victor Lemoine of France and Prof. A. P. Saunders of Clinton, New York. Lemoine worked in the nineties, Mr. Saunders not until the 1920s and these so far are the only tree peony hybridizers. The one criticism of their hybrids was weak stems. P. lutea and P. delavayi both hide or hang their blooms in the foliage. Lemoine made crosses with the double Chinese varieties producing huge flowers which weighted the stems down so they hung underneath the leaves. In crossing P. delavayi he produced Sang Lorraine, a wonderfully fragrant, single or semi-double, dark crimson. Prof. Saunders in using Japanese varieties produced smaller, single flowers like Argosy, introduced in 1928, which hold themselves up well. One of his introductions, a magnificent semi-double, Age of Gold, came from a Japanese variety and even though its weak stems allow the flowers to hang beneath the leaves, it is undoubtedly the most beautiful yellow peony today.

These early hybridizers made a wonderful start and increased the blooming season and earlier color range of white, pink, red and purple by adding yellow and the darker colored hybrids. We owe them a tremendous debt of gratitude for their foresight and developmment of the peony. Since their time, P. lutea ludlowi with large yellow flowers on strong stems which comes into bloom about two weeks before P. lutea has been introduced.

13

Tree Peonies in the Landscape

Few plants offer the landscape artist the opportunities presented by the tree peony. This beautiful and exotic plant is remarkable in its shrub-like habit, of convenient size, easy to grow, hardy and long-lived. Its woody stems carry attractive soft green foliage above which appear beautifully shaped flowers of supreme beauty which last long on the plant. The shrubs' graceful lines and delicately parted foliage have an Oriental look and older plants bearing scores of blooms make a striking focus. Once established they increase in size and number of blooms from year to year, their wide umbrella of foliage making a delightful plant even after blooming is over. More and more gardeners are making the acquaintance of the tree peony and finding it irresistible. No other bloom can compete with the tree peony when it is in flower and it blooms in advance of most garden perennials.

A show plant, grown primarily for its spectacular display of blooms, the tree peony should be given a place of prominence. Nothing else has quite the glamorous impact of a tree peony in full flower. The ethereal beauty of the plant with its delightful qualities and charm deserves close range inspection and should be planted so one may go up to and walk all around it to enjoy the detail of its beauty to the fullest. Plant it where you will enjoy it most. If possible, where you can enjoy it from indoors as well as out, where a window will frame it for you.

WHERE TO PLANT

Hillside Planting

In its native China the tree peony is found growing in the forest regions on the mountainside, a reasonable amount of high shade from the trees protecting the pale and delicate colors from the intense heat of the afternoon sun. The shade of the trees also keeps the temperature of the soil about the roots cool. Where terrain permits, this type of planting is ideal. At Swarthmore College Dr. John Wister has a hillside planting of tree peonies, a perfect setting and a beautiful sight when in flower. The trees also offer protection from severe wind and storms.

On Level Ground

On level ground where drainage is good, a grouping of tree peonies planted under trees several feet from the trunk to avoid the tree roots and too much shade makes an ideal situation. Dr. David Gurin on Long Island, New York, has such a planting. Picturesque gray birch trees furnish some high shadows, the dappled shade keeping the flowers fresh and playing interesting patterns on the lovely peonies.

Terraced Planting

In China tree peonies are grown on stepped terraces, or planted in high raised beds enclosed with stone or marble, a good idea in any country, supplying good drainage and pleasing landscape effects. The precious plants are also protected in China when in flower with bamboo shades or a cloth screening to keep off wind and sun and to prolong the blooming period.

As A Focus

When in flower the tree peony stands out in all its glory whether planned as a focal area or not. Why not place it to make the most of its natural eye catching beauty to accent the garden design and show off to best advantage. As a focal area on a wide sweep of lawn, in the garden border, in a terrace border, or along the garden path, the tree peony, when in bloom, attracts the major attention. Place it so it complements its companions and the garden as a whole. As specimen plants in front of a

TREE PEONIES IN THE LANDSCAPE 133

Gardens Featuring Tree Peonies

Tree peonies partially shaded by fence

Hillside planting partially shaded by trees

Raised bed or terraced garden featuring tree peonies

On two levels. Azaleas, tall growing in background, low growing in foreground

Garden Featuring Tree Peonies
also using some herbaceous

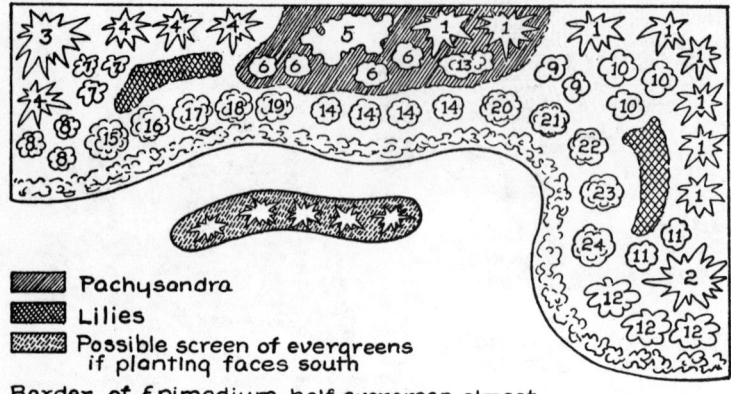

- ▨ Pachysandra
- ▩ Lilies
- ▧ Possible screen of evergreens if planting faces south

Border of Epimedium, half evergreen, almost woody perennial, 8"-12" high. Yellow and slightly red flowers, May-June

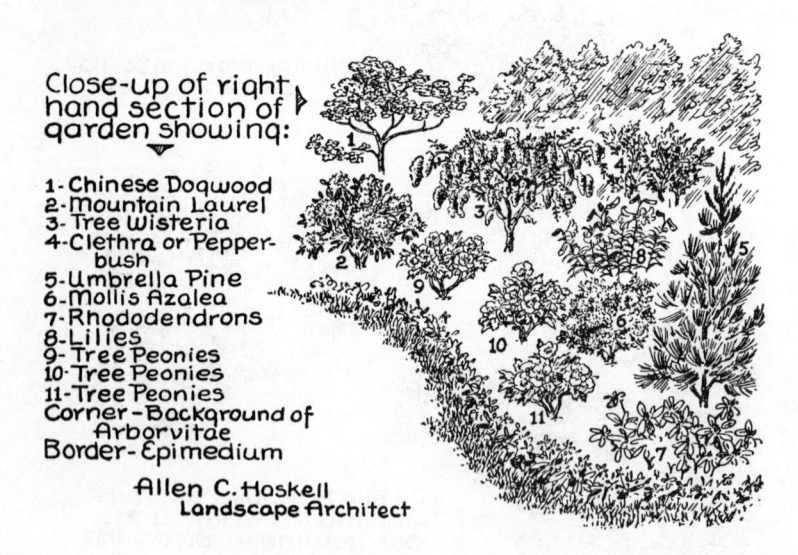

Close-up of right hand section of garden showing:

1. Chinese Dogwood
2. Mountain Laurel
3. Tree Wisteria
4. Clethra or Pepperbush
5. Umbrella Pine
6. Mollis Azalea
7. Rhododendrons
8. Lilies
9. Tree Peonies
10. Tree Peonies
11. Tree Peonies

Corner - Background of Arborvitae
Border - Epimedium

Allen C. Haskell
Landscape Architect

TREE PEONIES IN THE LANDSCAPE

This planting featuring peonies has seasonal interest, and is practical and easy to maintain.

Key to materials used in Allen C. Haskell plan.

1. Dark green arbor-vitae.
2. Umbrella pine (Sciadopitys verticillata).
3. Cryptomeria, Japanese evergreen tree of pyramidal habit.
4. Canadian hemlock.
5. Chinese dogwood (Cornus kousa chinensis) to 15 ft., flowers in June, red autumnal foliage.
6. Mountain laurel (Kalmia latifolia) 5 ft. to 6 ft., flowers in late May and early June—blush-pink clustered flowers.
7. Cotoneaster divaricata, 6 ft to 8 ft spreading.
8. Hypericum hidcote, low growing summer-flowering shrub 18 inches tall, bright yellow flowers, late June until frost.
9. Enkianthus campanulatus. Rather erect graceful shrub of narrow outline to 10 ft. or more. Dropping dainty bell-shaped yellow flowers in pendulous clusters on long slender stems in May. Striking orange-scarlet fall foliage.
10. Clethra alnifolia (Sweet Pepperbush)—Spikes of fragrant white flowers from late July through September.
11. Mollis or Chinese azalea, "Directeur Moerelands" to 5 ft., handsome clusters of soft golden yellow flowers in abundance in May and June.
12. Rhododendron hybrid 'Boule de Neige", white flowers, bushy, compact plant.
13. Tree wisteria, pale purplish-blue flowers.
14. Herbaceous peony, white, single, 4 plants.

TREE PEONIES (15-24)

15. Reine Elizabeth, bright salmon-rose, double.
16. Howzan, bright light pink, double.
17. Gabisan, large white, double.
18. Teikwan, enormous bright red, double.
19. Tama-fuyo, light pink, nearly full double.
20. Alice Harding, yellow, double.
21. Argosy, yellow, single.
22. Flora, immense white flowers slightly blotched violet-carmine in throat.
23. La Lorraine, large soft sulphur yellow with salmon tinge when opening, becomes lighter when expanded.
24. Ubatama, huge satiny black maroon.
25. Lilies for summer color.

backdrop of evergreens or flowering trees and shrubs, the tree peony shows off to excellent advantage.

To Accent Entrance

As specimen plants to accent the entrance to a home or to a garden, tree peonies are ideal. Their dignity and beauty when in flower are unequalled by any other plant, making them excellent specimen plants in the landscape.

A Picturesque Pergola

A pergola letting in plenty of sun yet offering some protection for the flowers from the afternoon's hottest rays makes an attractive and interesting garden feature.

In Small City Yard

A well drained and slightly high shaded location in a small city yard can be used successfully for the growing of one or two specimen plants, which may then be complemented with several dwarf evergreen azaleas, deutzias, roses, or any one of a number of plants suitable for such a situation.

Potted Tree Peonies

Potted tree peonies were used in China on a seasonal basis to grace the courts of the wealthy but in our climate pot culture for terrace or portable gardens as yet is not practical and is too costly. Sealed in heat and moisture destroy the roots at a time when these very roots have a heavy foliage to support. Then there is the problem of dormancy, which requires cold storage and handling, increasing labor costs.

JAPANESE INFLUENCE

Japanese influence is seen in many of our gardens today, especially in tree peony gardens. A well shaped pine, a few spring flowering trees, a garden bridge spanning a stream of water are all typical Japanese features. They make an ideal setting for a planting of tree peonies.

We may well consider some of the practical features of Japanese landscaping. Since for generations they have had to make the most of limited space, they have become masters in giving depth and a feeling of size within a small area. Security and privacy with an utter detachment from the outside world is a must in their gardens. The garden is a place for repose, meditation and quiet; a place to induce relaxation and provide seclusion from the hustle and bustle of life. It is not a garden until it is enclosed, although no opportunity is lost to take advantage of, capitalize on, and "borrow" the pleasing views of surrounding scenery, giving the small enclosed private garden a feeling of great space and distance.

A feeling of simplicity, restraint and quiet harmony prevails. The garden must appear natural, weathered and related to the entire setting. The architecture of the area is constructed from materials on hand and always an inconspicuous part of the plan. Symbolism plays an important role. Native rocks or stones, water and moss are basic. Moss is encouraged and cherished to suggest age.

A group of low growing pines located at the stream's edge indicates the symbolic tortoise island, the tortoise signifying a long life. Symbolic shapes of clipped shrubs resembling a tortoise or a crane also signify a long life. The three, five and seven combinations of arranging garden stones or shrubs, so often seen, signify holiness or happiness.

The stone lantern, of purely Japanese origin, illuminates and guides the way by night and also gives the feeling of age. A bamboo screening or thicket of growing trees conveys security and privacy for the owner.

Water is of intrinsic value in the Japanese garden and always featured, a stream or cascade making a pleasing sight. If not available, water is simulated. Carefully selected and carefully placed stones, gravel and sand are used to suggest a running stream. A simple garden bridge is a familiar sight even over a "dry-up" water stream. A simple garden gate and garden house are other typical features.

Primary and secondary paths of native stone are made taking one to a destination by the most interesting route. Along the path in the tea gardens are low type water-filled basins where one may rinse the mouth and hands, symbolic of spiritual cleansing or purifying oneself, before entering the tea room for the tea ceremony. Enough diversity is allowed to suit the needs of the individual owners and the Japanese gardens are as varied as our own even though they all follow a few basic principles. Ease of maintenance is an appealing feature of all Japanese gardens.

COMPANION PLANTS

A picturesque pine; the Japanese maple with its dainty, finely cut leaves; the dwarf Japanese larch, its new growth soft and delicate in texture; late flowering cherries and the plum; the azalea and wisteria all come to mind when thinking of Japanese gardens and tree peonies.

A tree peony garden can be planted with a wide variety of plants useful for both foliage and flowers. With judicious selection, wonderful garden effects may be achieved.

Flowering Trees

A flowering plum or late cherry covered with blossoms makes a fitting setting for the early season display of tree peonies. Pink blossoms of a crabapple somewhere nearby add interest and color. The Washington hawthorn, where space permits (20-30 feet), has profuse white flowers in May and June and lustrous scarlet small fruit in clusters in September and October. The Siberian pea-tree (caragana) grows from 15-20 feet, has bright green leaves and small, bright yellow pea-shaped flowers in June, a good background specimen and the yellow repeats the yellow centers of many of the tree peonies.

Flowering Shrubs

There are many fine shrubs that bloom with the tree peony including azaleas, rhododendrons, and the hybrid lilacs and shrub roses. Viburnum tomentosum grows about 8 feet tall, has creamy-white flowers in June and colorful dull red foliage in the fall. Deutzia kalmiaeflora grows 3 feet in height and is

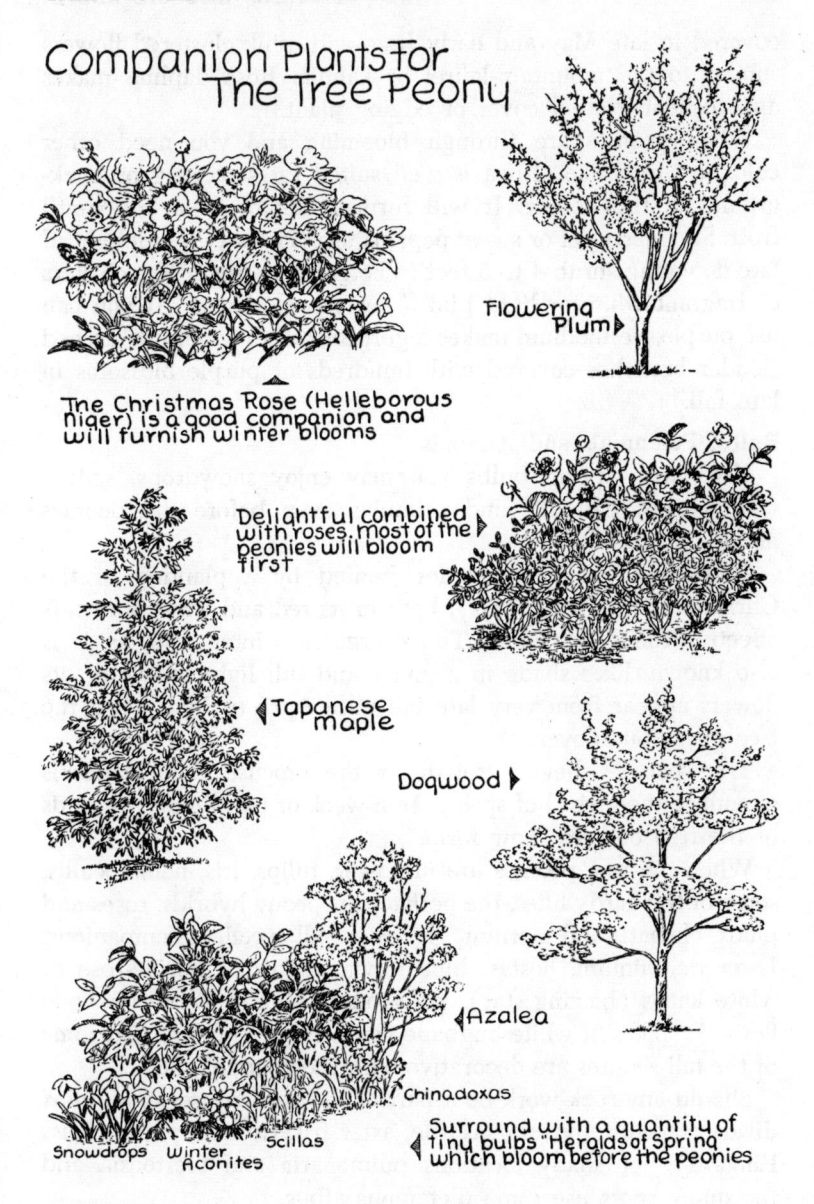

TREE PEONIES IN THE LANDSCAPE   139

Companion Plants For The Tree Peony

The Christmas Rose (Helleborous Niger) is a good companion and will furnish winter blooms

Flowering Plum ▶

Delightful combined with roses, most of the peonies will bloom first ▶

◀ Japanese Maple

Dogwood ▶

◀ Azalea

Snowdrops   Winter Aconites   Scillas   Chinadoxas

◀ Surround with a quantity of tiny bulbs "Heralds of Spring" which bloom before the peonies

covered in late May and early June with pink clustered flowers similar to the mountain-laurel or kalmia. Rose daphne makes an excellent ground cover or edging plant.

When peonies are through blooming and you need other color, a shrub like althea is well suited for screening or background in the border. It will furnish blooms from July until frost. Summersweet or sweet pepperbush (clethra) is a delightful late flowering shrub 4 to 5 feet in height with finger-like clusters of fragrant white or light pink (var. rosea) flowers. If you can use purple, desmodium makes a gorgeous display with its arched slender branches covered with hundreds of purple blossoms in late fall.

Bulbs, Perennials and Annuals

Used with spring bulbs you may enjoy snowdrops, scillas, chionodoxas, daffodils and primulas even before the peonies are in flower.

A grouping of tree peonies fronted by a planting of the Christmas rose (helleborus), both in its red and white forms, is effective the year round. The evergreen winter rose, as it is also known, likes shade in summer and full light in winter, its flowers appear from very late fall until April or May when the tree peony takes over.

Tree peonies begin growth as the crocuses and daffodils announce the arrival of spring. In a week or two the flower buds of the tree peonies show form.

When the tree peonies are in flower, tulips, iris, hemerocallis, some of the hardy lilies, the herbaceous peony hybrids, roses and phlox, clematis and morning glories are all excellent companions. Later delphinium, hostas, blue salvia, spikes of purple-rose or white liatris (blazing star); platycodon, blue or white (balloon flower); spikes of white bugbane (cimicifuga simplex) and some of the tall sedums are decorative with the peony plants.

Should any rock work be a part of the garden use some phlox divaricata with alyssum saxatile, aster frikarti with phlox (Miss Lingard); for shady locations pulmonaria and mertensia and for sunny spots use some dictamnus albus.

Edging Plants

There are many excellent edging plants that bloom with the tree peony. With a carpet of garden pinks (Old Spice) and white sweet alyssum at their feet tree peonies make a lovely picture in the spring. Pansies, iberis (candytuft), cerastium (snow-in-summer), arabis (wall cress), and arenaria (sandwort) are also good low, companions.

Heuchera (coral-bells) has slender, tall stems with loose clusters of small, bright-red flowers in May and June but the tufted plant with its well rounded attractive leaves is attractive throughout the season when not in flower and makes an excellent edging plant.

14

Making New Plantings

BUYING THE PLANTS

Although tree peonies are more expensive than herbaceous roots, improved propagating and growing techniques are bringing the price of this choice plant down nearer the reach of most gardeners. The cost should be considered as a long time investment since there are tree peonies in the Philadelphia area known to have been in the gardens of one family for over 100 years.

Tree peonies may be bought 2 or 3 years after they are grafted. Since the early years are the crucial ones, the beginner would do well to buy an older well established plant, one at least 3 years old or older, of blooming age. Results will be more certain and quicker. The plant should have some good new roots to give satisfaction. If immediate results are wanted, by all means buy an older established plant. Plants from seed are sold when they are 5 to 8 years old, when just ready to bloom for the first time.

Commercially most tree peonies are offered bare root. Some specially prepared pot-grown plants are now being offered guaranteed to bloom within the first growing season following planting. Also balled and burlapped specimen plants with 3 and 4 dozen buds on and close to the stem are now available for fall planting. To ball and burlap a tree peony successfully requires a knowledge of the type roots of each variety as the roots of some varieties are unsuitable for balling. At no time is spring planting advised for bare root plants. Fall planting of bare roots requires some winter protection the first year.

CHOOSING THE LOCATION

SUNLIGHT. Tree peonies love the sun as herbaceous peonies do, yet as a forest plant in its native China, it likes a reasonable amount of high shade to protect the pale and delicate flower colors from the heat of the afternoon sun and to keep the temperature of the soil about the roots cool.

The plants bloom most freely in full sunlight but a play of shadows intensifies the colors. The pink varieties need more shade, both to show off their sublety of color and texture and to preserve the flower, which by opening too wide in mid-day heat loses its lovely goblet shape so characteristic of the tree peony. Blooms last longer when not exposed to the hot sun all day.

ROOT COMPETITION. Plant at sufficient distance from trees and shrubs so the peony roots will not have to compete for water and food.

PROTECTION. A protected location sheltering the plant from heavy winds, rain and hail is advisable.

DRAINAGE. The limestone, mountainside forest regions from which the tree peony originated suggest good drainage. Although the peony will withstand drought, during a rainy season the water must move downward through the soil and not stand around the peony roots. Adequate drainage is a *must*.

PREPARE BEDS AND SOIL CAREFULLY

SOIL AND HOLE. Tree peonies like a deep sandy loam rich in humus (decayed organic matter: compost, leafmold or peatmoss) and enriched with a fertilizer like bonemeal. Decayed organic matter prevents heavy soils from packing and light sandy soils from rapid drying. Too heavy soil may also be lightened with sand or coal ashes.

Iron in the form of sulphate is of value in producing vigor in the plant and depth of color in the blooms. Too much nitrogen may produce soft growth, abnormally subject to botrytis. Roots should never come in direct contact with manure in any form. If the soil tests pH 5.5 or lower add one-half cup ground limestone or one-quarter cup white lime for each plant, to the soil, to decrease the acidity bringing it up to around pH 6.

Dig the border or holes for the plants 2' deep and 3' in diameter if you have the space and fill in with well-prepared soil a month or more before planting time. This will give the soil time to settle. Plants set in freshly dug soil may sink too deep for best results.

Preparation of the hole and soil for each plant is very important since the tree peony lives to such a ripe old age. A bushel of leafmold and a generous supply of bonemeal incorporated with the soil should get the plant off to a good start.

DRAINAGE. Tree peonies need both good air and water drainage and cannot take water standing around their roots as will happen in heavy soil. Excessive moisture encourages a fungus growth to which the tree peony is susceptible.

WHEN AND HOW TO PLANT

Late September or October is a good time to plant, a month later in the south. When planting, always examine the roots carefully for any fungus growth. Cut off any rotted parts and give the roots a soaking in a 5% solution of formalin. Unless the fungus is thoroughly removed, it will spread and eventually cause the death of the peony. This fungus disease can only be prevented not cured.

Set the plants the same depth they were in the nursery. Since most tree peony stock is grafted, the graft junction or union should come well below the ground level (4") so the scion can

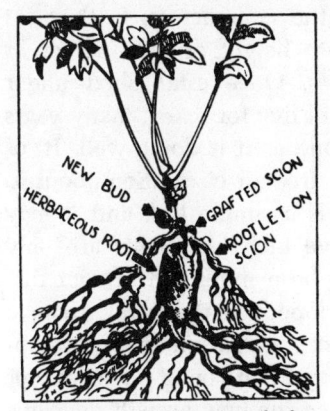

MAKING NEW PLANTINGS 145

This is a grafted plant on herbaceous peony root. Note new roots developing from the Tree Peony stock. This is 3-year graft.

Same grafted plant pruned and set in planting hole. Soil must be friable for good root growth. Note planting depth.

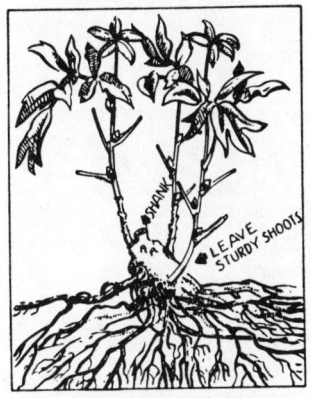

This seedling plant is about seven years old, as dug from the field.

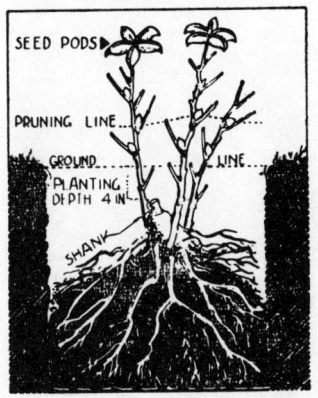

Same seedling set in hole. Note planting depth and pruning line.

How To Plant Tree Peonies
Courtesy of Toichi Domoto Nursery, Hayward, Cal.

develop its own vigorous root system. This in turn means a wealth of subterranean buds and consequently a strong growth above ground.

Space plants at least 4 feet apart. If there is ample room, keep in mind that a tree peony in 6 to 8 years should form a compact bush 2 to 3 feet high and the same across. In the next 10 years it should reach its ultimate height of 4 to 6 feet or more and the same distance across. Once established under favorable conditions a tree peony will live for many, many years and should never be disturbed as long as it is doing well. It, of course, needs enough space to enjoy free air circulation about it.

Planting a pot-grown tree peony is a simple task and it may be planted at any time. Four to five inch pot plants are only one or two years old, so there will be a minimum of root disturbance. If a flower bud has developed on the plant, remove it at the time of planting to insure strong root and top development. Do not cut back the woody growth on young plants except to remove dead or injured parts, since the new growth develops along these woody stems.

15

Caring for Established Plants

FOOD AND WATER

Fertilize as you do for herbaceous peonies (see page 110) applying a small feeding in the spring before the buds start forth, or just before the flowers open, and again in the autumn. If the soil has been properly prepared, very little fertilizer is necessary, perhaps ½ to 1 cup for each established plant in April and again in the fall. Bonemeal is the most effective fertilizer since most tree peonies have high phosphoric acid and potash demands. Wood ashes and superphosphate are good fertilizers. Manure should be avoided (or used with great care) as it may encourage botrytis. Never let it touch the roots.

Since tree peony roots are fairly shallow, in hot, dry weather during the blooming period, a good watering is beneficial.

CULTIVATION TO KEEP DOWN WEEDS

Tree peonies develop a strong system of feeder roots near the surface of the soil so the plant must be cultivated with great care to avoid injury to the shallow roots. Use the hoe with caution in keeping down the weeds.

PRUNING AND STAKING

With the exception of an occasional snipping here and there to shape and the removal of dead ends from the branches, pruning is not necessary. However, when old plants become ungainly or thin after several years, they may be cut to the ground in the fall to rejuvenate them. Strong healthy stems will sprout from below the ground level the following spring.

A fine specimen can also be hurried along by cutting the plant to the ground in early fall, 3 or 4 years after being set out. This gives a completely new set of vigorous, healthy stems. In Japan the plants are pruned rather severely, maybe only leaving 5 stems and flower buds, to increase the size of the flowers. As plants get older the structure may be controlled depending upon whether you want fewer stems with larger flowers or a massive display of smaller flowers.

Some older plants bearing 50 or more flowers may need their weight supported by staking some of the lateral branches.

MULCHING

In a climate like Massachusetts or New York summer mulching is not necessary. However, it has proven valuable in the Middle West and Southern states where the summers are hot and dry. Rather heavy mulching helps keep down ground temperatures and conserves moisture, both conducive to good root growth in tree peonies.

Use straw, hay, ground corncobs, buckwheat hulls, or peat. These mulches do make convenient shelters for mice and other small animals so traps or poison baits may be necessary. Mulches may also harbor spores of fungi, particularly botrytis, so spray mulch with bordeaux mixture or fermate which is an effective control.

The first winter after planting, mulch with a light covering to keep the roots from heaving as a result of frost. Once established, tree peonies are sufficiently hardy to withstand the rigors of the northern climate without protection in winter. Where temperatures are 10°-20° below zero for any length of time, with little snow covering, they do need protection however. In Minneapolis, for example, the Japanese tree peonies have to be boxed in with dry leaves and a wooden box. Even in Clinton, New York, they and the lutea hybrids kill back to the ground in winter and start again like the herbaceous from ground level or below in spring.

DISEASES AND PESTS

The sudden wilting of foliage or branches is an indication of botrytis blight which will not kill but will greatly weaken the plant, the only serious disease problem with tree peonies. This can be guarded against by providing good drainage and good garden sanitation. Botrytis can only be prevented, not cured, so spray plants from early spring at regular 10 day to 2 week intervals with bordeaux mixture, fermate or any good fungicide. Always cut away and burn or destroy any infected or wilted parts. For nematodes, ants and thrips see pages 117-118.

FORCING

Tree peonies may be forced into bloom in advance of their natural flowering time for flower shows or other special occasions. Here is the method employed by Mr. Marinus Vander Pol:

"Select plants at least five years old that have been grown out of doors, properly spaced, never crowded at any time, and well taken care of. They should have been transplanted at least two years and preferably not longer than three years prior to forcing.

"Dig in late fall with as large a ball of earth as possible without disturbing the roots. Place at once in a container large enough to hold the ball of earth without crowding the roots. Be sure there is ample drainage and be sure to fill in underneath the plant and around the edges with the best earth obtainable and pack firmly. Water thoroughly to wash the earth down around the plant. Store out of doors and leave plants to the weather until time to bring them indoors for forcing.

"Bring prepared plants in from six to eight weeks before the date on which they are to be in bloom. Allow three weeks longer for the lutea hybrids. Keep them in good light, but not direct sunlight, at a temperature of not lower than 45° nor higher than 55°. Plants brought along at the lower temperatures do best. Too much heat will cause the buds to come blind. Keep the soil moist, but not wet and never allow water to touch the leaves or flower buds.

"If the flowers come along too fast, they may be delayed by placing the plants in a temperature of not higher than 40° and not lower than 36° and then raising the temperature to 66° a day or two before use.

"Tree peonies may also be held back in order to have good flowers for exhibition at a later date than they normally bloom by following these instructions: dig the plant as soon as frost leaves the ground, pot as above and place immediately in a freezer. Six weeks before the time for the show, bring into a temperature of 40° and allow three days for thawing, then raise the temperature to 55° and keep at that temperature for 20 days, in good light but not brilliant sunshine. Buds will be showing. Again cool off for from six to ten days at 45°, to swell the buds. Return to 55° to 60° to bloom. These times may be slightly varied to suit the circumstances. Be sure to keep all top growth dry and the roots moist.

16

Propagating the Tree Peony

Most tree peonies are propagated by grafting, a slow process. Grafts made in August or September left undisturbed in cold frames, a cold greenhouse or planted in the field are ready for the average garden in 2 or 3 years. This is, however, the quickest, surest, and best method of propagating tree peonies and the method most commonly used.

Propagation by layering, laying a branch down on the ground while still attached to the plant and covering it with a few inches of good soil is not often used. After 2 or 3 years small plants may form somewhere along the branch, grown enough to cut off and transplant in permanent quarters.

Tree peonies are sometimes propagated by root division but this is much more difficult than with herbaceous peonies, since the wood is extremely hard and it is difficult to make the cuts. Root divisions should be set somewhat deeper than the plant from which they are made so the crown of the plant is 4″ to 6″ below the surface of the ground.

Propagation from seed, except in the species, never produces plants true to name and may require as long as ten years to get a flower. Frequently the percentage of germination is small.

GRAFTING

Here we should like to include a mild warning about mortality in grafting. A nursery that has less than 50% deaths the first year and another 50% the second counts that it is doing pretty well. This is what accounts for part of the expense of a tree peony.

The usual method of propagating the Japanese tree peony is by grafting a shoot or scion of the tree peony upon the fleshy root of a herbaceous peony (P. lactiflora). Choose a scion 2" to 3" long bearing 2 or more buds from the current year's growth. Select a good piece of root or understock ½" to 1" in diameter, at the large end and shortened to 4" to 6" in length.

When grafts are to be placed in the open field, they should be made early enough to allow scion and rootstock to knit before danger of freezing, mid-August in the north, a month later in the south.

The grafts may be left undisturbed in a cold frame or cold

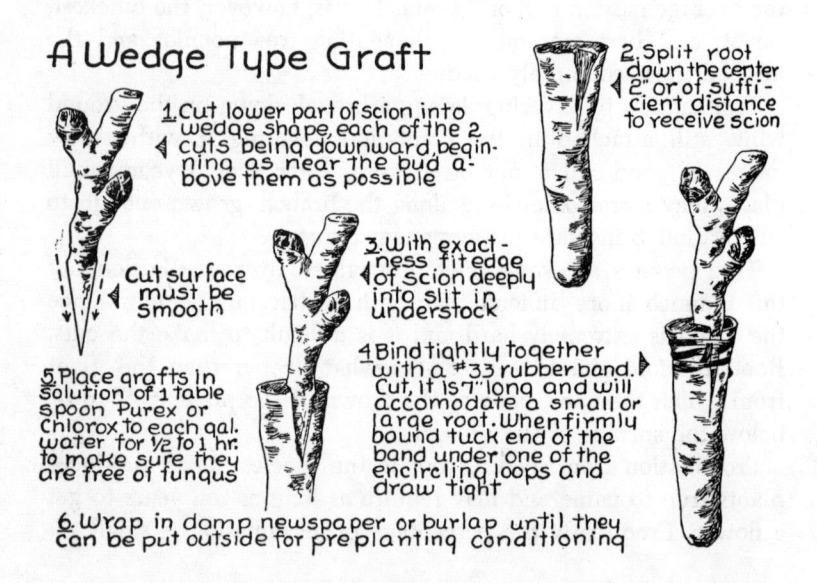

A Wedge Type Graft

1. Cut lower part of scion into wedge shape, each of the 2 cuts being downward beginning as near the bud above them as possible

Cut surface must be smooth

2. Split root down the center 2" or of sufficient distance to receive scion

3. With exactness fit edge of scion deeply into slit in understock

4. Bind tightly together with a #33 rubber band. Cut, it is 7" long and will accomodate a small or large root. When firmly bound tuck end of the band under one of the encircling loops and draw tight

5. Place grafts in solution of 1 tablespoon Purex or Chlorox to each gal. water for ½ to 1 hr. to make sure they are free of fungus

6. Wrap in damp newspaper or burlap until they can be put outside for preplanting conditioning

greenhouse for 2 or 3 years when they are ready for the average garden. To plant in the open field place the grafts horizontally on a layer of sawdust 2" deep on the ground, in any well shaded place. Pile 3 or 4 rows deep with sawdust between each layer and cover with a 3" layer. Water occasionally to keep entire bed damp but not wet. Evaporation keeps the sawdust cool. When the union of the scion and understock is well underway (they knit quickly in a cool, moist place) after 3 to 4 weeks, plant grafts in field in rows in a trench the width of a spade. Place vertically on each side of trench 3" to 4" apart with the top bud 2" to 3" below the surface. Level the ground and cover to a depth of 3" with sawdust. If the ground is dry, soak trench before it is completely filled. The grafts need no further attention until they are lifted 2 or 3 years later when the scions should have good roots. The sawdust is a protection from rapid temperature changes and minimizes weed growth. Planted in the open field, grafts should be made early enough to allow union before danger of freezing.

FROM SEED

Tree peonies grown from seed usually require 5 to 7 years to bloom, although the range varies from 3 to 10 years or more. No one can predict just what a seedling will be but the hope and thrill of getting a new and unusual plant spurs many peony lovers on to keep trying, demonstrating a wonderful degree of patience.

To grow seedlings harvest seeds at earliest stage of ripeness, just as they are beginning to turn black. There is no use in planting any soft seed, seeds that give when you pinch them between your fingers. Store in a cool place until you have collected all you want. Soak seeds in Purex or Clorox solution (1 tablespoon to 1 gallon of water) ½ to 1 hour to destroy any fungus. To stratify, choose a clay pot of convenient size. Use a 1" layer of friable, crumbly soil in the bottom of the pot, then a layer of seeds, alternate until pot is filled, being sure each seed is completely covered with soil.

Sink the pot in a well shaded, well drained location deeply into the ground, so the top of the pot rim is 18" below the surface of the ground. If the ground is dry fill the hole with water and let it soak in before placing the pot into it. Soak the pot in water before burying it. In six weeks lift the pot, invert and remove the seed and earth mass. A tiny rootlet will have formed at the open end of each seed that has germinated.

Prepare a trench as wide as your spade and 2½" deep, in half shade. The soil should be rich and well drained. Scatter sprouted seeds 1" apart. Refill trench, level ground, cover with 2" to 3" sawdust to conserve moisture and keep weeds and grass out when young tree peony shoots make their way up the following spring. In the spring, before growth starts, sprinkle with chlordane dust to discourage cutworms. When tiny plants show, spray with ½ strength solution of bordeaux or fermate. Repeat at 2 week intervals several times the first season. Do not disturb seedlings for two, or better still, three years. Transplant into rows 6" to 8" apart and leave until they have flowered. Seedlings perhaps never have the distinction of the fine selected plants but they give a sense of ownership and accomplishment to their grower. The lutea hybrids, being excessively sterile, never set seed, or almost never. If yours does, save and coddle it.

17

Selecting Varieties

EARLY AND LATE VARIETIES

It is possible to extend the blooming season by careful selection of varieties. Start the season with an early bloomer such as Tama-fuyo (Jeweled Lotus) which has very pale pink-blush, cup-shaped flowers of exquisite delicacy. Its semi-double flowers are early and it has deep rose carpels. Gessekai (Moonlit World) is a popular white variety which flowers early. Haku-raku-ten (Poetry of China), a single, has white flowers with reflections in its depth of shell-pink, stamens of gold and a purple pistil, a real beauty.

Shin-tenchi (Between Heaven and Earth) has lovely, semi-double, pink flowers and a dark exciting center. A beautifully shaped and colored flower is Shuchiuka (Flower in Wine). Its delicate pink petals have deep pink splashes at the base. Kintajio (Castle of Kinuta) has lovely pale pink single flowers.

Later comes a deep, dark maroon, Uba-tama, and Hatsu-garashu (First Crow of the Year) which is one of the finest of the dark varieties with crimson-maroon, semi-double flowers.

Usually the Japanese tree peonies are over before lutea hybrids begin though of course, in every season, there is a little overlapping. After the Japanese tree peonies are through blooming the lutea hybrids extend the season. Harvest, a semi-double

Tree Peony Blooms Are From 2" to 12" Across

Sizes differ depending upon culture, weather, etc. Among the smallest are P. lutea, single yellow and P. delavayi, single maroon, resembling the buttercup

P. lutea about 2" across

Most double flowering European types are of medium size, 5" to 8". Include a wide range of colors, many fragrant, most of superior lasting quality. Foliage broader and less finely cut than Japanese types

P. banksi, double flesh lavender-pink

Tremendous sized flowers among Japanese varieties. Broad petaled, tips crinkled with crepe paper like texture, central cushion of golden anthers. Gessekai (white) and Haru-no-akebono (white with divided petals shaded with crimson) sometime measure nearly 12" across

Ukaregi-ohi, semi-double, salmon-rose

lutea hybrid, has bronze gold flowers with petal edges flushed with rose. Age of Gold has a flat rosette flower with ruffled petals of bright gold. And last of all making about three weeks of bloom comes Argosy, one of the last P. lutea hybrids. It has clear sulphur yellow, single flowers 6"-7" wide, plum-colored flares.

ACCORDING TO COLOR GROUPINGS

The late Dr. A. P. Saunders, beloved Dean and Professor of chemistry at Hamilton College, Clinton, New York, showed his new tree peony "Argosy" in Boston in 1928. It was at a combined American Peony Society and Massachusetts Horticultural Society Peony Show and with it he won the President's cup. He established a special niche for himself in the peony world because of his great contribution in the field of hybridizing, both with herbaceous and tree peonies. Dr. Saunders' daughter Silvia is successfully carrying on his work.

Their choice Japanese tree peonies usually bloom in Clinton the second to the last or last week in May and on into June when the lutea hybrids start, followed by P. lutea itself, the last to flower. The blooming season covers three to four weeks. Two year grafts or older, some nursery grown plants are available at varying prices depending upon the size and quality.

Japanese tree peonies, P. lutea or P. delavayi hybrids bloom through the first half of June, in Clinton, sometimes longer. The above mentioned Argosy is a clear sulphur yellow, single, 6"-7" wide with plum-colored flares. Silvia Saunders lists her lutea hybrids under six groupings according to color and under each grouping are many fine named varieties. The six groupings are as follows:

1. "Roman Gold" group—Yellow, clear or almost clear, generally single.
2. "Golden Hind" group—Yellow, clear or almost clear. Generally semi- or fully double.

3. "Tea Rose" group—Generally yellow, but tinted and suffused rose. Single to double.
4. "Banquet" group—Generally red in color but with yellow undertones. Single or double.
5. "Black Pirate" group—Six darkest crimson and nine almost black maroon. Single to double.
6. "Mystery" group—Ivories, pearled shades, suffused mauves. Single to double.

EUROPEAN-CHINESE, JAPANESE AND HYBRIDS

European-Chinese
ALBERT CROUSSE—Large double, flesh-pink.
BANKSI—First tree peony variety brought to the new world from China. Large, double, flesh-pink flowers, good bloomer, hardy.
BIJOU DE CHUSAN—Large double, outer petals pure white, center petals cream tipped with green. Good bloomer.
FRAGRANS MAXIMA PLENA—Fine double, salmon-flesh.
OSIRIS—Double, velvety dark red, profuse bloomer. Dwarf grower suitable for rock gardens.
REINE ELIZABETH—A vigorous, free bloomer with large pink, almost rose-red flowers.
SOUVENIR DE DUCHER—Large double, deep violet flower with reddish tinge; outer flat layer of guard petals with a rounded bomb of petals on them.

Japanese Varieties
ANYO-NO-HIKARE (Light in the Dark)—Large double, rich deep crimson with crinkled petals.
FUJI-NO-MORI (Grove of Fuji)—Watermelon pink, deeper in center, crepe-like texture, semi-double.
FUSO-NO-TSUKASA (God of Japan)—Large, ball-shaped double white.
GABISAN (Mountain of the Arched Eyebrow)—Large white, double beautiful center.
GEKKYUDEN (Palace of the Moon Kingdom)—Large double white, shaded yellow.

SELECTING VARIETIES

GENKIMON (Gate of Genki)—Huge white shaded yellow, double.

GESSEKAI (Moonlit World)—Immense double, glistening white crinkled petals.

GODAISHU (Large Globe-like)—White with yellow center, large translucent petals beautifully curved. Double.

HAKU-RAKU-TEN (Poetry of China)—Single, white, reflections in its depth of shell-pink, stamens of gold, purple pistil.

HANA-DAIGIN (Minister of Flowers)—Lustrous deep purple, large full double.

HANA-KISOI (Floral Rivalry)—Large excellent deep cherry-pink, double.

HATSU-GARASHU (First Crow of the Year)—Huge double, rich glowing maroon.

HIGURASHI (Twilight)—Large double, bright pink.

HINODE-SEKAI (World of the Rising Sun)—Large brilliant rosy-red double.

HINO-TSUKASA (Ashes of the Setting Sun)—Big double, glistening fiery scarlet.

HIRA-NO-YUKI (Snow of Hira)—Semi-double white with yellow center.

HOWZAN (Treasure Mountain)—Full double, brilliant light pink, twisted petals.

IMA-CHOW-KOW (Name of Ancient Saint)—Large double, opens lemon-yellow and fades to white.

KAGURA-JISHI (Sacred Lion Dance)—Immense double, rich pink with rose-red center.

KAMADA-FUJI (Wisteria of Kamada)—Double wisteria purple with lavender shadings.

KINTAJIO (Castle of Kinuta)—Full double, blush-pink with fringed petals.

KOKAMON (Gate of Koka)—Double lustrous brilliant maroon.

MOMOYAMA (Mountain of Peach Orchard)—Large full double, fine pink. A favorite.

NISHIKI-NO-TSUYA (Beauty of Brocade)—Double of great size. Scarlet-crimson base.

NISSHO (Sunbeam)—Glistening scarlet, enormous double.

ORIHIME (The Weaving Princess)—Large double, exquisite Chinese-red.

SHIN-MOMO-ZOMA (New Bloom of the Peach Flower Garden)— Immense double, light pink. Coral branches and stems.

SHINTENCHI (New Heaven and Earth)—Large shell-pink, semi-double with thick satiny petals.

SHOGYOMON—One of the largest and best whites, bluish cast. Full double.

SHUCHIUKA (Flower in Wine)—Rose-pink large semi-double. Old favorite.

SUMA-NO-ICHI (Deepest Ink)—Immense satiny deep maroon.

TAMA-FUYO (Jeweled Lotus)—Early blooming blush pink, semi-double to double, establishes easily. Deep rose carpels.

UBA-TAMA (Beautiful Black King)—Huge satiny maroon.

YACHIYO-TSUBAKI (Long Hedge of Camellias)—Brilliant coral-pink double.

YAE-ZAKURA (Very Double Cherry)—Large double, soft cherry-pink.

Lutea (delavayi) Hybrids

French (Lemoine) originations:

ALICE HARDING—Bright lemon yellow, full double but shows stamens in its center when fully open.

SANG LORRAINE—Fragrant, semi-double, deep mahogany-red, black at base.

SATIN ROUGE—Vigorous but not floriferous, large, fragrant, fully double flowers, deep blood-red shade with broad satiny petals.

SOUV. DE MAXIME CORNU—Grows vigorously, large double yellow flowers edged with red.

American (Saunders) originations:

AGE OF GOLD—Like a ruffled camellia. Flat rosette of soft cream gold. Semi- or fully double. Central mass of stamens. Flower stems weak but one of the most beautiful of the yellow tree peonies.

ARGOSY—Single, cup-shaped, clear sulphur-yellow, red blotched at base. Free bloomer.

BANQUET—Shinny flat rosette of cherry red, brilliant dark center.

SELECTING VARIETIES

Single to semi-double.

BLACK PIRATE—Dramatic. Very dark mahogany red single with black flares.

CANARY—Dazzling yellow, one of the brightest, dramatic heart, very fine, single.

GOLDEN HIND—Fluffy 7"-8" blooms of bright yellow, flared dark. Fine variety. Double.

HARVEST—Color of ripe grain. Petals furled and rosy edged, semi-double. Decorative.

MYSTERY—Large flowers, pearled lavender with darker shading, varied with palest green.

PRINCESS—Semi-double dusky mauve suffused with golden sheen. Pale gold center. Gorgeous.

ROMAN GOLD—Cup-shaped single, brilliant warm yellow, flared dark. Fine form and substance. Seventy-two blooms reported on one plant.

TEA ROSE—Lovely flower of warm light amber.

THUNDERBOLT—Floriferous. Black crimson single streaked scarlet.

There are about seventy-five Saunders hybrid varieties. The flowers are smaller than the Japanese tree peonies but the colors are more unique and magnificent ranging from yellow through orange and blends of yellow and red to almost black. These colors do not exist except for the black maroons, in the European-Chinese and Japanese varieties so are doubly valuable in a collection for they bloom two or three weeks later than most other varieties.

MOST POPULAR TREE PEONY VARIETIES

(As voted by members of the American Peony Society—1958)

White:
Coronal, Rosy tints. S.
Flora, S.
Fuso-no-tsukasa, D.
Gabisan, D.
Genkimon, D.
*Gessekai, D.
Haku-banriu, D.
*Godaishu, D.
Kamikaze, D.

WHITE (continued)
*Renkaku, D.
Suisho-haku, SD.
Tama-sudare, D.
*Tsuki-sekai, D.
Okina-jishi, D.
*Yaso-no-mine, D.
*Yaso-okina, D.

Pink:
Akashigata, D.
Higurashi, D.
Howzan, D.
Momo-yama, D.
Sakura-gasane, D.
Sakura-jishi, D.
*Shintenchi, SD.
Suigan, D.
*Tama-fuyo, D.
*Yachiyo-tsubaki, D.
Yae-zakura, D.
Yomo-zakura, SD.

Cherry:
Beni-chidori, SD.
Hana-kisoi, D.

Rose Red:
Hinode-sekai, D.
Hodai, D.
*Mme. Stuart Low, D.
*Reine Elizabeth, D.
Shin-kagura, D.
*Ukaregi-ohi, SD.

Scarlet:
Impumon, D.
Kin-pukurin, SD.
*Nishiki-no-tsuya, D.
Nissho, D.
Robert Fortune, D.

Taiyo, SD.
Tama-fidori, SD.

Red (Crimson):
Charioteer, S.
Kokamon, D.
Satin Rouge, D.
Shugyo-kuden, SD.
Teikwan, D.

Black Red:
Black Douglas, SD.
Black Panther, SD.
*Black Pirate, S.
Kuro-botan, SD.
Ubatama, D.

Purple:
Hana-daigin, D.
Hatsu-garashu, D.
Hora-kumon, D.
Rimpo, SD.
Souvenir de Ducher, D.

Yellow:
Age of Gold, D.
Alice Harding, D.
Amber Moon, S.
Argosy, S.
Canary, S.
Chromatella, D.
Golden Vanity, S.
Goldfinch, SD.
Harvest, SD.
High Noon, SD.
Kinshi, SD.
La Lorraine, D.
Roman Gold, S.
Silver Sails, S.
Wings of the Morning, S.

SELECTING VARIETIES

Yellow with Reddish Markings:
  Banquet, SD.
  Chinese Dragon, S.
  Conquest, SD.
  Pastoral, S.
  *Souvenir de Maxime Cornu, D.

Other Colors:
  Aurore, terra cotta, S.
  *Kamada-fuji, wisteria, D.
  Princess, mauve and gold, SD.
  Savage Splendor, ivory, purple, and red, S.

Many listed as double (D) are perhaps semi-double (SD). Those * were voted "the best" tree peony. Gessekai received the most votes.

TREE PEONIES that do very well in the south.

Gessekai	White	Double	Early
Tama-fuyo	Blush	Semi-Double to Double	Early
Hana-kisoi	Cherry	Double	Early
Uba-tama	Dark Maroon	Double	Early

PART IV — PEONIES INDOORS

18

An Ancient and Modern Favorite for the Home

The Chinese in their ancient decorative arts frequently used two or more arrangements together, flowers in a tall vase with flowers or fruit beside it in a low basket or cut flowers with pot plants. The plant material was chosen because of its symbolic or religious significance or association with the season. The peony signified spring just as the unfurling leaves or blossoming branches were a symbol of spring, new strength and virility. Designs showing a branch of the Japanese plum, a spray of cymbidium, and the peony are found on screens and panels of old silk. Magnolia was combined with crabapple and flowers of the tree peony in seventeenth and eighteenth century woodblock prints. The designs were informal using a few perfect blossoms and branches of interesting shapes with the emphasis on the form, texture and color of a few well chosen subjects.

In Japan arranging flowers has long been a recognized art starting back in the sixth century when the first emissary to China is said to have brought back to Japan the idea of floral offerings for Buddhist altars. As in China, much folklore, symbolism and tradition are associated with the art. For centuries in Japan the peony has been known as the flower of prosperity and is highly prized by arrangers because of its symbolism and beauty. The Japanese decorative arts seen in paintings, ceramics and textiles, like the Chinese, show frequent pictorial use of the peony. Peach blossoms and sprays of orchids are frequently combined with them. A lacquered cart painted on a sixteenth and seventeenth century Japanese screen shows a basket of wisteria, tree peonies and blossoming fruit branches. In arranging flowers the Japanese have become masters of line design, practicing simplicity and restraint.

In both Europe and America in the eighteenth and nineteenth centuries the peony was a popular garden flower. A study of the Dutch and Flemish flower painters shows the tulip, rose, peony, and iris to be the four favorite flower subjects. The peony was used cut in combination with many other flowers of the day in large, lavish and colorful bouquets.

An abundance of material was used in contrast to the more frugal restraint displayed in the Orient.

Today American arrangers use what is best from the past to fit their present day needs. They use modified mass groupings of the eighteenth and nineteenth centuries, line designs, or a combination of the two, whatever best suits their purpose, depending upon the type home in which they live. If there is a harmony of materials: flowers, container, accessories and setting, a pleasing relationship with the surroundings, the results will be satisfying.

The answers from a couple dozen top arrangers, lecturers and accredited judges when asked how they like to arrange peonies may be summarized by the four following answers.

1. "When peonies are in season I always incorporate them into a lecture, usually in a simple Japanese manner."

2. "I'm not a period or mass arranger and as we have more or less a contemporary home, my choice of containers for peonies is heavy plain glass or pottery. I think they are excellent for practicing in the oriental manner of using just three graduated blossoms. Personally I prefer them with their own foliage but at least they should be in keeping in scale, feeling and visual weight."

3. "I use peonies in arrangements, mostly as a focal point since the large, beautiful flowers are so well suited to that purpose. I do use the tight buds for line in other arrangements. The foliage too is very interesting, especially when it has turned color late in the season."

4. "Peonies are wonderful for weddings or decorating the church, they have excellent carrying power. Use the buds and the full blown ones and don't overlook the tight green buds. Break them up using the various stages. When in the market use them in colorful, lavish bouquets with all the other lovely spring things. Use the foliage and the seed pods too. Tree peonies! Just float one of the exquisite flowers. What could be lovelier!"

19

Peonies In Floral Design

ALONE WITH OWN FOLIAGE

The peony tops the list of flowers that can effectively be arranged alone with its own foliage. Highly decorative it lends itself well to natural groupings which are quick and easy to do. In an arrangement try to capture something of the distinction and spirit of the flower as it grows in the garden, emphasizing its quality of richness and the individual beauty of the flowers, so lovely in both form and texture. Some of the beautiful ruffled white petals are translucent and ethereal in appearance. And the handsome blooms come in colors of surprising brilliance as well as delicate, soft hues. Some fascinating and exciting flowers have undertones of silver in their pink colorings, one lovely white is flecked with carmine and yet another pure white is blotched with purple at the base of the petals. Many have richly marked centers and beautiful stamens, usually of a bright canary yellow.

The fact a bloom may be as big as a saucer need not be a problem. If space is limited use only one, three or five blooms to avoid a bouquet that is too large for the space where it is to be used. Remember five peonies will perhaps equal in bulk a dozen other flowers. Graduate stem lengths letting one or two stand tall, cutting others short, placing each bloom so it can

Peonies Used Alone With Own Foliage

This simple grouping of peonies with their own attractive foliage has sparkle and richness

Peonies of varying heights, none crowded, the larger fuller types used at the base

Foliage concentrated at base adds weight to support height. Each bloom is distinct with a natural charm and beauty

Their own rich green foliage contrasts and shows off to best advantage the beautiful flowers

Cut to varying stem lengths, flowers faced in slightly different directions with largest blooms lowest, design is attractive from all sides

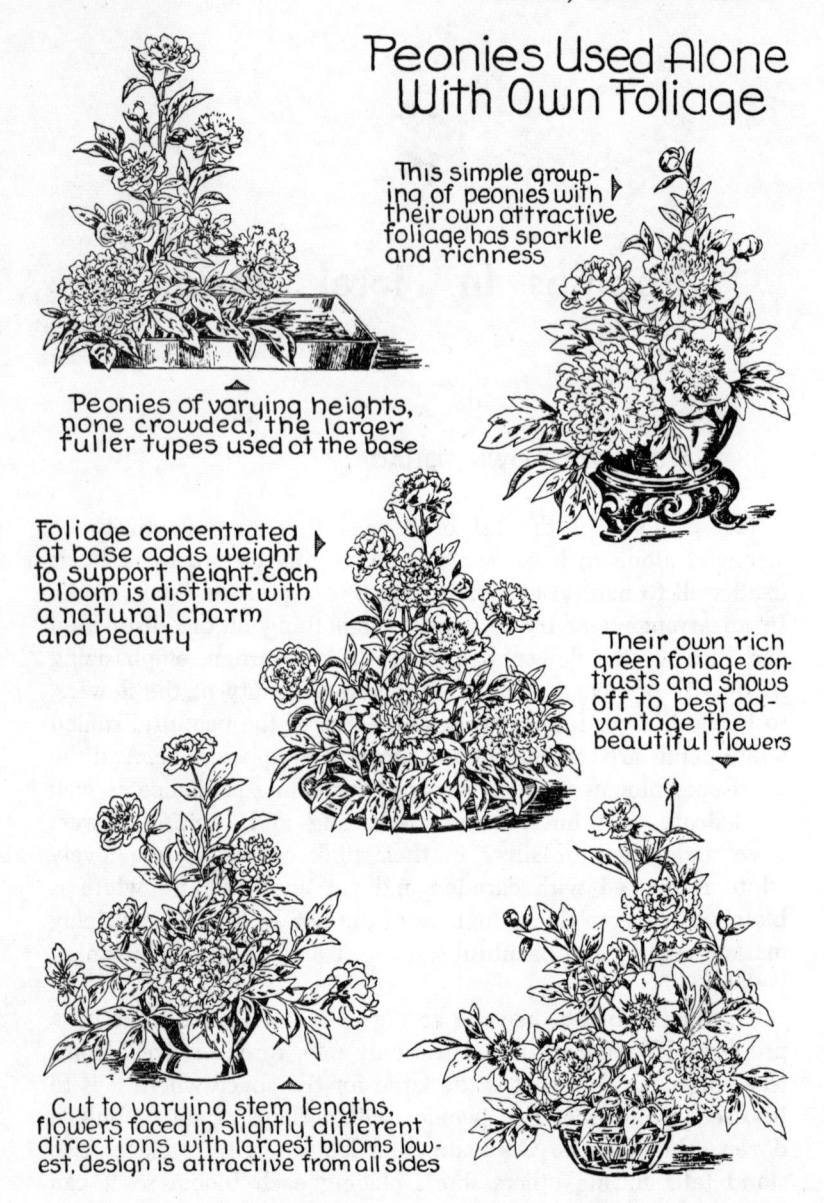

PEONIES IN FLORAL DESIGN 171

Peonies Used Alone With Own Foliage

Float a gorgeous flower. Anchor to holder. Leaves protect petals from water soaking

A handsome peony framed with its own attractive foliage

The tall bud and two shorter staggered stems seem to spring from one point and make a pleasing design ▼

Foliage frames lower flowers, accents taller ones, adds visual weight at bottom where needed

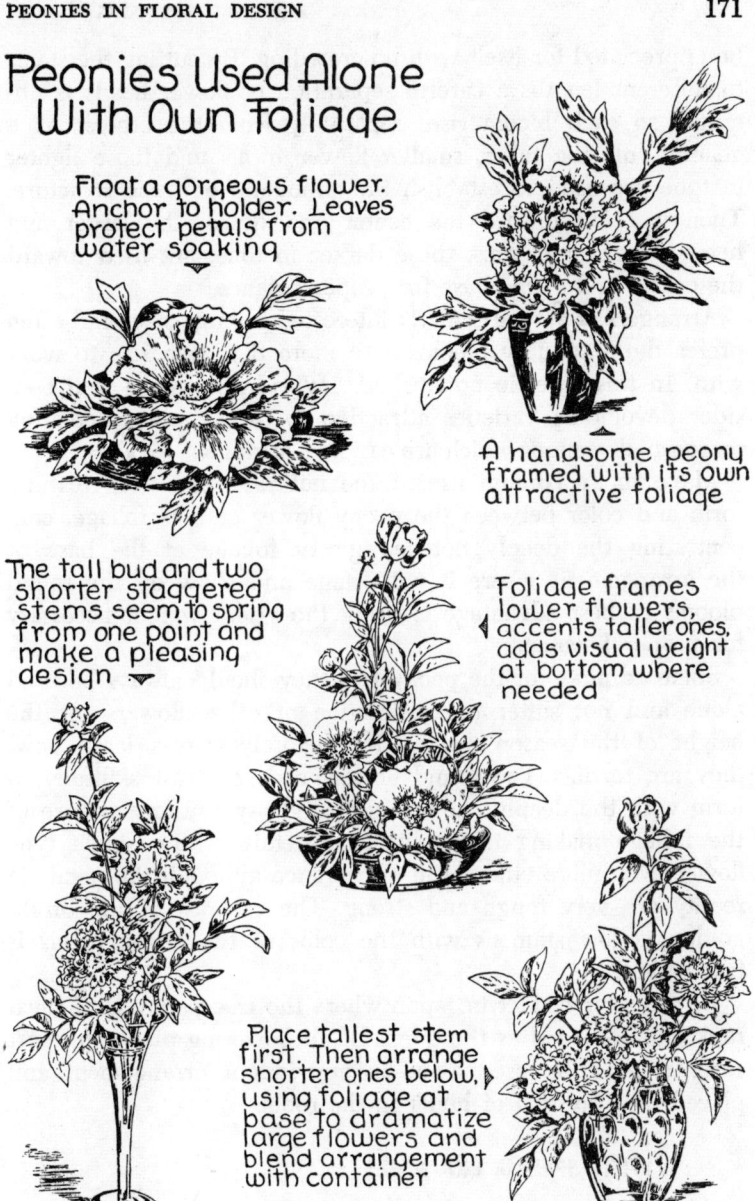

Place tallest stem first. Then arrange shorter ones below, using foliage at base to dramatize large flowers and blend arrangement with container

be appreciated for itself with no crowding. By cutting the stems to different lengths a careful separation of flower heads is obtained so each bloom rises separately from the others. As a general rule the taller, smaller flower forms and those lighter in tone are used to establish the silhouette or basic structure. Then working toward the center and down, the larger and heavier looking blooms, those darker in tone, are used toward the center and at the base for proper balance.

Arrangers aren't particularly interested in huge sizes and often prefer the secondary blooms as a more desirable size to work with. In this case do not disbud. Hybridizers might well consider developing varieties attractive to the arrangers, creating more small versions which are easier to arrange.

Make the maximum use of the natural contrast in texture, form and color between the peony flower and its foliage, concentrating the deeply notched glossy foliage at the base of the arrangement where it will frame and show off the round blooms to best advantage creating the visual weight necessary for proper balance.

Some admirers of the peony feel they should always be used alone and not suffer the distraction of other flowers. At the height of the season massed by themselves in a large bowl they are terrific. The round flower-heads contrast skillfully in form with the deeply cut leaves and glossy leathery texture of the foliage making the translucent petals of the single type flower even more ethereal in appearance although the petals in reality are very tough and strong. The contrast of the bright golden yellow stamens with the color of the satiny petals is fascinating.

As a matter of fact in Japan where the tree peony is of royal rank and regarded as the queen of all flowering plants, in most cases it must be used alone in any indoor arrangement and placed in a position of honor in the room.

WITH SPRING BRANCHES

A minimum of material is required for this type arrangement.

PEONIES IN FLORAL DESIGN 173

Peonies With A Few Well Chosen Branches

Choice and effective with a minimum of material

Siberian pea shrub adds airiness and height

Mock-Orange forms the outline. Peonies add interest and color

Long, sweeping branches bring Spring indoors

The lovely dogwood and peonies make delightful companions

If your peony plants are young or for any reason you do not want to cut many a very few flowers with short stems can be effectively combined with a few well chosen spring branches. Choose branches of apple, cherry, peach, plum, quince, redbud, spice bush, dogwood or whatever is at hand.

If you cut in the woods, observe the state conservation laws and never for a few branches or flowers do anything to harm or deplete our woodland treasures. If possible select branches with naturally lovely or interesting curves or bend them to the shapes needed. Branches lend themselves well to any size space, since they may be cut as short or long as necessary. If the space requires height branches may be cut three or more times higher than the container since their delicacy of line keeps the arrangement from appearing top heavy. In a low container always use a needlepoint holder of sufficient size and weight so it will not tip with the weight of the branches. Fill an opaque tall receptacle with crushed hen wire to anchor the placements. Start with the taller, lighter branches forming the outline of the design, then fill in, working toward the center and base, where the peonies, larger and heavier in appearance, provide the eye appeal and give the necessary balance. Replace the cut flowers at the base of the branches as necessary since the branches will usually outlast the cut flowers.

WITH OTHER PLANT MATERIAL

Since we do not share the feeling of association and symbolism found in the Orient we use the peony in any way that best suits our needs. We do not maintain an atmosphere of general elegance but dress the peony up or down to fit the situation. After all, in this country the peony is grown in the farm dooryard as well as on great estates. Blooming as it does with both the flowers of late spring and early summer, the most colorful time of the year in the garden, the peony season is the delight of arrangers. There is an endless source of forms, textures and colors from which to choose.

Mass Vertical Groupings

When flowers are abundant in the garden we can afford to be extravagant and use them generously in colorful buxom bouquets. Peonies lend themselves unusually well to this treatment. The big round forms are a natural center of interest. The open blossoms are excellent for emphasis and to focus attention, while the tight buds on longer stems supply line. Eighteenth century Williamsburg arrangements use peonies in mass with a wide variety of other garden flowers.

If one flower is to dominate, it sets the keynote and other flowers are selected to harmonize in color, or contrast, as is desired. Tall pointed or spiked flowers add interest and contrast. Spire-like flowers like the canterbury bell, delphinium, foxglove, lupine and thermopsis furnish height and line. The daylily, iris, madonna and regal lilies and tulips offer contrast in form and color and lend height if needed. Round forms, smaller and different in texture from the round peony, like coreopsis, pyrethrum and the rose add interest. The coral-bell and bleeding heart have graceful lines and add a touch of color.

Greens like ivy or artemisia foliage may be cut from the yard and used for graceful curves to soften any stiffness in the flowers themselves or to soften a severe silhouette. Use the decorative foliage of the peony if your plants are well established and you have enough to cut. It is particularly lovely used in fall arrangements with mums and other fall flowers after turning color late in the season.

Mass Horizontal Groupings

A massed horizontal grouping is practical for the dining, coffee or terrace table. The arrangement should be:

1. low enough not to interfere with the diners' view of one another.
2. attractive from every angle.
3. follow lines of table as round, oblong, square or oval. A longer table requires a longer container and arrangement. A small bouquet is lost on a large table, a large one overpowering on a small one.

4. considered as to total effect: colors, textures, atmosphere, table covering, china, accessories, etc. Must all make a pleasing, unified whole.

For the cocktail, tea or buffet table, plan a design to look down on as people will be standing. Depending on the placement of the table it may or may not be viewed from all sides. Viewed from only three sides it must have a feeling of depth, as though completed on the fourth side.

Generally speaking to arrange, start with the tallest and smallest flowers placing them horizontally in the needle holder, pointing some slightly upward, others downward to the length you want the finished design. Work in toward the center with the partially open blooms to those full blown with foliage or leaves at the base of the container to provide visual weight, interest and transition from flowers to receptacle making a harmonious unit.

For the Modern Setting

Simple uncluttered arrangements fit well in the modern surroundings. Large branches of whatever is available; apple, pear, plum, lilac or dogwood (forced or not) with the round peony blooms used as a focus can produce pleasing results. This is especially true against the large, plain surfaces in the modern home, stressing outline or silhouette, using a selective amount of plant material to obtain dramatic effects through simplicity.

Foliage having strong linear patterns which combine well with peonies for use in modern surroundings include such plants as aspidistra, bamboo, cryptomeria, Japanese holly, hosta, iris, juniper, ligustrum, magnolia, Japanese maple, nandina, narcissus, podocarpus, pothos, willow and wisteria. The hosta leaf is a favorite with peonies because of its strong, broad effects, glaucous sheen and strong veining. The variegated types are especially useful and interesting. Expose both the front and back of leaves for contrast and interest.

FOR LARGE SCALE DECORATIONS
(Platform, Hall, Church and Weddings)

Many of us associate the peony with Decoration Day, graduation or weddings. Because of its size and form it is ideal for large scale decorations. Placed in sturdy containers of pottery, metal or wood and combined with strong companions like the lilac, dogwood or large flowering fruit branches they make excellent pedestal arrangements for the platform or may be used equally well to decorate the church. Special attention must be given to scale in planning flowers for a large hall. Anything too small is out of proportion and ineffective. Cut larger, longer sprays or branches so they will be of sufficient size for the space where they are to be used.

Flowering spring branches are invaluable for large scale peony arrangements as they supply an airy, fairy-like silhouette or basic design for the peonies and add a fragrance, grace and lavishness in keeping with the peony itself. Often a selection of branches from two or three varieties of the same named plant add a subtle interest to the composition. To illustrate use the common, old-fashioned mock-orange or Philadelphus coronarius for the upper and outer branches. Remove the prolific foliage so the fragrant, white, single flowers may be better seen. The branches will last longer with most leaves removed and also appear lighter and less heavy. For the lower branches use P. splendens with its single flowers borne in groups of five and noted for their brilliant yellow stamens echoed in the peonies used in the arrangement and again in the soft gilt of the urn or container used. Cut the branches when ¼ the blossoms along the branch are open using both open flowers and buds.

If room permits and there is ample open space around the arrangement, large designs are effective placed on the floor. Use containers heavy and dark enough in appearance to give a sense of stability. The beauty of the lilac which blooms with the peony is especially lovely and effective viewed from above as is the peony. Cut the lilacs when ¼ to ½ the panicle is open.

Denude each flowering stalk of its leaves. If you want lilac foliage to break up the mass of flowers cut non-flowering branches which may easily be replaced as the leaves drop and wilt rather quickly.

Visibility

An arrangement designed for a large room should have carrying power to be enjoyed and seen by the people at the back. Good visibility is a must. Distinct, clean cut forms devoid of fussiness so the plant material will stand out in simplicity and elegance against a good solid background is important. Restraint is advisable and keep in mind one large arrangement or grouping is much more effective than several, small scattered decorations.

Lighter colors and white flowers show up best. Dark flowers and those in the blue to violet range become invisible at a short distance and look grey in subdued light. Always study the arrangement from the back of the hall or church, from the various entrances, and under artificial light if it is to be seen at night. Yellow loses its intensity under artificial light and becomes almost white. Blues and lavenders are scarcely noticeable and soft pastel shades lose their effectiveness under artificial light.

Flowers show up best with a natural light falling on them, however this is not always possible. A hidden, inconspicuous spotlight can highlight and add to the effectiveness of a decoration.

Church

As in all arrangements suitability and good taste are of first importance. Consider the interior decoration of the church and place the peony arrangements for best effects at the chancel steps or on either side of the altar, where they will enhance the decorations of the church leading the eye to a cross or some similar sacred object.

Plain interiors are easier to handle than the highly decorated as the situation is less complicated. A plain interior makes an excellent background for flowers which add warmth, cheer, color and relieve any bareness. If more than one arrangement is used space and group them so there will be a unity of design and interest using one or two predominant colors to tie the group together and create a unity and harmony.

Appropriate containers should have wide enough openings or tops for graceful arrangements and hold adequate water. Containers for the church are often used in pairs. They should be dignified and suitable, the larger more elaborate churches requiring more elaborate vases. Expensive silver or silver-gilt cups and chalices should have linings to avoid injury to the inside. Some excellent modern reproductions of good shapes and design in stone, lead and marble, carved wood and bronze are available. In a simple country church plain pottery or simple garden baskets are suitable. Peonies can be truly beautiful arranged properly in the chancel of any church. A well done church decoration is particularly rewarding because it is seen and enjoyed by so many people.

Weddings

June is the month of brides and peonies, which are much used and loved for weddings. Practical and lovely for either a home or church wedding with colors to fit any bride's color scheme they may be used in luxuriant decorations or for the simplest type ceremony. Nothing is lovelier than an all-peony wedding.

An arranger friend of ours who plans the flowers for top weddings discovered at the last minute that the bride had invited an extra bridesmaid and not informed her. Short one bouquet she rushed to the garden, cut two open double peonies and three bursting buds, made a collar of peony foliage designing an old-fashioned bouquet, which made an interesting contrast to the other bouquets which were all alike. It was the most admired of the bridesmaids' bouquets.

For mixed combinations featuring peonies there are endless choices, and for home or church decorations there is a wide choice to suit all tastes and pocketbooks.

WHITE. For the traditional white (or green and white) wedding white peonies in any of the five flower types or a combination of the differing forms may be combined with spiked white flowers such as canterberry bells, delphiniums, foxglove or gladiolus, hyacinths, iris, larkspur, lilies, lupines, narcissus, snapdragons, stock and tulips. White roses also combine well with peonies, the round forms contrasting in size, form and texture.

Materials to make up the silhouette or basic design may include any of the many white flowering branches available which supply lightness and a delicacy. Dogwood makes a fairy-tale background ideal for home or church weddings as do white lilacs, spirea or philadelphus. The fragrant, small, white flowers in short broad spikes at the end of branchlets on the fothergilla shrub are interesting and so are the large feathery pinacles of double white filipendula flowers.

Adding a tone of pink, apple blossoms, white lilacs and white peonies are a favorite combination for weddings.

PINK. Apple blossoms or any of the lovely ornamental fruit blossoms, pink dogwood, honeysuckle (Lonicera tatarica), beauty bush (Kolkwitzia) and the lovely magnolia blossoms used with pink or rose peonies and any of the white flowers listed above which come in pink (most of them do) offer a wide choice of materials from which to choose.

WHITE AND YELLOW OR GOLD. There are many possibilities with white and yellow or gold. Use yellow Siberian pea-shrub (caragana) and the more solid heads of white lilacs, to outline the design. Add some pale yellow or gold tulips and narcissus or yellow snapdragons, daylilies, aquilegia or iris using white peonies with yellow or gold centers lower in the arrangement near the base for focus. Use some buds and variegated ivy or pachysandra to soften the lines. Bold hosta leaves showing from behind the tulips will add character and interest to the design.

Possibilities are limitless. The lovely red peonies with yellow stamens have richness and great appeal and could be used with other peonies in all their various shadings from palest pink to deepest red.

HISTORICAL OR PERIOD DESIGNS

The peony was used through all the European historical and period styles as well as in our own Early American and Colonial Williamsburg days. Arrangements in "the spirit of" or characteristic style of these periods must contain the flowers typical of the period, the favored colors, prevailing style of design, preferred containers and accessories and conform in all the elements including plant material, furniture and the fabrics of the time.

For those who live in a period home or wish to enter Flower Show competition there are many fine helpful books available. *The Complete Book of Flowers and Plants for Interior Decoration* by Esther Wheeler and Anabel Combs Lasker is excellent. Visit museums and study the period rooms, paintings and tapestries to acquire knowledge and a feeling for the periods.

20

How to Cut, Condition and Dry

The beauty of the peony is as notable as its hardiness and many varieties are excellent cut for indoor decoration. The decorative flowers and ornamental foliage last well. The lovely satiny petals of the flowers reflect light and hold shadows enhancing their textural beauty. Newer introductions have a wide range of clear colors and intermediate tones and combinations such as a clear white with royal purple blotches at the center, a deep rose edged with silver and delicate lovely blossoms tinged with yellow.

Some of the breathtaking single, open forms add a richness and elegant touch to any arrangement. These forms hold themselves stiffly erect and lend themselves particularly well to Japanese type designs.

There are some almost cabbage-like doubles. These fat and full forms used in buxom bouquets need plenty of space and should be placed low in the arrangement where their apparent weight will focus attention so that balance is achieved. All arrangements must be well balanced or give a sense of stability, never appear lopsided or top heavy.

HOW TO CUT

Peonies may be cut at any time after the color shows in the

bud until they reach a fully open stage. Double varieties will last best however if cut when less than half open. Cut the buds of the double flowered types just as they are showing the first signs of color, as the sepals or green covering on the buds have separated enough to show the true coloring of the flower. This rule applies to the early varieties such as Edulis Superba, Mons. Jules Elie and to some late ones which have the so called "bomb" center. Practically all of these will open from a tight bud showing only a faint line of color. The late full petalled varieties usually have to be soft to the touch (like a marshmallow). Press down on them gently and if they feel soft to pressure they can be cut but if the center is still hard it should be left until it softens.

Cut tree peonies, single and Japanese types, when the blooms are just half open. If cut in tight bud they may fail to open in water. However if you need a tight bud for effect in an arrangement cut it the way you want it. Singles and Japanese often lock guard petals so tightly they will not open. Give them a little gentle help if they do.

When cutting peonies leave uncut at least one-third of the blossoms on the plant. Cut the stems no longer than needed for the arrangement leaving at least two sets of leaves on each stalk. If you must cut to the ground for a long stem then leave one-half the flowers uncut on the plant. In other words if you cut long stems cut correspondingly fewer blooms.

Remove the dead flowers as they fade to keep the garden neat and tidy in appearance. Do not cut away an excessive amount of foliage after flowering is over, some foliage is needed for good root growth and to aid in storing up the strength for next year's flower buds or blooms.

CONDITIONING

Observe the following procedure and if picked in the bud stage peonies will last 7 to 9 days. If newly cut conditioned blooms show signs of wilting, recut stem ends, place in water hot to the elbow (100°F) and recondition.

1. Cut peonies in the early evening or morning.
2. Take bucket or pail of water, at outdoor temperature, to garden.
3. Cut stems with a sharp knife.
4. Split ends a couple of inches and remove any unnecessary lower leaves.
5. Put directly into the water.
6. Bring indoors and set in a cool place away from drafts. Let condition overnight or at least several hours before arranging.
7. Some people add 3 tablespoons of sugar to each quart of water for better keeping. Chemicals such as Bloomlife and Floralife are quite effective in prolonging the life of cut flowers, but if too much is used the flowers turn brown. So be careful not to exceed directions, maybe a little experimentation is in order.
8. To hold the fragrance, while conditioning, cover the whole bouquet of blossoms loosely with a thin wax paper or cellophane, especially if exhibiting peonies in a class where fragrance counts.

STORAGE

Cut buds of double flowered varieties just as they are showing the first tints of color, pack in a box and put in cold storage. Stored in a cool room or cellar at 45°-50° F. the blooms may be held for several weeks. Bring out in advance of mid-June commencement or wedding and plunge into vessels of water. Keep in as cool a spot as you have, maybe the cellar, for two or three hours before bringing into a warm room, so change in temperature will be gradual. The flowers will explode into full bloom. These stored peonies will not keep very long once placed in warm rooms but long enough for the graduation or wedding for which they were held.

Peonies stored "dry" need at least a day to fill with water. Often when taken from storage "wet" and brought into a room to warm up and open they will wilt slightly but they will recover in an hour or so. If they do not, try hot water. If they do not respond to this they may as well be thrown out. Singles and Japanese are especially liable to flop when first brought out from storage. If they do not revive they were cut too late. As a matter of fact the proper time to cut a peony depends on the variety and is learned best by experience. Also if peonies are cut in the late afternoon, when they have begun to close for the night, as many do, it is almost impossible to tell when they are past the age for cutting. Hence morning is the best time to cut peonies, especially singles and doubles.

Commercially peonies are held for a month or two in cold storage. Thousands of blooms are cut each season and shipped from growers' fields to wholesale centers for sale, through local florists, for Decoration Day and later use. Growing chrysanthemums the year round, which are easier and cheaper to transport, and other changes in the flower industry have reduced the number of wholesale cut peonies in commerce today. However it was a thrill for us to walk into the Ritz in Boston June 1 of this year and see a gorgeous bouquet of Festiva Maxima in the lobby and a few days later to view a superb arrangement of Mons. Jules Elie as we entered a Statler dining room.

DRY FOR WINTER BOUQUETS

Buds and Blossoms

Dry peonies in both bud and blossom for they retain good color and form. The large, round double type flower is excellent in Victorian style winter bouquets and the lovely single Japanese and semi-double are equally effective used in modern designs.

The white, pink and red varieties keep their petal colors well enough to supply color in winter arrangements as do their bright yellow centers. The easiest way to dry buds and double flowers is to hang them upside down, one flower on a string by itself, fastened to a line, hook or coat hanger. In a dark, dry place they should be ready in two or three weeks.

Dried Arrangements Featuring Peonies

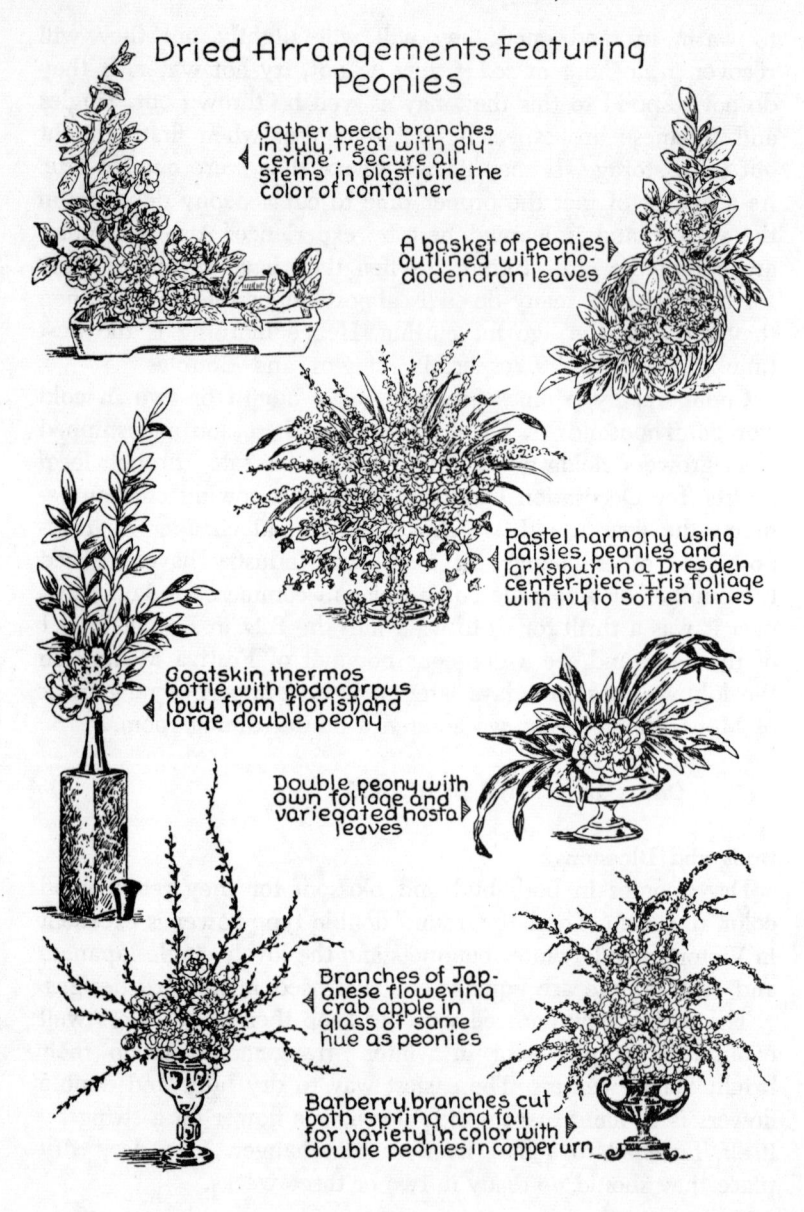

Gather beech branches in July, treat with glycerine. Secure all stems in plasticine the color of container

A basket of peonies outlined with rhododendron leaves

Pastel harmony using daisies, peonies and larkspur in a Dresden center-piece. Iris foliage with ivy to soften lines

Goatskin thermos bottle with podocarpus (buy from florist) and large double peony

Double peony with own foliage and variegated hosta leaves

Branches of Japanese flowering crab apple in glass of same hue as peonies

Barberry branches cut both spring and fall for variety in color with double peonies in copper urn

HOW TO CUT, CONDITION AND DRY 187

Drying Techniques
Dry Twice As Much As You Need To Allow For Breakage

Hanging:
Cut buds with foliage at stage you want them. Hang upside down, one to a string, in a dark, dry place. Should dry in 2-3 wks. Cut green foliage in spring, autumn colors in fall. Foliage dried by hanging has form and color.

Borax and sand or cornmeal:

Use box deep enough to adequately hold large flower. Place 2" drying mixture in bottom of box.
Face Down: Place single or Japanese type with petals smooth, in proper position. Gently cover with mixture.
Face Up: Make hole in center of box just large enough to push through stem of double type peony. Cover flower gently with mixture. Support box at each corner at least height of stem. Cut flowers at prime, when best color. Do not cover 6-8 days while drying in dark, dry place.

Foliage:

Pressing foliage keeps color but has no depth. Lay flat on absorbent paper, adjust to curves or shape desired. Do not overlap. Cover with absorbent paper, weight down, turn weekly until dry.

In container with 2" of water. Place stem end of foliage in container with water which will evaporate in week. Let foliage remain until dry. Has depth and form.

Store all dried materials in covered boxes properly labeled.

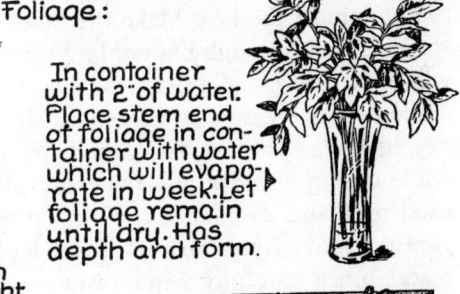

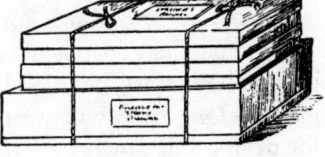

Better results are obtained with the single, Japanese and semi-doubles if dried in borax with sand or cornmeal, either face-down or face-up. Use fine builder's or thoroughly washed and sifted beach sand, well dried (using 1 cup borax to 2 cups sand), or mix one part of powdered borax with six parts of white cornmeal. Two tablespoons of uniodized salt to each quart of mixture will help maintain the brightness of the color.

Cut buds at stage you want them and flowers when they are at their prime, at their best in color. Never cut for drying after a rain, heavy dew or any extreme dampness. Shake off or get rid of any worms or bugs that might be present as they could destroy the dried flowers.

Use a box deep enough to adequately hold the large flowers placing 2 or more inches of the drying mixture on the bottom of the box.

(FACE-DOWN) Place single or Japanese type flowers, face down on the mixture, making sure the petals are smooth and in proper position. Gently work mixture around, up and over the flowers until they are lightly but completely covered.

(FACE-UP) Punch holes in boxes through which you push the stem with the double flower types remaining face-up, resting on the bottom of the box. Make the holes just large enough for the stems to push through but not large enough so the drying mixture will spill through. Support the boxes in some manner at each corner, high enough so the stems do not rest on the shelf or drying table. The flowers should dry in a week. Do not cover while drying and dry in a dark, dry place. The mixture may be used over and over again. When flowers seem thoroughly dry, gently remove from mixture. Never let them stay too long. With a soft brush carefully wipe away any borax and sand or meal.

If time is important flowers may be dried by laying them on newspapers and placing them in an oven turned to its *lowest* heat. They must be closely watched to retain their color. If left too long they will turn brown. It is the quickest procedure for drying but flowers become brittle and baking is only recommended if speed is essential.

Foliage

Peony foliage may be pressed for making flower pictures or hung upside down to dry. Dried upside down it maintains its form and depth. Decorative in form, dried peony foliage also retains its color well in the various shades of green. Since it turns to such wonderful colors as the season progresses toward autumn it is possible to dry many shades of foliage from May till frost for winter bouquets. Peony foliage may also be dried placed upright standing in a jar. Wash the foliage to remove any dust or dirt. Split the stem about 2". Then place stem ends in a jar with 2" of water which will evaporate in about a week. Do not add any more water. Let stand until thoroughly dry.

Peony Seed Pod
Useful in Dried Arrangements

As the seed pod develops the sections split open naturally to emit the seeds looking like the petals of a flower

As the seed cases dry they turn brown

Seed Pods

The sections of the peony seed pod as they develop and split open naturally to emit the seeds, look like the petals of a small flower. As the seed cases dry they turn brown. These exciting flower-like shapes add an interesting variety in form to small winter designs. Although you will remove faded flowers and will not allow all flowers to go to seed never hesitate to let a few develop on well established plants if you are interested in the seed cases for fresh or dried bouquets. The pale greenish-yellow seed pods of the peony are especially beautiful when newly formed.

Dried Petals

Remove petals from flower and spread on absorbent paper in a warm room, never in direct sunlight. Since the petals shrink as they dry start with about twice the volume you want. Carefully shuffle the petals daily. They should be dry in 4 to 5 days. Slightly sprinkle with salt and place the dried petals in a covered container until you wish to use them. Pink dried peony petals add a note of color and interest to potpourri and sachet.

Wax White Peonies

For those who are interested in old fashioned waxed Victorian bouquets, dry peonies at room temperature. With atomizer use a solution of 2 parts floral wax diluted with 1 part water mixed well. Use an egg beater. Let flowers drip to remove any surplus wax. Or peony may be gently but quickly dipped in solution if you have no atomizer.

Storage

Store all dried material in covered boxes, properly labeled, in a dry, cool place until needed. Label properly and keep delicate textures separated from heavy material. Have seed pods together in one box and foliage in another for easy finding.

TIPS FOR THE NOVICE

1. Plan simple, uncomplicated designs with a minimum of material.
2. Cut one, two or three well chosen branches for height and to outline the silhouette.
3. Use some tight green buds, some showing color, flowers half open and others well open for interest and contrast in form and size.
4. Combine various peony types as singles with doubles.
5. Cut varying stem lengths.
6. Avoid facing all flowers front or in one direction. Face some profile, others almost completely reversed as they grow in the garden.
7. Place the heavier looking flowers, those large or dark in

color low, with the lighter appearing buds and blossoms higher in the composition.

8. A congenial leaf or vine will soften harsh lines and at the base make a pleasing unity with the container. Vines are useful for their graceful curves.

9. For some arrangements to obtain proper visual balance a suitable base is necessary. Place the completed design on a small stand, pedestal or one, two or three blocks of wood, whichever number seems necessary. Paint the base a blending color or the color of the container. This often gives a nondescript vase or bowl character and distinction.

10. Use simple, well-proportioned containers in good neutral tones. Have at least two to start with; one a low type for the dining table or mantle and the other a taller urn-shaped, oval or upright rectangular for tall designs in the entrance hall or living room.

11. As a guide to good proportion when using a low container place the tallest stem 1½ to 2 times the length or diameter of the bowl, place the tallest stem in the tall container to extend 1½ to 2 times the height of the vase above its rim.

12. Work with these two pet containers, a good flower holder and a few blossoms until you are satisfied with the results you obtain. Then start to expand.

MECHANICS REQUIRED

To Gather Flowers

Pail, something to hold water and easy to carry.
Sharp knife.
Cigarette lighter or candle to sear stems.

To Make An Arrangement

Container.
Plant material.
Needle or pinpoint holders (assorted sizes and shapes).
Posey clay.
Sharp knife.
Wire cutter.
Florists' sticks, wire and tape.

Proper mechanical aids are essential to hold peony arrangements firmly in place and keep their stem ends always in water. The needle or pinpoint holder comes in assorted sizes and shapes and is excellent because stems may be arranged at an angle in this type holder. They are particularly good in shallow, open containers. The best ones have a heavy substantial base with firm brass points set close together to hold stems firmly.

For tall vases or any arrangement in an opaque container hen wire is especially helpful. The wire comes in a roll and may be purchased at a hardware store in any quantity you wish. Hen wire has larger holes and is softer and more easily crushed than chicken wire. Cut the wire with a wire cutter to the size you need. Crush it and fit it into the container. For a heavy flower like the peony use a needle holder with the hen wire crushed over it for a secondary holder.

Use "posey" clay which is non-hardening and insoluble in water to anchor the holder solidly in place. Apply the clay to the bottom of the holder, press it firmly into position securing it to the bottom of the container. The holder should never be visible and can easily be covered with plant material used in the composition.

In constructing large arrangements, using heavy flowers like the peony, especially for a church or public building, wire a florists' stick to the stem of the first placement and see that it is firmly anchored in the holder. This will help hold the entire design more securely.

Many people today like the plastic sponges in place of pinpoint holders, they are so easily used. You can arrange flowers at any angle and carry the arrangement about, to a friend in the hospital or wherever you wish without danger of it getting too much out of position.

21

Varieties Best for Cutting

Early in the season, in May, when peonies are not plentiful or only choice extra-early hybrids and singles or tree peonies are blooming, you may hesitate to cut many because you want them for garden display. Just one attractive flower with a collar of peony foliage is most decorative, since the various parts of the flower are so interestingly and beautifully formed and colored. There is much detail and variation to be observed and enjoyed in a single bloom, a choice centerpiece for a dining room table or a table near a favorite living room chair.

Later, when the June-flowering or so-called Chinese herbaceous peonies (P. lactiflora) come along, the last to bloom, you can cut all you want. They bloom profusely and are so plentiful you don't mind cutting them and taking them from the garden. Picked when in almost the tight bud stage they will open to perfection in water and last a surprisingly long time.

It would be sensible for you to select varieties whose colors, form and foliage suit the interior of your home. Double flowers open easily from tight buds, and commercial peony growers usually confine themselves to doubles. Singles, Japanese and semi-doubles are all attractive in home flower arrangements, but be sure not to cut them too soon because they do not open after cutting if in bud. See page 183.

HERBACEOUS REGULAR

Single

The singles resemble huge anemones in form and open three or five days earlier than the Japanese types. If singles are cut at the stage when they will shed the pollen they will show it and the flowers may be badly discolored. Graceful plants, they hold their blooms up well without support, offering very handsome subjects for flower arrangements. They are good peonies for the south. Following are some outstanding varieties. Also see variety list page 74.

ARCTURUS (Auten)—Extremely rich, clear red single. Tall and early.

HELEN (Thurlow)—Double row of broad, cupped petals of deep shell pink, surround a mass of gold stamens. Plant medium size and spreading. Stems very tall, strong and erect with broad foliage. Early.

IMPERIAL RED (Sass)—Large, single, early red. Won third place in the popularity contest for red singles. Really a dark pink but its effect is light red.

KRINKLED WHITE (Brand)—Small bud that expands into a large flower with great, broad pure white petals, like crinkled crepe paper. One of the best single whites. Mid-season. When first opening petals are blush, which fade white in sunlight but will not fade when cut early and kept in the dark.

LE JOUR (Shaylor)—Long overlapping pure white guard petals with a center of golden yellow, stamens pink tinged. Remarkable substance. Plant large, compact. Early mid-season.

PICO—Early white. Won second place in the popularity contest for white singles. Foliage extra large.

PRESIDENT LINCOLN (Brand)—Single, early red. Won second place in the popularity contest for red singles.

SEASHELL (Sass)—A lively delicate pink, slightly fluted, with a full center of golden stamens. Strong stems hold the large flowers erect. Outstanding variety. Distinctive. Mid-season.

Japanese

The Japanese type peony is graceful in growth and quite different in type of flower with wide flaring petals of exquisite coloring and texture. The centers are usually a more or less compact mass of tiny petalodes if anemone (Japanese) or staminodes if regular Japanese, usually a color contrasting with the main petal color. Very charming color effects are found among them. They are ideal for making striking flower arrangements. For cutting see variety list page 74 as well as the fine varieties listed below.

AMA-NO-SODE (Japan)—Bright rose-pink, cup-shaped guard petals surrounding a center of long, yellow staminodes, edged gold and faced with pink. Large flower, medium height, strong stems, good foliage. Mid-season.

HARI-AI-NIN (Babcock)—Dark maroon-red petals with center of broad stamens color of petals heavily tipped yellow. Late mid-season.

ISANI GIDUI (Japan)—Rounded guard petals of pure white, which surround a compact cushion of golden staminodes. Like a large white poppy. Mid-season. Lovely white and gold effect. Moderately tall.

LOTUS QUEEN—Second only to Isani Gidui in popularity vote for best white or blush, Japanese type. Mid-season bloomer. Stems strong.

NIPPON BEAUTY (Auten)—Rich deep garnet-red, center staminodes are garnet edged with golden yellow. Strong grower, tall and free bloomer. Late. Lovely for cutting.

NIPPON BRILLIANT—One of finest in its class, crimson and gold, tall, late.

TAMATE BOKU (Japan)—Also incorrectly known as Tomtabako. One of the largest of the Japanese type. Bright old rose China pink, center yellow and tipped pink, gold edges. Mid-season.

WESTERNER (Bigger)—Guard petals very large, beautiful shade of light rose-pink. Center filled with yellow staminodes extremely firm and erect. Cup-shaped form is gracefully poised and held rigidly erect. Mid-season.

Anemone

The anemone peony is listed in catalogs either under Japanese or doubles. It has several rows of guard petals, which are usually white or pink, with a center of small narrow petals (petalodes) of yellow or the same color as the guards, sometimes of a different shade. Many of these erroneously, since the yellow always fades to white, are called "yellow" peonies. Interesting and useful for cutting. In addition to the varieties listed below also see pages 74-75.

ADA PRISCILLA (Guille)—White petals with yellow center fading to white. Mid-season. (Listed under Doubles)

LAURA DESSERT (Dessert) (Listed under Doubles)—White guard petals with yellow center, fading to white. Early.

NIPPON GOLD (Auten) (Listed Japanese)—Dark pink guard petals with yellow center. Mid-season.

PRAIRIE AFIRE (Brand)—The guard petals are broad and a soft creamy-rose with good substance. These surround a great ball of brilliant fiery red staminodes. Listed as Japanese.

PRIMEVERE (Lemoine)—A flattish flower, medium size, with creamy white cupped guards rarely splashed with red, with center of deep sulphur-yellow becoming white with age. One of the best and yellowest of the "yellow" herbaceous peonies. Mid-season. Listed as a double. Tall, floriferous, stems lax, good dark green, rather coarse foliage.

Semi-Double

The center of the semi-double is made up of a greater or lesser number of broad petals but it never becomes fully double. Intermixed with the broad petals are many pollen bearing stamens, sometimes grouped together in the center and in other varieties forming rings among the petals, always a prominent and interesting feature of the flower. The group includes some of the most artistic of the peony blooms and are popular with arrangers. See varieties listed page 75 as well as the list that follows.

LADY ALEXANDRA DUFF (Kelway)—Nicely formed flowers with

broad petals of soft pale pink. Tall, robust and delightfully scented. Mid-season.

MARGARET LOUGH (Gumm)—A very fine white coming into bloom at mid-season. The flower shows tints of pink and its golden stamens add interest.

MILDRED MAY, one of the finest whites of all for arrangement where its triangular sprays of bloom can be used.

MINNIE SHAYLOR (Shaylor)—Several rows of fluffy crepe-like petals of clear light pink fading to white. Center of golden yellow. Stamens very attractive.

RED GODDESS—Won first place in the popularity vote for the best red, semi-double. Mid-season bloomer. Medium dark velvety red, about the purest red in the lactifloras.

SILVIA SAUNDERS (Saunders)—Cup-shaped, bright clear rose-pink, fading lighter toward center, which is filled with yellow stamens among which the very bright pink stigmas make a conspicuous pattern. Dwarf, good grower, abundant bloomer, not large. Extra early. The distinctive grey green carpels add greatly to its charm.

WHITE ROSE—Blooms late mid-season to late. Its broad white petals faintly veiled pink with the intermingled stamens make a flower of indescribable charm and lovliness.

Double

Doubles are still the most popular and widely grown and are long lasting and decorative used as cut flowers when properly conditioned. The following varieties are recommended as very fine cut flowers. Also see varieties listed pages 75-77.

Early Blooming
Edulis Superba—Light pink
Festiva Maxima—White
Kansas—Red
Kelway's Glorious (white), one of the longest lasting of all cut flowers.

Mons. Jules Elie—Pink
Mrs. F. D. Roosevelt—Pink,

Early to mid-season
Pfeiffer's Red Triumph—Red
Richard Carvel—Red, fragrant

Mid-Season
Annisquam—Pink
Karl Rosenfield—Red
La Lorraine—Blush
Le Cygne—Cream-white
Longfellow—Red
Loren Franklin—Dark pink, fragrant
Lottie Dawson Rea—Light pink
Mary Brand—Red
Minuet—Light pink
Myrtle Gentry—Light Pink
Sarah Bernhardt—Pink, fragrant
Souv. de Louis Bigot—Dark pink, mildly fragrant
Late
Avalanche—Creamy-white
Baroness Schroeder—Blush
Felix Crousse—Red
Nick Shaylor—Light pink

HERBACEOUS HYBRIDS

The herbaceous hybrid group includes some of the most striking and beautiful of all the peonies. Brilliant and beautiful in color they are stunning for indoor arrangements. Any of them are good cut. Following is a list of favorites. Also see pages 93-102.

ALEXANDER WOOLLCOTT (Saunders)—Large, flat cups, shining crimson. Brilliant color doesn't fade. Extra early.

CAMPAGNA (Saunders)—Pure white single with gold and green center (no pink tones at all). Blooms just ahead of the lobatas, end of May and first of June.

CHALICE (Saunders)—Large pure shimmering single white, 8"-9", with long silky stamens. On heavy stems 3' tall. Immense dark glossy leaves. Mid-May.

CHOCOLATE SOLDIER (Auten)—Maroon almost black semi- to full double.

CLAIRE DE LUNE (Dr. White)—Pale yellow single variety of great charm and distinction. Greatest success in achieving yellow single, herbaceous peony.

LAURA MAGNUSON (Saunders)—Large cup-shaped clear bright rose, semi-double. Late for this strain. Mid-June.

NATHALIE (Saunders)—Magnificent flat bloom, semi-double or more. Intense clear rose, smooth-edged petals.

ORIENTAL GOLD (Japan)—First true double yellow, origin not known. New, scarce and expensive. Lemon-yellow, fading lighter. Stems medium height, strong bright green with darker foliage.

Blooms with the late Japanese and early lactifloras. Flowers of memdium size. Wonderful for arrangements.

RED CHARM (Glasscock)—Rich ruby-red, bomb shaped double with tall, strong stems. Fine plant. Still scarce.

TREE PEONIES

Cut any of the tree peony blossoms you feel you can spare from the garden for indoor use. They are all highly decorative. A few favorites follow but also see pages 155-163 for others.

ALICE HARDING—Clear yellow, ball-shaped double. Fragrant.

ARGOSY—Clear sulphur-yellow, single, 6"-7" across. Plum colored flares.

CHARIOTEER—Satiny, deep maroon, single with great dark heart, flat, open bloom.

GESSEKAI (Kingdom of the Moon)—A glistening pure white, immense double, with crinkled petals. Vigorous grower. Spectacularly beautiful. Kamikaze is a seedling of Gessekai.

HANA-DAIGIN (Minister of Flowers)—Lustrous, dark purple double.

HANA-KISOI (Floral Rivalry)—Enormous, deep cherry-pink double. A beauty.

HODAI (Reign of Chinese Emperor)—Giant, rose-red double.

KAMADA-FUJI—Large, wisteria colored, double.

RIMPO—Large, deep brilliant purple, semi-double to double, with yellow center.

SHUGYO-KUDEN (Palace of Gems)—Brilliant scarlet-red, semi-double.

SOUVENIR DE MAXIME CORNU—Yellow, full double, with reddish markings (yellow-orange effect). Grows 3' to 4' high. Fragrant.

SUISHO-HAKU (Clear Crystal White)—Semi-double, snow white, incurved petals.

TAIYO (Great Emperor)—Bright-red, enormous, satiny.

TAMA-FUYO (Jeweled Lotus)—Large, exquisite, cup-shaped blush-pink, double.

UBA-TAMA (Brilliant Black King)—Beautiful huge, satiny black-red double, incurved petals. Outstanding.

22

Flower Shows

DATES

Setting dates for peony shows in any locality which will suit all peony growers is impossible for some peonies are early, others late and some gardens are early and others come later. The local show committee should endeavor to set a show date that best suits the majority of peony growers, a time when the most peonies can be brought from the garden to the show without need of holding the blooms in storage.

The peony shows start in the south in early May and gradually move northward, the date varying slightly each year depending upon the type of season. Following are some show dates for this season: Oklahoma May 10-11, Maryland and Nebraska late May, Ohio early June, New York and Massachusetts mid-June, Minneapolis, Minnesota a week later, Ottawa, Canada June 23, North Dakota late June and Duluth, Minnesota and Superior, Wisconsin, mid-July.

MANAGEMENT

No matter how small or large a show a good organization with an efficient director, chairman or manager and capable working committees, each with well defined duties, is essential.

The chairman acts as a coordinator and moderator maintaining a smoothly operating group, with a secretary or assistant keeping accurate records and files of all transactions; the final objective—staging an artistic, educational and successful show. A person who has had organizational experience working with others, who can delegate authority with discretion and then follow through will get the best results. Ability to select the best possible chairman for each committee is important.

The chairman in selecting co-workers must choose some person who knows peonies. He also needs a person with extremely good taste, preferably with a background in art. Sometimes these two qualifications can be found in one person. If there is available someone with show experience, even though in some other field, that will be helpful. Know-how and experience are valuable attributes. The secretary or assistant handling the office work and records must be accurate and dependable.

The number and size of the committees will vary depending upon the type and size show. The chairman should be able to have a voice in choosing his committee associates. Any show chairman will need someone to act as a good dependable secretary to take charge of the records and office work. This may be done from the chairman's home until show time. The secretary will send out all notices of meetings; keep a record of the minutes of each meeting; receive and record all entries in the entry notebook; type and file exhibitors' entry cards alphabetically and distribute them to the exhibitors the day of the show; prepare loose leaf notebook sheets for the judges; type any comments they may want posted with the awards; purchase necessary supplies such as ribbons, stickers, committee badges, etc.; prepare list of awards for the local newspapers; print or have printed labels or signs needed for the show and issue the permits for the exhibitor to remove belongings at the end of the show if this is necessary. In large shows this is important to protect the property of exhibitors. The permit slip must be shown at the door on leaving. At the close of the show the secretary should have a complete record of all transactions.

The show committee is made up of the general chairman, secretary and committee chairmen who are responsible for writing the schedule, staging, judging and hospitality, publicity, tickets and special projects. In a small show combine several of the jobs under one chairman. The show committee should meet from time to time as a group to make decisions, discuss problems, and to be informed on the progress of the show. A good flower show represents a lot of work and thought but it is a known fact that a more lively interest in good gardening, proper landscaping, local parks, conservation of natural resources, removal of unsightly billboards and the general beauty of the community is stimulated in localities where good shows are held annually.

After deciding upon the dates of the show, where it is to be held, and what it is to include the schedule chairman is ready to go to work.

It makes no difference whether the show is large or small. It is the quality of the exhibits and schedule that is important. The schedule should include enough variety in the classes to insure an interesting and worthwhile show.

SCHEDULE

In writing an intelligent schedule for a show, a knowledge of local material and talent is necessary. The schedule should be written to make the best possible use of what is available. You would include a 400 sq. ft. display only if you knew of a large grower with the necessary facilities and talent to set up such an exhibit. You would include an extensive arrangement section only if there were competent people to carry out such a schedule.

Include classes for both amateurs and commercial interests, also open classes for all who grow peonies, amateurs and professionals alike. Plainly indicate whether classes are open or for the amateur or professional so there will be no misunderstanding in making entries. In some cases a distinction between the novice and advanced amateur is made. If so, make sure the two classifications are clearly defined in the show rules.

At peony time it is possible to put on a very interesting and spectacular Flower Show, which in addition to peonies may also include other classes for material which blooms at the same time. Roses, bearded iris, perennials and annuals, rhododendrons and azaleas, other flowering shrubs, flowering house plants, strawberries, cherries and vegetables may all have classes included for entries.

The schedule must clearly state the name of the show, where it is to be held, the dates and hours it will be open, the sponsor of the show and person, with address and telephone number, to whom entry blanks should be mailed or to whom exhibitors may write or call for further information.

RULES

The rules for the show should be clear, concise, simply written and easily understood, to avoid misunderstandings. State the time exhibitors must be finished with their staging in readiness for the judging, removal time, whether the class is for amateurs or professionals. The show management can not be responsible for the property of the exhibitors, whether or not multiple entries are allowed in a class from the same garden by various members of the same family and whether an exhibitor is allowed more than one entry in a class. In other words anticipate any difficulties you may encounter ahead of time and avoid them by a fair, concise set of rules.

Use correct horticultural terms and define such terms as: amateur, novice, professional etc.

CLASSES

Horticultural Classes

The following flower show classes are offered merely as a guide in writing peony show schedules. Any schedule must be adapted to meet local requirements.

Displays

Include displays only if there is talent and material available for such classes. From the scale of points for judging (see page 210) you can see a display is judged both for quality of material and artistic effect with emphasis on the artistic effect. In larger shows classes are sometimes written to cover 100, 200 or 400 sq. ft. using any or all varieties as noted in the class, the number of varieties may or may not be restricted. A fine display is always an asset to any show but a poor one is very disappointing and poor publicity.

Collections

Always specify the number of blooms, square footage if limited, and in some cases length of stem. Include classes for the type peony flowers your exhibitors grow. If possible for a more attractive show provide uniform containers for the cut peonies entered in the collection classes.

Collections may include as few or as many classes as the material available for the show demands.

Small Collections of 3, 5, 6 or 10 may include classes which call for:

1. Specify number, all different varieties, any type, one bloom of each.

2. Specify number, all different varieties, any type, one color, indicate white, light pink, deep pink or red, one bloom of each.

3. Specify number, all different varieties, only one type, indicate double, single, Japanese or hybrids, one bloom of each. (Always show singles for display before the pollen sheds.)

4. Specify number, all different varieties, one type, indicate which; one color, indicate which, one bloom of each.

5. Specify number of blooms, one variety, one type, one color.

Larger Collections of 20, 25 or 50 usually call for a specified number of different varieties, any type, one bloom of each. In some cases in the larger collections the class may be modified to read: 25 different varieties, one bloom of each, not more than 10 blooms may be single and/or Japanese types or: collection of 25 different varieties, one bloom of each, not to exceed 50 sq. ft.

Specimen

Always specify the number of blooms and length of stem in some cases. If possible supply uniform vases for the specimen classes. For exhibition purposes cut stems not shorter than 15″.

1. Best in a type (specify), any color.
2. Best in a type (specify), one color (specify).
3. Best herbaceous hybrid, any type, any color.
4. Best species.
5. Best miniature, any variety, any color.
6. Best specimen in show.

In advising how best to cut and hold early blooms for specimen competition in shows George Peyton writes "Those who have extra early locations and those growing the extra early hybrids will have to resort to refrigeration to hold them till show time. In order to do this it becomes necessary to cut the peonies at the proper time and place them in storage. A temperature of 36 degrees is best but a temperature as high as 50 degrees is satisfactory if the blooms are to be stored for a week or less. Blooms can be kept for over a month when stored at 36 degrees. A very important point to keep in mind is that blooms should be chilled for several hours before being brought to the show room. This chilling prevents wilting. Peonies are best stored with the stems in about eight inches of water.

"Most new exhibitors are also troubled as to what stage of development buds should be cut. The following types may be cut when the bud is showing color or when the first petals begin to unfold: singles, Japanese, semi-doubles. The full double type such as Hansina Brand should not be cut until almost fully open. It is important to place in cold storage as soon as possible after cutting.

"It is a good practice to place the buds in paper bags before placing in storage. The procedure is this: cut a hole in the bottom of the bag and slip the stem thru the hole, the open end of the bag is then closed by twisting. The bag gives protection to the petals against bruising. The one pound bag is about the right size for singles, Japanese and semi-doubles while the two pound bag is more satisfactory for the larger and fuller blooms.

"Cut stems about sixteen inches long and remove all foliage except the top leaf. However the stems should be cut so that at least two leaves are left on the plant. When the buds are brought to the show room, cut off the ends of the stems about a half inch, place in water and carefully remove the paper bag. It's a thrilling sight to see the buds unfold into beautiful blooms and it is even more thrilling to see a ribbon pinned on your exhibit."

New Hybrids and Seedlings

Reserve space for recently introduced and new varieties. These should be judged for Awards of Merit or medals by qualified judges.

Tree Peonies

If you have tree peony exhibitors include specimen and collection classes to fit what they grow as: three blooms, one variety, any type or include an invitational class not for competition encouraging a collection of tree peony flowers from both amateurs and professionals alike.

Arrangement (without definite use being named)

Specify using peonies and peony foliage only or if other material is permissible state what. Also indicate container if you wish and size: not to exceed 6, 12 or 25 blooms, whatever you determine.

Gardens

If there is a nursery nearby or an estate that features peonies contact them and if interested in setting up a garden write a class into the schedule or classes specifying the type gardens they are qualified and equipped to stage. Explore other sources for garden possibilities. They add much to the interest of a show.

Arrangement Classes

Here again plan classes suitable for the talent from which you must draw. It is far better to have a few good, simple arrangements which display the true natural beauty of the peony than to attempt a schedule too difficult for the exhibitors to do well.

For arrangements it is very important to list the conditions under which they will be shown: height at which arrangement will be displayed, background color, size of space and any other pertinent information. It is also very important the exhibitor read the schedule and classes with utmost care. Many a good arrangement has been disqualified because it did not comply with the class requirements. A classification or passing committee or individual checking on entries in this section may catch an error before it is too late.

Some garden clubs include the flower show schedule in their year book. If not, it should be printed, typed or mimeographed and when mailed out to every possible exhibitor it should also contain an entry blank which the exhibitor will return, properly filled out, by a set date, in advance of the show.

Invitational classes can add to the interest and beauty of the show. A simple, well thought out theme will give unity and charm to an arrangement section as a pioneer theme in connection with a centennial celebration or "Peonies Go Modern" or "Fancy Free", themes which give the exhibitor a wide range of freedom in which to work.

Peony classes may be written into the schedule in many ways using peonies with own foliage only, peonies with other foliage allowed or in mixed bouquets. Type peony flower or color to be used may be designated. The following suggest only a few of some of the many possibilities.

"At Home" or *"June Glory"*. Use some peonies in each arrangement (otherwise free hand or list limitations). State dimensions of niches, shadow boxes or space, height from floor, background color.

1. In a man's den.
2. In a modern room with an oriental influence.
3. In a ranch type house.
4. In an Early American room.
5. In a Victorian room.

"Around the Clock"—For table arrangement classes featuring peonies. State whether informal, semi-formal or formal. Indicate

number of place settings, size table, in center of room or against wall. List properties show committee will supply, etc.
1. June breakfast on the porch.
2. Noon birthday party for the small fry.
3. Coffee or cocktail hour.
4. Supper at seven.
5. Stag party.
6. Buffet for twenty.

Mantel Arrangement for Home Wedding.
Church Arrangement.
Pedestal Arrangement for the Platform.
Any Design or Motif, peonies predominating.

Junior Classes and Awards

If there is sufficient interest to make it worthwhile a simplified schedule of classes and awards for juniors, in both the horticultural and arrangement classes, is a fine way to interest young folks in the peony and horticulture in general. This often may be done through contact with the schools, scouts or similar organizations.

Educational Exhibits

If possible, especially in a specialized show such as a Peony Show, some member or members should be on duty at all times during the show to answer questions intelligently, explain exhibits, varieties, etc.

Feature books, bulletins and garden magazines that tell about the peony. Explain what the American Peony Society is and what it has to offer and take subscriptions. A mimeographed sheet telling about the peony may be given free to all interested visitors. Encourage the state extension service, arboretums and similar groups to stage exhibits showing propagation, pest control, etc.

Get a landscape architect to demonstrate a simple right and wrong planting design using balled and burlapped plants.

ENTRIES

It is important to have all entries in writing to avoid any misunderstandings or arguments. Do not accept verbal entries. Buy a notebook. Cut up a show schedule pasting each class at the top of a separate page. As the entry blanks come in record them under the proper class in the notebook giving each an entry number and file the entry blanks alphabetically according to name for easy reference. From the notebook you will know just how many entries you have received and how much space to allot to each class. If a cancellation comes in cross it off the page.

The entry blank must include the name and address of the exhibitor with enough space to write or type in the number of entries. As these entry blanks come in the entry chairman can make out the entry cards in advance of the show. The day of the show the exhibitor picks up his entry cards and places them with his exhibits, never with the name showing. Uniform entry cards should be typed for each entry with the name and address of the exhibitor. This information is kept covered until after the judging either by use of an envelope or by placing the card face down. On the envelope or reverse side of the card type the class number and entry number which is all the judges should see.

STAGING

In a large show the chairman should find someone, perhaps a landscape architect, who can draw a floor plan of the hall showing any openings such as doors, windows and stairways or obstructions like posts or partitions, using correct measurements so the person responsible for staging the show can plan and lay it out accurately on paper. In keeping with the theme or type show the staging should be as creative and distinctive as the best talent available can produce. A planned unity or harmony throughout the show is pleasing and effective. With good quality material and the artistic know how the staging committee can do an outstanding job although it does involve a great amount of detail and work. The staging committee is responsible for all the properties necessary in setting up and dismantling the show, the lighting, supplying the necessary water for the exhibitors and for any trees or other decorations necessary in setting up the show. In large shows a decorator may be hired to cover posts with smilac and hang cloth backdrops where needed.

If the staging chairman goes to the hall and can accurately chalk off the exact space for the different classes and number them correctly, before the exhibitors arrive to start working, it will save much time and confusion.

A special clean up committee may be planned. If not the staging group is responsible for cleaning up the hall as well as storing any properties owned by the show committee. Store equipment in proper condition for use another time.

POINT SCALES FOR JUDGING

Suggested scales of points to help in judging flower show classes, especially useful if decisions are very close.

Display
Scale of points courtesy National Council of State Garden Clubs, Inc.

Arrangement and effect	30
Grouping of freshly cut peonies so arranged to create an artistic and pleasing overall picture or effect.	
Quality, distinctive or excellence of character	30
Variety, diversity	20
Condition, freshness of bloom	10
Correct labeling	10
	100

Collections
In collection classes arrangement is considered only in cases of equal scoring.

Courtesy American Peony Society

General Quality	40
Pleasing appearance. Uniform high quality, harmonious color combinations.	

Condition 30
   See "Condition and Freshness" under scale of points below
   for judging Specimen
Conformity to schedule 20
Labeling and display 10
   All labels legible from the aisle preferably written on
   both sides   100
Courtesy National Council of State Garden Clubs, Inc.
Cultural Perfection 45
Types and varieties 30
Staging 20
Correct and suitable labeling 5
                                                                                                  100

Specimen

A specimen bloom is judged on its cultural perfection, its merits as a good specimen of the variety it represents.

American Peony Society scale of points

Color 30
   Clear, harmonious, rich; true to variety, outstandingly
   beautiful
   Faults—fading, discoloration, blotches, streaks, defacing
   marks, unpleasant combination, lack of beauty.
Form and pattern 30
   Symmetrical, attractive, graceful, true to type and variety.
   Form of petals, attractive placement, depth of flower,
   form and development of center.
   Faults—lopsided, unattractive, abortive, poorly developed,
   petals notched and crimped, lack of uniformity in placement of petals, looseness, falling apart, any deviation from
   norm for type or variety. Coarseness.
Texture 10
   Silken sheen, velvety, suede-like, glistening, satiny petals.
   Faults—poor condition, poor sheen; lack of sparkle, irri-

descence, glow; coarse.

Stem and foliage 10

Stem adequate to support flower. One or two leaves.
Faults—No stem, weak, side buds, any damage to stem or foliage. (Flowers taken from storage not to be penalized for lack of or damage to foliage.)

Size 5

Normal for variety in the locality or slightly above. No penalty for oversize except for miniatures and at the expense of other qualities.
Faults—Undersize for variety and type. Big miniatures.

Distinctiveness 5

Novelty, rarity, difficult of culture, overall charm and quality. Well staged. Fragrance may be counted an asset.
Faults—Old, commonplace variety and characteristics. Poor staging.

Condition and freshness 10

Correct degree of maturity, healthy condition, cleanliness, without insects, spray residue, foreign matter. No pollen stains or fallen pollen. Turgid.
Faults—Water spotting, soil or spray residue, pollen stains, over or under age, indications of poor culture, wilted.

                                                                                    ───
                                                                                    100

Distinguish between single and Japanese types by pollen test. Japanese nearly or completely void of pollen.

New Hybrids and Seedlings

In judging new introductions the following characteristics should be studied.

1. Color, is it pure, clear and rich?
2. Form, does it have a pleasing shape and structure?
3. Substance, is it firm in texture?
4. Condition, is it fresh, not fading or shattering?
5. Stem, is it stiff and adequate to hold up the flowers.
6. Distinctiveness, important in a new variety! Does it have

vigor, charm or some other admirable characteristic that makes it stand out? Is it different from varieties already in the trade.

Only a peony authority with a wide knowledge of existing varieties is qualified to judge new hybrids and seedlings.

Arrangement without specific purpose or use being named
Courtesy American Peony Society

Conformance to schedule	10
Color	40
Quality of bloom	20
Design	30
	100

Scale of points—Courtesy National Council of State Garden Clubs Inc.

Design	30
relation of all parts to the whole, all 6 art principles considered	
Color, distinctive use of	20
Suitable relationship of materials	20
Distinction	10
through skillful craftsmanship in how materials are used	
Originality	10
not commonplace	
Condition of all materials	10
	100

Judging a Garden
Scale of points, courtesy Massachusetts Horticultural Society

1. Design and consistency to scale	30
2. Suitability and quality of plant material	25
3. Color harmony	10
4. Seasonability	10
5. Quality and suitability of accessories	10
6. Condition of plant material	10
fresh, fading or falling	
6. Correct and suitable labeling	05
	100

Arrangement Classes
Courtesy National Council of State Garden Clubs Inc.
Arrangement with a theme, title or purpose.

Design, relationship of all parts to the whole, all 6 art principles considered	25
Interpretation, suitability, conformity to schedule	20
Color, distinctive use of	15
Relationship, of suitable materials	15
Distinction, superiority in how materials were used	15
Condition, freshness, freedom from any injury to material	10
	100

Table setting for a special occasion or with a title.

Overall design	25
Relation of all materials	20
Color	15
Perfection of arrangement	15
Suitability or interpretation of schedule	15
Condition of all materials	10
	100

It goes without saying in a competitive flower show the judging must be honest and fair so great care must be used in selecting competent and qualified judges. If possible out of town judges who do not know the exhibitors are advisable.

JUDGING

It is customary to have three judges work together on the section of classes they are best qualified to judge. Each group of judges should have either an aid or a clerk or in a small show one of the three judges may act as the clerk. The office should supply the clerk with a judge's sheet from a looseleaf note book clamped to a cardboard or board firm enough to write on. This judge's sheet should have the scale of points to be used in judging the class with the class number and the number of entries registered in the class. The clerk should check to see the proper number of entries are in place. On the loose leaf judge's sheet the clerk records the decision of the judges and also

FLOWER SHOWS

records the prize winning entries with the judges comments. Record varieties shown in Specimen classes and in Collections if possible. After this has been completed the sheet must then be signed by the three judges, returned to the office, put in the looseleaf notebook according to the class number and kept there as the permanent official record of the judging of the show.

The office types a list of the awards and may either give the list directly to the local newspapers or to the publicity chairman, depending upon how you decided it should be done.

AWARDS

The question of awards, like report cards, always arises. In general, exhibitors seem to enjoy the competitive spirit and feel it adds to the interest of the show. The exhibitor who learns by his mistakes makes progress. Awards are usually stickers or ribbons with a blue for first, a red for second and yellow for third. An honorable mention may also be given. These stickers and ribbons may be obtained through a State Garden Club Federation Office or from a stationery or specialty shop. Medals may be given for outstanding exhibits; gold representing the highest recognition, silver second and bronze third.

National plant societies, Peony and Rose, have worked out "Point Scales" they use in judging. They also maintain a list of accredited judges who represent their Societies. If you are holding a show under their auspices you must of course use one of their judges to have the award recognized by them. The number of accredited judges in some cases is however limited so you may have to contact the best qualified person you can find to judge the class for you. Many good horticulturists are well qualified to judge in the Horticulture classes. Arrangements should be judged by persons trained and accredited as flower arrangement judges.

SPECIAL AWARDS may be given for special flower show achievements such as:

1. "*Sweepstake Award*" to the person winning the most blue

ribbons in the entire show or the largest number of points.

2. *"Award of Distinction"* to be earned by the highest scoring blue ribbon winner in the horticultural classes or in the arrangement classes or in the entire show.

3. *"Award of Merit"* to go to the exhibit judged the finest in the horticultural classes or in the arrangement classes or in the entire show.

4. *"Trophy"* for the best specimen bloom in the show.

5. A special prize may be offered for the best hybrid or seedling or both, if they are worthy.

A "Tricolor Award" to a top winner, "Cultural Certificates" for material unusually well grown or a "Vote of Thanks" certificate to some one who stepped in the last minute and helped out are all possibilities. Keep the standard for awards sufficiently high so they will have value and be treasured. Interested individuals, groups, organizations or business firms will sometimes offer a special trophy or cash in a specific class if contacted.

PART V — SUPPLEMENT

REGISTERED VARIETIES

What constitutes a registration? The peonies which have been submitted to the American Peony Society for registration (or which, in the case of varieties originated before the Society was organized, were accepted by the Society as valid names and have been published in bulletins). The following list (for which the library staff of the Massachusetts Horticultural Society deserves full credit) was compiled by going through the complete set of Bulletins published by the Society up to January 1, 1959. It is unfortunate that all hybridizers do not register their new varieties with the Society. Unregistered varieties are not included in this list, although many are mentioned elsewhere in the book.

The names albiflora, chinensis and sinensis are synonyms of lactiflora. They were in common use when many of the varieties were registered and are therefore printed as given in the American Peony Society Bulletins. Most of the varieties listed are lactifloras unless otherwise noted.

KEY
A — Anemone
AV — Average
D — Double
DW — Dwarf
E — Early
EM — Early mid-season
J — Japanese

L — Late
LM — Late mid-season
M — Mid-season
S — Single
SD — Semi-double
T — Tall
V — Very (as VL—very late)
X — No longer in commerce

A

ABBE (Lewis, 1921), J. Deep rose-pink. AV. M.
A. B. C. NICHOLLS (Nicholls, 1937), D. White, tint of flesh L. AV.
ABEEKINS (Guppy, 1929) D. VE. Ruby red. Albiflora singles x officinalis rubra plena. X.
ABRAHAM LINCOLN (Lanigan, 1935), D. White. X.
ACE (Smith-Krekler, 1954), J. Dark red. E. AV.
ACME (Franklin, 1931), D. Light pink. L. AV.
ADA PRISCILLA (Walter J. Guille, 1948), A. White and yellow. E. T.
ADDIELANCHEA (Brand, 1907), D. Pure white. LM. AV. X.
ADELE SAWYER (Nicholls—Wild & Sons, 1957) (Seedling no. 1177), D. Rose pink. M.

ADOLPHE ROUSSEAU (Dessert & Mechin, 1890), D. Dark red. EM. T.
ADONIS (Sass, 1930), D. Pink with yellow collar. L. T.
ADORATION (Lein, 1935), D. Dark red. M. to L. T.. X.
AGLOW (Nicholls-Wild and Son, 1959), D. White. L.
AILEEN BRETHOUR (Brethour, 1935), Pink. AV. M. X.
AKALU (Dessert—reg. before 1926), J. Dark rose-pink. M. AV.
AKBAR (Nicholls, 1941), J. Rose-red. T. Number 202 from Mikado. M.
ALASKA (E. Auten Jr., 1925), A. Salmon red. Fragrant. E.
ALBATRE (Crousse, 1885), Generally considered identical with AVALANCHE.
ALBERT CROUSSE (Crousse, 1893), D. Light rose-pink. L. T.
ALBERTA KELSEY (Kelsey, 1940), SD. Rose pink. Fragrant. EM.
ALBIFLORA, THE BRIDE see THE BRIDE
ALBUQUERQUE (Wild, 1955), SD. Dark red. M. AV.
ALEX. D. VORIES (Vories, 1924), D. American Beauty red. M. T.
ALICE (Krekler, 1955) (seedling no. AQ6), D. Red. LM. AV.
ALICE HARDING (Lemoine, 1922), D. Flesh-pink. M. AV.
ALICE REED BATES (A. B. Franklin, 1939), D. Rose pink. M. T.
ALLINE ROGERS (Nicholls-Wild and Son, 1959), D. Salmon pink. EM.
ALMA (Shaylor, 1916), J. Light pink. M. AV.
ALSACE-LORRAINE (Lemoine, 1906), D. Pure white tinted with cream and buff in center. LM. AV.
ALSTEAD (E. Auten Jr., 1939), J. Deep pink. Albiflora variety.
ALTAR CANDLES (Pleas, 1908), J. Flesh pink. M. AV.
AMANDA YALE (Brand, 1907), D. Flesh-white. M. AV.
AMA-NO-SODE (Japan), J. Rose pink. M. AV.
AMERICAN LEGION (A. L. Murawska, 1932), D. Rose pink. E. AV. X.
AMOSKEAG (Guppy, 1935), S. White. X.
A. M. SLOCUM (Franklin, 1920), D. Rose-pink. L. DW.
ANDY (E. Auten Jr., 1936), SD. Dark red. EM.
ANETTE CARSON (Risk, 1929), D. Blush pink, creamy white center. Fragrant. L. T.
ANGEL WINGS (R. H. Brant, 1939), "Flat Type". Ivory white. T. LM.
ANGELO COBB FREEBORN (Freeborn, 1943), D. Coral red. VE. T. Officinalis rubra x Madame Jules Dessert
ANGELUS (E. Auten Jr., 1933), S. Light pink. M.
ANNABESSACOOK (Guppy, 1935), J. White. X.
ANNA SASS (Sass, 1930), D. Deep pink. LM. T.
ANN COUSINS (Cousins, 1946), D. White. Rose fragrance. LM. AV.
ANN RUTLEDGE (Lanigan, 1936), D. Cream-white tinted light pink. L. D. X.
ANN ZAHLLER (Mains, 1956), SD. Red. E. officinalis x albiflora
ANNE BIGGER (Bigger, 1945), D. Pink. LM.
ANNE HARGROVE (Nicholls-Wild

REGISTERED VARIETIES

and Son, 1959), D. China pink. E. T. Mme. Calot x Nicholls no. 272

APOLLO (Sass, 1930), D. Pink with salmon blush center. L. AV.

A. P. SAUNDERS (Thurlow, 1919), D. Flesh pink, white in center. L. AV.

ARBUTUS PINK (Freeborn, 1951), S. Pink. E. AV. Officinalis rubra plena x Mme. Jules Dessert. VE.

ARCTURUS (E. Auten Jr., 1933), S. Dark red. E.

ARGENTINE (Lemoine, 1924), D. Purest white with creamy tint towards center. Fragrant. L. M. AV.

ARGOSY (Saunders, 1929), SD. Yellow stained deep purple red over small area at base of petals. Lutea x moutan. VE.

ARIEL (Lyman, 1939), J. Pale pink. X.

ARLEQUIN (Dessert, 1921), A. Pale rose-pink. Faintly fragrant. M. AV.

ASA GRAY (Crousse, 1886), D. Pale pink "powdered with minute rosy dots". Fragrant. M. AV.

ASSMANNSHAUSEN (Goos & Koenemann, 1912), D. Light pink, fading white. Fragrant. L.

ATHELSTANE (Brown, 1938), D. Lavender pink. Fragrant. M.

ATLANTA (Franklin, 1931), S. E. AV. White.

ATTAR OF ROSES (Murawska, 1951) (seedling no. 59), D. Dark pink. E. T.

ATTRACTION (Hollis, 1906), J. Red. Fragrant. M. AV.

AUGUSTE DESSERT (Dessert, 1920), D. Pink. Each petal edged with silvery border. M. AV.

AUREOLIN (Shaylor, 1917), A. Light rose-pink. Fragrant. LM. AV.

AURORE (Dessert, 1904), D. Creamy-pink. M. AV.

AUTEN'S PRIDE (E. Auten Jr., 1933), D. Light pink. Rose fragrant. L.

AVALANCHE (Crousse, 1886), D. Blush white. LM. AV.

AVE MARIA (J R. Mann-Van Steen, 1936), D. White. EM. AV.

AVIATEUR REYMOND (Dessert, 1915), D. Light crimson. M. T.

AZTEC (Nicholls, 1941), J. Scarlet rose. Number 200 from Mikado.

B

BABY KELWAY (Kelway, 1929), S. Flesh white. Not sold in U.S.A.

BALL O'COTTON (Franklin, 1920), D. White with wire edge of crimson. Fragrant. LM. AV.

BANDERILLA (Jones, 1957), J. Black-red. M.

BARBARA JEAN ROHE (Napier, 1937), D. White, reverse side blush rose. Fragrant. M. AV. X.

BARBARA UTTERBACK (Winchell, 1948) (seedling no. 91A), D. Red. M.

BARONESS SCHROEDER (Kelway, 1889), D. Flesh-white. Fragrant. LM. T.

BATTLE FLAG (Nicholls, 1941), J. Deep-red. Number 196 from Mikado.

BAYADERE (Lemoine, 1910), D. White. Pink marks on outer petals. Fragrant. M. T.

BEACON HILL (Auten, 1937), S. Dark red. E. T. Officinalis x chinensis

BEATRICE KELWAY (Kelway, 1929), D. Rose. Not sold U.S.A.
BEAUMARCHAIS (Lemoine, 1922), D. Pink-flesh-mauve. L. T.
BELLA DONNA (Nieuwenhuizen, 1935), Rose type. Light mauve pink. D.
BELLE (Field no. 2A3; reg. by Glasscock, 1931), chinensis var. Rose type. Shell pink. Fragrant. L. T.
BELLE CENTER (Mains, 1956), D. Red. E. Officinalis x albiflora
BELLE CHINOISE (Auten, 1935), D. White. Rose fragrance. AV. LM.
BEN HABERMAN (H. P. Sass, 1941), D. Rose type. Bright deep pink. M. AV.
BENJAMIN FRANKLIN (Brand, 1907), D. Dark crimson. Fragrant. M. T.
BERTRADE (Lemoine, 1909), D. White, shaded yellow at base of petals. LM. AV.
BERYL CROCKETT (Nicholls-G. H. Wild & Son, 1954) (Nicholls seedling 442), D. White. M. AV.
BESS BOCKSTOCE (Bockstoce, 1955), D. Light pink. E. AV. Officinalis x lactiflora.
BESSIE (Krekler, 1958), D. Silvery pink. M. T.
BETTY BLOSSOM (Thurlow, 1925), D. White, tinted yellow. LM.
BETTY CALVERT (Nicholls-G. H. Wild & Son, 1950) (Nicholls seedling no. 391), D. Blush. LM.
BETTY GROFF (Krekler, 1958), J. Light pink. M. T.
BETTY J. (Jones, 1957), D. Pink. M. AV.
BETTY MINOR (Nicholls-G. H. Wild & Son, 1954) (Nicholls seedling no. 1372), D. Light pink. L. AV.
BETSEY ROSS (E. Auten, Jr., 1931), D. White. Fragrant. L. T.
BIEBRICH (Goos & Koenemann, 1912), D. Soft pink fading white tinted flesh. Rose fragrance. M. to L. T.
BIG TOP (Jones, 1957), D. White. L. T.
BLACK HAWK (E. Auten, Jr., 1933) S. Dark red. E. AV.
BLACK KNIGHT (Glasscock, 1939), S. Scarlet with orange tint. E. Name changed to Bright Knight. T. Chinensis x Otto Froebel.
BLACK MAGIC (E. Auten, Jr., 1929), S. Black red. AV. E.
BLACK MONARCH (Glasscock, 1939), Rose type. Dark red. Officinalis rubra x Rosy Glow
BLACK PRINCE (Thurlow, 1915), S. Deep crimson. Fragrance not pleasing. M. AV.
BLACK VELVET (Murawska, 1957), D. Bright red. M. AV. Chippewa x Matilda Lewis
BLACK WARRIOR (Nicholls, 1941), D. Red Black. AV. M. Number 3 from M. M. Cahuzac
BLANCHE ELIE (Brethour, 1934), Bomb type. White. Fragrant. E. T.
BLANCHE KING (Brand, 1922), D. Dark pink with silvery sheen. LM. AV.
BLAZING STAR (Auten, 1937), SD. Dark red.
BLONDE (W. A. Dana, 1926), Bomb type. Light pink, bi-colored pink and cream. Fragrant
BLUSH (Nicholls, 1941), D. Rose type. Pink. AV. Number 1 from Othello. M.
BLUSHING BEAUTY (Franklin,

REGISTERED VARIETIES

1931), Rose type. Pale pink. Fragrant. L. AV.
BLUSH QUEEN (Hoogendoorn, 1949), D. White. M. AV.
BONNIE BECKER (Sass, 1942), Rose type. Pink. L. AV.
BONNIE WINSLOW (Winslow, 1951) (seedling no. 27), D. Light rose pink. Mildly fragrant. M. T.
BORDER GEM (Hoogendoorn, 1949), D. Red. E. DW.
BOULE DE NEIGE (Calot, 1867), D. White with yellow suffusion and crimson flecks on guards. Fragrance raw and pungent. EM. T.
BOWL OF BEAUTY (Hoogendoorn, 1949), J. Fuchsine rose. E.
BRAND'S MAGNIFICENT (Brand, 1918), D. Crimson with purplish cast. LM. AV.
BRIDESMAID (Kelway, reg. before 1926). The same as Marie Jacquin, which see.
BRIGHT KNIGHT see BLACK NIGHT.
BRIGHTNESS (Glasscock, 1947), albiflora x officinalis Sunbeam. S. Red. VE. AP. V.
BUCKEYE BELLE (Mains, 1956), SD. Red. E. Officinalis x albiflora
BUNCH OF PERFUME (Kelway, 1901), D. Rose. LM. AV.
BURMA RUBY (Glasscock, 1951), S. Red. E. AV. Albiflora x officinalis Sunbeam
BU-TE (Wassenberg, 1954), J. White. M. T. Tamate Boku x Isani Gidui

C

CALUMET (E. Auten, Jr., 1931), S. Red. E. T.
CAMEO (E. Auten, Jr., 1926), Low bomb type. Blush white. Fragrant. Name changed to Clorinda.
CANDEUR (Dessert, 1920), D. Light rose-pink, flushed darker outside. Faint fragrance. LM. T.
CAPRICCIO see FANTASIA.
CAPTAIN JONES see PINK GLORY.
CAPTAIN KIDD (E. Auten, 1934), SD. Dark red. T.
CARILLON (Richmond, 1951) (seedling no. 51-326), D. Rose pink. LM. T.
CAROL (Bockstoce, 1955), D. Red. E. AV. Officinalis x lactiflora.
CAROLINA MOON (E. Auten, Jr., 1940), Bomb type. White with yellow center, albiflora variety. AV. E.
CAROLYNE MAE NELSON (H. P. Sass, 1937). Dark crimson maroon. L. T.
CARRARA (Bigger, 1952) (seedling no. 59-37), J. White. M. AV.
CASABLANCA (Lins, 1942) (seedling no. R-5-242), D. White. L. T.
CATHEDRAL (Reg., before 1926, origin unknown) (also catalogued as Hana-no-sato), J. Dark rose-pink in combination with pale pink petaloids. Slightly fragrant. M. AV.
CATHERINE CRAIN (Nicholls, 1948), D. Pink. EM. T. Marie Crousse x Spring Beauty
CATHERINE EMMA (Mrs. C. E. Athrop, 1941), D. Strawberry guards, cream-yellow heart. LM. T. X.
CELESTIA LEWIS (Lewis, 1921), D. Clear pink with white petals intermixed. Fragrant. T. X.
CERISE BEAUTY (Risk, 1929), D.

Cerise, darker in center. LM. AV.
CHALICE (Saunders, 1929), S. White. E. T. Sinensis x macrophylla
CHAMINADE (E. Auten, Jr., 1933), J. Light pink. T.
CHARITY (Saunders, 1929), SD. Deep cherry crimson. Otto Froebel x sinensis
CHARLENE (E. F. Kelsey, 1938), D. White. L. AV.
CHARLES MAINS (Mains, 1956), seedling no. A18), D. Pink. E.
CHARLES NEIDEL (Wettengel, 1916), D. Rose form. Shaggy rose-pink. M. AV.
CHARLIE'S WHITE (Klehm, 1951) (seedling no. 69B), D. White. E. T.
CHARLOT (Doriat, 1924), D. M. T. Flowers silvery lilac with carmine base, silvery borders.
CHARM (Franklin, 1931), J. Dark red. L. AV.
CHASTITY (Brethour, 1935), Bomb type. White. Fragrant. T. X.
CHEROKEE (Franklin, 1931), Rose type. Pure white. L. AV.
CHERRY HILL (Thurlow, 1915), D. Dark maroon. Very early. T.
CHERRY RED (Glasscock, 1939), Rose type. Pure red. M. DW. Officinalis rubra x chinensis
CHESTINE GOWDY (Brand, 1913), D. Light rose. Creamy white collar. Excellent fragrance. L. T.
CHESUNCOOK (Guppy, 1935), J. White. X.
CHIEF (Franklin, 1931), Rose type. Light pink. Fragrant. L.
CHINA MAID (Murawska, 1943), J. Medium pink. M.
CHIPPEWA (Murawska, 1943), D. Dark red. M. T.
CHOCOLATE SOLDIER (E. Auten, Jr., 1939), J. Bomb type. Black-red. Officinalis hybrid
CINDERELLA (R. H. Jones, 1938), S. Apple blossom pink. EM. AV.
CLAIRE DE LUNE (White, 1954), S. Yellow. E. DW. Mons. Jules Elie x mlokosewitschi
CLAIRE DUBOIS (Crousse, 1886), D. Bright rose pink bordering on mauve-pink. L. AV.
CLAIRETTE (Dessert, 1905), S. Pink opening to white. M. T.
CLARA MAY BERNHARDT (Kummer, 1939), D. Rose type. Pure white. Fragrant. M. AV. Pollen parent unknown. Seed producing this white offspring is from Mons. Martin Cahuzac.
CLEMENCEAU (Dessert, 1920), D. Globular form. Glowing rose-pink. Rose fragrance. LM. T.
CLEOPATRA (E. Auten, Jr., 1939), albiflora variety, D. Dark red. Fragrant. L.
CLORINDA see CAMEO.
COATICOOK (Guppy, 1935), J. Light pink. X.
COBSECOOK (Guppy, 1935), J. Light pink. X.
COLONEL LINDBERG (A. E. Kunderd, 1927), D. Dark red. E. X.
COMMANDO (Glasscock, 1944), D. Red. E. T. Officinalis x albiflora
CONQUISTADOR (R. H. Jones, 1938), D. Pale pink with lavender sheen. Fragrant. L. T. X.
CONSTANCE MOORE (Mains, 1956), J. Red. E. Officinalis x abliflora

REGISTERED VARIETIES

CONTOOCOOK (Guppy, 1935), J. Deep pink. X.

CONVOY (Glasscock, 1944), D. Red. E. T. Officinalis x albiflora

COPY CAT (Freeborn, 1945), D. Brilliant blood red. E. Officinalis rubra plena x Mme. Jules Dessert

CORAL GLOW (Klehm, 1951), (seedling no. 781 Z), D. Pink. LM. T.

CORAL QUEEN (H. P. Sass, 1937), Blush pink. L. T. D.

CORDELIA (submitted by Interstate Nurseries, '37). No description supplied. Name never used.

CORINNE WERSAN (Krekler, 1955) (seedling no. AV4), D. White. M. AV.

CORINTH (Saunders, 1929), D. Light crimson. M. to L. AV. Officinalis x sinensis

CORNELIA SHAYLOR (Shaylor, 1917), D. Globular form. Opens pink becoming white. L. T.

CORNIE MOORE (E. F. Kelsey, 1940), S. Dark red. Fragrant. E T.

CORONATION (Kelway, 1902), D. Pale rose pink flecked with crimson on edges. Fragrant. LM. AV.

COUNTESS MARITZA (Nieuwenhuizen, 1935), Rose type. Pink to white, yellow at base. E. T.

COUNTRY DANCE (E. Auten, Jr., 1931), S. White. E. T.

COURONNE D'OR (Calot, 1873), D. White center. Petals tipped with crimson. L. AV.

CREVE COEUR (E. Auten, Jr., 1929), J. Dark red. Rose fragrance. T. M.

CRIMSON BOMB (Freeborn, 1943), D. Crimson. Officinalis rubra x Mme. Jules Dessert.

CRIMSON GLORY (submitted by Interstate Nurseries). No description furnished. Name never used.

CRODIE (Krekler, 1958), S. Deep red. EM. T.

CROWN IMPERIAL (Kelway, 1929). J. Imperial pink with large mass of orange-yellow petalodes.

CRUSADER (Glasscock, 1940), SD. Scarlet-red. E. Officinalis rubra x Ruby

CUPID (Glasscock, 1950), S. Pink. E. AV. Otto Froebel x albiflora

CYGNET (Nicholls-G. H. Wild and Son, 1951) (Nicholls seedling no. 35/12), S. White. E. T.

D

DAINTY (Nicholls, 1941), S. Lt. silvery pink. Number 270 from Lady Alexandra Duff. E. AV.

DAINTY LASS (Glasscock, 1935), J. Coral pink. E. Officinalis hybrid

DAISY B. (Nicholls-Wild & Son, 1957) (seedling no. 920), D. White. L.

DANA GARNOCK (Dana, 1920), D. White

DANCE CAPRICE (E. Auten, Jr., 1933), Flesh. SD. T.

DANCING NYMPH (E. Auten, Jr., 1933). S. Pink, crinkled. L.

DANIEL BOONE (E. Auten, Jr., 1931), D. Dark red. T.

DAPHNE (Earnshaw, 1922), D. Pure white. LM. AV.

DARK KNIGHT (Glasscock, 1941), S. Dark red. T. E. Fuyajo x officinalis Jap.

DARKNESS (Brand, 1913), S.

Dark maroon red. Fragrant. M. AV.

DARWIN (Winslow, 1951) (seedling no. 5), S. Dark red. M. AV.

DAVID HARUM (Brand, 1920), D. Clear light red. M. T.

DAWN PINK (H. P. Sass, 1946), formerly Pink Dawn (seedling no. 1-34), S. Pink. E. to M. AV.

DAY DREAM (R. W. Auten, 1939), J. Pink and yellow. Albiflora variety.

DAYLIGHT (Risk, 1929), J. White. M. AV.

DEARBORN (E. Auten, Jr., 1929), SD. Rose type. Dark red. LM. AV.

DEEDIE MAY (Vories, 1927), D. White with crimson threadline on edges of center petals. E. T.

DEER CREEK see MID-AMERICA.

DEFENDER (Saunders, 1929), S. Dark mahogany crimson. M. to L. AV. Sinensis x officinalis

DELIGHT (H. P. Sass, 1937), J. Apple blossom pink

DELPHI (Saunders, 1929), D. Bright dark crimson. E. Officinalis x sinensis

DENISE (Lemoine, 1924), D. Soft flesh white center flecked crimson. Fragrant. LM. AV.

DEPARTING SUN (origin unknown), J. Dark rose pink, touched with lilac at tips and edges. Slightly fragrant. M. AV.

DESIRE (Brand, 1923), D. Soft rose-pink. Suggestion of lilac. M. DW.

DIADEM (Franklin, 1931), Dark pink. Cup-shape. Fragrant. L. AV. D.

DIANA (Sass, 1930), D. Pure white. L. T.

DIANA PARKS (Bockstoce, 1942), S. Carmine red. Fragrant. T. Officinalis x chinensis

DIEPPE (Keagey, 1946), D. Pale lavender pink. LM. AV.

DIEUDONNE (Brethour, 1936), Pink and white. T.

DIXIE (Franklin, 1931), Bomb type. Dark red. L. AV.

DOLLY VARDEN (Brethour, 1937), J. Violet pink. T.

DOLORODELL (Lins, 1942) (seedling no. R-4-49), D. Pink. LM. AV.

DONALD (E. F. Kelsey, 1936), D. Rose pink. T. LM.

DONNA BERKLEY (H. P. Sass, 1942), Rose type. White. L. AV.

DOREEN (Henry E. Sass, 1949) (seedling no. 35-94), J. Pink. M. AV.

DORIS (Shaylor, 1920), D. Fresh pink. M. AV.

DORIS COOPER (Cooper, 1946), (seedling 35), D. Pink. L. T.

DOROTHY J. (R. H. Jones, 1938), D. Rose type. Blush white. L. T.

DOUGLAS MacARTHUR see GENERAL DOUGLAS MacARTHUR.

DRAGON'S NEST (E. Auten, Jr., 1933), J. Bright red guards. Bright yellow collar. Tuft red petals in center. M. AV.

DRESDEN PINK (Wild and Son, 1957), D. Pink. L.

DRESS PARADE (Auten, 1937), J. Light red. E.

DR. F. G. BRETHOUR (H P. Sass, 1938), Rose type. White. L. T.

DR. H. BARNSBY (Dessert, 1913), D. Globular. Dark old-rose, bordering on magenta. Fairly fragrant. L. Not sold in U.S.A.

DR. H. VAN DER TAK (Nieu-

REGISTERED VARIETIES

wenhuyzen, 1916), D. Crimson, lighter sheen on incurved tips. EM. Not sold in U.S.A.
DR. JEKYLL (E. Auten, Jr., 1936), J. Often with SD blooms. Dark red. L.
DUCHESSE DE NEMOURS (Calot, 1856), D. Cupped white guards. Center light canary yellow. E. AV.
DUCHESS OF SUTHERLAND (Kelway, 1929), S. Pure white. Not sold in U. S. A.
DULUTH (Franklin, 1931), Rose type. Pure white. L. AV.
DUNKIRK (Keagey, 1946), D. Pink. T.
DUNLORA (Leyton, 1943), S. White. E. AV.

E

EAU CLAIRE (Dana, 1926), S. Pink. X.
ECSTASY (Brethour, 1926). D. Large flower. White with yellow tone at base of petals. M. T.
ECSTASY (Nieuwenhiuzen, 1935), J. Pink. M.
EDGAR JESSEP (Bockstoce, 1958), D. Brilliant red. E. AV. Officinalis x albiflora
EDITH M. SNOOK (Snook, 1931), Rose type. Soft ivory, tinted coffee brown. Fragrant. L. AV.
EDITH R. STONE (Webb, 1958), SD. Pale pink. T.
EDMOND ABOUT (Crousse, 1885), D. Shell pink with rose tints. Fragrant. LM. AV. Not sold in U.S.A.
EDMOND LEBON (Calot, 1864), D. Dark pink becoming silvery with age at center. M. DW. Not sold in U.S.A.
EDNA (Winchell, 1941) (no. 3C), Light pink. Fragrant. M.
EDULIS SUPERBA (Lemon, 1824), D. Bright old rose pink. Very fragrant. Very E. T.
EDWARD (Lyman, 1939), S. Black-red. X.
EDWARD W. BECKER (Franklin, 1920), SD. Light pink shading to white. Fragrant. M. AV.
EDWIN C. SHAW (Thurlow, 1919), D. Light old rose with flesh pink tones in center and collar. Fragrant. LM. AV.
EEPLES (Guppy, 1922), D. Bright red. Albiflora single x officinalis rubra plena
EEWEE (Guppy, 1932), S. Deep red. T. Albiflora single x officinalis rubra plena. X.
E. G. KENDALL (Nicholls-Wild & Son, 1959), D. Pink. M.
EGLANTINE (Dessert, 1913), S. Flesh pink paling to white. M. AV. Not sold in U.S.A.
EGYPT (Risk, 1929), S. Dark red. E. AV. X.
EGYPTIAN (Brant, 1941), Jap. effect. Rich maroon. Someganoko seed
E. J. SHAYLOR (Shaylor, 1918), D. Dark rose-pink, petals tipped lilac. Globular form. Rose fragrance. LM. AV. X.
EL CAPITAN (Auten, 1937), SD. Light red. LM.
ELEANOR (Winchell, 1946), D. Bomb type. Deep old rose. Fragrant. M.
ELEANOR DANA (W. A. Dana, 1926), Bomb type. Silvery salmon pink. X.
ELFIN PINK (Auten, 1937), S. Pink. E.
ELISA (Dessert-Doriat, 1922), SD. Cup-shaped flower. Carmine-hydrangea pink shaded silvery salmon. AV. M.
ELISE (W. A. Dana, 1926), Rose type. Light clear pink. Fragrant. X.

ELIZABETH BARRETT BROWNING (Brand, 1907), D. Creamy blush paling white. Red marks in center and on outer petals. Very fragrant. L. T. X.

ELIZABETH HUNTINGTON (Sass, 1930), D. Pale pink. E. T.

ELIZABETH PRICE (Nicholls-Wild and Son, 1957) seedling No. 892. D. Pink. LM.

ELLA CHRISTIANSEN (Brand, 1925) D. Medium pink. Fragrant. M. T.

ELLA CHRISTINE KELWAY (Kelway, 1899), D. Lavender flesh color. X.

ELLA WINCHELL (Winchell, 1941), no. 32A. D. Albiflora. Red. M.

ELLENWILDER (Guppy, 1926), S. Salmon. Albiflora single x officinalis rubra plena. X.

ELMER J. WRIGHT (E. Auten, Jr. 1929), S. Dark red. T.

ELNA (H P. Sass, 1941), D. Rose type. Bright pink. M. T.

ELOISE (E Auten, Jr., 1934), D Cr. pink. L. T.

ELSA SASS (Sass, 1930), D. White. L. AV.

ELVINA (Krekler, 1958), J. Pink. M. T.

ELWOOD PLEAS (Pleas, 1900), D. Pale rose pink. Light flesh pink centers. L. AV. X.

EMALINE (Mrs. W. Wolfe, 1931), Pink. Fragrant. M. T.

EMILE HOSTE (Origin doubtful) Rated much too high and suppressed by unanimous vote of the Directors of the American Peony Society, January 1928.

EMILY D. PROCTOR (Freeborn, 1947), J. Old rose. E. AV.

EMMA KLEHM (Klehm, 1951), DW. Seedling no. 690. D. Pink. L.

EMPRESS OF BRITAIN (Norton, 1931), D. White. L.

ENCHANTERESSE (Lemoine, 1903), D. White with lemon tints. Slightly fragrant. Very L. T.

ENCHANTMENT (Hollis, 1907), D. Old rose with shell pink at center. Fragrant. M. AV.

ENGLISH ELEGANCE (Kelway, 1929), S. Flesh pink.

ENTICING (Hruby, 1955), seedling no. 06-C. D. Light pink. L.

ERIC THE RED (James Pillow, 1923), Dark red. S. X.

EROS (Glasscock, 1940), S. Salmon pink. E. No. B.5 x off. Sunbeam.

ESTELLE (Mrs. W. C. Lyman) S. Pink. X.

ESTHER MITTENDORFF (Lanigan, 1944), D. Light rose pink. Mildly fragrant. M. T. X.

E. ST. HILL (Kelway, 1929), S. Deep rose pink. E. T. Not sold in U.S.A.

ETHEL HALSEY (Hans P. Sass, 1952), seedling no. 13-27. D. Pink. M. T.

ETHEL MARS see MARS.

ETHEREAL (R. H. Jones, 1938), Rose type. Blush pink. Very fragrant. T. L.

ETIENNE BRULE (Brethour, 1934), D. Similar to Solange, white with pink and yellow tints. L. AV. Cut almost never opens. X. May be obtainable in Canada.

ETTA (Terry, 1904), D. Old rose pink with flesh pink center. Rose fragrance. L. AV.

EUGENE BIGOT (Dessert, 1894), D. Crimson with violet tinge with silvery tips. Slight fragrance. L. AV.

EUGENIE VERDIER (Calot, 1864), D. Rose pink with crimson near center. DW. L. X. Not a good variety. T.

EUNICE SHAYLOR (Shaylor, 1919), D. Outer petals cupped and wavy. Rosy flesh flushed with rose toward base. Tea rose fragrance. M. AV.

EUPHEMIA (Terry, 1910), Much overated and suppressed by vote of the Directors. X.

EVANGELINE (Lemoine, 1910), D. Dark but bright rose pink. Crimson edges on center petals. Rose fragrance. L. AV.

EVELYN BUECHLY (Buechly, 1923), SD. Light pink. AV. X.

EVELYN CLAAR (Glasscock, 1946), D. Cerise. E. AV. Officinalis x sinensis.

EVENING GLOW (Hollis, 1907), SD. Light shell pink, paling to white and old rose. E. T.

EVENING STAR (H. P. Sass, 1937), D. White with crimson edges occasionally. L.

EVENTIDE (Glasscock, 1945), S. Pink. E. T. Officinalis x albiflora.

EVERETT (Simpson, 1929), Crown type. Pink. M. to L. AV. X.

EXCELSA (Franklin, 1931), Rose type. Light pink. L. T.

EXELEE (Krekler, 1958) D. White with pale yellow and and pink petaloids. L. AP.

EXOTIC (E. F. Kelsey, 1940), SD. Deep pink.

EXQUISITE (Kelway, 1912), D. Bright rose pink, paling towards tips of petals. M. AV.

F

FAIR ELAINE (F. W. Auten, 1939), albiflora variety. J. Pink and yellow.

FAIRLEIGH (Brown, 1938), D. Blush Pink. Fragrant. M. T.

FAIRY DANCE (E. Auten, Jr. 1931), S. Pink. E. T.

FAIRY DREAM (Nicholls-Wild and Son, 1959), D. White, tapering to pink. L.

FAIRY PINK (A. B. Franklin, 1939), J. Light pink. M. AV.

FAIRY PRINCESS (Glasscock-Falk, 1955), seedling no. 816. S. Red. E. DW.

FAIRY QUEEN (E. Auten, Jr. 1931), S. Pink. AV. E.

FAITH (Saunders, 1929), D. or S.D. Light rose pink. Season of officinalis. AV. Otto Froebel x sinensis.

FALAISE (Keagey, 1946), This name reserved for future use.

FAMIE (Saunders-Krekler, 1955), D. White. E. Hybrid.

FANNIE HEATH (Cooper, 1946), AV. Seedling no. 1. SD. White. M.

FANNY LEE (Vories, 1924), American Beauty red. M.

FANTASIA (Lyman, 1939), J X. Pale pink. L. Name changed to Capriccio.

FANTASY (Auten, 1925), A. Outer petals deep pink, center yellow. Slight fragrance.

FASCINATION (Brethour, 1936), Rose type. White. Fragrant. T.

FELICIA (Gardner, before 1951), S. Deep pink. M. AV.

FELIX CROUSSE (Crousse, 1881), D. Crimson. LM. AV.

FELIX SUPREME (Kriek, 1955), seedling no. 6. D. Red. M. AV.

FESTIVA (Donkelaer, 1838), D. LM. DW. White. Much over rated and suppressed by vote of the Directors. X.

FESTIVA MAXIMA (Miellez, 1851), D. Globular. White with prominent crimson flakes. Fairly fragrant. E. T.

FINE LADY (Kelway, 1909) S. Cup shape. Blush white.

FIRE CHIEF (Auten, 1934), Novelty J. Deep red and yellow.

FIRELIGHT (Brant, 1931), S. Red. L.

FIREPLACE (E. F. Kelsey, 1940), D. Mahogany red. EM.

FLAMBOYANT (Origin unknown) Correct name Kamenokegoromo. J. Dark rose-red or light crimson. M. T.

FLAME (Glasscock, 1939), S. Red. E. Chinensis x officinalis Sunbeam.

FLASH (Glasscock, 1950), S. Bright red. E. AV. Albiflora x Sunbeam off.

FLASHLIGHT (Hollis, 1906), J. Dark rosy red. Pinkish staminodes tipped bright yellow creates terra-cotta effect to center of bloom. M. AV.

FLORENCE BRUSS (Franklin, 1953), seedling no. X474. S. Dark red. LM. AV.

FLORENCE ELLIS (Nicholls, 1948), D. Pink. M. T. Marie Crousse x Lady Alexandra Duff.

FLORENCE MACBETH (Sass, 1924), D. Pale shell pink, deepening toward center. Slightly fragrant. LM. AV.

FLORENCE NICHOLLS (Nicholls, 1938), D. Blush white with a scarlet suffusion. Very fragrant. EM. AV.

Seedling No. 1 from Mme. Calot.

FLORIZELL (Brant, 1941), J. Soft rose. Mikado is seed parent.

FLOWER GIRL (Auten, 1935), D. Blush, fading to white. Rose fragrant. DW.

FLOWER OF CHIVALRY (Kelway, 1928), SD. Rosy pink. Not sold in U.S.A.

FLOW'RET OF EDEN (Neeley, 1919), D. Light rose pink, shading to flesh pink at center. EM. AV.

FORTUNE TELLER (E. Auten, Jr., 1936), S. Light red.

FRAICHEUR (Lemoine, 1914), D. Pale flesh white with salmon undertone. Mildly fragrant. LM. AV. Not sold in U.S.A.

FRANCES MAINS (Mains, 1955), seedling no. H-3. D. Light pink. M. AV.

FRANCES SHAYLOR (Shaylor, 1916), D. White. Sometimes flushed with pink on opening. Fragrant. M. DW.

FRANCES WILLARD (Brand, 1907), D. Opens pale pink changing to white with yellow suffusion in collar. Bears few red lines in center. Mildly fragrant. LM. T.

FRANCOIS ROUSSEAU (Dessert, 1909), D. Rich crimson. Fragrant. E. AV. Not sold in U.S.A.

FRANK E. GOOD (Good & Reese, 1929), Semi-rose type. Flesh pink. L. T.

FRANKIE CURTIS (Vories, 1924), D. Delicate flesh changing to pure white. M. AV.

FRANKLIN'S PRIDE (Franklin, 1931), Rose type. Pink. Fragrant. L. T.

FRECKLES (Neeley, 1926), Full rose type. Flesh pink. M.

REGISTERED VARIETIES

FRIEND HARRY (Smith-Krekler, 1954), D. Dark red. M. AV.
FRIENDSHIP (Glasscock-Falk, 1955), seedling no. A1-A101. S. Pink. E. AV.
FRONTIER (E F. Kelsey, 1940), D. Pink. L.
FURNACE (W. J. Guille, 1951), D. Red. L. AV.
FURY (Bigger, 1955), seedling no. 9-47. D. Red. M. T.
FUYAJO (Origin unknown. Reg. before 1926), J. Dark purplish crimson. Slightly fragrant. M. T.

G

GAIETY (H. P. Sass, 1937), J. Bright red. L.
GALATHEE (Lemoine, 1900), D. Flesh with pink center. Very fragrant. Very L. T.
GARDEN SENTINEL (Freeborn, 1943), D. Brilliant pink. VE. AV.
Officinalis rubra x Madame Jules Dessert.
GARNET BEAUTY (B. B. Wright, 1935), S. Dark red. EM. to LM. T.
GAYBORDER JUNE (Hoogendoorn, 1949), D. Fuchsine rose. E. AV.
GAY PAREE (E. Auten, Jr., 1933), A. J. Guards deep cerise, center, flushing to white. M. AV.
GEISHA (Sass, 1930), seedling of MIKADO. J. Light pink:
GEISHA GIRL (Richmond, 1952), seedling no. 52-323. J. Rose pink. M. AV.
GENERAL DOUGLAS MacARTHUR (Rosefield, 1942), Semi-rose type. Pink. T. M. General now dropped.
GENERAL GORGAS (Van Leeuwen, 1924), SD. White with rose pink center. Guard petals streaked with red. Fragrant. M. AV.
GENE STRATTON PORTER (Rosefield, 1925), D. White. T. L.
GENE WILD (Cooper, 1956), seedling no. Cooper 6. D. Pink. M.
GEORGE J. NICHOLLS (Nicholls, 1948), D. White. L. T. Marie Crousse x Lady Alexandra Duff.
GEORGE W. PEYTON (Nicholls, 1938), seedling no. 2 from Lady Duff. D. Buff suffused with pink. M. AV. Slightly fragrant.
GEORGIANA SHAYLOR (Shaylor, 1908), D. Light rose pink, paler on backs of petals. Vivid crimson marks on ring of short center petals. Sweet fragrance. LM. AV.
GERMAINE BIGOT (Dessert, 1902), D. Light rose pink. M. AV.
GERTRUDE COX (Krekler, 1958), D. Light pink. LM. AV.
GERTRUDE GIBSON (Reno Rosefield, 1939), Rose type. White. AV. L.
GIANT JAP see JAP. GIANT.
GIGANTEA (Calot, 1860), (original name was Lamartine). D. Rose pink fading to light old rose with silver tipped petals. Fragrant. EM. T.
GILBERT H. WILD (Nicholls-Wild & Son, 1957), seedling No. 392. D. Rose pink. LM.
GINETTE (Dessert, 1915), D. Pale pink with faint old rose shading and crimson marks. Mildly fragrant. LM. DW.

GINNY (Freeborn, 1947), D. Brilliant red. E. AV. Hybrid.
GISMONDA (Crousse, 1895), D. Pale creamy pink with rose pink center. Rose fragrance. Very L. T. X.
GLAMOUR (Jones, 1957), J. Rose pink. M.
GLEAM OF GOLD (H. P. Sass, 1937), White with a broad yellow collar. LM. AV.
GLOBE OF LIGHT (Kelway, 1928), A. Silvery rose.
GLORY OF LANGPORT (Kelway, 1929), D. Rosy pink. Not sold in U.S.A.
GLORY OF THE GARDEN (Toedt, 1929), S. Dark red. X.
GOBLIN (E. Auten Jr., 1931), J. Bright red. T.
GOLDEN ARROW (Nicholls, 1941), J. Deep red. Number 173 from Mikado. AV. M.
GOLDEN DAWN (Gumm, 1923), A. High yellowish center with guard petals of ivory white. Fragrant. M.
GOLDEN DREAM see ORIENTAL GOLD
GOLDEN GLOW (Glasscock, 1935), S. Scarlet red with orange tint. E. Chinensis x officinalis Otto Froebel.
GOLDEN LIGHT (Murawska, 1944), J. White. L. T.
GOLDEN SUN (Rosenfield, 1934), J. Rose pink. AV. L.
GOLD MINE (Hollis, 1907), J. Dark rose pink. M. AV.
GOLD STANDARD (Rosenfield, 1934), J. White tinted yellow. T. M.
GOPHER BEAUTY (Franklin, 1933), S. Red. (Seedling no. R-300, selected 1926.) M. AV.
GRACE BATSON (Sass, 1927), D. Medium pink. M. to L.
GRACE GEDGE (Kelsey, 1934), D. Cream white. LM. AV.

GRACE KELSEY (Kelsey, 1940), D. Pink. M. AV.
GRACE LEWIS (Lewis, 1922), D. Deep blush, lighter toward center. Fragrant. M. T. X.
GRACE LOOMIS (Saunders, 1920), D. White with faint lemon tints in depths of petals. Mildly fragrant. L. AV.
GRACE OTT (Gumm, 1923), D. Brilliant dark crimson. M. T.
GRACE WILLE (Claar, 1955), S. Pink. E. AV. Albiflora x lobata
GRADUATION DAY (E. Auten, Jr., 1939), S. White. Albiflora var.
GRAND MASTER (Rosenfield, 1934), Rose type. Dark red. E. AV.
GRANDIFLORA (Richardson, 1883), D. Bright pink shaded old rose and white. Fragrant. VL. T.
GRANDIFLORA NIVEA PLENA (Lemon, 1824), D. Rose type guards faintly pink fading to white with prominent red marks. Sweetly fragrant. VE. T.
GREER GARSON (Payne, 1945), D. Pale rosaline purple. Fragrant. LM. AV.
GROVER CLEVELAND (Terry, 1904), D. Bright crimson. Mildly fragrant. LM. AV.
GUIDON (Nicholls, 1941), D. Rose type. Rose pink. AV. M. (Number 5 from Othello.)
GYPSY (Hollis, 1904), J. Guards dark wine red and cupped. Petalodes light at base, shading to dark wine red and creamy white on reverse. Bordered buff tips. M. AV.
GYPSY ROSE (Franklin, 1939), J. Rose pink. M. AV.

H

HABANERA (E. Auten, Jr., 1930), S. Light red. E. T.
H. A. HAGEN (Richardson, 1904), D. Globular. Dark rose pink. L. AV.
HANSINA BRAND (Brand, 1925), D. Dark flesh pink shading darker at base of petals with a salmon glow. L. AV.
HANS P. SASS (H. P. Sass, 1937), Blush white, suffused shell pink. L. AV.
HARBINGER (Saunders, 1929), S. Pink. E. AV. Otto Froebel x macrophylla
HARDY GIANT (Freeborn, 1943), D. Pink. L. T. Officinalis rubra x Madame Jules Dessert
HARGROVE HUDSON (Wild and Son, 1949), D. Pink. EM. AV.
HARMON (Smith-Krekler, 1957), no description. Name never used.
HARMONY (R. H. Jones, 1938), Pale rose darker at center. L. T. X.
HARRIET CORY (Lyman, 1940), A. J. Deep rose. Fragrant. X.
HARRIET OLNEY (Brand, 1920), S. Soft rose color. M. AV.
HARRY A. NORTON (Norton, 1939), D. Dark crimson. L. AV. X.
HARRY F. LITTLE (Nicholls, 1933), Rose type. White. L. AV.
HARRY L. RICHARDSON (Rosenfield, 1925), D. Bright red. Fragrant. VL. AV.
HARRY L. SMITH (Smith-Krekler, 1953), D. Dark red. LM. Note: Taller and later than Monsieur Martin Cahuzac
HARVARD CRIMSON (Smith, 1928), SD. Crimson. M. X.
HAZEL KINNEY (Brand, 1925), D. Light flesh pink. M. AV.
HEART OF KNOX (Auten, Jr., 1939), J. Red. T. Albiflora var. M. X.
HELEN (Thurlow, 1922), S. Dark shell pink. E. T.
HELEN DANCER (Dancer, 1935), S. Cream pink or rose cafe au-lait. Blooms earlier than tenuifolia. AV. Parentage uncertain.
HELEN HAYES (Murawska, 1943), D. Dark pink. L. T.
HELEN MATTHEWS (Saunders-Krekler, 1953), SD. Brilliant red. E. AV. Hybrid.
HELEN OF TROY (Pillow, 1923), S. Light red. X.
HELEN SEARS (Smith-Krekler, 1954), J. Light pink. M. T.
HENNEPIN (Auten, Jr., 1931), S. Black red. AV. E.
HENRIETTE CLARKE (MacDonald, 1948), D. White with scarlet splashes. M. AV.
HENRI POTIN (Doriat, 1924), J. Deep pink tinted carmine filament petals gradually turning white and vivid yellow at tips.
HENRY AVERY (Brand, 1907), D. Light pink mixed with shades of yellow and cream. Mildly fragrant. L. AV.
HENRY BOCKSTOCE (Bockstoce, 1955), D. Dark red. E. T. Hybrid.
HENRY M. VORIES (Vories, 1924), D. Light pink darker towards center. L. AV.
HENRY SWINDEN (Swinden, 1941), J. Dark red. M. to L. T.
HERMIONE (Sass, 1932), D. Pink. L. T.
HIAWATHA (Franklin, 1931), D. Rose type. Dark red. L. AV.
HIGH JINKS (Auten, Jr., 1929), A. J. Cerise red. L. T. X.
HIGHLAND LASSIE (Toedt, 1929), S. Center of petals

pink, crimson edges, rolled and widely ruffled. X.
HIGHLIGHT (Auten-Wild, 1952) seedling no. 930), D. Red. LM. AV.
HIS MAJESTY (Kelway, 1929), D. Maroon crimson surrounding scarlet central, petals.
HOARY (Krekler, 1958), D. White. LM. T.
HOLLYWOOD (Auten, 1937), J. Cerise pink. L. AV. X.
HONEYSWEET (A. B. Franklin, 1933) (seedling no. D-103, selected 1923), Rose type. White. T. X.
HOPE (Saunders, 1929), SD. Pink between salmon and cherry. VE. Otto Froebel x sinensis
HOTTENTOT (Dana, 1926), SD. Lilac and pink combined with stamens of various shades. X.
HOWARD R. WATKINS (Bockstoce, 1947), D. Red. VE. AV. Officinalis x chinensis
HUMORESQUE (Auten, 1925), D. Light pink with unusual markings of red. X.

I

IDEAL (Franklin, 1931). Rose type. Dark pink. L. AV.
ILLINI (E. Auten, Jr., 1931), S. Black red. T. X.
ILLINI BELLE (Glasscock, 1941), SD. Dark red. VE. AV. Chinensis x officinalis.
ILLINI WARRIOR (Glasscock-Falk, 1955) (seedling no. A1A1), S. Red. E. T.
IMPERIAL PINK (Sass), S. Dark pink. T. E. Name changed to Imperial Red, effect is light red.
IMPERIAL RED
see IMPERIAL PINK
INCA (Nicholls, 1941), S. Scarlet rose. T. Number 201 from Mikado. E.
INCA DEITY (McMurray, 1937), SD. White. E. AV.
INDIANA MOON (Rosenfield, 1933), Bomb type. Pink. T. AV.
INDIAN HILL (Glasscock, 1950), D. Black red. E. AV. Otto Froebel x albiflora
INDIAN MAID (Dana, 1926). Deep mahogany red. Fragrant. M. to L. X.
IN MEMORIAM (Brethour, 1929). Flesh pink, often a wide ring of red surrounding the center. M. Large flower.
INNOCENCE (Hollis, 1904), J. Light old rose guards. Center canary yellow fading to creamy white. LM. T.
INSPECTEUR LAVERGNE (Doriat, 1924), D. Globular. Crimson. M. to LM. T.
IROQUOIS (E Auten, Jr., 1931), J. Dark red. X.
IRVING FLINT (E. F. Kelsey, 1940), D. Rose pink. Fragrant. M.
ISANI GIDUI (Origin unknown), J. Guard petals pure white. Center buff-yellow. M. AV.
ISOLINE (Lemoine, 1916), A. Guards cuplike, cream white fading lighter. Center tuft canary-yellow fading almost white. M. AV.
IWO (Nicholls, 1946). Rose-red. AV.

J

JACOB STYER (Styer, 1948), D. White. L. T.
JACQUELINE HANRATTY (Gardner, before 1951), D. Red. E.
JAMES BOYD (Thurlow, 1919),

REGISTERED VARIETIES

D. Flesh pink. Buff center. very fragrant. L. AV.

JAMES KELWAY (Kelway, 1900), D. Pale pink, paling white. EM. T.

JAMES R. MANN (Thurlow, 1920), D. Rose-type. Dark rose pink. Crimson streaks in center and on outside guards sometimes noted. M. AV.

JAMES WILLIAM KELWAY (Kelway, 1929), SD. Deep purple rose. LM. AV.

JANES OLESON (Oleson, 1926), D. Red. VL. T.

JANET (Auten, 1940), D. Cerise red. T. Off. hyb. E.

JAPANESE BEAUTY (H. P. Sass, 1937). Carmine red. LM. T.

JAPANESE FAIRY (Secor, 1924), S. Pink with yellow center. M. X.

JAP. GIANT (Franklin, 1933), J. Rose pink. T. Seedling no. J-119, selected 1926. M. Often listed as Giant Jap.

J. BEENEY (Nicholls-Wild and Son, 1957) (seedling no. 1374), D. White. Fragrant. LM.

J. BOY (Jones, 1957), D. Bright pink. M.

J. C. LEGG (Wild, 1950), D. White and yellow. M. T.

J. C. NICHOLLS (Nicholls, 1948), D. White. EM. T. Marie Crousse x Spring Beauty

JEAN A. (Alexander, 1955), D. Light pink. LM. AV.

JEAN BRUCE (Chesher, 1941). Delicate pink. Fragrant. D. M. X.

JEAN COOPER (Cooper, 1946) (seedling no. 102), D. White. Very fragrant.

JEAN HARLOW (B. B. Wright, 1938). Pure white. EM. T.

JEANNE GAUDICHAU (Millet, 1902), D. Pale pink paling to white. Crimson edges in center. L. AV. Not sold in U.S.A.

JEANNOT (Dessert, 1918), D. Rose form. Pale rose pink. Old rose center. Overcast of pale violet. Faintly fragrant. L. AV.

JESSIE GIST (Nicholls-Wild and Son, 1953), D. Pink. EM. AV. Marie Crousse x Spring Beauty

JESSIE SHAYLOR (Shaylor, 1916), D. Blush white, darker outside with suffusion of yellow. Slightly fragrant. M. AV.

JEWEL (Glasscock, 1927), S. Red. E. AV. Officinalis hybrid.

J. N. DARLING (Reno Rosefield, 1939). Semi-rose type. Bright pink. T.

JOCELYN (Lemoine, 1923), D. Cup shape. Waved outer petals rose pink. Mildly fragrant. M. AV. Not sold in U.S.A.

JOEHANNA (Mrs. W. Wolfe, 1931). Rose type. Pink, tinged with lavender. X.

JOE HANRATTY (Gardner, before 1951), D. Deep pink. LM. T.

JOHANNA (Mrs. Wm. Karth, 1941), D. Soft rose ivory. LM. Name changed to Mary Jo.

JOHN ALDEN (W. A. Dana, 1926), Rose type. Rose pink. Fragrant. L. T. X.

JOHN GARDNER (Gardner, before 1951), J. Bright red. LM. AV.

JOHN HARVARD (E. Auten, Jr., 1939), S. Dark red. E. T. Officinalis hybrid

JOHN HOWARD WIGELL (H. E. Wigell, 1942), Rose type. Deep pink. EM. AV.

JOHN M. GOOD (Welsh, 1921), D. Outer petals pale pink shading to ivory white center — sometimes pure white. Yellow tint in depth of flower. Very fragrant. LM. T.

JOHN M. LEWIS (Lewis, 1921), D. Rose pink. Center flesh pink. Mild fragrance. LM. X.

JOHN RICHARDSON (Richardson, 1904), D. Flesh pink. Darker center. Pale tips. Fragrant. L. T. X.

JOHN SAYLOR (Krekler, 1958), S. Dark red. M. AV.

JOHN STARK (Freeborn, 1953), S. Deep crimson. E. T. Nippon Beauty x unknown

JOSEPH CHRISTIE (Rosefield, 1939), Rose type. White. AV. L.

JOSEPHELUS (Guppy), D. Bright red. X.

JOSETTE (Brethour, 1937), S. Pink with white centers. AV. E.

JOY (Saunders, 1928), S. Rose pink. T. Sinensis (Venus) x Otto Froebel. X.

JOYCE (Auten, 1938), D. Pink. L. AV.

JUBILEE (Pleas, 1908), D. White with greenish tinge. M. T.

JUDGE BERRY (Brand, 1907), D. Light rose pink of delicate shade. Slight fragrance. E. AV.

JUDGE ORR (Edlund, 1929), Pink. M. X.

JUDY BECKER (H. P. Sass, 1941), D. Rose type. Dark red. M. to L. AV.

JULIA (Auten, 1926), D. Pink. L. X.

JULIA (Glasscock, 1927), D. Pale pink. L. X.

JUNE BRIDE (Glasscock, 1939), Rose type. White. Fragrant. L. T.

JUNE BRILLIANT (Auten, 1938), D. Dark red. T. L.

JUNE DAY (Franklin, 1920), D. Light old rose pink. White outer petals. Crimson line in center of flower. Sweet fragrance. M. AV.

JUNE MOON (E. Auten, Jr., 1931), S. White. L. AV.

JUNE ROSE (R. H. Jones, 1938), D. Deep rose. E. AV.

JUNE WELCOME (Dana, 1926), S. Dark red. Yellow stamens. X.

K

KAHOKIA (E. Auten, Jr., 1931), S. Almost black. AV. E. X.

KAMENO-KEGOROMO see FLAMBOYANT

KANKAKEE (Auten, Jr., 1931), S. Dark red. L. AV.

KANSAS (Bigger, 1940), D. Red. AV. M.

KARL ROSENFIELD (Rosenfield, 1908), D. Bright crimson. M. T.

KASKASKIA (E. Auten, Jr., 1931), S. Dark red. E. DW.

KATE BARRY (Nicholls, 1938), D. Salmon pink. M. T. Seedling no. 214 from Ama-no-sode.

KATHALO (Kelsey, 1940), J. Pink-yellow. M. AV.

KATHARINE HAVEMEYER (Thurlow, 1921), D. Light rose-pink. Tinge of old rose. Mild rose fragrance. M. AV.

KATHRYN E. MANUEL (Phillips, 1953), S. Blush. E. AV.

KATE SMITH (Murawska, 1950), D. Dark pink. Fragrant. LM. AV. Seedling no. 53

KAW VALLEY (Bigger, 1944), D. Dark red. M. AV.

KELWAY'S BEAUTIFUL (Kelway, 1929), D. Silvery lavender. X.

REGISTERED VARIETIES

KELWAY'S CRIMSON BANNER (Kelway, 1929), D. Dark red.

KELWAY'S FAIRY QUEEN (Kelway, 1928), SD. Pink. Fragrant. DW. Not sold in U.S.A.

KELWAY'S GLORIOUS (Kelway, 1909), D. White, creamy suffusion in depths. Crimson on outside of guard petals, faint crimson edges in center. Strong rose fragrance. M. AV.

KELWAY'S GLORY OF JUNE (Kelway, 1928), SD. Pink. DW. Not sold in U.S.A.

KELWAY'S GORGEOUS (Kelway, 1929), S. Salmon rose. Not sold in U.S.A.

KELWAY'S LOVELY (Kelway, 1929), D. Light rosy red. Not sold in U.S.A.

KELWAY'S MAJESTIC (Kelway, 1929). J. Carmine. E. Not sold in U.S.A.

KELWAY'S PEACE (Kelway, 1929), D. Creamy white, almost a yellow tint. Not sold in U.S.A.

KELWAY'S PEERLESS (Kelway, 1928), S. Deep pink with large gold center. T. Not sold in U.S.A.

KELWAY'S QUEEN (Kelway, 1909), D. Bright rose pink, few red flakes. Strong rose fragrance. LM. AV.

KELWAY'S ROSE OF DELIGHT (Kelway, 1929), S. Rose pink. L. Not sold in U.S.A.

KELWAY'S UNIQUE (Kelway, 1917), D. Pink with golden petaloids. Not sold in U.S.A.

KEMANKEAG (Guppy, 1935), S. White. X.

KENDUSKEAG (Guppy, 1935), S. Light pink. X.

KEWANEE (E. Auten, Jr., 1930), S. Dark red. Long blooming season. E. AV.

KICKAPOO (E. Auten, Jr., 1931), S. Dark red. L. AV.

KILLINGTON (Freeborn, 1934), D. White. Tea-rose fragrance. L. AV. X.

KING (Krekler, 1958), D. Deep pink. LM. AV.

KING ALBERT (Kelway, 1929), S. Rosy violet.

KING BEE (B. B. Wright, 1935), D. Bomb type. Dark red. M. to LM. AV.

KING BOREAS (Wilkus, 1948) (seedling no. 1), D. White. LM. T.

KING GUSTAV (Rosenfield, 1934), Semi-rose type. Maroon. E. T.

KING MIDAS (Lins, 1942), D. Red. AV. M.

KING OF ENGLAND (Kelway, 1902), J. Dark red center. Buff staminodes streaked with dark rose-pink. EM. T.

KINNEY (Winchell, 1941) D. (no. K.2.A.). Red. M. D.

KINO-KIMO (Origin unknown), J. Dark rose pink petals. M. AV.

KIOWA (E. Auten, Jr., 1931), S. Light red. E. X.

KISSIMMEE (Jones, 1957), J. Rose. M.

KLONDIKE (Franklin, 1939), J. White. M. T.

KUKENI JISHI (Origin unknown), J. Delicate pink guard petals have pale rose shading on outside. Fragrant. E. M.

KURI (Jones, 1957), J. Rose. M. L.

L

LA CANADIENNE (Brethour, 1936), White. L. T. X. Note: form resembles Kelway's Glorious.

LADDIE (Glasscock, 1941), S. Bright red. E. DW. Officinalis Otto Froebel x tenuifolia

LADY ALEXANDRA DUFF

(Kelway, 1902), D. Pale blush pink, almost white. Slight fragrance. M. AV.

LADY BERESFORD (Kelway, 1893), A. Guards bright rose pink. Creamy white petaloids, edged crimson. Sweetly fragrant. M. X.

LADY EMILY (Pleas, 1907), D. Light rose pink, deep fringed shaggy flower. Fragrant. M. AV. X.

LADY KATE (Vories, 1924), D. Solid light pink. L. T.

LADY OF THE WEST (Kelway, 1912), D. Soft rose and creamy white. Light center. Not sold in U.S.A.

LADY ORCHID (Bigger, 1942), D. Lavender pink. LM. AV.

LA FEE (Lemoine, 1906), D. Light old rose pink. Creamy pink collar. Rose fragrance. EM. T.

LA FIANCEE (Dessert, 1902). Considered same as THE BRIDE, which see.

LA FONTAINE (Lemoine, 1904), D. Light old rose pink with pale violet tone. Notably fragrant. LM. T. X.

LA FRAICHEUR (Dessert, 1905), S. Light rose pink. Faintly fragrant. T. E. Not obtainable in this country.

LA FRANCE (Lemoine, 1901), D. Rose type. Light pink. Richer in center. Crimson splashes on outer petals. Fragrant. VL. T.

LAKE O'SILVER (Franklin, 1920), D. Light pink, silver tipped central petals dark pink. M.

LA LORRAINE (Lemoine, 1901), D. Cream white, tinted dark pink center. M. T.

LAMARTINE (Lemoine, 1908), D. Mixture of dark old rose pink and violet shades. Fragrant. L. AV. X.

LAMARTINE (Calot, 1860). The original name of GIGANTEA, which see.

LANGLEY (Bockstoce, 1955), SD. Pink. E. AV. Hybrid.

LANGPORT CROSS (Kelway, 1929), S. Rose turning to lavender. X.

LA PERLE (Crousse, 1886), D. Light old rose. Pink guards and collar. Center slightly darker, flaked with red giving whole flower lavender tone. Spicy fragrance. M. AV.

LA ROSIERE (Crousse, 1888), SD. White petals, yellow stamens. M. AV.

LA SALLE (E. Auten, Jr., 1931), S. Dark red. E. AV.

LASSIE (Glasscock-Falk, 1955) (seedling no. 10R1), S. Pink. E. AV. Hybrid.

LAST ROSE (Sass, 1930), D. Pale pink. L. AV.

LA TENDRESSE (Crousse, 1896), D. Almost white with slight lavender tone edged and flaked with crimson. Fragrant. M. T. Not listed in this country.

LA TULIPE (Calot, 1872), D. Flesh pink. Center creamy and often streaked with crimson. EM. T.

LAURA DESSERT (Dessert, 1913), A. Guards pale pink in bud—opening cream or pale lemon and becoming white. Moderately fragrant. EM. AV.

LAURA KELSEY (Kelsey, 1940), D. Blush white. LM. T.

LAURA MARCHES (Smith-Krekler, 1954), S. Deep pink. M. AV.

LAURA VORIES (Vories, 1924),

D. White with blush pink center. Mild fragrance. LM. AV.

LAVENDER PINK (Franklin, 1931), Rose type. Lilac. L. AV.

LAVERNE CHRISTMAN (Brand, 1925), D. Deep pink of varied shadings. T. LM.

LEADING LADY (Bigger, 1955), (seedling no. 16-47), D. White. M. AV.

LE CYGNE (Lemoine, 1907), D. White, tinged ivory, becoming pure white without markings as it develops. Moderately fragrant. E. AV.

LEE YOUNGBERG (Claar, 1955), S. Rose pink. E. AV. Albiflora x lobata

LEGEND (Jones, 1957), D. Deep rose. M.

LE JOUR (Shaylor, 1915), S. White with 2 rows of overlapping petals. Center a broad ring of golden yellow stamens. EM. AV.

LEONE GARDNER (Gardner, before 1951), D. Red. M.

L'ETINCELANTE (Dessert, 1905), S. Bright pink petals having a lighter border. Stamens bright golden yellow. M. T.

LETTIE (Nicholls-Wild & Son, 1957) (seedling no. 940), D. Pink. M.

LEWIS' AMERICAN BEAUTY (Lewis, 1921), D. Blood red. LM. T. X.

LIBELLULE (Dessert, 1922), D. Flesh colored flower, marked crimson. Fragrant. T. X.

LIGHTS OUT (Kelsey, 1934), D. Rose pink. L. AV.

LILLIAN GUMM (Gumm, 1921), D. Deep even rose pink suffused by chamois from the base of the petals. Fragrant. LM. T.

LILLIAN WILD (Wild Bros., 1930), D. Flesh color. LM. T. Marie Jacquin x albiflora

LITTLE GEM (Glasscock, 1940), J. Black-red. E. Fuyajo x officinalis Jap.

LIVINGSTONE (Crousse, 1879), D. Old rose pink, flaked on a lighter base. Few petals marked with crimson. Delicate spicy fragrance. L. AV.

LOIS (H. P. Sass, 1941), D. Bomb type. Chinensis. Medium pink. Fragrant. VE. DW.

LOIS Q. GAYLE (Wigell, 1944), D. Flesh. Mild fragrance. L. AV.

LONGFELLOW (Brand, 1907), D. Bright crimson. Fadeless. Fragrance is pleasing. M. DW.

LONG ISLAND (Guille, 1952), D. White. E. AV.

LORA DEXHEIMER (Brand, 1913), D. Bright crimson. M. AV.

LORCH (Goos & Koenemann), D. Outer petals snow-white incurving over a center of pale lemon and cream. Crimson lines on edges of petals near center. Rose fragrance. M. AV.

LORD AVEBURY (Kelway, 1929), D. Crimson maroon. X.

LORD KITCHENER (Kelway, 1929), S. Maroon crimson. E.

LOREN FRANKLIN (Franklin, 1931), Rose type. Dark pink. Fragrant. L. AV.

LORETTA FRANK (Franklin, 1953) (seedling no. H2), S. Dark pink. E. AV.

LOTHARIO (Wettengel, 1923), J. Bright violaceous pink. M. AV.

LOUIS JOLIET (E. Auten, Jr., 1929), SD. Dark red. AV. EM.

LOUISE M. Murawska, 1943), D. White. M. AV.

LOUISVILLE (E. Auten, Jr., 1940), S. Cerise pink. E. Officinalis hybrid.

LOVANCIA (Lyman, 1933), SD. or J. Pink. Fragrant. M. X.

LOVELINESS (Hollis, 1907), D. Pale flesh pink, center flesh white with few red markings. Mild fragrance. VL. AV.

LOVER'S DREAM (Rosenfield, 1934), Rose type. Bright pink.

LOWELL THOMAS (Rosenfield, 1934), Semi-rose type. Dark crimson. M. T.

LUCILE HARTMAN (Franklin, 1931), Rose type. Light pink. L. T.

LUCKY DAY (Auten, 1934), S. Deep pink. E. AV.

LUCKY STAR (Auten, 1938), D. Dark red. L. T.

LUCKY STRIKE (B. B. Wright, 1935), D. Rose pink. LM. to L. AV.

LUCY DUNN (Wettengel, 1924), D. Pink. X.

LUCY INEZ (Nicholls-Wild and Son, 1954) (Nicholls sedling no. 1305), D. Light pink. EM. AV.

LUCY SHAYLOR (Shaylor, 1920), D. Pure white outer petals. Many stamens in collar and center give it a pale yellow suffusion. M. AV.

LUCY WILLIAMS (Krekler, 1958), D. Light pink. LM. T.

LUETTA PFEIFFER (Brand, 1916), D. Pale pink paling to near white. Crimson fleck appears on center petals occasionally. Fragrant. E. T.

LULU CLIFFE (B. B. Wright, 1935), J A. Yellow petaloids, carpels bright green with pink stigmas. E. to EM. T. X.

LUXOR (Sass, 1933), D. White. EM. AV.

M

MABEL L. FRANKLIN (Franklin, 1920), D. Guards and center rose pink. Collar flesh pink or pale salmon. Strong lemon fragrance. M. AV.

MADAME BUTTERFLY (A. B. Franklin, 1933), J. Rose pink. M. AV.

MADAME CHIANG KAI-SHEK (Payne, 1943), A. White and yellow. E. T.

MAD CAP (Auten, 1931), S. Red, Flushed to white. L. T. X.

MADELEINE GAUTHIER (Dessert, 1908), S. Light flesh pink. EM. AV.

MADELON (Dessert, 1922), D. Silvery pink, flushed carmine. L. T.

MAFEKING (Kelway, 1929), S. Scarlet crimson.

MAHAL (Sass, 1934), Rose type. White. E. AV.

MAHOGANY (Glasscock, 1937), S. Deep mahogany. E. Chinensis x officinalis Otto Froebel

MAID OF ATHENS (Pillow, 1923), J. Pink. X.

MAID OF HONOR (Pillow, 1923), Semi-rose. Pink. X.

MAJESTIC ROSE (Franklin, 1953) (seedling no. A209P), D. Rose pink. L. AV.

MAJOR A. M. KREKLER (Johnson-Krekler, 1957), D. White. LM. T.

MANCHU PRINCESS (Harding, 1929), S. White tinged with coffee. E. Never in comerce.

MANDALEEN (Lins, 1942) (seedling no. R-4-7), D. Light pink. Rose fragrant. AV. M.
MANDARIN (E. Auten, Jr., 1933), Bomb type. Dark red. E. X.
MANOAH (E. Auten, Jr., 1933), D. Lavender. M.
MAN OF WAR (Saunders, 1929), S. Crimson. Season of officinalis. T. Sinensis x officinalis. X.
MARANACOCK (Guppy, 1935), J. Deep pink. X.
MARCELLA (Lins, 1952) (seedling no. A-6-25), D. White. M. AV.
MARCELLE DESSERT (Dessert, 1899), D Pale pink. M. T.
MARCHIONESS OF LANSDOWNE (Kelway, 1899), D. Brilliant rose pink. M. AV. X.
MARCIA (Lyman, 1933), D. Black-red. Fragrant. Never in commerce. Renamed Marcia Dewey.
MARDI GRAS (Winslow, 1951) (seedling no. 16), J. Dark red. M. T.
MARGARET (Sass, 1952), D. Blush white. L. T. (Note: formerly HANS' BLUSH WHITE)
MARGARET ATWOOD (Origin uncertain. Farr found this with no label in a shipment of roots from Holland.) J. White. M. AV.
MARGARET CLARK (Mains, 1956) (seedling no. A18), D. Dark pink. L.
MARGARET HAGERMAN (Hagerman, 1935), D. White, fairly fragrant. M. T. Never in commerce.
MARGARET VIERHELLER (Wettengel, 1920), D. Salmon pink. T. M.
MARGUERITE DESSERT (Dessert, 1913), S. White. Faint fragrance. M. T.
MARGUERITE GAUDICHAU (Millet, 1903), D. Light rose pink. Sweet fragrance. L. T. Not available in this country.
MARGUERITE GERARD (Crousse, 1892), D. Pale flesh pink to dark rose pink. M. AV.
MARIE (Calot, 1868), D. Pale old rose pink, changing to white. VL. VT. Not available in this country.
MARIE CROUSSE (Crousse, 1892), D. Pale pink. M. AV.
MARIE DEROUX (Crousse, 1881), D. Flesh pink, paling to white. L.
MARIE ELIZABETH (Guille, 1959), D. Red. M.
MARIE JACQUIN (Verdier), SD. Pale pink. M. AV.
MARIE LEMOINE (Calot, 1869), D. Lemon white. L. DW.
MARIELLEN (Guppy), S. White. X.
MARIETTA SISSON (Sass, 1933), D. Light pink. M. AV.
MARILLA BEAUTY (Kelsey, 1940), D. Blush white. L. T.
MARION CRAN (Kelway, 1929), SD. Flesh pink. Fragrant. T. X.
MARION PFEIFFER (Pfeiffer, 1929), D. Red. Rose geranium fragrance. T.
MARION TALLEY (Simpson, 1929), D. Rose type. Pink. D. X.
MARJORIE ALLISON (Shaylor, 1918), S. White. M. AV. X.
MARK TWAIN (Franklin, 1939), D. Crimson. M. T.
MARS (Murawska, 1943), SD. White. M. AV. Name changed to Ethel Mars.
MARTHA A. TWYMAN (Wetten-

gel, 1920), D. Pink. X.

MARTHA BULLOCH (Brand, 1907), D. Blend of bright old rose pink to pink. Rose fragrance. L. T.

MARTHA V. LANE (Wettengel, 1924), D. White. X.

MARTHA SHARP (Nicholls, 1949), D. Pink. M. AV. Marie Crousse x Lady Alexandra Duff

MARTHA WASHINGTON (Hollis, 1909). Suppressed by vote of Directors. X.

MARVEL (Secor, 1924), D. Light rose pink. Fragrant. L. T.

MARY AUTEN (E. Auten, Jr., 1933), D. White. Fragrant. L. AV.

MARY BRAND (Brand, 1907), Rose type. Crimson. Fragrant. M. AV.

MARY B. VORIES (Vories, 1924), D. Blush pink. Sweet fragrance. L. AV.

MARY C. WEDGE (Secor, 1924), D. Red. Fragrant. M. X.

MARY ELLEN (Franklin, 1931), Semi-rose type. Blush white. L. AV. LM.

MARY E. NICHOLLS (Nicholls, 1941), D. White. AV. Number 210 from Ama-no-sode

MARYGOLD (Mrs. Freeborn, 1931), J. Rose pink. Gold staminodes. X.

MARY J. HAWKE (Hawke, 1946), D. Dark red. M. T.

MARY JOAN CUMMINGS (Guppy, 1940), S. Pale pink. E. Solfatare x James Kelway. X.

MARY JO
see JOHANNA

MARY LENA (Lyman, 1936), A. Pale pink with white center. Never in commerce.

MARY L. HOLLIS (Hollis, 1907), SD. Bright pink. M. AV. X.

MARY LOUISE (Lyman, 1940), S. Pink. T. X.

MARY LOU KIMMEY (Edlund, 1929), Rose type. Light pink with splashes of carmine on center petals. Fragrant. T. X.

MARY M. FISCHER (Croix Farms, 1957) (seedling no. 15C), D. Light pink. LM. T.

MARY P. KING (Franklin, 1920), D. Flesh pink. Mild fragrance. M. AV.

MARY WOODBURY SHAYLOR (Shaylor, 1916), D. Flesh white. Fragrant. LM. DW.

MASSASOIT (White, 1954), S. Dark red. E. AV. Richard Carvel x officinalis anemone-flora aurea ligulata

MATADOR (Jones, 1957), J. Ruby red. M.

MATILDA LEWIS (Saunders, 1921), D. Dark maroon. M. AV.

MATTAWAMKEAG (Guppy, 1935), S. Deep pink. X.

MATTIE LAFUZE (Johnson, 1942), D. White. Fragrant. LM. AV.

MAUD E. TICKNOR (Ticknor, 1940), D. Pale rose pink. E. X.

MAUD L. RICHARDSON (Hollis, 1904), D. Light rose pink. Fragrance strong. VL. T. X.

MAURICE LOWE (Kelway, 1929), D. Rosy pink. Not for sale in this country.

MAURINE (Haupt, 1935), D. Light lavender. E. AV. X.

MAVOURNEEN (Lanigan, 1944), SD. Light rose pink. M. DW. X.

MAXINE ARMSTRONG (Sass, 1952) (seedling no. 21.29), D. White. M. T.

MAY DAWN (Glasscock, 1947), S.

Red. VE. Tokio x officinalis Sunbeam
MAY DELIGHT (Glasscock, 1941), S. Coral pink. E. D. White chinensis x officinalis Sunbeam
MAY MORN (Nicholls, 1952), D. Blush pink. M. T. Mme. Calot x unknown.
MAY OLESON (Oleson, 1924), S. Appleblossom pink. M. AV.
MEDICINE HAT (Auten, Jr., 1936), S. Dark red. AV. E.
MELLOW MOON (Jones, 1938), D. White. Very fragrant. M. AV.
MELODY (Auten, 1925), A. Pale pink. Pleasing fragrance. X.
MEMORIAL QUEEN (Rosenfield, 1934), D. Clear pink. E. T. A sport of Edulis Superba.
MEMORY (Jones, 1938), D. Blush pink with trace of tan at center. Slightly fragrant. L. AV. X.
MENTOR GRAHAM (Lanigan, 1938), D. Pale pink to white. LM. AV.
MENDOTA (Auten, 1937), SD. Red. T.
MERCEDES (Lins, 1956) (seedling no. M-L-96-B), D. Blush pink. LM.
MERRIGOLD (Wright, 1932), J. Violet pink. X.
METEOR (E. Auten, Jr., 1933), J. Red. M. AV.
MID-AMERICA (Bigger, 1952) (seedling no. 52-37), D. Pink. M. Renamed Deer Creek.
MIDNIGHT SUN (Murawska, 1954), J. Dark red. M. AV. Dignity x unknown
MIDSUMMER NIGHT'S DREAM (Pleas, 1906), D. Blush white. Fragrant. LM. AV. X.
MIGNON (Lemoine, 1908), D. Light flesh pink, paling to flesh white. Rose fragrance. M. AV. X.
MIKADO (Japan, 1893), J. Dark crimson. M. T.
MILDRED MAY (Murawska, 1943), SD. White. M. T. Note: changed from MRS. L. E. MAY
MILTON HILL (Richardson, 1891), D. Light shell pink. Faint fragrance. L. AV.
MINE (Krekler, 1958), S. Purplish red. E. T.
MINERVA (Sass, 1930), D. White. L. T.
MINNEAPOLIS (Dana, 1926), S. Pink. Fragrant. E. X.
MINNIE GERTRUDE (Glasscock, 1931), Rose type. Red. M. Officinalis hybrid. X.
MINNIE SHAYLOR (Shaylor, 1919), SD. Light pink. M. AV.
MINUET (Franklin, 1931), Rose type. Light pink. L. T.
MIRIAM MARSH (Freeborn, 1931), J. White with pale yellow center of stamenoids. X.
MIRIAM NAPIER ROHE (Sass-Napier, 1940), D. White. M. AV. Formerly Sass no. 42½. X.
MISCHIEF (E. Auten, Jr., 1925), S. Appleblossom pink. L. T.
MISS AMERICA (J. R. Mann-Van Steen, 1936), SD. White. E. AV.
MISS IDA CHAMBERLAIN (Kelway, 1929), S. Light rose. T. Not for sale in this country.
MISS MINNEAPOLIS (Franklin, 1931), Rose type. Pale pink. L. AV.
MLLE. JEANNE RIVIERE (Riviere, 1908), D. Blush white. Mild fragrance. M. T.

MLLE. LEONIE CALOT (Calot, 1861), D. Flesh pink. Sweet fragrance. LM. AV. X.

MLLE. ROUSSEAU (Calot, 1886), D. Pale creamy pink. Faint fragrance. M. AV. X.

MME. AUGUSTE DESSERT (Dessert, 1899), D. Old rose pink. Elderberry fragrance. E.M. AV. X.

MME. BENOIT RIVIERE (Riviere, 1911). Suppressed by vote of the Directors. X.

MME. CALOT (Miellez, 1856), D. Light old rose pink. Fragrant. E. T.

MME. DE VATRY (Guerin, 1863), D. Light pink. Fragrant. M. AV. X.

MME. DE VERNEVILLE (Crousse, 1885), D. White guard petals. Rose fragrance. Best in cooler climates. E. AV.

MME. D. TREYERAN (Dessert, 1889), D. Flesh pink. Pleasing fragrance. M. DW. X.

MME. DUCEL (Mechin, 1880), D. Pale old rose. M. DW.

MME. EDOUARD DORIAT (Dessert-Doriat, 1924), D. White, tipped crimson. T. LM.

MME. EMILE DUPRAZ (Riviere, 1911), D. Old rose pink. Rose fragrance. M. X.

MME. EMILE GALLE (Crousse, 1881), D. Light rose pink. Rose fragrance. L. AV.

MME. EMILE LEMOINE (Lemoine, 1899), D. White streaks on outer petals. Mildly fragrant. M. T.

MME. ESCARY (Lemoine, 1922), D. White. M. X.

MME. FOREL (Crousse, 1887), D. Pinkish-lavender. Fragrant. LM. AV. X.

MME. GAUDICHAU (Millet, 1902), D. Dark crimson, blackish sheen. LM. T. X.

MME. GEISSLER (Crousse, 1880), D. Light old rose pink. Crinkled petals. LM.

MME. JULES CALOT (Calot, 1868), D. Pinkish white, paling to white. M. DW. X.

MME. JULES DESSERT (Dessert, 1909), D. Flesh-white. Mild fragrance. LM. T.

MME. JULES ELIE (Calot, 1873), D. Old rose guards, cream white collar, pinkish crown. Mild fragrance. M. AV.

MME. LEMOINIER (Calot, 1865), D. Pale old rose pink, lavender tinge. Fair fragrance. M. T. X.

MME. MANCHET (Dessert, 1913), D. Pale old rose pink, distinct purple shading at base. VL. T. X.

MODELE DE PERFECTION (Crousse, 1875), D. Light old rose, tipped with silver. L. DW.

MODELLA (Betscher, 1920), D. Light pink guards. Creamy suffusion in the collar. Sweet fragrance. M. AV.

MODESTE GUERIN (Guerin, 1845), D. Dark rose-pink, slight violet tint. Rose fragrance. E. AV.

MOLLY STARK (Auten, 1927), D. Cream white, pink with red splashes. E. AV.

MONS. CHARLES LEVEQUE (Calot, 1861). Same as Mlle. Leonie Calot, which see. X.

MONS. DUPONT (Calot, 1872), D. White, with crimson blotches on central petals. Fragrant. LM. T.

MONS. JULES ELIE (Crousse, 1888), D. Light rose pink. E. T.

MONS. MARTIN CAHUZAC

REGISTERED VARIETIES

(Dessert, 1899), D. Maroon-crimson. EM. AV.
MONT BLANC (Lemoine, 1899), D. White. Fragrant. EM. AV.
MONTEREY (E. Auten, Jr., 1930), J. Light red, cerise and golden tints in center. M. AV.
MONTICELLO (E. Auten, Jr., 1931), S. White. T. X.
MOONGLOW (Rosefield, 1939), Rose type. Pale yellow. AV. L.
MOON MAGIC (E. Auten, Jr., 1939), A. Pink with yellow center. Albiflora var. M. AV.
MOON MIST (E. Auten, Jr., 1929), S. Pale pink. AV. M.
MOON OF NIPPON (R. W. Auten, 1936), J. White. T. LM.
MOONSTONE (Murawska, 1943), D. Blush pink. M. AV.
MORNING SONG (E. Auten, Jr., 1933), S. White. Crinkled. E. AV
MOROCCO (E. Auten, Jr., 1933), D. Red. VE. T.
MOSES HULL (Brand, 1907), D. Old rose pink. M. AV. X.
MOTHER'S CHOICE (Glasscock, 1950), D. White. M. AV.
MOULD OF FORM (Kelway, 1928). Cherry red. Not listed in this country.
MOUNT EVEREST (Sass, 1937), D. White. L. DW.
MOUNT PALOMAR (E. Auten, Jr., 1939), J. Dark red. E. T. Albiflora var.
MR. L. VAN LEEUWEN (Nieuwenhuyzen, 1916), D. Light crimson. LM. AV.
MRS. A. G. RUGGLES (Brand, 1913), D. Light pink, paling lighter. L. T. X.
MRS. A. M. BRAND (Brand, 1925), D. White. Fragrant. L. AV.
MRS. COL. LINDBERGH (Simpson, 1929), Rose type. Pink. Fragrant. M. T. X.
MRS. C. S MINOT (Minot, 1914), D Flesh pink, coppery tints. L. DW.
MRS. EDWARD BROMET (Kelway, 1929), D. White. Fragrant E. Not listed in this country.
MRS. EDWARD HARDING (Shaylor, 1918), D. White. M. AV.
MRS. E. J. SHAYLOR (Shaylor, 1920), D. Delicate pink. LM. X.
MRS. E. J. STREICHERT (Murawska, 1942), D. Deep pink. M. T. X.
MRS. EUGENE SECOR (Secor, 1924), D. White. Fragrant. L. T. X.
MRS. EVA BARRON (Glasscock, 1932), Rose type. Shell pink. Rose fragrance. M. T. Jules Elie x Georgiana Shaylor. X.
MRS. F. A. GOODRICH (Brand, 1925), D. Dark deep bright pink. LM. AV.
MRS. FRANK BEACH (Brand, 1925), D. Creamy white. L. DW.
MRS. FRANKLIN D. ROOSEVELT (Franklin, 1933) (seedling no. E-6 selected 1924), D. Rose pink. EM. AV.
MRS. FRED ATHROP (Athrop, 1941), D. White, sometimes edged with carmine. LM. T.
MRS. GEORGE BUNYARD (Kelway, 1898), D. Bright rose pink. Fragrant. M. T.
MRS. GEORGE RAWSON (Allison, 1931). Light pink. Fragrant. L. T.
MRS. HARRIET GENTRY (Brand, 1925), D. Pure white. L. AV.
MRS. HARRY A. NORTON (Norton, 1939), Semi-rose

type. Cochineal carmine. M. AV. X.

MRS. J. F. ROSENFIELD (Rosenfield, 1934), Rose type. White. E. T. X.

MRS. J. H. NEELEY (Neeley, 1931), Rose type. White. L. T.

MRS. JAMES KELWAY (Kelway, 1926), D. Flesh white. EM. AV. Almost identical with Kelway's Glorious.

MRS. JOHN M. GOOD (Good & Reese, 1929), Rose type. White. M. T.

MRS. JOHN M. KLEITSCH (Brand, 1925), D. Light violet rose. AV. L.

MRS. JOHN M. LEWIS (Lewis, 1920), D. Dark crimson, fragrant. M. AV.

MRS. JOHN SMYTHE FOGG (Hollis, 1907), D. Pale rose pink. M. T. X.

MRS. J. V. EDLUND (Edlund, 1929). White. Fragrant. L. T.

MRS. LIVINGSTON FARRAND (Nicholls, 1935), D. Rose type. Pink. T. LM.

MRS. PHILIP RUNCIMAN (Kelway, 1928), D. Rose. Not listed here.

MRS. R. M. BACHELLER (Vories, 1930), D. Pink. M. AV.

MRS ROMAINE B. WARE (Brand, 1925), D. Light flesh pink, shading lighter. Rose fragrance. T. L. M.

MRS. R. T. WHITAKER (Reineke, 1936), D. Light pink. Fragrant. M. AV. X.

MRS. SHAYLOR FORCE (Shaylor, 1919), D. Creamy white, tinge of lemon. M. AV.

MRS. SPRINGER BROOKS (Edlund, 1934), SD. White. M. AV.

MRS. TELFER MAC ARTHUR (Murawska, 1940), D. Blush fading to white. M. AV. X.

MRS. WILDER BANCROFT (Nicholls, 1935), J. Deep red. AV. M.

MUSKOGEE (Jones, 1957), J. Dark red. M.

MYRTLE GENTRY (Brand, 1925), D. Rose white, tints of flesh and salmon. Fragrant. LM. AV.

MYRTLE ROSENFIELD (Rosenfield, 1934), Rose type. Pink. AV. X.

MYRTLE REINEKE (Reineke, 1936), D. White, with cast of pink. M. AV. X.

N

NANCY (White, 1954), S. Peach pink. E. DW. Officinalis rubra plena x Saunders 4710

NANCY DOLMAN (Vories, 1924), D. Pale rose pink. L. T.

NANCY NICHOLLS (Nicholls, 1941), D. White flushed rosy pink. No. 116 from YESO.

NANCY NORA (Bernstein, 1942), D. Pink. M. AV. Walter Faxon x Lady Alexandra Duff

NANTICOOK (Guppy, 1935), J. Bright red. X.

NAOMI (E. Auten, Jr., 1933), D. Creamy flesh pink. M. AV.

NATANIS (Guppy, 1929), D. Crimson. Fragrant. T. Albiflora single x officinalis rubra plena. X.

NAUVOO (Auten, 1937), D. White. Fragrant. L. T.

NEHUMKEAG (Guppy, 1935), S. Bright red. X.

NELLIE (Kelway, 1915), S. Rose pink. M. DW.

NEON (Nicholls, 1941), J. Rose-pink. No. 208 from Ama-no-sode. M. AV.

REGISTERED VARIETIES

NEW ERA (A. Franklin, 1939), D. White. M. T.

NICK SHAYLOR (Allison, 1931), Rose type. Pink. L. AV.

NINA SECOR (Secor, 1922), D. Pure white. M. AV.

NIPPON BEAUTY (Auten, 1927), J. Dark red, staminodes flushed yellow. M. AV.

NIPPON BRILLIANT (E. Auten, Jr., 1933), J. Red. T.

NIPPON CHIEF (E. Auten, Jr., 1931), J. Dark red. L. T.

NIPPON GOLD (Auten, Jr., 1929), J. Pink. L. T.

NIPPON MAID (E. Auten, Jr., 1931), J. Dark red. AV. to DW. L.

NIPPON PARADE (Auten, 1935), J. Red. AV. M.

NIPPON PRINCESS (E. Auten, Jr., 1931), J. Cerise pink. X.

NIPPON RED (E. Auten, Jr., 1931), J. Red. AV. X.

NIPPON SPLENDOR (E. Auten, Jr., 1931), J. Deep red. T. M.

NIPPON TRIUMPH (E. Auten, Jr., 1937), J. Red. Renamed War Hawk. M.

NIPPON WARRIOR (E. Auten, Jr., 1933), J. Red. Center tipped yellow. M.

NOKOMIS (Franklin, 1920), D. Light pink. Fragrant. X.

NORSEMAN (Pillow, 1923), S. Light red. X.

NYMPHAEA (Thurlow, 1919), D. Cream white, flushed pale rose pink. Fragrant. M. AV.

O

OCTAVIE DEMAY (Calot, 1867), D. Light old rose pink guards. Darker crown. E. DW.

ODALISQUE (Lemoine, 1923), D. Outer petals tinted pink, center cream white. Rose scent. LM. AV. X.

OHIRAMA (Origin unknown), J. Guards, bright rose pink. Fragrant. DW.

OLD HUNDREDTH (E. Auten, Jr., 1933), D. Creamy white. L. T. X.

OLD IVORY (Glasscock, 1950), S. White. E. Sunbeam x albiflora

OLD MAIN (E. Auten, 1939), Bomb type. Red. T. (off. hyb.) E.

OLD SIWASH (E. Auten, 1939), D. Flesh fading to white. M. Fragrant. T. Albiflora var.

OLIVER P. BAYNE (Smith-Krekler, 1954), D. Dark pink. E. DW.

OPAL (Pleas, 1908), D. Pale rose pink, becoming white. M. AV. X.

OPAL HAMILTON (Nicholls-Wild & Son, 1957) (seedling no. 1355), J. Pink. M.

OPAL IRIS (Pleas), SD. Light pink, salmon shading. M. T. X.

OPHA (Wild & Son, 1950), S. White. E. AV.

ORIENTAL GOLD (Japan, 1954), D. Yellow. M. AV. Also listed as Golden Dream and Yokihi.

OWEN F. HUGHES (Phillips, 1953), S. Light pink. LM. DW. Mischief x Clio

OZARK BEAUTY (Wild Bros., 1950) (seedling no. 4), D. Dark pink. L. AV.

P

PALLAS (Terry), SD. Flesh pink. EM. DW.

PANDORA (Guille, 1952), D. Rose pink. E. T.

PARADISE (Hollis, 1907), D. Flesh pink, paling to white center. Fragrant. EM. AV.

PARTY GIRL (Jones, 1957), J. Pink. M.
PARTY GOWN (Kelsey, 1940), D. White. LM. T.
PASSADUMKEAG (Guppy, 1935), S. Dark red. X.
PASTEL (Nicholls, 1941), Rose type. Light salmon pink. AV. M. No. 217 from WALTER FAXON
PASTEUR (Crousse, 1896), D. Pale pink outer petals, center almost white with green center. Faint fragrance. LM. T. X.
PATHFINDER (E. Auten, Jr., 1939), D. Pink. Fragrant. M. Albiflora var.
PATIENCE (E. Auten, Jr., 1933), D. Cream-white. E. T. X.
PATRICIA (E Auten, Jr., 1931), SD. Blush. E. T.
PATRICIA HANRATTY (Gardner, before 1951), J. Rose red. M.
PATTY (E. Auten, Jr., 1939), A. Near salmon pink. DW. LM. Albiflora var.
PAUL BUNYAN (Lins, 1955), D. Rose. LM. T.
PAULINE HENRY (Nicholls-Wild & Son, 1957) (seedling no. 436), D. White. LM.
PAUL REVERE (E. Auten, Jr., 1939), D. Dark red. LM. T. Albiflora var.
PEACE (Murawska, 1955), D. White. Not yet introduced.
PEACHBLOW (Shaylor, 1938), SD. & D. Peach pink. E. AV.
PEDRO (G. Richmond, 1951), S. Bright red. M. T.
PEGGY (E. Auten, Jr., 1931), D. Deep pink. AV. LM.
PEG OF MY HEART (G. Richmond, 1949), D. Cerise pink. E. AV.
PELHAM (Auten, 1935), D. White. Fragrant. LM. T.
PENNACOOK (Guppy, 1935), J. Dark red. X.
PEORIA (E. Auten, Jr., 1931), S. Red. DW. E. X.
PERRETTE (Dessert, 1921), D. Faint pink, paling to white. Fragrant. LM. AV.
PETITE D'OR (Murawska, 1944), S. Blush fading to ivory white. E. T.
PERE MARQUETTE (E. Auten, Jr., 1933), S. Dark red. E. AV. X.
PERFECT JOY (Kelway, 1929), D. Coral pink turning nearly white. Not listed in this country.
PERFECT PICTURE (Kelway, 1928), SD. Pink. L. Not listed in this country.
PERLE BLANCHE (Dessert, 1913), S. White. Golden yellow stamens. EM. T.
PETAGRA (Franklin, 1920), D. Light red. Fragrant. X.
PETER OLESON (Oleson, 1924), S. Red. M. AV. X.
PETER PAN (Hollis, 1907), D. Old rose. Rose fragrance. L. AV.
PETITE (Falk-Glasscock, 1956), SD. Red. E. DW. Officinalis x albiflora
PHILIP G. CORLISS (Claar, 1955), S. Red. E. AV. Albiflora x lobata
PHILIPPE RIVOIRE (Riviere, 1911), D. Very dark crimson. Rose scent. E. AV.
PHILOMELE (Calot, 1861), A. Guards, dark old rose; collar buff. Fragrant. E. AV.
PHOEBE CARY (Brand, 1907), D. Old rose pink. Rose scent. VL. T.
PHYLLIS KELWAY (Kelway, 1908), SD. Rose pink, paling to white. M. AV.
PICO (Freeborn, 1934), S. White. M. AV. T.

REGISTERED VARIETIES

PIE PLATE (Wright, 1935), S. White. EM. to LM. T. X.

PIERRE DUCHARTRE (Crousse, 1895), D. Rose pink. Rose scent. L. AV.

PINK ANGEL (Christenson, 1948), S. Pink. VE. T. Tomentosa x F2 hybrid

PINK BEAUTY (Risk, 1929), D. Bright pink. Fragrant. M. T. X.

PINK CAMEO (Bigger, 1954) (seedling no. 6-45), D. White, shaded pink. LM. AV.

PINK FORMAL (Nicholls-Wild and Son, 1953) (Nicholls seedling no. 877), D. Light pink. LM. AV.

PINK GEM (Mann-Van Steen, 1936), S. Pink. EM. to LM. AV. X.

PINK GLORY (Jones, 1938), S. Dark pink with yellow center. EM. T. Name changed to Captain Jones.

PINK JEWEL (Winslow, 1951) (seedling no. 1), S. Bright pink. E. AV.

PINK LEMONADE (Klehm, 1951), D. Pink and yellow. M. T.

PINK MONARCH (E. Auten, Jr., 1933), D. Bright pink.

PINK MOUND (Klehm, 1952), (seedling no. 780A), D. Pink. M. DW.

PINK O'DAWN (Cooper, 1953), D. Dark pink. L. Not in commerce yet.

PINK OPAL (Sass, 1934), Full rose type. Light pink. M. T. X.

PINK PEARL (Submitted by Interstate Nurseries.) No description. Never listed.

PINK PERFECTION (Risk, 1929), D. Pink. Fragrant. L. T. X.

PINK POMPOM (Freeborn, 1943), D. Clear pink. E. Officinalis rubra x Madame Jules Dessert

PINK RADIANCE (Allen Wild, 1959), D. Pink. M.

PINK SOLANGE (E. Auten Jr., 1933). Fine pink. L. AV.

PIRATE FLAG (E. Auten, Jr., 1933), S. Dark red. VL.

PITTI SINN (Vories, 1924), D. Pink guard petals, yellow petaloids, pink center tuft. L. AV.

PIXIE (E. Auten, Jr., 1931), J. Red. T. X.

PLYMOUTH (E. Auten, Jr., 1931), D. White. Fragrant. AV. L.

POLAR STAR (Sass, 1932), J. White. T. M.

POMPILIA (Earnshaw, 1920), D. Ivory-white. M. AV.

PORPENTINE (Guppy), D. Red. X.

POTTSI ALBA (Buyck, 1840). Much overrated. Suppressed by vote of the Directors. X.

PRAIRIE BELLE (Bigger, 1945), D. Cream fading to white. EM. AV.

PRESIDENT FRANKLIN D. ROOSEVELT (Franklin, '33) (seedling no. X-24, selected 1923), Rose type. Dark pink. L. T.

PRESIDENT POINCARE (Kelway, 1929), D. Ruby crimson, spice scented. Not available here.

PRESIDENT TAFT (Blaauw, 1909). Considered same as REINE HORTENSE, which see.

PRESIDENT WILSON (Thurlow, 1918), D. Rose pink. Spicy fragrance. L. AV.

PRESTO (Auten, Jr., 1925), S. Red. E. AV. X.

PRIAM (Sass, 1930), D. Dark maroon red. M. T.

PRIDE OF ESSEX (Thurlow, 1916), D. Rose pink guards,

blush-white center. Fresh fragrance. M. T.
PRIDE OF HUISH (Kelway, 1928), S. Peach pink. E. Not avvailable here.
PRIDE OF LANGPORT (Kelway, 1909), S. Pale rose pink. M. T.
PRIDE OF PAULDING (Neeley, 1920), D. Flesh pink. Rose fragrance. L. X. Not good.
PRIDE OF SOMERSET (Kelway, 1928), S. Deep crimson. E. Not available in U.S.A.
PRIMA DONNA (Franklin, 1939), D. Light pink. E. M.
PRIMEVERE (Lemoine, 1907), A. Creamy white. Moderately fragrant. M. T.
PRINCE CHARMING (Glasscock-Falk, 1955) (seedling no. A1A46), J. Red. E. T.
PRINCE OF JAPS (Lewis, 1927), J. Oxblood red. M. AV.
PRINCESS DULEEP SINGH (Kelway), J. Dark old rose pink, center buff. Fragrant. EM. AV.
PRINCESS IMPERIAL (Kelway, 1929), S. Rosy pink, edged lighter. E. Not available in U.S.A.
PRISCILLA ALDEN (Originator: Roberts, 1926), Reg. by: A. H. Fewkes. Rose type. White. E. AV.
PRUDENCE (E. Auten, Jr., 1933), D. Lavender. Fragrant.
PURITAN MAID (E. Auten, Jr., 1933), S. White. AV.
PURPLE CUP (Secor, 1924), S. Red. E. X.

Q

QUEEN OF HAMBURG (H. P. Sass, 1937). Bright pink. LM. T.
QUEEN OF SHEBA (H. P. Sass, 1937), Bomb type. Bright rose. LM. AV.
QUEEN OF THE BELGIANS (Kelway, 1929), S. Creamy white. AV.
QUEEN OF THE WEST (Kelway, 1929), D. Rosy peach. E. Not listed in this country.
QUEEN VICTORIA (Kelway, 1929), D. Cream flesh. X.

R

RACHEL (Lemoine, 1904), D. Light rose pink. LM. AV.
RADIANCE (Brant, 1931), S. Dark red. T. E. X.
RAGGEDY ANN (Krekler, 1958), D. Light pink. LM. AV.
RALPH (Pleas, 1913). Much overrated. Suppressed by vote of the Directors.
RAMONA LINS (Lins, 1942) (seedling no. S-1-4), D. Pink. ML. T.
RAOUL DESSERT (Dessert, 1910), D. Shell pink. Rose scent. L. AV.
RARE CHINA (Kelsey, 1940), SD. White. M. AV.
RASHOOMON (Japanese origin), J. Rose-red. Good fragrance. M. AV.
RED BALL (Murawska, 1950), D. Red. L. T.
RED BIRD (Franklin, 1921), A. Rose-red. M. AV.
RED CHARM (Glasscock, 1944), D. Red. E. T. Officinalis x albiflora
RED CLOUD (Jones, 1941), D. Red. LM. AV.
RED CROWN (E. Auten, Jr., 1931), J. Red. T. X.
RED DAWN (Kelway, 1929), SD. Dark maroon red. Not available in U.S.A.

REGISTERED VARIETIES

RED ELIE (Winchell, 1948), D. Red. M.

RED EMPEROR (E. Auten, Jr., 1931), J. Light red. AV. M.

RED ENSIGN (E. Auten, Jr., 1940), SD. Black-red. L. DW. Off. hyb.

RED FEATHERS (Jones, 1941), Bright red. LM. T.

RED GIANT (Glasscock, 1939), Semi-rose type. Chinensis. Dark red. M. T.

RED GLORY (Auten, 1937), S. Dark red. Officinalis x chinensis. VE. T.

RED HARMONY (Freeborn, 1941), S. Deep crimson. M. AV.

RED JACKET (Krekler, 1955) (seedling no. J19), D. Red. E. DW.

REDKEY (Smith-Krekler, 1953), S. Deep black-red. E. AV.

RED MONARCH (Auten-Glasscock, 1937), Bomb type. Red. T. Officinalis x chinensis

RED SATIN (Sass, 1937), Rose type. Cerise. LM.

RED SIGNAL (Freeborn, 1941), S. Scarlet. Officinalis hybrid. E. AV. X.

RED SPLENDOR (Mann-Van Steen, 1936), J. Deep pink. M. T.

RED STAR (Nicholls, 1941), J. Vermilion. T. M. No. 80 from KARL ROSENFIELD

REGAL (Lyman, 1933), S. Black-red. Never in commerce.

REINE BARONET (Millet, 1924), D. Pink. M. AV.

REINE HORTENSE (Calot, 1857), D. Rose pink. M. T.

RELIANCE (Glasscock, 1950), D. Bomb type. Pink. E. AV. Otto Froebel x albiflora

REMEMBRANCE (Lyman, 1939), A. Rose pink. Never in commerce.

RENEE MARIE (Dessert, 1920), D. Flesh white, shading to pale pink. M. AV.

RESPLENDENT (Franklin, 1931), Rose type. White. M. to L.

REVERIE (Jones, 1938), D. Rose type. Pink with flush of lavender. LM. T. X.

RICHARD CARVEL (Brand, 1913), D. Bright crimson. Slight fragrance. E. T.

RICHFIELD WHITE (Franklin, 1939), Rose type. Midseason Festiva Maxima. T. Seedling G279

RIO GRANDE (Nieuwenhuizen, 1935). Dark red. M. AV.

RITA (Dessert, 1922), D. Rose pink outside, flesh pink within. Fragrant. L.

ROBERT (Gardner, before 1951), D. Deep pink. LM. T.

ROBERTA (E. Auten, Jr., 1936), J. White. LM. T.

ROBERT LEE DAVIS (Vories, 1924), D. Soft light pink. M. X.

ROBIN HOOD (E. Auten, Jr., 1939), SD. Red. M. AV. Albiflora var.

ROMEO (Rosenfield, 1934), S. Bright red. E. T.

ROSABEL (Sass, 1937). Rose red. M. AV.

ROSA BONHEUR (Dessert, 1905), D. Old rose pink. Rose scent. L. AV.

ROSADA (Nicholls, 1942), D. Rose type. Rose pink. T. LM.

ROSALIE (Auten, 1927), D. Similar to American Beauty Rose. DW. M.

ROSALIE (Glasscock, 1927), Rose type. Medium red. DW. X.

ROSAMOND (Lewis, 1922), D. Rose pink. Fragrant. AV. X.

ROSANNA SHRADER (Shrader, 1940), D. Rose type. Rose pink. M. T.

ROSE BEAUTY (Richmond, 1949), D. Old rose pink. L. T.

ROSE BOWL (Keagey, 1946), S. Pale pink, fading to white. M. T.

ROSEDALE (E. Auten, Jr., 1936), SD. Dark red. E. DW. Officinalis x chinensis

ROSELLA MAY (Glasscock, 1927), Rose type. Deep pink. M. to L. T. Chinensis var. X.

ROSE MARIE (Auten-Glasscock, 1936), D. Dark red. Officinalis x chinensis. E AV..

ROSE MARIE LINS (Lins, 1958), D. Light pink. LM. T.

ROSE OF HEAVEN (Mann-Van Steen, 1936), D. Pink. AV. M.

ROSE OF MIAMIS (Jones, 1957), D. Blush white, some petals crimson edged. M.

ROSE SHAYLOR (Shaylor, 1920), D. Flesh pink, fragrant. M. T.

ROSE TRIUMPH. Submitted by Interstate Nurseries, 1937. No description. Never introduced.

ROSETTE (Dessert, 1918), D. Light shell pink. EM. AV.

ROSE VALLEY (Scott, 1925), J. Pink with yellow center. M. AV.

ROSINE (Lemoine, 1913), D. Bright rose pink. Rose fragrance. LM. AV. Not listed here.

ROSY DAWN (Barr), S. White, tinged pale pink. E. AV. Not listed here.

ROXANA (Auten-Lake, 1946), S. Pink red. E. DW. Richard Carvel x tenuifolia simplex

ROY ROBINSON (Winchell, 1941), no. 7A. Red-pink. M.

R. P. WHITFIELD (Richardson), D. Pale rose pink. Rose fragrance. L. T. X.

RUBIE BATTEY (E. Auten, Jr., 1933), J. Rich red. Yellow lines and dots on center petaloids very scanty. L. T.

RUBIO (Nicholls, 1941), D. Red. T. No. 135 from Torpilleur. M.

RUBY (Glasscock, 1927), D. Dark red. EM. Former No. 173. X.

RUBY KING. Submitted by Interstate Nurseries, 1937. No description. Never introduced.

RUSSELL EMRICK (Krekler, 1957) (seedling no. AT19), D. Blush. M. T.

RUTH FORCE (Shaylor, 1921), J. Cerise-pink. M. to L. AV.

RUTH GALLAGHER (Cooper, 1946) (seedling no. 10), Bomb type. Cream-colored. T. M.

S

SABLE (Glasscock, 1943), S. Red. Almost black. E. 2d generation OTTO FROEBEL hybrid.

SALEM (E. Auten, Jr., 1931), D. Red. Fragrant. X.

SALMON BEAUTY (Glasscock-Auten, 1939), D. Pink with salmon cast. E. T.

SALMON GLORY (Glasscock, 1947), D. Salmon pink. VE. T. Officinalis rosea plena x albiflora

SALMON GLOW (Glasscock, 1947), S. Salmon pink. VE. AV. Albiflora x officinalis Sunbeam

SAMUEL HILL (Berneche, 1932), S. Pink. E. AV.

SANCTUARY (E. Auten, Jr., 1933), D. Cream white. T. M.

SAN DIEGO (E. Auten, Jr., 1931), J. Light red. M.

SANS SOUCI (E. Auten, Jr., 1930), A. Light violaceous pink. X.

SANTA FE (Auten, 1937), SD. Red. E.

SARAH (Pleas, 1913), D. Light pink. M. X.
SARAH BERNHARDT (Lemoine, 1906), D. Dark rose pink. L. AV.
SARAH CARSTENSEN (Terry, 1901), D. Light rose pink. M. DW. X.
SARAH K. THURLOW (Thurlow, 1921), D. Pure white. Rose fragrance. VL. AV.
SCARF DANCE (Auten, 1927), SD. Light pink and white. M. AV.
SCARLET O'HARA (Falk-Glasscock, 1956), S. Red. E. Officinalis x albiflora
SEASHELL (Sass, 1937), S. Pink. EM. AV.
SEBASTICOOK (Guppy, 1935), J. Dark red. X.
SECRETARY FEWKES (Shaylor, 1916), D. Pale rose pink, paling to white. M. T.
SEIHIN IKEDA (Harding, 1935), J. Reddish purple. M. T. Never in commerce.
SEIRIU SOMAE (Origin unknown), J. Creamy white. M. AV.
SENORITA (E. Auten, Jr., 1931), J. Deep cerise red. L. X.
SENSATION (Sass, 1937). Light pink. L. AV.
SENTINEL (E. Auten, Jr., 1931), J. Red. T. X.
SERENE (Franklin, 1921), D. Rose-pink. L. DW. X.
SHAWNEE CHIEF (Bigger, 1938), D. Dark red. L. AV.
SHAYLOR'S DREAM (Shaylor, 1918), D. Pale flesh pink, paling to white. Fragrant. M. AV.
SHAYLOR'S SUNBURST (Allison, 1931), J. Pure white. Pond lily fragrance. LM. T.
SHIRLEY ANN (Winchell, 1941), No. 12A. Red. LM.

SHO-YO (Harding, 1935), Semi-rose. Flesh-blush. Fragrant. LM. AV. Never in commerce.
SHIRINE (Brethour, 1936). Pink. T. LM.
SHY MAID (E. Auten, Jr., 1930), A. Pale lavender pink. E.
SIBELIUS (Rosefield, 1939), Rose type. Light pink.
SIGNAL STATION (Auten, 1938), J. Red. AV. VL.
SILOAM (E. Auten, Jr., 1933), D. White. L. DW.
SILVER CERISE (Porter, 1927), S. Cerise with silver-tipped edges. M. T. X.
SILVER KING (E. Auten, Jr., 1933), D. White. L.
SILVER WEDDING (Lyman, 1939), S. White. Never in commerce.
SILVER SWAN (Rosenfield, 1934), D. Rose type. White. L. T. Never in commerce.
SILVIA SAUNDERS (Saunders, 1921), SD. Rose pink. Extra E. DW.
SIR JOHN FRANKLIN (Franklin, 1939), Rose type. Red. Fragrant. L. T.
SISTER MARGARET (Cooper-Wild and Son, 1953), D. White. EM. AV.
SISTIE (E. Auten, Jr., 1933), D. Pink, fades white. Rose fragrance. L. AV.
SKY PILOT (E. Auten, 1939), J. Deep pink. T. LM.
SLEEPY HOLLOW (Auten, 1935), S. Blush white. E. T.
SMILES (Nieuwenhuizen, 1935), D. Light mauve, yellow petaloids. M. T.
SMOKE SIGNAL (Jones, 1957), J. Deep rose. M.
SNOWBALL (Franklin, 1933), Rose type. White. Seedling No. X-5, selected 1925. M. AV.

SNOW BOUND (E. Auten, Ir., 1931), S. White. X.
SNOW CLOUD (Hoogendoorn, 1949), D. White. E. AV.
SNOW MOUNTAIN (Bigger, 1946) (seedling 22-37), D. White. M. T.
SNOW SPRITE (E. Auten, Jr., 1930), S. White. DW. E.
SNOW WHEEL (Origin unknown), J. White. M. DW.
SOLANGE (Lemoine, 1907), D. Cream white, suffusion of buff and pale salmon pink. L. AV.
SOME GANOKO (Origin unknown), J. Dark crimson, fragrant. DW. M.
SOPS OF WINE (Secor, 1922), D. Dark red with purple. L. DW. X.
SOUVENIR DE A. MILLET (Millet, 1924), D. Amaranth. LM. T.
SOUVENIR DE LOUIS BIGOT (Dessert, 1913), D. Rose pink. M. AV.
SOWADABSCOOK (Guppy, 1935), J. Dark red. X.
SPARKLES (Glasscock, 1946), SD. Scarlet red. AV. E. Hybrid.
SPARKLING STAR (Bigger, 1953), S. Dark pink. E. AV. Mary Brand x unknown
SPLENDIDA (Guerin, 1850), D. Light old rose pink. L. T.
SPLENDOR (Sass, 1929), Rose type. Dark red. L.
SPOON RIVER (E. Auten, Jr., 1931), D. Creamy magenta. Rose fragrant. AV. X.
SPRING BEAUTY (Nicholls, 1933), D. to SD. Rose pink. E. AV.
STANDARD BEARER (Hollis, 1906), D. Dark old rose. E. DW. X.
STANLEY (Crousse, 1879), D. Light old rose pink. M. T. Not listed here.

STEPHANIE (Terry, 1891), D. Pale pink. M. T. X.
STONEY EDWARDS (Kelway, 1929), D. Rose and pale cream center. Not listed here.
STRASSBURG (Goos & Koenemann, 1911), D. Pale old rose. M. T. X.
SULLY PRUDHOMME (Crousse, 1898), D. Light flesh pink. M. AV. X.
SUNBEAM (Hollis, 1906), J. Pale old rose, fading bluish white. M. AV. X.
SUNBRIGHT (Glasscock, 1939). Red. E. AV. Chinensis x officinalis Sunbeam
SUNCOOK (Guppy, 1935), J. Dark red. X.
SUN FAST (Freeborn, 1945), D. Bright red. E. Officinalis ruba plena x chinensis
SUNMIST (Nicholls, 1942), Blush. M. AV.
SUNRISE (Franklin, 1931), SD. Rose pink. L. AV. X.
SUNSET (Risk, 1929). Light pink, gold center. M. T. X.
SUNSET GLORY (Lyman, 1939). J. Deep rose pink or red. M. X.
SUN-UP (Auten, 1937), S. Dark red. L.
SUZETTE (Dessert, 1911), D. Rose pink. Fragrant. M. AV.
SWEET GENEVIEVE (Richmond, 1949) (seedling no. 201-327), D. Deep lilac pink. M. AV.
SWORD DANCE (E. Auten, Jr., 1933), J. Rich red. M. T.
SYLVIANE (Lemoine, 1924), A. White guard petals, pale canary yellow petals in center. M. Not sold in U.S.A.
SYMPHONY (Brethour, 1929). Light salmon pink. Fragrant. EM.

T

TAMATE-BOKU (Origin unknown), J. Old rose pink. M. AV.

TANAGER (Sass, 1934). Red. L. D. T. Note: formerly registered as VESUVE, 1934.

TANYA (Jones, 1957), D. Dark red. L.

TARANTELLE (E. Auten, Jr., 1929), J. Brilliant light red or deep cerise pink. AV. X.

TAR BABY (E. Auten, Jr., 1931), SD. Dark red. L. DW.

T. B. TERRY (Pleas, 1911). Suppressed by vote of Directors. X.

TECUMSEH (White, 1954), S. Réd. F. AV. Marie Crousse x lobata

TEMPEST (E. Auten, Jr., 1931), SD. Dark red. T. M.

THE BARON (Auten, 1934), J. Red and yellow. M.

THE BRIDE (Dessert, 1902), S. Pure white. E. AV. Also listed as Albiflora, The Bride.

THE FLEECE (Kelsey, 1940), D. White. M. AV.

THE GEM (Pleas, 1909), D. Dark crimson. M. T. X.

THE JEWEL (Pleas). Considered the same as OPAL, which see. X.

THELMA BARNES (Franklin, 1933), Rose type. White. Seedling No. D-66, selected 1923. X.

THE MIGHTY MO (Wild, 1950), D. Red. M. T.

THE QUEEN (Kelway, 1902), S. White petals, flushed pink. M. AV. Not listed here.

THERESA GARDNER (Gardner, before 1951), D. White. L.

THERESE (Dessert, 1904), D. Old rose pink. M. AV.

THOMAS C. THURLOW Thurlow, 1919), D. Flesh pink, paling to cream white. Fragrant. M. AV.

THOR (Sass, 1937), D. Deep maroon. M. AV.

THURA HIRES (Nicholls, 1938) (seedling no. 8), D. White. Fragrant. LM. AV.

TILLIENOONE (Guppy, reg., 1932), S. Deep bright red. X.

TINKA PHILLIPS (Phillips, 1953), D. Rose salmon. EM. T.

TIRA (Franklin, 1939), Rose form. Pink. LM. T. X.

TO KALON (Kelsey, 1936), D. White. LM. AV.

TOKIO (Origin unknown), J. Rose pink. M. T.

TOM BERKLEY (Sass, 1941), D. Light pink. M. to L. AV.

TOM TINKER (E. Auten, Jr., 1930), S. Dark red. E. AV. X.

TONDELEYO (Lins, 1942) (seedling no R-2-101), D. Dark pink. ML. T.

TONTI (E. Auten, Jr., 1933), S. Light red. T. E.

TOP FLIGHT (Nicholls-Wild and Son, 1959), D. Blush. LM. T.

TOPEKA (Auten, 1938), Bomb type. Bright red. Officinalis x chinensis. E. AV.

TORCHLIGHT (Lyman, 1939), A. Deep rose pink or red. Never in commerce.

TOREADOR (Wettengel, 1923), S. Light red. Very L. T.

TORO-NO-MAKI (Origin uncertain), J. Blush white. Fragrant. M. AV.

TORPILLEUR (Dessert, 1913), J. Deep rose red. Fragrant. M. AV.

TOURANGELLE (Dessert, 1910), D. Light pink. Fragrant. L. AV.

TOWN CRIER (E. Auten, Jr., 1939), S. Light red. Albiflora var. E.

TRAGEDY (Hollis, 1909), D. Dark crimson. M. T. X.

TRANQUILITY (Nicholls-Wild & Son, 1957) (seedling no. 960), D. White. M.

TRINKET (Nicholls, 1941), D. White with yellow underglow. AV. LM. No. 72 from Laura Dessert

TRUMPETER (Sass, 1949), D. Dark red. M. AV. Fuyago x red seedling no. 10-31

TWO-IN-ONE (Bockstoce, 1955), D. Red. E. T.

U

UNA HOWARD (Kelway, 1929), SD. Carmine. Not listed here.

UNCLE BILL (Klehm, 1954) (seedling No. 77B), D. Dark rose pink. M. T.

UNCLE REMUS (E. Auten, Jr., 1931), SD. Black red. T.

V

VANDALIA (E. Auten, Jr., 1939), D. White. Rose fragrance. LM. Albiflora var.

VAUGHN DELEATH (Lanigan, 1945), D. Dark rose pink. M. T. X.

VENUS (Kelway, 1888), D. Old rose pink. Fragrant. M. T.

VERA (Gumm, 1923), S. Dark maroon-crimson. Fragrant. EM. AV.

VERITAS (E. Auten, Jr., 1939), D. Dark red. E. AV. Officinalis hybrid.

VESTA CLAUSSEN (Claussen, 1936), D. Pink. T. X.

VESUVE (Sass, 1934). Red. L. Changed to Tanager.

VESUVE (Dessert, 1905). Red. (Sym. 1921) E. AV.

VICTOIRE DE LA MARNE (Dessert, 1915), D. Dark pink. M. AV.

VICTORY (Thompson, 1944), D. White with a dash of pink. L. T.

VICTORY CHATEAU THIERRY (Brand, 1925), D. Clear pink. Fragrant. M. DW.

VIKING (E. Auten, Jr., 1936), D. Dark red. L. X.

VIMY RIDGE (Brethour, 1937), D. Bright pink. X.

VINCENNES (E. Auten, Jr., 1939), D. White, flushed pink and yellow. E. T. Albiflora var.

VIRGINIA LEE (E. Auten, Jr., 1939), D. Pink. L. AV. Albiflora var.

VIRGINIA LOUISE (Walter J. Guille, 1948), D. Blush. M. to L. AV.

VIVID ROSE (Klehm, 1952) (seedling no. 76A), D. Bright rose pink. LM. AV.

VOGUE (Hoogendoorn, 1949), D. Rose. M. AV.

W

WABASH (Smith-Krekler, 1955), D. Pink. M. DW.

WALLY Z (Nicholls-Wild and Son, 1959), D. Light pink. EM.

WALTER (Krekler, 1958), D. Light pink. LM. T.

WALTER CAMPBELL LYMAN (Lyman, 1933), D. Shell pink. Fragrant. L.
Never in commerce.

WALTER E. WIPSON (Murawska, 1956), D. White. L. AV. Le Cygne x Frances Willard

WALTER FAXON (Richardson, 1904), D. Shell pink, mild fragrance. M. AV.

WALTER MAINS (Mains, 1957), J. Dark red. E. T. Albiflora x officinalis, anemoneflora aurea ligulata rosea

REGISTERED VARIETIES

WAR HAWK
see NIPPON TRIUMPH
WATCHMAN (E. Auten, Jr., 1933), S. White. L. T.
WATER LILLY. Same as MARIE JACQUIN, which see.
WATERLILY (Brant, 1931), SD. Pure white. Fragrant. M.
WAUKEAG (Guppy, 1935), S. Dark red. X.
WEDDING DAY (E. Auten, Jr., 1933), S. Flesh white. T.
WEE PHILIPPE (Smith-Krekler, 1954), D. Dark red. M. DW.
WENONAH (Franklin, 1920), D. Dark pink, tipped with white. X.
WEST ELKTON (Krekler, 1958), J. Dark red. LM. AV.
WESTERNER (Bigger, 1942), J. Pink. M. AV.
W. F. CHRISTMAN (Franklin, 1921), D. Blush white, shaded with pink. Rose fragrance. M. AV.
WHISKERS (Jones, 1957), J. Red with bicolor plume center. M.
WHITE BEAUTY (E. Auten, Jr., 1931), D. White. Fragrant. M. T.
WHITE CAP (Winchell, 1956) (seedling no. J-3-CJ), J. Dark pink. M. T.
WHITE CLOUD (Auten, Jr., 1931), J. White. E. T.
WHITE COCKADE (Keagey, 1946), S. White. M. AV.
WHITE CRANE (E. Auten, Jr., 1939), J. White and yellow. T. Albiflora var.
WHITE DELIGHT (Auten, 1935), D. White. Fragrant. T. E.
WHITE EAGLE (Sass, 1937), Rose type. White. EM. AV.
WHITE EMPEROR. Entered by Interstate Nurseries, 1937. Never introduced. No description.
WHITE GOLD (Mann-Van Steen, 1936), J. White. T.
WHITE JADE (Harding, 1935), Rose type. Rose fragrance. White. M. Never in commerce.
WHITE LADY (Kelway, 1900), J. White. LM. DW.
WHITE MOTH (E. Auten, Jr., 1933), S. Flesh white. T. X.
WHITE PEARL (E. Auten, Jr., 1931), D. Shell pink with lavender cast. E.
WHITE PERFECTION (E. Auten, Jr., 1931), S. White. AV. M.
WHITE PRINCE (Risk, 1929). White with cream center. Fragrant. L. AV. X.
WHITE ROSE (Shrader, 1942), SD. White. LM. AV.
WHITE SWAN (Pleas, 1913), S. White. E. AV.
WHITE WATER (Kelsey, 1940), D. White. M.
WHITE WINGS (Hoogendoorn, 1949), S. White. M. AV.
WHITLEYI MAJOR (Origin unknown.) S. Blush. E. AV.
WIESBADEN (Goos and Koenemann, 1911), D. Flesh pink paling to white. LM. AV.
WILBUR WRIGHT (Kelway, 1909), S. Dark crimson-maroon. M. AV.
WILD ROSE (Kelway), S. White. Speckled pink. M. AV.
WILLA GIRL (Nicholls-Wild and Son, 1959), D. Creamy white. M. to ML.
WILLIAM F. TURNER (Shaylor, 1916), D. Very dark crimson petals. Blackish sheen. EM. T.
WILLIAM H. PARK (Freeborn, 1945) (seedling Chugai no. 29), J. White. M. AV.
WILLIAM SHERADEN

(Bockstoce, 1955), D. Light pink. E. T. Officinalis x lactiflora

WILL ROGERS (Franklin, 1935), D. White. AV. DW.

WILTON LOCKWOOD (Shaylor, 1915), D. Light rose-pink. Fragrant. M. T.

WINNEFRED DOMME (Brand, 1913), D. Dark maroon-red. M. DW.

WINNIE WINKLE (Franklin, 1931), Rose type. Pink. L. T.

WINNIKENNI (Thurlow, 1915), D. Rose-pink. VL. X.

WITCHES' DANCE (E. Auten, Jr., 1931), S. Dark red. T. L.

W. W. BLACK (Nicholls-Wild and Son, 1957) (seedling no. 1033), D. Pink. LM.

Y

YOKIHI
see ORIENTAL GOLD

YONDER LEA (Fletcher, 1942), S. American Beauty. M. AV. Unknown red double x Festiva Maxima. X.

YONG-LO (Harding, 1935), Rose type. Lilac rose. Fragrant. M. T. Never in commerce.

YORK AND LANCASTER (Kelway, 1928), S. Red and white. E. X.

YUKON (Auten, 1937), D. White. Fragrant. L. T.

Z

ZIP COON (E. Auten, Jr., 1931), SD. Dark red. DW. M.

ZULIEMA (Brant, 1941), D. Red. Fragrant.

ZULU BRIDE (E. Auten, Jr., 1933), SD. Dark black-red. M.

ZULU WARRIOR (Glasscock, 1939), S. Dark red. E. T. Chinensis x Otto Froebel

ZUZU (Krekler, 1955). Bluish pink. SD. M. AV.

INDEX

A

A. B. Franklin, 75
Accessories, 167
Acid soil, 107, 122
Aconitum, 28
   fisheri, 59
Ada Priscilla, 34, 75, 83, 196
Adolphe Rousseau, 79, 84, 89
Aerie, 75, 78, 83
Age of Gold, 129, 157, 160, 162
A. G. Perry, 75
Akashigata, 74, 162
Albert Crousse, 158
Albuquerque, 75
Alesia, 72, 75, 82
Alexander Woolcott, 78, 84, 97, 96, 98, 102, 198
Alice Harding, 36, 70, 72, 75, 82, 135, 160, 162, 199
Alma Hansen, 71, 82
Althea, 140
Alyssum saxatile, 140
   compactum, 63
Amalia Olson, 89
Ama-no-sode, 34, 69, 74, 84, 86, 195
Amberglow, 81
Amber Moon, 162
American Peony Society, 38, 46
   lists of hybrids, 98, 99
   lists of most popular herbaceous peonies, 71-77
   lists of most popular tree peonies, 161-163
   recommended lists for buying, 68-92
Anemone, 17, 28, 34, 70, 74
   cutting of, 196-199

Angelo Cobb Freeborn, 77, 97, 99
Angelus, 74
Anne Bigger, 84
Annisquam, 81, 83, 197
Annuals, 40, 64, 140
Anomala, 90
Ants, 45, 87, 118
Anyo-no-hikare, 158
Aphids, 87
Aphis, 118
Apple blossoms, 180
Aquilegia, 28, 180
Arabis, 59, 141
Arasan, 117
Arbutus Pink, 83
Archangel, 70, 97
Arcturus, 33, 69, 74, 85, 194
Arenaria, 141
Argosy, 129, 135, 157, 162, 199
Arientina, 90
Arizona, 38
Armeria, 59
Arrangements, 33, 45, 166-185
   for flower shows, 206-207
Artemisia, 175
Aruncus sylvester, 59
Aspidistra, 176
Aster frikarti, 140
Auguste Dessert, 35, 75, 84, 88
Aurea, 90, 95
Aureolin, 74
Aurore, 163
Auten, Edward, Jr., 94
Auten's Pride, 76, 83
Avalanche, 202
Avant Garde, 94
Avelyn, 98
Ave Maria, 75
Azaleas, 136, 138

259

B

Ballerina, 85
Bamboo, 176
Banksi, 158
Banner Bright, 75
Banquet, 160, 163
Baptisis australis, 61
Baroness Schroeder, 76, 82, 88, 198
Beauty bush, 180
Beds, 127, 133
   for herbaceous peonies, 107
   for tree peonies, 143-144
Beetles, 118
Bellis perennis, 63
Beni-chidori, 162
Better Times, 63
Big Ben, 85
Bijou de Chusan, 158
Birthday, 83
Black Douglas, 162
Black Panther, 162
Black Pirate, 161, 162
Blanche King, 36, 72, 76, 4, 88
Blazing Star, 75
Bleeding-heart, 64, 175
Blooming times
   of herbaceous, 77-86, 100-101
   of tree peonies, 155
Blue Rose, 90
Blush, 88
Bockstoce, W. S., 94
Boltonia, 59
Bonanza, 71, 84
Bonemeal, 46, 107, 144, 147
Borax, 187, 188
Bordeaux mixture, 44, 115, 117, 148, 149, 154
Borders, 52-60, 77, 132
   herbaceous peonies for, 63, 78, 79
Borders
   tree peonies for, 131-141
Botrytis, 44, 46, 87, 113, 116, 117, 118, 148, 149
Bouquets, 175, 182

Branches, 173, 174, 176, 177
Break O' Day, 74, 80
Bright Knight, 97, 102
Broteri, 90
Buckwheat hulls, 148
Buds, 123
Bugbane, 140
Bulbs, 140
   spring-flowering, 61
Burning foliage, 46, 87, 113, 116, 149
Bu-te, 74
Buttercup family, 27
Buying, 63, 64
   herbaceous roots, 103
   tree peonies, 142-143

C

California, 38, 39
Camellia, 82, 102
Campagna, 97, 198
Canada, 38, 39, 124
   herbaceous peonies for, 86-88
Canary, 161, 162
Candytuft, 63, 141
Caragana, 180
Cardinal's Robe, 78, 98
Care
   of herbaceous peonies, 43-47, 110-115
   of tree peonies, 43-47, 147-149
Carina, 78, 85, 96, 97, 98
Carolina Moon, 34, 83
Carrara, 74
Cathedral, 34, 75
Ceceilia, 99
Cerastium, 141
   tomentosum, 63
Chalice, 82, 97, 99, 100, 198
Champlain, 79, 81
Charioteer, 162, 199
Charm, 70, 74, 85
Cherry Hill, 85, 89
China, 23, 126, 127, 166
Chinese Dragon, 163

INDEX

Chinese varieties, 42, 43, 89, 91, 93, 100, 126, 127, 128, 155, 157-162, 197
Chionodoxa, 61, 140
Chippewa, 35, 75, 85
Chlordane, 45, 118, 154
Chocolate Soldier, 72, 78, 85, 96, 97, 98, 102, 198
Christmas rose, 140
Chromatella, 162
Chrysanthemums, 59, 126, 175
Church arrangements, 178, 179
City gardens, 40
Claire de Lune, 70, 78, 83, 95, 96, 97, 99, 102, 198
Classification, 27, 28
Claudia, 101
Clematis, 28, 140
Climate, 38, 39, 40, 106, 123
  for mulching tree peonies, 148, 149
Clusi, 90
Coal ashes, 144
Cold frames, 119, 152
Colonial Williamsburg arrangements, 181
Color
  herbaceous peonies by, 82-86, 97-98
  in flower arrangements, 172, 175
  tree peonies by, 157-161
Columbine, 28, 61
Companion plants
  for herbaceous peonies, 54, 56-64
  for tree peonies, 134-135, 138-140
Compost, 107, 113, 144
Contesse de Tudor, 63
Conditioning, 183-184
Conquest, 163
Containers, 167, 174, 176, 177, 179, 191
Coral-bells, 63, 141, 175
Cereopsis, 61, 175
Corn cobs, 111, 148

Cornmeal, 187, 188
Coronal, 161
Couronne d'Or, 83, 88
Crocus, 61, 140
Crowfoot family, 27
Crusader, 97, 102
Cryptomeria, 176
Cultivation, 44
  of herbaceous peonies, 111
  of tree peonies, 136, 147
Cut flowers, 18, 35, 41, 45, 122
Cutting, 172, 177, 186-187, 188, 197-203
Cymbidium, 166

D

Daffodils, 61, 140
Dainty Lass, 97, 102
Dancing Nymph, 74
Daphne, 140
Daurica, 91
Dawn Pink, 70, 74, 79, 84
Daylily, 61, 175, 180
Daystar, 97, 99, 100
DDT, 118
Deciduous shrubs, 60
Delphinium, 28, 61, 140, 175, 180
Desmodium, 140
Deutzias, 60, 136, 138
Diana Parks, 99
Dianthus, 59, 63
Dicentra spectabilis, 64
Dignity, 34, 74, 85
Disbudding, 111, 112 illus.
Diseases, 44, 87, 115, 116-121, 123, 129
Displays, 204
Division of clumps, 113, 114, 122
Dogwood, 180
Dolorodell, 71, 83
Doreen, 74, 80
Doris Cooper, 71, 76, 83
Dormancy, 39, 123, 136
Dorothy J., 82
Do Tell, 34

Doubles, 17, 31, 32, 35, 38, 44, 70, 71, 75
Dragon's Nest, 80
Drainage, 122, 132
　for herbaceous peonies, 106
　for tree peonies, 143, 144
Dr. J. H. Neeley, 75, 82
Drying, 185-190
Duchesse de Nemours, 83
Dunlora, 74

E

Early American arrangements, 181
Earlybird, 100
Early-flowering varieties, 35, 38, 61, 63, 155-157, 201
Early Windflower, 82, 100
Echinops ritro, 59
Edulis Superba, 76, 81, 84, 88, 89, 93, 197
Elfin Pink, 74
Elizabeth Foster, 97
Ella Christiansen, 72, 76, 83
Elsa Sass, 36, 70, 72, 73, 75, 79, 82, 86, 89
Emblem, 101
Emodi, 91
England, 23, 126
English daisy, 63
Ensign Moriarity, 84
Entrance, 136
Eros, 97
Eupatorium rugosum, 59
European varieties: see Chinese varieties
Eventide, 97
Evergreens, 46, 55, 109, 124
Exhibition flowers, 64, 111, 121
Exhibitions, see flower shows
Exquisite, 33, 74
"Eyes,' 113, 122, 123

F

Fairy Princess, 68

False dragonhead, 59
False indigo, 61
Fancy Nancy, 75
Felix Crousse, 36, 37, 73, 77, 85, 89, 198
Fermate, 44, 115, 117, 148, 149, 154
Fertilizers, 46, 107, 110, 147
Festiva Maxima, 25, 36, 42, 55, 63, 70, 72, 73, 78, 82, 88, 89, 197
Feverfew, 61
Filipendula, 61, 180
Fillers, 59
Firelight, 100
Flame, 78, 84, 97
Flamingo, 81
Flander's Field, 74, 85
Flora, 135, 161
Florence Ellis, 71, 81
Florence Nicholls, 76, 82, 86
Flore pleno, 41
Florida, 38
Flower
　parts of, 29, 30, 31
Flowering branches, 177
Flowering bulbs, 61
Flowering shrubs, 55, 60, 138-140
Flowering trees, 138
Flower shows, 64, 69, 200-216
Flower shows
　for tree peonies, 206
Foliage, 45, 169, 170, 171, 176, 179
　herbaceous peonies noted for, 81
Food
　for herbaceous peonies, 110, 111
　for tree peonies, 147
Forcing, 120, 121, 149, 150
Formaldehyde, 117
Formalin, 147
Fortune Teller, 74
Fothergilla, 180
Foxglove, 61, 175, 14
Fragrans, 89, 93, 158
France, 24, 25, 126
Frances Mains, 71

INDEX

Frances Willard, 76
Freeborn, Mary E. G., 94
Freezing, 123
Fruit branches, 167
Fuji-no-mori, 158
Fungicide, 44, 87, 115
Fuso-no-tsukasa, 158, 161

G

Gabisan, 135, 159, 161
Garden design
  herbaceous peonies in, 51-65
  tree peonies in, 131-140
Gardenia, 76, 82, 101
Garden Peace, 77, 82, 101
Garden pinks, 141
Garden Princess, 80, 81
Gardens, 33, 40, 41, 50-65, 133-134
Gardens
  for display, 206
  for tree peonies, 136, 137
Gay Cavalier, 97
Gay Paree, 34, 75
Gekkyuden, 158
Genkimon, 159, 161
Genus, 27, 28
Georgia, 38
Georgiana Shaylor, 88
Gessekai, 155, 159, 161, 163, 199
Gladiolus, 61, 180
Glassock, Lyman D., 94
Gleam of Gold, 83
Globe thistle, 59
Goatsbeard, 59
Godaishu, 159, 161
Goddess, 74
Gold-Dust, 63
Golden Bracelet, 83
Golden Dawn, 83
Golden Dream, 71, 90, 95
Golden Glow, 85, 97, 99, 102
Golden Hind, 161
Golden Vanity, 162
Goldfinch, 162
Graduations, 181

Grafting, 153
  of tree peonies, 151-152
Greece, 22
Greek legend, 21
Greenhouse, 121
Green Ivory, 85
Grootendorst, 60
Growth requirements, 38-40
Guppy, Col. Benjamin M., 94
Gypsophila, 64

H

Haku-banriu, 161
Haku-raku-ten, 155, 159
Hana-daigin, 159, 162, 199
Hana-kisoi, 159, 162, 163, 199
Hansina Brand, 36, 72, 73, 76, 88
Hargrove Hudson, 63
Hari-ai-nin, 34, 74, 85, 195
Harriet Olney, 84
Harvest, 155, 161, 162
Hatsu-garashu, 155, 159, 162
Hay, 148
Helen, 33, 74, 84, 88, 194
Helen Hayes, 76, 84
Helen Matthews, 78, 97
Heliotrope, 59
Hemerocallis, 61, 140
Herbaceous peony, 28, 29, 37, 38, 49-124
  hybrids, 42, 43, 93-101, 140
  for cutting, 198
  plants as companions with, 60-63
  most popular, 71-77
Hermione, 84
Heuchera, 63, 141
High Noon, 162
Higurashi, 159, 162
Hinode-sekai, 159-162
Hino-tsukasa, 159
Hira-no-yuki, 159
History, 21, 23-25, 127, 128, 166, 167
Hodai, 162, 199

Holders, 191
Hollyhock, 59, 113
Honeysuckle, 180
Hora-kumon, 162
Horizon, 102
Hostas, 140, 176, 180
Howzan, 135, 159, 162
Humei, 93
Humilis, 91
Humus, 107, 144
Hyacinth, 61, 180
Hybridizers, 24, 25, 93-96, 129, 130

I

Iberis, 141
  sempervirens, 59, 63
Illini Belle, 97
Illini Warrior, 77
Ima-chow-kow, 159
Imperial Red, 33, 74, 85, 86, 194
Impumon, 162
Indoor arrangements, 33, 35, 166-185
Insects, 116-121
Insulation, 87
Iris, 59, 61, 113, 140, 175, 176, 180
Iron, 144
Isani Gidui, 30, 70, 72, 74, 86, 88, 89, 195
Ismene, 61
Ivy, 175, 180

J

James Kelway, 70, 79, 82
Janice, 97, 99, 101
Japan, 24, 126
Japanese
  arrangements, 33
  art, 127
  gardens, 136
  holly, 176
  larch, 138, 139
  maple, 138, 139, 176

Japanese (continued)
  plum, 166
  varieties, 32, 33, 70, 74, 126, 127, 128, 155, 157-162, 199
Japonica, 91
J. C. Legg, 34, 75
Jean E. Blockstoce, 99
John Harvard, 97, 102
John Howard Wigell, 80
Joseph Christie, 79, 83
Josette, 74, 83, 88
Judging
  for flower shows, 210-212, 214-215
June Brilliant, 63
June Rose, 84, 84
Juniper, 176

K

Kagura-jishi, 159
Kalmia, 140
Kamada-fuji, 159, 163, 190
Kamikaze, 161
Kansas, 63, 71, 73, 77, 78, 85, 197
Karl Rosenfield, 36, 72, 77, 85, 86, 89, 197
Kaskaskia, 74
Kelway's Glorious, 36, 70, 71, 73, 76, 78, 81, 82, 86, 88, 89
Kewanee, 74
Kickapoo, 33, 74
King Midas, 85
Kin-pukurin, 162
Kinshi, 162
Kintajio, 155, 159
Kokamon, 159, 162
Kolkwitzia, 180
Krinkled White, 33, 69, 72, 74, 80, 82, 88, 194
Kukenijishi, 88
Kuro-botan, 162

L

Labeling, 91, 190, 191

INDEX

Laddie, 85, 97
Lady Alexandra Duff, 35, 75, 79, 83, 88, 198
Lady Aroostock, 55, 81
La France, 88
La Lorraine, 36, 70, 73, 76, 135, 162, 197
Landscape, 17, 50-65
 herbaceous peony in, 50-60
 tree peonies in, 131, 132
Largo, 34, 74, 80, 81, 84, 88
Larkspur, 180
Late-flowering
 tree peonies, 155-157, 201
 varieties, 31, 35, 38, 42, 63
Late Windflower, 100
Laura Dessert, 34, 75, 83, 196
Laura Magnuson, 84, 97, 99, 198
Lavender, 85, 90
Leaf Curl virus, 87
Leafmold, 107, 144
Leaf spot, 115
Le Cygne, 36, 72, 73, 76, 82, 88, 89, 197
Le Jour, 33, 69, 74, 82, 86, 194
Lemoine's disease, 87, 117
Lemoine, Victor, 25, 94, 129
Le Printemps, 94
L'Etincelante, 33, 74, 84, 88
Leto, 34
Liatris, 140
Light
 for arrangements, 178
 for forcing tree peonies, 150
 for herbaceous peonies, 104
 for tree peonies, 143
Ligustrum, 176
Lilacs, 60, 177, 180
Lilies, 59, 61, 140, 180
Limestone, 122
Lindane, 87
Line designs, 167, 191
L'Institeur Dorian, 89
Loam, 110, 119, 144
Location, 122
 for herbaceous peonies, 105
 for tree peonies, 143

Longfellow, 73, 77, 85, 197
Lonicera tatarica, 180
Loren Franklin, 70, 76, 84, 197
Lottie Dawson Rea, 63, 198
Lotus, 126
Lotus Bloom, 97
Lotus Queen, 33, 74, 82, 195
Louis Joliet, 36
Lovely Rose, 83, 96, 97
Lowell Thomas, 81, 85
Ludovica, 84, 96, 97
Lupines, 61, 180
Lycoris, 61

M

Mme. Butterfly, 34
Mandaleen, 63
Magnolia, 176, 180
Mallow, 64
Margaret Lough, 196
Mary Brand, 198
Materials
 for arrangements, 191, 192
Medicinal use of, 22
Mertensia virginica, 64
Messagere, 94
Midnight Sun, 74
Midseason varieties, 31, 35, 63, 201
Midway Island, 74
Miellez, 25
Mighty Mo, 35, 75
Mikado, 34, 74, 89
Mildred May, 35, 55, 71, 75, 80, 81, 82, 89, 197
Milton Hill, 88
Minnesota, 38
Minnie Shaylor, 35, 75, 82, 86, 201
Minuet, 72, 76, 81, 83, 198
Mischief, 33, 74, 83
Miss America, 35, 75, 79
Mlokosewitschi, 81, 91, 97
Mock-orange, 60, 173, 177
Modern arrangements, 176
Moles, 118

Mollis, 91
Momo-yama, 159, 162
Monkshood, 28, 59
Mons. Jules Elie, 36, 68, 70, 71, 73, 76, 78, 79, 84, 86, 89, 197
Mons. Martin Cahuzac, 63, 77, 89
Montezuma, 102
Moonglow, 83
Moon of Nippon, 34, 74, 82
Moonrise, 83, 97, 99
Moonstone, 36, 71, 72, 76, 83
Morning glories, 140
Moss, 137
Mother's Choice, 71
Mountain-laurel, 140
Mount Palomar, 70
Mrs. A. M. Brand, 38
Mrs. Deane Funk, 75
Mrs. Edward Harding, 82, 88
Mrs. F. D. Roosevelt, 36, 63, 68, 70, 73, 76, 83, 89, 197
Mrs. J. V. Edlund, 72, 76
Mrs. Livingston Farrand, 71, 72, 76, 84, 89, 90
Mrs. L. Van Leeuwen, 75
Mrs. R. M. Bacheller, 81
Mrs. Wilder Bancroft, 34, 74
Mrs. W. L. Gumm, 78
Mulching, 39, 43, 46, 123
   of herbaceous peonies, 87, 109, 111, 113
   of tree peonies, 148
Myrtle Gentry, 36, 72, 76, 82, 88, 198
Mystery, 161

N

Nadia, 102
Nancy Nicholls, 72, 76, 82
Nandina, 176
Nanette, 75
Narcissus, 176, 180
Nathalie, 96, 97, 128
Native of Japan, 90
Neilla sinensis, 60
Nemas, 117, 118

Nematodes, 117, 118
Nepeta mussini, 59
Nick Shaylor, 36, 38, 70, 71, 73, 76, 79, 83, 89, 198
Nicotine sulfate, 45
Nippon Beauty, 195
Nippon Brilliant, 34, 68, 73, 74, 80, 85, 195
Nippon Gold, 34, 75, 84, 196
Nishiki-no-tsuya, 159, 162
Nissho, 159, 162
Nitrogen, 107, 111
North, 39, 45
Nutrients, 123

O

Obovata, 91
Obovata willmottiae, 91
Octavie Demay, 79
Okina-jishi, 162
Old Main, 99
Orange Glory, 99
Orchids, 167
Organic matter, 107
Oriental Gold, 71, 77, 83, 90, 95, 99, 202
Orihime, 160
Osiris, 158

P

Pachysandra, 180
Paeon, 21
Paeonia
   alba plena, 41
   albiflora, 29, 42, 43, 74, 93
   arborea, 128
   cambessedesi, 90
   chinensis, 42, 93
   delavayi, 42, 128, 129, 157
   lactiflora, 23, 25, 28, 29, 93
   lutea, 25, 31, 42, 128, 129, 155, 157, 160
   ludlowi, 130
   moutan, 29, 128
   officinalis, 23, 24, 29, 41, 91, 93
   alba plena, 93

INDEX

Paeonia (continued)
  rosea plena, 85, 89, 93
  rosea superba, 84, 93
  rubra plena, 85, 93
  onaepia, 28, 29
  rosea superba plena, 41
  rubra plena, 41
  sinensis, 42, 93
  suffruticosa, 23, 25, 28, 29, 42
  tenufolia, 40, 41
  wittmanniana, 25, 41, 92
Pageant, 101
Pansies, 63, 141
Pastoral, 163
Peach blossoms, 166
Peatmoss, 107, 119, 144, 148
Peregrina lobata, 91
Perennials, 64, 140
Pergola, 136
Period designs, 185
Pest control, 149
Pests, 116-121, 149
Pfeiffer's Red Triumph, 201
Philadelphus, 180
  coronarius, 60, 177
Philippe Rivoire, 37, 70, 71, 77, 79, 82, 85, 86, 89
Philomele, 75
Phlox, 59, 61, 140
Phyllis Kelway, 35, 75, 88
Physostegia virginiana, 59
Pico, 33, 63, 70, 72, 74, 80, 81, 194
Pine, 138, 139
"Piney," 41
Pink Wonder, 84
Plainsman, 34, 74
Planting, 44, 45, 46, 122, 123, 124
  of herbaceous peonies, 103-109
  of seeds, 119, 120
  of tree peonies, 131, 143-146
  for arrangements, 174, 177
Plant Research Institute, 86
Plastic forms, 192
Platycodon, 140
Playmate, 100
Plum, 126
Podocarpus, 176

Pollination, 120
Poppies, 61, 64
"Posey clay," 195, 196
Potanini, 128
Pot culture, 136
Pothos, 176
Potpourri, 190
Prairie Afire, 34, 75, 196
Prairie Belle, 75, 83
Prairie Rose, 84
Pres. F. D. Roosevelt, 84
Pres. Lincoln, 33, 74, 85, 194
Pride of Langport, 74, 83
Primevere, 34, 70, 75, 83, 196
Primulas, 140
Princess, 161, 163
Propagation
  of herbaceous peonies, 113, 119-120
  of tree peonies, 151-154
Pruning
  of tree peonies, 148
Pulsatilla, 28
Pyrethrum, 61, 175

Q

Queen of the Dawn, 99
Queen Rose, 97

R

Rabbits, 118
Ramona Lins, 89
Ranunculaceae family, 27
Rare herbaceous peonies, 70, 71
Rare China, 75, 88
Rashoomon, 63, 74
Rebecca, 74
Recipes, 23, 25, 26
Red Charm, 70, 72, 73, 85, 97, 99, 96, 102, 198
Red Goddess, 35, 75, 85, 99, 197
Red Red Rose, 97

Red Signal, 99
Refrigeration, 205
Regions
　for growth, 38
Registered varieties, 236
Reine Baronet, 88
Reine Elizabeth, 63, 135, 158
　162
Reine Hortense, 36, 70, 76, 83
Renkaku, 162
Requiem, 97, 101
Reward, 101
Richard Carvel, 77, 85, 197
Rimpo, 162, 199
Ring Spot virus, 87
Robert Fortune, 162
Robert W. Auten, 97
Rock-cress, 59
Rock gardens, 40
Rocks, 137, 140
Roman Gold, 161, 162
Root division, 103, 119
Root knot, 117
Root rot, 117
Roots
　of herbaceous peonies, 103-109
Rosalie, 35, 75
Rosa rugosa, 60
Rose chafers, 118
Rosedale, 99
Roselette, 97, 100
Rose Marie, 97, 99
Roses, 59, 60, 136, 138, 140, 184
Rotting, 116
Round forms, 175
Royal Horticultural Society, 127, 128
Rushlight, 97
Russi, 91
Ruth Clay, 85
Ruth Elizabeth, 73, 77, 85

S

Sable, 90, 95
Sakura-gasane, 162
Sakura-jishi, 162

Salmon Beauty, 84, 97
Salmon Glow, 84, 97
Salt, 188, 190
Salvia, 140
Sanctuary, 78
Sand, 144, 187, 188
Sandwort, 141
Sang Lorraine, 129, 160
Sarah Bernhardt, 36, 70, 73, 76,
　84, 88, 198
Satin Rouge, 160, 162
Saunders, Prof. A. P., 94, 129, 157
Savage Splendor, 163
Sawdust, 111, 152
Scilla, 61, 140
Sea-pink, 59
Seashell, 33, 69, 72, 74, 83, 86,
　194
Season
　herbaceous peonies by, 77-86,
　　100-101
　tree peonies by, 155
Seasonal care, 43
Sedums, 140
Seedlings, 44
　of tree peonies, 153-154
Seed pods, 45, 119, 189
Semi-doubles, 17, 31, 32, 34, 35,
　70, 71, 75
Shaylor's Sunburst, 70, 74, 82, 86
Shell Pink, 83
Shin-kagura, 162
Shin-momo-zoma, 160
Shin-tenchi, 155, 160, 162
Shogyomon, 160
Sho Yo, 23
Shuchiuka, 155, 160
Shugyo-kuden, 162, 203
Siberian pea shrub, 173, 180
Silver Sails, 162
Silvia Saunders, 35, 70, 75, 80,
　83, 88, 197
Sinbad, 75
Singles, 31, 32, 33, 38, 69, 70, 74
Sir Thomas Lipton, 60
Sistie, 82
Size, 17, 18, 44
Sky Pilot, 74, 84

INDEX

Snakeroot, 59
Snapdragons, 180
Snowdrops, 61, 140
Snow-in-summer, 63, 141
Soil, 123
 for herbaceous peonies, 107, 108, 109, 110
 for tree peonies, 143-144
 for trenches, 154
Solange, 36, 63, 72, 76, 82, 88, 89
Sophie, 78, 97, 99
South, 38
 herbaceous peonies for, 85-89
Souvenir de Ducher, 158, 162
Souv. de Louis Bigot, 76, 198
Souvenir de Maxim Cornu, 160, 163, 203
Space
 for herbaceous peonies, 54, 55, 103, 104
 for tree peonies, 144, 145, 146
Sparkling Star, 74, 80
Species, 28, 29
Specimen plants, 132, 136
Specimens, 205
 of herbaceous peony, 104
Spiked forms, 61
Spireas, 61, 180, 184
Spraying, 115, 117, 118, 123, 148, 149
Spring Beauty, 68, 75
Staking, 44, 112
 of tree peonies, 148
Staminodes, 33
Starlight, 97, 101
Stock, 180
Stone lantern, 137
Stones, 137
Storing, 136, 188-189
 dried materials, 190, 191
 for flower shows,
Straw, 46, 109, 124, 148
Suigan, 162
Suisho-haku, 162, 203
Sulphur, 113
Suma-no-ichi, 160
Summersweet, 140
Sunlight, 97

Superphosphate, 46, 107, 147
Supports, 112
Susan B. White, 75
Sweet alyssum, 141
Sweet pepperbush, 140
Sword Dance, 80, 85, 86
Symbolism, 137
Syringa vulgaris alba, 60

T

Table arrangement, 175, 176
Taiyo, 162, 199
Tama-fidori, 162
Tama-fuyo, 135, 155, 160, 162, 163, 199
Tama-sudare, 162
Tamate boku, 34, 74, 84, 88, 195
Tea Rose, 161
Tecumseh, 99
Teikwan, 135, 162
Temperature, 17, 39, 40, 41, 46, 123, 124, 132
 for conditioning, 184
 for drying, 188
 for forcing, 121
 for forcing tree peonies, 150
 for storing, 185, 205
Tempest, 72, 77, 85
Tenuifolia hybrids, 79, 81, 91
Terraces, 104, 132
Texture, 172, 175
Therese, 36, 70, 72, 76, 83, 86
Thermopsis, 61, 175
Thrips, 118
Thunderbolt, 161
Tibet, 127, 140, 175
Titania, 78
Tokio, 88
Tondeleyo, 84
Topeka, 99
Toro-no-maki, 74, 88
Torpilleur, 75
Tourangelle, 76, 83, 88
Transplanting, 44, 46
 of herbaceous peonies, 106
 seedlings, 119

Tree Peonies, 29, 37, 38, 126-161
    flower shows for, 206
    for cutting, 203
    hybrids, 42, 127-129
    most popular, 161-163
Trench, 154
Tsuki-sekai, 162
Tulips, 61, 180

U

Uba-tama, 135, 155, 160, 162, 163, 199
Ukaregi-ohi, 162
United States, 123, 126

V

Valeriana officinalis, 59
Vanity, 74, 83
Varieties
    blooming times of, 39-42
    buying of, 63
    by color, 82-85, lists
    by season, 77-85, lists
    care of, 43, 47
    for fragrance, 81
    parts of, 30, 31
Veitchi
    woodwardi, 91
Vera, 74
Veritas, 97, 99
Vermiculite, 119
Veronica latifolia, 59
Vertical design, 61, 175
Viburnum
    carlesi, 60
    tomentosum, 138
Victoria Lincoln, 97, 99
Victorian, 185
Victorian bouquets, 190
Victory, 71, 72, 76, 82, 83
Vines, 191
Viola, 59
Virginia-bluebell, 64
Virginia Dare, 74
Virginia Lee, 83

W

Wall cress, 141
Walter Faxon, 36, 70, 72, 76, 84, 88, 89, 90
Walter Mains, 97
Watchman, 74
Watering, 44, 123
    of herbaceous peonies, 106, 110, 111
    of tree peonies, 147
Waxing, 190
Weddings, 168, 179-180
Weeds, 111
Weigela, 60
Westerner, 34, 70, 74, 83, 195
Westhill, 83
White, Earle B., 94
White Gold, 82
White Innocence, 77, 82, 97
White Rose, 35, 71, 75, 82, 89, 197
Whitleyi, 89, 93
William F. Turner, 75
Williamsburg arrangements, 175
Willow, 176
Wilting, 149
Windflower, 68, 100
Wings of the Morning, 162
Winter bouquets, 185
Winter care
    of herbaceous roots, 109
Winter protection, 39, 46, 124, 149
Winter rose, 140
Wisteria, 167, 176
Wonder Lily, 61
Wood ashes, 110, 147

Y

Yachiyo-tsubaki, 160, 162
Yae-zakura, 160, 162
Yaso-no-mine, 162
Yaso-okina, 162
Yellow King, 74, 83
Yokihi, 71, 90, 95
Yosemite, 71, 81, 83

Es hora de decir adiós

Literatura Mondadori, 148

Es hora de decir adiós

DALE PECK

Traducción de Catalina Martínez-Muñoz

MONDADORI

Barcelona, 2001

El editor quisiera expresar su agradecimiento por el permiso para reproducir fragmentos de «Bad, Bad Leroy Brown», con la autorización de Denjac Music Co. © 1972 Denjac Music Co./MCA Music Publishing (ASCAP). Gestionada por Denjac Music Co. Letra de Jim Croce.

Quedan rigurosamente prohibidas, sin la
autorización escrita de los titulares del
copyright, bajo las sanciones establecidas por las
leyes, la reproducción total o parcial de esta obra
por cualquier medio o procedimiento,
comprendidos la reprografía y el tratamiento
informático, así como la distribución de ejemplares
de la misma mediante alquiler o préstamo públicos.

Título original: *Now It's Time to Say Goodbye*
Traducido de la edición original de Farrar, Straus and Giroux, Nueva York, 1998
© 1998 Dale Peck
© 2001 de la edición castellana para todo el mundo:
MONDADORI (Grijalbo Mondadori, S.A.)
Aragó, 385. 08013 Barcelona
www.grijalbo.com
Primera edición
ISBN: 84-397-0383-X
Depósito legal: M. 828-2001
Impreso y encuadernado en Artes Gráficas Huertas, S.A.,
Fuenlabrada (Madrid)

No le dedico a nadie este libro
salvo, quizá, a Robbie Powell y Vaughan Jenkens

1

1.01

JUSTIN

Ha pasado la medianoche. Es mi cumpleaños.

Una vez hojeé una novela que empezaba así, pero algo me distrajo después de haber leído las primeras líneas. Aunque recuerdo la librería donde la encontré –hoy cerrada–, y también lo que me distrajo –medía aproximadamente un metro noventa–, no recuerdo nada más sobre la novela, ni el título, ni el autor, ni lo que ocurría a continuación, mas por alguna razón nunca he olvidado esta frase. No sé por qué. *Ha pasado la medianoche. Es mi cumpleaños.* Puede que sea evocadora, pero no tiene el menor sentido. Y sin embargo, no he podido olvidarla; me venía a la cabeza de vez en cuando, y la recordé de nuevo poco después de marcharme de Galatea. Durante el año que pasé allí fui testigo de una violación, varios asesinatos y algo que, fuera de contexto, solo puedo calificar de tumulto, pero en aquellos doce meses nadie celebró su cumpleaños. La ciudad era la única que celebraba su cumpleaños; solo ella, como insistía Rosemary Krebs, era importante. Y con esa idea en mente me atrevo a afirmar que la historia que están ustedes a punto de leer es la historia de un lugar, no de una persona. Es como un desfile: aunque todos los participantes dan un paso al frente y declaran ser la estrella, lo que finalmente registra la memoria es el espectáculo en sí. Por eso, para empezar, me apartaré a un lado; pero quiero dejar en ustedes esta impresión: la de un palimpsesto oculto bajo estas palabras. Ha pasado la medianoche. Es mi cumpleaños. En cierto sentido les estoy proponiendo un trato: si consiguen encontrar sentido a esta frase, les prometo ocuparme de todo lo demás.

1.02

MELVIN CARTWRIGHT

Abrió los ojos.

El resplandor de la luz del porche latía entre la lluvia que lavaba la ventana de su dormitorio. Su mirada podía elegir entre diversas cosas —el espejo que colgaba de la pared, el montón de novelas policíacas leídas y releídas apilado en una esquina, las fotografías de sus padres y de su hermana—, pero se posó finalmente en el retrato de Cristo que había pintado en el campamento evangélico cuando tenía ocho años. La luz empapada de lluvia hacía que los ojos del Salvador, vueltos hacia el cielo, llorasen sombras de lágrimas.

Volvió a sonar el teléfono.

Antes de contestar sabía qué sería. No quién. Qué. No había otra razón para que nadie llamara a una hora tan infame.

Descolgó el auricular y se lo acercó al oído sin hablar. Una pausa y luego, una voz anunció quedamente:

—El cadáver de John Brown está pudriéndose en la tumba.

Melvin contuvo un sonido que era al mismo tiempo risa y jadeo. La risa la provocó lo absurdo del mensaje; el jadeo era fruto de la sorpresa y el reconocimiento. No podía ser. Pero tenía que ser. Era.

Compuso su voz lo mejor que pudo.

—Su verdad sigue su curso.

Cuando la voz habló de nuevo, su tono resultó más familiar; se percibía en ella la fuerza de la exhortación capaz de hacer que el mero hecho de pedir un vaso de té helado suene como un mandamiento divino.

—Pasé por el bar de Cora a primera hora de la noche —dijo la voz.

—¿Probaste el guiso? —preguntó Melvin.

—Por supuesto.

—Yo también lo he probado —dijo Melvin. Se detuvo un momento, asombrado por lo fácil que resultaba, lo natural que parecía, como si el guión estuviera escrito de antemano.

Él nunca habría usado la palabra «guión».

Melvin se aclaró la garganta y dijo:

—Un guiso prodigioso.

—Cierto —dijo la voz; y con una sola palabra otorgó a la carne con patatas, zanahorias y cebollitas francesas la categoría de ambrosía. Una pausa y luego—: DuWayne Hicks pasó por allí a la misma hora que yo. Dijo que Vera le había contado en el IGA, el nuevo supermercado, que Eddie Comedy se ha mudado.

—¿DuWayne compra en el IGA? —preguntó Melvin. Para entonces había salido de la cama. Estaba junto al escritorio, abriendo un cajón. El largo cable amarillo del teléfono se balanceaba detrás de él como una comba para hacer ejercicios de calentamiento, o tal vez se enredaba.
—Bueno, eso es otra historia —rió la voz entre dientes, y, por un momento, las cosas parecieron casi normales. Luego, tornándose profunda y grave, añadió—: Vera dijo que no encontraba trabajo. Me refiero a Eddie Comedy.
—Las cosas están difíciles —asintió Melvin. Se había puesto los pantalones y la camisa; y llevaba el revólver.
—Así es —dijo la voz—. Uno tiene que aceptar condiciones extremas para mantener a la familia. —La voz rompió en pedazos la palabra «ex-tremas», y la lanzó enfatizando lo extremo—. Sí, había estado tomando unas copas de despedida en el bar de Sloppy Joe. Se despidió de todos diciendo que volvería por la mañana. La furgoneta está cargada y aparcada en el garaje.
—Metalizada, ¿verdad? —dijo Melvin—. ¿Con la parte de abajo azul y la parte de arriba plateada?
—En dos tonos. Creo que así es como llaman a ese tipo de pintura.
Melvin asintió en silencio. Se miró en el espejo: vio la cabeza rasurada de un hombre negro de treinta años que no iba a ninguna parte. El reflejo de la lluvia hacía que su imagen llorase las mismas lágrimas falsas que el retrato de Cristo. Nunca le había gustado el nombre de Melvin. Su madre se llamaba Malvernia y a él le habían puesto el nombre por ella. De pronto sintió deseos de preguntarle de dónde venía aquel nombre, pero estaba muerta. Llevaba muerta un año.
La voz llenó sus oídos:
—Bueno, tengo que marcharme.
Un nombre que sí le gustaba era Malcolm. Malcolm Cartwri... Carter. Malcolm Carter.
Ex-tremo.
—¿Nos veremos el domingo en la iglesia?
Melvin se volvió hacia el retrato del hijo de Dios. Con una buena iluminación se apreciaban las tenues sombras de los números escritos bajo el pelo castaño claro, la tez rosada y pálida, el blanco inmaculado de la vaporosa túnica —555 666 777—, pero bajo aquella luz el rostro parecía casi real. Al menos tan real como el suyo, en el espejo, en la oscuridad.
Las lágrimas se deslizaban secamente.
Melvin habló despacio:

—A decir verdad, yo también he estado pensando en largarme. El trabajo me importa un bledo. En esta ciudad ni siquiera encuentras una mujer.

—En el bar de Cora desde luego que no —dijo la voz, y los dos hombres compartieron de nuevo una risa y, de nuevo, por un instante, las cosas parecieron casi normales.

—He estado pensando en marcharme al oeste —dijo Melvin, y mientras lo decía casi llegó a creer que realmente lo había pensado. A fin de cuentas nunca había cruzado la frontera del estado en dirección oeste, aunque esta se encontraba escasamente a ciento sesenta kilómetros. Un hombre tenía derecho a ver mundo. Derecho, si no la obligación.

—¿Conque al oeste, eh? —dijo la voz—. Hay todo un mundo en el oeste. —Hubo una pausa—. Creo que Eddie Comedy dijo que se iba al este. A Missouri, creo.

Melvin asintió con la cabeza.

—El este es bonito —dijo a continuación, pero lo cierto es que él habría preferido el oeste—. La veinticuatro va hacia el este.

—Y al oeste también —dijo la voz—, pero creo que Eddie Comedy dijo que se iba al este.

Melvin pensó que ya era suficiente, que casi era demasiado. Una sola cosa más y no se sentiría capaz de hacerlo. Eddie Comedy se había cubierto de mierda durante toda su vida, pero nunca le había hecho nada a Melvin, salvo aquello, claro está. Y en realidad no se lo había hecho a Melvin. Bien, se dijo, nadie podría impedirle darse la vuelta cuando todo hubiera acabado, darse la vuelta para dirigirse al oeste y llegar hasta donde quisiera.

Se miró en el espejo por última vez para comprobar que todo estaba en orden, pero al verse la cara comprendió que en realidad no sabía qué quería comprobar, y desvió la mirada hacia el reflejo de Cristo. Entonces, por primera vez en muchos años, recordó que Sawyer Johnson había pasado por alto deliberadamente los números cuando pintó el mismo cuadro. El Cristo de Melvin tenía la tez oscura y el pelo negro, y su túnica era verde, roja y azul. Sawyer solo había usado el rosa para las llagas en las palmas de las manos de Cristo y había prescindido del blanco por completo. El reverendo Abraham fingió reprender a Sawyer por esta infracción, pero veinticinco años más tarde el Cristo de Sawyer aún seguía en la pequeña oficina del reverendo, en el sótano de la iglesia.

Melvin se preguntó dónde estaría Sawyer Johnson en ese momento.

—Siento mucho que tú también vayas a dejarnos —dijo la voz, interrumpiendo los pensamientos de Melvin, pero su pátina de tristeza

era tan fina como la pintura que cubría las mejillas del Señor–. ¿Te gustaría que enviara a Grady Occonnor para que te ayude a recoger tus cosas? Por la mañana, quiero decir. No ahora mismo.
–No, no ahora mismo –dijo Melvin, y pensó: Grady Oconnor. No había pensado en Grady.
–De acuerdo –interrumpió nuevamente la voz, como para recordarle que de nada servía especular, al menos en ese momento–. Supongo que esto lo arregla todo.
Hubo una larga pausa y luego Melvin oyó la voz por última vez:
–Te deseo toda la suerte del mundo, hijo –dijo la voz–. De este mundo... y del mundo futuro.
Melvin empezó a dar las gracias, pero advirtió que su interlocutor había colgado. Imaginó la escena: un pulgar marrón pulsando un botón blanco, una mano marchita con la piel del color y la textura de una vieja bolsa de papel que depositaba en silencio el auricular en su receptáculo para no despertar a los que dormían en la casa. Melvin colgó el teléfono igual de silenciosamente, aunque no había en la casa nadie a quien despertar. Su madre había muerto el año anterior, su padre perdió la vida en el incendio de Kenosha cuando Melvin era un adolescente. Más tarde se le ocurrió lo siguiente: esa era la razón por la que lo habían elegido esta vez. Nadie preguntaría adónde se había ido, ni por qué. Nadie lo echaría de menos. Nadie esperaba que se despidiese antes de partir.

1.03

JUSTIN

Colin dice que toda acción responde a dos motivaciones. Por un lado está la razón que se manifiesta expresamente, y por otro, la que se oculta bajo las palabras, la razón que, si llegara a desvelarse, revelaría la inutilidad, la distracción, el movimiento en falso, tanto de las palabras como de la propia acción. Por eso Colin decidió empaquetar todo lo que poseemos y mudarse a otra parte, a cualquier parte, lejos de la ciudad: cuando la quingentésima persona que conocíamos murió de sida, Colin informó a todo el mundo, incluido a mí, de que nos marcharíamos de Nueva York y no regresaríamos hasta que la epidemia hubiera pasado. No podía soportarlo un momento más, dijo; sencillamente no podía. Luego sacó de sus archivos –Colin lo archiva todo– su vieja agenda telefónica. «Andrew», leyó en voz alta, y junto al número uno yo escribí: «Andrew». «Barney», «Christopher», «David», «Edward», «Franklin», «Gregory», «Henry», «Isaac», todos aquellos nombres cristianos sin abreviar. Cuando terminó de leer habíamos anotado más de doscientos nombres, y luego yo rastreé en mi memoria para recordar los nombres de los chicos, las chicas y casi-chicas con quienes había trabajado: «Jamal» y «Kareem», «LaRhonda», y mi lista casi llegó a igualarse a la de Colin. Entonces comenzamos la búsqueda. Colin tenía un único criterio –mil seiscientos kilómetros–, de modo que empezamos por la costa este y Europa. Viajamos a Johannesburgo y Sydney, a Calcuta y a São Paulo, recorrimos el mundo entero. Se nos fue un año entero buscando y durante ese tiempo, en algún momento caí en la cuenta de que mi deseo de salir de Nueva York era tan grande como el de Colin, aunque mis razones fueran diferentes. Pero, aun así, acabamos regresando a la ciudad convencidos de que ninguno de los lugares que habíamos visitado era adecuado para nuestra huida. A nuestro regreso comprobamos que los fallecimientos habían continuado inexorablemente, y casi a diario sonaba el teléfono o llegaba el correo o leíamos en el *Times* el nombre de otro fallecido, fulano o mengano, un colega, alguien a quien habíamos conocido en una fiesta, un artista cuya obra Colin había comprado o un viejo y querido amigo, mas para entonces la cifra de fallecimientos era tal, que los muertos quedaban reducidos a simples nombres que Colin redujo aún más, hasta convertirlos en meros números, y los números aumentaban de manera imparable. Teníamos ya diez para empezar cuando un marchante a quien Colin conocía nos habló de cierto pintor al que representaba, un pintor llamado Painter, Wade Painter, que vivía en una pequeña y delirante ciudad de Kansas. ¡Kansas! Colin rió con ganas. ¡Kansas!, repetí, aunque sin reírme. Entonces recordé otro número, otro apellido, y lo añadí a nuestra lista. «Martin», escribí. El apellido parecía fuera de lugar y pensé si no debería haber escrito primero el nombre: «John». Bien. Unos escogen el lugar de donde vienen y otros el lugar a donde van; los más afortunados escogen las dos cosas y los más desgraciados ninguna de ellas. Colin y yo habíamos elegido ambas, aunque no creo que nadie nos considere afortunados.

1.04

BIENVENIDOS A GALATEA
EN EL PINTORESCO CONDADO DE CADAVERA
343 HABITANTES
MUNICIPIO DESDE 1976

1.05

JUSTIN

El enorme bloque de hormigón donde vivía el pintor llamado Painter parecía de lejos una nube de humo solidificado. Más que haber sido construido daba la impresión de haber caído del cielo y, cuando Colin y no nos acercamos a él por primera vez, casi sentí que el suelo aún vibraba a consecuencia del impacto. El filo del tejado cortaba un cielo azul grisáceo como la hoja de un cuchillo, y las paredes estaban completamente desprovistas de otro detalle o elemento decorativo que no fuera la oscura perforación ocasional de puertas o ventanas, de tal modo que el conjunto parecía un gigantesco bloque de escoria, el comienzo de una superestructura destinada a cobijar a una estirpe de gigantes o las ruinas de una fortaleza colosal. Habría destacado en cualquier parte, pero allí, en aquella llanura de granjas con costados de aluminio y techumbres de conglomerado asfáltico, todas ellas coronadas por una buhardilla y una chimenea ciega, era sencillamente una monstruosidad, y la idea de hogar quedaba reducida a un mínimo intolerable: en lugar de seguridad, impermeabilidad; en lugar de estabilidad, estancamiento.

—¿No es exactamente *La casa de la pradera*, verdad?

—Creo —dije entonces, aunque no a Colin— que me va gustar mucho este tío. Voy a adorarlo o a aborrecerlo de veras.

Antes de que pudiéramos llamar, la puerta se abrió bruscamente. El chico que salió a recibirnos no era Wade Painter; lo supe porque había leído su currículum vitae y sabía que Wade Painter tenía cuarenta y ocho años, mientras que aquel muchacho tendría unos dieciocho. Tenía el rostro acalorado y brillante, casi temblaba de emoción, y también era negro, cosa que, debo admitir, me sorprendió un poco porque Yonah no había mencionado que Painter tuviera un novio y desde luego no había dicho nada de un novio negro, y esos no eran detalles que Yonah Schimmel pasara por alto, a menos que lo hiciera deliberadamente. «Me llamo Divine —declamó el muchacho—. ¡Bienvenidos a Galatia!» Habló como si nos diera la bienvenida a Xanadú, y luego, lanzándome una rápida mirada, le dio a Colin el más largo repaso visual que yo había presenciado en mi vida. Luego chasqueó la lengua, sacudió la cabeza y dijo: «Vaya, vaya, vaya».

De los chulos —como de los locos, las brujas y los hombres sabios— suele decirse que solo quienes lo son pueden reconocer a los que son como ellos, y lo cierto es que, después de aquella mirada, Divine evitó mirarme a los ojos durante el resto de la noche. E chico muy guapo, puede que incluso fuera hermoso, pe marca de la vanidad grabada en cada uno de sus rasgos. Su piel cobriza había adquirido una pátina untuosa y reluciente tras muchas horas de rayos UVA; el pelo, decolorado y moldeado con ondas muy marcadas, aparecía tieso y brillante a causa del gel fijador. Llevaba la ropa muy ceñida con la intención de acentuar las largas y esbeltas piernas, y al hablar ponía ese tono propio de estar entre colegas, de modo que no tardé más que un segundo en comprender que Divine era una especie de actor, un actor que no estaba del todo seguro del papel que interpretaba, si negro, reina de la fiesta o chico provinciano, y por eso intentaba interpretarlos todos al mismo tiempo.

Nos condujo hasta una enorme habitación desprovista de muebles que a simple vista parecía un cubo perfecto. La tarima del suelo era oscura como la tierra húmeda, pero las paredes y el techo eran tan blancas y yermas como la niebla de medianoche. Justo en el centro de cada pared había una puerta, y en una de estas puertas apareció, vacilante, una mujer: apoyó una mano en el marco y se quedó allí, con un pie dentro y otro fuera de la habitación, como si esperase autorización para entrar. Me había sorprendido que la persona que había salido a recibirnos fuera negra, pero al ver que la segunda también lo era mi sorpresa se convirtió en recelo, y entonces caí en la cuenta de que las tres o cuatro personas que había visto en el pueblo también eran negras. ¿Adónde nos has enviado, Yonah?, me dije, y me volví para saludar a este nuevo personaje que se presentaba en voz baja.

—Soy Webbie —dijo, y su tono de voz me hizo preguntarme cuántas veces había repetido estas palabras—. Webbie Greeving —añadió, alzando ligeramente la voz; luego muy despacio, avanzó hacia mí poniendo las manos como parapeto, tal como uno se acerca a un perro desconocido y acaso temible. Aquel gesto me sobresaltó: era la primera vez en mucho tiempo que me sentía como un individuo peligroso.

Cuando se hubo acercado lo suficiente, tomé una de sus manos para estrechársela.

—Me llamo Justin Time —dije, y continué estrechándole la mano durante el torpe momento que invariablemente sucede a esta declaración. Webbie tenía la mano seca y ligera, y apenas pude sentirla en la mía.

—Justin...

—Time —dije, asintiendo y sin soltarle la mano.

Webbie mantuvo la boca abierta un momento y luego, sobresaltándose, la cerró y apartó su mano de la mía.

—Perdona... —Sacudió levemente la cabeza y me dirigió una sonrisa nerviosa—. Disculpa —dijo, y luego, con voz más serena, añadió—:

Bienvenidos a Galatia. —Advertí que en su boca la palabra tenía claramente las tres sílabas; en la de Divine apenas llegaba a las dos.

Webbie Greeving tenía unos de treinta años, y se veía que su cuerpo comenzaba a deslizarse por la pendiente de la madurez: el pelo, informal y con rizos suaves, le llegaba hasta los hombros y se mantenía apartado de la cara con ayuda de una cinta de cuero marrón; aparecía salpicado de largas canas y alguna que otra trenza muy fina, pero en su cara, redonda, brillante, oscura como una castaña, no había una sola arruga. Ni siquiera cuando sonreía —y en ese momento estaba sonriendo, insegura, burlona, ante mi mirada— llegaba a fruncirse, como si los labios, más pálidos y rosados que el resto de la piel, se expandieran en el interior de un metal semisólido como el mercurio.

Una de las manos flotó entonces hasta su cara. Se sirvió de ella para taparse la boca, aunque solo por un momento; luego la dejó reposar sobre el esternón y, mientras yo la observaba, deslizó inconscientemente un dedo por uno de sus pechos, y fue esa mano la que de pronto despertó en mí un sentimiento de cariño por ella. Aquel gesto significaba muchas cosas, pero era inequívoca, inconscientemente sexual, y al ver que yo miraba aquella mano, Webbie la apartó del pecho como si se quemara, aunque la mano volvió de inmediato, instintivamente, a la boca, y advertí que temblaba mientras Webbie decidía qué hacer con ella. Finalmente, se la guardó con resolución en el bolsillo de la falda de ante marrón y, cuando volvió a sonreírme, su boca pareció desnuda, sin una mano que la cubriera.

—Gracias —dije—. Yo, bueno, nosotros, nos alegramos de estar aquí.

Webbie parpadeó una sola vez, como si no valiera la pena esforzarse siquiera en fingir que me creía; pero también sonrió, y me pregunté cuánto se alegraría ella de estar allí.

—Estaréis agotados después de tantos viajes —dijo, metiéndose en el papel de la anfitriona—. ¿Os apetece tomar algo? ¿Té helado, un poco de vino?

—Yo tomaré vino tinto, guapa —dijo Divine casi gritando; y me habría reído de no ser porque Webbie dio claras muestras de sentir vergüenza ajena al oír la voz del chico.

Vi entonces que Divine había cogido a Colin del brazo y se lo llevaba a alguna parte. Webbie me miró, se encogió de hombros y me indicó que los siguiéramos a otra habitación igualmente cúbica. Cuatro sillones perfectamente alineados flotaban en un espacio por lo demás vacío; Colin ya se había sentado cuando entramos en la habitación, y Divine, apoyado en el brazo de madera del sillón, sostenía entre sus manos la cabeza de Colin. No era una ocurrencia en absoluto extraña: mi amante tenía la cabeza bastante grande y además estaba completamente calvo, y la gente, incluso gente que apenas lo conocía, sucumbía a la tentación de tocarla, incluso de acariciarla. Aun así, me impresionó el atrevimiento de Divine. Deslizó los dedos por el cráneo de Colin sin el menor atisbo de timidez y luego comenzó a frotarlo con fuerza, casi con violencia, como haría una adivina con su bola de cristal.

La mirada de Webbie revoloteó del rostro de Colin al mío. Los dos le sonreímos, pero ella seguía pareciendo preocupada. «No pasa nada», dije. Colin se limitó a cerrar los ojos. Webbie se dio la vuelta y cogió una botella de vino tinto.

No había ninguna mesa en la habitación, así que la botella y los cinco vasos se alinearon en el suelo, junto a la pared.

Se volvió hacia mí diciendo:

—Espero que os guste —dijo, sosteniendo el vaso con una mano y sirviendo el vino torpemente con la otra—. El club de enólogos suele mandar buenos vinos. —Sonrió y se encogió de hombros—. La verdad es que no es fácil, quiero decir que en el supermercado de Vera no encuentras...

Mostró entonces la botella y me dispuse a alcanzarla con la mano derecha, pero de pronto retrocedí, exclamando:

—¡Dios mío!

—¿Qué pasa?

—Esta copa es de vino blanco.

Webbie me miró, miró la copa y, comprendiendo que se trataba de una broma, se echó a reír, pero apenas un segundo después se le congeló la expresión. Miraba detrás de mí; me di la vuelta y vi a Wade.

Es importante mencionar que no lo había oído entrar en la habitación. De hecho, creo que es el dato más importante que puedo ofrecerles acerca de Wade Painter, además de que no era negro. Wade Painter era la primera persona que yo conocía cuya presencia en este mundo parecía incluso más inmaterial que la mía. Parecía no bastar con un solo sentido para ubicarlo en el espacio. No bastaba con oír: había que verlo también. Al instante sentí deseos de cogerle la mano, no fuese a desaparecer. Pero llevaba las manos en los bolsillos, lo que confería a su cuerpo la forma de un huevo inclinado, y se quedó junto a la puerta, sin abrir la boca, sin sonreír. Wade es blanco, pero después de ver a Webbie y a Divine me pareció sencillamente incoloro: pensativo, pálido, quizá gris, no exactamente antipático o poco cariñoso, sino fundamentalmente resignado. No había en él una sola gota de pintura, aunque aún olía a pintura, a una mezcla química de pintura, aguarrás y un tercer ingrediente que al principio no reconocí pero que más tarde pude identificar como el jabón que usaba, no para lavar los pinceles o la ropa, sino para lavarse la piel: Lifebuoy; lo recordé porque de pequeño yo siempre lo llamaba Lifeboy.

Todo pareció detenerse cuando Wade entró en la habitación y todo pareció ponerse de nuevo en funcionamiento, cuando al fin habló. De unos labios que tenían el color y la textura de la piedra pómez salió una voz tan árida como las páginas de un libro de historia. Nos dio la bienvenida, igual que Divine y Webbie, pero no a Galatia, sino, tal como indicaba el cartel del Departamento de Obras Públicas de Kansas, a Galatea. Me dio la mano. Aceptó la copa de vino que Webbie le ofrecía. Luego, fijando su atención en Divine, cuyas manos se habían quedado congeladas sobre la cabeza de Colin desde que Wade reveló su presencia en la habitación, dijo:

—No es un melón, Divine. No hace falta que compruebes si está maduro antes de abrirlo. —Luego, dándose bruscamente la vuelta, salió de la habitación.

Por un momento me pregunté si de verdad había estado allí o si solo lo había soñado. Pero mientras lo pensaba sentí que me dolía la mano y supe que Wade Painter, o quienquiera que fuese, había estado allí, pues no era de esa clase de hombres con los que se sueña o a los que uno se imagina.

1.06

EL AGENTE BROWN

El sheriff Eustace Brown —por favor, no lo llamen agente, al menos no se lo digan a la cara— ocupó su coche patrulla y su coche patrulla ocupó el risco pelado. Había apagado los faros antes de subir a la montaña, pero aun así, el maldito esquisto crujía y saltaba con tal fuerza a su paso por la llanura que antes de que el coche se hubiera detenido, los otros tres vehículos que estaban allí aparcados arrancaron e intentaron escapar como si los persiguiera el diablo (nosotros ya estábamos a punto de marcharnos, de todos modos): el Camino de Howard Goertzen, el Chevelle de Blaine Getterling y un Monte Carlo rojo del 76 que Brown no conocía. El agente Brown anotó el número de matrícula del Monte Carlo, por si pudiera necesitarlo en el futuro —era bonito aquel modelo del 76, el último de los grandes Monte Carlo— y tomó nota mentalmente para no olvidar decirle a Rosemary Krebs que Howard Goertzen había estado en el risco. Howard Goertzen era, en la más amplia acepción del término, el pretendiente de Lucy Robinson, y todo lo que concerniese a Lucy Robinson concernía a Rosemary Krebs, y todo lo que concerniese a Rosemary Krebs concernía al agente Brown.

No se molestó en comprobar lo que había estado haciendo Blaine Getterling, aunque había pensado preguntarle si tenía idea de adónde podía haber ido Melvin Cartwright. Cuando un chico como Melvin desaparece en plena noche puedes estar seguro de que no está tramando nada bueno.

Se preguntó de quién sería el Monte Carlo del 76. Si estaría en venta.

La cabina del coche patrulla olía a coche limpio y a café recién hecho, ambas cosas por cortesía de Nettie Ferguson, y cuando el agente Brown se hubo quedado solo en el risco, se desabrochó el cinturón para aliviar la opresión del vientre, suspiró cuando aquellos cinco kilos, ¿cómo cinco?, de acuerdo, veinte, que había engordado durante las últimas Navidades quedaron libres de la atadura que los oprimía y empezó a tomarse el café bebiendo directamente de la tetina del termo. Se llamaba así porque tenía la forma de un biberón: tenía una boquilla a un lado, con un diminuto agujero, y para extraer el líquido del recipiente había que tirar de ella, había que poner los labios alrededor de la tetina y succionar el café. El agente Brown tuvo que ir hasta el almacén de accesorios y maquinaria del Big M para conseguir un termo así, y una vez lo hubo conseguido lo llenaba siempre con el café que Nettie Ferguson preparaba en la gasolinera o se pasaba por el Café Sumnertime, de Elaine Sumner.

Al pensar en ello pensó también en Eddie Comedy, cliente habitual del café de Elaine: sin trabajo, sin mujer, ¿qué otra cosa podía hacer? Eddie Comedy era un buen chico, dispuesto a defender con ahínco aquello en lo que creía, no como la mayoría de los chicos de ahora, que solo piensan en follar. Eddie Comedy siempre llamaba a las cosas por su nombre —incluso en presencia del agente Brown— y al agente Brown le parecía una vergüenza que un chico como Eddie Comedy tuviera que marcharse de la ciudad, mientras que otros, como Melvin Cartwright, desaparecían durante varios días cuando les venía en gana y volvían apestando a alcohol barato y a mujeres aún más baratas y contando a todo el mundo lo que habían hecho, aunque a nadie le importara.

Después de dar unas chupadas a la tetina, el agente Brown sacó la pistola de la cartuchera y la depositó sobre el regazo. El largo cañón apuntaba hacia abajo sobre el muslo de sus holgados pantalones, y el agente Brown pensaba en sacar un trapo para limpiar el cañón cuando la voz de Nettie Ferguson cloqueó en la radio: «Eustace, ¿me oyes? Sé que me oyes, Eustace. Rosemary Krebs dice que aún no has averiguado nada sobre los visitantes de Wade Painter. ¿Eustace?». ¿Eustace? Era una absoluta desgracia, pensó el agente Brown, considerar a Nettie Ferguson una confidente policial cuando en realidad no era más que una maestra jubilada, y para colmo solo de segundo grado; y en lugar de responder apagó la radio, dio un sorbo al café y se sacó el pañuelo del bolsillo para abrillantar su pistola. No tenía prisa por visitar a Wade Painter, de eso no cabía la menor duda; se ponía malo solo de pensar en lo que aquellos tres personajes hacían en esa casa, e intentaba no pensar en ello; prefería sacarle brillo a su pistola.

«Patrullando» es lo que diría si Rosemary Krebs le preguntara cómo había pasado la noche. «Patrullando». Ella no tendría nada que objetar a eso.

A sus pies, Galatea era un pequeño espacio de luz en la llanura, con sus calles rectas, trazadas como una cuadrícula, como cualquier gran ciudad del este. La cuadrícula solo quedaba interrumpida por esa especie de signo más en espiral que se formaba en la confluencia de la carretera 24 y la autopista 9, y el agente Brown llevaba el mapa tan grabado en el inconsciente como las líneas de su mano, ocultas bajo un guante de cuero. Levantó la mano izquierda, mientras con la derecha sujetaba el termo, y guiñó un ojo para formar con ella una línea hasta la ciudad, de modo que Galatea parecía descansar en la palma de su mano.

Patrullando. Todo en orden.

Se centró por un momento en la imagen y luego cerró el puño como si sujetara un micrófono imaginario; después, al principio en voz baja, pero elevando progresivamente el tono, empezó a cantar con voz mucho más profunda de lo normal en él: «Es malo, muy malo, el agente Brown es el hombre más malo de esta maldita ciudad», y al pronunciar la palabra «maldita» se sonrojó ligeramente, pero siguió cantando.

1.07

JUSTIN

—¿Dónde estoy?
Colin no habló hasta que nos sentamos a la mesa redonda colocada justo en el centro del vacío salón de Wade Painter, y, a juzgar por la expresión de su cara, casi me atrevería a decir que había estado esperando ese preciso instante para hacer su pregunta. Colin tiene un

don especial para la frase inicial; una escena se construye o se destruye en la primera frase, me dijo en cierta ocasión, lo cual es cierto siempre que la escena avance, pero Colin tiende a olvidar que la frase inicial no es la totalidad de la escena: algo debe sucederla. Algo debe ocurrir a continuación.

Webbie, sentada frente a Colin, parecía confusa, y dijo:
—¿Perdón?
—Están ustedes en el salón. Aquí es donde comemos normalmente.

Colin, comprendiendo que su frase había fracasado, intentó borrarla con una carcajada. Tomó un sorbo de vino y dijo:
—Disculpadme. —Colin nunca dice lo siento; siempre dice discúlpame; siempre hace que su error parezca responsabilidad del otro—. Mi pregunta ha sido demasiado vaga. Lo que quería era preguntar por Gala... Gala...
—Galatea —dijo Wade.
—Galatia —añadió Divine, dándole tal efecto a la palabra que sonó como «glacier».
—Galatea —repitió Wade, sin intención de insistir, pero en tono inexorable, como el hielo fundido—. Quizá podríamos responder mejor a tu pregunta si supiéramos qué te interesa exactamente.
—Me interesa Gala...
—... tea —concluyó Wade.
—Está buscando un tema para su novela —intervine, pero Colin me interrumpió.
—Estoy pensando en instalarme aquí.
—Está bloqueado —dije—. Lleva veinte años bloqueado. Piensa que aquí encontrará un tema literario.

Hubo un breve silencio; luego, Wade dijo:
—No creo que Galatea tenga nada que ofrecerle a un escritor como tú.
—No sé qué es lo que ofrece —dijo Colin—. Pero el hecho de mudarme, si es que finalmente nos mudáramos, no tiene nada que ver con mis novelas.
—Entonces... ¿por qué? —preguntó Webbie, en tono de incredulidad.
—Nueva York —dijo Colin. Y apretó los labios—. Nueva York ya no es lo que era.
—Quiere decir que todos nuestros conocidos han muerto.

Divine soltó el tenedor. El tenedor chocó contra el suelo, y después de fijar en mí una expresión de absoluto terror, Divine desapareció debajo de la mesa.

—¿Y... Yonah? —preguntó Wade. Había un ligero temblor en su voz, y recordé que hacía mucho, mucho tiempo, hubo entre Yonah y Wade algo más que una relación meramente profesional, según había oído decir–. ¿Cómo está Yonah?

–Creo que está bien –dijo Colin con cautela–. Todo lo bien que cabe esperar. –Se encogió de hombros–. Hemos pasado la mayor parte del año fuera.

Advertí que mi copa estaba vacía y me acerqué para coger la botella.

Esta se tambaleó torpemente en mi mano derecha y tuve que concentrarme para no derramar el líquido púrpura sobre el blanco mantel de Wade.

–No creo que esté tan mal –dije, cuando hube terminado de servirme–. Nos ha mandado aquí, ¿no?

Mientras hablaba miraba a Webbie, que se llevó una mano a la boca y dijo:

–No entiendo.

–Yonah puede ser un poco… intolerante –dijo Wade en voz baja.

–Yonah es un cerdo racista –dije yo–, y estoy seguro de que ahora mismo se está partiendo el culo de risa. Lo que le queda de él.

–Justin –dijo Colin en voz baja.

–Yonah está muy delgado.

–Justin.

–No me hagas callar, Colin –dije, y mientras lo decía recordé algo que Yonah había dicho cuando nos mandó aquí, algo que entonces no alcancé a comprender–. ¡Coño! Yonah había llamado a este lugar Shvartzville.

–No pretendía hacerte callar –dijo Colin, cuando hube terminado–. Solo estaba diciendo tu nombre.

–¡Hola! –La voz de Divine llegó de debajo de la mesa. Luego apareció de nuevo, tenedor en mano, y me miró, diciendo–: ¿De dónde has sacado ese nombre? ¡Hay que joderse! ¿Time Justin?

–Verás, Divine, creo que esa pregunta debería responderla el señor Nieman.

Divine se volvió hacia Colin y dijo:

–¿Y bien?

Colin guardó silencio durante un momento, luego se encogió de hombros y explicó:

–Es un chiste malo. Un chiste malo que se ha quedado para siempre.

–Eso parece –dijo Divine; y volviéndose hacia mí preguntó–: ¿Cuál es tu verdadero…?

–Bueno, deja que te sirva un poco de vino. –Me incliné sobre la mesa para llenarle la copa y, esta vez, derramé el líquido sobre el mantel; Divine se levantó de un salto para evitar que le cayera en los pantalones. Mientras volvía a ocupar mi asiento, Colin me acercó su copa vacía y la llené con más cuidado, evitando mirarlo a los ojos.

−Volviendo a tu pregunta anterior −le dijo Wade a Colin.

Si aún hubiera tenido la botella en la mano se me habría vuelto a derramar el vino, porque casi me había olvidado de que Wade estaba presente.

−Mi...

−Galatea −dijo Wade, en voz tan baja que tuve que esforzarme para oírla.

−¡Galatia! −exclamó Divine, casi gritando.

−¡Ah, sí! −dijo Colin. Hizo una pausa, sopesó la cuestión−. Galatia.

−Iba a decir −dijo Wade− que Galatea tiene una historia bastante... pintoresca −en este punto sonrió brevemente, muy brevemente−, pero no soy la persona más indicada para contarla. Webbie lo hace mucho mejor. Es casi la historiadora oficial del pueblo.

−Bueno, mi padre...

−¿Pintoresca? −preguntó Colin, volviéndose hacia Webbie.

Webbie lo miró dubitativamente, dio un sorbo de vino y sostuvo la copa contra su pecho.

−Galatia −dijo, asintiendo hacia Wade− es en realidad dos pueblos.

−¿Dos? −se extrañó Colin−. Si apenas parece que haya gente suficiente para uno.

−Trescientos cuarenta y tres...

−Según ese cartel −interrumpió Divine−, que hace como mínimo dos años que ya no indica nada. ¿Sabes? Este pueblo se reduce cada minuto que pasa. Se está convirtiendo en un puto pueblo fantasma delante de tus narices −añadió, mirando a Colin.

Webbie esperó hasta que Divine hubo terminado y luego, en una voz que intentaba seguir pareciendo tranquila, continuó diciendo:

−De esos trescientos cuarenta y tres habitantes, ciento cuarenta y siete viven al este de la autopista nueve, en un pueblo al que llaman Galatia, desde hace ciento veinticinco años. Los otros ciento noventa y seis −dijo, y se detuvo para dar un sorbo de vino− viven aquí, en Galatea, desde hace unos veinte años.

−¡Eh, eh, venga ya! −exclamó Divine−. ¿Es que nadie va a poner freno a esta cacería de los cojones? Todos nos hemos criado aquí, no hay necesidad de andarse con rodeos. Quiero decir que a este paso nos moriremos antes de que vayas al grano.

Webbie tomó un largo trago de vino, se llevó una mano a la boca y luego la apoyó sobre su pecho. Divine no esperó a que terminara de tragar.

−A este paso nos darán las uvas −dijo−. Lo único que necesitáis saber es esto: todos los que viven en Galatia son negros, como yo y como aquí mi hermana, que es de color seta. Y todos los que viven en Ga-la-la-la son… –hizo una pausa y, señalando a Wade, concluyó–: como él.

Wade bajó los ojos ante la mirada colectiva, como si le incomodara ser el blanco de un escrutinio tan directo. Luego, con el mismo pésimo sentido del humor que junto con este nombre me ha tocado en suerte, Colin, colocando una mano sobre el pecho, dijo:

–¿Pintores?

1.08

WEBBIE

Hay dos ventanas en el archivo. El archivo está en el ático donde mi padre atesora la historia de su pueblo; una de las ventanas mira al sur, hacia Kenosha, la otra mira al norte, hacia la calle Matthew, el molino, los sauces, el campanario que hay en el centro del pueblo –me refiero a Galatia, no a Galatea– y, aún más allá, hacia la reluciente calva del risco pelado; esta vez quiero empezar por aquí y no por Kenosha, como hago normalmente. No tardaremos en llegar a Kenosha.

Galatia limita al norte con una pequeña sucesión de montañas conocidas colectivamente como los riscos. El nombre no se escribe con mayúscula y no figura en ningún mapa; de hecho, las gentes de Galatia rara vez lo emplean, y solo el más alto de los riscos tiene su propio nombre. Se conoce como el risco pelado, porque no tiene pelo, con lo cual quiero decir que carece de vegetación; es una meseta de esquisto blanco, quebradizo y llamativo. Las carretas que circulaban por allí en el siglo pasado debían de producir un sonido como el de los cañones, pero ahora solo los coches hacen crujir el terreno, y solo de noche, porque el risco pelado se ha convertido en el refugio de los enamorados de Galatia. Yo lo prefiero de día, especialmente por la mañana. Se ve desde cualquier parte del valle donde se asienta el pueblo –un valle tan poco profundo como pequeños son los riscos–; por la mañana, no solo atrapa la luz sino que la retiene y la libera produciendo un extraordinario estallido de oro líquido. En este monótono paisaje es como una joya, y me gusta pensar que fue la imagen del risco pelado por la mañana, y no solo la presencia del agua, lo que animó a las Cinco Familias a detenerse aquí. Pero esto es una ficción histórica, tan romántica como la idea de que un pionero arrastró su carreta por el risco solo para oír el crujido de la pizarra bajo las ruedas, en lugar de abrirse camino entre el fango del valle.

Las gentes de Galatea, dada su propensión a cambiar los nombres de las cosas, llaman al más alto de los riscos risco «desnudo», en lugar de «pelado».

Está escrito, al menos eso dice mi padre, que las Cinco Familias –los Greeving, los Deacon, los Johnson, los Getterling y los Rochelle– se detuvieron allí al ver el barro. Fue en el mes de marzo de 1859, dieciséis meses antes de las elecciones presidenciales de 1860; era un frío y seco día de marzo, y las Cinco Familias sabían que siempre que encontraban agua durante el viaje, también encontraban gente. El barro se hallaba en el fondo de un pequeño valle encerrado por los riscos al norte y que daba paso a una serie de cavidades y manantiales en todas las demás direcciones. El reverendo John Greeving cavó un pozo en el lugar donde encontraron el barro; los habitantes le cambiaron el nombre, y para cuando todo el mundo lo llamaba reverendo Alpha, ya había construido un molino hidráulico que permitió a las gentes del pueblo extraer el agua de ese pozo durante décadas. En el archivo de mi padre hay una fotografía de un grupo de robustas mujeres y niños inquietos que hacen cola con cubos de metal y de madera para coger su ración diaria de agua; esta fotografía está colgada en la pared y a veces la veo cuando mi padre entra o sale de la habitación. También hay otra fotografía de los veintitrés hombres, mujeres y niños negros que fundaron Galatia. Los siete hombres están de pie, las siete mujeres sentadas en sillas y ocultas por sus vestidos, y los ocho niños sentados sobre la tierra desnuda y removida. Pese a la pétrea expresión que tienen los retratos de esa época, se advierte en los rostros cierto orgullo y temor, pero sobre todo determinación. Una de las mujeres sostiene a un niño en los brazos, y el hombre que aparece tras ella es el único que lleva sombrero. Como en el famoso mural de John Brown que hay en el edificio del capitolio de Topeka –pintado años después de que se tomara esta fotografía y restaurado hace treinta y cinco años por Wade Painter–, el hombre del sombrero lleva una Biblia en una mano y un rifle en la otra, aunque ambas armas reposan tranquilamente en sus costados. Este hombre es Alpha Greeving –bautizado con el nombre de John pero más tarde llamado reverendo Alpha–, el abuelo de mi tatarabuelo y el hombre que construyó la primera Iglesia Baptista del Sur en Galatia, y que ofició en ella por primera vez. Galatia, como verán, se diferencia en un aspecto fundamental de los otros pueblos negros desperdigados en el norte, por lo demás escasos. La mayoría de estos asentamientos fueron fundados después de la guerra civil por antiguos esclavos que anhelaban forjarse una nueva vida, pero Galatia –bautizada con el nombre de la tierra bíblica de la abundancia– fue fundada durante el turbulento período anterior a la guerra.

Se instalaron allí un grupo de negros firmemente decididos a que Kansas se incorporase a la unión como estado libre, y todavía hoy algunos de sus habitantes, especialmente mi padre, insisten en que ningún miembro de las Cinco Familias había sido esclavo; tampoco eran refugiados o vagabundos llegados del otro lado de la frontera. Eran peregrinos, y no es de extrañar, pues, que sus descendientes se convirtieran en puritanos.

Un pueblo negro, como algunos blancos llamaban a Galatea, cuando no lo llamaban directamente Niggerville. Niggerville junto a Bigger Hill.

Bigger Hill es el pueblo más cercano a Galatia y se encuentra situado a cuarenta y cinco kilómetros en dirección suroeste. Hasta 1974 existió Kenosha, a menos de quince kilómetros al sur. Kenosha contó en su día con una población de cinco mil blancos, cosa que en sí misma carece de importancia: hay docenas de pequeños pueblos mayoritariamente blancos en Kansas, y Kenosha solo merece un lugar en esta historia porque el lugar fue arrasado por un incendio en 1974, incendio del cual nació Galatea.

Yo tenía catorce años cuando ocurrió y lo recuerdo bien. Fue en julio, en la época de la recolección, y llevaba semanas sin llover; hasta el rocío era escaso y hacía tanto calor que si hubiera habido aceras en Kenosha se habría podido freír un huevo en ellas. Todo el que no haya nacido en un pueblo de granjeros lo encontrará siniestro, mas para un granjero este tipo de condiciones climáticas son las óptimas para cultivar el trigo. No obstante, también tienen sus riesgos: el aire alrededor del granero estaba cargado de briznas de paja, y alguien o algo prendió fuego allí. Según la creencia popular, el responsable de la catástrofe fue Gene Zwemmer, el borracho oficial de Kenosha, aunque nadie sabe cómo empezó la leyenda. En cualquier caso, el efecto inmediato –una explosión cuya bola de fuego pudo verse a cien kilómetros de distancia– destruyó doce de las catorce torres del granero, de treinta metros de alto, matando a cinco personas, entre las que figuraba Gene Zwemmer. La explosión derribó los álamos de Virginia, situados a más de siete kilómetros de distancia y, a pesar de que en la llanura siempre soplaba el viento, lo que quedó de la ciudad permaneció cubierto por una nube de humo y ceniza por espacio de tres días.

Lo cierto es que no quedó mucho: la llamarada de fuego que salió del granero devoró casi todos los edificios de la ciudad en menos de una hora; otras dos personas perdieron la vida. La gente había salvado la vida, pero nada más, y cuando llegaron los bomberos se limitaron a evitar que el fuego se extendiera por la pradera. Al día siguiente no quedaba más que humo y los carbonizados esqueletos de los edificios, además de algunas estructuras de ladrillo –el banco, la escuela, la nueva tienda de comestibles–, y recuerdo que en Galatia se hacían todo tipo de especulaciones sobre el futuro de los supervivientes. La respuesta no tardó en llegar: menos de dos semanas después del incendio los habitantes de Kenosha –auténticos refugiados, sin hogar, sin un céntimo y sin perspectivas– comenzaron a instalarse al oeste de Galatia en las tierras de los Krebs. Llegaron grandes camiones, se levantaron viviendas y se construyeron carreteras. Al final, la mayoría de los habitantes de Kenosha se marcharon, pero quienes carecían de mejores perspectivas aceptaron la oferta de Rosemary Krebs de comprar a buen precio tierras donde empezar una nueva vida, y como hija de Galatia imagino lo irresistible que semejante oferta debió de ser para un bracero o un dependiente de la tienda de ultramarinos: ¿cuántas personas podían decir que habían fundado y bautizado el pueblo donde vivían? Durante diecinueve años celebraron una fiesta popular para conmemorar su victoria. El 4 de julio, el Día de la Independencia, es fiesta en todas partes, pero aquí, en «Galatea», la fiesta es el Día de los Fundadores.

Supongo que podría defender la idea de que un nombre puede transformar el carácter de un lugar, o de una persona, si vamos a eso, pero no voy a hacerlo. Sé lo sugestionable que es la naturaleza humana. Puede que un nombre no altere el carácter de lo nombrado, pero a menudo influye bastante en la gente que lo emplea, y eso es lo que importa en el caso de Galatia, y en el de Galatea, y también en el mío. Aunque nunca se me ha permitido ver la partida de nacimiento de mi padre –un «documento histórico» que por razones de seguridad se conserva en el archivo–, sí he visto la mía. Mi nombre es Webbie Greeving. Mi padre me dio este nombre y también una historia. Supongo que todo padre considera esto una responsabilidad, pero mi padre se lo tomó mucho más en serio que la mayoría. Mi madre murió cuando yo nací; mi padre quería un hijo. Enumero estas tragedias según mi orden de prioridades, aunque no me atrevería a jurar que el orden sea el mismo para mi padre. Mi padre quiso llamarme W. E. B. Greeving: quería que yo fuera maestra, predicadora, profeta de la raza, y no una simple historiadora, que es lo que soy (al menos estudié para eso). El nombre de Webbie no refleja la idea de compromiso con la realidad que tiene mi padre, sino que es más bien un chiste; mi segundo nombre es Martina. Pero antes del nombre de Webbie, en mi partida de nacimiento aparece una letra –no una inicial, sino una sola letra seguida de un gran espacio, como si mi padre quisiera dejar sitio por si en algún momento reconsiderara su decisión– y esta letra es, legalmente, mi primer nombre. La letra es una A, pero nadie me ha dicho nunca lo que esa letra representaba para mi padre. «A.» A veces, cuando me siento optimista, la considero como un comienzo que nunca tendrá fin, pero normalmente la entiendo como lo que es: una historia que nunca llegó a contarse. «A.» Mi nombre no es Aaron, ni Alá, ni Alah, ni Arthur, ni siquiera Art. Mi nombre es Webbie, pero no llego a entender si esta historia no es más que una pequeña aunque inextricable parte de la historia del pueblo de mi padre o si, como espero, puede existir de manera independiente y tan solo espera, como yo, el momento de poder liberarse. Debo decir también que me irritaba, que me llenaba de rabia, el hecho de que alguien como Colin Nieman hablara con tanta ligereza de instalarse aquí, cuando a mí ni siquiera se me permitía marcharme. Advertirán que estoy personificando mi rabia, aunque no la dirijo exclusivamente contra Colin. Justin apenas dijo nada cuando conté esta historia. Picoteó perezosamente la insípida comida que le ofreció Wade y derramó grandes cantidades de vino, pero dejó traslucir de todos modos que no sentía el menor interés por estar en Galatia y mucho menos por vivir aquí, por eso, mucho antes de que nos hiciésemos amigos, ambos sabíamos lo que teníamos en común, y en cierto modo nos convertimos en aliados.

Al terminar la cena había cinco copas de vino vacías a la espera de ser llenadas. Justin, borracho, llenó la suya primero y luego, después de mirar alrededor, vació en mi copa lo que quedaba en la botella. Y brindó conmigo, aunque sin decir nada.

1.09

JUSTIN

—¡Mirad! —dijo Wade, frenando bruscamente.
—¿Qué pasa? —preguntó Divine, asomando la cabeza desde el asiento trasero. ¿Que miremos qué?

Íbamos hacia el este, por la carretera 24, la misma por la que Colin y yo habíamos viajado el día anterior; resultó ser la única carretera asfaltada que permitía salir y entrar al pueblo en dirección este. Wade estaba enseñándonos los alrededores.

—Parece que ha habido un accidente —dijo, y mientras hablaba vi largas huellas de neumáticos impresas sobre el asfalto, un poste de teléfono con un trozo de madera arrancado, como mordido por un tiburón, y cristales rotos esparcidos sobre la sucia hierba que crecía en la cuneta.

—¡Mierda! —dijo entonces Divine—. A mí no me parece que haya habido ningún accidente.

–Dos –dijo Wade, mientras se detenía en el arcén–. Ha habido dos coches implicados.

–¿Y cómo lo sabe, eminencia?

Wade le habló como se le habla a un niño, aunque sin condescendencia. Supongo que Divine era un niño.

–Porque hay dos tipos de huellas. Aunque…

–¿Y? –preguntó Colin.

–Las huellas van en la misma dirección –dijo Wade–. Parece que… –Y de nuevo dejó la frase en suspenso.

–Venga, señor detective –dijo Divine–, cuéntanos qué has «detectado».

–Lo que parece –dije, en un tono más brusco de lo que pretendía–. Lo que parece es que un coche ha sacado al otro de la carretera.

Wade me miró y dijo:

–Parece que un coche ha empujado a otro contra el poste.

–¡Joder! –dijo Divine, volviendo a acomodarse en el asiento–. Habéis visto muchas películas últimamente. ¿Creéis que habéis descubierto un misterio o algún rollo por el estilo?

Wade no respondió de inmediato. Arrancó el coche de nuevo y enfiló la carretera.

–Estuve aquí el miércoles pasado –dijo–. Y no había habido ningún accidente.

–Venga ya, tío, ¿por qué no llamas al agente Brown para que haga un informe oficial? Olvídate del asunto.

Wade asintió con la cabeza, pero no dijo nada. Luego murmuró, casi para sus adentros: «Mi padre murió en un accidente de tráfico». Después de decir eso me miró, y como yo también lo estaba mirando, nuestras miradas se cruzaron y asentí.

–Mi madre murió de muerte natural –dijo Wade–, pero mi padre murió en un accidente de tráfico.

Asentí de nuevo y miré por la ventanilla.

–Mi madre murió por culpa de mi padre. No sé de qué murió mi padre; ni siquiera sé si ha muerto.

–¿Qué? –dijo Colin, estirando la cabeza y echando todo el cuerpo hacia delante–. ¿Qué has dicho?

No respondí.

Un momento después, Divine dijo:

–¿Por qué no vuelve a sentarse bien, señor Colin Nieman? Relájese, disfrute de las vistas. Créame estamos a medio camino entre ningún lugar y ninguna parte, y aún nos queda un buen trecho hasta llegar a casa.

Era domingo, creo que ya es hora de decirlo. Llevábamos veinticuatro horas en Galatea, o en Galatia, o dondequiera que estuviésemos. Habíamos dormido en una cama cuadrada situada justo en el centro de una de las habitaciones cúbicas de Wade: finalmente supe que había nueve en la casa, todas trazadas según la rígida simetría del tres en raya. Al final de la velada, Divine se despidió de Webbie en voz alta, indicando que ella se marchaba y él no, pero antes de dejar que se fuera, Wade le dio un largo y fuerte abrazo; al principio me pareció cariñoso, pero luego vi una horrible expresión de angustia en el rostro de Webbie. En cuanto Webbie se hubo marchado, cogí mi cepillo de dientes y decidí abordar a Wade justo en la puerta del cuarto de baño, para preguntarle, a bocajarro, qué hacía Webbie allí.

Una expresión de algo parecido al pánico surcó fugazmente el rostro de Wade.

—¿Perdón?

—Es evidente que no quiere estar aquí.

—La he invitado a cen...

—Me refiero a Galatia, o Galatea, o como llaméis a este sitio. ¿Por qué no se marcha?

Wade guardó silencio antes de responder.

—Ya se marchó una vez —dijo al fin.

Yo pensé evasivamente: «Se fue a Nueva York. A Columbia. Quería escribir su tesis doctoral sobre la historia de Estados Unidos».

—¿Y?

—Y a su padre le dio un ataque. Estuvo postrado durante un año, y tiene el lado derecho parcialmente paralizado. Ella lo cuida desde entonces.

—¿Cuándo...?

—Hace ocho años —dijo Wade, y luego, pasó un dedo largo y calloso sobre mi cepillo de dientes—. Cuando tenía cinco años y no tenía pinceles, pintaba con el cepillo de dientes. Me lavaba los dientes por la mañana y luego lo usaba para pintar todo el día; por la noche lo lavaba y me volvía a cepillar los dientes. Una vez me intoxiqué por el plomo de la pintura y tuvieron que hospitalizarme; cuando mis padres descubrieron el cepillo de dientes manchado de pintura me prohibieron volver a pintar. —Wade guardó silencio, esbozó una de sus tenues sonrisas, y luego, en lugar de continuar su historia o la de Webbie, me preguntó por la mía.

—¿Qué te pasó? —dijo, sujetándome la mano derecha.

Me miré la mano que él sujetaba. Ya casi nunca me fijaba en ella, pues apenas quedaban huellas de la lesión, pero una vez, hacía mucho tiempo, me la habían aplastado de tal modo que se puso como una pelota roja y durante años, después del accidente, estuvo retorcida, rígida, inflamada. El tiempo y el dinero de Colin lograron reparar el daño, al menos desde el punto de vista estético; el único signo externo que aún resultaba visible era su tamaño, ligeramente superior al de mi mano derecha; eso y cierta torpeza en los movimientos, sobre todo cuando estaba borracho. Solo un ojo sagaz, quiero decir, el ojo de un pintor, podría apreciar la diferencia; aunque para advertir que aún me dolía, especialmente cuando llovía o hacía frío, se requería otro tipo de visión. Algunos días no sentía absolutamente nada con ella, pero esa noche percibí con claridad el sudor y la fuerza de la mano de Wade, que tiraba ligeramente, como si intentara sacar de mí un pasado que yo ya había preferido borrar, y por primera vez en muchos años permití que otra persona sintiera el peso de aquella historia aunque solo fuera un momento; luego, con un recelo que me sorprendió, aparté mi mano de la suya.

Siempre me extrañaba que alguien se fijara en mi mano, pero casi me asustó que lo hiciera Wade: el vacante, ausente, quiero decir, «vacío» Wade Painter. No se me había ocurrido que aún quedara algo de él, en él, para ser tan perspicaz, pero antes de que pudiera indagar en su pasado oculto, Wade suspiró y, por el rabillo del ojo, vi que abría y cerraba el puño con fuerza; luego se encogió de hombros y, sonriendo, dijo: «Buenas noches, Justin Time –sin el menor atisbo de incomodidad–. Nos veremos por la mañana».

Y por la mañana empezó la excursión. Wade nos enseñó primero su estudio, una granja remodelada que había sido el hogar de sus padres –muertos, dijo, cuando Colin le preguntó dónde estaban, muertos–; después, en el polvoriento cascarón de un viejo Galaxie 500 verde, nos condujo por la desangelada zona nueva del pueblo que él llamaba Galatea, y luego por la desangelada zona antigua del pueblo que Divine llamaba Galatia, sin que ninguno de los dos hiciera el más leve comentario sobre la blanca pared del granero que dividía las dos mitades del pueblo, con un solo nombre escrito en ella. Las letras negras comenzaban en un lado del pueblo y continuaban describiendo una curva hasta el otro: GALATEA. En esa parte del pueblo había un banco, una iglesia, un pequeño restaurante, una ferretería, un IGA, una oficina de correos, una biblioteca, una escuela y, según Wade, noventa y siete casas, treinta y dos de las cuales eran caravanas desperdigadas como colillas en un aparcamiento al cual, en un asombroso alarde de falta de imaginación, se le había dado el nombre de Prairieview. En Galatia había setenta y ocho casas –no caravanas–, una iglesia de madera, debo admitir que bastante bonita, un supermercado, un café y un largo parque rectangular que contenía diez enormes sauces y un molino, alto y herrumbroso. La larga y sinuosa curva de la calle principal dividía el pueblo, esta calle se dividía a su vez en dos calles, como los cabos de una cuerda deshilachada, y el granero semejaba una isla en un río de asfalto negro y uniforme; la carretera 24, más estrecha, pasaba junto al paso elevado que comunicaba las dos alas del granero. No había en ninguna de las dos mitades del pueblo otra carretera asfaltada, aunque para compensar esta carencia las sucias calles de Galatea llevaban el nombre de los presidentes: Washington, East Adams, Jefferson, Monroe, West Adams; mientras que las sucias calles de Galatia aludían piadosamente a los libros del Nuevo Testamento: Mateo, Marcos, Lucas y Juan.

Ambas mitades del pueblo contaban con numerosas casas vacías. Para ser exactos –para ser tan exactos como lo era Wade Painter a la hora de describir su pueblo–, había dieciséis en Galatea y trece en Galatia, y la visión de las casuchas me alegró un poco, pues sabía que Colin jamás se rebajaría a vivir en ellas. Colin tenía armarios más grandes que aquellas casas.

–Con esa hacen catorce –dijo Wade cuando pasamos junto a otra casa con un cartel de SE VENDE en el jardín. El cartel parecía recién instalado; la tierra alrededor del poste aún estaba fresca, lo que indicaba que había sido removida muy poco antes.

La cabeza de Divine asomó desde el asiento trasero, como impulsada por un resorte:

–¿No era esta la casa de Melvin Cartwright? No sabía que Melvin se hubiera marchado.

Wade asintió:

–Se fue la semana pasada. El mismo día que Eddie Comedy.

Divine volvió a reclinarse en el asiento, pero su voz llegó flotando hasta la parte delantera del coche:

–Siempre se fugan en pareja. Esto está jodido, tío. Un par de años más y aquí no quedará nadie.

Cuando volvimos a casa de Wade ocurrió algo curioso: salí del coche, miré la imponente masa gris del edificio y tuve la clara sensación de estar en casa. Me irritó tanto que le agarré a Colin de la muñeca para mirar el reloj, pero tardé un buen rato en darme cuenta de que quedaba menos de una hora para que saliéramos hacia el aeropuerto.

–Menos de una hora para marcharnos –dije en voz alta, tanto para situarme como para subrayarlo. Me di la vuelta para no ver la casa, pero no vi más que un horizonte lejano, una tenue mancha de tierra y un cielo tan vasto que preferí mirar la casa de Wade. El hormigón era original y parecía seguro. Resultaba sólido y preciso en aquella inmensidad vacía, y tuve que hacer un esfuerzo para recordar que la casa estaba tan vacía por dentro como ese cielo al que no dejaba entrar.

–Bueno, Wade –dijo Divine–. Tengo cosas que hacer. Me largo.

—Ten cuidado —dijo Wade en voz baja, con seriedad, y Divine le lanzó una rápida mirada antes de volverse hacia Colin.
—Señor Colin Nieman —dijo, tendiéndole la mano—. Ha sido un verdadero placer conocerlo y espero verlo pronto por aquí. Recuerde que «la puerta trasera siempre está abierta». —Y entonces casi me da un ataque de risa, porque Colin se puso tan colorado que ni siquiera pudo responder a Divine, que se metió en su coche y salió a toda velocidad sin molestarse en despedirse de mí.
—Bueno —dijo Wade cuando Divine se hubo marchado—, creo que aún os falta algo por ver.
Me volví hacia él, pero la imagen de la inmensa pradera que se extendía a su espalda me distrajo de nuevo. Costaba creer que aún quedase algo por ver: ¿era posible esconder algo en aquel paisaje yermo y plano?
Wade se había quedado mirando la estela de polvo que levantó Divine en su retirada; luego, volviendo en sí, dijo:
—¿Vamos?
Colin asintió y se sentó en el asiento delantero del coche. Yo estaba a punto de sentarme detrás cuando noté que Wade me miraba fijamente. Nuestras miradas se cruzaron un instante; él aclaró la voz y dijo:
—Creo que cabemos todos delante.
Esta vez fuimos hacia el sur, por un camino estrecho y polvoriento, lleno de curvas. Yo iba tarareando la canción de *Gilligan's Island*, pero Colin me dio un codazo en las costillas y a partir de ese momento guardé silencio y clavé la vista en el suelo. Entonces Colin me dio una palmada en la rodilla.
—¡Eh! No he dicho nada…
Colin me interrumpió:
—¿Eso es un incendio?
Levanté la vista y vi una enorme nube negra pegada al horizonte. Era achatada y baja y, aunque parecía humo, pensé que no podía ser, porque el humo asciende y aquella nube flotaba a escasa distancia del suelo, como un peinado caído por falta de laca.
—Eso es Kenosha —dijo Wade en voz baja.
No recordé la palabra hasta que Colin dijo:
—¿Esa ciudad? ¿Esa de la que nos habló Webbie ayer por la noche?
—Cuando hace viento las cenizas se esparcen por el aire y parece que la ciudad aún está ardiendo —explicó Wade. Luego hizo una pausa y añadió—: Aquí hace viento casi todos los días.
Siguió conduciendo mientras hablábamos —no podía ser de otro modo—, luego, sin previo aviso, giró bruscamente y se metió por el hueco abierto en una hilera de cedros que se alzaba a nuestra izquierda. Antes de que girase yo pensaba que lo que nos quedaba por ver

era Kenosha, pero cuando hubimos entrado en el recinto rodeado de cedros, supe que era otra cosa lo que Wade tenía en mente.

Una casa.

Una casa enorme, una señora casa, en forma de cruz griega, con cuatro brazos de dos plantas cada uno y un tejado muy pronunciado. Era abrumadora, simple y sólida como un dato y, al verla, me sentí repentinamente cansado, como si, una vez más, aquel paisaje me robara la imaginación, dejándome indefenso, incapaz de relacionarme con el mundo que me rodeaba, solo capaz de describirlo.

Las paredes de la casa estaban construidas con grandes bloques de caliza de un amarillo muy pálido, el tejado era de tejas negras y, en el vértice, asomaba tímidamente una pequeña cúpula. El jardín, plano y sin vegetación, brillaba bajo el sol poniente, y me pareció pavimentado como un aparcamiento, hasta que advertí que la casa estaba rodeada por un foso de lascas de obsidiana que absorbía la luz y parecía profundo y grasiento. El sol entraba por otro hueco en el seto de cedros perfectamente alineados con una de las alas de la casa —supongo que sería el ala oeste— y una franja de luz que trepaba por la pared de caliza, con la anchura de una espaldera, iluminaba directamente el edificio. Allí donde se hundía en la roca, la luz confería a la pared una pátina amarilla y húmeda, de un amarillo líquido y transparente como la mantequilla derretida. Ese color me recordó primero al papel viejo, pero luego me di cuenta de que era el mismo que había visto en algunos cuadros de Wade.

Observamos el espectáculo en silencio. Era grandioso, tan artificial que casi parecía natural. Era, en cierto sentido, la casa más hermosa que había visto en mi vida, pero también la más opresiva... incluso más que la de Wade. No parecía permitir que nadie dejara su impronta en ella: era ella quien la dejaba en ti.

—¡Vaya...! —exclamó Colin, después de carraspear.

Wade lo interrumpió antes de que pudiera decir nada.

—Lleva cinco años deshabitada.

—¿Sí? —preguntó Colin, pero Wade volvió a interrumpirlo.

—Sí —dijo; y lo dijo con nostalgia—. Está en venta. —Guardó silencio y, cuando volvió a hablar, detecté un matiz distinto en su voz, casi una amenaza—. No sé por qué os la enseño. Rosemary Krebs nunca os la vendería a vosotros.

Me incliné hacia delante. Me sorprendía lo deprisa que Wade había comprendido que Colin jamás rechazaría semejante reto, y me sorprendió aún más que Wade lo lanzara. Pero lo que más me sorprendió fue el hecho de que Wade me hubiera sorprendido, y empecé a darme cuenta de que no era tan insensible como fingía o pretendía ser. Me miró a los ojos y vi en su mirada un deseo tan evidente como el que Divine sentía por Colin, y me recosté rápidamente en el asiento.

Me quedé un buen rato mirando la casa antes de hablar.

—¿Por qué no vives aquí?

Por el rabillo del ojo vi que Wade apartaba la vista de la casa; Colin no había dejado de mirárla ni un segundo.

—Porque —dijo Wade al cabo de un rato— la añoranza y el deseo dieron paso por primera vez a la tristeza aquel fin de semana. Porque —repitió, y pensé que no iba a decir nada más. Pero luego añadió—: ya he construido mi propia casa.

1.10

WEBBIE

No hay sótanos en Galatia. Ni uno solo.

Las cuevas subterráneas se inundan en Galatea todas las primaveras, y las casas se asientan en sesgados ángulos sobre sus agrietados y hundidos cimientos, pero en Galatia, todas y cada una de las casas, hasta las más pequeñas, se elevan sobre pilares de madera introducidos en sólidos cimientos de hormigón, quedando así protegidas del agua que aflora a la superficie de la tierra. Pero no siempre fue así. De hecho, las Cinco Familias perdieron sus hogares una primavera especialmente lluviosa, solo dos años después de establecerse aquí, y al construirlos de nuevo decidieron elevarlos, aunque la más alta de todas es la vivienda situada en el número uno de la calle Matthew. Diez escalones de piedra conducían hasta la puerta de nuestra casa, y cuando yo tenía cinco años y ya podía subir los escalones sin ayuda de nadie, le pregunté a mi padre por qué nuestra casa tenía el doble de escalones que las de nuestros vecinos. Mi padre, ese hombre delgado y resuelto, me contestó sin mirarme, como hacía siempre. Cada uno de estos diez escalones, le dijo al aire, nos acerca un poco más a Dios, y al oírle decir esto me pareció que en realidad no le hablaba al aire, sino al propio Dios, y pensé que si fuera tan alta como mi padre también yo podría verlo desde el último escalón.

Pero desde que mi padre cayó enfermo, cada uno de estos escalones se convirtió para él en un pedazo de infierno. Un infierno que es suyo pero también mío, pues en el interior de la casa está Madre Mabel —así es como yo llamo a la silla-ascensor que permite a mi padre subir los tres pisos de nuestra casa—, pero fuera está la congregación del reverendo Abraham, y al buen reverendo le parece impropio que el representante de Dios se presente ante sus feligreses sentado en un torpe y lento aparato mecánico. Por eso, todos los miércoles por la noche y dos veces el domingo, una por la mañana y otra a última hora de la tarde, mi padre me dice: «Préstame tu brazo, hija», petición que pronuncia con voz retumbante, de manera que todos los que se han reunido para recibir al reverendo cuando sale de casa para dirigirse a la casa del Señor son testigos de este cordial intercambio entre padre e hija, entre reverendo y feligreses, entre amo y criada.

Más cerca del cielo, me dijo cuando yo tenía cinco años. Si miras por la ventana del archivo verás que Dios te está mirando. Pero en el archivo no entraba nadie más que mi padre, y si alguna vez hubo alguna visión divina, jamás la compartió conmigo. Préstame tu brazo, hija, me decía ahora tres veces a la semana, y yo se lo habría regalado gustosamente si hubiera podido, pero él necesitaba tanto el cuerpo al que ese brazo estaba unido como el propio brazo.

El domingo que vinieron Colin y Justin no fue distinto de otros domingos, salvo por el hecho de que yo tenía resaca y el estentóreo grito de mi padre me retumbó en los oídos, doliéndome más de lo habitual.

—¡Préstame tu brazo, hija! –gritó. Llevaba el bastón colgado en su debilitada muñeca derecha y se agarraba a mí con la mano izquierda. Me clavó los dedos en el brazo cuando nos preparamos para bajar la escalera, apretándome con tanta fuerza que su mano me pareció no la de un inválido, sino la de un carcelero, como si no fuera yo quien escoltaba a mi padre, sino él quien me escoltaba a mí.

Tres ancianas esperaban al reverendo al pie de la escalera. Creo recordar que él se había referido a ellas como sus «Damas», y lo cierto era que se llamaban Faith, Hope and Charity. Tan triste reunión de nombres solo podía atribuirse a una misma madre en exceso devota, aunque lo cierto es que Faith Jackson, Hope Rochelle y Charity Getterling, las tres únicas supervivientes de las Cinco Familias de la generación de mi padre, no estaban emparentadas.

—Buenos días, reverendo Abraham –dijeron al mismo tiempo, como tantas otras veces. Estaban debajo de nosotros, tres mujeres negras, ya ancianas aunque todavía fuertes, con relucientes vestidos de poliéster salpicados de migas de pan, que olían a jabón, perfume y beicon a partes iguales.

Mi padre colgó de mi brazo todo el peso de su nada desdeñable mole, amenazando con desencajármelo; luego, emprendimos el descenso con cuidado.

—El Señor nos ha dado otro hermoso día. –Su voz, el único rasgo de su persona, además de su peso, que no se había alterado con la enfermedad o con los años, tronó en mis oídos, y las Damas manifestaron su asentimiento.

—Un día realmente hermoso, reverendo —afirmó Faith Jackson—. No hay más que pájaros en el cielo.

Mi padre no respondió. Desplazaba con mucho cuidado la pierna izquierda de un escalón a otro; cuando la pierna derecha la seguía, todo el peso de su cuerpo reposaba sobre el mío.

Entonces, en un tono no tan alegre y reverente como era habitual en ella, Charity Getterling dijo:

—Puede que haya una pequeña nube en el cielo, reverendo.

—No tanto en el cielo, como en el horizonte —aclaró Hope Rochelle.

—Pero está alejándose —apostilló Faith Jackson—, y el cielo está tan despejado como antes.

Mi padre se detuvo, tambaleándose, y casi caemos los dos al suelo; consiguió no soltarse de mi brazo, aunque a mí me pareció casi imposible.

—Cuéntenme las novedades, señoras.

—Melvin Cartwright —dijo Charity Getterling.

—Se ha marchado —explicó Hope Rochelle.

—Y también Eddie Comedy —añadió Faith Jackson, esbozando una sonrisa forzada en su rostro marchito.

Mi padre me apretó el brazo. Las uñas me atravesaron la piel y la carne y llegaron hasta el nervio; tuve que hacer un esfuerzo para no gritar.

—Melvin Cartwright era un buen chico, y Galatia lo echará de menos —dijo, tras una brevísima pausa.

—Claro que sí, reve...

—Pero no tanto —interrumpió mi padre a Charity Getterling—, no tanto como él echará de menos a Galatia.

Las mujeres guardaron un notorio silencio, el silencio de quienes se reúnen para recordar a un hermano devoto y descubren que el difunto practicaba cierto vicio secreto.

Mi padre miró a las sufridas mujeres como si se apiadara de ellas:

—Recordaremos a Melvin Cartwright tal como fue y rezaremos para que la vida no lo trate con excesiva dureza. Tal vez —dijo, reanudando el descenso con un nuevo tambaleo— un día recuerde la sencillez y la piedad del lugar que lo vio nacer y regrese a nosotros.

—Seguro que lo recuerda, reverendo —dijo Charity Getterling.

—Y nosotros también lo recordaremos, reverendo —se apresuró a decir Hope Rochelle.

—Recordar y recordar y recordar —repitió Faith Jackson mientras el polvo crujía bajo mis pies y los de mi padre.

Se hizo el silencio entre el actor y el público cuando concluimos esta primera etapa del viaje. Las mujeres nos observaban con inquietud, y comprendí que si mi padre tropezaba, las tres se lanzarían al suelo para protegerlo de los escalones erosionados por el tiempo. Para entonces, se me había quedado la mano fría, casi insensible, y el hombro me ardía a cada paso que dábamos.

Finalmente, mi padre apoyó el pie malo en la acera y, con una última sacudida, colocó también el bueno. Jadeé, sudorosa y mareada por el esfuerzo, mientras la charla de las mujeres volvía a estallar como un zumbido.

—Hay que ver, hermana Webbie, cada día te pareces más a nuestra difunta Emily —dijo Charity Getterling.

—Era una buena mujer, Dios la tenga en su gloria —respondió por mí Hope Rochelle.

Y Faith Jackson concluyó, como hacía siempre:

—Todo el mundo sabe lo mucho que ayudas a tu padre.

—Eso hay que agradecérselo a la hermana Emily —dijo entonces mi padre con esa voz (que las Damas habían llamado un don de Dios) segura, exenta de temblor—. Con el paso de los años, va desapareciendo un poco más de Webbie y va apareciendo un poco más de su madre.

Pronunció este discurso sin mirarme; en lugar de ello, levantó el bastón con la mano derecha y lo clavó en la tierra. Luego, con tanto garbo como su tullido esqueleto le permitía, dio un paso en dirección al parque. Las mujeres se arremolinaron de inmediato en torno a él. Hacía tiempo que mi padre había dejado de insistir en que lo acompañara a la iglesia, pues la visión de mi cara bostezando era más fastidiosa que mi ausencia.

Ahora habría otra ausencia más en la iglesia: la de Melvin Cartwright. Una vez, cuando tenía dieciséis o diecisiete años, permití que Melvin Cartwright me besara. Logré mantener los labios cerrados hasta que me hizo cosquillas en el vientre y, cuando abrí la boca para reírme, me metió la lengua hasta el fondo. Fue la curiosidad, más que nada, lo que me hizo no apartar a Melvin de inmediato, como ahora apartaba también su recuerdo. Pero mi cuerpo, más nostálgico que mi mente, no se liberaba tan fácilmente: advertí que, inconscientemente, había puesto la mano sobre las costillas, justo debajo del pecho, justo encima del punto donde me había tocado Melvin Cartwright. Pero al bajar la vista y ver la mano, cuando intenté recordar el roce de Melvin, o el de cualquier otro hombre, solo sentí el abrazo de despedida que me había dado Wade la noche anterior.

Me dio un escalofrío, a pesar de que el sol apretaba con fuerza, y con el escalofrío lo expulsé todo de mí, volviéndome hacia mi padre y su séquito. Parecían no haberse movido y me asombró el contraste entre la velocidad del pensamiento y la lentitud de la vida: mi padre y las mujeres caminaban tan despacio que un diente de león los adelantó, perdiéndose en un rayo de sol. Iban al encuentro de su congregación, que ahora contaba con un miembro menos y menguaba tan lenta pero inexorablemente como ellos mismos, y la tierra que pisaban, bien apretada bajo la maleza, se negaba a grabar la huella de sus pies. Solo el agujero que hacía el bastón de mi padre aparecía a intervalos regulares, dejando un hoyuelo diminuto, tan inocuo como inútil, aunque en aquellos hoyuelos perfectamente grabados yo veía la historia de Galatia, igual de diminuta, igual de inocua y, supongo, igual de inútil, pero también hermosa, casi perfecta, teniendo en cuenta el país que la había producido, y de pronto me invadió un profundo sentimiento de ternura por el pueblo donde nací. Creo que fue la presencia de Colin y Justin la que produjo esta oleada de nostalgia, casi de amor, hacia un lugar que de ordinario me parecía una prisión más que un hogar, o puede que fuera la ausencia de Melvin.

Aún sentía que el hombro me abrasaba, por el peso que había cargado, y la cabeza me estallaba por aquella última copa de vino, pero nada me pertenecía, ni siquiera esa sensación de dolor, y por un momento todo quedó desplazado por la visión de esas cuatro frágiles figuras que avanzaban despacio, midiendo bien sus pasos, hacia la casa del Señor; y me quedé mirándolas hasta que hubieron entrado en la iglesia.

1.11

JUSTIN

El viaje hasta el aeropuerto duró tres horas. Es una exageración llamar autopista a la franja gris por la que circulábamos: era una simple carretera. Sentías la distancia que habías recorrido y los kilómetros que aún quedaban por recorrer; y al mismo tiempo, tenías la sensación de estar suspendido entre dos puntos, entre dos decisiones. Aunque desde el momento en que nuestro avión salió del mar de nubes el día anterior supe que ese lugar no era en absoluto adecuado para nosotros, me cuidé mucho de no decir nada en todo el fin de semana, e incluso en ese momento dejé que los indicadores de la carretera hablasen por mí: Russell, Waldo, Paradise, Natorna, Codell, Plainville.

Plainville. ¿Qué podía decir a eso?

Cuando al fin llegamos al aeropuerto la moderna imagen de los aviones que se elevaban pesadamente en el aire me sacó de mi estupor y pude volver a pensar con claridad, hacer juicios, sacar conclusiones, comprendiendo entonces que todo Kansas, y no solo esa estrecha e interminable carretera que conducía hasta Galatea, me había producido la impresión de estar a medio camino entre un lugar y otro, de hallarme en un estado de letargo. La diferencia es relativa. La diferencia entre una duna de arena y el océano Atlántico es elemental, pero los cinco veranos pasados en la casa que Colin tenía en Pines no habían sido suficientes para enseñarme esto; había bastado con la difusa monotonía de un fin de semana en Kansas, donde la hierba de la pradera da paso a los trigales y los trigales a la tierra parcheada, para que al fin se me revelase con nitidez. Kansas era una región de amplias vistas, pero mis ojos no se habían apartado en ningún momento del suelo, como si hubiera algo fascinante en la tierra granulosa o algo aterrador en su infinita monotonía, en la distancia por recorrer hasta alcanzar el horizonte.

El coche tembló ligeramente cuando despegó otro avión, con sus alas que parecían batir entre un velo de humo.

También Colin tembló ligeramente antes de depositar un billete de veinte dólares entre el parasol y el techo del coche. Cabía pensar que solo estaba dejando una propina desproporcionada a la persona encargada de limpiar nuestro coche de alquiler, pero lo cierto es que aquel gesto iba dirigido a mí. Los veinte dólares equivalían a la frase inicial de una obra literaria. Era el modo que tenía Colin de comenzar una nueva escena.

Se volvió hacia mí lanzando un suspiro. Se quedó mirándome, pero yo fingí no darme cuenta y preferí mirar a los aviones que aterrizaban o despegaban, o al cielo vacío. El aeropuerto de Wichita no tiene demasiado tráfico, y yo miraba principalmente al cielo vacío.

Al cabo de un rato, Colin dijo despacio, cautamente, con esa voz que solo yo tenía el privilegio de oír, esa voz frágil, la voz de su infancia, una voz que solo sirve para preguntar:

—¿Jus-tin Time? ¿Tu padre mató a tu madre?

Fingí estar enfadado, aunque en realidad estaba sorprendido: después de tantos años, lo único que le interesaba era mi historia; y en aquel momento, al pensar de pronto en ello, me enfadé de verdad, y le dije:

—Vete a la mierda, Colin.

Hubo otro largo silencio hasta que Colin sacó su cartera, extrajo de ella otro billete de veinte dólares y, con dedos ligeramente temblorosos, como si no reparara en que ya había dejado una propina, lo puso donde había puesto el otro. Luego volvió a suspirar y comprendí que no se había olvidado del primer billete, sino que estaba actuando. Estaba repitiendo la escena.

Esta vez habló con su voz de adulto, la que solo sirve para afirmar. Y dijo:

—Esa casa era muy bonita.

—Vamos a perder el avión —dije, pero cuando me disponía a abrir la puerta, Colin activó el bloqueo electrónico de las puertas. Supongo que podría haber desbloqueado el mecanismo, pues había otro botón idéntico a mi lado, pero no lo hice. Me quedé allí sentado. Esperé. Pero esta vez Colin tuvo más paciencia, y cuando sentí que ya no podía soportar el silencio, dije—: Ese pueblo me mataría.

Hubo una tercera pausa, pero esta vez Colin no añadió otro billete de veinte dólares a los dos primeros. En lugar de ello, desbloqueó el cierre de las puertas y abrió la suya, pero antes de salir del coche dijo:

—Esta mañana ingresan a Yonah en el hospital. —Luego se levantó y habló de nuevo, como si se dirigiera no solo a mí sino a Kansas, a aquel aeropuerto, y al mundo con el que se comunicaba mediante sus miles de tentáculos aéreos, y dijo—: Dos. Solo dos.

1.12

DIVINE

Érase una vez un viejo cobertizo situado aproximadamente a medio kilómetro del aparcamiento de camiones, del Big M. No tenía nada de especial: había sido construido con planchas de madera barata antes de que yo llegase a este mundo, y cuando lo vi por primera vez el tejado estaba hundido como el lomo de un buey viejo. Dentro, todo estaba lleno de polvo y de mierda, o de humedad (alguien me dijo una vez que la mierda era humedad, pero da lo mismo lo que fuera). Si lo saco a colación es porque podría decirse que por culpa de ese cobertizo algunos de nosotros acabamos convenciéndonos de que todo se había ido definitivamente a la mierda en Galatia. Quiero decir que todos sabíamos que las cosas estaban jodidas de antemano, pero después, bueno, después, comprendimos que no había marcha atrás.

Yo iba mucho por ese cobertizo. El Big M está en el cruce de la I-70 con la nacional 288. Existe de verdad —pueden buscarlo en un mapa— y hay un montón de surtidores de gasoil alrededor del aparcamiento, que es tan grande que a su lado un campo de fútbol parecería el patio trasero de una casa. Lo que quiero decir es que había un montón de plazas de aparcamiento, pero yo siempre dejaba el coche en el cobertizo, pues a nadie le convenía ser visto en el Big M dos o tres veces a la semana, aunque os sorprendería saber cuántos granjeros miserables eran capaces de conducir durante media hora solo para ahorrarse diez centavos en cada galón de combustible y comerse un trozo de ese rancio pastel de limón y merengue que sirven en la cafetería. Pero yo no iba por gasolina, ni a comer. Preguntadle a Wade, o a Webbie; ellos decían que yo iba allí para timar a la gente, pero no tienen ni puta idea. Yo iba en busca del Rata.

Esa vez, la vez de la que hablo, cuando llegué ya había un vehículo aparcado; una furgoneta metida en el cobertizo. Lo supe sin necesidad de abrir la puerta porque las paredes estaban llenas de agujeros y mierda; parecía un Chevy destartalado, pero no sé si había alguien dentro porque estaba demasiado oscuro y no quise entrar para averiguarlo. No creo en los espíritus ni en gilipolleces por el estilo, pero lo peor que le puede pasar a un negro es que alguien lo sorprenda en el granero de un blanco... y mi padre me había dado un buen consejo: que si no ves escrito en ninguna parte el nombre de un negro es porque pertenece a un blanco. Supongo que en condiciones normales me habría vuelto a casa de Wade, pero aquel no era un día normal. Nada normal. Ese día, Colin Nieman había estado en Galatia y todavía, horas después de que se hubiera marchado, me bastaba con pensar en él para sentir un ligero escalofrío en la columna, y necesitaba hacer algo para quitármelo de la cabeza, por eso, con furgoneta o sin ella, aparqué el coche a un lado del cobertizo, lo cerré y me dirigí al aparcamiento.

Debo decir una cosa. Nunca había tenido que esperar demasiado en el Big M, pero ese día ni siquiera me habría dado tiempo a terminar un cigarrillo, si lo hubiese encendido, antes de que aquel tío bajase la ventanilla y me preguntara —esta era nueva, incluso para mí— si quería patatas fritas.

Que él llamó papas fritas.

Tenía un camión que olía a tabaco y a café barato mezclado con whisky aún más barato, y toda aquella mierda estaba como envuelta en quinientos kilómetros de polvo y sudor a través de Kansas, y lo mismo le pasaba a él, por cierto, y por eso se convirtió en un camionero más. Era un hombre agitanado, quizá mestizo, con sangre mexicana; tenía la cara áspera, con barba de varios días, llevaba las uñas sucias, y las uñas sabían como las patatas fritas con sal y vinagre, las papas fritas, o lo que fueran, pues al parecer no comía otra cosa. Hablaba un inglés aún peor que los espaldas mojadas, aunque no hablaba mucho. Sabía que no se desnudaría, solo se abriría la bragueta:

todos suspiran cuando se abren la bragueta, tío, siempre, y a mí me entran ganas de decirles: «Cómprate la ropa más grande, cabrón, cómprate una ropa que no te apriete»; y este tío, por supuesto, se abrió la bragueta, pero también se desabrochó la camisa de franela y me sentí afortunado. Yo llevaba puesta una camiseta, unos vaqueros viejos y una gorra de béisbol, y la tenía a punto, ya me entendéis, la tenía levantada, y como Harry Houdini, salí de mi ropa con toda facilidad; entonces, el tío se me echó encima y empezó a restregarme toda la mierda que llevaba incrustada como si fuera un puto estropajo de aluminio y quisiera limpiarme bien; los sobacos le olían a leche agria. Y el tío no paraba de decir: «Quiero romperte el culo», como un personaje salido de una película del Conde Chócula, el de los cereales y las barrita de cereales; y entonces encontré los pantalones, los atrapé por el bolsillo y saqué un condón y lubricante, para fastidiar, ya me entendéis, más que nada para fastidiar, porque aquí no hay que tomar demasiadas precauciones, pero tampoco me gusta tener que meterme la perilla cada vez que lo hago, me deja seco, sí, seguro que alguien sabe lo que quiero decir, por eso le di la mercancía, y luego me di la vuelta y suspiré. El suspiro los pone a cien; el suspiro combinado con la visión de un culo desnudo, sobre todo cuando el culo es tan bonito como el mío. Ese suspiro equivale a decir: «Tengo un escape en la cañería, chato, a ver si encuentras el agujero y lo sellas».

Y ahora, prestad atención, chicos y chicas, porque Divine os va a decir cómo se hace. Mi consejo es muy sencillo: no lo hagáis en casa, aunque en casa sería mucho más fácil que en la cabina de un tráiler. Pero no olvidéis que requiere práctica, además de flexibilidad en la columna, coger una polla más corta que la tripa bajo la que asoma y darle placer al tío, y mucho más sentir tú un poco de placer. Quiero decir que la mayoría de estos gordos gitanos o mexicanos, o lo que coño fuera aquel tío, te agarran de la cintura, cierran los ojos y buscan el agujero entre las nalgas tanteando con una polla ridícula, y se comportan como si fueran Jeff Stryker, la estrella del cine porno, como si ¡venga, venga!, ¡te estuvieran dando una lección, los hijos de la gran puta! Te cagas del aburrimiento. Pero Divine lleva muchos años practicando, y resultó que Vlad el Empalador también estaba acostumbrado a entrar por la puerta de atrás, y lo pasamos muy bien. Y os diré otra cosa: Webbie nunca se lo ha creído, pero aunque haya folleteo, no soy yo quien se folla sus miserables culos. Estos pobres chicos buscan lo que no encuentran en el culo de sus mujeres; aunque a mí solo me dan enfermedades venéreas. Pero no os preocupéis por Divine. Sé cuidar de mí mismo. Ya sé que estamos en los noventa, y todo ese rollo, pero el tiempo avanza un poco más despacio aquí, en el puto medio de la nada, y no tienes que preocuparte por tu culo tanto como en Nueva York. El caso es que Webbie, después de pasarse veinte años estudiando, decía que no entendía por qué Colin Nieman quería conocer Galatia y mucho menos vivir allí, aunque yo le di cinco razones que había descubierto yo solito. La primera era el sida, y la quinta, que en Galatia no lo había.

Por eso. Algunos fingen que no se enteran de nada mientras lo hacen, pero otros no pueden cerrar la boca entre bocado y bocado, y hablan del rollo gay. Unos fingen que yo soy la mujer y otros que ellos son la mujer, y a veces quieren acunarme como a un bebé cuando hemos terminado, y debo reconocer que siento debilidad por ese rollo. Casi todos me dan algo, con suerte veinte pavos, aunque normalmente tengo que conformarme con una cerveza o un paquete de tabaco, que siempre acepto aunque ya no fumo. Una vez, un tío me dio una lata de aceite de motor; dijo que era lo único que tenía. Yo acepto lo que me ofrecen, porque así ellos se sienten más cómodos, sobre todo los blancos: puedes follar, pero no pagar por ello; aunque en este país todo el mundo sabe que cualquiera puede comprar a cualquiera, y eso facilita las cosas. ¿Me entendéis? Es como si tú eres tú y yo soy yo, y con veinte dólares las cosas pueden seguir siendo así. Lo que hizo Vlad fue devolverme la vaselina y también el condón cubierto de mierda; me lo ofreció con una sonrisa, como si fuera una rosa de chocolate, y yo hice como si me diera igual y lo cogí con dos dedos, y luego, por postre, o algo así, me metió cuatro asquerosos dedos en la boca, y yo se los chupé, pero solo sentí mi sabor, y lo aparté de un empujón.

−¡Eh! −dije, tirando el condón detrás del pequeño colchón del tráiler−. ¿Te has cruzado alguna vez con un tío que se hace llamar el Rata?

−¿El Rati?

−El Rata.

Vlad negó con la cabeza y los carrillos le colgaron a ambos lados de la boca como a un cerdo. Cuando todo hubo terminado me di cuenta de que era un pobre diablo, de eso no cabía duda.

−¿Y qué me dices de Lamoine?

−¿La-qué?

−Lamoine −dije, como diciendo: ¡Qué cojones, es que ya nadie sabe hablar inglés!−. Bajito, blanco, con cara de chiste y dientes de conejo.

Esta vez se rascó la barriga, que era aún más fea que su temblorosa cabeza, y dijo que no.

Entonces salí del camión de un salto, desnudo como vine al mundo. Que se fuera a la mierda, no me servía de nada. Me vestí debajo del camión. Antes de terminar de vestirme oí un crujido y un gemido por encima de mi cabeza, y sentí una especie de orgullo profesional ante la idea de que estuviera masturbándose, pues sabía que mientras lo hacía pensaba en lo que acababa de hacer conmigo. Y entonces me dio un ataque de risa al pensar en el condón usado que su mujer encontraría cuando limpiase el camión. Y me dije: ¡A ver cómo se lo explicas a esa zorra, cabrón!

Bien. Hablemos de algo realmente espeluznante. Espeluznante es la noche sin estrellas en la pradera, un paseo de medio kilómetro en una noche más negra que el conejo de Webbie, con nubes que oprimen como una sábana empapada en sudor. Antes de que hubiese recorrido la mitad del camino hasta el cobertizo empezaron los relámpagos, y ¿sabéis?, su resplandor encendió un fuego debajo de mi negro culo, ya me entendéis. Pero ni siquiera el negro que quedó en segundo lugar en el *cross* del estado –de no ser porque me había torcido un tobillo habría ganado yo– puede derrotar a una tormenta en Kansas, y en menos que canta un gallo estaba calado hasta los huesos. Entonces, no sé qué pasó, de pronto vi la imagen fugaz del Rata y yo encima del granero. A veces nos encontrábamos allí, nos emborrachábamos y nos lo hacíamos, pero la vez que estaba recordando no habíamos hecho nada, porque alguien o algo le había partido la cara al Rata y tenía los labios demasiado hinchados como para besar a nadie. Luego empezó a llover, y yo sentí que me congelaba y quise marcharme, pero el Rata se quedó allí, sin moverse, y yo me quedé también. Siempre hacía lo que él hacía, cuando tenía agallas. Entonces, el Rata me dijo: «Bésame». Y yo le dije: «Pero con los labios así...», y de pronto vislumbré en la oscuridad que la inflamación se había reducido. La lluvia, ya sabéis, esa maldita lluvia helada debió de curarlo, y lo besé, y aunque ninguno de los dos dijo nada creo que los dos estábamos pensando en lo mismo: que algo, la lluvia o algo, siempre acudiría para resolver las cosas, pero hoy estoy aquí para deciros que nos equivocamos; nos equivocamos esa noche encima del granero y volvimos a equivocarnos otra noche junto al Big M, cuando arrastré mi culo empapado hasta el viejo cobertizo y casi me rompo la rótula al chocar contra la rejilla de la furgoneta de Eddie Comedy, aunque al principio no me di cuenta, porque lo único que sentí fue el olor.

Habréis leído en los libros todo ese rollo; es como en las películas, cuando unos tíos entran en una habitación y arrugan la nariz como diciendo: ¡Coño, aquí huele a mierda!, pero os diré una cosa: no todos los muertos huelen igual. Quiero decir que hay algo en un ser humano que puede explicar la diferencia entre un perro o un gato, o una vaca muerta, que todos hemos olido alguna vez, y una persona muerta, que yo no había olido antes, y lo único que pensé fue: ¡Mierda, lo que me faltaba!

Al principio pensé en largarme, sin molestarme siquiera en averiguar lo que había pasado; abrir la puerta del cobertizo, meterme en el coche y volver a Galatia a toda hostia, pero entonces pensé en las huellas dactilares y todo el rollo, y en que alguien podría haberme visto en el Big M, y entonces pensé: Vale, tranqui, tío, como si fuera peor largarse, y eché un vistazo. Al principio no vi a nadie, solo la furgoneta, pero luego reconocí que era la de Eddie Comedy. Galatia no es un pueblo tan pequeño como para saber qué coche tiene todo el mundo, pero yo había estado un par de veces en la parte trasera de la furgoneta de Eddie Comedy, ya me entendéis, y, además, seguía acordándome de Eddie Comedy, porque lo había hecho con él por primera vez y todo ese rollo. La furgoneta de Eddie Comedy, súper guapa, pintada a dos colores, parecía como si hubiera metido el morro en un poste de teléfono. La rejilla tenía un agujero más grande que mi cuerpo, y pensé que había que abrirse de allí al instante.

Juro por Dios que pensé en todo ese rollo, quiero decir que al principio no me acordé del poste de teléfono caído en la carretera 24, al este del pueblo, y ni siquiera se me ocurrió mirar detrás del volante, porque sentía que Eddie Comedy era alguien conocido, no un extraño que se pudre en un cobertizo en mitad de un campo.

Pero nadie puede quedarse mucho rato mirando una rejilla rota, así que al final levanté la vista y lo primero que vi fue que la furgoneta de Eddie Comedy había perdido el parabrisas. No tenía cristal.

Lo segundo que vi fue a Eddie Comedy.

Un cadáver no cambia tanto en tres o cuatro días, o en una semana. Al menos no bajo esa luz. Tenía la cara como... como hinchada, como si tuviera los carrillos llenos de comida o algo así. Estaba hinchada, pero también caída, como si en algún momento hubiese estado más hinchada que cuando yo la vi, y tenía el lado izquierdo manchado, con una especie de porquería oscura y seca en el pelo y el pelo tieso y pegado en la sien. Por lo demás, se parecía bastante a Eddie Comedy. Quiero decir que Eddie Comedy nunca había destacado precisamente por ir bien arreglado y tal, siempre había sido un cerdo. Tenía la boca abierta y los ojos cerrados, y si hubiera oído ronquidos habría creído perfectamente que estaba durmiendo la mona.

Pero entonces vi el agujero. Estaba en el lado izquierdo, justo debajo del ojo, y era como una mancha oscura. Pensé que debería haber sangre alrededor, pero no había sangre, solo una especie de costra negra, aunque tampoco era exactamente una costra. Tenía un tamaño como si alguien le hubiera arrancado un trozo de piel con la uña del dedo meñique; luego le miré el lado derecho de la cara, el pelo cubierto de sangre seca y pegado en la sien, y después miré el asiento del pasajero. Tardé un rato en reconocer lo que había, porque era viscoso y estaba cubierto de mierda y, entonces eché a correr para meterme en el coche, pensando «¡La he cagado!», y volví a pensar «¡La he cagado!» cuando arranqué el coche y doblé la esquina a toda velocidad, y otra vez «¡La he cagado, la he cagado!» al notar que el coche rozaba contra la pared del cobertizo y que se me arrancaba el retrovisor lateral igual que una bala le había arrancado la oreja a Eddie Comedy y había aterrizado sobre el asiento después de atravesarle la cabeza.

Y os diré una cosa, he leído libros y he visto películas. Sabía que lo que tenía que hacer era volver en busca del retrovisor y no dejarlo allí para que alguien lo encontrara, pero lo cierto es que miré a Eddie Comedy y él me miró y que solo tenía una oreja. Yo tenía dos, dos orejas monísimas que mi madre me sujetaba con cinta adhesiva por las noches para que siguieran siendo bonitas y no se separaran de la cabeza, y estaba decidido a conservarlas a toda costa. Pisé el acelerador a fondo y no levanté el pie del pedal hasta que llegué a casa de Wade, pero entonces salí del coche y vi el hueco donde debía estar el retrovisor. Toqué con el dedo el pequeño trozo de metal partido. Había pasado media hora y el agujero aún estaba caliente, como si arrancar el retrovisor hubiese requerido un gran esfuerzo. No es que quemara, pero aparté el dedo bruscamente y me lo metí en la boca, y mientras me lo chupaba se me pasó por la cabeza la idea de que dejar allí ese espejo había sido un gran error. Entonces pensé en el agente Brown, aunque luego resultaría que fue el cartero quien volvió a introducir ese espejo en mi vida, aunque mucho tiempo después, tanto que ya casi me había olvidado por completo, y todo ocurrió de un modo que jamás habría imaginado.

1.13

JUSTIN

Al principio estaba en todas partes. Detrás de mí, a mi lado, delante de mí. Me abría todas las puertas y me encerraba todas las noches en lugar seguro. Me abría las piernas, jugaba conmigo. Nunca había recibido tanto dando tan poco. Su amor era hambriento, voraz. Me comía, aunque yo siempre salía intacto. Su amor era indigente, pero era a mí a quien necesitaba y solo a mí. A veces me asustaba y me sentía como un cordero sacrificado para la ofrenda, degollado y ensartado en el asador; pero normalmente me sentía como algo dorado, como un icono o un altar. Era él, Colin, el que estaba escindido, el que al mismo tiempo veneraba y era venerado. Sus dos mitades se comunicaban a través de mí. No es solo que estuviese en todas partes, es que además estaba... dentro de mí. Era omnipotente, pero... yo me sentía iluminado.

Colin quería comprar la casa de caliza. Yo esperaba a ver si lo conseguiría. Para entonces, ya me había acostumbrado a esperar a Colin; la espera era lo que había caracterizado nuestra relación desde el primer momento, aunque ninguno de los dos empleábamos el término «espera». Colin lo definía casi siempre como «explorar nuestras opciones»; aunque mi expresión favorita era «estar aburrido». Colin exploraba nuestras opciones, asunto: la casa de caliza; hacía llamadas telefónicas, asunto: Rosemary Krebs; comprobaba si allí había una historia, asunto: Galatea; y yo me aburría mientras él hacía estas cosas. Yo me limaba las uñas mientras él hundía los dedos hasta el hueso. Me gastaba a lo loco el dinero que me daba. Me refugiaba en los recuerdos mientras él planeaba nuestra vida futura. Estas últimas frases son de Colin, son opciones que él fue explorando una por una, hasta que al final las desechó todas, porque todas se reducían a lo mismo: yo esperaba y Colin esperaba a ver qué pasaría a continuación.

Así son las cosas. El amor es como una flor. El amor es como una guirnalda de madreselvas blancas, una dulce abundancia de hojas acorazonadas, un manto de perfume vespertino. El amor es como una parra, un zarcillo que se agarra y trepa, algo envolvente, que se abre camino centímetro a centímetro por entre los listones de una espaldera o sobre una fachada de ladrillo. Un desasosiego interno, una tibieza, un llanto externo, un rayo de luz que se niega a ser liberado, que no sabe cómo salir. Una transformación, un brillo, un ocultamiento y, luego, un cambio, una sustitución, un balanceo en el abismo, una pierna arriba, un paso abajo, estancamiento, avance, revolución y, finalmente, vuelta a abarcarlo todo, a trepar, a aferrarse. Sí. Todo ser vivo tiene su primavera, todo tiene su invierno. Ese es el problema: el amor es como una flor, pero no es perenne. Una vez muere, muerto está.

Una semana después de nuestro viaje a Kansas murió Yonah. Colin llamó a Wade para darle la noticia. Cuando colgó el teléfono, le pregunté qué había dicho Wade, y Colin dijo: «Ha dicho, no me sorprende. —Y luego añadió, no tuvo más remedio—: Ya solo queda uno».

Lo había agredido por primera vez. Yo llevaba una pulsera de pinchos —aún me iba el rollo punk— y le di un golpe a traición cuando intentó largarse en mitad de una pelea. Aún conserva la cicatriz, como un pequeño relámpago en la base del occipital. Yo también tengo una cicatriz debajo del ojo: me cortó con el anillo de diamantes que le había regalado su padre; me devolvió la agresión. La tercera vez me corté yo solo. Esperé hasta que se quedó dormido y me hice un corte en la muñeca, en la derecha, claro, la que estaba unida a mi mano tullida; empecé a sangrar y me deslicé sigilosamente hasta nuestra cama, donde él estaba durmiendo, y dejé que la sangre le goteara en la boca abierta hasta que se despertó, ahogándose. Primero escupió y luego vio que era sangre; entonces gritó y finalmente se quedó sentado como paralizado, su cuerpo y el mío envueltos en una neblina roja. «No tragues», le dije. «Practicas una buena higiene bucal, ¿verdad?» Lo seguí mientras avanzaba tambaleándose hacia el cuarto de baño. «Camina como un hombre», le provoqué. «¡Ni que te hubiera disparado!» Colin abrió el armario, los cajones, lo tiró todo por el suelo. «¿Qué buscas? ¿Elixir? ¿Alcohol? ¿Quieres que te traiga un poco de lejía?» Al final hizo gárgaras con agua oxigenada porque no encontró otra cosa. Cuando salió de la ducha estaba más colorado que cuando entró, pero aun así, temblaba de arriba abajo, y supo cuál era la apuesta: por mí y, mientras pudiera tenerme, por él.

Parece que nos hemos perdido el principio de algo, me decía Colin todos los días, después de que Yonah muriera. Un camionero descubrió anoche una furgoneta accidentada, dijo Colin, al parecer el mismo vehículo que se estrelló contra el poste de teléfono que nos había enseñado Wade, solo que la furgoneta estaba aparcada en un cobertizo a cuarenta y cinco kilómetros del poste. Restos de pintura, dijo Colin, respondiendo a una pregunta que yo no había formulado, por eso supieron que era la misma furgoneta. Y continuó tras una pausa: Dentro de la furgoneta había un cadáver. Otra pausa y luego: Lo extraño es que el hombre no murió en el accidente. Alguien le voló los sesos. Otra pausa, en voz más baja: El tío tenía un nombre gracioso, ¿cómo era?, Carmody, no, Carmody no, Comedy, sí, eso es, Comedy. Un nombre gracioso, ¿verdad? Esta vez Colin no volvió a hablar, y al cabo de un rato yo dije: Creo que tengo fiebre, y Colin respondió: Vete a la mierda, Justin. Quieres vivir en el pasado, pues muy bien, por mí como si te revuelcas en él. ¡Vete a la mierda!

Zach era amigo de Colin. Había hecho una promesa: sobrevivir a su gato. Eso es lo que Colin me había contado: cuando Zach supo que era seropositivo, se fue a casa y la gata le saltó al regazo. Y pensó:

¡Dios mío!, este gato va a vivir más que yo. Y se dijo que todo el mundo se compraba un gato sabiendo que un buen día el gato se moriría y que se sentiría triste durante un tiempo, y luego se compraba otro gato o un pero o cualquier cosa, un periquito, o un lagarto. Pero el gato de Zach tenía ocho años, y por lo tanto, la esperanza de vida del animal era mayor que la suya. Entonces juró que el gato se iría a la tumba antes que él. Durante cinco años no pasó nada. Luego, Zach empezó a enfermar. Después se puso más enfermo. Y al final se puso muy enfermo. Para entonces la gata ya era vieja, no estaba tan ágil como antes, pero aún tenía buena salud. Zach dejó de darle de comer, pero entre los amigos y el asistente social siempre pasaba alguien por allí a diario y alimentaba a la gata. Zach intentó matarla en una ocasión, pero la gata fue más rápida y logró subirse a una estantería. Así pasaron varios años. Nadie estaba seguro de cómo lo conseguía Zach, a qué se aferraba. Pero había llamado la noche anterior. Y había dicho: Un año en un gato equivale a cinco en un hombre. El sida es así, con la diferencia de que un año para un seropositivo equivale a diez o veinte, o treinta, en una persona sana. Y luego dijo: Se ha muerto, la muy puta. Y él también había muerto cuando llegamos a su casa esa mañana.

Esta gente está como un cencerro, dijo Colin. La propietaria de la casa de caliza había manifestado en su testamento la voluntad de que ningún miembro de la familia Krebs pudiera comprar la casa o las tierras, pero cuando le pregunté al agente por qué, lo único que pudo decirme fue que Rosemary, supongo que se refería a Rosemary Krebs, que Rosemary y Bea no eran precisamente buenas amigas. Y esa Krebs, Rosemary, que al parecer es propietaria de casi todo lo que hay aquí, en lo que se conoce como el condado de Cadavera, había logrado transferir la finca de Bea a la mayor agencia inmobiliaria de San Luis, es decir, la empresa que vendió por cuatro perras los terrenos donde se construyó el dichoso puente Arch, a más de setecientos kilómetros de aquí. No es precisamente la máxima prioridad, ya me entiendes. Y para colmo, esa bruja ha apelado a todas las instancias habidas y por haber para que califiquen el lugar como monumento histórico y que no pueda venderse. Parece que hay un túmulo funerario en algún lugar de la finca, un agujero en el suelo del tamaño de un vestidor que contiene un esqueleto, un esqueleto y unos fragmentos de cerámica antigua, sin esmaltar siquiera, y el caso es que ahora nadie tiene ni puta idea de dónde está el esqueleto. Bueno, y ya que preguntas, Señor Curiosidad, dijo Colin, no, no ha habido movimientos en el frente Eddie Comedy. El agente Brown no ha descubierto ninguna pista, según Wade. Colin calló. Me ha preguntado por ti. ¿El agente Brown?, pregunté. No, dijo Colin; Wade. ¿Y qué le dijiste?, pregunté. Le dije que estabas bien, dijo Colin. Le dije que seguías igual.

Les das la espalda, pero eso es lo que les permite entrar en ti. Ya sabéis lo que quiero decir, ¿verdad, chicos?... y también muchas de las chicas, seguro que vosotras también lo entendéis. Te das la vuelta, apartas la cara, los ojos, la boca, la nariz, incluso los oídos, los oídos apuntan hacia delante, y cuando te tumbas boca abajo se unen a todos los demás sentidos para «rechazar al hombre que está a punto de follarte»; y no creáis que él no lo sabe. Pero fingirá y dirá: «Es una muestra de confianza por tu parte que lo hagamos así», y tal y cual, eso es lo que dirá cuando te hayas dado la vuelta, tras un momento de silencio, mientras contempla tu cogote sin rostro, la espalda sin pezones, mientras desliza un dedo por la abertura de las nalgas, sintiendo, probando, dirá: «Podría hacerte cualquier cosa, pero ¿confías en mí, verdad?», siempre la misma pregunta en tono cantarín al final del discurso, siempre la petición, por favor, afírmame. Y tú suspiras, agachas la cabeza, levantas un poco el culo, separas las piernas: «esa» boca no habla y, frente a su silencio, también él guarda silencio, ocupado como está, y su pregunta sin responder queda suspendida en el aire. A veces acerca tu cabeza a la suya: para eso tiene que tirar de ti, del pelo, si es que tienes, o de una oreja, o del cuello, echarte la cabeza hacia atrás hasta que una de tus mejillas entra en contacto con la suya, y entonces intenta comprobar adónde estás mirando antes de besarte, esa maniobra para la que tiene que retorcer el cuello de un modo que recuerda a la mantis religiosa devorando al macho. Casi siempre su lengua busca tu oído; una especie de incomprensible sonido de succión ocupa el lugar del lenguaje entre vosotros y, lejos, muy lejos, otro ojo ciego busca algo que sabe que está ahí, pero que no puede ver ni tocar. La primera vez, cuando Colin terminó de follarme –la primera vez que lo hicimos, casi dos años después de conocernos, porque Colin quiso asegurarse de que yo era legal–, se levantó de la cama para ir al baño en busca de una toalla, y yo lo observé, Colin, memoricé la forma de la espalda y el culo de Colin, los muslos y las pantorrillas, el balanceo de los brazos, Colin, la redondez del cráneo, Colin, Colin, Colin, lo observé porque quería saber lo que se ocultaría bajo la ropa cuando finalmente me abandonara.

Pero me sorprendió. Esperó hasta que a mí se me agotó la paciencia, como hace a veces.

Fue la tarde del funeral de Zach.

Colin dijo:

–He cerrado el trato de la casa esta mañana. Es nuestra.
–Es «tuya». Que la disfrutes con salud.
–Justin…
De pronto sentí que no podía soportarlo.
–Se acabó, Colin, se acabó. Escúchame bien. Solo hay un modo de que te libres del sida, y es librándote de mí.
–Justin…
Entonces lo agarré con la mano insensible y lo atraje hacia mí. Me habría gustado razonar con él, pero las cosas nunca funcionaron así entre nosotros: la chabacana escena que representamos requería primero gritos, luego silencio, luego lágrimas, hasta que le dije al oído:
–Considero que mi misión en esta vida es derribar todos los muros que tú construyas, ya sea con palabras, con distancia o con dinero. Mientras esté contigo, no olvidarás de qué estás huyendo.
–Justin…
–Ese no es mi nombre.
Entonces fue Colin quien me agarró a mí, con las dos manos; casi me levanta del suelo tirándome de la pechera de la camisa.
–¿Cuál es tu nombre, entonces?
Dejé que mi silencio respondiera, pero no dijo nada. Mi nombre es nada.

1.14

WADE

Divine estaba dormido.
Dormía desnudo, esa noche y todas las noches que pasaba conmigo. Siempre lo había visto dormir desnudo, salvo la primera vez, en las escaleras de la nueva biblioteca. Dormía desnudo en mi habitación con la calefacción encendida en invierno y el aire acondicionado apagado en verano, para no tener que meterse dentro de las sábanas, porque, incluso cuando dormía, Divine organizaba su vida sobre la base de que alguien lo vigilaba. Si esto es lo que algunos entienden por vanidad, en el caso de Divine era vanidad condicionada, pues siempre había estado expuesto a la contemplación de los demás: un hermoso bebé que se convirtió primero en un niño guapo y luego en un adolescente cautivador, cuando yo lo conocí. Una vez me contó que, cuando tenían visita, sus padres no le decían: ¿Por qué no le sirves un té helado al reverendo Abraham? Le decían: ¿Por qué

no le cantas al reverendo «Swing Low»? O ¿por qué no bailas como Michael Jackson? Divine debutó primero en la sala de estar de su casa y luego en el escenario del instituto, en el equipo de atletismo, en el Big M y en mi dormitorio: dormía desnudo, encima de las sábanas y boca abajo, con la espalda arqueada y el culo ligeramente levantado. Hundía la cara entre dos abultados montones de almohada, y lo único que quedaba oculto bajo el cuerpo era el pene, y también las manos, debajo de la almohada, y cuando le pregunté por qué escondía las manos y el pene, frunció el ceño y dijo: «A Dios no le gusta ver a los vagos y a los desocupados», y se tapó la cabeza con la almohada.

Era por la mañana. La noche antes, Colin Nieman me había llamado para decirme que había logrado superar los obstáculos puestos por Rosemary Krebs y que había comprado la casa de caliza, que se trasladaría en pocos días.

Apoyé una mano en el hombro de Divine. Su piel cobriza resultaba suave y cálida, ligeramente húmeda, como si una tubería de agua caliente lo recorriese por dentro, y la dejé descansar allí un momento, sacudiéndolo luego con suavidad.

—No estoy de servicio —bramó Divine, tan deprisa que comprendí que ya llevaba un rato despierto—. Lárgate.

—Tengo que dibujarte antes de que se estropee la luz —dije.

—Es el sol, no un trozo de carne. No se pondrá malo.

—Hace un día espléndido. Ni siquiera hace falta que te vistas. Solo ven conmigo al estudio. Puedes volver a dormirte allí si quieres.

—¿Y por qué no puedo volver a dormirme aquí?

—Ya lo sabes. Tengo que dibujarte en tu habitación.

—¿«Mi» habitación? ¿Cómo voy a llamarla mi habitación si la tienes cerrada con llave y no me dejas entrar?

—Divine...

—Venga, Wade, déjame en paz por una puta vez en tu vida. Casi no he dormido esta noche.

—¿Y quién tiene la culpa de eso?

Divine tenía los ojos cerrados, pero en la ceja arrugada y en los labios se apreciaba el esfuerzo que hacía por apretarlos.

—Así de pronto yo diría que la tienes tú. A menos que haya sido otro quien me folló anoche.

—Colin vuelve el sábado. Viene para quedarse.

Los ojos de Divine se abrieron como activados por un resorte.

—¿Vuelven de verdad? ¿Se mudan aquí?

—Solo Colin. Just... Justin no viene.

Una sonrisa se dibujó despacio en el rostro de Divine y allí permaneció hasta que le llegó de oreja a oreja.

—¡Cojonudo!

—Venga, levántate. Vamos.

—Me levanto y vamos —dijo Divine. Y se sentó, se levantó, hizo varias flexiones, estiró los brazos hasta el techo y hundió los dedos de los pies en el suelo de madera. Mantuvo la postura hasta que dijo—: ¿Seguro que no quieres follarme? Podría ser tu última oportunidad.

Me di la vuelta y eché a andar hacia el estudio. Me alejé de él no solo porque no estaba seguro de no querer follármelo, y no solo porque sabía que podría ser mi última oportunidad, sino también porque Colin Nieman había dicho que Justin Time no vendría a Galatea. Al cabo de un momento oí que Divine me seguía, sus pisadas produjeron un rápido *staccato* cuando me adelantó, desnudo, abrió la puerta y salió bailando bajo la fina llovizna de la mañana.

—¡Mierda! —gritó, deteniéndose, dándose la vuelta, mirándome fijamente—. ¡Dijiste que hacía buen día...! — Entonces se puso a dar saltos y todos los músculos de su cuerpo se revelaron como cuerdas tensas bajo la piel erizada por el frío y tachoneada por las gotas de agua, mientras la resbaladiza gravilla asomaba bajo sus pies cada vez que saltaba, pero antes de que pudiera contestarle, un breve y agudo toque de sirena rasgó el aire de la mañana.

Divine dejó de dar brincos y se volvió hacia el patio. Tenía la boca abierta, mas no salió de ella ningún sonido.

Más tarde me dijo que el asunto había empezado para él dos semanas antes, cuando se encontró con el cadáver de Eddie Comedy en el cobertizo junto al Big M., aunque para mí no empezó hasta esa mañana, cuando entre la lluvia y la neblina vislumbré un par de escobillas que oscilaban sobre el opaco parabrisas del coche patrulla del agente Brown. El agente Brown, sentado, enmarcado por el esqueleto vacío de la casa de mis padres, en el centro del patio trasero. No había huellas sobre la hierba plateada y húmeda, por lo que supe que llevaba allí un buen rato, seguramente desde la madrugada, y nos estaba esperando. El hecho de que esperara en la puerta de atrás también significaba algo, pero no se me ocurrió pensar en eso hasta más tarde.

La escasa luz del sol se reflejaba en el parabrisas, haciendo invisible el interior del vehículo, pero, mientras lo mirábamos, la puerta se abrió lentamente y apareció la cabeza calva del agente Brown, seguida por una mano en la que sostenía el sombrero que se caló antes de ponerse en pie y echar a andar hacia nosotros, con una mano apoyada en la culata de la pistola y la otra en su voluminosa barriga.

Divine se quedó inmóvil sobre la gravilla, desnudo, temblando ligeramente. Tenía la piel tan pulida que la lluvia se posaba sobre ella como si fuera un coche recién encerado, formando gotas perfectamente redondas y separadas, y por un momento lamenté no tener a mano un trozo de papel y un carboncillo, para dibujarlo allí mismo, con el cuerpo salpicado de gotas de agua, aunque luego comprendí que no podría dibujarlo bajo la lluvia.

Cuando el agente Brown se hubo acercado lo suficiente como para que me oyera sin necesidad de gritar, dije:

—Buenos días, agente.

Avanzó unos pasos más antes de responder.

—Me llamo Eustace y soy el sheriff, y te agradecería, Wade, que me mostraras el respeto que mi cargo merece.

—Buenos días, sheriff Brown —dijo entonces Divine, y me sorprendió su tono adulador. Lo miré y vi que seguía temblando, aunque no de frío. Comprendí que estaba aterrorizado.

—Buenos días, Reggie.

Al ver que Divine no decía nada supe que algo pasaba, pues Divine no permitía que nadie lo llamase por el nombre que sus padres le habían dado.

—Hace un poco de frío para tomar el sol, ¿no te parece, Reggie? Además está un poco nublado. Pero ¡qué digo, la gente como tú no...! El ala del sombrero del agente Brown se inclinaba exageradamente a derecha e izquierda. No veo por aquí ninguna piscina climatizada, así que supongo que no pensabas bañarte en cueros. —Hizo una pausa y añadió—: ¿Qué pasa, Reggie? ¿Dónde has dejado la ropa?

Divine me señaló con su temblorosa cabeza.

—Quería dibujarme.

—¿Dibujarte?

—Más vale que vayamos al grano, Eustace, todos tenemos cosas que hacer.

—¿Y así es como se viste Reggie para trabajar? —El agente Brown señaló con la cabeza primero hacia Divine, luego hacia mí; después, volviéndose de nuevo a Divine, preguntó—: ¿No estarías por casualidad... trabajando en el Big M hace unas tres semanas, verdad?

—Nunca voy al Big M —dijo Divine—. ¿Para qué iba a ir yo allí?

—Creo que fue un domingo por la noche —dijo el agente Brown, y luego dijo una fecha.

—Eustace —dije—. Divine estuvo aquí esa noche. Esa noche tuvimos invitados, por eso lo recuerdo. Webie Greeving y dos hombres de fuera del pueblo.

Por primera vez desde que salimos de la casa, Divine se tapó los genitales con las manos. La lluvia corría por su cuerpo justo hasta ese punto y allí se filtraba entre sus dedos; tuve la clara impresión de que el líquido derramado era sumamente precioso, y que estaba perdiéndose para siempre.

—Webbie estuvo aquí el sábado, no el domingo —dijo entonces el agente Brown—; y sus invitados se marcharon el domingo a las dos y media. Yo me refiero concretamente al domingo por la mañana. Big M, aparcamiento noroeste. Seguro que no…

—¡Has encontrado el espejo! —gritó Divine—. Solo fui a comprar comida y a echar gasolina, agente, Wade necesitaba comprar algo en la tienda de pintura de Bigger Hill y, yo… ¡mierda!, ¡maldita sea!, ¡ese puto espejo!

—Reggie, te agradecería que no blasfemes y te recuerdo que mi cargo no es agente, sino sheriff, soy el sheriff Brown, y te agradecería que…

—¿A qué coño viene todo esto, Eustace?

—Y te agradecería, Wade, que te abstengas de interferir en la labor policial, lo cual, debo recordarte, es un delito castigado por la ley. Vamos a ver, Reggie —dijo el agente Brown, moviendo rápidamente la cara, cada vez más roja y sacudiendo con la mano el agua acumulada en el ala de su sombrero—, ¿de qué espejo hablas?

Divine parecía confundido.

—¿Es que no lo has encontrado? Pensé que sabías que estuve allí, porque el retrovisor lateral…

—Ya basta de cháchara, Reggie —le interrumpió el agente Brown. Se estiró, revelando claramente su estatura, se aclaró la garganta y, en su mejor representación de acto oficial anunció—: Reginald Packman, estoy aquí para llevarlo bajo custodia policial al efecto de ser interrogado en relación con el asesinato de Eddie Comedy. No está usted detenido, repito, no está usted detenido, pero tengo que hacerle algunas preguntas. Tiene cinco minutos para entrar y cubrir su desnudez. Luego iremos a la comisaría.

Divine miró un momento al agente Brown y luego volvió hacia mí su rostro congelado por el pánico. Tenía la boca abierta, implorando salvación, pero también, y con idéntica intensidad, invitando a la traición.

—¿Wade?

—Vístete —le dije. Me habría gustado decirle que me ocuparía de todo, pero no sabía por dónde empezar. No sabía de qué tenía que ocuparme. Hay gente capaz de hacer esta promesa a ciegas, pero yo nunca he sido así. Sentí que me encogía, que me alejaba de la escena que estaba presenciando.

—¿Wade? —repitió Divine. La palabra se alejó de mí flotando, como si yo no estuviera allí.

—Vístete —dijo el agente Brown. Te quedan cuatro minutos y medio.

Entonces me quedé a solas con el agente Brown. No hablamos.

No nos miramos. El sol aún estaba bajo, a espaldas del policía; me quedé mirando la densa nube gris que aquel teñía de amarillo y naranja, de ocre crepuscular, y me pareció que el agente Brown estaba en otra parte. Pasó un minuto, dos minutos, tres minutos, cuatro. Cinco.

El agente Brown carraspeó. No estaba seguro de si aquello era el preludio a una conversación o sencillamente que tenía una flema. Escupió y se instaló de nuevo en su silencio.

—Pasaron otros cinco minutos.

El agente Brown volvió a carraspear.

—¿Eh, Wade?

Aparté la vista del sol para mirarlo. El color grabado en mi retina pintó su rostro de amarillo hepático.

—¿Quieres ir a ver por qué tarda tanto?

Una vez, cuando íbamos juntos al instituto, yo pinté una cara sonriente en el asiento del agente Brown. El niño Eustace, regordete y lleno de granos, se sentó sin darse cuenta, y se pasó el resto del día andando por ahí no con una, sino con dos muecas aleladas, una delante y otra detrás. Aunque nunca pudo demostrar que había sido yo, se mostró huraño conmigo desde entonces, pero sin la acobardada presencia de Divine su bravuconería se esfumó, y pasó a ser tan solo un policía gordo con debilidad por los donuts.

—¿Eh, Wade?

—Estás en tu casa, Eustace. Al fin y al cabo eres el sheriff.

Lo dejé allí y me marché al estudio. Me encontró, quince minutos más tarde, en la habitación de Divine. Estaba sudoroso y sin aliento, y llevaba el sombrero torcido.

—¡Se ha ido! —exclamó—. ¡Se ha escapado!

—Pareces sorprendido.

—Escucha, Wade. Doce personas han visto a ese chico rondando por el cobertizo donde encontraron a Eddie Comedy. No digo que tenga algo que ver con ello, pero en todo caso, puede saber algo importante. Él...

Se le quebró la voz cuando su mirada, que había estado recorriendo las paredes de la habitación, finalmente reconoció lo que había en ellas.

—¿Es... Divine?

En otro tiempo, la habitación en la que nos encontrábamos había sido mi dormitorio. Durante años yo había pintado sus paredes blancas con escenas imaginarias de huida y de venganza, de liberación con respecto a mis padres, a Galatea y a todo Kansas. Treinta años más tarde esa habitación se había convertido en un monumento a Divine. Estaba completamente cubierta de dibujos de él: había dibujos en el techo, en el suelo y en las cuatro paredes. Día tras día, había hecho posar a Divine desnudo en el centro de aquella habitación, y había dibujado hasta el último trozo de su cuerpo que no quedaba oculto por la luz del sol. Había dibujado sus manos, había dibujado un solo dedo. Había dibujado su cuerpo sin rostro, su rostro sin cuerpo. Lo había dibujado todo de él. Una vez dibujé solo su sombra, y dejé el cuerpo fuera del cuadro. Ahora, cuatro días antes de que Colin Nieman regresara a Galatea, había más de doscientos dibujos en esa habitación; solo queda espacio para uno más, y era el que pensaba dibujar esa mañana cuando desperté a Divine; ese era el espacio que me proponía llenar.

De pronto, se me ocurre que mis dibujos de Divine guardan un siniestro parecido con la lista que Colin y Justin habían elaborado. Ofrezco esta información como dato ilustrativo, aunque no estoy seguro de qué es lo que ilustra, si ilustra algo sobre mí, o sobre Divine, o sobre Colin y Justin. Podría parecer que eso me molesta, pero lo cierto es que no. Hay personas —Colin Nieman era una de ellas, y Divine también— que creen en el significado de las cosas y en la importancia del significado, y hay otras, gente como yo, gente como Justin, que no ven en las cosas un significado intrínseco sino solo el significado que los demás les atribuyen. Y hay un tercer tipo de personas —Rosemary Krebs era una de ellas, como lo era también la persona que orquestó el asesinato de Eddie Comedy— a las que no les interesa el origen del significado, de la información, sino el modo en que esta se usa o puede usarse. Webbie Greeving pertenecía a esta tercera categoría, aunque jamás lo admitiría.

—¿Eh, Wade?

Tenía en la mano una hoja de papel en blanco. Antes de responder al agente Brown, la pegué en el hueco que quedaba en la pared. Observé la lluvia entre los pequeños trozos de ventana que asomaban bajo mis dibujos de Divine y, sin apartar la vista de allí, dije:

—¿Dónde se refugiaron los animales cuando cayó el diluvio?

—¿Eh, Wade?

—La lluvia desciende, las aguas suben, ¿te acuerdas de esa canción, Eustace? ¿Adónde fueron los animales?

—Se metieron en el arca y...

—¿En qué arca?

—En la de Noé...

La voz del agente Brown se quebró al comprender a qué me refería. La habitación estaba en silencio, salvo por el leve tamborileo de la lluvia en el exterior. Escuché la llovizna, intenté sentirla y ver qué aspecto tenía al salir de las nubes, al caer por el cielo y golpear contra el suelo para mezclarse con la lluvia caída anteriormente, y entonces una leve brisa entró por la ventana agitando los dibujos de Divine, y fue este sonido el que me incitó a hablar. Y dije:

—Creo que sabes dónde encontrar lo que buscas, Eustace —pero cuando me di la vuelta para mirarlo vi que ya se había marchado.

1.15

JUSTIN

Habían muerto quinientas personas y, como respuesta a ello, Colin había comprado una mansión de caliza situada a menos de setenta y cinco kilómetros del centro exacto del país, lo que equivale a decir en el punto más alejado del epicentro de la plaga del sida sin necesidad de salir del país. Dijo que se marchaba, que se iba a Kansas, conmigo o sin mí.

Quinientos uno si contamos a un hombre llamado Eddie Comedy, a quien yo no contaba, pero Colin sí. Yo no contaba a Eddie Comedy, no porque no hubiese muerto de sida, sino porque no tenía nada que ver con el hecho de que yo me fuera o me quedara, mientras que Colin lo contaba porque sí tenía que ver con él. Tenía algo que ver con sus ganas de marcharse. Quiero decir que, Eddie Comedy, según dijo Colin, iba a escribir la nueva novela de Colin, y cuando yo le dije que eso iba a ser un poco difícil, porque Eddie Comedy estaba muerto, Colin dijo que «estaba empleando una metáfora», y yo intenté recordar la expresión que Colin usó para decir esto, que «estaba empleando una metáfora», intenté recordar qué hubo en la expresión de Colin que a mí me asustó hasta el punto de obligarme a salir inmediatamente de la casa.

Mientras avanzaba hacia el norte por la Séptima avenida, intenté recordar los grises e inexpresivos ojos de Colin, la luminosidad de su piel y la fina línea horizontal que dibujó su labio superior al pronunciar las palabras «estaba empleando una metáfora». Caminaba por la acera derecha de la calle, entre la calle Doce y la calle Trece; sin proponérmelo, me había encaminado hacia San Vicente, pero esta vez no había entrado, porque todo el mundo estaba muerto, por eso pasé de largo junto a la puerta de la capilla en la calle Doce, la entrada de urgencias en la Séptima avenida y la entrada principal en la calle Trece, y, al cruzar esta última calle, comprendí que habría cogido el metro en la Catorce para irme lo más al norte posible de no ser porque de pronto descubrí lo que había en la expresión de Colin que tanto me había inquietado cuando dijo que «estaba empleando una metáfora».

Y se me ocurrió también, mientras cruzaba la calle Trece, que el norte era la única dirección que Colin jamás había tenido en cuenta. El sur, sí; el este y el oeste, de acuerdo; pero el norte no era una opción. Era un cálido día de otoño, pero se me puso la carne de gallina al pensar en Toronto, Anchorage, Vladivostok, y comprendí que lo que tanto me había inquietado en la expresión de Colin cuando dijo que «estaba empleando una metáfora fue precisamente la ausencia total de expresión. Colin se había mostrado irritado y decidido cuando dijo que se marchaba a Kansas, conmigo o sin mí, y una encendida expresión de culpa había velado su rostro cuando dijo que Eddie Comedy iba a escribirle su nueva novela, pero cuando dijo que «estaba empleando una metáfora» su rostro se transformó en una máscara vacía, y entonces comprendí que Colin se iba a Kansas, no para escribir una novela sobre Eddie Comedy y lo que quiera que fuese que lo había matado, y tampoco para alejarse de la epidemia de sida. Colin se iba a Kansas para alejarse de mí. La metáfora que estaba usando Colin era la muerte de Eddie Comedy, y lo que esa metáfora representaba, la cosa elidida, era yo.

Decidí coger el metro de todos modos. Llegaría solo hasta el Bronx y luego daría la vuelta. Lo cierto es que no había razón alguna para coger el metro, a menos que decidiese bajarme en algún punto del trayecto y buscar otras vías de escape, pero no tenía intención de hacerlo, al menos no hasta que hubiese regresado al punto de partida.

Entonces vi a lo lejos a un hombre gordo y blanco que entraba en el metro en la estación situada en la esquina de la calle Catorce y la Séptima avenida, y por alguna razón, inconscientemente, esperé hasta verlo aparecer de nuevo, pues en esa esquina de la calle no hay entrada al metro: solo hay salida. Pero el hombre no salía y, al acercarme más al cruce, vi que otras personas bajaban por las mismas escaleras, pero ninguna volvía a salir. Miré los otros tres accesos: vi ríos de gente que entraba precipitadamente en el metro, gordos y delgados, jóvenes y viejos, negros y blancos, hombres y mujeres, sanos y enfermos: todos bajaban con decisión aquellas escaleras y desaparecían, uno tras otro, sin que ninguno de ellos volviera a aparecer. No quiero decir que la gente a la que veía bajar las escaleras no volviera a subirlas, lo que digo es que nadie –ni uno solo– regresó, y supe que si yo bajaba aquellas escaleras tampoco regresaría.

¿Qué es lo que había dicho Divine? Siempre van de dos en dos.

Cuando llegué a casa, tiré al suelo los periódicos que había sobre el escritorio de Colin y lo obligué a follarme allí mismo, en el lugar donde escribía, o quizá debería decir, donde no escribía su segunda novela; cuando empezó a correrse lo aparté de un empujón y le dije:

No me dejarás nunca. Puede que yo te deje algún día, pero tú no me dejarás nunca. Se despatarró en la silla: un Colin absolutamente atónito, con el pene aún erecto, cubierto por un condón negro y manchado con mi mierda y mi sangre; y cabría pensar que en su rostro se reflejaría cómo le afectaba todo aquello, pero no. Se mostró tan inexpresivo como cuando dijo que «estaba empleando una metáfora», y de pronto me asaltó el temor de que Colin me convirtiera en un mentiroso. Tengo que hacer las maletas, dije entonces. Si nos vamos este fin de semana, más vale que vaya empezando.

1.16

DIVINE

Debo deciros algo: nunca he conocido en Galatea a nadie que hubiese oído hablar del arca de Noah y mucho menos que supiera lo que es. Me parece que ya ni siquiera se puede confiar en que los negros guarden sus secretos, y no me vengáis con historias sobre la vieja Beatrice. La muy zorra estaba tan cascada cuando apareció por aquí que casi no podía subir las escaleras de la casa que le había comprado a Donald Deacon, de manera que no me vengáis con el rollo de que daba paseos de quince kilómetros por el campo. La gente dice que la única razón que tenía Donald Deacon para vender la casa a una pareja de blancos era pagar las deudas que contrajo su hermano cuando se construyó una barca del tamaño de Texas en mitad de un prado de vacas en Kansas. La gente dice que si no hubieran sido Bea y Hank habría sido Rosemary Krebs, y teniendo en cuenta todo esto a la mayoría le pareció bien que la vieja aprovechase la oportunidad de hacerse con un artículo insólito.

Yo creo que fue Webbie. Quiero decir que fue ella quien contó la historia de Noah Deacon y el arca en la que derrochó su vida entera y el dinero que había ganado en el negocio de la construcción. Hay gente que tiene la necesidad de contar historias, y Webbie Greeving es de esa gente. Webbie se lo contó a Wade y Wade se lo contó al agente Brown, ese hijo de puta, y yo fui a dar con el culo en la cárcel. Aunque debo decir que el agente Brown no se sorprendió al encontrarme en el arca. Lo cierto es que, al parecer, había habido bastante movimiento en el arca desde la última vez que estuve allí; encontré condones, latas de cerveza y mierda por todas partes, hasta latas de comida y cenizas de las hogueras que habían encendido para calentarlas. Bueno, yo habría hecho lo mismo, menos lo de la comida. No creo que sea precisamente una buena idea encender fuego en el interior de un gran cajón de madera seca, pero supongo que comiendo se combate el puto frío.

Preguntas. Dijo que me llevaba para hacerme unas preguntas. Los negros se conocen muy bien este rollo. ¿Yo qué coño sabía sobre Eddie Comedy, aparte de que tenía el pelo del pubis tan negro y rizado como el mío y de que lo que asomaba entre aquella mata de pelo era una polla ridícula? Eso y que el agujero de salida de la bala era bastante más grande que el de entrada. ¿Es necesario que me metan en la cárcel para preguntarme eso?

Pues el agente Brown me metió en la cárcel, y allí me dejó. Una puta jaula de hierro en un puto sótano, y os diré una cosa: el fluorescente no es la iluminación más adecuada para mi cutis. No había ni una mísera ventana para saber si era de día o de noche, solo un camastro con un colchón mugriento más fino que la manta que lo cubría, y un váter de esos sin asiento, y nada que comer. Ni siquiera me dejaron hacer una puta llamada de teléfono.

—No estás detenido —fue lo que dijo el agente Brown—. Si no estás detenido no estás autorizado a llamar por teléfono. Además —añadió, y estoy seguro de que lo hizo para joder—, ¿a quién piensas llamar? ¿A los «cazafantasmas»?

—¿Que a quién pienso llamar? Espera y verás, agente Brown; pasas tanto tiempo con los negros que empiezas a hablar como ellos.

Eso le picó, pero luego me arrepentí de haberlo dicho, porque se puso de muy mala hostia y me dejó encerrado allí abajo. No podía hacer nada más que sentarme y comerme el tarro, porque no había manera de apoyar mi hermoso culo en aquel puto váter sin asiento y lleno de meadas. No sabía que en la nueva prisión de Rosemary Krebs hubiese tanto movimiento, pero a juzgar por el estado del váter había un trasiego continuo de prisioneros, todos ellos con la misma puntería que una vieja ciega que sale a cazar cuervos a medianoche. ¡Qué difícil era acertar en el puto agujero!

Cuando oí el tintineo de las llaves en la cerradura de la puerta que había al final del pasillo —las paredes de la celda eran de hormigón, pero delante había barrotes, de manera que podías ver lo que tenías enfrente—, supuse que era el agente Brown que volvía para molestarme con más preguntas estúpidas. Pero antes de que pudiera ver nada se me hizo la boca agua, porque percibí un delicioso olorcillo a jamón recién cocido.

—¿De verdad eres tú, Cora Johnson, o estoy alucinando?

En ese momento vislumbré su figura. Creo que tenía unos treinta y siete años, uno o dos más que Webbie, pero podría pasar por cincuenta. Mi madre siempre decía que eso es lo que hacen las preocupaciones: llenarte la cara de arrugas y el pelo de canas mucho antes de tiempo, pero supongo que Cora tenía motivos para preocuparse, por ser madre soltera y tener que criar a un hijo que se pasaba la vida entrando y saliendo del hospital a cuenta del asma, y además llevando un bar ella sola... aunque supongo que Rosa estaba en el ajo. Siempre me olvidaba de Rosa.

Cora llevaba una cesta de tamaño suficiente para alimentar a una familia de cinco y me miró un momento antes de dejarla en el suelo e incorporarse. Parecía un poco tensa; no es que le doliera la espalda sino que se comportaba con mucho formalismo, aunque supongo que eso le pasa a todo el mundo cuando va a ver a alguien que está en la cárcel.

—¿En qué lío te has metido ahora, mi niño? —dijo al fin.

—No he hecho nada, Cora. Nada de nada.

—El agente Brown —continuó Cora, carraspeando—, el sheriff Brown pensaba que te vendría bien un cambio de aires, ¿es eso lo que me estás diciendo?

Me quedé un rato mirándola y ella bajó la vista, pero antes torció la mirada hacia la izquierda, y comprendí que el agente Brown estaba allí, al final del pasillo. Entonces dije en voz bien alta:

—¿Desde cuándo el agente Brown necesita una buena excusa para encerrar a un negro?

—No intentes jugar conmigo, Reginald Packman. Ese tío no es amigo mío. —Cora volvió a carraspear y luego continuó en tono normal—: No es amigo mío, pero nunca he tenido noticia de que se metiera con los negros. Sin razón. —Al decir esto sonrió, esbozó una leve sonrisa con la comisura derecha de la boca, y yo se la devolví.

—Me llamo Divine —le dije.

Cora frunció el ceño, pero luego recuperó la sonrisa.

—Sí, ya lo sé —dijo, y debo decir que su risa sonó muy extraña al retumbar en aquel sótano de cemento vacío—. Divine. Lo había olvidado, Divine.

—¿Es para mí lo que hay en esa cesta? ¿O es para algún huérfano al que yo no conozco?

—Tú eres casi huérfano —dijo Cora—. ¡Ay!, lo siento, Reg... Divine. No debería haber dicho eso. —No respondí. Al cabo de un minuto, Cora dijo en voz alta—: Bueno, técnicamente se supone que debo incordiarte un poco, conseguir que respondas algunas preguntas antes de darte lo que hay en la cesta, pero... —Se encogió de hombros, sacó una silla plegable y se dejó caer sobre ella como hace la gente que se pasa de pie doce horas al día. Abrió la cesta de un manotazo y después de rebuscar un buen rato, sacó una loncha de jamón, de jamón rosado, tostado y blanco, con una deliciosa corteza—. El agente Brown dice que no puedes usar cuchillo y tenedor, lo siento. Ni siquiera platos. No puede arriesgarse a que el prisionero se autolesione.

—Tú pásame el jamón, Cora Johnson. No necesito cuchillo y tenedor para comerme esa mierda.

—Cuidado con lo que dices, chico —dijo Cora. Había empezado a pasarme el jamón, pero se detuvo, sosteniéndolo fuera de mi alcance.

Le sonreí y dije:

—Lo siento, señorita Johnson, quiero decir, señora. Por favor, ¿puede pasarme el jamón?

Sonrió y me lo ofreció.

—En realidad sigo siendo señora, para ser exactos.

No respondí porque para entonces ya tenía la boca llena de jamón. Aún estaba caliente y me lo comí de tres o cuatro bocados. Cora tenía otra loncha preparada cuando terminé, y luego otra, y cuando terminé la tercera me ofreció una servilleta y me limpié los dedos y la boca llenos de grasa. Cora me miraba con gesto divertido, y le dije:

—¿Qué pasa, Cora? ¿Aún tengo comida en la cara?

—¿Eh? No, no, estás limpio. —Metió la mano en la cesta y sacó una patata asada—. Acabo de cortarla y untarla con mantequilla antes de bajar, así que, ten cuidado, aún está caliente. —Yo intentaba tragarme la patata quitándole al mismo tiempo la piel sin parecer un cerdo cuando Cora se aclaró la voz y dijo—: Bueno, verás... el agente Brown quiere que te pregunte por esos dos hombres.

—¿Qué dos hombres? —pregunté, entre bocado y bocado.

—Los que estuvieron en casa de Wade. Creo que dijo que venían de Nueva York.

—Colin y Jason. Justin, quiero decir. Justin.

—¿Se llaman así? No me lo dijo. Solo me dijo que te preguntara por ellos.

—¿Por qué? ¿Piensa que ellos también se han cargado a Eddie Comedy? ¿O aún sigue convencido de que fui yo?

—Vamos, niño; nadie piensa que tengas nada que ver en la muerte de Eddie Comedy.

—Eso es fácil de decir cuando se está al otro lado de estos barrotes.

Cora sacó más comida. Pan de maíz, con mantequilla y aún caliente.

—Bueno, ¿qué sabes de esos hombres?

—No mucho más que tú. Ricos. Blancos. Prodigiosamente blancos. El más mayor, Colin, es escritor.

—¿Y son?

—¿Qué? ¿Gays?

—¿Como tú y Wade?

Me eché a reír y antes de pensar en lo que decía, dije:

—No, Cora, no son para nada como Wade y yo. —Pero en cuanto lo dije, comprendí que no era verdad—. Aunque son gays, si es eso lo que preguntas.

Cora me pasó un trozo de tarta de cereza.

—¿Qué tal está Sawyer?

Cora normalmente preguntaba qué Sawyer cuando alguien le hacía esta pregunta, pero esta vez se limitó a decir:

—Está bien. Respira sin dificultad.

—¿Y Rosa?

Cora me miró un buen rato antes de responder, y luego dijo en voz baja:

—Está bien. Le diré que has preguntado por ella.

Después se quedó allí sentada, sin más comida y sin más preguntas, o sin más preguntas que quisiera formular con palabras, y ya estaba a punto de preguntarle qué sabía sobre Colin y Justin, pues quizá el agente Brown le había contado algo, cuando me interrumpió el sonido de las llaves en la cerradura. Cora dio un respingo y volvió la cabeza, luego metió la mano en la cesta, sacó unas servilletas y me las pasó por los barrotes.

—Límpiate con esto —dijo, en voz alta—. Mañana vendré a traerte el desayuno. —Se sacudió la falda, como si fuese ella la que estaba llena de migas—. Pórtate bien, todo esto terminará antes de que te des cuenta —dijo, y se marchó corriendo.

—Adiós, Cora —le grité, y luego añadí algo que no suelo decir—: Gracias.

Oí que la puerta se cerraba al final del pasillo, pero no el ruido de la llave. Esperé, pero no oí nada.

—Déjate ver, agente Brown. Sé que estás ahí. De todos modos, no pienso decirles a las paredes nada que me incrimine.

El agente Brown esperó un momento, como si aún se estuviera choteando de mí, y luego se puso a tararear esa puta canción, ¿cómo se llama?, «Leroy Brown». Cuando llegó junto a la celda dejó de cantar y me miró de arriba abajo, como si no me hubiera visto en la vida.

—Me llamo...

—... Eustace, y eres el sheriff. Me conozco ese rollo, agente, ahórratelo conmigo. ¿Cuánto tiempo piensas tenerme aquí sin cargos?

—Según la ley puedo retenerte hasta setenta y dos horas —dijo el agente Brown, dándose palmaditas en el estómago—. Sin cargos. Tres días.

—¡Tres días!

—Claro que podrías ver la luz del sol mucho antes si resulta que estás limpio.

—¿Si estoy limpio de qué? Ya te he dicho mil veces que no sé nada, cabrón.

—¿Qué hacías entonces en el Big M?

—Ya te lo dije. Estaba buscando a un tío.

—Buscando a un tío, ¿eh? ¿Como, por ejemplo, a Eddie Comedy?

—A Eddie Comedy ya lo tenía muy visto. Estaba buscando a alguien nuevo.

El agente Brown pareció a punto de decir algo, luego solo dio la impresión de que iba a escupir.

—La gente como tú me pone enfermo. ¿Sabes? Enfermo.

—Creo que antes decías que los que estábamos enfermos éramos nosotros. ¿Ahora resulta que eres tú? No te entiendo, agente, siempre estás cambiando de rollo.

—¡Sabes muy bien lo que quiero decir! Eres… —Se le trabó la lengua en ese momento y se quedó un buen rato con la boca abierta. Luego echó mano directamente al arma (en la vida había visto a nadie a quien le gustara toquetear tanto su arma como al agente Brown) y empezó como a balancearse sobre los talones—. Dime una cosa, Reggie —dijo al fin—, ¿a quién buscabas si no buscabas a Eddie Comedy?

—Buscaba a…

—No me vengas con el cuento del Rata. Ya estoy harto de ese rollo.

—Buscaba a Lamoine. A Lamoine Wiebe.

—Lamoine Wiebe. ¿El mismo Lamoine Wiebe que se largó hace dos años?

—Tú dices que se largó; yo digo que se lo llevó uno de esos camioneros.

—¿Y qué? ¿Es que crees que si se lo preguntas van a decírtelo? Sí, yo me llevé a ese chico, lo corté en pedazos y esparcí su cuerpo desde aquí hasta el monte Rushmore. —Se echó a reír—. Sigue intentándolo, Reggie.

—Seguro que sirve más que lo que haces tú. Porque tú no haces nada.

—Escucha, cuando un delincuente juvenil de dieciséis años desaparece es asunto suyo. He hablado con Carol; por su parte dice que adiós y buen viaje. Yo digo lo mismo. Galatea está mucho mejor sin gente como él.

—Ahora tiene dieciocho años. En agosto fue su cumpleaños.

—Sí, claro. Si es que aún sigue con vida. —El agente Brown dio un paso a la derecha, acercándose a los barrotes—. Si todavía no se lo ha cargado algún pervertido se lo cargará el sida. Si es que no se lo ha cargado ya.

—Crees que tu culo no corre peligro, hijo de puta; pues ya verás lo que te espera. Todas las noches oscurece, cabrón; todas las putas noches oscurece.

El agente Brown se inclinó entonces sobre los barrotes. Su panza asomó entre ellos, y pocos centímetros más abajo la pistola.

—No tengo miedo a la oscuridad, Reggie.

—Sí, bueno, más vale que le tengas miedo a lo que se mueve en ella.

—Estás hablando mucho, Reggie, pero no dices nada. ¿Por qué no dices algo de lo que quiero oír? Algo que me venga bien.

—Lo que te vendría bien es un buen polvo. A lo mejor te animaba un poco.

—Ya te has pasado bastante, Reggie.

—Discúlpeme, sheriff Brown. No estoy acostumbrado a llenarme la boca de palabras.

El agente Brown abrió entonces los ojos con expresión de asombro. Y volvió a poner cara de ir a escupir, pero no escupió.

Mientras hablaba con el agente Brown tenía en la mano la servilleta que me había dado Cora antes de marcharse, y entonces la solté. El silencio era tal que se oyó el ruido de la servilleta al caer al suelo, entre dos sonoros suspiros del agente Brown.

—¡Vaya, qué tonto! —dije, en voz muy baja—. Se me ha caído la servilleta. —Y me arrodillé para recogerla.

Luego solo se oyó la respiración del agente Brown, el aire que entraba y salía por la nariz cada vez más deprisa. Los hombres respiran de un modo especial cuando se encuentran en esta posición, y cuando aprendes a escucharla puede decirte mucho más que las palabras. Cuando oyes esa respiración sabes que ni siquiera la vergüenza o la ofensa puede echarlos atrás. Y el agente Brown era un hombre soltero, que no faltaba a misa los domingos. Llevaba mucho tiempo esperando ese momento.

Apoyé las manos en los fríos barrotes de acero. La mano izquierda quedó a quince centímetros de la culata de la pistola del agente Brown, pero preferí usar la derecha. Quería asegurarme de distraerlo antes de…

—¡Eh, Eustace!

Los dos dimos un salto. Yo caí de espaldas y me golpeé con la cabeza en el váter, mientras el agente Brown tropezaba con la silla en la que se había sentado Cora. El ruido retumbó en las paredes de cemento durante mucho rato; pareció que pasaban horas hasta que se extinguió por completo.

—Solo he venido para ver si Reggie quería comer algo.

Reconocí entonces la voz de Nettie Ferguson. Dios la bendiga; nunca había pensado que se preocupara por mí.

El agente Brown se dispuso a levantar la silla como si se tratara de un desafío ineludible.

—El prisionero ya ha comido, Nettie —dijo, sin darse la vuelta, para ocultar lo que yo aún seguía viendo.

—Te has dejado las llaves en la puerta, Eustace —dijo Nettie, y las oí tintinear. Nettie volvió a agitar las llaves, pero no entró en el pasillo.

La prueba incriminatoria, ya me entendéis, había desaparecido para entonces y el agente Brown se volvió hacia Nettie Ferguson.

—Te agradecería mucho, Nettie, que no obstaculices la acción de la justicia. Tus tareas administrativas deberían bastar para mantenerte ocupada.

—Y eso incluye un filete de pollo frito.

—Dame las llaves, Nettie. No hay razón para seguir reteniendo a este chico más tiempo.

Enderezó la espalda, aunque sus pantalones también necesitaban un buen estirón, mientras Nettie Ferguson se acercaba a la celda renqueando. Al verme en el suelo me miró bizqueando con sus ojos de gato. Ni adrede habría tenido más pinta de profesora de primaria.

—¡Madre mía, Reggie, cuánto has crecido!

Intenté reírle la gracia, pero no funcionó.

—Buenas tardes, señora Ferguson.

—Es de noche, Reggie. Son casi las once. —Se quedó un rato mirándome y luego dijo—: ¿Qué haces en el suelo, Reggie?

—Se me había caído la servilleta. —La cogí y la agité ante ella, pero ya se había dado la vuelta para entregarle las llaves al agente Brown, y tiré la servilleta al váter.

Cuando me volví el agente Brown ya estaba metiendo la llave en la cerradura. La miraba fijamente. No me miró en ningún momento.

—¿Puedo irme a casa? —dije, en mi tono más amable.

El agente Brown me miró entre los barrotes antes de girar la llave y luego hizo exactamente el mismo sonido que había hecho cuando me encerró por la mañana.

—Umpf —dijo—. Eso es lo que te falta. Puedes tener muchas cosas, Reggie Packman, pero no tienes familia, ni amigos ni casa.

1.17

JUSTIN

Casi habíamos terminado de embalar nuestras pertenencias. Las pocas cosas que quedaban, cosas que en otro tiempo nos habían parecido imprescindibles, resultaban ahora simples trastos, artículos secundarios y en su mayoría prescindibles. «¿Quieres esto?», pregunté. Sostenía en la mano un candelabro de ocho brazos, danés, fabricado en los años veinte, con los finos brazos de hierro cubiertos por una polvorienta pátina de óxido. Era pequeño y solo soportaba velas pequeñas; Colin me había leído bajo aquella luz los *Sonetos* de Shakespeare, el *Grendel* de Gardner, *Utopía* de Tomás Moro... «No», dijo; y lo aparté. «¿Quieres esto?», preguntó Colin. Sostenía la gran pecera esférica que durante tres años había albergado a mis peces de colores japoneses. Una avería eléctrica, una ola de frío y unas vacaciones se habían aliado contra ellos: al volver a casa los encontramos flotando en un bloque de hielo. «No», dije; y Colin lo apartó. «¿Quieres esto?», pregunté. Sostenía entonces diez hojas de papel en las que había escritos quinientos y un nombres (alguien llamado Nolan había sido tachado y sustituido por alguien llamado Oren; Nolan no había muerto). «No», dijo Colin tras una larga pausa, y aparté la lista. Poco después oí el tintineo del metal al chocar contra el vidrio y, al levantar la vista, vi que Colin intentaba meter el candelabro dentro de la pecera. Había encontrado velas en alguna parte y las había encendido; luego había metido las páginas llenas de nombres dentro del acuario y lo había cerrado con su tapa de metal. El papel ardió con fuerza un momento, pero no tardó en ponerse negro y romperse en pedazos minúsculos. Los papeles revolotearon en el aire caliente atrapado en la pecera, prendiendo ocasionalmente con breve pero intensa llama. Luego, cuando las velas se apagaron al fin, los trozos de papel quemado se posaron en la base del acuario y allí quedaron formando una capa de cenizas frías, secas y mudas. Me pareció que todo lo que se pudiera decir estaba allí, en aquellas cenizas, pero a Colin no le bastó con eso. Le oí carraspear, le oí contener el aliento. Me sorprendió ver que tenía lágrimas en los ojos, y cuando habló comprendí que a veces es necesario, por fútil que el esfuerzo pueda parecer; que a veces hay que decirlo en voz alta. Habló mirando a las cenizas, y lo que dijo fue: «Adiós».

2

2.01

JUSTIN

El segundo de los seis primeros días lo pasamos desembalando... digo el segundo y no el primero; tardé dos días en reaccionar. Abrí una puerta que creí haber abierto en otras ocasiones y encontré algo que no era nuestro, sino que, según supuse, había pertenecido a la gente que vivió en la casa de caliza antes que nosotros: una pareja de blancos llegados «de fuera», como nosotros, que le compró la casa a la familia negra a la que había pertenecido desde los tiempos de la fundación de Galatia. No estaba seguro de lo que había encontrado. No sabía si se trataba de una piedra o de un trozo de cerámica sin esmaltar. Tenía un tacto más parecido a la piedra pómez que a la porcelana y un aspecto también como el de la piedra pómez: era gris, esférica, ligeramente más pequeña que una pelota de béisbol, y al tocarla se deshizo en cenicientos terrones entre mis dedos. Sin embargo, parecía... demasiado «redonda» para ser natural y, cuando la levanté –estaba en el suelo, en el centro de una habitación vacía–, dejó escapar una especie de tintineo, aunque no encontré ninguna grieta en ella, ningún indicio de que la hubieran abierto para guardar algo en su interior y vuelto a cerrar después. El objeto, fuera lo que fuese, me pareció de repente sumamente valioso: era enigmático y, aunque plano, estaba al mismo tiempo preñado de posibilidades; además, era una de las pocas cosas que había en la casa que no llevaba escrito el nombre de Colin, y me la guardé en el bolsillo. Es decir, me apropié de ella y la escondí. Me apropié de ella para que no se la quedase Colin y la escondí de él; luego la envolví en un trozo de tela para amortiguar el tintineo, pero seguí llevándola en el bolsillo y no me cambié de pantalones en cuatro días, hasta que encontré un lugar mejor donde ponerla a buen recaudo.

Terminamos de desembalar a primera hora de la noche del sexto día y cenamos por primera vez en el comedor. Una de las ventanas estaba situada justo frente a un hueco del seto, y a través del hueco se veían seis de las Pléyades. No estaba seguro de si los desiguales bordes del seto sin recortar oscurecían la séptima estrella; recordé vagamente algo sobre una Pléyade perdida, pero no sabía si era solo parte del mito o si en realidad correspondía a la constelación. Seguro que Colin lo sabía, pero no se lo pregunté; en lugar de ello, después de cenar salí al jardín con la intención de localizar la séptima estrella. Me abrí camino entre las afiladas y resbaladizas piedras, mientras el objeto que reposaba en mi bolsillo me golpeaba ligeramente en el muslo. Al cabo de cuatro días aún seguía considerándolo como eso, un objeto; aún no le había dado un nombre, quizá porque intuía que ya lo tenía y que, a su debido tiempo, acabaría por descubrirlo. Dejé atrás el seto y enfilé hacia los campos. La brisa fría traía un leve aroma a madera quemada. Subí un promontorio —incluso «colina» sería un término excesivo para esa pequeña protuberancia del terreno—, pero nada más bajar por el lado contrario la luz de la casa de caliza desapareció y no vi más que la pradera oscura, tan informe como la niebla, que se extendía hasta el infinito en todas las direcciones; y una imagen de Catherine perdida en los páramos llenó mi mente. Ya lo sé, ya lo sé: piensan que él conoce las constelaciones, que no necesita señales. Pero yo no conocía las constelaciones como los marinos antiguos; para mí eran un simple ornamento celestial. Aunque podía quedarme absorto en la contemplación de las estrellas por espacio de un momento, ellas jamás me ayudarían a encontrar nada. Lo que quiero decir es que jamás me ayudarían a encontrarme a mí mismo y, dándome la vuelta, volví corriendo a la casa.

Y en la casa estaba Colin. O, mejor dicho, su voz que llegaba desde arriba. «Justin —me llamó—. Justin, ven aquí.» Subí al segundo piso; no estaba allí. «Justin —volvió a decir—. Mira lo que he encontrado.» Subí al ático; no estaba allí. «Justin, Justin, Justin», le oí llamarme, y al ver las escaleras que conducían hasta la cúpula del tejado me pregunté cómo era posible que la voz de Colin, la voz de Colin hablando en tono normal, hubiese podido llegar desde allí arriba hasta las lejanas habitaciones del piso de abajo. Pero como eso es algo que no está al alcance de nadie comprender, decidí subir, ladeándome ligeramente —las escaleras eran más estrechas que mis hombros— y rozando con los brazos esa ilusoria humedad que desprende la piedra muy, muy fría. En la habitación del tejado encontré mucho polvo, una sola bombilla de baja potencia y a Colin, que me sonrió cuando abrí la puerta y dijo, como siempre, «Just-in-time»; pero yo me aparté de él, de su sonrisa y de su nombre. Había angostas ventanas en cada una de las ocho paredes de la habitación, decorada con un fresco agrietado y desvaído que representaba cientos de pájaros y, sin embargo, parecía intensa y extrañamente colorido a pesar de la pobre iluminación, aunque por el momento no hice caso de los pájaros y me dirigí a una de las ventanas. Busqué las Pléyades. La ventana era más alta que el seto y la constelación brillaba nítidamente en el cielo despejado. Las conté: seis estrellas. Un parpadeo ocasional insinuaba la posible existencia de una séptima, aunque ninguna de ellas resistía una mirada directa. Finalmente, tuve que admitir que solo había seis estrellas y una vez hube llegado a esa conclusión bajé la mirada, por un momento, hasta la tierra que yacía bajo ellas, y entonces, al observar la inmensa pradera desde la seguridad de la cúpula, comprendí que no era la casa lo que me asustaba. Era la tierra sobre la que esta había sido construida. Era la pradera. La casa de caliza era grande, aunque no tanto como para perderse en ella. En la pradera sí podías perderte.

—¿Justin?

Colin intentó que su voz sonara normal, pero advertí su impaciencia. A Colin no le gusta que las ensoñaciones de los demás se prolonguen más que las suyas. En todo caso, su voz me sacó del ensueño, y me volví hacia él.

El polvo, el reflejo de la luz en el polvo y los pájaros que rodeaban a Colin, desnudo, hirsuto, guapo, hacían que apareciera como flotando en el espacio. Me impresionó la escena y, al mismo tiempo, me provocó cierto rechazo, pues supe que Colin lo había planeado minuciosamente: siempre encuentra el marco adecuado para sí, para su belleza. Pero la pradera lo desplazaba a un segundo plano. A través de la ventana que había detrás de él vislumbré un centelleo, demasiado grande y demasiado pegado al suelo como para ser una estrella.

—¿Justin?

Lo empujé sin responder. Al momento habló de nuevo y reconocí que sus palabras eran las mismas que pronunció cuando vimos la cortina de humo de Kenosha en el horizonte.

—¿Es un incendio?

Era un incendio. La noche y lo anodino del terreno hacían que resultara imposible determinar si era grande o pequeño, si estaba cerca o lejos, pero estaba claro que un fuego ardía en algún punto, situado entre la casa y el horizonte, que se veía a través de un hueco en el seto.

Lanzando una mirada a las llamas distantes, Colin salió corriendo de la habitación, pero yo me quedé un momento junto a la ventana, paralizado por algo que no podía definir. Luego caí en la cuenta: el fuego quedaba perfectamente enmarcado por la ventana y el seto. Fuera lo que fuese lo que ardía, no cabía duda de que había sido algo importante para alguien que había vivido en esta casa. Y no pude sustraerme a la sensación de que ardía para que nosotros lo viéramos.

Entonces me aparté de la ventana y me dirigí hacia la puerta. Antes de llegar a ella vi una vieja y enorme llave metida en la cerradura. Como había ocurrido con el objeto que guardaba en el bolsillo, no recordaba haber visto antes esa llave. Saqué la piedra del bolsillo y cogí la llave. Desenvolví el trapo, agité el objeto y lo deposité en medio de la habitación. Se quedó inmóvil. Resultaba muy pequeño en el suelo, aún sin nombre, aún desconocido, pero mientras lo miraba se transformó en una especie de huevo, un solo huevo rodeado por los miles de pájaros pintados en la habitación. Apagué la luz y el huevo, y los pájaros desaparecieron; cerré la puerta, eché la llave y me la guardé en el bolsillo. Luego, en voz alta, pero sin dirigirme a nadie en particular, dije: «A partir de ahora esta es mi habitación». Y luego me marché, con Colin —y con todos los demás habitantes del pueblo— en busca del arca de Noah.

2.02

WEBBIE

Algunos pensaban que seguía siendo un secreto, pero ya no lo era. Cuando digo «algunos» me refiero en concreto a los negros, y cuando digo «secreto» me refiero a que ellos pensaban que eran los únicos que lo sabían, aunque lo cierto es que nunca había sido un secreto. Mi padre me lo contó cuando yo era muy pequeña y, cuando le pregunté por qué no era un secreto, se echó a reír y dijo: «¿De dónde piensan que sacó la madera?».

Esa madera tenía setenta años y estaba medio hueca tras haber sido roída durante décadas por las termitas y los ratones, únicos seres vivos que había albergado siempre. Además, estaba seca y polvorienta, por el granero. Probablemente bastó con una sola cerilla.

Aunque Noah Deacon le hubiese comprado la madera a una empresa negra, es imposible construir un granero en mitad de un pasto en Kansas sin que nadie se dé cuenta, sobre todo si el granero mide treinta y seis metros de largo y cinco de alto, y tiene un tejado tan pronunciado. Noah Deacon construyó un gigantesco cascarón hueco: no empleó más madera que la necesaria para edificarlo, pero eso fue una enorme cantidad de madera para aquella zona y aquella época. La gente no se pone de acuerdo sobre el año en que Noah comenzó su «empresa secundaria», como la llamaban, si en 1925, en 1924 o quizá en 1923, pero eso da lo mismo; lo que importa es que, una vez terminada, el arca se convirtió en el segundo hito, natural o artificial, más alto del condado de Cadavera. El primero era el risco pelado. Desde la cima de uno se veía la cima del otro, pero solo si sabías dónde mirar y lo que estabas buscando. Muchos sabían dónde mirar, pero muy pocos sabían lo que buscaban, y es posible que la gente de Galatia se refiriera a esto cuando decían que el granero, y la barca que este ocultaba en su interior, era un secreto, aunque en tal caso el secreto era tanto suyo como de los blancos. Se alzaba directamente sobre la tierra y allí reposaba, plano como la mano que cubre la cara... pero, como decía mi padre, hasta tu propia mano es invisible cuando cierras los ojos.

La noche que se incendió el arca subí al risco pelado. Todo el mundo, la gente de Galatia y la gente de Galatea, y la mayor parte de ellos por primera vez, cruzaron la propiedad de Colin Nieman para ver la construcción que desde siempre había formado parte de la tradición local. Pero yo me fui al risco. Como la mayoría de la gente, hasta entonces no había sabido dónde mirar, pero ahora tenía una pista, una bandera al viento, una baliza, y la vi parpadear en la distancia: una luminosa bola de fuego situada a unos quince o veinte kilómetros. Una sombra oblonga se extendía sobre la pradera entre el fuego y yo, y aunque me gustaba imaginar que la sombra era el gentío atraído por el incendio, quizá no fuera más que lo que parecía: una sombra que se extendía sobre la pradera.

El granero —su tamaño y su situación— ya era de por sí bastante extraño, pero lo que hizo que la gente empezara a hablar fue que, una vez terminada su construcción, siguiese llegando madera. Camiones cargados de madera, de vigas gruesas y oscuras, tan largas como los nuevos postes del teléfono que comenzaban a verse en el camino de Bigger Hill, solo que aquellas eran cuadradas y muchas estaban combadas, según decían los que veían pasar los camiones en dirección a la autopista. Los camiones transportaban su misteriosa carga hasta el granero hueco de Noah Deacon, y regresaban vacíos, traqueteando, al lugar de donde habían venido. Los hombres a los que Noah Deacon contrató para que lo ayudaran a construir el granero ya se habían marchado para entonces, y nadie sabe quién lo ayudó a construir luego la barca.

Lo que sí se sabe es que hace unos sesenta años la inundación anual de primavera fue más severa que en años anteriores, tanto es así que el brazo sur del río Solomon se desbordó, arrasando a su paso el pueblo de Galatia dos años después de haber sido construido y descubriendo por azar la entrada a la cueva de Bellystones. Noah Deacon, que tenía un año menos que el pueblo donde vivía, afirmaba recordar perfectamente esa inundación, y poco después comenzó a anunciar que vendría otra aún mayor, una inundación como el diluvio universal del Génesis. El sucesor del reverendo Alpha, el segundo reverendo Greeving, el reverendo Able, lo reconvino por hacer esa premonición: el Señor había prometido que nunca más volvería a destruir el mundo con agua. ¿No se acordaba Noah del pacto del arco iris al terminar el diluvio? Pero Noah Deacon había tenido una visión y pensaba mantenerse fiel a ella. Si la gente prefería ignorarlo allá ellos; ya habían pasado por alto la primera de sus advertencias y él, impertérrito, puso manos a la obra. Su familia consintió la aventura, si es que no colaboró activamente en ella, en primer lugar porque tenía dinero y en segundo lugar porque ese dinero lo había ganado él. Y aunque es cierto que Noah Deacon invirtió una enorme cantidad de tiempo y dinero en su empresa secundaria, no lo es menos que trabajó con igual ahínco en su empresa principal: las cosechas y el ganado; lo que permitió que las posesiones de los Deacon crecieran de manera imparable gracias a la buena gestión de Noah. Su suerte parecía casi mágica: producían el doble de fanegas de trigo por acre que sus vecinos y saturaban el mercado con su ganado, haciendo que los precios se desplomaran. Por más dinero que costara la empresa secundaria de Noah –la gente la llamaba así porque no era fácil llamarla el arca de Noé sin echarse a reír–, siempre parecía haber dinero de sobra para seguir adelante.

Es más, mientras Noah construía el granero, su hermano Donald se ocupaba de ampliar la casa de caliza, añadiendo las dos alas que le confieren su actual forma de cruz. Noah Deacon compró cuatro mil metros cúbicos de madera de pino para asegurarse de que su barca fuese completamente hermética, mientras que Donald Deacon revistió las frías paredes de piedra de su mansión con paneles de caoba, teca y árboles frutales; Noah Deacon construyó diversas hileras superpuestas para albergar a los animales a los que se proponía salvar, mientras que Donald Deacon construyó grandes y opulentas habitaciones, y dio fiestas de disfraces a las que asistieron todos los habitantes del pueblo; pero en las fiestas de Donald nadie hablaba de Noah ni de su arca, por la creencia general de que este proyecto, que cabía considerar como una excentricidad de hombre blanco, empezara a entenderse como prueba de la locura de un hombre negro, y si llegara a oídos de los blancos que dirigían el resto de la finca el pobre Noah Deacon sería encerrado en un manicomio y la fuente de la prosperidad de su familia –y de la prosperidad de Galatia– se secaría para siempre.

He de confesar que nunca entendí esta estrategia: cómo el silencio de los negros, entre los negros y sobre los negros, podía evitar que los blancos descubrieran los secretos. ¿De dónde pensaban que sacaba la madera, los clavos y las docenas y docenas de parejas de animales? Pero esa no era, o al menos no es, la cuestión: la cuestión era que Noah Deacon construyó su arca y Donald Deacon construyó su mansión, y que Galatia decidió no apartar la vista de aquel monumento visible, de aquella estructura que era un emblema de la industriosidad y la prosperidad afroamericanas, y la burbuja no explotó hasta que Noah Deacon murió a la avanzada edad de ciento nueve años, momento en el que salieron a la luz la segunda y la tercera hipoteca, la inmensa deuda, la fragilidad de aquella empresa. Más tarde se dijo que la mayor parte de esa deuda había sido acumulada por Donald Deacon y su hijo, Donald junior. Que el arca de Noah, por más que hubiese costado, se terminó de construir antes del fin de la Gran Depresión, y que durante sus restantes cuarenta años de vida, Noah Deacon se había limitado a hacer pequeños retoques o adquirir algún que otro raro trofeo, como un dodo o una paloma mensajera. Fueron los excesos arquitectónicos de Donald Deacon primero los que sumieron a la familia en una deuda creciente, y fue Donald Deacon tercero quien heredó este embrollo a la muerte de su tío abuelo. Donald Deacon tercero hizo un último esfuerzo por salvar la granja: perforó en busca de petróleo, pero no encontró nada. La suerte de la familia Deacon pareció morir junto a Noah y, pocos años después de la muerte de este, Donald hubo de enfrentarse al siguiente dilema: vender o dejar que el banco de Rosemary Krebs se quedase con todo. Vendió y se marchó. O tal vez debería decir, vendió y huyó.

Pero mucho antes de eso el arca de su tío ya formaba parte de la leyenda. Supongo que había razones para ello, una de las cuales era el hecho de que casi todos los que aún vivían cuando Noah Deacon comenzó a construir el arca murieron antes que él. Quienes lo sobrevivieron eran niños cuando comenzó la construcción del arca y la mayoría se comportaba como si todas aquellas viejas historias no fuesen más que eso, historias que ellos o sus padres habían inventado para distraerse. Además, había cosas más importantes de las que ocuparse. Estaban, por un lado, los nuevos propietarios de la finca Deacon: Beatrice y Henry. Por otro, Rosemary Krebs. Frente a eso la excentricidad de un viejo carecía por completo de importancia.

Myra Robinson le había contado a Wade, y Wade me había contado a mí, que no creía que Beatrice tuviera la menor idea de dónde estaba el arca, que ni siquiera sabía de su existencia. Me extraña. Puede que, como yo, sencillamente evitara buscarla. Rosemary Krebs, según supe más tarde, también lo evitó. El día del incendio, Rosemary se quedó en casa; envió a Phyneas y al agente Brown, y se conformó con el testimonio de estos.

Noah Deacon, por su parte, dejó de hablar del arca y del futuro diluvio mucho antes de morir. Lo cierto es que dejó de hablar de casi todo. Lo recuerdo sentado en la iglesia los domingos, con la boca cerrada mientras se entonaban los himnos, un ligero alzamiento de sombrero por todo saludo y una nueva colocación del mismo por toda despedida. Solo lo oí hablar en una ocasión. Fue una tarde oscura y triste de finales de primavera, con el cielo encapotado y el aire cargado de polvo y hojas arrastradas por el viento. Volvía a casa desde la iglesia, corriendo, con la cabeza baja para protegerme del polvo, cuando tropecé con las piernas de Noah Deacon, delgadas como postes, pero igual de fuertes, y antes de que pudiera disculparme, Noah me sujetó la barbilla con sus viejas y secas manos, me miró primero fijamente a los ojos, luego miró al cielo, volvió a mirarme y dijo con aire solemne: «Más vale que te vayas a casa, Webbie. Parece que se acerca una tormenta. Parece que va a llover».

El fuego ardió durante tres horas antes de ser localizado. Era una noche clara y se veía la nube de humo que ascendía por el cielo, ocultando las estrellas. Al día siguiente, cuando vino a buscar a mi padre, Alice Gunderson dijo que gracias a Dios la noche anterior no hizo viento, pues podría haber sido mucho peor. Quincy Cross y George Oconnor fueron hasta allí con un par de tractores y se pusieron a segar la hierba seca. Alma Kiehler me dijo que una llama podía separarse de la masa de fuego y prender sobre los campos —como los tentáculos de una mata de fresas—, pero el aire estaba tan quieto que los hombres armados con extintores y sacos de barro y arena lograron sofocar todos los brotes antes de que resultaran peligrosos. Victor Bradfield me dijo días más tarde, cuando me lo encontré en el IGA, que se limitaron a vigilar. Era la primera vez, dijo, la primera vez que él recordara, que el pueblo entero se había reunido, y aunque normalmente era yo quien se ocupaba de hacer ese tipo de comentarios, Vera Gatlinger se me adelantó. «¿Qué me dices de Eric Johnson?», le preguntó Vera a Victor, pero Victor se quedó mirando el carrito de la compra y al cabo de un rato se volvió hacia mí y dijo: «No recuerdo haberla visto allí, señorita Webbie». No encontré las palabras para explicarle que no, que no había estado allí, que no había querido presenciar la destrucción de otro de los iconos de mi pasado, y me limité a decir: «Tampoco me viste en el linchamiento de Eric Johnson».

2.03

JUSTIN

—Usted debe de ser el señor Nieman —dijo Rosemary Krebs al abrir la puerta de su gran casa, rodeada de columnas blancas. Habló con el típico falsete sureño que a mí siempre me parece transmitir cierto disgusto, y después de que Colin pasara junto su cuerpo, asombrosamente menudo y contenido en una especie de colmena amarillenta, me dijo—: Y usted debe de ser su hijo.

Intenté contener una carcajada.

—Si Colin fuera mi padre estaría infringiendo dos leyes de este estado, en lugar de una sola.

Esperé, mientras Rosemary Krebs nos miraba alternativamente intentando establecer una relación filial. La observé asombrado. Medía menos de un metro cincuenta. No debía de pesar más de cuarenta kilos. Tenía los dedos tan pequeños como colines.

—Les ruego que me disculpen —dijo al fin—. Reginald me hizo creer que eran ustedes parientes.

—¿Reginald? —preguntó Colin.

—¿Parientes? —dije yo.

Rosemary Krebs se frotó las manos en el inmaculado delantal que cubría su blusa de seda blanca y su falda de lana gris. Luego, dirigiéndose a Colin, explicó:

—Reginald Packman. El amigo de Wade. Me dijo que venía usted a instalarse aquí con su chico.

2.04

DIVINE

Puta enana blanca. ¡Que se vaya al carajo! ¡Como si yo tuviera tiempo de cenar en su casa! Y Wade que se vaya también al carajo. Quiere tener a Webbie atada como si fuera un perro (como si alguien pudiera creer que se la está follando); ese es su problema, ya me entendéis. Tengo cosas más importantes que hacer.

Wade siempre me está diciendo que un día de estos voy a pillar algo chungo. ¿Y sabéis?, a veces me gustaría pillar algo, para pasárselo a él. El muy cabrón. ¿Os imagináis a Wade Painter rascándose las ladillas? Pues yo no.

A T. V. Daniels le costó un paquete de tabaco salir del bar de Sloppy Joe. Sé que he dicho que ya no fumo, pero a veces hay que hacer ciertas concesiones. En el aparcamiento hacía un frío de mil demonios y me sentaba bien sentir el aire caliente en los pulmones. Aunque en realidad eso no te hace entrar en calor, y estaba tiritando, a punto de largarme, cuando vi que T. V. salía bamboleándose de la sala de billar. Parecía que no cabía dentro de su uniforme de cartero, y eso que según decía la gente, siempre lo llevaba puesto porque la compañía de correos era la única empresa que hacía ropa de su talla.

Ese tío engordaba dos kilos cada día.

Me pasé la lengua por la boca para quitarme el sabor a nicotina y escupí –lo único que T. V. Daniels no se metería nunca en la boca es un cigarrillo, ya me entendéis–, y luego lo llamé:

–¡Eh, T. V.!

Se sobresaltó tanto que casi se cae al suelo; eso sí que habría estado bien. Iba comiendo una bolsa de Cheetos, y se desperdigaron por todas partes.

–Me has asustado –dijo, mirando al suelo como si pensara recoger los Cheetos.

Como si pudiera agacharse.

Entonces apoyé un pie en el coche, me saqué la polla y me aseguré de que se fijara bien en ella.

–¡Toma! –dije entonces–. Seguro que se lo cuentas a todo el mundo.

2.05

JUSTIN

Un viejo famélico entró en el comedor dando brincos. Cinco mechones de pelo repeinado le cubrían la calva como un pentagrama sin escribir.

–Hola-aa –dijo, anunciando con tres sílabas que estaba loco de atar. Movía las manos como un bailarín sin pareja–. Soy el alcalde Krebs –añadió, apretándole el brazo primero a Colin y luego a mí–. Phyneas es mi nombre, pero todos me llaman alcalde. Supongo que es más fácil. ¿Estáis inscritos en el censo electoral?

Parpadeé y comprendí que esperaba una respuesta.

–En Nueva York –dije–. Colin sí, pero yo no.

–¿Qué os pareció el lío de la otra noche? –preguntó el alcalde–. Fue estupendo, ¿verdad?

Colin se aclaró la garganta.

–A mí me pareció muy bonito.

–Bueno, supongo que en la gran ciudad siempre hay incendios –continuó el alcalde, sonriendo y asintiendo con la cabeza; luego se volvió hacia mí y observó–: ¡Tienes el ojo a la funerala, chico!

Miré primero a Colin y luego al alcalde.

–Un accidente durante la mudanza. Me di con una...

–Ja, ja, ja –rió el alcalde–. La gran ciudad. La gran ciudad. La política de la gran ciudad. Y la primera palabra sonó a «película» en su boca, como si dijera la «película de la gran ciudad»–. Bueno, no os preocupéis, os cuidaremos bien. Galatea no es más que un pueblo, pero tiene mucho que ofrecer en lo que a política se refiere.

–Phyneas –dijo entonces Rosemary Krebs, con una entonación tan lenta y esmerada como un adiestrador de animales–. ¿Por qué no cierras la puerta mientras acompaño a nuestros invitados al salón?

Un conjunto de muebles victorianos adornados con brocados y borlas doradas se amontonaban en el salón, como temerosos de la tela roja y verde que cubría las paredes. Sobre un confidente de madera oscura y acanalada como la concha de Venus aparecía la versión lugareña de una muchacha: estaba sentada muy erguida, y aunque en su rostro se leía el esfuerzo por parecer refinada, sus maneras eran más propias de una *majorette* que de una debutante. Un sillón similar ofrecía asiento a una mujer similar, que era a todas luces la madre de la muchacha. Ambas tenían el pelo oscuro y rizado con permanente, el rostro demasiado bronceado –aunque en el caso de la madre el bronceado parecía efecto del tiempo y en el de la hija de una máquina de rayos UVA– y unos pechos pequeños que asomaban casi con desafío por el escote de sus vestidos.

Una vez más tuve que contener la carcajada; no por las mujeres, sino por las intenciones que habían movido a Rosemary Krebs a invitarlas a su casa esa noche.

–Myra Robinson –anunció Rosemary Krebs– y su hija Lucille. Myra, Lucy, os presento a Colin Nieman y Justin…

–Time –terminé por ella.

–Justin Time –repitió Rosemary Krebs, controlando el tono de voz. Lucy –dijo, aún dirigiéndose a mí– es la Reina del instituto.

–Lo siento –dije, pero mis palabras quedaron ahogadas por el frufrú del vestido de baile de satén rojo cuando la joven se levantó.

–¡Encantada de conocerlo! –dijo, sacando del costado una mano enfundada en un guante blanco.

–Lucy –dijo Rosemary Krebs en voz baja–. Se trata de dar la mano, no de devolver la pelota en un partido de voleibol.

Al oír estas palabras Lucy retiró la mano y su brazo extendido cayó ligeramente, pero antes de que llegara al costado, Colin dio un paso al frente, le tomó la mano y la besó diciendo:

–*Enchanté*.

El rostro de Lucy se tiñó de un tono rojizo que contrastaba horriblemente con el de su vestido, y apartando bruscamente la mano se volvió hacia mí casi con desesperación. Pareció fijarse en mi ojo derecho y me pregunté si estaba mirando el moratón reciente o la vieja cicatriz. Sus palabras, cuando habló, sonaron perfectamente ensayadas:

—La señora Krebs me ha informado de que vienen ustedes de Nueva York. ¿Son ustedes originariamente de allí?
—¿Originariamente?
Titubeó un momento.
—Quiero decir si es allí donde han nacido…
Sentí que Colin me miraba con insistencia, pero yo me dirigí solo a Lucy:
—No. ¿Y usted?
Sus ojos parecieron velarse:
—¿Yo qué?
—Si ha nacido aquí.
Lucy era lista; al momento aplaudió con deleite y dijo:
—¡Me toma usted el pelo! —Luego miró a Rosemary Krebs, que parecía complacida con esta respuesta, y acto seguido volvió a sentarse sin decir palabra. Se le arqueó la espalda un instante, pero enseguida la enderezó, tensando la columna como un arco.
Colin le ofreció entonces la mano a Myra que, en lugar de estrechársela, se sirvió de ella para levantarse. A juzgar por la tensa expresión de Colin, Myra no era tan delgada como su hija, e incluso de lejos noté que el aliento le olía a Binaca y a whisky.
—Encantada de conocerlo —dijo, con la boca pastosa, y luego, sin molestarse en saludarme, volvió a ocupar su asiento. Al levantarse, el bolso que llevaba colgado del hombro se balanceó bruscamente y al sentarse chocó contra el brazo del sillón, produciendo un gran estrépito. Myra lo sujetó contra el vientre, acariciándolo con expresión satisfecha.
—Bueno, creo que ya nos conocemos todos —dijo Rosemary Krebs en tono aliviado—. ¿Alguien quiere beber algo antes de cenar?
—Yo tomaré lo mismo que la señora Robinson —dije.
Rosemary Krebs esbozó una ligera sonrisa y dijo:
—¿Phyneas?
—No, no, yo no quiero nada, gracias —dijo el alcalde, pero al ver que su mujer seguía mirándolo se dio una palmada en la frente y dijo—: ¡Sí, sí, claro, ¡qué tonto!, ¿en qué estaría pensando? —Y volviéndose hacia la madre y la hija preguntó—: Myra, Lucy, ¿Coca-Cola para todos?
Myra se limitó a mover la mano, pero Lucy exclamó animadamente:
—¡Sí, gracias!
Colin, algo inseguro, dijo:
—Yo preferiría un gin tonic, por favor.
Hubo un breve silencio y Rosemary Krebs explicó:
—En esta casa somos abstemios, señor Nieman.

—Claro —dijo Colin, y vi que Myra volvía a tocar el bolso, esta vez con sonrisa más abierta. Colin carraspeó y dijo—: En ese caso tomaré agua de Seltz.

—¿Qué? —preguntó el alcalde.

—Agua —suspiró Colin—. Solo agua.

Pareció que pasaban años hasta que al fin llegaron Webbie y Wade. Para entonces me había arrancado todos los pelos de la cabeza, hasta quedarme tan calvo como Colin, y Myra se había levantado varias veces para ir al cuarto de baño. Por más que lo intenté, no logré salir al mismo tiempo que ella, y tuve que conformarme con inhalar la embriagadora estela de whisky y elixir que dejó en el cuarto de baño.

En lugar de darle la mano a Webbie la cogí del brazo y dibujé con los labios la palabra «¡Socorro!». Pero ella parecía no encontrarse bien y se limitó a esbozar una débil sonrisa al tiempo que me daba un apretón en el brazo.

La voz de Wade cobró vida bruscamente. Ya había aprendido que cuando Wade Painter hablaba sin que nadie se hubiera dirigido a él era casi siempre para decir algo importante.

—Rosemary —dijo Wade—, ¿qué es lo que ese inútil culo de sebo al que tú llamas sheriff ha descubierto sobre el incidente de Eddie Comedy?

Entonces comprendí que Wade, igual que Myra Robinson, asistía a la cena debidamente pertrechado.

Rosemary Krebs dejó que un largo silencio siguiera al exabrupto de Wade, y luego, en un tono que excluía toda réplica, respondió:

—Nada. Absolutamente nada.

2.06

DIVINE

Cuando T. V. me miró con el ceño fruncido su cara me recordó a una patata pelada, o algo así, una patata arrugada y llena de picaduras, que había que limpiar con esmero. Se me quitó el apetito de cuajo, ya sabéis a qué me refiero, pero nadie ha dicho que la vida sea fácil.

—¿Qué, fuiste tú quien provocó el incendio la otra noche? —le pregunté.

—No.

—Claro que no. ¿Por qué ibas a ser tú? —dije sonriendo—. Creo que fue un gran espectáculo.

—¿Acaso fuiste tú?

—Tengo cosas más importantes que hacer que quemar un granero viejo. Además, yo he estado allí montones de veces.

Supongo que en ese momento T. V. me miró de reojo, aunque más bien pareció como si metiese los ojos en la cabeza.

—Entonces, ¿es verdad? ¿Era verdad? ¿Había un, un, un arca allí dentro?

—Arca, barca, granero, lo que sea. A mí nunca me pareció gran cosa.

T. V. se quedó un buen rato mirando dentro de su bolsa de Cheetos vacía, como si por mirar con atención acabara encontrando alguno, luego suspiró y tiró la bolsa al suelo.

—He oído que unos chicos de Bigger Hill estuvieron de juerga por allí; eso me han dicho. Hicieron fuego para calentarse y lo quemaron todo.

—¿De juerga? ¿Qué quieres de mí? —dijo entonces T. V.—. Tengo que irme a casa.

—¿Que qué quiero? No quiero nada. Tengo todo lo que quiero.

—Entonces, ¿por qué me molestas?

—¿Te estoy molestando? Creía que solo estaba saludando a un viejo conocido al que no veo desde hace tiempo.

—Me viste la semana pasada.

—Conque encendieron fuego para calentarse, ¿eh? No creo que armaran mucha juerga si necesitaban encender fuego para calentarse.

—Vamos, no me vengas con ese rollo. No quiero saber nada de eso.

—¿De qué rollo me hablas, T. V.?

Noté entonces que T. V. estaba sudando. ¿Os imagináis la escena?: cinco grados, un viento gélido del noroeste y T. V. sudando de tal modo que intentó secarse la cara con la manga del abrigo. Pero no lo lograba, porque cuando intentaba levantar el brazo y agachar la cabeza al mismo tiempo, una especie de bulto asomaba entre el hombro y el cuello.

Tuve que bajar la vista para no mirar.

—Bueno, supongo que ya nadie podrá ir de juerga por allí.

—Mira, tengo que irme a casa. ¿Tienes algo que decirme o solo quieres fastidiarme?

—¿No te parece que eso está un poco lejos de Bigger Hill para ir de juerga?

—Eso es lo que he oído —dijo T. V.—. No sé si es verdad o...

—¿Cómo te va en el trabajo, T. V.?

T. V. intentaba parecer receloso, pero como eso implicaba fruncir el ceño y mirar de reojo, no lo consiguió. Tenía la cara tan gorda que apenas podía gesticular.

—Esos dos tíos, los nuevos vecinos, reciben un montón de correo. Y también envían mucho.

—Seguro —dije—. El señor Colin Nieman es un escritor importante. Una de las cosas que hacen los escritores es escribir cartas.

Cuando T. V. miraba de reojo parecía un muñeco de nieve con los ojos hundidos.

—Tengo una corazonada sobre esa cena —dije. Y luego, con aire despreocupado, mientras me desabrochaba el abrigo, añadí—: ¿Sales con alguien, T. V.?

—¿Qué?

—Ya sabes a qué me refiero, T. V. Estás en esa edad en que los chicos empiezan a interesarse por las chicas. Se afeitan por la mañana, se ponen un poco de colonia de su viejo. Ya sabes, T. V. Se van de juerga. Se calientan. —Y tiritando ligeramente concluí—: ¡Qué frío hace esta noche!

T. V. me miró; eso sí podía hacerlo porque no necesitaba mover la cara. Tendría treinta años como mucho y, ¡qué coño!, he de admitir que ese comentario acerca de su viejo fue de muy mal gusto teniendo en cuenta que el pobre hombre había comprado la granja un año antes de que pasara lo de su madre, de modo que solté una risita, me encogí de hombros y puse cara de arrepentimiento.

—Solo quería saber si sales con alguien.

Su voz sonó bastante áspera, incluso enfadada, cuando dijo:

—No salgo con nadie.

—Bueno, no te preocupes. Tienes un carácter agradable y estoy seguro de que pronto encontrarás a alguien. —Y volví a tiritar.

T. V. se recostó entonces en el capó del coche, y el cacharro estuvo a punto de volcar. Os juro por Dios que una de las ruedas traseras se levantó del suelo.

—Bueno, ya vale. ¿Qué quieres? —dijo T. V., casi con desesperación—. Es tarde, estoy cansado y mañana trabajo.

—Ya te he dicho que no quiero nada, T. V. Solo he venido para ver si puedo ayudarte en algo. Ya sabes, de amigo a amigo.

—¿Has venido solo para verme?

—Expresamente, T. V.

—Bueno, no necesito nada.

Intentó que su voz sonara despreocupada, pero no podía engañar a nadie. No dejaba de mirarse los pies. Aunque no sé lo que miraba, porque no creo que pudiera verse los pies. A lo mejor buscaba su bolsa de Cheetos.

Me incorporé y me aparté del coche como si quisiera estirarme un poco, y luego, como por casualidad, avancé hacia él. Caminé muy despacio, como paseando, como si contemplara el paisaje que rodeaba el metro y medio escaso que separaba mis pies de la panza de T. V., como si fuera a detenerme en cualquier momento. Y entonces algo se infló de pronto debajo de su panza, como si una tienda de campaña saliese volando en plena noche, y no os equivoquéis, no me refiero solo a un montón de grasa. Cuando llegué a su lado, T. V. estaba hiperventilando, y cuando le apoyé una mano en el hombro me pareció que si hubiera podido habría dado un salto.

Luego le estrujé el hombro con fuerza.

—Ya sabes, T. V. Todo el mundo necesita algo. —Volví a estrujarle el hombro, porque me gustaba cómo se le movían las carnes. ¿Estás seguro de que no puedo hacer nada por ti?

T. V. evitó mirarme.

—No soy amigo tuyo.

—Vaya, T. V. Eso me ofende.

—Te desprecio.

—Eso ya lo sé. Pero también me necesitas. ¿No tienes frío? Yo estoy helado.

—Odio a los negros en general.

«Y ellos te odian a ti —pensé, aunque no lo dije—. Si es que llegan a fijarse en ti.» Pero no dije nada. Era mejor no decir nada.

T. V. tampoco dijo nada, pero intentó secarse el sudor de los ojos. Sentí lástima de él, tengo que reconocerlo, y si hubiera tenido un pañuelo le habría secado el sudor de los ojos y me habría marchado sin más. Sí, sí, es un pensamiento bonito, pero... Pero como no tenía un pañuelo no pude hacerlo. Adelanté el muslo izquierdo hasta rozar con él el interior de la rodilla derecha de T. V. Intenté rodearle la pierna izquierda como mi pierna derecha, pero era demasiado gorda para abarcarla.

—No lo consideres una ayuda, T. V. Piensa que es como repartir el correo. Es algo que haces por los demás. Es tu trabajo. Y el mío es este. Esto es lo que yo hago por los demás.

Y os diré una cosa: T. V. era capaz de moverse muy deprisa cuando quería, teniendo en cuenta lo gordo que estaba. Ni siquiera lo vi venir; de pronto me hizo agachar la cabeza de un empujón. Yo habría preferido hacerlo con la mano, ya sabéis lo que quiero decir, pero tenía las dos manos ocupadas apartando su panza —temía que si no la sujetaba se me cayera encima y me aplastara—, y todo terminó en menos de un minuto.

¿Qué más puedo decir? Que para ser tan gordo disparó muy poca carga.

Luego T. V. se buscó la polla con las manos por debajo de la panza para metérsela otra vez en los pantalones, y yo rebusqué en el bolsillo para sacar la última carta que le había escrito al Rata.

—Eh, T. V., ¿puedo darte...?

—Y ahora, ¿qué más quieres? —rugió T. V., con tanta fuerza que debo admitir que me asustó. Miré alrededor, pero no vi que nadie saliera del bar de Sloppy Joe. T. V. seguía tanteando a ciegas por allí abajo y pensé si debía ayudarlo a encontrarla, pero me pareció que lo mejor era esperar.

Cuando hubo terminado de arreglarse, dije:

—Es solo una carta, T. V.

—Las cartas se echan en el buzón.

—Ya lo sé, ya lo sé, no quiero darte trabajo de más. Solo pensaba que, como estamos los dos aquí y...

Pareció cambiar de humor entonces y, como acabo de decir, a veces podía ser muy rápido. Me arrancó la carta de la mano como si fuera un bocadillo de jamón. Se quedó un rato mirando la dirección y luego volvió a mirarla otro buen rato. Al fin me miró.

Le devolví la mirada.

—No te preocupes, Divine. Me ocuparé de que llegue a su destino.

En el remite ponía Divine.

Intentó meterse la carta en el bolsillo de los pantalones, pero no lo encontraba, y acabó guardándosela bajo la cinturilla del pantalón. Pensé que debería darle alguna explicación, pero me encogí de hombros y dije:

—Sabía que podía contar contigo, T. V.

T. V. esbozó una especie de sonrisa. Incluso eso le costaba. Resultó que llevaba un pañuelo en el bolsillo de la camisa, y se secó el sudor de la frente.

—Pues claro que puedes contar conmigo, Divine. ¿Para qué están los amigos, si no?

2.07

JUSTIN

Rosemary Krebs se quedó de pie junto a su silla. Los ornamentos de la parte superior del respaldo, tallados en forma de bellotas, eran casi tan altos como ella, y cuando se sentó pareció por un momento como si los dos palos de la silla se le hubieran clavado en los hombros.

—Bueno, ¿ya estamos todos? —dijo.

—Ahora sí —observó Myra, entrando precipitadamente en el salón. Acababa de empolvarse la nariz y el escote (también el vestido púrpura) y tenía los labios húmedos y brillantes. Se sentó sin mirar a nadie.

Vi por el rabillo del ojo que Lucy hacía una mueca de disgusto. Lucy, que era mi «acompañante», estaba sentada a mi izquierda, mientras que yo me encontraba a la izquierda del alcalde; Colin, que era mi «padre», estaba sentado frente a mí, a la derecha del alcalde, con Myra a su derecha. Webbie estaba al lado de Myra, aunque apenas la veía por culpa del enorme candelabro que ocupaba el centro de la mesa, y Wade estaba frente a ella. El candelabro, que presidía la estancia, producía mucho calor, y el parpadeo violeta de las velas desbarataba el cursi peinado de Rosemary Krebs.

Colin carraspeó antes de decir:
—Esto, bueno, no me gusta echar sal en las heridas.
—¿Cómo dice? —preguntó el alcalde.
—¿Señor Nieman? —Rosemary Krebs se miró las manos, como si buscara algún tipo de laceración.

Colin esbozó una atribulada sonrisa.
—Lo que quiero decir es que yo, como Wade, siento bastante curiosidad por la historia de Eddie Comedy.

El rostro del alcalde se iluminó fugazmente para oscurecerse al momento igual de súbitamente, y asintió con tal solemnidad que pensé que por una vez iba a decir algo sustancial. Pero siguió asintiendo un rato hasta que sacudió la cabeza, como para despejarla, y dijo:
—¿Quiere servirse un poco de pollo, Justin, para que podamos empezar?
—El sheriff Brown me ha llevado a creer —comenzó Rosemary Krebs, pero luego se detuvo—. El sheriff Brown nos ha llevado a creer a mi marido y a mí que está investigando cualquier posible... —La voz se perdió cuando, con gran delicadeza, se sirvió tres trozos de remolacha en el plato y le pasó la fuente a Wade.
—Creo que la palabra que buscas es «pista», Rosemary —dijo el alcalde, sirviéndose a su vez dos trozos de pollo frito—. Aunque tal vez deberías preguntarle al señor Nieman, puesto que él es el escritor.
—Creo que «pista» es la palabra...
—Phyneas, antes de repetir deberías esperar hasta que todos nuestros invitados se hayan servido.

El alcalde pareció avergonzado y volvió a dejar uno de los trozos de pollo en la fuente.
—Cualquier pista posible —continuó entonces Rosemary Krebs, sonriendo a Colin, que en ese momento se servía un muslo de pollo—. Como pueden imaginar, un incidente como este no es en absoluto común en Galatea, no obstante, el sheriff Brown es un policía con mucha experiencia, y tanto el alcalde como yo tenemos una

enorme fe en su capacidad para resolver este caso con celeridad y eficacia.

—¿Con celeridad y eficacia? —repitió Wade—. Madre mía, Rosemary, eso sí que es confianza. —Hizo una pausa hasta que ella le pasó la fuente de puré de patatas y, gesticulando aparatosamente, a causa del alcohol, consiguió servirse dos enormes montones de puré antes de pasarle la fuente a Lucy—. No pretendo insinuar que hayas depositado tu confianza donde no debes, Rosemary, pero lo cierto es que ese Eustace Brown sería incapaz de encontrar su propia... mano si esta no estuviera unida a su cuerpo.

—¿Judías verdes? —invitó Rosemary Krebs, ofreciéndole a Wade la fuente, pero antes de que ninguno de los dos pudiera decir nada, el alcalde rió con ganas y dijo:

—No me gusta nada llevarle la contraria a mi mujer, Wade, pero he de admitir que no entiendo qué es lo que Rosemary ve en ese hombre.

—Supongo que yo podría decírselo, señor alcalde. Eustace Brown es un hombre de imaginación limitada, y los hombres así resultan muy eficientes para una cosa: acatar órdenes.

—Señor alcalde, ¿eh? —dijo el alcalde, reteniendo la fuente de judías verdes—. Eso no lo había oído nunca. «Señor alcalde.»

—Phyneas —dijo Rosemary Krebs—. Seguro que el señor Nieman quiere un poco de verdura.

—Sí, claro, claro —admitió el alcalde, pasando la fuente de inmediato.

—Llamó a papá —dijo entonces Webbie.

—¿Eddie Comedy? —preguntó el alcalde.

Webbie se cubrió la boca con una mano:

—No, no. El agente Brown. Le preguntó si sabía dónde estaba Melvin Cartwright.

—Tal vez, señorita Greeving, puesto que el sheriff Brown ha hablado con el reverendo, deberíamos dejar el asunto en manos de ambos.

Webbie cogió entonces la servilleta para limpiarse los labios, aunque aún no había probado la comida.

—Bueno —dijo, en voz baja aunque insistente—. Papá lo estuvo discutiendo luego con sus Damas, de manera que no creo que siga siendo secreto.

Myra Robinson lanzó entonces una carcajada; Lucy emitió una risita ahogada después de mirar a Rosemary Krebs.

—¿Sus Damas? —preguntó Colin—. ¿Melvin Cartwright?

—Melvin Cartwright —explicó el alcalde arrastrando las palabras, con la voz llena de oficialidad y pollo— era un muchacho negro de la edad de Webbie aproximadamente, un negro muy educado, a decir verdad, que casualmente se marchó del pueblo más o menos cuando desapareció Eddie Comedy. El agente Brown parece haber reparado en la posible relación entre ambos hechos, lo cual me resulta…

—Creo que la palabra que buscas es «ridículo», Phyneas.

—En realidad pensaba en «memez», pero gracias, Rosemary, creo que «ridículo» encaja bastante bien.

Sobrevino un largo silencio roto tan solo por el ligero tintineo de la plata contra la porcelana y el chasquido ocasional de un hueso de pollo. El salón de los Krebs era grande, pero los sólidos y oscuros muebles, con sus superficies talladas ocultas bajo una nebulosa de encajes, se comían el espacio. Todo estaba adornado con cenefas blancas —las ventanas, la mesa, los aparadores— y había pañitos de encaje bajo todos los objetos decorativos de cristal, plata o porcelana. El conjunto parecía salido de una obra de Ibsen: solo faltaba el disparo en la habitación contigua.

Wade dejó caer los cubiertos con gran estrépito.

—Pero ¿no os parece?… —dijo, sin que estuviera nada claro a quién se refería—. ¿No os parece una extraña coincidencia que el caso Eddie Comedy-Melvin Cartwright se parezca tanto al caso de mi padre y Gary Gables?

—Wade —dijo Webbie, con una brusquedad que yo no le había oído hasta entonces—. Gary habló de mudarse meses antes de la muerte de tu padre. —Dicho lo cual bebió un trago de agua y se limpió la boca con el dorso de la mano.

—Creía que tu padre había muerto en un accidente de tráfico —dijo Colin.

—Sí, murió en un coche. Lo del accidente no lo sé.

—No entiendo.

—Claro que no entiendes —replicó Wade bruscamente—. ¿Por qué ibas a entenderlo si no eres de aquí?

—Wade —repitió Webbie, esta vez en tono suplicante—. Por favor…

Wade la interrumpió de inmediato:

—Hace nueve años el coche de mi padre, igual que el de Eddie Comedy, se estrelló contra un poste de teléfono, casualmente en la carretera Veinticuatro, a unos cuatro kilómetros al este del pueblo. Mi padre salió despedido por el parabrisas. Murió, aunque no a consecuencia de las heridas, que en todo caso resultaron fatales, ni tampoco de un disparo, sino por falta de ayuda. Estuvo casi veinticuatro horas tirado en la cuneta. Pero lo que a mí me preocupó, lo que, tal vez debería decir, preocupó a mi madre, puesto que yo no estaba aquí en ese momento, fue el hecho de que además de las heridas que le provocó el impacto contra el poste, había una abolladura en un costado del coche y manchas de pintura color turquesa, que parecían indicar que el coche de mi padre había colisionado con otro, presumiblemente antes de estrellarse contra el poste.

—Wade —intervino Webbie una vez más—. Era azul. Azul. Hay montones de cosas azules...

—¿Creéis que ese Gary...?

—Gables —dijo Webbie.

—¿Creéis que Gary Gables...?

—Pedí que analizaran la pintura, Webbie. Era un pigmento usado por la General Motors, concretamente de la marca DuPont, y más concretamente llamado «turquesa Cherokee», que se usó en modelos como los Buicks, los Pontiacs y los Cadillacs entre mil novecientos setenta y ocho y mil novecientos ochenta y cuatro. Gary Gables tenía un Pontiac Le Sabre del ochenta y dos.

—Le Sabre es un Buick —dijo Webbie, casi susurrando— y el Cherokee no se pintaba de turquesa. —Juntó las manos delante de la boca y las dejó allí.

—¡Crees que Gary Gables echó a tu padre de la carretera! —exclamó Colin, esforzándose por borrar la sonrisa de su rostro, aunque por sus ojos se veían pasar palabras, párrafos, capítulos enteros—. ¿Cómo es que tardaron veinticuatro horas en descubrir el accidente?

—Fue al este del pueblo —dijo Wade.

—Quieres decir de Galatia.

—Lo que quiero decir es —respondió Wade, lanzando una rápida mirada a Rosemary Krebs— al este del «pueblo». Lo que quiero decir es que mi padre era un hombre ruin. No solo abusaba de sus hijos, no solo maltrataba a su mujer, sino que además era un racista cruel. Mi padre intentó impedir en cierta ocasión que Abraham Greeving pudiera votar en las elecciones municipales, y cuando alguien se lo echó en cara dijo, en voz bien alta, públicamente, que por lo que él sabía los «negros» ya no eran propiedad de nadie, pero que tampoco tenían derecho a votar.

—Pero votó de todos modos —dijo el alcalde—. Yo vi cómo el reverendo Greeving introducía la papeleta en la urna —explicó con una risita—. Aunque perdió a pesar de todo.

—Y usted ganó, señor alcalde. Sí, todos lo sabemos.

—¿Creéis —preguntó Colin— que la gente pasó por alto el accidente de manera deliberada?

—Fue Howard quien lo encontró. Howard encontró a tu padre.

Era Lucy quien había dicho esto y, al oír sus palabras, Wade se volvió bruscamente hacia ella.

—Sí, Lucy. Howard encontró a mi padre, pero dime, ¿dónde está el tuyo?

Lucy se quedó sin aliento y se tapó la boca con la mano.

La sala quedó en silencio tras esta última intervención de Wade y en ese silencio Colin susurró una única palabra:

—Fascinante.

Myra, sentada frente a Lucy, agachó la cabeza. Acariciaba anhelantemente el bolso con una mano, mientras con la otra se tapaba la boca. Y, sin embargo, parecía que estaba riéndose.

—Lo que le pasó a tu padre fue una tragedia, Wade —intervino Rosemary Krebs, adoptando un tono político, tranquilizador, de esos que a mí me ponen loco de rabia—. Sé que hablo también en nombre del alcalde cuando digo que a todos nos afecta profundamente esta pérdida.

—Veinticuatro horas —dijo Wade—. Mi padre se rompió las piernas, la pelvis y el brazo derecho en el siniestro. También se dislocó el brazo izquierdo, se partió dos costillas y se perforó el hígado; tenía veintitrés fragmentos de cristal incrustados en la cara, uno de los cuales le atravesó el ojo derecho, pero a pesar de todas estas heridas consiguió arrastrarse exactamente tres metros y medio desde el lugar donde había aterrizado. Logró meterse en la cuneta, pero no pudo salir, y estuvo veinticuatro horas allí tirado hasta que Howard, muchas gracias, señorita Robinson, hasta que Howard Goertzen decidió pararse para ver qué pasaba.

Lucy, sentada junto a mí, habló sin quitar la vista de su regazo:

—Howard dijo que vio el coche por la mañana. Dijo que lo vio por la mañana, pero que no pensó que hubiera ocurrido nada hasta la noche, cuando vio que aún seguía allí. —Levantó la vista de repente y, en lugar de mirar a Colin, me miró a mí—. Howard es «blanco».

—Vamos, Wade —dijo Webbie—. Gary llevaba meses diciendo que se marchaba antes de que muriera tu padre. Meses.

—Sí —dijo Wade—. Se pasó meses diciendo que se marchaba, pero no parecía tener intención de hacerlo. Hasta el día en que ocurrió el accidente de mi padre. —Guardó silencio. Lanzó una lenta mirada alrededor, como desafiando a que alguien hablara, pero nadie aceptó el desafío. Al final, su mirada se cruzó con la mía por encima de la cabeza de Lucy, y me miró con tan franco deseo que, al instante, bajé la vista—. ¡Hay que ver, todo este lío y nadie ha mencionado aún a Eric Johnson!

Alcé la vista y vi que Rosemary Krebs se levantaba.

—¿Alguien quiere postre? —preguntó, al tiempo que sonreía.

Vi que tenía el plato vacío, aunque no recordaba haberla visto comer nada.

2.08

DIVINE

Lo que pasa con el sexo es que enseguida se acaba. Quiero decir que si lo que se pretende es matar el tiempo, más vale poner la tele o cualquier cosa, porque follar no lleva más de una o dos horas, eso contando con los preámbulos y el epílogo, y chupársela a un cartero seboso en el aparcamiento de una sala de billar no lleva más de diez minutos, contando con la charla y la limpieza. Lo que quiero decir es que cuando T. V. Daniels y yo dimos por terminado el asunto, ni siquiera eran las nueve. Lo que quiero decir es que todos mis conocidos seguían cenando en casa de Rosemary Krebs, todos menos mis padres, que lo último que sabía de ellos era que estaban en Florida, y yo estaba sentado en mi coche más solo que la una. No es que me sintiera solo. Solo que tenía un muermo del copón.

Por eso decidí ir hasta el arca de Noah.

Pero Noah había construido su barca y su granero de madera y solo de madera; ni siquiera usó clavos, pues al parecer en la Biblia no tenían clavos, pero si eso es cierto, ¿cómo coño le clavaron a Cristo las manos y los pies cuando lo crucificaron? Además, Noah lo llenó todo de paja. De paja, como si quisiera alimentar a todos los animales que había metido allí dentro. Ahora bien, admito que no tengo demasiado sentido común, pero hasta yo podría decir que fue un «milagro» que aquello no se hubiera quemado mucho antes.

Ese negro estaba loco, de eso no cabe ninguna duda. Ya pueden decir lo que quieran de él –que era un buen granjero, padre de familia y constructor de barcos–, pero Noah Deacon estaba como una puta cabra.

Creo que eso que dijo T. V. de que unos chicos de Bigger Hill habían prendido fuego es una gilipollez, pero sé de más de uno en Galatia que ha estado en el arca un par de veces. Aunque debo decir que a nadie le entraban ganas de volver. Un granero lleno de paja es muy probable que esté también lleno de ratas y ratones, y cualquier lugar lleno de ratas y ratones es muy probable que esté lleno de serpientes, incluso de serpientes de cascabel. La única vez que estuve allí creo que fue con Lyle Goertzen. No, no pudo ser con Lyle, porque Lyle era blanco y yo nunca habría llevado a un blanco al arca de Noah. Fue con Bruce Cardinal, creo, en nuestro segundo asalto, si mal no recuerdo, pero no me acuerdo de casi nada más que del olor a verdura podrida y el sonido de cosas que crujían entre la paja, lo cual es una pena, porque Bruce tenía una polla del carajo, hummm, eso sí que lo recuerdo bien, y recuerdo que entre nuestro primero y nuestro segundo encuentro había aprendido a usarla muy bien. Pero con todo, ni siquiera por un buen polvo vale la pena correr el riesgo de que te pique una serpiente, y lo que más me asustó fueron todos aquellos animales disecados; me refiero a animales de granja normales y corrientes: caballos, vacas, cerdos y gallinas, aunque Noah había comprado también una pareja de búfalos y otra de longhorns de Texas –bueno, todos estaban en parejas, ¡para eso era el arca de Noé!– y todos estaban pudriéndose. Te daban ganas de vomitar, y se te cortaba la erección, y después de esa visita con Bruce, creo que yo tenía trece o catorce años, nunca me molesté en volver por allí hasta la semana pasada, cuando intentaba huir del agente Brown.

No tengo ni idea de cómo Wade pudo saber adónde había ido. A veces ese tío me deja perplejo.

Estaba tan absorto pensando en todo esto que casi me olvido de ella, quiero decir del arca, o lo que quedaba, que eran principalmente cenizas. No podía haber recorrido más de siete kilómetros en una hora, no había carretera que llevase hasta allí y, además, la oscuridad era casi total, y no os podéis imaginar lo deprisa que un coyote te puede poner las pilas. Iba mirando al horizonte, como si esperara ver el arca a lo lejos, pero el arca ya no estaba, y luego, de repente, fue como si me hubiera metido dentro de una nube o algo por el estilo. Eran las cenizas que levantaba el coche, pero me cagué de miedo. Pisé el freno, pero antes de detenerme del todo me dije: Tranquilo, Divine, solo son cenizas. Y las cenizas seguían volando por debajo del coche, pero como llevaba los faros encendidos la escena me recordó a una película de extraterrestres y naves espaciales. Estaba acojonado, y hacía mucho frío.

Al cabo de un rato apagué el motor, aunque dejé los faros encendidos. Las cenizas tardaron un minuto en posarse, pero yo seguía cagado de miedo. Los faros estaban encendidos y la tierra aparecía cubierta de polvo blanco. Era, no sé, como estar en medio del desierto o algo así, como estar en la luna. Era muy bonito, pero también un poco triste, porque todas esas cenizas no estarían allí si el arca no hubiera ardido, y era como si el hecho de que el arca hubiese ardido hiciera en parte que las cenizas fueran tan bonitas. Quiero decir, saber por qué había pasado y por qué estaba allí. Era como si el arca fuera mucho más interesante ahora que ya no existía. Creo que me conozco muy bien la historia: mamá y el Rata, y hasta Eddie Comedy, todos se habían ido, y ahora que no estaban me importaban mucho más que antes.

De vez en cuando, una ligera brisa removía y levantaba las cenizas. Era una noche muy tranquila y la brisa también era tranquila, quiero decir que no hacía ruido, pero el aire tan pronto estaba despejado y oscuro como se llenaba de ceniza, y como los faros del coche calentaban la ceniza, el aire parecía lleno de chispas. Y creo que me quedé colgado mirándolas un buen rato, porque cuando al fin me di cuenta de que había alguien más no supe decir si habría llegado mucho antes sin que yo me diera cuenta: Colin Nieman estaba a pocos metros, iluminado por la luz de los faros. Sabía que era Colin Nieman por su estatura, pues no había en Galatia nadie tan alto como Colin Nieman, y también por su ropa, concretamente por el abrigo, un gran abrigo negro, tipo trenca, que los hombres de Galatea no suelen usar, y, además, por su cabeza, grande y calva, tan redonda y blanca como una bola de billar.

Al verlo salí del coche de un salto.

—¡Colin! —grité—. ¡Colin, soy yo, soy Reggie! —Supongo que me había quedado pasmado al verlo, de lo contrario no habría usado mi nombre de pila.

La capa de cenizas era muy profunda. Era como correr por la nieve. Y juraría que aún estaban tibias. Hacía un frío del carajo, pero tenía los pies calientes hundidos en aquella masa seca y blanda.

Colin sacó una de las manos del bolsillo. Pensé que iba a saludarme, pero se puso algo en la cabeza, una especie de gorro de lana, y una vez se lo hubo puesto, no se distinguía dónde terminaba el gorro y dónde empezaba la piel. Pero no pensé demasiado en eso. Hacía un frío polar. Luego me acerqué un poco más y, al ver que Colin se tapaba también la cara con el gorro pensé que se trataba de un pasamontañas, pero después de dar unos cuantos pasos vi que no era un pasamontañas sino una capucha; una capucha blanca con un par de agujeros para los ojos, y entonces —no soy el negro más tonto del mundo—, entonces se me ocurrió pensar que tal vez no era Colin Nieman. Se me pasaron varias cosas por la cabeza. Aún seguía corriendo hacia él, hacia quien había tomado por Colin Nieman, aunque no tenía la seguridad de que fuera Colin Nieman, sino más bien, corría hacia mi idea de Colin Nieman, y esa idea me atrapó como si fuera un pez. Y en lo primero que pensé entonces fue en el Rata, en la vez que volvió del Big M con el cuerpo lleno de quemaduras de cigarro, y luego en Eddie Comedy, con la cabeza reventada y la oreja arrancada sobre el asiento de la furgoneta, y luego en Justin Time. Había visto a Justin hacía un par de días, en casa de Wade, y tenía un ojo morado, y dijo que se había dado contra una puerta mientras hacía la mudanza. Y luego volví a pensar en Colin Nieman. Para entonces, estaba casi delante de él, y dejé de correr.

Seguía sin saber si quien estaba allí era Colin Nieman o no. Había tenido mucho tiempo para pensar en ello, pero seguía sin tenerlo claro. Lo único que sabía, por si estáis pensando en eso, es que la cena de Rosemary Krebs debía terminar a eso de las nueve o nueve y media, y calculaba que serían más o menos las diez. Quiero decir, me gustaría poder decir que no era Colin —y estoy casi seguro de que no lo era—, pero, si lo dijera estaría tergiversando las cosas. Normalmente no me preocupa tanto la verdad, pero esta vez quiero contar los hechos tal como ocurrieron.

Quienquiera que fuese no se movió mientras yo corría hacia él. Se cubrió la cara con el saco, pero luego metió las manos en los bolsillos y no hizo nada más. Y acto seguido se desvaneció en la noche, con su abrigo negro, sus pantalones y sus botas; quiero decir que se me metieron cenizas en los ojos, y me hicieron llorar un poco; todo se volvió borroso y durante un rato no vi más que la mancha blanca de su cabeza flotando en el aire, y tardé un momento en descubrir a qué me recordaba, hasta que supe que me recordaba a una piedra ventral, pero entonces se me aclaró la visión y avancé un paso más, antes de detenerme. Noté una cosa más: que había algo, unas letras, aunque podría haber sido un dibujo, bordadas en la capucha con hebras oscuras y brillantes. Estaba casi seguro de que eran letras. El hombre no se movió cuando yo me detuve. Me gustaría poder decir que me estaba mirando, pero estaba demasiado oscuro para verle los ojos.

—¿Colin?

No sé cuánto tardé en decir esto, pero entonces el hombre dio una especie de respingo, como si se hubiera olvidado de que yo estaba allí.

—¿Eres tú, Colin?

No respondió; no dijo nada; no movió la cabeza, ni asintió. Se quedó quieto, pero me pareció que rebuscaba en uno de los bolsillos con la mano izquierda. Estaba tan oscuro que resultaba difícil saberlo.

—Soy yo, Divine. ¿Eres tú, Colin?

Entonces se me acercó y, por el modo en que movió los pies, os aseguro que sus intenciones no eran buenas, fuese o no fuese Colin. Pero yo estaba paralizado. Parecía como si las cenizas fuesen arenas movedizas o algo así, pero también pensaba en el incendio que las había producido. Me entraron ganas de desaparecer, igual que el arca de Noah, igual que Noah. Daba igual que aquel hombre fuese Colin Nieman o el coco o el diablo; sabía que tarde o temprano se desvanecería con su abrigo negro y sus pantalones negros y sus botas negras, dejando tras de sí la imagen de la cabeza encapuchada, y luego también esta imagen desaparecería, y yo me sentiría mucho más solo.

Intenté llamarlo por última vez, pero cuando abrí la boca no logré emitir ningún sonido. Era como cuando, en sueños, quieres hablar pero no te sale la voz. Exactamente igual.

Entonces, sacó la mano derecha del bolsillo. Vi que llevaba algo en ella, puede que fuera de metal, o de cristal, algo brillante y plateado, de aspecto duro, según me pareció al principio, pero de pronto algo hizo clic en mi cabeza y vi que lo que llevaba en la mano era el retrovisor que yo había perdido la noche que encontré a Eddie Comedy en el Big M, pero no tuve tiempo de pensar en nada más, porque tras realizar otro suave movimiento, levantó la mano por el aire y ¡bam!, me golpeó con el espejo en la cabeza, y se apagaron las luces para Divine.

2.09

JUSTIN

Una vez hubo terminado no estaba seguro de qué había pasado. De lo que se había dicho y de lo que se había dejado implícito. Durante la cena todo parecía tener sentido, pero cuando terminamos de comer, Wade se marchó con Webbie dejando tras de sí una vaga sensación de tensa inquietud. Parecía bastante claro que Wade acusaba al tal Gary Gables del accidente de su padre, y también parecía claro, aunque menos, que acusaba a toda Galatia de la muerte de su padre, e incluso a Galatea. Era difícil distinguir a qué se refería cuando hablaba del «pueblo». Y luego estaba el asunto de Eddie Comedy y el de Melvin Cartwright. Y el de Howard Goertzen, fuera quien fuese, y el de Eric Johnson. Y el agente Brown. Y el reverendo Greeving, y las Damas de la iglesia: ¿quién coño eran las Damas? Quería irme a casa para aclarar todos aquellos nombres e historias que habían surgido durante la cena, todos aquellos retazos de historias, pero Colin aceptó el café que nos ofreció Rosemary Krebs. «En la salita –dijo–, allí estaremos más cómodos.»

Camino de la salita Myra Robinson anunció que tenía que ir al cuarto de baño, y yo me quedé el último para poder seguirla por el pasillo y esperarla a la salida del baño.

Estaba cerrando la cremallera del bolso cuando abrió la puerta, y yo le ofrecí la mejor y más desesperada de mis sonrisas.

—Por favor —le dije—, sería capaz de matar por un trago de lo que lleva en el bolso.

Myra vaciló un momento, luego me metió de un empujón en el cuarto de baño. La petaca era de metal barato, igual que el whisky.

—Espero no causarle una mala impresión —dijo Myra—. En realidad no soy una alcohólica. Pero es el único modo de soportar una velada con Su Alteza Real.

—Por favor —le dije, dando un largo trago por tercera vez—. No tiene que darme ningún tipo de explicaciones.

Myra sonrió y dijo:

—Claro que, sabiendo que usted bebe, podría negarme a que salga con mi hija.

—No creo que eso sea un problema.

Myra pareció no comprender, luego me quitó la petaca de la mano y se la llevó a los labios. Bebió, le puso el tapón y se la guardó en el bolso.

—¡Vaya! Estaba pensando que… ¿Significa eso que me he emperifollado tanto para nada?

—Bueno —dije—. Retiro lo dicho.

—¿Usted…? —Myra se estiró los pechos, el escote.

—No, no, no —añadí—. No me refiero a eso. Los dos somos maricones perdidos. Retiro lo dicho sobre las explicaciones. Me gustaría que me explicara algunas cosas. Algunos huecos en la historia de Wade.

—¿Huecos?

—Lagunas, omisiones, evasiones, lo que sea. Tenía la sensación de estar oyendo una versión abreviada.

—¿Cómo dice?

—Creo que estaba ocultando algo, ¿no es cierto?

—¡Ah! —dijo Myra. Y abriendo mucho los ojos se apartó de mí—. Supongo que hay muchas cosas que Wade no ha dicho, pero yo no soy la persona más indicada para hablar de eso. —Se miró con atención en el espejo y luego, como inconscientemente, se retocó el pelo—. Creo, esto, creo que deberíamos volver.

—Myra. —Le puse una mano en el hombro y casi dio un salto. Me miró y comprendí que no solo estaba evadiéndose sino que estaba aterrorizada.

—¿Sí?

—Lo digo en serio —dije, sonriendo—. Creo que está usted fabulosa.

—¡Fabulosa! —me imitó Myra, y entonces soltó una risa que desprendió un olor ligeramente amargo por el alcohol, y añadió—: De todos modos usted no querrá salir con Lucy. A decir verdad, no es más que una cursi y una estirada a quien le gustaría que su madre se pareciese a Rosemary Krebs —explicó, haciendo pinzas con los dedos; luego buscó en el bolso y sacó un pequeño pulverizador.

—Viene usted realmente preparada.

—Pues no ha visto ni la mitad. Ahora abra bien la boca y ruegue que no sea gas de defensa personal. —Antes de que pudiera pensar si estaba bromeando sentí el picor del elixir en la lengua. Se detuvo cuando hubo terminado, sin dejar de mirarme. Se estaba fijando en mi ojo—. Ya sé que no es asunto mío, pero ¿fue él quien…?

—¿El ojo morado? No, me di con una puerta. —Me miró con aspecto divertido y añadí—: En serio. Esa casa está llena de puertas.

—Sé exactamente cuántas puertas hay en esa casa. La he estado limpiando durante veinte años.

—Usted...

—No me refería al moratón. Me refería a la cicatriz.

—La cicatriz —dije, sorprendido de que la hubiera visto, y me la toqué con la mano, esa mano en la que, sorprendentemente, Wade había notado algo raro, y me pregunté si todos mis secretos eran igual de transparentes—. No, no fue Colin. Colin intentó curarme. ¿De modo que limpiaba usted nuestra casa? —dije, sonriendo.

—Durante veinte años, pero ya estoy retirada. Bea me dejó un pellizquito en su testamento. Lo suficiente para ir tirando, aunque a veces le echo una mano a Elaine Sumner en el café.

—Otra historia —dije.

Myra sonrió con aire cómplice.

—No venga pisándome los talones, para no levantar sospechas. Los talones —repitió, mirándose las varicosas piernas y los zapatos con plataforma de madera—. Mis pobres tobillos —se lamentó, y luego dijo—: ¡Fabulosa!

Cuando al cabo de varios minutos regresé a la salita, Lucy le estaba contando a Colin que había quedado finalista en el concurso de Miss Kansas.

Pobre Lucy. Estaba peligrosamente sentada en el borde de la silla, y en la rigidez de su columna se advertían sus futuros problemas de espalda.

—Supongo que te refieres al concurso de Miss Culo Dulce —estaba diciendo Myra cuando entré en la habitación. Y Lucy la miró con un desprecio que la habría descalificado en «Elegancia».

—¡Mamá! —exclamó, pero se recuperó de inmediato—. Bueno, más vale que no hablemos de eso —dijo, e intentó suavizar sus rasgos con un gesto que le arrugó el vestido—. De lo contrario, descubrirían una faceta mía que no les resultaría demasiado agradable. Ja, ja —añadió, como si a nosotros nunca se nos hubiera ocurrido pensar que pudiera tener un lado desagradable.

Advertí entonces que Phyneas Krebs se había quedado dormido en una punta del sofá. Rosemary Krebs estaba sentada en silencio junto a su marido. Miraba fijamente a Colin y, al volverse, su mirada se cruzó con la mía.

—Espero que usted y el señor Nieman hayan pasado una grata velada.

—Claro que sí —me apresuré a decir—. Grata compañía, grata velada, es lo que digo siempre.

—Me alegro —dijo—, porque me gustaría invitarlos a una repetición de la actuación.

—¿Repetición? ¿Actuación? —indagué.

—El alcalde y yo vamos a dar una pequeña fiesta —explicó Rosemary Krebs. No miró a su marido, que roncaba ligeramente—. Creo que la gente joven lo llama «baile».

Lucy Robinson rió con ganas.

—¿Con qué motivo?

Y entonces Rosemary Krebs hizo algo, aunque tardé un rato en comprender que estaba riéndose.

—¿Es que hace falta un motivo para celebrar? —Siguió riendo con aquel sonido raro, como si tuviera dificultades para respirar—. El alcalde y yo celebramos la fiesta del Día de los Fundadores todos los veranos, pero este último otoño ha sido muy… complicado. Parecía que todo el mundo aprovechaba la menor oportunidad para desaparecer. La fiesta será este fin de semana. Sé que no los aviso con demasiado tiempo, pero me gustaría extender personalmente esta invitación a ustedes cuatro.

—Será un placer —dijo Colin al punto, y me volví hacia él, pero él miraba a Lucy. Parecía a punto de preguntar algo, pero Rosemary Krebs intervino antes que él:

—Por favor —dijo—, si me lo permiten me gustaría abordar un asunto un poco… delicado.

Colin se volvió hacia ella.

—Por supuesto —dijo, siempre impecable cuando se trataba de respetar la etiqueta—. Hable con entera libertad, por favor.

—Nuestro amigo, Wade Painter —dijo Rosemary Krebs.

—Nuestro amigo —repetí.

—El caso —continuó Rosemary Krebs en voz más baja— es que el agente Brown no llegó a encontrar nunca a Gary Gables. Pero, aparte de la extraña coincidencia temporal, nada podía indicar que Gary Gables o alguien de Galatia tuviera algo que ver en la muerte de Odell. Es triste que aquí muera más gente de la que nace.

—¿Odell? —preguntó Colin.

—¿Galatia? —pregunté yo.

—Perdónenme. Odell era el nombre del padre de Wade. —Rosemary Krebs se permitió tragar saliva discretamente y, cuando volvió a hablar, lo hizo casi susurrando—. Me disgusta hablar con tanta… franqueza, pero debo decirles que todo el mundo sabía que Odell… El accidente fue a causa del alcohol. De hecho, el juez de instrucción llegó a insinuar que Odell estaba tan borracho que casi ni se dio cuenta de que había sufrido un accidente.

—Pero ¿y lo de la pintura? —dije, sin poder contener el fuerte eructo que siguió a mis palabras.

Rosemary Krebs se volvió hacia mí.

—Señor Time.

Lucy soltó una risita y yo rechacé aquel nombre. Nadie me había llamado nunca «Señor Time», y no me gustaba cómo sonaba.

—Lo siento —dije—, es que...

—No, no lo sienta. Su preocupación es absolutamente comprensible. —Se detuvo un momento—. Pero, sin embargo, es infundada. Eustace pudo determinar que, por aquel entonces, hace nueve años, había cuarenta y seis automóviles en Galatea, todos ellos pintados de Cherokee turquesa.

—¿Eustace? —inquirió Colin.

—El agente Brown —le recordó Myra. Se echó a reír, pero con risa nerviosa—. Estuvo husmeando por todas las casas en plena noche y tomó una pequeña muestra de pintura de todos los coches, hasta que el doberman de Vern Gatlinger le dio un buen mordisco en el trasero, y a partir de ese momento se limitó a preguntar a la gente por radio. ¡Qué hombre! —exclamó, riendo de nuevo.

—Galatea es de la General Motors —intervino Lucy.

—¿En oposición a qué? —pregunté, volviéndome hacia ella.

Me miró con expresión confundida:

—Pues a la Ford. O a la Chrysler, supongo; aunque en realidad aquí nadie tiene un Chrysler.

—En todo caso —dijo Rosemary Krebs—, me pareció que debía aclarar... los recelos de Wade.

—Sí, claro, gracias —dijo Colin, y volviéndose hacia Lucy añadió—: Me parece, señorita, que estábamos hablando de usted.

—¡Eh! —exclamó Lucy, levantando la vista y con las mejillas arreboladas. Tensó la espalda, produciendo un chasquido casi audible. Se volvió con aire nervioso hacia Rosemary Krebs, suspiró con fuerza y sonrió primero a Colin, luego, más abiertamente, a mí—. Este año debía elegir entre primer tambor y animadora, y lo que hice fue inventar una nueva ovación.

Miró alrededor acobardada y, al ver que nadie decía nada, sonrió y se puso en pie. Cerró los ojos y movió los labios como si pronunciara las palabras para sí, luego abrió los ojos, sacudió con las manos unos pompones imaginarios —el frufrú de su vestido imitaba bastante bien el sonido— y empezó a cantar:

> *Galatea, Galatea,*
> *¡eres la mejor!*
> *Galatea, Galatea,*
> *¡derrótalos!*
> *Galatea, Galatea,*

¡a cargar!
Galatea, Galatea,
¡vamos a ganar!

Terminó, colorada, con un grito y un salto, y luego nos miró a todos en busca de aprobación. Como nadie hizo ningún comentario, dejó caer ligeramente los hombros y dijo:

—Supongo que sale mejor cuando somos cinco. —Y en tono suplicante añadió—: Es para el fútbol. Al final hago el spagat. Soy la única que puede hacerlo —concluyó, casi con un susurro.

2.10

DIVINE

Recuerdo que tenía calor. Recuerdo que tenía casi calor, y de pronto empezó a hacer frío, empezó a hacer mucho frío, un frío glacial, y todo estaba oscuro. Oscuro como boca de lobo. Estaba tan oscuro que no veía nada, por más que me esforzaba, y recuerdo que me dolían los ojos de tanto escudriñar en la oscuridad con la intención de ver algo, cualquier cosa, y al abrir los ojos vi que todo seguía oscuro. Seguía oscuro, pero no tanto como antes. Vislumbré unas nubes tenues y alargadas, y detrás, las estrellas, un millón de estrellas que parecían estar justo encima de mi cabeza, como si pudiera cogerlas con solo levantar un brazo. Pero no lo hice. No levanté el brazo. Sabía que no podría. Sabía que aunque las estrellas estuvieran al alcance de la mano, se alejarían de mí si intentaba cogerlas, de manera que seguí allí tumbado, dejando que ocuparan mis ojos durante un buen rato. Además, estaban las cenizas. Al principio no sentí más que olor, sequedad, quemadura, podredumbre, todo mezclado; pero luego también sentí un sabor: todas esas cosas, secas, quemadas, podridas, se me mezclaron en la boca y, mientras intentaba reunir fuerzas para escupirlas, se levantó una brisa suave y el aire se inundó de pronto de cenizas brillantes, como si las nubes hubieran descendido y me hubiesen devorado, o como si hubiese subido flotando hasta meterme dentro de ellas, y durante un minuto, solo durante un dulce minuto, me pareció flotar entre los ángeles, rodeado de viento y estrellas por encima y por debajo y a mi alrededor, y pensé: «¡Ay, Dios mío! ¡Ay, Dios mío! Estoy muerto».

2.11

JUSTIN

Colin se pasó la noche trabajando. No paró de escribir a máquina, como un periodista de pacotilla, solamente con dos dedos. Aporreaba las teclas de su anacrónica máquina de escribir manual –una Remington, como el rifle–, produciendo un sonido como… bueno, como el que hacen las viejas máquinas de escribir. Colin vivía para ese sonido. Decía que le emocionaba, y cuando cogía carrerilla tecleaba durante horas, llenando de tinta negra páginas y páginas de ese papel color crema que Colin había pedido por correo a una papelería de París, cada resma empaquetada por separado en una bolsa de algodón, con sus iniciales bordadas. A veces Colin llenaba páginas enteras de letras sin sentido, hasta que la inspiración acudía de nuevo, pero esa noche su escritura era real, tenía un ritmo sincopado de caracteres, espacios y retornos, y yo sabía que estaba trabajando de verdad, escribiendo, transformando o, al menos, transcribiendo la conversación de la cena en un nuevo intento de comenzar su segunda novela. Me preguntaba si esta vez lo conseguiría, si se pasaría la noche escribiendo para luego quemarlo todo por la mañana o si se dejaría llevar y escribiría durante varias semanas o meses o años hasta que tuviera un buen taco de páginas sobre su enorme escritorio de caoba, como una nube, densa y solitaria, posada sobre la tierra plana. Me preguntaba qué terminaría antes, si la historia que contaba Colin o la historia que Webbie había comenzado el día de nuestra primera visita y que Wade había continuado esa misma noche, la historia de Galatea. Puede parecer que lo convierto en una carrera, pero es porque sabía que se trataba de una carrera, y Colin también sabía que en cuanto hubiera terminado su novela habría terminado con Galatea, y aunque por un lado yo esperaba que terminase pronto, también esperaba que Galatea lo derrotara. Me sentía atrapado contra mi voluntad. Quería conocer el resto de la historia. Y podía limitarme a desear únicamente eso, porque pensaba que la historia de Galatea había terminado, igual que nuestra historia, la mía y la de Colin, había terminado, y todo era ya cuestión de encajar las piezas. De haber sabido lo que aquel pueblo nos tenía reservado, esa noche me habría levantado de la cama para destruir el manuscrito, habría destruido hasta la última hoja de papel que hubiera en la casa y habría tirado la máquina de escribir por las escaleras. ¿Y por qué no? Ya lo había hecho en otra ocasión y nos había salvado, al menos momentáneamente. Nos había salvado para esto.

2.12

WEBBIE

—Es tuya.
—¿Tú crees?
—¿Es que nadie se ha molestado en decírtelo? Es de tu propiedad.
—Ya. —Justin me miró y dijo—: Es de Colin.
Miró hacia los trozos de piedra ventral de mi padre que tenía en las manos. El borde petrificado de una vieja vaina de semillas rodó por el hoyuelo de la palma de su mano izquierda.
—Encontré una igual, en la casa de caliza.
—¿De veras? No sabía que Beatrice tuviera una piedra ventral.
—¿Una qué?
—Se llaman piedras ventrales. Bueno, algunos las llama perlas de la pradera, pero casi todo el mundo las llama piedras ventrales.
—¿Algunos?
—Los blancos —dije, encogiéndome de hombros.
—Pero ¿qué son? —rió Justin.
—Nadie lo sabe. No se sabe si son naturales o artificiales. No hay ninguna mención anterior a su descubrimiento. Ninguna de las tribus indígenas americanas dispone de información al respecto. Tampoco —añadí, sonriendo irónicamente— el hombre blanco.
Una corona de largas ranuras invasoras rodeaba las dos mitades de la piedra ventral en la mano de Justin, y este las recorrió con un dedo, un dedo que, pude notar, parecía ligeramente torcido.
—Vaya —dijo—. ¿Y qué hacía tu padre...?
—¿Mi padre?
—¿Cómo las abría?
—Con un destornillador y un martillo.
Justin se estremeció, como si los golpes fuesen dirigidos contra su propio cuerpo, y hubo algo en ese gesto que me hizo fijarme en su ojo morado. Fue entonces cuando advertí por primera vez la leve sombra de la cicatriz que lo rodeaba. Solo se veían pequeños fragmentos de la cicatriz, minúsculas marcas rojizas sobre la piel blanca, pero parecía que, en algún momento, la cicatriz había rodeado el ojo por completo. No era fácil de distinguir, por el moratón que tenía en la sien, pero de todos modos me pregunté qué habría provocado una cicatriz como esa. El cuello de una botella rota, quizá, la pezuña de un caballo sin herrar, una hebilla de cinturón en manos de su agresor. Luego me pregunté quién podría haberle hecho una herida así.
Justin no pareció reparar en mi observación.

—¿Quieres decir que todas salen de una mina o algo así que hay en nuestra finca?

—Lo llaman cueva. La cueva de las Piedras Ventrales.

Se le iluminó el rostro de repente.

—Quiero verla. Llévame.

—En realidad no es una cueva —dije—. No es más que un agujero, un pozo cavado en la tierra, con una pila de piedras encima.

—Son muy bonitas.

—No. Son misteriosas, pero eso no es lo mismo. —La acaricié con un dedo—. Mírala bien. No es más que un pedrusco gris. Lo único que tiene de interesante es de dónde ha salido y cómo llegó hasta allí.

—¿De dónde ha salido?

Me encogí de hombros, aunque inútilmente, porque Justin parecía absorto en la piedra ventral.

—Algunos piensan que pudo formarse en la garganta de uno de los mamíferos acuáticos que vivieron aquí hace millones de años, cuando la llanura era un mar interior. Otros creen que una tribu de indios desaparecida conocía una técnica de trabajar la cerámica sin fisuras, aunque este tipo de innovaciones en el tratamiento de la cerámica se asocian más con las tribus del suroeste. La mayoría se decanta por la teoría de la ballena.

—Me muero por ver esa cueva. Vamos ahora mismo.

—Tu piedra, la piedra de Bea, ¿está entera?

—Sí.

—Wade también tiene una entera. Todas las demás, creo que había cien en total, se han abierto. Se supone que Noah Deacon encontró un trozo de oro dentro de la primera que abrió, y a partir de ese momento todo el mundo... —Sacudí la cabeza—. Lo siento, no puedo ir. Tengo que estar aquí para ayudar a mi padre a subir las escaleras.

—Quieres decir que tu padre quiere que estés aquí para que lo ayudes a subir las escaleras.

—Es lo mismo.

—No. Dijiste que cuando tú no estás entra por la puerta de atrás y coge la silla-ascensor.

—Se llama Madre Mabel. Quiero decir, la silla.

—Pues claro. Madre Mabel, y Faith y Hope y Bestialidad. —Puso los ojos en blanco—. ¡Hay que ver los nombres que tiene la gente en este pueblo!

—Pues tú no eres precisamente el más indicado para decir eso. «Justin Time».

—¿Cómo dices? ¿William Edward Burkhardt Du Bois Martina Greeving?

Me eché a reír. Por primera vez en la vida mi nombre me parecía más una bendición que una maldición, una broma compartida, más que una broma que alguien me gastaba.

—En mi partida de nacimiento solo pone Webbie. Y no es culpa mía. Yo no lo elegí.

—Quizá deberías cambiar de nombre. Aunque Webbie me parece muy bonito.

—Estoy firmemente convencida de que la gente no puede cambiar de nombre a la ligera.

—Claro que puede. Mira Divine.

Entorné los ojos.

—Venga, venga. ¿No pensarás que mis padres me pusieron de verdad «Justin Time»? —dijo Justin.

Me quedé un poco cortada. Lo cierto es que sí lo había pensado, aunque descarté la idea de inmediato. Sacudí la cabeza como para situar esta nueva información en su correspondiente departamento, y al hacerlo me vinieron más palabras.

—Empiezo a pensar que te he contado demasiadas cosas.

Justin seguía sujetando la piedra ventral y, gesticulando con ella, dijo:

—Yo no me preocuparía por eso. Todo el mundo hace lo mismo.

—¿Te has creído que eres una especie de confesor?

—Nadie me ha acusado nunca de ser paternal, pero te sorprendería saber las cosas que me cuenta la gente.

Se apartó de mí bruscamente, de un modo que empezaba a resultarme familiar. Miró la piedra ventral e intentó encajar las dos mitades. Y mientras lo hacía me pareció que se perdía muy lejos, mucho más allá de esa tarde de domingo en la sala de estar de mi padre. Sostenía la piedra en la mano completamente inmóvil, como si estuviera llena de agua, y en sus ojos pude ver el momento prehistórico de su formación. La raya de unión de la piedra ventral desaparecía tras los ojos de Justin, el agua inundaba la casa, las paredes de la sala de estar se convertían en el vientre de una gigantesca ballena, y la piedra ventral rodaba en su interior, aumentando lentamente su masa a medida que la viscosa sustancia que revestía las paredes del estómago se adhería capa tras capa, año tras año. Pasó el tiempo. La ballena murió, posada sobre el fondo del océano; el agua se alejó del cadáver. La carne se pudrió, se marchitó, se secó, se convirtió en polvo, dejando tan solo un esqueleto y luego ni siquiera eso. Solo más polvo y la piedra ventral que Justin abría ahora aún más despacio de lo que la había cerrado.

—La mayoría de la gente —dijo entonces, sin mirarme ni dirigirse a mí— siente una necesidad imperiosa de confesarse. —Entonces me miró con el rostro absolutamente inexpresivo, como si esperara que algo se grabara en él–. Pero algunos, por desgracia, necesitamos confesiones. Unos cuentan secretos y otros los escuchan. Y la mayoría de la gente, si te fijas bien, deja tras de sí una especie de crónica. Y en este preciso instante –dijo, borrando de pronto su ausencia de expresión con una sonrisa– quiero conocer el secreto de la cueva de las Piedras Ventrales.

Acabé cediendo, y fuimos en mi coche a su casa. Justin me pidió que aparcara fuera del seto, y lo rodeamos en dirección a los campos.

–Esas piedras –dijo, con un estremecimiento.

–Sé exactamente lo que quieres decir. De pequeña leí ese cuento aterrador que hablaba de los pozos de alquitrán de La Brea, de cómo en ellos se consumieron miles y miles de dinosaurios durante eones, y desde entonces no he sido capaz de andar sobre ese foso sin miedo a ser devorada igual que los dinosaurios.

Justin se echó a reír y asintió con la cabeza, pero su risa fue distante. Rastreó el horizonte hasta que un halcón que planeaba llamó su atención; al momento, se distrajo con el plateado resplandor de las hojas marchitas de un álamo de Virginia que se cimbreaba bajo el frío viento.

Vi que miraba alrededor, consciente de que el paisaje no llegaba a atraparlo. Me pareció asombroso que, aun disponiendo de tanto espacio, su mente necesitara ir más lejos, marcharse a otra parte. Quise preguntarle adónde, pero no lo hice. En lugar de ello, le pregunté por Colin.

Cómo le iba con su novela.

–Está escribiendo.

La añoranza que antes había detectado en la voz de Justin desapareció entonces; endureció el tono y, aunque se metió las manos en los bolsillos, vi que apretaba los puños con fuerza.

–Me llamó la atención algo que dijo la otra noche durante la cena. Cuando estábamos hablando del padre de Wade y de Gary.

–¿Qué dijo?

–Cuidado –le advertí, cuando vi que estaba a punto de tropezar con una maraña de alambre de espino. El alambre formaba espirales sobre una serie de postes podridos y derribados por el suelo–. Creo que... sí. Debemos seguir esta alambrada –dije– o lo que queda de ella. Creo que nos llevará hasta allí. –Y haciendo una pausa, añadí–: Dijo «fascinante».

–Fascinante, ¿eh? –Justin lanzó un bufido. Fue un sonido extraño, agresivo. Fue entonces cuando reparé por primera vez en el grado de animosidad que había entre él y Colin. Echó a andar a grandes zancadas junto a la serpenteante línea de la valla que cruzaba el prado, y tuve que apresurarme para alcanzarlo–. Lo que me parece fascinante en la literatura de Colin es que nadie haya advertido nunca la diferencia entre *La Bella* y *La Bestia*.

Fingí frivolidad.

—Me estremezco cada vez que oigo mencionar esos títulos —dije. Justin no respondió, de manera que añadí—: ¿Cuál es la diferencia fundamental entre *La Bella* y *La Bestia*?

—¿Los has leído?

—Claro. Era una alumna aplicada.

—¿Cuál es la primera frase de *La Bella*?

Sonreí y, con voz bronca, entoné:

—Me llamo Colin Nieman.

—¿Y?

—¿Y? Vale, de acuerdo. «Me llamo Colin Nieman y juro que lo que voy a contar es la verdad.»

—Perfecto —aprobó Justin—. ¿Y la primera frase de *La Bestia*?

—Estooo....

—«Porque la bestia no tiene nombre —recitó Justin—, siempre está huyendo.»

—«Se mueve en la oscuridad —terminé—, porque no soporta la luz del sol.» —Me eché a reír—: ¿No te parece un poco engolado? —Esperé, pero Justin no dijo nada. Me pareció que lo que quería era un análisis, no un juicio, de manera que me quedé pensando y dije—: Uno empieza con un nombre y el otro con la ausencia de nombre.

—No es solo la ausencia de nombre —dijo entonces Justin—, sino la afirmación de lo que no se puede nombrar.

—Creo que deberías avanzar un poco más en la lectura —dije, pero Justin parecía extrañamente empeñado en sus palabras, y pasó por alto mi observación.

—Vuelve a leer el libro y verás como tengo razón.

—Vale —dije—, pero eso sigue sin explicarme a qué te refieres.

Justin suspiró, un leve sonido que, como mis palabras, pareció perderse en la pradera. Caminaba con resolución, y yo me rezagué un poco intencionadamente para dejarle que aclarara las ideas.

Me di la vuelta y vi que la casa de los Deacon resultaba ya casi invisible, que su cúpula coronaba una pequeña elevación del terreno. Enfrente de nosotros, una nube baja y gris indicaba la posición de Kenosha.

—¿Qué es un nombre? —preguntó entonces Justin. Pero antes de que pudiera contestarle, dijo—: Un nombre es una declaración. Un nombre dice: «Creo en el poder de las palabras para describir el mundo».

Guardé silencio. Estaba pensando: «pradera», «cúpula», «ceniza», «viento», «vallado». Esas eran las palabras que tenía en la cabeza, las palabras que usaba para describir el mundo. Y parecían cumplir debidamente sus fines.

—¿No te das cuenta? —continuó Justin, levantando las manos, ahora vacías, en las que aún se advertía el espíritu de la piedra ventral—. Un nombre y lo que este nombra son la correspondencia más sencilla entre las palabras y las cosas. Esto —dijo, simulando una balanza con las manos—, es igual a esto. Esto «significa» esto. —Esperé, y Justin continuó de inmediato—: Hay fe en *La Bella*, fe en el hecho de que las palabras, de que sus palabras, tengan un significado y resulten útiles. Pero esa fe no está presente en *La Bestia*.

La alambrada se adentraba entonces en un vado y el sonido de nuestras pisadas cambió al esforzarnos por no resbalar sobre la tierra seca. Las cenizas de Kenosha desaparecieron; sabía que la cúpula de la casa se habría vuelto invisible. Torcer, girar, resbalar, desaparecer, invisible. ¿No era eso lo que estaba ocurriendo, lo que estábamos haciendo?

—¿Y qué pasó? —pregunté en voz alta—. ¿Qué fue lo que hizo que Colin perdiera la fe?

Justin me miró, y por su expresión supe que no me estaba contando la historia completa y que nunca me la contaría. Justin Time, Webbie Greeving, Colin Nieman. Galatia, Kenosha, Galatea.

—Nada —dijo Justin—. A Colin no le pasó nada.

Sus palabras respondían a una pregunta que aún no se había formulado, pero había en su voz algo que me hizo callar, y guardamos silencio por espacio de varios minutos. Pensaba que aún estábamos lejos de la cueva cuando llegamos a la cima de una colina, pero allí estaba.

—¡Dios mío! —exclamé.

—¿Qué? ¿Qué pasa?

—¿Cómo que qué pasa? ¡Mira!

—No sé lo que estoy mirando. ¿Hay algo extraño?

—¿Que si hay algo extraño? ¡Han construido una cerca alrededor! Un sombrero. Como, como, como… un gorro de hechicero.

—Espera un momento. ¿Quieres decir que esta construcción no es la entrada?

La entrada a la cueva de las Piedras Ventrales era originariamente una pila cónica de piedras, no de piedras ventrales, sino de piedras ordinarias, aunque toscamente cortadas en forma de esferas. Estas piedras eran en su mayoría arenisca, pero también había esquisto blanco y pedernal gris, y algún que otro fragmento de caliza con incrustaciones de cristal que destacaba por su brillo del resto de la roca, más blanda y apagada. La pila de piedras tenía unos seis metros de alto y quizá la mitad de ancho, y estaba dividida en dos por una abertura que conducía hasta el interior. Pero el cono de piedras estaba ahora cubierto de tablones. Los tablones se parecían más a un tipi que a un sombrero de bruja, y en medio de la rabia que sentía me pregunté si eso es lo que intentaría representar el cono. Siempre había optado por una interpretación ligeramente más freudiana: montículo, abertura, agujero en la tierra; pero a veces un montón de piedras no es más que un montón de piedras.

—¿Webbie?

Tenía los puños apretados y tuve que esforzarme para abrir las manos antes de hablar. Respiré con fuerza. Intenté relajarme.

—¡Ay, Justin —exclamé, casi gritando—, la han destrozado!

No necesitó preguntar quién. Había una pintada que decía: PELIGRO. PROHIBIDO EL PASO POR ORDEN DEL DEPARTAMENTO DE POLICÍA DE GALATEA.

Los tablones estaban descoloridos y gastados. Comprendí que debieron de ponerlos cuando me marché a estudiar fuera de Galatea. Llevarían allí unos diez años, puede que más. De pronto caí en la cuenta: tenía treinta y cuatro años. Cora Johnson tenía treinta y siete. Cora tenía un hijo de ocho años enfermo de asma y estrías en el pecho de la época de la lactancia. En verano, cuando llevaba blusas sin mangas, se le veían las estrías.

Justin se había acercado hasta la puerta y estaba zarandeándola; suavemente al principio, luego con fuerza. Un gran candado chocó contra la puerta de metal. Justin miró alrededor en busca de algo que le sirviera para abrir el candado. Solo había piedras y algún que otro cactus lleno de espinas. Ni siquiera crecía la hierba en el arenoso suelo del vado donde se encontraba la cueva. No había más que viento, que se metía allí y parecía quedar atrapado, que se arremolinaba fútilmente y se calmaba derrotado, dejando en la arena una huella en forma de espiral, como si una serpiente gigantesca se hubiera enroscado sobre ella.

Justin se dio por vencido y se volvió hacia mí. Me miró con una sonrisa divertida.

—Me siento ofendido. Esto es de mi propiedad.

Me reí para quitar importancia al asunto.

—Bueno, supongo que si ella lo hizo es porque era legal. Peligro público para los niños, el ganado, lo que sea —dije.

—Lo que sea —repitió Justin, encogiéndose de hombros—: Da lo mismo. —Me miró un momento, se volvió de nuevo hacia los tablones y se apoyó en ellos con las palmas de las manos—. Dime una cosa —dijo, apretando aquí y allá—, ¿qué hay aquí dentro? ¿Qué estoy perdiéndome?

—¿Ahora? —pregunté—. No demasiado. Un olor seco, un techo

más bajo que tú y nichos rectangulares cavados en las paredes de tierra. Puede que un par de serpientes o un montón de ratas.

—Pero no las dos cosas.

—No, las dos cosas seguramente no.

—¿Qué es lo que impide que el techo se hunda?

—Las raíces de la hierba. Como en las casas de adobe.

Justin miró alrededor y dijo:

—Aquí no hay hierba.

—Ahora no.

Justin echó a andar hacia mí.

—¿Y qué más había aquí? Antes de que lo vaciaran y lo sellaran.

—Mantas —dije, en tono distante—. Había mantas y los chicos follaban en ellas. La oscuridad era absoluta. Total. Era más íntimo que masturbarse.

Seguía avanzando hacia mí.

Noté que me ruborizaba y me sentí incómoda por el hecho de sentirme incómoda. Justin avanzaba hacia mí. Ya debería haberme alcanzado, pero aún estaba lejos.

—¿Y tú, Webbie? ¿Tú también follabas aquí?

—¿Que si yo follaba aquí? Nunca he follado en Galatia; ni siquiera en Kansas. Me parecía que si follaba en el mismo estado donde vivía mi padre podría... explotar.

—A lo mejor usabas otro nombre.

—¿Otro nombre? —pregunté. Pensando al principio que se refería a un seudónimo—. ¿Quieres decir para follar?

Justin no respondió. De pronto estaba justo delante de mí, y allí se quedó, sin hablar; su silencio parecía arrancarme las palabras.

—No le pusimos ningún nombre. No podíamos ponerle ningún nombre.

Justin seguía sin responder. Había pasado de estar imposiblemente lejos a estar demasiado cerca de mí.

—¡Dios mío! —exclamé—. Lo escribiste tú, ¿verdad? Tú escribiste el segundo libro de Colin. *La Bestia*. Lo escribiste tú.

Me miró un momento, y comprendí dos cosas: que quería que yo descubriese su secreto, pero no quería que lo divulgara. Entonces, se apartó de mí y echó a andar hacia su casa.

—¿Justin?

No dijo nada. Me gustaría poder decir que su silencio era respuesta suficiente, pero esperaba algo más concreto, y dije:

—Justin, contéstame.

Siguió andando.

—Te he traído aquí. Te he enseñado la cueva, te la he ofrecido. Ahora tienes que darme algo a cambio.

Esta vez se detuvo y se dio la vuelta.

—Todo es mercadeo, ¿verdad?

—¿Cómo dices?

Entonces se puso a gritar. Se puso a gritar, pero no importaba, porque la tierra era grande.

—¡Todo el mundo quiere comprar las cosas! Nadie da nada a cambio de nada. Todo el mundo quiere dinero…

—Justin, yo…

—Sí, yo escribí el puto libro. Y sí, es un poco excesivo. Tenía dieciséis años, y él me lo robó. Yo se lo habría dado, le habría dado cualquier cosa, pero él tenía que quitarme lo único que era mío y hacerlo suyo. Y ahora os quitará a Galatia; os quitará a Eddie Comedy y a Odell Painter y a Melvin Cartwright y a Gary como-coño-se-apellide, y descubrirá quién es ese tal Eric Johnson y por qué nadie quiere hablar de él, y también se quedará con Divine, y con Wade y contigo. ¿Vale? Se apropiará de todos vosotros. ¿Ya estás contenta? ¿Te vale con eso?

Se dio la vuelta para marcharse, pero volví a detenerlo.

—¿Y el ojo? —pregunté—: ¿Fue él quien te hizo eso?

Rozó con un dedo las huellas de la cicatriz, invisibles bajo la intensa luz de la tarde, y luego el moratón. Me sonrió, no sin regocijo.

—Sí —dijo, apretándose el moratón con tanta fuerza que me hizo cerrar los ojos—. Pero yo le pegué primero.

Esta vez no impedí que se marchara. Me quedé mirándolo mientras emprendía el largo camino de vuelta a casa. Una casa que en realidad era de Colin, que había sido de Bea, que había pertenecido a los Deacon durante un siglo y nunca a los millones de indígenas americanos, durante muchos milenios antes. Pero comprendí que esa historia importaba bien poco: lo único que contaba era el presente; el aquí y ahora. Millones de indios muertos, una familia de negros, una puta vieja y blanca: todos ellos habían sido suplantados por un maricón calvo y blanco y su lacayo, herido, marcado, pero también ellos desaparecerían algún día. Me volví para mirar la entrada de la cueva de las Piedras Ventrales. Quizá no se parecía tanto a un tipi como a un cobertizo. Pero eso tampoco importaba, ni lo que en otro tiempo había pasado al otro lado de esa puerta, ni si la puerta estaba abierta o cerrada. En aquel momento era una puerta y estaba cerrada, pero sabía que si algún día lo necesitaba, podría abrirla.

2.13
JUSTIN

Vigas de acero sostenían la fláccida piel de latón del gimnasio, y el suelo aparecía cubierto de charcos de luz. Líneas rojas y negras ofrecían el cianotipo de un partido de baloncesto, pero los únicos interesados eran las parejas de Galatea, las parejas heterosexuales de Galatea, las parejas de heterosexuales blancos de Galatea. Hombres arrastrados por sus grandes barrigas conducían a sus mujeres o a sus novias; ellas dejaban a su paso una estela de perfume. En el escenario, cuatro hombres calvos y barrigudos interpretaban un tema de «La reina del Caribe», y el oscuro y mudo zambombazo de la música se cernía sobre el gimnasio y sus ocupantes. Lucy, sentada a mi lado, suspiró. Fue un suspiro de alegría.

—¡Qué bonito!

Se refería, supongo, a las serpentinas metálicas que caían del techo formando arcos desiguales, a los globos multicolores colgados de cuerdas de diferente longitud, inclinados por las corrientes de aire caliente que, por desgracia, no llegaban a caldear el suelo del gimnasio, gélido y con olor a espacio cerrado. Lucy estaba muy guapa, vestida con un traje corto de color púrpura, medias blancas y zapatos de salón a juego con su vestido. Sus ojos, cargados de maquillaje también a juego con el vestido y los zapatos, eran como mínimo dos centímetros más altos que los míos, y su densa mata de pelo, recogido en un moño alto, la hacía parecer quince centímetros más alta. Noté que se había pintado las uñas de un tono azul claro que desentonaba con el resto de su indumentaria, y cuando Lucy me vio mirarlas, escondió las manos detrás de la espalda.

—No tenía nada mejor a mano —se excusó, con risa caballuna—. ¿A cuántas chicas conoces que compren el esmalte de uñas en la ferretería?

—Creo que no te gustaría saber la respuesta.

Lucy seguía el ritmo de la música con los pies, aunque le costaba mantenerlo. Vio que le miraba los pies y volvió a reír.

—No tardarán en elevarse —dijo.

—¿Elevarse? ¿Como si levitaran?

Me miró con expresión de no entender y luego, al ver que la observaba atentamente, borró esa expresión con una risa.

—¡Cómo eres! —dijo, y me dio un golpe con el bolso.

—¡Ay! —exclamé—. ¿Qué llevas ahí dentro? ¿Un ladrillo?

—Cosas de chicas —dijo—. No lo entenderías.

—Te equivocas —dije, y Lucy me miró.

—¡Cómo eres! —repitió, pero esta vez logré esquivar el golpe.

—¡Eh, chicos! —La voz de Myra llegó por detrás de nosotros—. ¿Por qué no bailáis? —La pregunta resultaba surrealista, a la vista de la orquesta, de la música que tocaba y de cómo la tocaba.

—¡Mamá! —protestó Lucy, lanzando el bolso, pero Myra parecía estar acostumbrada a esquivarlo.

Las manos de Colin reptaron entonces por mi espalda.

—¡Eh! —le dije, queriendo decir «hola», pero se metió las manos en los bolsillos antes de que pudiera cogérselas.

—Ya que no estáis dispuestos a salir a la pista, el señor Nieman y yo os enseñaremos cómo se hace.

—¡Ni se te ocurra, mamá! ¡Me muero de vergüenza!

—Me parece una buena razón. ¿Señor Nieman?

—Por favor —dijo Colin—, si voy a avergonzar a la hija de alguien, sobre todo si se trata de la guapa hija de una guapa mujer, insisto en que me llame Colin.

—¡Anda, anda! —dijo Myra, soltando una risita. Colin la cogió de la mano, pero antes de marcharse se volvió hacia mí.

—¿Has guardado tú mi abrigo negro en alguna parte?

—Estará en el armario del dormitorio.

—Es curioso. Lo he buscado y no está allí. Bueno. —Se encogió de hombros, le dio un achuchón a Myra y se alejaron bailando justo cuando la orquesta se lanzaba a tocar algo que se suponía era «Brown Sugar».

—¡Dios mío! —exclamó Lucy—. Espero que no la vea nadie.

Señalé hacia la pista vacía del gimnasio y el pequeño círculo de parejas:

—Es difícil no verlos, ¿no te parece?

—¡Oh, no! —dijo Lucy—. Ahí están Brenda, Lee Anne y Shelly. Baila conmigo, por favor.

Me eché hacia atrás antes de que pudiera cogerme del brazo:

—Lo siento, yo no bailo.

Lucy me miró como si hubiera dicho que respiraba agua.

—Seguro que bailas muy bien. Vamos.

—Lo siento, perdí una pierna en un accidente náutico, y desde entonces no ha vuelto a ser igual.

—¿Cómo? ¿Qué pierna...? ¡Ah! —Lucy soltó una risita. El brazo que sujetaba el bolso tembló ligeramente, pero no llegó a moverse.

—No es momento para bromas. Venga, vamos. —Esta vez me cogió del brazo, pero conseguí mantenerme firme.

—No lo tomes a mal —dije, intentando soltarme—, pero esta intriga de comedia de situación no va conmigo. Además, yo no bailo.

Lucy dejó de tirar, pero no me soltó el brazo.

—No lo entiendo.

—Verás; hay algo que debes saber —me oí decir, y también yo tuve que reírme: ¿quién de los dos creaba un ambiente de comedia de situación? Lucy me apretó el brazo, como si todo fuera una estratagema mía para distraerla, pero antes de que pudiera continuar una chillona voz femenina me interrumpió.

—¡Lucy! Esa que está ahí con el calvo, ¿es tu madre?

—¡Dios mío! —suspiró Lucy—. Nunca me dejarán en paz. —Se encogió visiblemente mientras las tres chicas se nos acercaban; las seguían tres chicos que parecían conscientes de que esa noche el gimnasio no era lugar para ellos, y noté que se fijaban en mí desde detrás del círculo de muchachas.

—¡Hola, chicas! —dijo Lucy con fingido entusiasmo—. ¡Hola, chicos! —Saludó a los muchachos. Tomó aire, se estiró el vestido y anunció—: Este es Justin.

—Hola —dije, y luego, alzándome un poco añadí—: ¿Qué tal? —Pero alzarme no sirvió de nada, porque las chicas seguían siendo más altas que yo. Me sorprendía la estatura de las hijas de los granjeros del Medio Oeste, aunque supongo que subrayar el gigantismo no era lo más adecuado para aquella canción de los Beach Boys.

—¿Dónde está Howard? —le preguntó Lee Anne a Lucy con sonrisa maliciosa.

—Vamos, por faaavor —replicó Lucy, apretando los dientes con disgusto—. Este es Justin —repitió con firmeza—. Acaba de venir de Nueva York para instalarse aquí.

—¡Ah! —exclamó Brenda. Sospeché que las chicas ya lo sabían. Me examinaron atentamente; me miraron de arriba abajo como si de ese modo pudieran detectar algún rasgo extraño: tres orejas, dedos sin uñas o pantalones con dobladillo.

Lee Anne se mordió un labio, manchándose las puntas de los dientes de color fucsia:

—Es guapo —dijo con vacilación.

—Es mucho más guapo que Howard —replicó Shelly.

—Y mucho más joven —dijo Brenda.

—Y mucho más delgado —añadió Lucy; y entonces las chicas se pusieron histéricas.

—Los hombres sois muy malos —dijo Anne Lee; y sin tomar aliento continuó—: ¡Eh, Lu, ¿quién es el calvo que está bailando con tu madre?

Lucy se ruborizó.

—Es el señor Nieman. También es de Nueva York. Él y Justin han comprado la casa de caliza.

—¡Ya! ¿Es tu padre?

—No desde hace tiempo.

Las chicas parecieron no comprender, y Lucy soltó otro de sus «¡Cómo eres!». El círculo de chicas me cerraba la vía de escape, y el bolso de Lucy se estrelló contra mi estómago.

—Es escritor —dijo Lucy, mientras me reponía del golpe—. Quiero decir, el señor Nieman. Tú no eres escritor, ¿verdad?

—No desde hace tiempo —volví a decir, pero esta vez mi comentario no pareció merecer un nuevo bolsazo.

—Es muy famoso —dijo Lucy—. Quiero decir, el señor Nieman.

—Oye, Lu —dijo Brenda rápidamente—, Shelly va a llevarnos al Big M el lunes por la noche. —Se inclinó hacia delante y dijo en tono confidencial—: Vamos a ver el cobertizo donde encontraron a Eddie Comedy.

—¡No me digas! ¡Qué genial!

—¡Vamos, Lu, no te pases! —dijo Shelly—. ¿Sabes lo que dice mi madre? Mi madre dice que ha sido Melvin Cartwright. Por eso ha desaparecido. Dice —Shelly hizo una elocuente pausa—, dice que ha sido una venganza.

A Lucy se le ensombreció el rostro al oír esta última palabra. Me pareció que estaba a punto de desmayarse.

—¿Venganza? —se extrañó Lee Anne—. ¿Por qué?

—Buah —respondió Brenda—. Por Eric Johnson.

—Ya basta —protestó Lucy—. No quiero oír nada más.

—Lu...

—¡He dicho que ya basta! Además —dijo Lucy, conteniendo el aliento—, el lunes hay ensayo de animadoras, así que no puedo ir. —Se llevó las manos a la cabeza, y noté que le temblaban, pero se calmaron al tocar el pelo como si ciñeran una tiara.

Entonces me levanté. Introduje un dedo en el peinado de Lucy. No sabía bien si pretendía ser tierno o cruel, pero tiré de uno de los rizos de Lucy y un largo mechón negro le cayó sobre la frente hasta rozarle la punta de la nariz. Lucy se quedó antinaturalmente quieta mientras yo la tocaba, y cuando terminé casi se pone bizca para mirarse el pelo. Como si lo que le hubiera soltado fuese una culebra.

—Así está mejor.

—¿Qué?

—Mucho más sexy —dije, y Lucy soltó el aliento muy despacio, produciendo un curioso silbido—. Eso es, tú sigue así y acabarás encontrándote con un hombre de verdad —dije. Y luego, sin esperar a que pudiera darme otro bolsazo, me abrí paso entre las chicas. En Nueva York podría haberme perdido entre el gentío, pero aquí tenía que poner tierra por medio, y me alejé del grupo lo más que pude.

2.14

WEBBIE

Cuando entré en el gimnasio me quedé en un rincón. Enseguida vislumbré a Justin. También estaba solo, balanceándose suavemente dentro de una chaqueta demasiado ligera para el frío que hacía fuera. Al verlo, su fragilidad volvió a llamar mi atención. Estaba demasiado delgado, pensé, demasiado flaco. Pensé que debería llevárselo a Cora para que le hiciera engordar un par de kilos. Incluso de lejos advertí que tenía una espinilla en la barbilla, grande y roja, y de pronto caí en la cuenta de que había ido al baile exclusivamente para verlo a él, porque no solo sabía que se sentía extraño aquí, sino que sabía que no podría sobrevivir. No tardaría en marcharse y yo volvería a quedarme sola, acorralada entre mi padre y sus Damas y Wade y Divine.

Vacilé un momento, sopesando qué hacer, pero Justin volvió la cabeza y me vio. Sonrió y salió a mi encuentro, estrujando un vaso de plástico vacío. Me besó en la mejilla y noté el olor del alcohol en su aliento.

Levantó el vaso y dijo:

—Puede que en casa de esa mujer no haya bebidas, pero al menos es lo suficientemente lista para servirlas cuando da una fiesta.

—Eso debes agradecérselo al alcalde. Él es el político. —Hice una pausa y sonreí—. ¿Cómo te va?

—He venido acompañado.

—Ya he visto a Colin…

—No es Colin —dijo Justin, y sacudió la cabeza.

—¿Cómo?

Volvió a sacudir la cabeza y dijo:

—Es que no quiero darme la vuelta, pero… —Y sacudió la cabeza por tercera vez.

—¡Ah! —dije, y observé a la gente—. ¿Sabes?, creo que nunca he visto hacer eso a nadie en la vida real. Eso de mira-hacia-donde-muevo-la-cabeza. Es cosa del teatro, o del cin… ¡Ah!

Mi mirada se cruzó con la de Lucy Robinson, y esta se ocultó de inmediato detrás de Shelly Stadler.

—¿Has venido con Lucy Robinson?

—Somos la comidilla del pueblo. Gracias a Rosemary Krebs.

Entonces vi a Colin y Myra en la pista de baile.

—¿Tú crees que de verdad se hace ilusiones? Tiende a tener delirios de grandeza, pero no es tonta.

—Sospecho que lo ha planeado todo —dijo Justin—. Sospecho que todo esto es por el bien de Lucy, aunque no entiendo nada.

—Pobrecito —dije, dando un golpecito a su vaso vacío—. ¿Quieres tomar algo?

—Me encantaría —dijo Justin, poniendo los ojos en blanco—. Esperemos que él no aparezca por aquí.

—Te refieres a Divine…

—¿Hummm?

—El otro día estuve hablando con Wade. Dice que Divine está muy raro últimamente.

Justin jugueteaba con el vaso vacío, frotándolo entre las manos. Con aire ausente dijo:

—¿Raro?

—Bueno, para empezar tiene una brecha en la cabeza —dije y, tras un momento de vacilación, toqué la mancha verdosa que Justin tenía en la sien—. Y estuvo tres días sin querer levantarse de la cama. Wade dice que ha vuelto a escribir cartas.

—¿Que Divine escribe cartas? —preguntó Justin, apoyando una mano en mi hombro para conducirme hacia el bar.

—Lleva tres días escribiendo sin parar.

—Creo que estoy perdiéndome algo importante. Además de una bebida, quiero decir.

Para entonces ya habíamos llegado al bar y le pedí un whisky a Dave Helman, que hacía de camarero esa noche.

—Mira —le dije a Justin cuando le sirvieron la copa—, Divine tiene la costumbre de hacer eso. —Hice una pausa al ver que Justin ponía los ojos en blanco—. Quiero decir, además de lo otro. Lleva varios años escribiéndole cartas a alguien a quien él llama el Rata. Dice que las cartas son como una póliza de seguros.

—¿El Rata? ¿Una póliza de seguros? Ahora sí que me he perdido.

—En lo del Rata no puedo ayudarte. Pero la póliza de seguros es, por lo que yo sé, chantaje.

—Chantaje.

—Bueno, lo que hace Divine está a medio camino entre lo que hacía Joe McCarthy y lo que hacía la mujer que salía en ese programa de televisión, el de la *Habitación mágica*, que miraba en su espejo mágico y leía los nombres de todos sus amigos. —Justin me miró inexpresivamente, de manera que seguí diciendo—: Divine dice que ha escrito el nombre de todos los hombres con los que se ha acostado en Galatia. No solo los nombres, sino todos los detalles: marcas de nacimiento, tatuajes y…

—¿Tamaño del pene?

—Gracias. Dice que lo ha escrito todo y que se lo ha mandado al tal Rata para garantizar su propia seguridad. Dice que mientras esas cartas estén a buen recaudo nadie se meterá con él.

Justin bebió un sorbo de whisky.

—Debo admitir que me sorprende bastante la cantidad de maricones que hay en un pueblo como este. Da un poco de miedo. —Justin sonrió—. Cartas. ¡Qué anacronismo tan bonito! ¿De verdad cree que eso puede funcionar?

Estaba a punto de responderle cuando alguien me llamó por mi nombre.

—¡Pero si es Webbie Greeving! Nunca me imaginé que te encontraría en un sitio así.

Entonces, me di la vuelta y vi a Cora Johnson que se acercaba hacia nosotros. Parecía más alta de lo que recordaba, un poco más gorda, pero seguía teniendo esa piel tan bonita, de color cobrizo, de la que siempre se había sentido tan orgullosa. Sawyer arrastraba su cuerpo fofo detrás de Cora, resollando ligeramente y aferrado al inhalador antiasmático que colgaba de su cuello.

Sentí que se me tensaba el rostro.

—¡Cora! —exclamé, con excesivo entusiasmo.

Nos dimos un abrazo. Cora aplastó mi cabeza contra su pecho mientras yo intentaba saludar a Sawyer, pero este se escondió detrás de su mamá, asomándose solo tímidamente.

—Cora, te presento a un buen amigo mío, Justin… Justin Time. —Mis ojos se cruzaron con los de Justin, y él sonrió y se encogió de hombros—. Justin, esta es una vieja amiga de la infancia, Cora Lewis… quiero decir… Cora Johnson, y ese pequeño que se esconde detrás de sus faldas es su hijo Sawyer.

—¡Cuidadito con llamar vieja a nadie! —dijo Cora, estrechando cordialmente la mano de Justin—. Porque no tienes muchos menos que yo. Sawyer, saluda a este señor. No muerde.

Sawyer se acercó solo lo justo para poner una mano rechoncha en la delgada mano de Justin, y entonces volví a notar que tenía los dedos, quiero decir Justin, ligeramente torcidos. Me fijé en la cicatriz y en el moratón.

—Justin acaba de mudarse aquí —dije—. El que está bailando con Myra Robinson es su amigo, Colin Nieman.

—Supongo que lo habría adivinado aunque nadie me lo hubiera dicho. No hay tantas caras nuevas en Galatia como para no saber quién es quién. —Cora le lanzó a Justin una sonrisa maliciosa—. Tu amigo está completamente calvo.

—Hablando de caras nuevas —dije, soltando una risa nerviosa—, ¿cómo está Rosa? ¿Ha venido?

—Rosa está bien —dijo Cora, volviendo a estrecharle la mano a Justin. Y entonces me di cuenta de que estaba igual de nerviosa que yo—. Se ha quedado en casa. Tiene que madrugar.

—Sí, ya lo sé.

Hubo un largo silencio, y vi que Justin tampoco sabía cómo actuar. Yo también me sentía incómoda.

—¿Has oído lo último? —dijo entonces Cora.

—¿Lo último...?

—Parece ser que ese cobertizo donde encontraron a Eddie Comedy ha ardido.

—¿Cómo? ¿Cuándo?

Cora miró el reloj.

—Hace un par de horas. El sheriff Peterson, de Bigger Hill, llamó a la comisaría. Nettie Ferguson cogió la llamada.

—En ese caso, me sorprende no haberme enterado antes —dije. Y Cora se rió un poco. Justin nos miraba primero a uno y luego a otro, pero sin decir nada—. Bueno, bueno. Primero el arca de Noah y ahora esto. ¿Sabe el sheriff Peterson quién lo ha quemado?

—Al parecer nadie sabe nada de nada —dijo Cora, negando con la cabeza—. Rosa dice que vivimos tiempos muy raros, y empiezo a estar de acuerdo con ella. Realmente muy raros. —Se produjo un paréntesis y luego Cora dijo—: Bueno, no quiero entreteneros. Parecíais muy enzarzados en la conversación.

—No —dije yo, quitándole importancia.

—Ya nos veremos —se despidió Cora. Me sobresalté al sentir su mano en la mía, y tuve que contenerme para no echarme atrás.

—Pronto. Pasaré por el café un día de estos, si el reverendo me deja desaparecer de su vista.

—Creo recordar que se te daba muy bien dar esquinazo al reverendo cuando querías —dijo Cora. Busqué en sus palabras cierto reproche, pero no lo había—. Vamos, Sawyer —dijo Cora, y se marchó con el niño de la mano.

Cuando Cora ya no podía oírnos, Justin dijo:

—No sé por qué me parece que aquí hay otra historia.

Me reí, haciendo un gesto de desinterés con la mano.

—Esta te la dejo para ti —dijo Justin.

—Vamos, Justin —dije, y al mirarlo vi que había fijado en mí una expresión tan afligida que me llevé las manos a las mejillas para comprobar si estaban mojadas de lágrimas. ¡Es terrible cómo se alejan las personas unas de otras!

Justin no me respondió inmediatamente, sino que se quedó mirando algo que estaba detrás de mí. Me di la vuelta y vi que Colin hacía girar a Myra en peligrosa pirueta por la pista de baile y, al echarla hacia atrás, casi hasta tocar el suelo, Myra dio un grito que resonó en todo el gimnasio.

Se volvió hacia mí y dijo:

—Creo que te entiendo.

Vi cómo se alejaba Cora.

—Ha sido una tontería venir aquí —dije—. Ni siquiera me gusta bailar. Perdóname por dejarte colgado, pero creo que voy a irme a casa.

Justin asintió con la cabeza y dijo:

—Relléname la copa antes de irte.

Me reí y le quité el vaso.

—Hace tiempo que no tengo resaca, pero creo recordar que la leche con cacao iba muy bien. —Nos reímos juntos un momento, y si hubiera sabido que esa risa sería el último sonido suyo que yo volvería o oír, le habría contado un chiste tras otro para que no parara de reírse. Pero me froté los ojos y dije—: Dejaremos la historia para otro momento. Ahora mismo te traigo tu copa.

2.15

JUSTIN

La cabeza me daba vueltas, y no solo por el alcohol. La tenía llena de nombres, de pequeños retazos de historias —Webbie Greeving y Cora Johnson, Divine y el Rata, Lucy Robinson y Eric Johnson— y todos esos nombres se mezclaban en torbellino con los que ya estaban allí; pese a mi resistencia, sentí que una poderosa fuerza me impedía salir de la espiral de Galatea.

Webbie Greeving y Cora Johnson.

Divine y el Rata.

Lucy Robinson y Eric Johnson.

Y entonces, en el sopor de la duermevela, capté el mensaje. Webbie y Cora, Divine y el Rata, Lucy y Eric. Todos habían sido amantes. Supe con quién había estado Webbie en la cueva de las Piedras Ventrales, supe quién le había roto el corazón a Divine y le había puesto a la caza de hombres como Wade y Colin, supe por qué Lucy Robinson veía un mechón de su propio pelo como si fuera una serpiente que le crecía en la cabeza. Eso es algo que toda prostituta aprende tarde o temprano: que todo el mundo tiene un solo secreto y que ese secreto es lo que verdaderamente aman.

Me permití decir el nombre del mío en voz alta: «Martin».

2.16

WEBBIE

La luz del archivo de mi padre estaba encendida cuando volví a casa, pero en la habitación, como siempre, reinaba el silencio. Mi padre había pasado mucho tiempo allí durante las últimas semanas, y más de una vez me había llamado por teléfono. Mi padre odiaba los teléfonos y a veces amenazaba con cortar la línea de casa, y el hecho de que ahora lo usara a todas horas, de día y de noche, era un claro indicio del estado de agitación en que se encontraba.

En algún momento había llegado a pensar que mi padre se encerraba en el archivo para masturbarse, pero sostener esa idea implicaba imaginar la erección de mi padre, y eso no estaba bien, no estaba nada bien.

Entré en mi habitación, me desnudé, me puse el camisón y me metí en la cama. Sentí un leve rastro de perfume en mi blusa, del perfume que usaba Cora, y me acordé entonces de sus muñecas y de su cuello, del espacio de detrás de las orejas, de sus «puntos de latido», como ella me había enseñado a llamarlos años atrás, cuando me explicó cómo había que perfumarse.

La persiana estaba bajada, las cortinas cerradas, y no había farolas en Galatia: la habitación estaba sumida en la oscuridad. Miré al techo y casi sentí el olor a tierra seca, el penetrante aroma del sexo viejo.

Toda la gente del pueblo había estado allí. Era un lugar que había que visitar al menos una vez, igual que los neoyorquinos acuden en peregrinación al Empire State Building o los parisinos a la Torre Eiffel. Yo había evitado ir durante años. El enigmático pasado del lugar me daba miedo: durante mi niñez, mi padre me había inculcado la actitud del historiador, y me desagradaba pensar en algo que suscitaba preguntas pero no ofrecía respuestas. Cuando al fin me decidí a ir tenía once años, y fui por la insistencia de mi mejor amiga, Coretta Beech Tree Lewis.

Cora era tres años mayor que yo, alta y guapa, con las caderas redondeadas y los pechos bien formados, y una piel cobriza que revelaba sus orígenes indios. A veces, Cora llamaba a ese color sombra, borgoña, sepia, siena. No soy solo negra, soy sienesa. Su abuelo paterno había sido medio cherokee —Cora llevaba como segundo nombre supuestamente el de su bisabuela— y era, con mucho, la chica más guapa del pueblo. Tenía los ojos grandes y almendrados, aún más negros que los míos, y ningún hombre, ni siquiera mi padre, podía resistirse cuando esos ojos se posaban en él. Encendía a los hombres con una mirada o un guiño, y si con eso no conseguía sus propósitos, no tenía más que abrir la boca y cantar. Mi padre la llamaba nuestra Mahalia, pero Cora, que fumaba, bebía cerveza y me llevaba a la cueva de las Piedras Ventrales para mostrarme dónde perdió su virginidad con Sawyer Johnson, Cora se llamaba a sí misma sirena. «¡Pobre del hombre que oiga mi voz!», solía decirme a espaldas de mi padre. ¡Pobre, pobre, pobre de él! Yo la adoraba.

—¿Qué te has creído, niña, que solo lo tenemos para sangrar?

Cora me instruía sobre el coño. Kenosha era una nube en el horizonte, un olor tangible. A nuestras espaldas, el humo salía por las tres chimeneas en casa de la señora Bea. Estábamos en mitad del verano.

—¿Qué te has creído, que es una calle de sentido único? Dentro y fuera, cariño, dentro y fuera.

Yo me ponía tan roja como lo era ella. Sentía el rubor hasta en las palmas de las manos. Antes de que pudiera contestar, Cora se reía de mí.

—Te parecerá una guarrería, pero algún día lo comprenderás. El sexo no es solo guarro; es divertido. Es risa. La primera vez que veas a un chico con la cara contraída porque está a punto de llegar, seguro que te mueres de risa. Yo le dije a Sawyer que parecía como si se hubiera bebido un vaso de limonada pensando que era leche. Un ponche caliente en vez de una cerveza fría, un Harvey Wallbanger en lugar de una Shirley Temple.

—¿Y qué dijo él?

—Dijo que hablar de bebidas le daba sed.

Me ruboricé por cómo pronunció Cora la palabra «sed», y ella volvió a estallar en carcajadas. Dejó volar la mano y la posó en mi hombro; tenía la palma sudorosa. Esa palma había tocado el culo de Sawyer, su pene; esos dedos habían dibujado el espacio entre los finos labios y las oscuras encías de Sawyer. Intenté fingir naturalidad, pero le aparté la mano en cuanto pude.

—Vale, chica —dijo Cora—. Dejaré de reírme de ti, pero primero tienes que decirlo.

—¿Decir qué?

—Coño.

—¿Se supone que eso me liberará? A lo mejor basta con que queme mi sujetador en el parque.

—¿Llevas sujetador? Eso está bien.

Me sonrojé; Cora se rió y dijo:

—Solo quiero que lo digas para que sepas cómo tienes que poner los labios cuando hagas una mamada.

Yo nunca había oído esa palabra, pero daba igual. Me tapé la boca con la mano y Cora rió con ganas.

—Venga, dilo. Coño.
Suspiré por la nariz, lanzando un largo silbido.
—Eso también está muy bien. Venga, dilo ya.
—Coño —dije, en voz baja.
—Más alto.
—¡Coño! —grité. Para eso sirve un gran espacio abierto y un viento fuerte: para gritar palabras que nos avergüenzan—. ¡Coño! —volví a gritar, e imaginé que la palabra se escapaba—. ¡Coño!
—¡Polla! —gritó Cora.
—¡Polla!
—¡Polla!
—¡Picha!
—¡Picha!
—¡Rabo!
—Bueno, ya vale —dije. Hubo un silencio: el viento, el crujido de la hierba, el zumbido de la tensa alambrada. Luego le pregunté—: ¿Cómo es que hay tantas palabras para la cosa del hombre… para eso?
—¡Webbie!
—Vale, vale, para la polla; pero solo hay una para las mujeres.
—Eso tiene dos respuestas —dijo Cora—. Por un lado, podríamos decir que este es un mundo de hombres, y dejarlo ahí.
—Ya, ya.
—Por otro lado puedes decir, chocho, chumino, almeja, conejo…
—Vale, vale. Ya me he enterado.
—Y eso es solo para el agujero. Todavía no hemos llegado al clítoris.
—Vale.
La alambrada se hundía en una depresión del terreno. Pisábamos sobre la tierra seca y suelta. Las cenizas de Kenosha desaparecieron, pero el olor se intensificó. Polla, picha, rabo, pija. Solté una risita. Coño, chocho, chumino, almeja, conejo. Más que sexo lo que yo quería era un rotulador y una pared en un cuarto de baño. Quería ser «mala». No «ser» mala.
—¡Oye, Cora!
—¿Qué?
—¿Tú lo has visto?
—¡Webbie!
—No, no, no digo la polla de Sawyer, digo el bebé de Marsha.
Habíamos llegado al fondo de la hondonada. La tierra estaba empapada y saltábamos de montón en montón de hierba para no hundirnos en el barro.
—Sí —dijo Cora, pisando con cuidado—. Lo he visto.
—Entonces, ¿es verdad?

Cora echó a andar monte arriba antes de responder, y luego dijo:
—¿Qué es verdad?

Comprendí por qué no me había entendido. A mí también me costaba decirlo.

—¿Que si… que si es…?
—¿Blanco?
—¡Sí! —casi grité, sobresaltada por la palabra—. ¿Es… blanco?
—Más blanco que un blanco —dijo Cora—. Con los ojos rosados, el pelo como un estropajo de aluminio y hambriento a todas horas.
—¿Sí? —Estábamos casi en la cima del monte—. ¿Y tampoco tiene padre?

Cora se rió un poco.

—Eres la niña más inocente que he visto en mi vida. Que Marsha no esté casada no significa en absoluto que el bebé no tenga padre. Es un albino, no Jesucristo. Y llámalo por su nombre. Se llama Eric. Eric Johnson. Y si algún día me caso con Sawyer Johnson, ese niño será mi sobrino.

2.17

JUSTIN

Myra me sacudió con una mano para despertarme. En la otra llevaba dos vasos, con los dedos metidos en el borde, las uñas sumergidas en el líquido oscuro.

—Mi heroína —dije, frotándome los ojos.
—No te entusiasmes tanto. Es Coca-Cola. Creo que ya has bebido demasiado por esta noche. —Le entró hipo, soltó una risita y dijo—: Igual que yo. —Luego, bebió un poco de Coca-Cola y me preguntó—: ¿Te has asustado de Lucy?
—Bueno… ya sabes —respondí, encogiéndome de hombros.
—Eso espero —dijo Myra, y volvió a beber.
—No te preocupes, la acompañaré a casa.

Myra sonrió agradecida, pero se limitó a decir:

—No te tomes demasiadas molestias por ella. Lucy es para mí como un dolor de muelas, pero sabe cuidar de sí misma.

Entonces, vi a Colin en la pista, bailando solo. La figura solitaria que había al otro lado del gimnasio podría ser Wade, o podría no serlo.

—¿Qué? ¿Te estás divirtiendo?

Myra bailoteó un poco.

—Es divertido bailar con gente de vez en cuando, en vez de bailar en casa sola.

Asentí.

—Mándame a paseo si me meto en lo que no me importa, pero ¿dónde está el señor Robinson?

—¿El señor Robinson?

—Tu marido. El padre de Lucy.

Myra me miró un momento con el rostro inexpresivo y luego dijo:

—El padre de Lucy —esbozó una sonrisa triste y enigmática; luego, la ira la endureció por un momento, y al fin dijo—: Supongo que nadie te ha enseñado aún el lado oscuro de la brillante historia de Galatea. La cara oculta de todo este asunto. —Señaló con el pulgar hacia los que bailaban y el resto de los invitados.

—¿El lado oscuro?

—Oscuro no es la palabra —dijo Myra—. Eso es lo curioso de este pueblo. Que todo está cargado en exceso. De todos modos, ¿sabes cómo se fundó Galatea?

—Webbie me lo ha contado —asentí—. Galatia y Galatea.

—Eso es —dijo Myra—. Bueno, la situación se mantiene tranquila desde hace tiempo. A la mayoría de los negros no les gustan los blancos, por regla general, y a la mayoría de los blancos tampoco les gustan los negros, pero no llegan a tirarse los trastos a la cabeza. Como esta noche, por ejemplo. —Señaló hacia la gente reunida en el gimnasio: ya no eran todos blancos, había una docena de negros—. En fin, podría explicártelo mejor, pero es preferible ir al grano. Hace diez años mi marido participó con una banda de, de, de, hijos de puta, en el linchamiento de un chico negro de trece años. Lo colgaron de los pulgares y lo dejaron allí toda la noche; por la mañana, unos cuantos hombres, mi marido entre ellos, volvieron para rematar la faena.

La miré un buen rato sin poder hablar. Al fin, logré decir:

—¿De los pulgares?

Myra lanzó un suspiro.

—El chico era un ladrón. En cualquier otro lugar le habrían llamado ratero y le habrían dado una bofetada en la mano, pero en Galatea un ladrón es un ladrón y…

—Ojo por ojo…

—Diente por diente, y pulgar por un bote de guisantes. Y… —Myra ahogó un sollozo, suspiró y bebió un largo trago de Coca-Cola— y mi hija, Lucy…

—¿Lucy? —Me vino entonces a la memoria el sueño que había tenido—. ¡Dios mío! ¡Lucy!

—Lucy dijo que aquel chico le había metido las manos en las bragas.

Iba todo demasiado deprisa tras un mes de silencio y equívocos. Necesitaba rebobinar.

—¿Una lata de guisantes?

—Guisantes, caramelos, bocadillos, lo que fuera —dijo Myra, encogiéndose de hombros—. Algunos dicen que solo robaba comida. No lo sé. A mí nunca me robó nada.

Esperé, intentando procesar la información, y dije:

—¿Rematar la faena?

—Stan dijo que lo bajaron del árbol a palos, como si fuera una pin... pin... pin...

—Una piñata.

—Luego enterraron sus pedazos. Eso dijo Stan. A saber dónde. Y luego, después.... después, Stan tuvo tiempo de recapacitar sobre lo que había hecho.

—Y se marchó.

—Se marchó.

Myra no volvió a hablar.

—Hay algo más que no me estás contando —dije. Lo mismo que dije sobre Wade la otra noche, en casa de Rosemary Krebs, y Myra me respondió igual que entonces:

—Hay muchas cosas que prefiero no contar. Preferiría que Stan no me hubiera contado tantas cosas. De todos modos, lo que pasó, en resumidas cuentas, es que mi marido y un puñado de hombres del pueblo cometieron un asesinato en nombre de la justicia, pero al menos mi marido tuvo el valor de sentirse culpable, y por eso se marchó.

—¿Sabes dónde?

Myra pareció no oírme.

—Bueno —dijo—. No te he dicho una cosa. El chico era blanco.

—¿El chico?

—Se llamaba Eric Johnson. Y era blanco. Era, ¿cómo se dice?, albino. Era la cosa más fea que he visto en mi vida.

—¡Ah! —dije, y como no se me ocurrió nada más que decir, repetí—: ¡Ah!

—Ahora entenderás por qué digo que las cosas están muy cargadas por aquí.

—Creo que empiezo a entenderlo. Creo que sí. —Volví a mi pregunta anterior—. ¿No tienes idea de dónde fue tu marido?

—No lo sé. No quiero saberlo. Me avergüenza haberme casado con un hombre que fue capaz de hacer una cosa así.

La conversación parecía haber terminado. Lo único que pude decir fue «Vaya»; nos quedamos los dos callados, y al cabo de un buen rato apareció Lucy.

—Mamá —dijo la chica por la que se había matado a un niño. No pareció reparar en nuestra mirada de extrañeza–. ¿No te basta con un hombre por día? —Y volviéndose hacia mí añadió–: Espero que no estés pensando en abandonarme. Lee Anne, Brenda y Shelly ya han planeado una excursión conmigo y el señor Nieman.

Lucy sacudió la cabeza, y el mechón de pelo que yo le había soltado le cayó sobre la cara.

—¿Intentas ponerme en un aprieto? Tengo diecisiete años. No puedo permitir que me vean volver a casa con mamá.

—Pues entonces vete sola —dijo Myra—. Y no quiero que te lleve en coche ninguno de esos chicos. Están tan borrachos como Justy.

Lucy puso los ojos en blanco y exclamó:

—¡Como si yo quisiera!

—Myra —dije—. ¿Señora Robinson?

Se volvió hacia mí.

—¿Sí?

—Me llamo Justin. Just-in.

—Entendido —dijo, sonriendo; y dirigiéndose a Lucy concluyó–: Hagas lo que hagas, quiero que estés en casa a la una. —La besó apresuradamente antes de que Lucy pudiera marcharse, y luego volvió a la pista de baile. Es quizá melodramático por mi parte señalar que, durante los meses siguientes, Myra Robinson no tendría más que ese beso por todo recuerdo de su hija, pero lo señalo de todos modos, porque la propia Myra nunca dio muestras de recordarlo.

2.18

WEBBIE

No llevábamos linterna. Nada más entrar en la pila de piedras todo estaba muy oscuro, y no teníamos luz de ninguna clase. El sol desapareció a nuestras espaldas en una curva del camino, y sentí que Cora me tomaba de la mano.

—Agárrate a esto —dijo.

Me puso en los dedos algo duro, redondo, seco, y me reí sin querer.

—No seas tonta, niña. No quiero que te caigas y te rompas una pierna.

Me puse seria rápidamente.

—¿Qué hago?

—El suelo está lleno de agujeros; más vale que te quites esos ridículos zapatos que llevas. Es como una escalera, solo que más resbaladiza.

—No entiendo nada, Cora.

—Pues tanto mejor. Vamos.

Me quité los zapatos empujando con los dedos. El derecho cayó al suelo, pero el izquierdo cayó en el vacío. Un segundo después oí un ruido sordo. Dos segundos, mejor dicho.

—Ha tardado dos segundos, Cora. Hay seis metros.

—No hay seis metros, hay tres. Además, ¿qué importa? No te caigas y no te pasará nada.

Dejé de protestar, pues comprendí que si seguía así conseguiría ponerme de verdad nerviosa. Y quería ver lo que había allí abajo. Más que verlo quería sentirlo, oírlo, experimentarlo. Me acordé de Jimi Hendrix y su cara llena de granos. Mi padre me había dicho que Jimi Hendrix tomaba drogas y que por eso tenía acné incluso siendo adulto. Por eso se había muerto. Intenté imaginarme al bebé de Marsha Johnson. A Eric Johnson. Algunos decían que el padre era blanco, pero mi padre me dijo que Eric había nacido fuera del matrimonio y que por eso era así.

—¿Webbie?

Sujeté el palo con las dos manos. Avancé un paso, busqué a tientas con el pie derecho hasta que encontré el palo y un agujero donde meterlo. El golpe. Adelanté el pie izquierdo y me quedé colgando del palo.

—Allá va nadie.

—Allá vas tú —dijo Cora. Su mano encontró mi cabeza; un dedo se posó justo en la fina línea de piel que me separaba las trenzas.

Me deslicé hacia abajo y la mano de Cora perdió el contacto con mi cabeza. Bajé despacio. No era difícil. Primero ponía los pies, luego las manos. Pies, manos, pies, manos. Ya había hecho algo parecido en las barras del gimnasio, con ayuda de una cuerda que colgaba del techo. Era delgada, ágil. Llevaba pantalones cortos. Podía conseguirlo.

El palo vibró cuando Cora se colgó de él por encima de mí. La oí bajar. Algo se rasgó.

—¡Me cago en...! —dijo Cora.

—¡Ni se te ocurra!

—Me he roto el vestido.

—No habértelo puesto.

—¡Cómo te atreves! —dijo Cora. Luego se hizo el silencio. Se oyó un segundo desgarrón y el ruido que hacía Cora al seguir descendiendo.

Al fin, el suelo. Al principio no me fiaba demasiado; tanteaba con los pies sin soltar el palo, pero el suelo parecía sólido, no resbalaba ni se hundía; tampoco se oía crujir de huesos. Me alejé del palo, tropecé con algo blando y grité al caer de culo. Sentí un intenso olor a cenizas y sudor, tan rancio que volví a gritar.

—¿Qué pasa? —gritó Cora—. ¿Qué pasa, Webbie? —La oí bajar por el palo. Avanzar hacia mí. Por un momento me sentí indefensa y necesitada de protección—. ¿Dónde estás, Webbie?

No me había dado cuenta de lo oscuro que estaba hasta que Cora habló y comprendí que estaba conmigo, en el suelo. No veía nada. Absolutamente nada. En voz baja dije:

—No sé.

Pero Cora estaba allí. Caminó hacia mí y uno de sus pies tropezó con mi tobillo; volví a gritar y Cora cayó a mi lado. Me puso una mano en la tripa y apretó, como para asegurarse de que no era un fantasma.

—Oye —empezó a decir, pero una carcajada ahogó sus palabras. Yo también me eché a reír y luego nos quedamos allí tumbadas un buen rato, riéndonos, respirando pesadamente, riéndonos y respirando.

Al fin dije:

—¿A qué huele?

—Cada cosa a su tiempo, niña. Cada cosa a su tiempo. Primero, ¿estás bien?

—Bueno, me has aplastado el tobillo, pero creo que estoy bien.

—Vale —dijo Cora, en voz seria y pensativa—. Huele —dijo, olfateando— a cenizas. Y huele también —volvió a olfatear— a sexo. Tropezaste con una manta y aterrizaste con el culo justo en la fogata que alguien encendió.

—¡Madre mía! ¿Quieres decir que estoy llena de ceniza? Mi padre me matará.

—No eres la única que lleva un vestido blanco. ¡Mierda! —dijo Cora—. Roto y sucio. Menudo espectáculo. Bueno, yo me ocuparé del reverendo Abraham.

—Cora... —empecé a decir, pero ella me interrumpió.

—Mis pecados se han lavado en la sangre del Señor. Ahora me visto con la belleza de su palabra.

Su voz inundó la cueva, rebotando en las paredes, con más fuerza que el coro de la iglesia. Esperé hasta que se restableció el silencio y dije:

—No conozco ese himno.

—Acabo de inventármelo —dijo Cora con una risita—. El reverendo tampoco lo conoce, pero no se atreverá a admitirlo.

Me reí al imaginarme a mi padre burlado. Me reí con ganas, echando la cabeza hacia atrás, con la boca abierta, sintiendo las cenizas en la lengua. Tenía los codos apoyados sobre algo blando; supongo que serían cenizas, aunque tenía una textura viscosa. Sentía la mano de Cora, caliente y pesada, sobre mi estómago, y tenía el tobillo derecho atrapado por su pierna izquierda. Moví la pierna.

—¿Eres tú, o es un espíritu indio que vuelve para vengarse?
—No estoy haciendo nada —dije, inocentemente.
—En ese caso... —La arena se movió a mi lado. Antes de que pudiera darme cuenta de lo que pasaba, la mano que antes reposaba en mi estómago me sujetó el tobillo. Volví a gritar, de miedo y de placer, mientras Cora me agarraba el tobillo, obligándome a girar para alejarme de ella.
—¡Cora!
Cora rió. La oí moverse por la cueva. El eco hacía que resultara imposible seguirle el rastro al sonido.
—¿Dónde estás, Cora?
Más risas. El sonido parecía flotar en el aire, como una capa de humo. Me levanté despacio con la intención de oírlo mejor, pero antes de que pudiera incorporarme del todo, mi cabeza chocó con algo blando pero implacable. Sentí que la tierra fría y seca se me metía por la espalda. Volví a gritar.
—¡Cora!
Nada. Nada de nada. Solo oía su respiración, a pesar de mis jadeos.
—Cora, por favor. Tengo miedo.
Silencio. Silencio y nada. Sabía que si no me movía de inmediato me echaría a llorar. Sabía que la cueva era pequeña, apenas más grande que el cuarto de estar de mi casa, más pequeña que el altar de la iglesia. Me lo habían dicho. Las piedras ventrales habían desaparecido; el esqueleto se lo habían llevado. Lo peor con lo que podía tropezar era una lata de cerveza sin terminar, rancia y llena de colillas. Lo sabía.

Avancé despacio. Más que andar, ponía un pie temblando detrás del otro, agachando la cabeza para no tocar contra el techo, paso a paso. Intenté avanzar arrastrando una mano por encima de la cabeza, pero el pelo y la nuca se me llenaban de tierra, de manera que extendí las manos como haría una ciega —en ese momento estaba ciega— y seguí adelante.

Paso a paso. Cora no emitía sonido alguno. Me parecía que la oía pensar. Ven por aquí, estaba pensando. Quiero que me encuentres.

No la llamé. No dije nada. No era eso lo que ella quería. Lo que quería era que la encontrara. Y la estaba buscando. Mis manos tropezaron con una pared, o, mejor dicho, la mano derecha tropezó con una pared, pero la izquierda siguió avanzando un par de pasos más. La moví, encontré los límites del habitáculo. Tenía el tamaño de una panera. Sabía lo que era. Ahora estaba vacía, pero sabía que había contenido una piedra ventral.

Continué junto a la pared hasta que encontré una esquina. La cueva era rectangular. Cuatro paredes; me encontraba en la intersección de dos de ellas. Recorrí la segunda pared. Tropecé con algo duro, metálico, redondo; crujió y se cascó al pisarlo: una lata de cerveza sin terminar, llena de colillas.

Llegué a la segunda esquina. Recorrí la tercera pared. Mis manos pasaban sobre nichos vacíos. Unos eran pequeños, del tamaño de tostadores, otros grandes como hornos. No necesitaba comprobar que estaban vacíos. Sabía que estaban vacíos. Me entristeció un poco, no el hecho de que estuvieran vacíos, sino el hecho de que ni siquiera pudiera imaginar que contenían una piedra ventral.

Una tercera esquina. Una cuarta pared. Giré. Antes de avanzar unos pasos noté que había algo donde no debería haber nada; nada que formara parte de la cueva.

—¿Cora?

No dijo nada, pero sentí el movimiento de sus tripas en mis manos. Oí el sonido de su respiración. Estiró las manos y me sujetó los pechos por debajo, pero sin decir nada.

—Cora —dije. Esta vez no era una pregunta. La primera vez tampoco lo había sido. Era una petición, aunque no sabía lo que estaba pidiendo.

—Hola —se limitó a decir; no necesitaba decir más. Su voz sonó densa y áspera, y no necesitaba decir más. Pensé en el pobre Sawyer.

Mis manos seguían sobre su estómago. Cuando dijo «hola» sentí el temblor, las vibraciones como burbujas que subían y bajaban.

—¿Es aquí donde lo hiciste, Cora? ¿Es aquí donde follaste?

Sus manos pasaron bruscamente de mis pechos a mis muñecas. Las sujetó con fuerza, pero solo dijo: «¡Niña!».

—¿Follaste aquí, Cora? ¿Es aquí donde follaste? —No necesitaba preguntarlo. Ya lo sabía, como sabía cuál era la forma y el tamaño de la cueva, como sabía que no había ningún tesoro oculto y que las manos que habían sujetado mis pechos y ahora me sujetaban las muñecas habían sostenido alguna vez la polla de Sawyer Johnson, su picha, su rabo, su pija.

Pobre Sawyer, volví a pensar. Pobre Sawyer, pobre Marsha, pobre Eric, pobres de todos aquellos que sintieran este horrible deseo.

Moví las manos hasta que pude sujetar las muñecas de Cora. Me retorcí la piel. En el colegio lo llamábamos fuego indio, porque la piel se te ponía roja, pero Cora ya tenía la piel roja.

—¡Auuu, Webbie!
—Tienes que decírmelo, Cora. Dímelo y te soltaré.

Era más grande que yo, mayor y más fuerte, pero no ofrecía demasiada resistencia.

—¡Webbie, por favor!
—Dímelo, Cora. Te he encontrado y ahora tienes que decírmelo.
—¡Sí! —dijo—. ¡Sí, vale, sí!

Entonces se apartó de mí. Me había respondido. Estábamos en paz y podía fingir que volvía a la carga. El sonido de nuestra respiración inundaba la cueva. Cuando apartó las manos de mí, supe que así serían las cosas para mí en lo sucesivo. No las haría. Las conocería. Las descubriría.

—Vámonos —dijo Cora.
—Tengo que encontrar mi zapato.

Buscamos por el suelo. Cora se dio por vencida al cabo de un rato. Dijo que no lo encontraríamos, pero yo sabía cuál era el tamaño de la cueva, sabía todo lo que contenía. Seguí buscando por el suelo, despacio, atentamente; sabía que podría encontrar lo que quisiera si buscaba con cuidado. Mi zapato intentaba esconderse. Estaba medio enterrado en la tierra, oculto bajo una manta, pero lo encontré y lo vacié. No podía ponérmelo mientras trepaba por el palo y tampoco podía metérmelo en el bolsillo de los pantalones, de manera que me lo guardé en la cintura. Sentí la suela de goma fría en el vientre, pero en lo que tardé en agarrarme al palo —«Vamos, Cora, por aquí»— ya se había calentado, incluso despedía más calor que mi cuerpo. El otro zapato esperaba arriba, y me los puse los dos; uno frío, el otro caliente. Al principio resultó un poco extraño, pero durante el camino de vuelta los zapatos volvieron a la normalidad, un poco aplastados, quizá, pero por lo demás igual que siempre.

2.19

JUSTIN

Escucha: la noche era fría y el cielo estaba despejado; el suelo helado se quebraba bajo nuestros pasos. Escucha: los caminos eran rectos y angostos, como cabía esperar que fueran los caminos en Galatea, y nos conducían inevitablemente hacia nuestro destino. Escucha: me llamo Justin Time, y es hora de decir adiós.

—Estás borracho —dijo Lucy.

—Sí, estoy borracho —dije, secamente.
—No tienes edad suficiente para beber.
—Sí la tengo.
—No sé por qué me hablas así. Yo no soy tan, tan...
—Ingenua.
—Tan ingenua como te imaginas.
Intenté quitar aspereza a mi voz, pero dije:
—Sí lo eres.
—Bueno, ¿y qué? ¿Acaso es tan malo?
—Tú eres la única que puede responder a esa pregunta.
—Es horrible —dijo entonces Lucy—. Quiero aprender, quiero hacer cosas. Quiero divertirme un poco.
—¿Crees que el conocimiento y la acción son necesariamente divertidos?
—¿Eh?
—A ver, por ejemplo, ¿qué pasa si buscas conocimiento y te encuentras con un hombre que es muy cariñoso contigo, que te besa en el cuello y te compra perfumes, ropas y joyas, y luego te pide que vivas con él para siempre?
—¡Estupendo!
—Y luego saca un cuchillo, y te viola y te hace un corte en forma de X en los pezones, no tan profundo como para dejar una cicatriz, solo lo suficiente para que sangres un poco.
Lucy seguía sonriendo cuando terminé de hablar, pero luego, un momento después, su rostro se ensombreció y dejó escapar un leve suspiro.
—Estás enfermo. Estás loco de remate.
—Y tú has aprendido algo.
—Eso no es lo que quiero aprender. Quiero la primera mitad de la historia, no la segunda.
—Sé lo que quieres. Quieres heredar una fortuna sin necesidad de que nadie muera. Quieres construir un castillo sin haber cogido un ladrillo en tu vida. Quieres tener hijos sin parir.
—Retiro lo dicho. No estás loco. Eres realmente malo.
—Y tú aprendes deprisa.
Lucy volvió a suspirar.
—¿Por qué estás siendo tan malo conmigo? Pensaba que esta era nuestra primera cita. No me importa si no quieres hacer nada conmigo, pero...
—Lucy, soy maricón.
Lucy levantó los hombros, pero intentó disimular el movimiento con un temblor. Fingió despreocupación, lo que en su caso equivale a decir que fingió aburrimiento.

—Ya lo sé.
—Colin es mi amante.
—Ya lo sé —repitió; y luego, abrió los ojos como platos—. ¿Te hizo eso? ¿Lo del cuchillo?
—¿Crees que seguiría con él si me lo hubiera hecho?
—Bueno, vale. —Casi parecía decepcionada—. Pero ¿eso pasó de verdad? ¿Alguien...?
Asentí.
Apartó su mirada de mí.
—A mí también me ocurrió algo malo una vez —dijo, en voz tan baja que sus palabras casi se perdieron entre el ruido de nuestros pasos. Entonces levanté la vista y comprobé con asombro que habíamos salido del pueblo. Los campos helados se extendían en todas las direcciones; la casa de Lucy se encontraba a medio kilómetro hacia delante, la casa de caliza a medio kilómetro hacia atrás.
—Tu madre me lo ha contado.
—¿Te lo ha contado?
—Lo de Eric Johnson.
—¿Te ha hablado de Eric Johnson?
—Me contó que mentiste.
—¡Serás maricón!
Me acertó con el bolso en plena cara. Casi me caigo al suelo. Me tambaleé hacia atrás, cubriéndome la cara con las manos.
—¡Zorra! —grité a través de los dedos, y cuando me aparté las manos de la cara vi que Lucy estaba frente a mí, con los brazos en jarras, los pechos pequeños palpitando bajo el abrigo, lanzando vapor al respirar y brillando bajo la luz de la noche. Estaba llorando—. ¡Joder! ¡Lo siento! No quería culparte de... Sé que no imaginaste que pudiera ocurrir una cosa así. —En realidad no lo sabía, pero quería concederle el beneficio de la duda.

Me miró un momento y se secó los ojos con el dorso de la mano. Sacó un pañuelo de papel del bolso y se sonó la nariz. Luego se dio la vuelta y echó a andar; la seguí. Permanecimos sin hablar durante varios minutos. La luz del porche de la casa de Lucy y Myra brillaba en la distancia. Las ramas de las moreras sin hojas que crecían junto al camino crujían y chocaban entre sí, y el viento se colaba entre la hierba en las zanjas y en los campos. Y nosotros avanzábamos sobre un suelo que parecía de cristal roto, mientras el eco de nuestros pasos resonaba entre los árboles.

Me coloqué un paso por detrás de Lucy para observar sus largas piernas, cubiertas por medias blancas, que temblaban cada vez que el tacón de su zapato se hundía en la suciedad del camino; hasta que volví a ponerme a su lado, ella no dijo nada.

—No sé qué esperaba que ocurriera —dijo, con la voz ligeramente temblorosa—. Tenía siete años y no entendía lo que él me hizo… lo que podría haberme hecho. Lo único que sé es que no me gustó, e intenté impedirlo.

Me hubiera gustado hacerle preguntas, el tipo de preguntas que le haría a cualquiera en Nueva York, pero de pronto, clarísimamente y por primera vez, sentí el terrible peso del silencio que parecía atenazar a todos los habitantes de Galatea. De todos modos, luché contra esa sensación y dije:

—Estás diciendo que ocurrió realmente.

Lucy no me contestó al momento. Cuando al fin habló, pronunció las palabras muy despacio:

—Era la cosa más fea que puedas imaginarte. Pregúntale a cualquiera. Hasta mi madre dijo una vez que tenía la cara como un plato de patatas aplastadas y podridas. Y ese día yo lo miré; no podía soportar su fealdad; los labios grandes y llenos de grietas rebosantes de pus; los ojos pequeños, como inyectados en sangre, y el pelo… era como el de esas chicas negras que se tiñen el pelo de naranja, pero mucho más feo, y más encrespado. Y esa piel… Pregúntale a cualquiera y te dirán que Eric Johnson… ¡ay!

Lucy se inclinó hacia delante, como si la hubiesen empujado. Cayó, rodó y quedó tendida en la hierba. Me volví y vi una forma humana que parecía el doble de grande que la mía, y entonces recibí un puñetazo en la cara. No recuerdo que me cayera al suelo. Solo recuerdo que una bota con remaches de acero se me clavó en las costillas, y en el silencio las oí crujir bajo el abrigo y la piel. Me quedé sin respiración, pero no perdí la conciencia, y vi que la misma bota golpeaba a Lucy. Le asestó un puntapié en el pecho, luego en el estómago, luego en la entrepierna… y me fijé en la bota porque la había reconocido. Esa bota era de Colin. Igual que yo, Lucy era incapaz de hablar o respirar; lo único que se oía era el ruido de la bota de Colin golpeando el cuerpo de Lucy. Lucy se revolvía con cada patada y el gran abrigo que ese hombre llevaba puesto volaba al viento como las alas de un ángel cojo. El abrigo era como las alas de un murciélago, de un dragón, la brillante cola de un avión surcando el cielo. El abrigo era de Colin. De pronto recuperé el aliento con un largo aullido de dolor, como el llanto de un recién nacido, y el hombre se dio la vuelta al oírlo. Vi que Lucy se retorcía y, por primera vez, vi la cabeza del agresor: la llevaba cubierta por una capucha blanca con dos agujeros abiertos a la altura de los ojos. Las manos del hombre —enfundadas en los guantes de Colin, unos guantes de piel de cordero, suaves como una mejilla recién afeitada— me agarraron como tenazas; una en la garganta, la otra en los testículos; me apretó con fuerza, ahogándome, aplastándome los huevos. Intenté escapar, intenté golpearlo, pero mi cuerpo no respondía. Mi cuerpo nunca había respondido ante Colin. En cuestión de segundos, la noche se llenó de brillantes puntos de luz púrpura. Estaba casi inconsciente cuando me levantó por encima de la cabeza como si fuera un trofeo. Sentía un dolor insufrible en los testículos, un dolor que, en cierto modo, parecía más viejo que mi cuerpo. Y no recordaba lo que significaba respirar. Por un momento no vi más que ramas dibujadas contra el cielo como un encaje roto, y detrás, las estrellas. Luego sentí que mi cuerpo se liberaba del torpe agarre de mi agresor, y vi una luna creciente, larga y fina, donde la negrura de la tierra se unía con la negrura del cielo. En lugar de intentar sujetarme, me tiró al suelo, y casi no me di cuenta de que volaba, de tan ocupado como estaba en respirar; luego aterricé sobre el suelo helado y perdí el conocimiento.

 Al abrir los ojos noté que tenía algo en la boca y que las piernas no me respondían, y vi al agresor tumbado encima de Lucy. Parecía apoyar todo el peso de su cuerpo sobre la mano derecha, que atenazaba la garganta de Lucy como antes lo había hecho con la mía, mientras metía el pulgar en la boca abierta de ella. Lucy tenía el abrigo abierto; su vestido había desaparecido, y tenía los muslos magullados y la piel desgarrada. El hombre ya la había violado, y aunque el pene aparecía cubierto por algo negro y brillante —supongo que era sangre, sangre de Lucy—, era la única parte de su cuerpo que resultaba visible: era blanco; reconocí, a pesar de todo, que había cambiado mucho desde que llegué a Galatea, porque antes jamás me habría fijado en el color de su pene, a menos que no fuera blanco.

 El agresor abofeteó a Lucy con la mano izquierda. La abofeteó lo suficiente para mantenerla despierta. Debí de emitir algún sonido, porque el hombre volvió hacia mí su cabeza encapuchada, pero no dejó de violarla, y aún seguía mirándome cuando su cuerpo se contrajo y tembló en el momento del orgasmo; luego se desplomó sobre Lucy y se puso a darle cabezazos, produciendo un sonido horrible, como el que hacen dos trozos de madera al chocar entre sí, y demostrando con ello que no era precisamente un espantapájaros con la cabeza rellena de paja. Se incorporó y aplastó el cuerpo de Lucy contra el suelo. Luego se detuvo bruscamente y, en el silencio, oí mis propios sollozos entrecortados. Descabalgó lentamente —Lucy no se movía—, introdujo las palmas de las manos abiertas por debajo del cuerpo de ella y la cargó sobre su hombro derecho. Caminó entonces hacia mí tambaleándose, con las botas de Colin y los pantalones de Colin, y cuando llegó a mi lado se detuvo un momento, con la camisa de Colin y el abrigo de Colin, balanceándose ligeramente, con los guantes de Colin y la corbata de Colin, como las ramas de los árboles sobre su cabeza, Colin, Colin, Colin, y supe que estaba llamado a recordar ese momento. Rebuscó entonces en un bolsillo y sacó algo. Sacó un espejo, el retrovisor lateral de un coche. Lo movió hasta que algo le indicó que podía verme la cara reflejada en el espejo, la cara que él quería que yo viera por última vez, la cara que yo estaba mirando cuando cayó sobre mí. Me clavó la rodilla en la ingle con todas sus fuerzas, y creo que vomité y me atraganté al mismo tiempo cuando aplastó el espejo contra mi sien, justo donde Colin me había dado un puñetazo recientemente, y volví a perder el conocimiento. Lo peor de todo fue que nadie dijo una sola palabra durante el ataque, ni él, ni Lucy ni yo. Lucy y yo lo habíamos intentado sin éxito, pero nuestro agresor ni siquiera se había molestado en intentarlo: ni una palabra, ni un suspiro, ni una súplica. Ni siquiera un gruñido.

2.20

WEBBIE

Siempre, desde niña, fui consciente de la fragilidad de las cosas y de su imparable decadencia. Esto no es normal; semejante conocimiento es, así lo creo, una preocupación más adulta que juvenil. Los niños, vagamente conscientes de su propia debilidad frente a un mundo hostil, se vuelcan en sus padres en busca de apoyo y protección. Poco a poco, a medida que van madurando, pierden esta sensación y se hacen más fuertes; aprenden que los objetos que los rodean, ya sean tazas de porcelana o muros de caliza, están tan sujetos a la erosión del tiempo como ellos mismos.

Pero yo era diferente. Siempre supe que era fuerte; «superior», era la palabra que empleaba mi padre cuando quería castigarme; «orgullo» era la favorita de las Damas de la Iglesia. Pero mi orgullo o mi superioridad o mi fuerza eran relativos, estaban más arraigados en mí misma que en una conciencia clara de la fragilidad de los objetos que constituían nuestro entorno familiar. Recuerdo el ciclo vital de los trapos de cocina: primero nuevos y almidonados; más tarde, llenos de manchas pero aún válidos para secar los cacharros, y finalmente, llenos de agujeros y solo aptos para limpiar el polvo, antes de arder en la chimenea (los residuos de productos de limpieza acumulados en ellos los convertían en un excelente material para encender el fuego: bastaba con una cerilla para que estallaran en llamas), como si el proceso en su conjunto, que había durado años, avanzara a cámara rápida. Recuerdo perfectamente la vajilla de porcelana que compramos cuando yo tenía ocho años y que usábamos en combinación con la antigua. La porcelana antigua, llena de grietas y desportilladuras, llevaba dibujada una tetera azul en el centro de cada plato, fuente o cuenco; la nueva era más sencilla —mi padre me permitió escogerla— y solo tenía tres rayas doradas alrededor del borde. A Hope Rochelle le parecía un poco sosa, pero yo insistía en poner la mesa con ella. Mi padre y yo nunca comíamos solos durante los últimos y felices años anteriores a la llegada de Rosemary Krebs; siempre nos acompañaban las Damas y a veces algún miembro de sus numerosas familias, u otros miembros de la congregación; después de que mi padre enfermara, y después de que yo volviera de Columbia, empezamos a comer solos. Pero la vajilla nueva, igual que la vieja, se fue deteriorando. Las rayas doradas se desdibujaron y se desconcharon, los bordes se desportillaron, las piezas cayeron y se rompieron en pedazos. Pronto —demasiado pronto en mi memoria mezclada— solo quedaron algunos restos de la vajilla nueva y aún menos de la vieja, y llegó el momento de renovar otra vez la porcelana.

Yo tenía once años; lo recuerdo porque fue solo unas semanas después de que visitara la cueva de las Piedras Ventrales con Cora Lewis. Recuerdo haber limpiado los armarios para acomodar la nueva vajilla y recuerdo que en un rincón oscuro y seco de uno de ellos, donde guardábamos los sacos de patatas y de cebollas, encontré un plato lleno de polvo incrustado, que, al lavarlo, reveló un dibujo desconocido. Una corona de rosas, antaño roja y ahora de un tono rosa pálido, rodeaba el borde del plato junto a una vid verde que en su día debió de ser un círculo continuo y que ahora aparecía intermitentemente fragmentado, tras haber perdido su color. Me quedé mirando el plato: lo había sumergido en el fregadero lleno de agua caliente, y brillaba entre el vapor y el líquido. Lo saqué del agua y lo puse con los otros —la antigua porcelana nueva, la antigua porcelana antigua, y esta otra, la antigua antigua porcelana antigua: la de mi madre—, luego volví a cogerlo y lo sostuve entre las manos durante un buen rato, lo miré, lo memoricé, cómo era y cómo imaginaba que podía haber sido, con sus colores vivos, incluso chillones, ofreciendo raciones de pollo con especias y gambas rebozadas; luego lo tiré al suelo. Amontoné los pedazos y los aplasté con un martillo, y cuando conseguí hacerlo añicos, lo trabajé con el rodillo hasta convertirlo en polvo, en polvo fino, casi tan fino como el talco. Un polvo como el que se me adhería a los dedos cuando tocaba la piedra ventral de mi padre.

Cuando terminé estaba llorando. Tenía once años y acababa de perder a mi mejor amiga —nada volvió a ser igual entre Cora y yo después de nuestra visita a la cueva— y me pareció que al romper el plato perdía a mi madre por segunda vez. Barrí el polvo, llena de remordimientos, y lo metí en una bolsa de plástico. Durante mucho tiempo pensé que debía hacer algo con ese polvo; mezclarlo con agua hasta formar una pasta y convertirlo en masa de modelar para hacer... ¿qué? ¿Un cenicero? ¿Una taza? ¿Otro plato? Al final no supe decidirme y dejé el polvo en la bolsa. Está guardado en algún cajón. Espera, como espero yo, como espera Lucy Robinson, a ser descubierto para volver a ser pleno, para volver a ser algo.

3

3.01

COLIN

¿Cómo empezar? ¿Por dónde? Tucídides comienza su relato de las guerras del Peloponeso situándolas con precisión en el tiempo, registrando las cosechas, la estación del año, el reinado de ciertos monarcas y la validez de ciertos tratados. Cuando leí su historia me sorprendió el contraste entre su enorme esfuerzo de precisión y la sencilla frase que aparece en la cabecera de la página, añadida por los editores del libro quince siglos más tarde: «Comienzo de la guerra, año 431». Tal vez deba empezar por ahí: por el 11 de noviembre de 1994, ciento treinta y cinco años después de la fundación de Galatia, dieciocho años después de la incorporación de Galatea, diez años después del linchamiento de Eric Johnson, nueve años después de la muerte de Odell Painter y la desaparición de Gary Gables, ocho años después de que el reverendo Abraham Greeving quedara impedido por un ataque y de que su hija Webbie regresara a Galatia, seis años después del regreso de Wade Painter, ocho años después del nacimiento del hijo de Cora Johnson, cuatro años después de la llegada de Rosa Stone, dos años después de la muerte de la anciana Beatrice, dos meses después de la muerte de Eddie Comedy y de la desaparición de Melvin Cartwright, un mes después de la llegada de Justin y mía a este pueblo, y catorce años después de que estallara la epidemia de sida, una muchacha de diecisiete años, Lucy Robinson, fue secuestrada por un desconocido que intentó acusarme del secuestro. Creo, por naturaleza, que la frontera de las historias la marcan los nacimientos y las muertes, pero por una vez pasaré por alto mi tendencia natural y diré que esta historia, como la de Tucídides, comienza con una declaración de hostilidad. No sé dónde terminará.

3.02

AGENTE BROWN

Se quedaba hasta muy tarde, haciendo las cuentas.

Al principio se proponía ser una presencia habitual en la empresa de Rosemary Krebs, pero ella cortó la iniciativa de raíz. Dijo que en su opinión la gente tenía menos posibilidades de relajarse y desconectar si «estaba de guardia», y al agente Brown no le gustó cómo sonaba aquello, pero resultó que, transcurridos unos meses, pudo tomarse la noche libre.

Las matemáticas nunca habían sido su fuerte, aunque en este caso las cuentas eran muy sencillas. Más o menos así:

Cinco menos tres igual a dos.

En el colegio, las cuentas más difíciles de resolver eran las que llamaban problemas de historia. Eran más difíciles porque mezclaban los números con un montón de palabras, de modo que lo primero que tenías que hacer era separar los números de las palabras y luego repasarlos y ver la relación que había entre los números, con el fin de hacer una cuenta elemental. Según este planteamiento, las matemáticas serían más o menos así:

Cinco hombres salen al campo una noche. Los cinco van encapuchados y los cinco portan antorchas. Los cinco llevan zapatos también, pero veamos cómo intentan confundirnos: introducen pequeños detalles, aunque eso no tiene demasiada importancia; no solo en lo que se refiere a los zapatos, sino también a las antorchas, las capuchas y algunas escopetas, lo cual no afecta al hecho principal, que es que son cinco hombres.

Había una sexta persona esa noche; no era un hombre, sino un niño, pero no figura en esta ecuación. De manera que tenemos cinco hombres. La sexta persona también va encapuchada, pero a diferencia de los otros encapuchados, su capucha no tiene agujeros, cero, aunque las capuchas de los demás hombres sí tenían agujeros; dos agujeros en cuatro de los casos y tres agujeros en uno de los casos, y por este agujero extra, que según los cálculos del agente Brown hacía el agujero número once, llegó la voz que se oyó esa noche, y la voz dijo: «Esto va por Lucy, muchachos. No lo olvidéis. Esto va por mi hija».

Se suponía que Stan Robinson no debía decir nada; se suponía que ninguno de los cinco hombres debía saber quiénes eran los demás. Pero Stan no paraba de hablar de su hija, de su Lucy, y aunque nadie hubiera podido reconocer su voz o su cuerpo alto y delgado dentro de aquel traje de fantasma, Lucy no tenía más que un padre, y así se descubrió todo. Y después de lo ocurrido, Stan tampoco se esforzó en guardar el secreto. Al contrario, le contó a todo el mundo lo que había pasado esa noche, en los campos, con las antorchas, las capuchas, las escopetas y la soga; por eso, todo el mundo lo sabía.

Como verán no es fácil sacar las cuentas cuando el problema se plantea como una historia. La historia tiende a superponerse. Pero el agente Brown tuvo diez años para ir resumiendo esta historia, todas las historias diferentes, hasta quedarse solo con los números.

El primer número era, definitivamente, cinco.

Lo que no estaba tan claro eran los nombres que acompañaban a ese número. Al menos, no todos. Solo tenía a Stan Robinson. Y Stan Robinson había contado a todo el mundo que él era el número uno. Y luego, bueno, es muy probable que el número dos fuera Odell Painter. Y que el número tres pudiera ser otro asesinado: Eddie Comedy era el número tres.

Menos tres.

Esa era la información de que disponía hasta el momento, y eso significaba que aún le faltaban dos nombres, dos números.

Cinco menos tres igual a dos.

Lo escribió. Ya lo había escrito antes, pero volvió a escribirlo; lo anotó claramente en una columna:

Stan Robinson
Odell Painter
Eddie Comedy

Dejó dos espacios en blanco para los nombres que le faltaban y se quedó un rato mirándolos, como si pudieran rellenarse solos por arte de magia, y al ver que tal cosa no ocurría hizo algo que nunca había hecho: escribió el nombre de Melvin Cartwright junto al de Eddie Comedy. Y luego escribió el nombre de Gary Gables junto al de Odell Painter. Y, de pronto, tuvo una iluminación y escribió otro nombre, y dos nuevos espacios en blanco. Este fue el resultado:

Stan Robinson – Sawyer Johnson
Odell Painter – Gary Gables
Eddie Comedy – Melvin Cartwright

La verdad es que aquello era para volver loco a cualquiera; mirar la lista y caer de pronto en la cuenta de lo que había estado pasando subrepticiamente, con todo tipo de subterfugios, delante de sus narices, pero tan despacio que ni siquiera él, el hombre encargado de evitar que tales cosas ocurrieran, se había dado cuenta.

Pero ¿quién podía pensar en Sawyer Johnson? Sawyer Johnson era un chico que caía bien a todo el mundo: trabajador, hombre de familia y buen feligrés... Era un chico por el que casi sentías pena cuando tenías acceso a ciertos documentos a los que solo el agente Brown y acaso el reverendo Greeving tenían acceso, documentos en los que se contaba que su mujer lo había abandonado y que nada tenían que ver con la otra cuestión. Pero, de todos modos...

Le distrajo el timbre del teléfono. Siempre había algo que lo distraía.

3.03

CORA

De noche: hora de cenar y luego hora de acostarse, así todos los días desde hacía cuatro años. A veces, ella me lleva directamente al sueño. Es así, como si me tomara de la mano para conducirme a alguna parte y me llevara al sueño. El día ha sido agotador, entre Sawyer y el café, y ninguna de nosotras es tan joven como antes: a veces el sueño es lo único que nos hace felices. Pero otras veces emprendemos ese largo camino, no como lo hacíamos Sawyer y yo, aunque tampoco es tan distinto de como lo había imaginado. En todo caso, nunca hay preocupación de noche, en la cama. Nunca con Rosa.

Pero la noche en que ocurrió por primera vez —la noche antes de que todo el mundo se enterara, la noche en la que aún podíamos defender nuestra inocencia— Rosa se quedó en el café y me tuvo varias horas esperándola. La oía trajinar en el piso de abajo, sacando brillo a lo que ya brillaba, tirando por el fregadero un caldo del día anterior, hasta que al final oí el ruido que hicieron las contraventanas al cerrarse, pero sabía que Rosa nunca se molestaba en cerrarlas a menos que estuviera preocupada por algo. Ahora, volviendo la vista atrás, casi me gustaría decir que Rosa sabía que algo se estaba gestando, aunque supongo que lo que ocurrió es que yo volví del baile de Rosemary Krebs oliendo a tabaco y alcohol. Tenía la ropa impregnada de humo —yo no había fumado—, pero me olía el aliento a alcohol, y en eso Rosa se parece un poco a Rosemary Krebs: no soporta que la gente beba, y supuse que necesitaba tomarse un poco de tiempo hasta que se le pasara el enfado.

Cuando al fin apareció Rosa, la grasa que había en su taza de té se había separado del agua y flotaba sobre la superficie formando pequeños círculos. Me había quedado dormida, pero me desperté cuando entró en la habitación. Debía de estar muy enfadada porque se puso el camisón encima del vestido y luego se desnudó por debajo, quitándose el vestido, las medias y el sujetador, pero se dejó puestos los calcetines gordos que usaba a modo de zapatillas, y cuando le pregunté por qué, dijo que tenía los pies fríos.

Una vez en la cama, apagó la luz, puso una mano fría en mi mano caliente, y me dio un pequeño apretón, que yo interpreté como una especie de invitación.

—Rosa —dije—. Rosa, cariño, siento lo que ha pasado esta noche, pero dijiste que no te importaba.

—Eso no es verdad —dijo Rosa.

—Sí lo es, lo dijiste, dijiste que...

Rosa me apretó la mano, como pidiéndome que me callara.

—No es por eso. No es por el baile. Es por...

—¿Por qué, cariño? ¿Qué pasa?

La mano de Rosa ya había entrado en calor. Le acaricié la palma con la uña del dedo índice. Se rió un poco, pero sabía que lo hacía para complacerme.

—No me hagas caso, Cora. Ya sabes cómo me pongo a veces.

—Sí, lo sé. Pero saberlo no me sirve para sentirme mejor.

—Ay, Cora. Mi Cora. Ya se me pasará. Solo estoy un poco disgustada.

Volvió a apretarme la mano, un apretón largo y fuerte, pero esta vez no me callé. No dije nada de inmediato, pero al fin hablé:

—A lo mejor podría ayudarte a sentirte mejor; a lo mejor podría sentirme un poco mejor si al menos supiera de dónde vienes. ¿Qué te pasó y por qué apareciste por aquí?

—Llevas años preguntándome lo mismo. Cuatro años. ¿Por qué no hablas más claro? —Su voz sonó casi normal en la oscuridad. Había que conocerla bien para notar que faltaba algo, y había que conocerla mejor de lo que yo la conocía para saber qué era lo que faltaba.

—¿De dónde vienes? —volví a preguntar.

—¿Quieres decir adónde voy?

—¿Vas a alguna parte?

—No voy a ninguna parte.

—Entonces, ¿de dónde vienes?

—De ninguna parte —dijo, suspirando. Se dio la vuelta y me miró.

—De ninguna parte —repetí—. Entonces ¿no piensas volver al lugar de donde viniste?

—No. No pienso volver.

Con eso bastaba, al menos por esa noche. En todo caso, no me diría nada más. No quería perder a Rosa como había perdido a Sawyer, pero si por alguna razón llegaba a perderla, no quería que fuera por el pasado. Que se alejara de mí, que continuara su camino sin mí. Eso decía Rosa cuando soplaba un diente de león. Decía que lo había aprendido cuando era niña. Pero ya me entendéis. Continuar su camino sin mí.

3.04

COLIN

No quiso sentarse en una silla. Se sentó en el suelo. Se apoyó en la pared. Se apoyó en una de las cuatro paredes; y estaban también el techo, el suelo y Justin. Lo encontré allí, con los brazos cruzados sobre el vientre, la pierna doblada debajo del cuerpo y la cabeza apoyada en la pared. Tenía la boca cerrada y los ojos abiertos, y estaba cubierto de sangre. Una bombilla desnuda iluminaba la escena, una lágrima brillante y cálida colgada de un cable negro y pelado que parecía seguirle el rastro como una raya de rímel. Justo debajo de la bombilla estaba Justin, golpeando en el suelo con un pie. El pie proyectaba una sombra minúscula cada vez que subía, pero la sombra desaparecía cuando el pie volvía a tocar el suelo. No oí ningún ruido.

El hombre al que todo el mundo llamaba agente Brown era alto y corpulento. Casi tan alto como yo y el doble de grande, y su mano derecha nunca se apartaba de la pistola durante más de un par de segundos; la otra mano tenía la costumbre de apoyarse en la tripa. El agente Brown suspiraba de vez en cuando, fuerte y entrecortadamente, mientras paseaba por la comisaría; rebuscaba entre los papeles, abría cajones, tarareaba una canción, pero no decía nada.

La canción era «Leroy Brown».

Yo no quería ser el primero en hablar. Quería que el agente Brown marcara el tono de la escena; quería que me explicara qué estaba pasando, pero la visión del apaleado cuerpo de Justin, sumada al incesante sonsonete del agente, me obligó a hablar finalmente.

—Disculpe, sheriff Brown. Creo que hay que llevar a Justin a un hospital.

El agente Brown levantó la vista de la mesa. Me escudriñó, como si intentara recordar quién era yo y por qué estaba en su oficina. Luego bajó la mirada hacia la mesa y continuó ordenando los papeles desperdigados sobre ella.

—Enseguida lo llevaremos al hospital —dijo. Cogió una tarjeta, la leyó y volvió a tirarla sobre el escritorio. Entonces se incorporó y, al mirarme, detecté en su mirada cierta acusación—. Primero tiene que contestar algunas preguntas, luego lo llevaremos al hospital.
—Pero ¡por Dios!
—Señor Nieman. Señor Nieman, le agradecería que se abstuviera de pronunciar el nombre de Dios en esta comisaría.
—¿Quiere hacer el favor de mirarlo? Está temblando, parece estar a punto de tener convulsiones. Está empapado en sangre.
—Lo que yo veo —dijo el agente Brown sin mirar a Justin— es a un chico tembloroso con unos cuantos rasguños y heridas. —Se encogió de hombros—. Le sorprendería la cantidad de sangre que contiene el cuerpo humano, señor Nieman. Pero le diré una cosa. A quien no veo por ninguna parte es a la chica de diecisiete años que fue vista por última vez con su... «amigo», aquí presente.
—Conque ¿se trata de eso? Le advierto que si me veo en la obligación de llamar a mi abogado, por Dios que se quedará usted sin esa insignia que lleva en el pecho...
—Señor Nieman. Señor Nieman. Ya le he advertido que no pronuncie el nombre de Dios. Por favor, no me obligue a repetírselo. Puede llamar a su abogado mañana por la mañana, cuando lo desee, pero yo que usted lo dejaría descansar esta noche, pues va a necesitarlo en pleno uso de sus facultades. Y por lo que respecta a esta insignia... —Retiró la mano de la culata de la pistola para llevársela a la insignia un momento y volvió a dejarla en su lugar habitual—. El único hombre que puede quitarme esta insignia del pecho es el juez Jackson Jameson Culpepper tercero, y puedo decirle que J. J. no vendrá por aquí hasta el lunes después del Día de Acción de Gracias, cuando se abre la veda del faisán. De manera que yo que usted...
Por primera vez detecté en su tono algo más que maldad.
—¿Adónde quiere llegar?
El agente Brown se detuvo un momento, luego se dirigió hacia un armario de metal gris, lo abrió y sacó de él un montón de ropa oscura. La estiró y dijo:
—Señor Nieman, ¿reconoce usted esta prenda?
—Por supuesto. Es mi abrigo. —Se trataba, en efecto, del abrigo que no había podido encontrar cuando salí de casa para ir al baile. Estaba sucio, cubierto de manchas húmedas y oscuras.
—¿Está seguro?
—Pues claro que estoy seguro.
—¿Puede aportar alguna prueba?
—Bueno, no llevo el recibo, si se refiere a eso, pero puedo asegurarle que es un abrigo de dos mil quinientos dólares comprado en

Giorgio Armani, en Beverly Hills. Sinceramente, dudo de que alguien de Galatia tenga una prenda similar.

El agente Brown asintió, como señalando que también él dudaba de que pudiera haber en Galatia una prenda similar, y luego dijo:

—Señor Nieman, este abrigo se encontró a unos tres metros del lugar donde estaba su amigo.

—Se lo habrá puesto esta noche.

—Llevaba su propio abrigo.

—Quizá lo cogió para Lucy.

—La señorita Robinson fue vista al salir de la fiesta con un abrigo que no era este.

Empecé a decir algo, pero me interrumpió.

—Señor Nieman, no quiero ser desagradable, ni mucho menos. Lo que quiero decir es que no deseo detenerlo por el momento, porque no me apetece nada ponerme a rellenar formularios esta noche. Pero le agradecería mucho que se sentara y cerrara la boca hasta que termine de interrogar a Justin, aquí presente.

—¡Cómo se atreve, pedazo de mierda pueblerina!

—Señor Nieman. No sabe cuánto me alegra que diga eso. Ahora ya no tengo necesidad de seguir fingiendo que usted me cae bien. Permítame decirle algo. Si este chico me proporciona la menor prueba de que usted ha tenido algo que ver en la desaparición de la pequeña Lucy Robinson, le aseguro que le haré desear no haber oído jamás el nombre de Galatea. Y permítame recordarle —siguió diciendo, y por primera vez detecté cierto nerviosismo en su voz— que la sodomía es un delito en el estado de Kansas.

Se dio la vuelta y volvió a guardar el abrigo en el armario, lo cerró y se marchó a la habitación contigua, donde estaba Justin.

Transcurridos unos minutos oí gritos procedentes de la sala de interrogatorios. Quien gritaba era el agente Brown, no Justin. A Justin no se le oía.

Me acerqué a la mampara de cristal, pero el agente Brown había echado las cortinas por dentro. Los gritos cesaron, y me alejé de la ventana en busca de un teléfono. Al fin encontré el cable: conducía hasta el interior del armario cerrado. Hijo de puta, pensé. Lamenté no tener un teléfono móvil, pero entonces pensé que aunque lo tuviera lo habría dejado en casa para ir al baile. En aquella habitación de pequeñas dimensiones, con Justin separado de mí y encerrado en otra estancia, sentí que todo aquello era una tremenda derrota para mi imaginación, y me dejé caer en una silla. Hundí la cabeza entre las manos, a punto de echarme a llorar, pero la idea de que el agente Brown podía regresar en cualquier momento me disuadió de hacer tal cosa. Por primera vez en la vida era incapaz de imaginar una solución, una vía de escape: todas las pequeñas historias que lograba construir conducían directamente a la habitación en la que me encontraba, y al cuerpo apaleado de Justin, en la habitación contigua. No sé si esto es indicio de mi error o de mi desesperación, pero lo único que podía haber evitado lo ocurrido esa noche –no haberme instalado nunca en Galatia– en ningún momento se me pasó por la cabeza.

Pasó el tiempo. Minutos, horas, no sabría decirlo exactamente. Al final, desesperado, saqué el diario que llevaba en el bolsillo. Tenía la intención de escribir algo ese día –parecía importante registrar los acontecimientos–, pero al abrirlo encontré las siguientes palabras:

La mayoría de la gente tiene siete agujeros en la cabeza.

Era una frase que le había oído decir a Divine noches antes, cenando en casa de Wade. Había dicho: «La mayoría de la gente tiene siete agujeros en la cabeza, pero Eddie Comedy tenía ocho». Y luego añadió: «Quiero decir, nueve». Y entonces le dio un ataque de risa. Divine estaba muy borracho esa noche, y yo también, pero recuerdo la frase porque me pareció un buen comienzo de capítulo, y al volver a casa la anoté en mi diario. Entonces, al leerla de nuevo, me puse a escribir sin darme cuenta:

Yo solo tengo seis.

En realidad tenía siete agujeros en la cabeza, como todo el mundo; tenía dos ojos, dos orejas, dos orificios nasales y una boca. Lo que quiero decir es que, cuando escribí «Yo solo tengo seis», no me refería a mí. No conocía a nadie que tuviera solo seis agujeros en la cabeza; ni siquiera estaba seguro de que alguien pudiera vivir en tal estado de deficiencia genética, pero de todos modos lo escribí. «Yo solo tengo seis.» Y luego añadí:

Podría presentarme de otra manera.

Para entonces el «yo» no se refería a mí ni siquiera remotamente. «Yo» no era Colin Nieman, y «yo» no estaba atrapado en una comisaría a las dos de la mañana en el centro de Kansas, con el cuerpo ensangrentado de mi amante encerrado en una sala de interrogatorios, a solo tres metros de distancia. «Yo» estaba en otra parte. No sabía bien dónde estaba «yo», pero no tenía más que decidirlo. Y entonces arranqué a escribir:

La mayoría de la gente tiene siete agujeros en la cabeza. Yo solo tengo seis. Podría presentarme de otra manera. Podría decir mi edad, mi estatura, mi peso o el color de los ojos. Podría describir dónde nací o cómo me gano la vida, o podría decir mi nombre, pero dado que ninguna de estas características es inmutable o especialmente relevante, al menos no para la historia que me propongo contar, tal vez debería limitarme a escribir que en lugar de los habituales siete agujeros de la cabeza humana, yo solo tengo seis, y aunque esto no es especialmente relevante para la presente historia, como ya he dicho, les contaré cómo llegó a ocurrir tal cosa. Resumiendo: la adicción a la coca me destruyó el tabique nasal, de tal modo que, a todos los efectos, solo tengo un orificio en la nariz...

Un ruido metálico me sacó de mi ensoñación. El agente Brown salía de la sala de interrogatorios. Se aseguró de dejar la puerta bien cerrada y dio un tirón del pomo para demostrar —supongo que tanto a mí como a él— que la puerta estaba cerrada. Tapé la pluma en cuanto lo oí y cerré el cuaderno. La tinta aún estaba húmeda y probablemente se emborronaría, pero me pareció preferible que el cuaderno estuviera cerrado. Aunque no tardaría en comprobar que lo mismo daba si lo hubiera dejado abierto.

El agente Brown había cerrado la puerta y observaba el cuaderno que descansaba sobre mi regazo.

—Qué bonito cuaderno, señor Nieman.

Me encogí de hombros.

—Y bonita pluma también. —Me dirigió una breve sonrisa; no entendí por qué—. Nunca había visto un cuaderno así, señor Nieman. ¿Qué hace con un cuaderno así?

—Es un libro de notas. Lo uso para tomar notas —dije, e intenté guardármelo en el bolsillo, pero el agente Brown levantó una mano.

—No, no, no, señor Nieman; no lo guarde todavía. ¡Un cuaderno tan bonito! Me gustaría verlo un poco mejor.

Echó a andar hacia mí. Tenía, como siempre, una mano en la pistola, y llevaba la otra extendida.

—Quizá incluso me deje tocarlo. ¿Es piel auténtica, verdad?

Asentí.

—Seguro que es una piel suavísima. ¿Me permite?

—Supongo que no tengo elección.

—Todo el mundo tiene elección, señor Nieman. Su amiguito prefiere no decir nada mientras usted no esté presente. En este momento estoy intentando decidir si le permito entrar con él o si dejo que Justin siga sopesando sus opciones un rato más, por ejemplo, hasta que salga el sol y todo el mundo pueda tomarse una taza de café y no necesite preocuparse de volver a dormir. Y ahora usted está intentando decidir si me deja ver ese cuaderno tan bonito que tiene en la mano o si prefiere echar una cabezadita en el piso de abajo.

Le entregué el cuaderno.

El agente Brown lo cogió sin hacer comentarios. No perdió el tiempo examinando la calidad del cuero: pasó directamente a la última entrada. Entrecerró los ojos al leer y se palpó los bolsillos, por lo que supuse que buscaba unas gafas, pero no las encontró y siguió leyendo. Tardó varios minutos en leer lo que había escrito –le concedí el beneficio de la duda y supuse que la tinta se habría corrido–; de vez en cuando apartaba la vista del cuaderno y me miraba. Finalmente, cerró el diario de un manotazo.

–Bueno.

–¿Sí?

–Bueno –repitió el agente Brown–. Lo que ha escrito es muy interesante. Dada la hora y las circunstancias.

Me encogí de hombros. Era lo primero que decía en toda la noche a lo que yo no tenía nada que objetar, y no veía razón para discutírselo.

El agente Brown volvió a mirarme y comprendí con sobresalto que estaba mirándome la nariz; cuando me la froté automáticamente, levantó las cejas y asintió con la cabeza. Sin molestarse en preguntar, metió el cuaderno en el armario de metal, lo cerró y se volvió hacia mí.

–Bueno, nunca... –dijo, y tuvo que abrir de nuevo el armario para llamar por teléfono a Nettie Ferguson.

Cuarenta y cinco minutos más tarde Nettie Ferguson entraba en la comisaría, gorda, vieja y artrítica. Llevaba unas gafas con la montura en forma de ojos de gato colgadas del cuello por una cadena, y una bolsa lo suficientemente grande para meter en ella a un niño bien alimentado, y al verla me sentí aliviado, porque el agente Brown llevaba más de media hora tarareando «Leroy Brown» y empezaba a sentirme capaz de cometer un asesinato después de todo.

Al verme se presentó:

–Nettie Ferguson; encantada de conocerlo –dijo. Tiró la bolsa sobre una mesa y se puso a rebuscar en su interior–. Normalmente deja que la gente descanse por la noche, él, yo, y todo el mundo, y se ocupa de los asuntos por la mañana. Me refiero a ti, Eustace, cuando digo que nadie ha podido contestar nunca a ninguna pregunta con el estómago vacío y sin haber pegado ojo. –Se dio la vuelta; sostenía una vieja grabadora incongruente marcada con el eslogan «Peligro-Prohibido el paso por orden del Departamento de Policía de Galatea»–. Bueno, vamos a acabar con esto cuanto antes. Cuanto antes empiece a hablar antes terminará y todos podremos volver a la cama. Pero, bueno, Eustace, ¿qué te pasa? Creo que no te había visto tan angustiado desde que te quitaron la medalla de plata en el instituto de Kenosha.

El agente Brown había escuchado en silencio el discurso de Nettie Ferguson; luego carraspeó nerviosamente y dijo:

–Nettie, más vale que te prepares. Este no es un caso típico de conducción en estado de embriaguez o de alboroto en el bar de Sloppy Joe.

Nettie Ferguson se volvió hacia mí y me hizo un guiño:
—He visto de todo en la vida, señor...
—Nieman —dije.
—¡Ah! —exclamó, fingiéndose sorprendida—. Es usted el señor Nieman. Tenía ganas de conocerlo desde que oí decir que había comprado la casa de caliza. No lo dejaré marchar sin que me haya respondido antes a unas cuantas preguntas.
—Nettie —dijo el agente Brown—. Se está haciendo muy tarde.
—Yo diría que muy temprano. Pero da lo mismo.
El agente Brown vaciló, giró sobre sus talones, produciendo un sonido chirriante, y nos condujo a la sala de interrogatorios. Introdujo la llave en la cerradura y el pomo giró sin hacer el menor ruido.
—Bueno —dijo—, señor Time, ya estamos todos aquí.
En presencia del cuerpo magullado y ensangrentado de Justin, hasta el agente Brown parecía sentirse cohibido. Tuve que hacer un gran esfuerzo para no acercarme a Justin: sabía que el agente Brown lo haría sufrir aún más si me acercaba. Justin no dio muestras de haber oído al agente Brown. Tenía la vista clavada al frente, miraba fijamente las robustas piernas que asomaban bajo el vestido de flores de Nettie Ferguson. Al ver a Justin, Nettie se quedó sin aliento y, tras una larga pausa, se agachó con mucho cuidado, sentándose pesadamente en una silla y sin dejar de mirar al cuerpo de Justin.
—Nettie —dijo el agente Brown—. Puedes empezar cuando quieras.
Nettie se puso las gafas con un dedo tembloroso —aunque creo que le temblaba igual cuando no estaba nerviosa— y, tras sopesar la situación, puso en marcha la grabadora con un dedo gordo e hinchado.
El agente Brown dijo:
—Cuando quiera, señor... Time. Empiece por el principio y cuéntelo todo tal como ocurrió.
Justin levantó la vista. Fue un gesto idéntico al que había hecho cinco años antes, cuando nos conocimos, y me pareció que recordaba ese momento, igual que yo. Miró al agente Brown como me había mirado a mí, inexpresivamente, inconscientemente, y luego volvió sus ojos ausentes hacia Nettie. Sonrió y Nettie se estiró en la silla; si hubiera sido católica estoy seguro de que habría hecho la señal de la cruz, pero como era baptista tuvo que contentarse con lanzar varios suspiros.
La grabadora aulló como un perro alrededor de un corral, y Justin comenzó su declaración. Sus ojos no habían cambiado, pero sonrió y las palabras salieron de su boca como canicas de un tarro volcado.
—Escuchen con atención, porque solo voy a contarlo una vez y no pienso repetirlo. Tenía las manos más grandes que he visto en mi vida,

y el cuerpo más grande que he visto en mi vida, y llevaba puesta tu ropa, Colin. No hizo el menor ruido. Se movía al abrigo de nuestros ruidos hasta que nos silenció por completo. Nuestras pisadas eran sus pisadas, nuestros gritos sus gritos, pero nuestros gritos eran mudos. Salió de detrás de nosotros, pero fue como si saliera de dentro de nosotros. Como si nosotros lo hubiésemos creado.

Al oír las palabras de Justin, tan evidentemente elaboradas, pese a la angustia que había en su tono y lo desesperado de su aspecto, me puse en pie.

—¡Maldita sea, Justin! —grité—. ¡No hagas esto! —Pero el agente Brown me volvió a sentar de un empujón, y Justin continuó hablando como si yo no existiera.

—Pegó a Lucy. Me pegó a mí. Me dio patadas. Le dio patadas. Me levantó por los aires. Me subió hasta el cielo. Me lanzó desde arriba. Se deshizo de mí. Siguió con Lucy. Se puso encima de ella. La cubrió y se cubrió a sí mismo. Nos cubrió a todos. Guantes negros, botas negras, pantalones negros, y una capucha gris en la cabeza, pero su polla, su polla era blanca.

Nettie Ferguson emitió un sonido ahogado, pero Justin no dejó de hablar.

—Terminó con Lucy. La dejó acabada, arruinada, rota, la levantó por los aires y la exhibió, y se exhibió ante mí y me obligó a exhibirme ante mí mismo, nos exhibió a todos y luego se me echó encima, él y Lucy, porque la llevaba en brazos, y yo estaba tirado en el suelo y entonces perdí el conocimiento y cuando abrí los ojos se había marchado, y Lucy se había marchado y yo me había marchado, todos nos habíamos marchado para siempre.

Se volvió hacia mí. Me miró fijamente a los ojos y los abrió con expresión de sorpresa, creo, o de terror, o de recuerdo del amor.

El agente Brown nos miraba a los dos.

—¿Qué intentas decir, Justin? ¿Intentas decir que el señor Nieman...? ¿Qué, Justin, qué?

Justin no apartó sus ojos de los míos, pero aquella expresión, fuera lo que fuera, acabó por desvanecerse, y no detecté en ella nada comprensible. En su último acto de comunicación, sacudió la cabeza de un lado a otro.

—Ese hombre olía a cenizas —dijo; y eso fue lo último que le oí decir.

3.05

DIVINE

Voy a contaros algo. La primera vez que ese tío me dio por culo lo entendí todo. No hizo un solo movimiento en falso; me tumbó en el suelo de baldosas de su despacho como si fuera un colchón de plumas en el que echarse una siestecita, pero lo más raro de todo es que, cuando me la metió, me di cuenta de que era diferente. Era... ¿cómo era? Era como si estuviera tirando de un guante, o algo así. Todo mi cuerpo, desde la punta de la cabeza hasta los dedos de los pies, se sentía tan cerca de él como mi culo, con perdón, y era como si todo él estuviera dentro de mí y yo fuera la piel que él estiraba para ponerse sobre la suya... como si yo siguiera siendo el colchón y él fuera las plumas, o algo así, como si los dos juntos estuviéramos haciendo algo completamente nuevo. Cuando todo hubo terminado, me dijo: Espero que nunca te arrepientas de esto, y la verdad es que me flipó bastante. Supongo que tendría que haberme largado en ese momento. Maldita la hora en que me quedé.

3.06

CORA

Al despertarme esa mañana noté por primera vez que había llegado el invierno. Lo cierto es que faltaba cosa de un mes para las Navidades, pero el otoño había sido suave ese año. En octubre hizo calor, y los niños andaban por ahí en pantalón corto y sin zapatos, y Maven Getterling seguía vendiéndome naranjada, bellotas, espaguetis y castañas bien entrado noviembre. Pero esa mañana, cuando me desperté y desde el piso de abajo me llegó el olor del café de Rosa, lo primero que pensé es que ya no bastaba con una sola manta. Había escarcha en la ventana, y las ramas heladas de los árboles crujían al chocar contra la pared norte del dormitorio, indicando que la savia ya se había helado bajo la corteza, y por primera vez tuve el deseo típicamente invernal de no querer salir de la cama. Nunca he sido de mucho dormir —el reloj de arena de la vida no se detiene mientras estás ahí tumbada, sorda, muda, ciega a todo—, de manera que cuando Cora Johnson se da la vuelta para acurrucarse cuando suena el despertador es porque fuera hace muchísimo frío.

Al cabo de un rato abrí los ojos y la cálida cadera de Rosa me

rozó un brazo. Aún era de noche, pero la oscuridad empezaba a teñirse de gris, como el pelo de Rosa.
—Café —dijo.
—Café —dije, tomando la taza que me ofrecía. Era un café fuerte, pero casi tan pálido como ella, pues estaba mezclado con leche condensada—. Hummm, gracias señora —dije. Y después de dar varios sorbos noté que me miraba de un modo extraño—. Parece como si te hubieras tropezado con el perro de los vecinos. ¿Qué te pasa, cariño?
—Ha venido Grady Oconnor. Dice que se encontró con Nettie Ferguson, que volvía de la comisaría.
—¿Cómo? —Miré el reloj—. ¿A las cinco de la mañana?
—Esa chica blanca de la que me hablaste una vez —continuó Rosa—, esa que...
—Lucy. Lucy Robinson.
Rosa asintió:
—Ha desaparecido. Creen que los hombres de la casa de caliza, creen que la han... —Suspiró profundamente—. Al más mayor lo tienen en arresto domiciliario, según dijo Nettie, que no es exactamente lo mismo que detenido. Dijo que no le está permitido salir del pueblo hasta que todo se... aclare. El joven está en el hospital de Bigger Hill.
El viento se calmó en ese preciso instante; las ramas dejaron de arañar la pared. En el silencio, oí a Sawyer roncando en la habitación de al lado. Sawyer tiene asma y vegetaciones, por eso ronca de un modo muy peculiar, pero a mí me tranquiliza ese sonido, porque eso significa que respira.
Al principio no quise aceptarlo.
—¿Desaparecido? ¿Quién lo dice? Se habrá marchado con sus amigas, o a lo mejor ella y Howard al final...
—No lo creo —dijo Rosa—. Ese hombre, quienquiera que fuera... —Sacudió la cabeza como si le pesara—. Grady dice que, bueno, que están rastreando la carretera en busca de pruebas.
Sawyer roncó, las ramas volvieron a crujir contra la ventana. Abajo, en el café, sonó un timbre: panecillos, maíz y salvado. Un día de invierno normal.
—¿Pruebas?
—Pruebas forenses. —Pareció como si necesitara distanciarse de sí misma para pronunciar esas palabras—. Sangre. Semen. Tejido.
—¿Tejido? —Al principio pensé que se refería a un trozo de tela, pero hablaba de algo muy distinto.
—Fragmentos de piel —dijo Rosa—. Están buscando muestras de Lucy Robinson en la carretera.

3.07

COLIN

Además de mi abrigo, la carretera en la que encontraron a Justin y desapareció Lucy albergaba otros tesoros: huellas de botas desperdigadas, grandes y lo suficientemente profundas como para quedar grabadas en la tierra helada, muestras de fibra mezcladas con filamentos de las medias de Lucy, jirones de su vestido púrpura, gruesas hebras negras de mi abrigo, y también muestras de pelo, de un pelo negro y encrespado que se correspondía claramente con el de Lucy, y de otro pelo, castaño y más corto, que era el de Justin. Al agente Brown le pareció significativo no encontrar indicios de un tercer tipo de pelo, y dijo: «Señor Nieman, me parece que usted no tiene pelo». Había también cenizas, tantas que parecían haber sido esparcidas deliberadamente, y encontraron los zapatos de Lucy, sin desabrochar. Había sangre, brillantes y endurecidas gotas marrones desperdigadas por la carretera, como filtradas a través de un trozo de encaje roto, y había otras gotas de líquido congelado, pero no eran marrones. No eran sangre. El semen se separa al congelarse; la parte más densa del esperma se adhiere a la tierra formando una fina capa blanca, y el fluido prostático se queda en la superficie, formando una película lechosa. El agente Brown se sirvió de una navaja para recoger las tres muestras de semen y guardarlas en sendas bolsas de plástico, y cuando le pregunté por qué separaba las muestras, el agente Brown me miró como si lo hubiera insultado y dijo bruscamente: «Por si acaso». Tardé un rato en adivinar qué quería decir con eso, pero luego comprendí que era por si había habido más de un agresor. Guardaba las muestras de semen en bolsas separadas «por si acaso» Justin y yo lo habíamos planeado todo juntos.

3.08

DIVINE

Que conste: declaro mi inocencia en este asunto. No planeé nada; sencillamente ocurrió. Pasé por allí con la intención de ver si podía ayudar en algo, a cualquiera de los dos. Vale, vale, yo tampoco me trago todo ese rollo, pero la verdad es que no tengo ninguna razón para haber pasado por allí. Quiero decir que no fui para que me jodieran, ni nada por el estilo. Pero Colin abrió la puerta, y nada más verlo supe que estaba tan furioso, tan loco, tan herido, que no pude contenerme; me quedé sin aliento, y entonces Colin me agarró, me metió en la casa y me empujó hasta su despacho. La verdad es que al principio me asusté; quiero decir que nadie sabe usar el teléfono como Nettie Ferguson, y a mediodía todo el pueblo sabía lo del abrigo de Colin, y además estaba lo del arca de Noah; seguía sin saber qué había pasado exactamente, pero dos semanas después aún tenía un chichón en la cabeza del tamaño de una pelota de golf, que gracias a Dios quedaba oculto por el pelo. El caso es que llevaba tiempo con ganas de ponerle las manos encima a ese hombre y, bueno, cuando él me puso las manos encima, sentí como si estuviera diciéndome que no aceptaba una negativa.

¡Como si yo pudiera negarme!

Bueno, vale, lo admito. En parte quería que pasara precisamente allí, precisamente entonces, quiero decir inmediatamente después. No estoy orgulloso de lo que pasó, pero pasó. En cierto modo me imaginé que yo era Lucy Robinson y que al apoyar la cabeza en aquel suelo de baldosas —baldosas caras, no pude evitar pensarlo, pues había oído decir que la vieja Bea las había traído de no sé qué castillo de Europa—, me imaginé que el suelo era una carretera helada, y no me fue difícil cerrar los ojos para evocar la cabeza de Colin oculta bajo una capucha. Alma Kiehler, que fue quien me contó la historia, no dio muchos detalles sobre la capucha. A Alma se lo había contado Cora Johnson, y a Cora se lo había contado Rosa Stone, a quien se lo había contado Grady Oconnor, quien, junto con DuWayne Hicks, fue el primero en enterarse por Nettie Ferguson. De manera que os podéis imaginar que la cosa se había distorsionado bastante al pasar de boca en boca. Alma llegó a decir que fuera quien fuese aquel hombre, llevaba una capucha del Ku Klux Klan, y cuando le pregunté por qué razón iba alguien a ponerse una capucha del Klan para violar a una chica «blanca», no supo qué responder; se encogió de hombros y dijo que creía que eso era lo que había dicho Cora, pero que tal vez... Y yo le dije a Alma que esperaba que encontrasen la capucha y vieran que era blanca y pequeña, muy ajustada, con dos agujeritos para los ojos, no muy grande y puntiaguda como las del Klan.

No mencioné lo de las letras porque no sabía qué significaban, ni siquiera estaba seguro de que fueran letras.

Alma me preguntó cómo lo sabía, y yo le dije que lo sabía, sin más. De todos modos.

Prefiero hacerlo boca abajo, ya me entendéis. Pero Colin me tumbó boca arriba, con las piernas en el aire, y estaba claro que no lo hacía para que estuviese más cómodo, ni para facilitar el encaje, ni nada de eso. Quería que lo mirara. Quería que viese cómo me follaba, y así lo hice; él no dejó de mirarme, y juro por Dios que no parpadeó ni una sola vez. Las luces del despacho estaban apagadas, y aunque fue en pleno día, la casa proyectaba sus propias sombras, y en la penumbra daba un poco de miedo, como si todo fuera al mismo tiempo lo que era y otra cosa distinta, y una parte de mí se imaginó que estábamos en aquella carretera helada, mientras otra parte de mí se imaginaba que estábamos en el piso de arriba, ya sabéis, en la cama de Colin, con sábanas de seda, almohadones mullidos, gruesas mantas y todo ese rollo. Y luego, como ya he dicho antes, Colin dijo: Espero que nunca te arrepientas de esto, y entonces me asusté, temblé de miedo, y si no fuera porque estábamos en noviembre me habría largado en pelotas y habría corrido por todo el pueblo como las recién casadas que antiguamente colgaban la sábana manchada de sangre en la ventana después de la noche de bodas. Pero no me moví del sitio, como si estuviera hipnotizado, o algo así, y un momento después Colin dijo: Me voy al hospital a ver a Justin; se me había olvidado por completo. Colin no me preguntó si me quedaba o me marchaba; no me preguntó si necesitaba algo. Se quedó de pie, se dio la vuelta y se marchó, y yo me quedé allí tumbado, mirándole el culo hasta que salió de la habitación. Lo oí subir al piso de arriba, lo oí bajar, lo oí abrir y cerrar la puerta principal. El coche levantó al arrancar un montón de piedras que salpicaron contra la pared blanca, y se acabó todo. Silencio. El sol de invierno al final de la tarde. Una ráfaga de aire frío en mi piel, una especie de tirón en el vientre, donde el semen, mi semen, se secaba. El de Colin lo llevaba dentro de mí.

Fue el zumbido lo que me hizo levantarme. Fue uno de esos ruidos sordos que parecen amplificarse en los oídos hasta que no puedes pensar en otra cosa, como el tictac de un reloj o el goteo de un grifo a medianoche. Me levanté, miré alrededor y, tengo que decirlo: ¡qué habitación! Era tan grande como toda la casa de mis padres, y solo había en ella un enorme escritorio, supongo que de caoba, con la superficie de mármol negro y blanco, y un sillón de cuero al otro lado; al verlo pensé: ¿Por qué no me has follado ahí, gilipollas, en lugar de arañar mi delicado cuerpo con el suelo de baldosas frío? Noté entonces que tenía el cuerpo cubierto de motas doradas y al mirar el suelo vi que todo estaba cubierto de trocitos de oro, como si fueran confeti, y al principio pensé: ¿Qué clase de imbécil rocía el suelo de polvo dorado?, pero luego se me ocurrió mirar al techo y vi que estaba revestido de vigas de madera oscuras, y que las motas doradas caían de allí; supongo que la vieja Bea las había cubierto de pan de oro, pero ahora la mitad de la capa dorada estaba en el suelo, y al parecer Colin no se molestaba en barrer. Como digo, ¡qué habitación!

Volví a oír el zumbido y entonces descubrí de dónde venía: una máquina de escribir eléctrica sobre el escritorio de Colin. Supongo que eso no tiene nada de raro, pero junto a la máquina de escribir había una vieja máquina manual, y en las dos había un papel, y junto a la máquina manual había un cuaderno, y el cuaderno estaba abierto, y había una pluma encima del cuaderno. ¿Qué haríais en mi lugar?

Esto es lo que había en la máquina de escribir eléctrica:

Más tarde tuve que llevar un pequeño candado colgado de la nariz. No sé si la coca habría bastado para destruirme el tabique por sí sola, pero lo cierto es que alguien me ayudó. Era un hombre alto y calvo; dijo que me daba mil pavos si le dejaba el candado, y antes de que pudiera sacar la billetera yo ya estaba buscando la llave. Dijo que nada de llaves. Sujetó el candado con la mano y dejó que lo que quedaba del tabique aguantara el tirón.

Al leerlo pensé: ¡Madre mía! No había leído los dos libros anteriores de Colin, porque Webbie había dicho que eran bastante aburridos, pero aquello me gustaba. Luego eché un vistazo al papel que había en la máquina manual, y esto es lo que decía:

Sucedió en un callejón. Me había metido allí para mear, y aún no había terminado cuando alguien me agarró por detrás. Me aplastó contra la pared que acababa de mojar y luego tiró de mí con la misma fuerza, y cuando me volví para ver a mi agresor, me puso una capucha en la cabeza, y, al sentir la tela sobre la piel, me entró un ataque de pánico, cometí el tremendo error de levantarme y me golpeé la coronilla contra el techo de piedra del callejón.

Luego leí lo que había escrito en el cuaderno:

Justin – hospital, llevar Bactrim
Gasolina
Agente Brown
Wade
Ira y Wyn – ¿a cuánto está el gramo de coca?
¿Instalarse? ¿Aquí? ¿En Mississippi? ¿En Marruecos?
¿Motivo?
Arma
Harrod's – más papel
IGA – bombillas, lejía
¿Cena en «Big M»? ¿Roast Beef?

Había una pequeña marca junto al nombre del agente Brown y otra junto al de Ira, y otra junto a lo de la coca, y otra junto a la palabra «arma», y me pregunté qué sería aquello, si sería una lista de la compra o una lista de cosas pendientes o de notas para lo que Colin estaba escribiendo o una mezcla de las tres cosas... y si era una mezcla, ¿dónde terminaba lo real y dónde empezaba lo inventado? Y aún seguía intentando descifrarlo cuando vi junto al cuaderno una bolsita de la que asomaba algo que parecía papel de escribir; pero no era una bolsa normal, era –lo reconocí con toda seguridad, como uno reconoce los pasos de su madre cuando sale de la habitación– una bolsa idéntica a la que cubría la cabeza de quien estuvo en el arca de Noah, la misma bolsa que cubría la cabeza de quien se había llevado a Lucy Robinson en esa carretera desierta, donde seguramente hacía mucho más frío que en el suelo del despacho de Colin. Quiero decir que era una bolsa blanca con una pequeña cinta en la parte inferior; y arriba había también unas puntadas, gruesas y oscuras hebras de seda que indicaban BORDE SUPERIOR, con unas letras tan raras que si resultaban difíciles de leer en la brillante luz de la tarde, ni te cuento en mitad de un campo a medianoche.

Al lado de la bolsa había un par de tijeras, y eso fue lo último que vi, porque al verlas me largué de allí, me esfumé, adiós, pensé, lárgate ahora mismo; más vale que no descubras nada más.

3.09

CORA

El sol se puso la noche siguiente a la desaparición de Lucy Robinson. El sol se pone todas las noches, pero ya sabéis lo que quiero decir. Esa noche la oscuridad pareció en cierto modo una bendición y en cierto modo una maldición. Nunca hay demasiada animación en las calles de Galatia, pero esa noche estaban desiertas. El pueblo parecía más muerto que una ciudad fantasma. Estaba definitivamente muerto.

Rosa volvió a cerrar las persianas. Las cerró despacio, muy despacio, una a una, y luego se dirigió a la puerta. Se quedó un buen rato mirando por el cristal y después, de mala gana, puso el cartel de cerrado. Echó el cerrojo con un leve y pequeño movimiento que siempre terminaba produciendo un chasquido. Siempre cerraba despacio, lanzando largas miradas al exterior, como si esperara la llegada de otro cliente. Eso pensaba yo, hasta que un día le pregunté, y me dijo que detestaba el ruido que hacían las puertas al cerrarse. Dijo que nunca sabía a qué lado de la puerta debía colocarse. Pero esa noche, esa noche parecía claro que el mejor sitio en el que se podía estar era dentro. Era extraño, era directamente espeluznante que yo tuviera que agradecerle a Lucy Robinson el hecho de poder pasar otra noche con Rosa.

Sawyer estaba sentado a la mesa, jadeando por el esfuerzo de empujar los coches de juguete sobre su superficie. Al acercarse a mí, Rosa extendió una mano para acariciar la cabeza de Sawyer, y, al retirarla, uno de los coches le corrió por el brazo. Sawyer lanzó un escupitajo al imitar el sonido del motor, y yo le ofrecí a Rosa una taza de café. Así eran nuestros días: ella me preparaba el primer café de la mañana y yo le preparaba el último café de la noche.

—¿Qué pasa? —me preguntó, como yo le había preguntado esa mañana—. Parece que algo te está rondando en la cabeza.

—Nada —negué con un gesto.

Rosa me tomó una mano, la sostuvo un momento y la dejó sobre la barra.

—Cuéntamelo.

—He estado pensando.

—¿Qué has estado pensando?

—He estado pensando que la gente no podrá seguir diciendo mucho más tiempo que él tuvo algo que ver con lo ocurrido. Quiero decir que no hay pruebas. No hay ninguna prueba. Un abrigo no es una prueba.

—Brrruummm, brruummm —dijo Sawyer. Lo miré y vi que había habido un accidente en la mesa—. Uuuu, uuuu, uuuu —dijo Sawyer, enviando una ambulancia al rescate.

—Pero está… lo otro —dijo Rosa, sonrojándose ligeramente.

La ambulancia se abrió camino entre los coches siniestrados. Los coches rodaron.

—Putt, putt —dijo Sawyer; y otra vez «Brrruuummm», cuando volvieron a ponerse en marcha, reparados, sin arañazos ni abollones.

—Sí —dije—. Es verdad. Pero no me parece importante.

—¿Qué quieres decir?

—He oído que estuvo con Myra Robinson hasta medianoche, y según todo el mundo el ataque ocurrió más o menos a esa hora. En ese caso solo pueden pasar dos cosas. O estaba con Myra o Myra está mintiendo para proteger al hombre acusado de hacerle eso a su hija. Y ya sabes lo que te conté. La última vez… la última vez que pasó yo aún no tenía a Sawyer y podría haberme creído lo que decía la gente, que quizá Myra y Stan, también Stan, que quizá los dos estaban inventándoselo para proteger a su hija. Pero ahora sé que no puedes hacer una cosa así cuando se trata de carne de tu carne y sangre de tu sangre… ¿Por qué me miras así?

Rosa tenía una expresión mitad alegre, mitad triste, y no sabía cuál de las dos mitades era la verdadera.

—Cora, cariño, ya sé que piensas que todo el mundo quiere a sus hijos tanto como tú quieres a Sawyer. Pero...

—Pero...

Rosa no concluyó su argumento, ni yo tampoco. Supongo que sabía muy bien lo que quería decir.

Al cabo de un rato Rosa volvió a tomarme la mano. Removió su café, pero no se lo bebió.

—¿Qué crees que pasará si tienes razón? Quiero decir, ¿qué pasará con Colin Nieman?

—¿Se llama así, Nieman?

—Nieman. Significa «nadie» en alemán.

No le pregunté a Rosa cómo lo sabía.

—Vamos, Rosa, lo sabes tan bien como yo. Los blancos nunca culpan a los suyos, ni siquiera cuando... cuando son gays. No tardarán en investigar al otro lado del pueblo.

Supongo que puede parecer gracioso que yo le dijera una cosa así a Rosa. Porque ella era blanca. Y no es que yo me olvidara de que era blanca, hablara como hablase. Pero lo único que dijo fue: Ya lo sé, ya lo sé, como si las costumbres de los blancos le resultaran tan extrañas como a mí.

—Ya no se le puede echar la culpa a Eric Johnson —dije—. Ya no hay un pobre chico al que nadie está dispuesto a defender. Y tengo miedo. Esta vez se pondrán todos en contra de nosotros. Esta vez será como, como, como...

—Como una guerra.

Un «infierno», era lo que yo estaba pensando, pero «guerra» encajaba mucho mejor.

—Pumm, pumm —decía Sawyer, haciendo chocar los coches que tenía en la mano—. Uuuu, uuuu, uuuu —hacía la ambulancia, lanzándose veloz al rescate.

Rosa se sobresaltó al oír el ruido.

—Bueno, bueno, bueno. Ha sido un día agotador. Creo que voy a darlo por terminado.

—¿Por qué no te llevas a Sawyer arriba mientras yo termino de recoger?

—¿Cora?

Rosa volvió a tomarme la mano.

—No pasa nada, cariño. Estoy bien. Solo —suspiré—, solo necesito un poco de tiempo para asimilar las cosas.

Rosa asintió. Sonrió. Me soltó la mano, pero despacio.

—Vamos, Sawyer.

Y se marcharon.

Un restaurante es un lugar perfecto para pensar cuando está cerrado. Todas esas mesas y sillas vacías: necesitan gente. Cuando la gente no está, la imaginación la crea. Y yo podía elegir. Había más de una persona en la que deseaba pensar. Pero un muchacho se abría camino entre todas ellas ahora que estaba muerto, igual que cuando estaba vivo.

Ese muchacho era Eric Johnson, el sobrino de Sawyer. Era feo, olía mal y, al parecer, solo sabía hacer una cosa: comer. Nunca he visto a nadie capaz de comer tanto como aquel chico, salvo T. V. Daniels, claro, pero esa es otra historia, incluso podría ser una gran novela. Decían que Eric era un ladrón, y supongo que era verdad, pero por lo que sé nunca robó nada más que comida. Cierto que rondaba por aquí a todas horas, porque sabía que siempre había comida. El restaurante aún no estaba abierto —no lo abrí hasta que se marchó Sawyer, y Sawyer no se marchó hasta que se marchó Eric—, pero siempre me había gustado cocinar y muchas veces, cuando me daba la vuelta, me encontraba con aquel fantasma que salía corriendo de la cocina con un pastel o un montón de galletas. Una vez se llevó una fuente de pollo frito que debía ser la cena y la comida de Sawyer y mía, y me entraron ganas de retorcerle el pescuezo en cuanto volviera a ponerle la vista encima, pero no podía, porque era demasiado gordo para mis manos. Era un chico grandullón, aunque tranquilo: no tardó en aprender que era mucho mejor para él pasar desapercibido. De cuando en cuando oías contar algo raro que había hecho, como cuando DuWayne Getterling lo sorprendió en una tumba abierta —en la que horas más tarde enterrarían a la tía de DuWayne—, pero yo le pregunté a DuWayne si estaba comiendo algo, y, claro, resultó que se estaba comiendo una fuente de macarrones que se había llevado del velatorio. Bueno, dije yo, si tienes que esconderte en mitad de una llanura, un agujero en la tierra me parece un buen sitio.

A veces lo sorprendía antes de que pudiera escapar, y entonces se quedaba como paralizado, con las manos llenas de lo que fuera. Recuerdo que una vez fue una fuente de manzanas asadas que yo había preparado para hacer una tarta.

—El tío Sawyer me dijo que podía coger unas cuantas —dijo, sin parecer asustado, poniéndome a prueba. No dejaba de parpadear, pero era porque sus ojos rosas no soportaban la luz del sol. No me gusta describir su aspecto, porque no me parece justo. Él no tenía la culpa de ser tan feo.

Sawyer estaba entonces a quince kilómetros de allí, en pleno campo, y tanto Eric como yo sabíamos que no había dicho nada por el estilo. Pero me limité a decir:

—Esta cocina no es del tío Sawyer, ¿verdad?

—Él dijo que podía coger lo que quisiera.

—Nadie pude coger lo que quiera, chico. Pero si quieres unas manzanas lo que tienes que hacer es pedirlas. Aunque creo que estarán mucho más ricas cuando haga la tarta.

—No quiero tus manzanas —dijo, y después de tirar la fuente sobre la mesa se marchó corriendo.

Siempre que me daba la vuelta me lo encontraba robando algo. Pero debo decir una cosa en su favor: siempre devolvía la fuente. No sé si lo hacía por educación o porque sabía que de lo contrario no habría más comida. Pero siempre devolvía la fuente.

En todo caso, supongo que lo que intento decir es que era un chico extraño, pero, dadas las circunstancias, nunca me llamó la atención de un modo especial. La vida nunca había sido fácil para él en Galatia, pero cuando Rosemary Krebs y sus secuaces dejaron bien claro que no solo tenían la intención de quedarse donde se habían instalado, sino de ocupar el pueblo entero, fue como si todos los que vivían a ambos lados de la autopista 9 necesitaran un chivo expiatorio. Pobre Eric: era como un bolo a la espera de ser derribado. Y sé que el reverendo Abraham no querrá admitirlo, pero el hecho de que los hombres anduviesen por ahí con mujeres menores que ellos no es fácil de guardar en secreto, ni siquiera en un pueblo adormecido como Galatia... pero nunca se supo quién era el padre de Eric, porque Marsha, la hermana de Sawyer, la madre de Eric, siempre estaba demasiado ocupada bebiendo como para contárselo a nadie. De manera que Eric tuvo desde el principio dos cosas en contra, aunque no tenía un pelo de tonto: sabía lo que podía llevarse y lo que no. Si merodeaba tanto por aquí era porque sabía que Sawyer y yo éramos blandos, que estábamos demasiado absorbidos el uno con el otro como para preocuparnos porque faltase una lata de judías verdes o un pan de maíz.

Como veréis, intento tenerlo todo en cuenta, igual que entonces, pero también igual que entonces la respuesta sigue siendo la misma: no es que Eric Johnson no pudiera molestar a Lucy Robinson, pero creo que nunca haría una cosa así. Eric Johnson podía tener la piel blanca, mas para los blancos seguía siendo un negro, y todos los negros saben de qué lado sopla el viento cuando te cuelgan de un árbol para lincharte. Sopla adelante y atrás, adelante y atrás, y una vez que empieza a soplar, no cesa nunca.

3.10

COLIN

Antes de hacer nada más con Divine tengo que asegurarme de algo. Estuvo unos días sin dar señales de vida y al final se presentó sin avisar; llamó a la puerta y se quedó en silencio, con expresión avergonzada y la mirada puesta en mi abdomen.

—Quiero leerte una cosa.

Divine levantó la vista y, en un primer momento, me pareció detectar cierto temor en sus ojos, pero enseguida se desvaneció. Miró el libro que yo tenía en las manos, carraspeó y dijo:

—Lee.

—«Me llamo Colin Nieman y juro que esta es la verdad. Hace mucho tiempo...»

—Espera un momento —me interrumpió Divine—. ¿Lo estás leyendo o me lo estás contando?

Me limité a mirarlo, sin responder.

—Ya sé —dijo—, este es tu libro, ¿verdad?

—Es mi libro —asentí—. *La Bella*.

Divine no dijo nada y, al cabo de un momento, volví a fijar la vista en la página, aunque me la sabía de memoria.

—«Me llamo Colin Nieman, y juro que esta es la verdad. Hace mucho tiempo aún tenía pelo en la cabeza. Mi madre decía que era un rubio auténtico: tenía el pelo del color del oro blanco, y ella me animaba a llevarlo largo, más largo que todos los chicos, e incluso más largo que la mayoría de las chicas. Creo que le daba tanta importancia a mi pelo para distraerme del resto de mi persona, pues era el niño más feo que hayan visto en la vida: gordo, bizco, con los dientes saltones, los pies metidos hacia dentro y poseído por una torpeza solo comparable a la de ciertos invertebrados. La adolescencia no hizo sino agravar esta infeliz situación, y durante aquellos años mi pelo fue mi único consuelo. Era largo y no demasiado denso, y lo llevaba peinado con raya al medio y recogido en una coleta que colgaba en medio de la espalda. Otras veces lo llevaba suelto y el viento me lo enredaba. Se me venía a los ojos y, si me quedaba muy quieto y dejaba que mi visión se tornara borrosa, llegaba a convencerme de que, como Jesucristo, estaba rodeado por un halo de luz.

»Mis padres se separaron cuando yo tenía doce años; mi padre obtuvo legalmente mi custodia y lo primero que hizo fue enviarme a una academia militar. Fue allí donde hice una serie de descubrimientos sobre los que reflexionaba durante los largos paseos, y más tarde carreras, que daba todas las mañanas. Las primeras horas de la mañana eran el único momento del día en que podía practicar, pues no soporto que la gente vea mi voluminoso cuerpo moviéndose y contoneándose, jadeando y resoplando en su tortuoso avance. Una de las primeras cosas que descubrí fue que cuando me tocaba el pene, este se ponía duro, y que cuando me lo tocaba durante un rato obtenía un placer que no creo necesario describir. Más tarde, descubrí que si pegaba a los demás chicos me dejaban en paz, y que si les pegaba más de una vez me hacían favores. Finalmente, descubrí que si los obligaba a tocarme el pene —y a chupármelo y a metérselo en el culo–, primero, el placer era mayor que cuando me lo tocaba yo solo y, segundo, los chicos se mostraban aún más dispuestos a hacerme favores que cuando les pegaba. Por aquel entonces me pareció que tal estado de cosas resultaba agradable, aunque no necesariamente útil, pues lo cierto es que no necesitaba que los demás hicieran nada especial por mí. Lo único que les pedía era que siguieran haciendo lo que hacían: masturbarme, chupármela y metérsela por el culo.

»Todos estos descubrimientos tuvieron lugar en la misma época en que mis brazos, mis piernas, mi pecho y mi entrepierna empezaron a cubrirse de pelo oscuro, y el pelo rubio de mi cabeza empezó a desaparecer. Cuando llegó el momento de elegir entre ir a la universidad o a la guerra, estaba completamente calvo y tenía un harén de muchachos dispuestos a hacer todo lo que les pidiera. Durante la última semana que pasé en la academia militar cada uno de estos chicos se me acercó por separado para preguntarme adónde pensaba ir, con la intención de seguirme; y a todos les di la misma respuesta: ¿Por qué quieres venir conmigo? Porque eres guapo, dijeron ellos, cada uno a su manera y con sus palabras; pero yo no los creí. Había perdido el único rasgo que me adornaba —mi pelo–, o, al menos, el único que yo estimaba; y los mandé a todos a hacer puñetas. No fui a la universidad, ni tampoco a la guerra, sino que, con el dinero de mi padre, me marché a Londres.

»Pero nunca olvidé lo que los chicos me habían dicho —lo que todos me habían dicho–, y comprendí algo importante. ¿Han pensado alguna vez en lo que le ocurrió al patito feo el día que descubrió que era un hermoso cisne? Esto fue lo que le ocurrió: quedó condenado a pasar el resto de su vida nadando en un estanque maloliente, repleto de trozos de pan lanzados por grupos de niños sucios cuyo único deseo parecía ser el de retorcerle el pescuezo al pobre animal. Pero el peculiar modo de descubrir mi belleza me permitió, además, adentrarme en el verdadero secreto de la hermosura. Para la mayoría de la gente la belleza es una fuente de debilidad, una situación de esclavitud en el interior de la propia piel hacia una adulación ciertamente odiosa. Pero la belleza puede ser una fuente de poder: confiere poder a quienes odian precisamente ese aspecto de sí mismos que a los demás les resulta hermoso. Cuando, años más tarde, entré en el mundo gay, aprendí a considerar esta relación en otros términos: los que viven prisioneros de su belleza se ponen debajo, los que la utilizan para cazar a los demás se ponen encima, y los que no poseen belleza alguna, para bien o para mal, no se ponen en ninguna parte.»

Divine se sobresaltó cuando cerré el libro bruscamente. Lo miré y vi que estaba temblando, pero antes de dejarle entrar necesitaba saber algo más.

—¿Lo has entendido?

Divine movió rápidamente los ojos a derecha e izquierda, como si la respuesta acertada pudiera estar escrita en las paredes de la casa de caliza.

—A lo mejor podría llegar a...

—¡¿Lo has entendido!?

—¿Tenías el pelo rubio? —soltó Divine.

—Tenía el pelo rubio.

Intentó reír, pero no lo consiguió.

—¿Eras gordo?

—Era gordo. No paraba de comer.

—¿Y llevabas gafas?

—Ahora uso lentillas.

—Nunca habría...

—¿Has entendido algo de todo esto?

Divine se atragantó.

—Ni una palabra.

Entonces, lo agarré de la camisa y lo metí en casa de un empujón. Mi deseo por él había aumentado con cada palabra, mientras leía, y lo tiré sobre la alfombra del vestíbulo. Pero Divine me detuvo. Con una mano me quitó el ejemplar de *La Bella* y con la otra comprobó mi erección a través de los pantalones. Mientras me besaba, oí el ruido del libro al chocar contra el suelo, detrás de Divine, y cuando terminó de besarme dije:

—El suelo está muy bien, pero ¿qué tal si esta vez lo hacemos en el sofá?

3.11

DIVINE

Querido Rata:
Ace tiempo que no tengo noticias tuyas, pero ya sé que siempre andas metido en un montón de historias y estás muy ocupado manteniéndote ocupado, así que supondré que las cosas te ban bien. Y por aquí todo bien, ya sabes que en G. no cambia nada, o alomejor debería decir que cuanto más cambian las cosas más se quedan como estaban. Ya sabes: un poco de esto y un poco de aquello, pero nada que balga la pena contar. Ja, ja.
    Seguro que adivino lo que estás pensando. Estás pensando <u>quién</u> fue esta vez. Pues te diré que esta vez no fue un cerdo como Howard Goertzen, no. Tampoco un negro muy mono pero tonto del culo como Melvin Cartwright... por cierto que, como te decía en mi última carta, cada vez está más claro que fue él quien le metió esa ~~vala~~ bala en la cabeza a Eddie Comedy y luego se escondió en paradero desconocido. Bueno, puede que sí halla habido cierta animación por aquí, pero ya sabes que ninguno de los 2 era tan excitante como para hecharlo de menos ahora. Pero bueno, yo te estaba contando quién fue esta vez. <u>Vale.</u> ¿Te acuerdas de ese hombre del que te hablé, el nuevo que acababa de mudarse? ¿Colin Nieman? (Creo que la última vez escribí Neeman, o algo así, pero se escribe N-I-E-M-A-N). <u>Bueno.</u> Cuando lo pienso casi no puedo escribir; me tiembla la mano y parece que se me va ha caer el boli, y hasta el culo me suda, y creo que lo único que puedo decir es que ha sido el mejor desde ti, Rata, el primero que ha sabido qué quería y cómo conseguirlo, y espero que no te enroyes pensando que ahora me olvidaré de ti o cosas así, porque cuando digo que fue bueno quiero decir que fue casi tan bueno como tú, valla, no sé cómo describirlo, alomejor diciendo que fue tan bueno que me hace hecharte mucho más de menos. Ya sabes que siempre serás el número 1 en mi lista, y espero que me escribas, por favor, o te pongas en conexión conmigo pronto (¿se dice así?).
    Un fuerte apretón,
                       Divine (alias Reggie, para que no te olvides)

3.12

CORA

Ahora algunos secretos, conocidos y desconocidos:
    Hace nueve años, cuando yo tenía veintiocho, dejé al hombre con el que llevaba diez años casada porque no me daba un hijo. Ese

hombre era Sawyer Johnson y, durante diez años, yo le había preparado el desayuno, le había empaquetado la comida y le había tenido la cena lista cuando volvía de trabajar en el campo. Lavaba sus platos, su ropa, incluso su cuerpo, cuando estaba demasiado cansado para hacerlo por sí solo. Y no creo que hiciera nada de eso movida por cierta idea del deber conyugal. Lo hacía porque lo amaba. Si no lo hubiera querido no me habría casado con él, pero tampoco me habría casado con él si no hubiera pensado que algún día me daría hijos. Pero él decía que era joven, que primero envejeciéramos un poco, que era pobre, que primero nos enriqueciéramos un poco, y que estaba disfrutando demasiado. Ese hombre me daba placer todas las noches; y a veces también por la mañana. Y no solo placer. Me reconfortaba. Me frotaba las manos cuando me dolían, y los pies, y el cuello y los hombros, y todas las primaveras cogía la primera flor para regalármela. A veces me sentaba en sus rodillas durante las oscuras horas de la noche, y sentía su pene en mi espalda, unas veces duro, otras blando, y me llenaba el pelo de trenzas que terminaban en una hilera de siete cuentas de cobalto que me refrescaban las mejillas con su cristalina redondez cada vez que volvía la cabeza. Pero debo decir que nunca –ni una sola vez– plantó su semilla donde tenía que plantarla, y un día después de nuestro décimo aniversario, después de tenerme toda la noche haciendo el amor inútilmente, hice las maletas y cogí el dinero que hasta ese día, sin darme cuenta, había estado ahorrando justo para ese momento, y me fui en autobús a Kansas City. Me pasé siete días encerrada en una habitación de motel que tenía más tipos de chinches diferentes que gente hay en Galatia, hasta que llegó mi hora, y entonces pasé las siete noches siguientes con siete hombres diferentes. Los conocía en los bares de blues, y debo reconocer que a veces me costaba abandonar la música por un hombre que seguramente no duraría más de lo que tardaba en repetirse el estribillo. Pero hice lo que tenía que hacer y volví a casa, y cuando volví, Sawyer no me preguntó nada. Pero meses más tarde, cuando las cosas empezaron a ser evidentes, metió su bonito pero inútil rabo entre las piernas y nadie en Galatia volvió a verlo o a saber de él. Antes de marcharse dijo una cosa. Dijo: «Nunca te he hecho nada malo». Y que conste en acta: Sawyer Johnson nunca me hizo nada malo, y para demostrarlo le puse su nombre a mi hijo. Y Dios sabe cuánto deseaba que aquel hijo hubiera sido suyo. No sé si habrá sido por el nombre o por mi buen ojo en Kansas City, pero el caso es que Sawyer se parece bastante a mi marido, de manera que la gente puede ahorrarse las preguntas. No es que pregunten: nadie pregunta cosas así en Galatia. Se limitan a mirar las tres fotografías que hay encima de la barra: el primer Sawyer, sonriendo, y a mí, mirándolo con unos ojos que quizá parecen haber visto más de lo que debería haber visto una mujer decente; y el segundo Sawyer, aún demasiado joven como para que nadie lo acuse de nuestros errores. Y entonces recogen los cincuenta centavos que pensaban dejar de propina y esconden un billete de dólar bajo la taza de café.

Después de Sawyer, Rosa. Dicen que algunas personas no pueden vivir con los demás y que otras no pueden vivir sin ellos. Yo sé de qué clase soy.

Nunca sabré por qué Rosa acabó apareciendo por aquí, a menos que un día cambie de opinión y se decida a contármelo. Se presentó una noche a finales de invierno, hace unos cuatro años. Llevaba una maleta en la mano y no estaba más cubierta de polvo que el que se puede coger caminando desde el IGA hasta el café. No había ningún coche a la vista, y espero que nadie piense que el tren pasa por este pueblo. ¿Llego demasiado tarde para cenar?, me preguntó, como si viniera todas las noches.

Como si yo la estuviera esperando.

Hice lo que cualquiera habría hecho en mi lugar. Le pregunté cómo se llamaba y me dijo que Rosetta Stone —Rose Etta Stone, así se escribía, según supe más tarde—. No es que yo lea la Biblia todas las noches, ni nada de eso, pero había oído hablar de la piedra Rosetta, aunque antes de que pudiera preguntarle nada ella me preguntó cuál era mi nombre. Bueno, dije, y luego me quedé pensativa un buen rato. Mi nombre completo es Coretta Beech Tree Johnson, Lewis es mi apellido, pero de eso puedes olvidarte ahora mismo, y de lo del Beech Tree, de lo del haya, también. Eso no fue más que la idea sentimental de un viejo que hizo que su hija le diera a su hija el nombre de su madre, como si con ello pudiera honrar a una mujer y a una tradición que nosotros, los vivos, ni siquiera conocíamos. Me gustaría pensar que esa mujer había sido una buena mujer, pero también es cierto que podría haber tenido tres ojos y afición por la sangre de niño, y no estaba dispuesta a cargar con esa historia en mi carnet de conducir. Además, ¿quién ha visto una haya en Kansas? Me pareció que tenía tanto derecho a preguntarle a Rosa de dónde había sacado ese nombre como ella a preguntarme de dónde había sacado yo el mío. Pero aún no estaba preparada para eso; no había pasado mucho tiempo desde que Sawyer se marchó, y me limité a decir: Puedes llamarme Cora, muchas gracias. ¿Quieres la carne con salsa o solo con patatas fritas?

Sawyer no me dejó nada más que la casona de su abuela. Todo el mundo me decía que abrir un café no era una buena idea, porque al otro lado de la carretera estaba el de Elaine Sumnertime y en Bigger Hill el de Art Penny, pero supuse que a la mayoría de mis conocidos no les importaría gastar veinticinco centavos aquí y cincuenta allá, y a fin de cuentas estaba en lo cierto. De todos modos, ciento cincuenta personas no gastan tanto dinero en comer fuera de casa, y cuando colgué el cartel de SE ALQUILA HABITACIÓN me dijeron que estaba aún más loca que cuando se me ocurrió abrir el café. En un pueblo en el que la gente intentaba alquilar casas enteras por cien dólares al mes, ¿quién iba a querer alquilar una habitación en una casa en la que vivía una madre soltera y su hijo de cuatro años? Bueno, muchas gracias, señorita Rosetta Stone, por ayudarme a demostrarles que estaban equivocados.

He aquí lo que escribió en el pequeño contrato que le hice firmar:
Domicilio: *ninguno.*
Duración de la estancia: *¿?*
Edad: *no consta.*
No fumadora.

Al principio, sencillamente vivía aquí. Se mantenía al margen. Compró una radio para su habitación y sintonizaba la emisora de gospel de Bigger Hill. Y se pasaba el día tricotando. Tricotaba mantas suficientes para abastecer un hospital militar. A veces me detenía junto a su puerta, escuchando el tintineo de sus agujas. Mi madre también tricotaba sin parar mientras yo crecía, pero la diferencia entre ella y Rosa es que esta lo hacía al ritmo de la música, cosa que a mí me parece una proeza.

Cuando la relación se fue estrechando, Rosa empezó a echarme una mano en el café. Nada de dinero, gracias; lo hago por gusto. Me enseñó unos cuantos trucos de cocina: sabía más que nadie de cocina caribeña y me enseñó a usar el curry, el cardamomo y la cúrcuma sin que el guiso supiera a remedio contra la difteria. ¿Me importaría que cultivara algunas hierbas en el jardín? Claro que no, dije; no había ningún problema.

Había un viejo seto muerto en el patio. Supongo que resultaba útil: impedía que se metiera la nieve y nos proporcionaba cierta intimidad, a pesar de lo feo que era. Bueno, Rosa no se limitó a plantar algunas hierbas, sino que además plantó campanillas de todos los colores del arco iris que acabaron cubriendo el seto por arriba y por abajo, por dentro y por fuera; en cuestión de pocas semanas lo vi completamente verde por primera vez en la vida, y poco después se llenó de pequeños brotes. Incluso mi hijo Sawyer, a quien solo le gustan los perritos calientes, la Coca-Cola y los dibujos animados de los sábados por la mañana, dijo que Rosa había convertido el patio en un lugar donde daba gusto estar.

A mí simplemente me pareció que era bonito, como casi todo lo que hacía Rosa. Como la propia Rosa.

Rosa había plantado todo lo que puede crecer en el clima de Kansas, y también cosas impropias de este clima, como albahaca, eneldo, romero, salvia y tomillo. Aprovechaba los huecos del jardín. Yo cultivaba tomates, maíz y patatas, bonitas hileras de productos útiles plantadas en sensatos rectángulos de tierra, pero ella sembraba sus hierbas en zigzag y en espiral, y a veces casi parecía que dejaba que las semillas cayeran de su mano al azar y arraigaran donde quisieran. Nunca había imaginado que un huerto pudiera ser tan bonito, fuerte tal vez, y exuberante, y eso que yo siempre me había sentido orgullosa de mis verduras, pero los finos tallos verdes de las hierbas de Rosa acabaron por eclipsarlas, hasta que un día, cuando me pidió que fuera a ver el jardín, me pareció como si lo viera por primera vez.

—Tus hierbas están creciendo muy bien —dije—. ¿Dónde has aprendido tanto de hierbas?

Fue entonces cuando aprendí que a Rosa se le puede hacer cualquier pregunta con tal que esta no empiece por «dónde». Más tarde aprendería que tampoco se le pueden hacer preguntas que empiecen por «cuándo».

Domicilio: *ninguno.*

Rosa no respondió. En lugar de ello, cogió un ramito de eneldo y, al abrigo de aquel seto muerto y rebosante de flores, tomó un mechón de mi pelo para hacerme una trenza, entrelazando el eneldo con el pelo, y, cuando hubo terminado, la trenza me rozó la mejillas.

Duración de la estancia: ¿?

Rosa me acarició la mejilla. En una mejilla sentía su mano y en la otra las briznas de eneldo acariciando mi piel, pero las dos cosas olían igual; las dos olían a eneldo dulce y fresco, aunque había otro olor más débil, el de la tierra de donde se había arrancado el eneldo, y otro aún más débil, y aunque puedo ponerle un nombre a ese olor, no puedo describirlo. Ese olor era Rosa.

Rosa dijo:

—Para entender una cosa hay que vivirla. Eso no se aprende en los libros. No se encuentra en ninguna enciclopedia; no se estudia. Hay que verla, sentirla, olerla, oírla y saborearla; hay que experimentarla con los sentidos.

Rosa tenía los ojos negros y el pelo negro, casi tan enroscado como el mío, y, para describir ese olor con exactitud, he de volver una vez más a mi madre. Mi madre se apellidaba Rochelle, era prima de Emily, la madre de Webbie Greeving, y cuando el reverendo Amias aún vivía, dejaba que mi madre usara una habitación en el sótano de la iglesia para sus reuniones sociales de los sábados por la tarde. Era una pequeña habitación llena de café y pasteles, de frutas dulces, como fresas y melocotones, y de mujeres negras; y al respirar aquel olor me preguntaba si Rosa sería, bueno… Rosa tenía la piel color aceituna, lo cual no significa exactamente verde sino que se puede poner de un color o de otro. Es curioso que una cosa así pueda producir timidez, pero ya ven.

No pude decirle nada a Rosa. Hice un gesto de asentimiento con la cabeza, y Rosa sonrió.

–Si observas cómo crece una planta, cómo crece y cómo no crece, acabas sabiendo qué es lo que la hace crecer mejor –dijo Rosa.

Y ahora, cuando llega el verano, soy feliz. Todo se llena de flores, de enredaderas verdes, de hierbas delicadas que se mezclan en este jardín nuestro que es como un muestrario de especies vegetales. Pero cuando llega el otoño, Grady Oconnor rotura la tierra, y cuando llega el invierno el seto queda cubierto por una nueva capa de enredaderas muertas que se retuercen por todos lados, asomando como las venas en las piernas de una anciana blanca. En marzo y abril, Rosa siembra su surtido de semillas para el año siguiente, a la espera del deshielo, y entonces siento que respiro mejor. Una vez le dije que me parecía un poco torpe, y entonces me explicó lo que era la fe. A veces, dijo, uno cree en lo que ve, pero la verdadera fe solo llega cuando uno comprende que los ojos nos engañan, y aprende entonces a creer sin más. Sin ninguna razón. Bueno, me pareció tan bonito que me entraron ganas de sentarme y echarme a llorar… y me eché a llorar, pero no porque creyera en lo que ella me había dicho. Lloré porque no creía. No tenía fe. Solo creía en lo que mis ojos me mostraban. Sawyer, Rosa, las burbujas de una tortita que indican que es el momento de darle la vuelta.

Con un billete de cinco dólares aún se puede cenar en mi café, y también con cinco billetes de un dólar, o con quinientos centavos.

Yo le enseñaba a Sawyer. Un plato limpio es un plato feliz.

Por el humo se sabe dónde está el fuego; eso me enseñó mi madre.

Pero sabía que no era eso lo que Rosa deseaba oír, y me limité a sonreír y a pronunciar su nombre. Rosa, dije; y eso fue todo. Eso fue suficiente por ese día. Por aquel entonces los problemas estaban en el pasado –Eric Johnson y el primer Sawyer–, pero nadie imaginaba el nuevo problema que se avecinaba: Colin Nieman y su joven amigo, ese que tenía un nombre tan raro. Y Lucy Robinson. Otra vez.

3.13

COLIN

No había en Galatia ninguna calle asfaltada, pero la tierra parecía más dura que el asfalto. Formaba una superficie irregular, tan llena de pliegues como una tabla de lavar; iba yo dando botes en el coche por una de esas calles, Adams, creo que se llamaba, East Adams, cuando un montículo de tierra se desmoronó justo delante de mí. No tuve tiempo de apartarme. Sentí un fuerte impacto, un nudo en el estómago, y la música de *Las valquirias* que sonaba en el cd del coche quedó ahogada por un aullido atroz y penetrante. Salí del coche rápidamente y la vi con absoluta claridad, tendida en la calle. Mil cosas me bullían en la mente: Justin, que acababa de salir del hospital de Bigger Hill, mi impaciencia por tener los resultados del laboratorio, que, según creía, demostrarían mi inocencia, mi novela, que había despegado al fin tras esa noche en la comisaría. Todas estas cosas bullían en mi mente, y lo que vi en un primer momento no fue el cuerpo que en realidad estaba tendido en la calle, sino el cuerpo de Lucy Robinson; su piel sonrosada llena de magulladuras, su vestido púrpura hecho jirones. La alucinación duró un segundo; en un segundo, la carne se transformó en pelo duro, las heridas en pegotes de barro seco, el vestido hecho jirones en las marcas que cubrían el lomo, el vientre y las patas de una pequeña cerda de orejas caídas. La cerda no paraba de aullar; movía convulsivamente las patas delanteras intentando levantarse, pero las patas traseras, enredadas, no le respondían. Era evidente que se había partido el lomo; pero, a pesar todo, el alivio que sentí al ver que no era una persona —que no era Lucy Robinson— fue tan grande que me eché a reír. No había soltado más de un par de carcajadas cuando una voz humana, tan aguda y desesperada como el aullido del animal, me interrumpió.

—¿Qué coño te hace tanta gracia?

El hombre que pronunció estas palabras iba sin abrigo y su enorme panza rebotaba como una pelota mientras corría hacia mí; me miró con malevolencia, pero antes de que pudiera decir nada, se quedó mirando a la cerda.

—¡Charlene! —exclamó, suavizando el tono—. Charlene, cariño, ¿qué te ha pasado? —Se hincó de rodillas y sujetó con cuidado la cabeza del animal. Al contacto con el hombre, la cerda dejó de aullar, pero se quedó con la boca abierta y jadeando entrecortadamente, lanzando bocanadas de vapor; seguía moviendo las patas delanteras con la intención de huir. El hombre me miró y dijo—: ¡La ha matado! ¡Ha matado a mi Charlene! ¿Qué le hace tanta gracia?

—P-perdóneme —dije, balbuceando. Moví las manos a modo de excusa, pero la etiqueta de asesino de cerdos me parecía demasiado—. Estaba tumbada en la carretera. No la he visto. Por favor, perdóneme.

El hombre me espetó:
—Siempre está tumbada en la carretera. ¡Siempre está ahí tumbada!

Retiró una mano de la temblorosa cabeza de Charlene y señaló hacia un bache que había debajo del Rover. Miré el agujero de bordes redondeados y cuando me di la vuelta vi que el hombre había apoyado la cabeza sobre la cabeza del animal. Era un hombre joven, no tendría más de veinticinco años, aunque empezaba a quedarse calvo y la barba roja de varios días que cubría sus mejillas estaba salpicada de canas. No pude evitar fijarme en que tenía las mejillas fofas, los ojos pequeños y cerdunos, y las botas cubiertas de pegotes de mierda seca. De todos modos, bajo la ceñida camisa de cuadros, asomaban unos músculos fuertes, sólidos y redondeados, cubiertos por una gruesa capa de grasa que los hacía parecer aún más voluminosos. Un gran cuchillo colgaba de su cinturón en una funda de cuero.

De pronto levantó la vista y dijo:
—Darrell, Grady, ¡ha atropellado a Charlene!

Me di la vuelta y vi a dos hombres; uno negro y uno blanco, que se acercaban a nosotros. Llevaban las cazadoras abiertas y el blanco llevaba en la mano una cazadora vaquera forrada de lino.

—Mirad lo que ha hecho —dijo el blanco, arrastrando las palabras tanto como el paso. El negro asintió y luego se llevó una mano a la boca, no sin antes esbozar un atisbo de sonrisa.

Luego nadie volvió a decir nada. El silencio era tal que se oía la música de la radio del coche, y Charlene volvió a lanzar un grito atroz.

—Mire cómo grita —dijo su propietario—. Mire lo que le ha hecho.

—Vamos, Howard —dijo el blanco—. Estoy seguro de que ha sido un accidente. Este hombre es extranjero. No puedes pretender que conozca las costumbres de Charlene.

El hombre tenía un acento sumamente peculiar, y resultaba mucho más fácil fijarse en su acento que en lo que decía, pues la única mirada que me dirigió dejaba traslucir cierta simpatía en sus palabras. Le ofreció a Howard la cazadora, pero este la rechazó.

—¿Un accidente? ¿Extranjero? —gritó Howard—. Primero, me, me, me roba a mi Lucy, y ahora a mi Charlene. ¿Un accidente?

Al oír que Howard mencionaba a Lucy, comprendí la hondura del drama que estábamos escenificando. Comprendí que aquellos hombres habían compartido en cierto modo mi visión del cuerpo magullado de Lucy tirado en la carretera, delante de mi coche. Pero nadie respondió a las acusaciones de Howard. El negro parecía fascinado por el diseño del coche, aunque seguía tapándose la boca con la mano, y el blanco se interpuso un momento entre Howard y yo, mirándonos alternadamente con la regularidad propia de un metrónomo. Luego, posó en mí su mirada y una amplia y falsa sonrisa se dibujó en su rostro, mostrando unos dientes marrones de tanto mascar tabaco. Se limpió la mano en los pantalones antes de ofrecérmela.

—Soy Darrell Jenkens. Con dos erres y dos eles. Y este es Grady Oconnor —añadió, señalando al negro con el pulgar—. Sin apóstrofo. Ese es Howard Goertzen y esa es Charlene.

Seguía con la mano extendida, una mano que pareció aún más sucia después de limpiársela en los polvorientos pantalones, pero se la estreché de todos modos.

Me apretó con fuerza y yo le devolví el apretón; apretó aún con más fuerza, pero yo había estudiado artes marciales con un monje budista capaz de pulverizar una bola de billar con una mano mientras con la otra sujetaba tranquilamente una taza de té. Los nudillos de Darrell Jenkens crujieron con un sonido parecido al que hace el plástico de burbujas al estallar, y la sonrisa desapareció de su rostro.

—Soy Colin Nieman —dije; aunque sin dar aclaraciones ortográficas.

Darrell Jenkens seguía estrechándome la mano.

—Sé quién es usted.

—Por favor, perdónenme por atropellar a Charlene. Pero es que estaba tumbada en medio de la carretera.

Darrell Jenkens se detuvo un momento y luego se guardó las manos en los bolsillos de la cazadora. Vi que me miraba de arriba abajo, fijándose en mi chaquetón de marinero y en la almidonada camisa blanca que llevaba debajo, en mis chinos bien planchados, en mi cabeza sin sombrero y sin pelo; Darrell era un hombre alto, delgado y sucio, con la piel cubierta de pecas. Luego se encogió de hombros.

—Tenía que pasar —dijo, y al principio no quedó claro si se refería a Charlene, a mí o a otra cosa—. Todo el mundo le decía a Howard que no dejara a la cerda suelta por la calle.

—Darrell —dijo Howard Goertzen—. Mírala. Dios mío, Darrell, se está muriendo.

Darrell Jenkens se acercó entonces a Howard Goertzen y, un momento después, Grady Oconnor —sin apóstrofo— dio un paso hacia mí.

—Howard no tiene muchos amigos.

Se esforzaba por hablar en un tono normal, pero era evidente que la situación provocaba en él más diversión que angustia. Charlene volvió a lanzar varios aullidos, pero Grady Oconnor se limitó a escucharlos.

—El padre de Howard tiene una granja de cerdos al oeste del pueblo. Un buen negocio. Charlene fue el lechón más pequeño de una camada que nació hace un par de años, más o menos cuando se marchó Lyle, y Howard se encariñó con ella. Seguro que la madre se la habría comido, pero Howard se la llevó y la alimentó con biberón; la ha criado como si fuera un animal doméstico.

—¿Lyle?

—Lyle era el hermano de Howard. Se alistó en el ejército. Murió en la guerra de Iraq.

—¿En la guerra del Golfo?

—La misma —asintió Grady.

—¿Y Charlene?

Grady seguía asintiendo.

—Sí, creo que le puso ese nombre por la cerda del cuento.

—¿Se refiere a *La telaraña de Charlotte*?

—El mismo.

—El cerdo se llamaba Wilbur.

—Bueno. Howard no lee demasiado.

—Y la araña se llamaba Charlotte.

—Así es Howard.

—¡Grady Oconnor! —interrumpió Howard—. ¿Piensas quedarte ahí todo el día cotorreando con ese hombre o vas a hacer algo?

Grady me miró un buen rato, y noté que una emoción, cierto fastidio quizá, o algo más fuerte, ensombrecía su rostro. Luego se volvió hacia Howard.

—¿Qué quieres que haga Howard? —preguntó. Y volviéndose hacia mí dijo—: ¿Lleva un arma en el coche?

—¿Un arma?

—Hay que ahorrarle sufrimiento al animal.

Volvió a pronunciar estas palabras con su acento peculiar. Dije que no llevaba ningún arma.

—¿De verdad? —replicó Grady, y la poca confianza que yo había depositado en él se desvaneció en ese momento—. Hace frío hoy —dijo—, y se subió la cremallera de la cazadora.

Hacía frío, aunque no me había dado cuenta. Howard Goertzen, que seguía en mangas de camisa, tiritaba junto a Charlene, y el vapor del aliento del animal formaba una mancha húmeda de color rojizo sobre los pantalones del hombre. Tenía las orejas tan frías que sentía latir el pulso en ellas.

Volví a oír la música de *Las valquirias* y después otro ruido de gravilla levantada por los neumáticos de un coche, seguido por la breve ráfaga de la sirena policial. Cuando el agente Brown salió de su todoterreno, su rostro se mostraba tan estólido, arrugado e inexpresivo como un tronco de madera. Se acercó hacia el grupo, con una mano en la barriga, la otra en la protuberante culata de su pistola; también su panza era protuberante. Iba tarareando «Leroy Brown», melodía que, al parecer, era para él como una especie de himno, y por un momento Jim Croce compitió con Wagner, pero luego, gracias a Dios, tanto el agente Brown como el cd quedaron en silencio al mismo tiempo.

Cuando vivíamos en Nueva York teníamos un Mercedes descapotable, pero cuando nos trasladamos a Galatia guardé el Mercedes en un garaje y compré un Range Rover; y fue la parrilla del Rover lo que primero llamó la atención del agente Brown al entrar en escena. Fingió no ver a Charlene, y tampoco pareció reconocer a Howard, Darrell o Grady; rozó con un dedo enfundado en el guante una de las placas de acero de la parrilla y, cuando hubo terminado, asintió con aprobación. Luego se volvió hacia nosotros.

—Y bien, caballeros, ¿cuál es el problema?

—¿Qué cuál es el problema? ¡Qué cuál es el problema! —gritó Howard Goertzen—. Este de aquí —torció la boca al no encontrar las palabras adecuadas—, este hombre ha atropellado a mi Charlene.

El agente Brown se volvió hacia mí.

—Señor Nieman.

—Sheriff Brown.

—Parece que tiene usted el don de aterrizar justo en medio de los problemas, señor Nieman.

—En este caso, sheriff, fue Charlene. Estaba tumbada en medio de la carretera.

Señalé el agujero que había debajo del coche, pero el agente Brown no me quitó la vista de encima.

—¡Howard! —dijo—. ¿Estaba Charlene otra vez echando una siesta en mitad de East Adams?

Como si pudiera haberla atropellado en la calle Jefferson y arrastrado una manzana en dirección oeste.

—Siempre duerme aquí, agente Brown. Todo el mundo lo sabe.

—Mi nombre, Howard, es Eustace. Mi título es sheriff.

Grady Oconnor se cubrió rápidamente la boca con una mano.

Howard Goertzen acercó a Charlene sus frías y sonrosadas mejillas.

—Estaba esperando a que yo terminara de almorzar.

Hubo un largo silencio, y todas las miradas se fijaron en el agente Brown. Sentí que empezaba a tiritar de frío y quise coger el abrigo del coche. El agente Brown tenía el rostro tenso, pero su pecho se infló ligeramente bajo nuestra mirada. Supuse que era uno de esos hombres que se creen muy importantes y disfrutan siendo el centro de atención —y en ese momento, sin duda lo era—, pero la razón de que se le hinchara el pecho se reveló un momento después, cuando un eructo hizo que se le hincharan los carrillos y el pecho se desinfló al expulsar los gases de su cuerpo al tiempo que lanzaba un largo suspiro y apretaba los labios.

Después de eructar sacó el arma de la cartuchera. No lo hizo con gesto teatral, pero yo di un respingo de todos modos y tuve que contener las ganas de agazaparme detrás del Rover.

—Me temo que no puedo hacer mucho más por ti, Howard —dijo el agente Brown, volviéndose hacia el hombre y la cerda—. Todos te hemos dicho mil veces que la cerda no podía andar suelta por una calle tan transitada.

No había pasado ningún coche. Pensé que lo de «transitada» era bastante relativo.

—¡Ay, agente Brown!

El sheriff no lo corrigió.

—Apártate, Howard. Vamos a ahorrarle a Charlene este sufrimiento. Y ponte algo encima antes de que te congeles.

Howard Goertzen miró un momento la pistola del agente Brown, luego me miró a mí, miró su cazadora y volvió a mirar al agente Brown.

—Me apartaré, pero que lo haga él. Que termine lo que ha empezado.

La maldad que había en su voz dotó de un nuevo significado a sus palabras. Howard Goertzen acariciaba tiernamente la cabeza de Charlene, y entonces recordé que alguien, Divine o Wade o Webbie, había mencionado que Goertzen había sido uno de los principales pretendientes de Lucy Robinson.

—Supongo que Howard tiene razón. ¿Sabe manejar un arma de fuego, señor Nieman?

—Solo he disparado una vez en mi vida —dije. Extendí la mano para coger la pistola.

El agente Brown me miró la mano y luego, sin hacer ningún comentario, se fue al coche patrulla y volvió con una escopeta. Pero no guardó la pistola en la cartuchera. Mientras me pasaba la escopeta, me vino a la cabeza la escena de *La Bella* en que cazan a un ciervo, y aunque me esforcé por recordar el incidente real, las palabras que empleé para describirlo desbordaron mi memoria:

Disparé y el ciervo corrió y el ciervo saltó y el ciervo se quedó quieto mientras sonaba el disparo, y la bala le reventó la garganta y la vida del animal quedó desparramada por el suelo del bosque, corriendo, saltando, quedándose quieto. Volví a disparar y un asta de su cornamenta se quebró como una rama;

uno de sus ojos explotó, mientras yo corría, saltaba, me quedaba quieto. El ciervo era mío, lo tenía atrapado, y al hundir las manos en el agujero de la garganta sentí que la vida se le escapaba, a falta de una piel que pudiera contenerla, repelerla, repeler la vida, repeler la muerte; por un momento, los dos habíamos huido de la muerte, corriendo, saltando, quedándonos quietos, pero luego, para siempre jamás, solo quedaría yo, mientras la sangre se enfriaba en mis manos, la noche caía y los demás ciervos corrían, saltaban; pero nosotros permanecíamos inmóviles.

Charlene parecía casi muerta; parpadeaba sin cesar, el pecho le temblaba como a un pájaro. Di un paso al frente, y Howard Goertzen apartó su gordo cuerpo, cogiendo su cazadora en el último momento. Sostuve la escopeta con una mano, puse el dedo en el gatillo, apoyé la culata en el antebrazo y doblé el codo. Y mientras el agente Brown decía «No crea que...», sonó un disparo y tras la oreja de Charlene apareció un pequeño agujero del que no brotó sangre; la cerda murió sin retorcerse. No salió sangre de la herida, pero un pequeño hilo de vapor ascendió desde el orificio de la bala.

Al volverme hacia el agente Brown, la escopeta, claro está, se volvió conmigo, y el agente Brown empuñó rápidamente la pistola para apuntarme. Comprendí entonces que me había instalado en un lugar donde los hombres adultos siempre van armados.

Bajé la escopeta y se la entregué por la culata al agente Brown.

—Es una escopeta del veintidós, con un solo pasador. No lleva más que una bala.

Howard Goertzen parecía como ido, y vi que algo, espero que solo fuera el aliento de Charlene, le había manchado la bragueta de los pantalones. Darrell Jenkens parecía muy ocupado sacudiéndose el polvo de los pantalones, y la sonrisa se había esfumado en el rostro de Grady Oconnor.

El agente Brown miró a Charlene; luego, sacudiendo ligeramente la cabeza, se volvió hacia mí.

—¿No conocería usted por casualidad a Eddie Comedy, verdad?

Sonreí y negué con la cabeza, pero entonces comprendí por qué Darrell Jenkens había pronunciado ese nombre. Había pronunciado ese nombre porque sabía que yo era escritor, y quería asegurarse de que lo escribiera bien en mi libro.

Dos erres y dos eles. Sin apóstrofo.

Supongo que quería asegurarse de que también escribía bien el nombre de Grady Oconnor.

3.14

WEBBIE

Me resultaba imposible guardar silencio ante el silencio de Justin, pero aprendí a no hacerle preguntas. Hablaba siempre con aseveraciones: Hace frío, o hay una oferta especial de carne en el supermercado, o Wade te envía saludos. La casa de caliza siempre estaba limpia y ordenada, pero a veces yo hacía un esfuerzo adicional. A veces cocinaba para él, aunque Justin apenas comía. Tienes que comer, le insistía, hasta que un día Colin apareció cuando estábamos sentados a la mesa.

—Ya ha comido —dijo.

—¿De verdad?

Colin venía de hacer la compra.

—Come todos los días. No ha dejado de comer. Solo ha dejado de hablar.

No me gustó que Colin dijera una cosa así tan a la ligera, como si Justin hubiese hecho una renuncia voluntaria, y, muy enfadada, le solté:

—¿Has matado algún cerdo hoy?

Colin levantó la vista de la bolsa de la compra. No sonrió con sarcasmo, pero tampoco con amabilidad.

—¿Sabes?, señorita Greeving, creo que te prefiero en presencia de Wade. En casa de Wade. Hay algo en él que te... baja los humos.

—No metas a Wade en esto.

Lo dije con una vehemencia que hasta yo misma me sorprendí, y Colin amplió su sonrisa con aire triunfal.

—No, señorita Greeving. Hoy no he matado ningún cerdo. He corrido ocho kilómetros, he escrito dos mil palabras y he comprado comida en una tienda muy agradable que ofrece un amplio surtido de productos envueltos en elegantes paquetes blancos y negros (una buena metáfora, ¿no te parece?), e incluso he comprado algo en la carnicería, creo que es búfalo, aunque no estoy seguro, pero me pareció interesante.

En algún momento, mientras Colin lanzaba su breve discurso, me volví hacia Justin, y cuando Colin hubo terminado, dije:

—Míralo. Está delgado.

Colin lanzó un suspiro exasperado.

—Es delgado.

—Está peligrosamente delgado —dije—, y no entiendo cómo puedes tomarte a broma...

—Siempre ha estado peligrosamente delgado, Webbie. Es parte de su atractivo.

—¿De su atractivo? ¿Cómo puedes ser tan cruel?
—Creo que la cuestión, Webbie, es cómo puedes tú ser tan ingenua.

Empecé a responderle, a protestar, pero Colin me pasó por encima como una apisonadora.

—¿Sabes una cosa, Webbie? Eres un puro cliché. Una paleta con un diploma de la Ivy League. Te sientes superior a la gente de tu pueblo, a los blancos y a los negros, por algo tan ridículo como haber estudiado en Columbia, pero eres tan sectaria como ellos para lo que quieres y para lo que no quieres.

Hubo algo en las palabras de Colin que me dejó muda, y lo único que pude hacer fue tartamudear.

—¿Q-q-qué?
—Míralo, Webbie. Míralo.

No quería mirarlo, pero me sentí obligada. Me volví y miré a Justin. Pero era como si allí no hubiera nada. Just, just... Justin Time, un nombre inventado para una entidad desconocida, una clave cubierta de heridas y cicatrices.

—Justin es un prostituto, Webbie, un chulo, un niño malnutrido con una imaginación exagerada y tendencia a ponerse melodramático; una vez se escapó de lo que probablemente era una situación familiar insoportable y acabó en las calles de Nueva York, donde vendía su culo a perdedores como yo que se sentían atraídos por su aspecto. Eso es todo, Webbie. No hay nada más. No es ni un mártir ni un santo; es uno de tantos, los hay a patadas como él. A cincuenta pavos la hora, para ser exactos.

Justin no se movió mientras Colin hablaba, pero mis manos volaban como globos atados con cuerdas y atrapados en una tormenta de viento.

—Yo, yo, yo —tartamudeé—, no te creo.
—No, Webbie, no me crees. Prefieres no creerme. Puedes aceptar el hecho de que Divine sea un chulo, porque Divine es un negro sin educación, como lo fuiste tú en algún momento. Pero piensas que Justin es diferente. Justin habla como un hombre educado. Justin es blanco. Pero no es diferente de Divine, Webbie, solo ha leído más. ¿Por qué crees que él y Divine no pueden verse? Porque son exactamente iguales.

Al fin, me ofrecía algo a lo que aferrarme.

—Yo pensaba que era porque estaban luchando por ti.
—¿Por mí? —Colin esbozó una sonrisita, pero detecté cierto nerviosismo en su voz—. No hay nada por lo que luchar.

Vi entonces que Colin tenía un moratón en el cuello, un mordisco amoroso. No me parecía que Justin pudiera haberle hecho eso.

–¿De verdad? No creo que Divine lo sepa.

Colin suspiró:

–Escúchame, Webbie, por favor. Justin tomó una decisión, una decisión estúpida, pero una decisión de todos modos, y ya va siendo hora de que lo admitas. Puede renunciar cuando quiera, pero nosotros no podemos hacerlo por él.

No dije nada. Colin me miró un momento, y luego siguió desempaquetando lo que había comprado. Sacó una bandeja de poliestireno cubierta de celofán. Sacudí la cabeza.

–Es carne de búfalo –dije–, búfalo mezclado con ternera picada. –Me encogí de hombros–. Solo intento ayudar.

Colin habló con amabilidad:

–Y estoy seguro de que Justin te lo agradece. –Sonrió, y habría resultado convincente si no se hubiera fijado en dónde tenía yo puestos los ojos; y se tapó el moratón del cuello tirándose de la camisa.

–¿Qué tal está Divine?

Colin empezó a decir algo, pero luego se detuvo.

–Creo que será mejor que no vengas por aquí hasta que Justin quiera verte. Por el bien de todos.

Habló en tono neutro, pero volvió nerviosamente la mirada hacia Justin, y yo lo miré. Justin miraba fijamente al espacio vacío que había entre Colin y yo. Seguía sosteniendo el tenedor con la mano, y al ver que nadie decía nada, se lo llevó a la boca y volvió a sacárselo. Masticó despacio y tragó. En el tenedor no había nada.

3.15

CORA

La primera vez que lo vi estaba sudando a chorros. Llevaba un chándal gris y unas zapatillas de deporte muy caras, y pensé que por eso se atrevía a encharcar el suelo con su sudor a las nueve de la mañana del primer día de diciembre. Como ya he dicho, no lo había visto antes, pero no hacía falta que nadie me dijera quién era y que él no había hecho nada. Hay cosas que saltan a la vista.

Esa primera mañana apenas hablamos, pero vino al día siguiente, y al otro, y al otro. Hasta que llegó el fin de semana, y luego vino también el lunes. Tenía que conocerlo, conocerlo en todos los aspectos que pudieran ser importantes, al menos en lo que a mí respecta: ni beicon, ni café, ni papas con cebolla o sémola de maíz. A veces se tomaba un par de huevos escalfados y una torta de trigo, aunque normalmente solo pedía la torta y un zumo de uva. Tomaba el zumo sin azúcar. Y de uva roja, por favor: tiene diez veces más vitaminas que la verde. Fue Grady quien me contó la otra parte, lo de que era escritor y venía de Nueva York y era rico como Creso. Grady llegó a decir que Nettie Ferguson le había contado que tenía problemas con la cocaína, pero yo lo dudaba, pues nunca había oído hablar de un drogadicto que se levantara a las seis de la mañana y corriera ocho kilómetros sin sufrir un infarto. Grady me contó también lo de este hombre con Reggie Packman, quiero decir, con Divine, y también me habló del otro, el que tenía un nombre tan raro y se pasaba el día sentado en el ático de la casa de los Deacon sin decir palabra. Grady es un hombre tranquilo, aunque enseguida te das cuenta de que anda poniendo la oreja por todas partes. Pero eso no era asunto mío, como tampoco lo era que Grady se colara furtivamente en esa casa por la noche ni lo que allí veía, si es que veía algo, y al final le dije que no me contara más chismes. Si Colin Nieman quería desayunar en el café del bando contrario era cosa suya. Sus asuntos eran suyos y los míos, y más valía que siguieran siéndolo.

A pesar de todo, enseguida me di cuenta. Intentaba sobreponerse. Llevar una vida lo más normal posible. No es que quisiera fingir que no había pasado nada, pero prefería dejarlo correr, y debo admitir que el hecho de saber que alguien está analizando tu sangre y tus tejidos con un microscopio es para ponerle los pelos de punta a cualquiera. Quiero decir que ahora saben lo que bebes y lo que comes con solo analizar una gota de tu sangre, y también si consumes drogas y si tienes alguna enfermedad, y supongo que también pueden saber si has cogido a una chica en una carretera polvorienta y te has despachado a gusto con ella. Yo, en su lugar, tomaría doble ración de beicon y huevos solo para soportar la espera, y me asombraba que él se las arreglara con un zumo de uva sin azúcar. Pero le dibuja una raya en la espuma de la leche del café. No hay nada como la espuma de la leche de la cafetería de Cora.

Así pues, ese lunes le serví el desayuno, si es que se le puede llamar así.

—¿Le importa que me siente?

Apartó el libro que estaba leyendo.

—Por favor.

—¿Se toma los fines de semana libres?

—¿Cómo dice?

—Si no sale a correr los fines de semana.

—¡Ah! Sí, pero no tan temprano, y corro un poco menos. Los domingos nunca corro.

—Eso está muy bien, porque yo no abro los domingos —dije—. ¿Sabe cómo le llaman al *jogging* por aquí?

—¿Eh...?

—Correr sin ninguna necesidad.

Pareció hacerle gracia. Se rió y luego dijo:

—¿Ha corrido usted alguna vez?

—¿Me está tomando el pelo?

—No, solo me parecía que debía preguntárselo.

—El culo me colgaría hasta las rodillas. Correr no va conmigo. Me gusta más estar sentada.

—Yo corro desde hace treinta años. Todas las mañanas. Esté donde esté. Si no lo hago, siento que me falta algo.

Lo que yo quería preguntarle era por qué diablos había decidido instalarse aquí, pero pensé que no era asunto mío. Y me limité a decir:

—A mí me pasa lo mismo con mi taza de café. Más vale que nadie se tropiece conmigo antes de que me haya tomado un café.

—Más vale que nadie se tropiece conmigo antes de haber corrido un rato.

—Bueno, yo preferiría verlo después de haberse duchado. No se ofenda, señor Nieman, pero está claro que suda usted mucho.

Poco después apareció Rosa con una fuente de macarrones con queso, lista para meterla en el horno, y por la dureza con que miró a Colin pareció que estaba a punto de volcarme la fuente encima de la falda.

—No es un marciano, niña —le susurré, pero no le quité la vista de encima. Rosa nunca hacía las cosas accidentalmente.

—Perdóneme, Colin, me parece que todavía no conoce usted a Rosa.

Levantó la vista del libro. Me gustaría poder decirles qué estaba leyendo, pero el libro estaba en latín, y eso lo sabía porque él me lo había dicho.

—No, creo que no la conozco.

—Pues esta es la señorita Rosa Stone —dije. Hubo un extraño silencio. Sabía que debía añadir algo más, como «Es una buena amiga» o «Trabaja aquí conmigo», pero ninguna de las dos cosas era del todo cierta. Miré que Colin nos miraba repetidamente y luego, no sé cómo, pero estoy segura, se dio cuenta de todo.

Se levantó, y antes de que se dirigiera a Rosa, esta dejó la fuente de macarrones encima de la barra y se acercó a él.

—Encantada de conocerlo, señor Nieman.

Creo que en cuatro años nunca había visto a Rosa acercarse para saludar a nadie, y me quedé atónita.

—Encantado de conocerla, señorita Stone.

Rosa se limpió la mano en el delantal antes de ofrecérsela.

—Llámeme Rosa, por favor —dijo, poniéndose colorada como un tomate.

—Iba a decirle a Colin que venga cuando quiera a comer o a cenar —dije—. No desayuna más que un zumo de uva y una torta.

—Cora es una cocinera maravillosa, señor Nieman. Debería venir a comer un día.

Me fijé en que habló sin mirarlo; no apartó la vista de la mesa. Del libro de Colin.

Colin parecía un poco cohibido.

—La verdad es que nunca almuerzo.

Me eché a reír.

—En ese caso, señor Nieman, espero que al menos cene usted.

—Sí —dijo—. Cenar, ceno siempre.

—Entonces, espero que un día de estos se pase por aquí y me deje prepararle una comida como Dios manda. Una cocinera no se siente valorada si no cocina especialmente para alguien.

—Lo haré. Le prometo que vendré pronto.

—Las cenas empiezan a las cinco —dije—. La cocina cierra a las ocho y media, aunque casi siempre queda algo caliente hasta las nueve. —Pero apenas me fijaba en lo que le estaba diciendo, porque seguía muy ocupada observando a Rosa. Rosa movía los labios muy despacio sin dejar de mirar el libro de Colin, como si pronunciara las palabras.

Cuando Colin se volvió hacia ella, Rosa dio un respingo.

—Discúlpeme, señor Nieman —dijo, poniendo un dedo en la página y moviéndolo sobre el papel—: ¡Qué escritura tan hermosa!

—¿Lee usted en latín, señorita Stone?

—Rosa —corrigió ella. Y volvió a sonrojarse—. Me refería a la forma de las palabras. A su aspecto sobre la página. Es precioso. Precioso.

Más tarde, cuando Colin se hubo marchado, Rosa fue a meter la fuente de macarrones en el horno, y yo intenté retenerla detrás de la barra; el espacio era tan estrecho que no podían pasar dos personas a la vez sin que una de ellas se apartara un poco.

—Dime qué pasa.

—¿Qué? —se extrañó Rosa. Clavó la vista en el suelo—. ¿Qué quieres decir?

—Te he visto. Estabas leyendo el libro. No estabas mirando el aspecto de la página. Estabas leyendo.

—Cora, el libro estaba escrito en latín.

—Eso ya lo sé. En latín. ¿Por qué piensas que te lo pregunto? Y no me vengas con que eres católica.

—Virgilio.

—¿Qué dices?
—Estaba leyendo a Virgilio. Estaba leyendo la historia de la fundación de Roma.
—¿Y eso qué tiene que ver?
—Cora, te he dicho mil veces que no me hagas preguntas. No preguntes y no te sorprenderás. Así es mucho mejor; confía en mí.
—¿Mejor para quién? ¿Para mí? ¿O para ti?
—Solo digo que no hagas preguntas —repitió, lanzando un largo suspiro—. Esto estará listo dentro de tres cuartos de hora. —Y al principio no entendí que se refería a los macarrones. Luego, me empujó para salir de detrás de la barra y la oí subir corriendo las escaleras y cerrar de un portazo la puerta de la habitación por la que seguía pagándome cincuenta dólares al mes.

El portazo me dejó helada, tanto que tuve que sentarme, hundir la cabeza entre las manos y reprimir el llanto para que no se me derritiese el cerebro. Sawyer había dado el mismo portazo, no la noche que se marchó, no, esa noche salió a hurtadillas, sino otra noche; la noche que fue a buscar el cuerpo de Eric Johnson. Ese chico era su sobrino, y Marsha, como ya he dicho, no le hacía ningún bien, ni a Eric ni a nadie. Recuerdo que alguien llamó por teléfono a Sawyer; Sawyer no dijo quién había llamado. Sonó el teléfono y Sawyer contestó, y después de decir hola se quedó callado muchísimo rato; luego dijo: Ahora mismo voy; se despidió, colgó el auricular y me abrazó con fuerza. Luego se marchó. Cuando volvió era casi de día; olía a sudor y estaba sucísimo, pero además estaba... cansado no es la palabra precisa, pero es la que más se aproxima. Estaba tan cansado que ni siquiera se molestó en lavarse o desnudarse. Se tumbó en la cama junto a mí, y entonces fui yo quien lo abrazó, en la riqueza o en la pobreza, en la salud o en la enfermedad, en la suciedad o en la limpieza, lo abracé mientras él lloraba. No decía nada; solo lloraba. No dijo nada hasta que se hartó de llorar, y luego dijo: Lo he enterrado donde nadie pueda encontrarlo. Donde nadie pueda volver a meterse con él. Mi pobre Sawyer. Casi sentía en mis manos su suciedad y el dolor de sus huesos, pero Sawyer se dio la vuelta y, de repente, se me subió encima, y aunque no tenía una erección, sentí su pene a través de los pantalones, y entonces me dijo: ¿Quieres saber por qué no quiero tener hijos, Cora? ¿Quieres saber por qué? ¡Por esto! Juro que en mi vida había pasado tanto miedo como esa noche. Yo no había dicho palabra y mi marido se me subió encima como si fuera un extraño, y yo lo aparté y me di la vuelta, y oí que se levantaba, que cruzaba la habitación y salía por la puerta. Pero no fue la puerta de nuestra habitación la que cerró de un portazo, sino la de la habitación de al lado.

La puerta de la habitación de Rosa.
Duración de la estancia: ¿?

Entonces sonó el timbre; levanté la vista, y no me habría sorprendido en absoluto que Sawyer regresara después de tanto tiempo. Porque tenía esa sensación. Sentía que algo, alguien, como Colin y Lucy Robinson, incluso Rosa en cierto modo, hacía que el pasado volviera, aunque no estaba segura de qué era lo que volvía exactamente; no podría decir si ellos me llevaban hasta allí o si, de alguna manera, lo cual resultaba mucho más aterrador, lo empujaban todo al presente. Sonó el timbre, pero no había nadie en la puerta. Será el viento, pensé; pero el timbre seguía sonando. Y entonces me di cuenta de que lo que sonaba era el reloj que me avisaba de que los macarrones de Rosa ya estaban listos. Me levanté, apagué el reloj y el horno, saqué los macarrones y los dejé encima de la barra. No podía hacer nada más, ni por Sawyer, ni por Eric Johnson, ni por Rosa, ni por Colin Nieman ni Lucy Robinson. Lo único que podía hacer era impedir que los macarrones se quemaran. Y eso fue lo que hice.

3.16

COLIN

Era evidente que sopesaba la situación. Por las mañanas, al despertarse, me tocaba; a veces incluso me besaba en el hombro, pero si le decía buenos días se tensaba de inmediato, luego se relajaba y salía de la cama. Se sobresaltaba cada vez que sonaba el teléfono; si yo no respondía, él bajaba el volumen del contestador automático, para no oír el mensaje. También bajaba el volumen del televisor, después de mirarlo un momento. A veces lo sorprendía revolviendo los cd, ojeando los cuadernillos, pasando los duros bordes de la caja por la palma de la mano; pero nunca volvió a poner el estéreo. Una vez lo oí tararear. Yo estaba en mi despacho; él estaba en la otra habitación, y no sabía si él sabía que yo estaba allí. Tareó un minuto una melodía que me resultaba muy familiar, aunque no conseguí recordar el título. Luego, cuando logré recordar parte de la letra de la canción, dejó de cantar. ¡Ay, Justin!, pensé. Pero yo tampoco hablaba. Pronto habré terminado, Justin, y entonces nos marcharemos. Aunque primero debo concluir lo que he empezado.

3.17

DIVINE

Esa vez no llamé a la puerta. Supuse que ya no era un extraño y entré directamente, sin hacer ruido, pero tampoco de puntillas; crucé el vestíbulo y el pasillo hacia la luz que salía del estudio de Colin.

No entendía qué sentido tenía vivir en una casa de veinte habitaciones si solo se usaba una, y esa olía a libros cubiertos de moho. ¿Sabéis?, si yo viviera en la casa de los Deacon, me pasearía por todas partes.

Justin también parecía tener su propia habitación, y como estaba arriba, era casi como si no estuviera. Se pasaba el día encerrado en el ático. Colin me dijo cómo se llamaba esa habitación, pero no me acuerdo. A veces lo veía allí arriba, junto a la ventana, observando el mundo como la anciana señora Bates en esa película, *Psicosis*; y debo recordaros, por si acaso, que la vieja estaba muerta.

Pero al menos estaba Colin, o tal vez debería decir el escritorio de Colin, que tenía más de tres metros de largo y la mitad de ancho, y era tan alto que incluso Colin, que era altísimo, tenía que sentarse en una silla especial para poder escribir allí; decir que ese escritorio era una antigüedad no le haría justicia; era más bien como una estatua, un… un monumento, todo tallado y con incrustaciones de oro o algo así; al menos era dorado, con la superficie de mármol, y encima del mármol había un tapete de cuero rojo, pero apenas se veía, porque estaba cubierto por montones y montones de papeles. A veces los montones no tenían más de dos o tres hojas, pero otras veces me parecía que había en ellos papel suficiente para varios libros, y en medio de todos los papeles estaban las dos máquinas de escribir; la eléctrica, plateada y reluciente, siempre emitiendo un ligero zumbido; y la manual, negra y silenciosa; y entre medias atisbé la calva de Colin, inclinada sobre el escritorio.

Estaba roncando.

Creo que nunca se me había ocurrido pensar que Colin Nieman pudiera tener problemas, como todo el mundo. Siempre me había parecido que en la vida solo hay un par de cosas por las que preocuparse: cómo pagar las facturas y quién te calentará por la noche. Y estas eran cosas de las que Colin Nieman, con su dinero y su aspecto, podía desentenderse más o menos. ¿No era eso lo que quería decir aquel pasaje que me leyó? Pero supongo que tenía el problema de qué hacer con el resto del día, cuando no estaba firmando cheques o follando. Ya sabéis que Webbie fue a la universidad y que Wade pinta, y al ver a Colin dormido sobre el escritorio, comprendí que había decidido llenar sus días escribiendo, aunque creo que eso no significaba demasiado para él, que solo era una manera de evadirse de lo demás.

Colin levantó la cabeza de repente. Tenía el ceño fruncido, pero no sabía si lo frunció al verme o si ya lo había fruncido antes.

—Reggie —dijo.

—No se te ocurra meterte ahí. No cuelgues el cartel de cerrado. Me llamo Divine.

Colin sonrió, pero su sonrisa no bastó para reconfortarme, porque no parecía que su humor hubiese cambiado.

—¿Has venido a verme?

—Como verás no llevo un azadón en la mano. No soy un bracero negro que viene a la Casa Grande para decir que ha terminado su trabajo. ¿Que si he venido a verte? ¡Hay que joderse!

—Quítate los pantalones.

—¿Qué?

—Que te quites los pantalones y te des la vuelta.

—Directo al grano. Un hombre con el que me identifico plenamente.

—Lo que quiero es tu culo. Quítate los pantalones, date la vuelta y cierra la boca.

Bueno.

Primero cerré la boca, luego me di la vuelta y luego me desabroché los pantalones y empecé a bajármelos.

—No del todo —dijo Colin—. Así está bien.

Tenía los pantalones por debajo de las caderas. Sentía el aire frío en las piernas, pero el culo aún seguía cubierto por los faldones de la camisa.

—Levántate la camisa. Solo... así vale.

Entonces me fijé en que la puerta estaba abierta y quise ir a cerrarla, pero supuse que no debía moverme. Y me quedé allí, esperando y confiando en que a la señorita Justin no se le ocurriera venir en ese momento para preguntar a Colin qué le apetecía cenar.

¡Como si fuera a hacer tal cosa!

«Cúpula». Entonces lo recordé. Cúpula era como Colin llamaba a la habitación donde Justin se pasaba el día entero. Quédate allí, supliqué, quédate en la cúpula.

Luego oí que la silla de Colin crujía cuando él se movió. Ya viene, me dije, pero en lugar de pisadas lo que oí fue el ruido de la máquina de escribir, y confieso que al oírlo se me cortó la erección, se evaporó como el agua en el desierto, y me quedé de pie frente a la puerta abierta, con ganas de cerrarla, no porque temiera que Justin pudiera verme, sino por miedo a que viera lo que Colin estaba haciéndome, aunque en realidad no era nada.

La máquina de escribir seguía sonando a mis espaldas, pero Colin no decía nada, y yo pensé en aquel saco, en aquella funda de tela elegante llena de papel de escribir, pero lo imaginé con los agujeros de los ojos ya recortados, y miré la superficie de mármol de la mesa y luego a Colin, y vi que Colin la miraba como si fuera humana, como si estuviera conversando con ella, y entonces caí en la cuenta de lo que pasaba: estaban hablando de mí.

3.18

WEBBIE

Hijos míos, resonaba la voz de mi padre por toda la casa, *mil plagas han amenazado a nuestra tierra.* Hijos míos, interpelaba, *la tierra, como sabéis, no es fácil compañera: nos pone a prueba con sequías e inundaciones, nos abrasa de calor y nos congela de frío. Nos envía granizadas y plagas de langostas, incendios y tornados; nos sostiene sobre la palma de su mano y se considera con libertad para cerrar el puño cuando quiera, atenazándonos con su furia.*

En ese momento sonó el teléfono, como si se tratara de una pequeña bendición. Aplasté el auricular contra un oído y me tapé el otro con un dedo para no oír la voz de mi padre.

—¿Sí?
—Webbie.
—Hola, Wade.

En la pausa que se produjo hasta que Wade volvió a hablar la voz de mi padre penetró en mis oídos: *Hemos luchado con ahínco para llegar hasta aquí, hemos luchado con ahínco para domesticar a esta tierra y hacerla nuestra...*

—¿Cómo te va? —preguntó Wade.
—Como siempre. El reverendo está a punto de volverme loca con sus sermones contra los infieles, aunque por lo demás no puedo quejarme.
—Hace tiempo que no nos vemos. Demasiado.

No respondí de inmediato, pero mi silencio solo sirvió para que la voz de mi padre resonara de nuevo en mi cabeza: *Estos enemigos no son nada comparados con lo que ahora nos amenaza...*

—¿De qué enemigos habla?
—Ya puedes imaginártelo —dije, intentando reír—. Los cristianos siempre ven al diablo por todas partes.
—Ya, ya. —Hubo una pausa brevísima, una palabra se coló bajo: *insidioso,* y Wade dijo—: ¿Qué has estado haciendo?

—Wade, por favor, no me lo preguntes. No puedo...

... *el león disfrazado de cordero*...

Bajé la vista y vi que tenía la mano apoyada en el pecho. Me pregunté qué efecto produciría en los demás esta postura, en alguien que me viera por la ventana, en alguien que no supiera con quién estaba hablando o incluso en quien lo supiera.

—Webbie, estoy muy solo. Divine nunca está en casa; se pasa el día por ahí. Y Colin y Justin no vienen nunca. Y... Webbie, por favor. Me quedo mirando los enormes lienzos vacíos y lo único que deseo es hablar con alguien.

... *que las ciudades de la llanura no cayeran en la perversidad nacida del lujo*...

—Hablar —repetí, en tono ausente.

—Solo hablar, Webbie. Solo... una comida, un poco de vino, una velada agradable.

... *la senda recta es angosta, pero es la única que conduce hasta el Señor. No os dejéis distraer por los placeres de esta tierra*...

—¿Webbie?

—Wade, no puedo. Tengo que prepararle la cena a mi padre.

—Son las dos...

—La comida. Una comida con cierto retraso.

Colgué el teléfono justo a tiempo de oírle decir a mi padre: *Alejad de vuestro lado la tentación, de lo contrario perderéis para siempre esos tesoros.* Me quedé como paralizada por sus palabras. ¿Cuáles, me pregunté, eran mis tentaciones? ¿Cuáles mis tesoros? Hacía mucho tiempo que todo quedaba reducido al tira y afloja entre estos dos hombres. Wade y mi padre. ¿Cuál era la tentación? ¿Cuál el tesoro? ¿O era todo una construcción absurda, un intento por encajar dos variables en una ecuación a la que no pertenecían? Recordé lo que dijo Colin sobre las cosas que me negaba a reconocer.

Bajé la vista y vi que mi mano seguía apoyada sobre el pecho. Y la aparté bruscamente, como si me quemara. Otra vez el mismo dilema: ¿qué era lo que quemaba y qué era lo quemado?

Mi padre no había reanudado su discurso, pero yo seguía atrapada en sus palabras. El teléfono estaba al lado del frigorífico y en el frigorífico había un imán con la siguiente inscripción: *Porque Dios amaba tanto al mundo que*... El resto de la cita se había borrado con el paso de los años, y parecía como si el Señor amase tanto al mundo que me entregara las notas que mi padre pegaba en el frigorífico con el imán. Porque el Señor amaba tanto al mundo que *limpia a fondo el cuarto de baño*. Porque el señor amaba tanto al mundo que *visita a Alma Kiehler para ver por qué no fue a la iglesia el domingo pasado*. Porque el Señor amaba tanto al mundo que *prepara el traje azul y la corbata roja*. Hoy el Señor amaba tanto al mundo que le había entregado una lista de ingredientes para preparar un guiso de carne, y al final de la lista mi padre había escrito: «Estoy cansado de hurgar en la basura en busca de comida. Si no tienes ganas de cocinar, prepara un buen guiso y podrás ahorrarte la molestia de verme unos cuantos días».

Le di la vuelta a la nota sin pararme a pensar en ello. «Esta noche, sobras —escribí—, si no te basta, llama a una de tus Damas. No volveré a casa hasta mañana.»

Cuando me ponía el abrigo me pregunté: «¿A casa?» Y antes de salir volví a entrar en la cocina, taché la palabra «casa» y dejé solo el «volveré». Luego salí corriendo y me metí en el coche; arranqué y me fui de allí. No iba a casa de Wade; tampoco a casa de Justin. Iba en busca de un hombre. De un hombre negro, para ser más exacta. Colin tenía razón. Ya iba siendo hora de sacar a la luz unas cuantas cosas.

No me acosté con nadie durante el año que pasé en Howard. La desenvoltura de los demás estudiantes me intimidaba, y también su conocimiento del mundo; de manera que opté por competir en la arena académica. Pero cuando me trasladé a Columbia me metí en un atolladero. Hice amigos, salí con varios hombres. Todos tenían sus puntos fuertes y sus debilidades; ninguno de ellos produjo en mí un sentimiento parecido al amor, aunque supongo que la culpa era más mía que suya. Ninguno de estos hombres era negro, cosa en la que ya reparé en su momento, pero entonces no le di ninguna importancia. Ya habrá tiempo, me dije; y ciertamente, ya habría tiempo.

Pero no lo había, ni entonces ni ahora; no había tiempo que perder, tiempo que esperar. Cuando salí de casa de mi padre, cuando salí de Galatia y dejé atrás a Wade y a Justin, e incluso a Lucy Robinson, lo hice con la intención de llegar hasta Kansas City, pero finalmente me quedé en Wichita, una ciudad anodina cuya red de carreteras parece sugerir que viven allí millones de habitantes, aunque su población real no pasa de doscientos cincuenta mil. Entre esos miles de personas había una abundante población negra, barrios, parques, clubes, iglesias, calles y calles llenas de viejos Chryslers y Buicks relucientes y Caddys muy cuidados que circulaban como gigantescos escarabajos acorazados. Pensaba en ir a un bar, escuchar la música que mi padre tenía en casa pero que nunca oía: Ella, Sarah, Mahalia; pero resultó que no necesité esperar tanto.

Eran más de las cinco cuando vi un pequeño parque donde dos niñas negras, que vestían largos anoraks, jugaban a la pelota con mitones en las manos. Le pedí un café a una camarera imperturbable, que pareció no reparar en mi presencia, y me senté en un banco del parque para observar a las niñas. Me gustaba no saber sus nombres. En

Galatia todo el mundo sabe cómo se llama todo el mundo, y a qué se dedica. Las niñas ni siquiera me miraron.

—Disculpe, señorita, ¿espera usted a alguien por casualidad?

Levanté la vista y vi a un hombre alto, ligeramente entrado en carnes, pero bien formado. Tenía la piel suave y cremosa como el interior de la cáscara de una castaña, y las mejillas salpicadas de pecas, tan oscuras y redondas que parecían pintadas con rotulador. Igual que yo, llevaba una taza de café en la mano.

—No conozco a nadie en esta ciudad.

—Entonces, permítame que me presente —dijo, y esperó un momento, como para darme tiempo a impedírselo—. Me llamo Wallace Anderson. —Me ofreció la mano, y yo se la estreché.

—Yo soy Webbie. Webbie Greeving. —Me retuvo la mano hasta que hube dicho mi apellido.

—Es el nombre más bonito que he oído desde Navidad —dijo, y los dos nos echamos a reír. Pero algo me incitó entonces a decirle mi nombre completo.

—William Edward Burghardt Greeving —dije—. A. William Edward Burghardt Martina Greeving.

Me miró un momento, luego soltó una carcajada y dijo:

—Webbie. Un nombre bonito para una mujer bonita. —Dio un sorbo a su café, volvió a reír y, tras deliberar un momento, se sacó una petaca del abrigo—. ¿Le molesta si...?

Levanté mi taza.

—En absoluto.

—De modo que no es usted del barrio.

Me eché a reír.

—¿Acaso me había visto alguna vez por aquí?

—Bueno, es un barrio grande.

—Soy del norte. De Galatia.

—Es la primera vez que conozco a alguien de Galatia.

—No somos muchos.

—Entonces, mi suerte es aún mayor, ¿no le parece? Ustedes son pocos, nosotros muchos, y soy yo el privilegiado.

Estaba sentado en un banco del parque, vuelto hacia mí, con la rodilla a pocos centímetros de la mía. Hablaba con naturalidad. Me preguntó por Galatia, me habló de su barrio, que era plano como una tortita a la plancha pero que aún llevaba el nombre de Tower Hill. Cuando nos terminamos el café, volvimos a la cafetería para tomar otro y compartimos un plato de rosbif con puré de patatas y salsa. Aún no habían quitado la decoración de espumillón y guirnaldas, y había también un pequeño naranjo con bombillas de colores, como los que se ven en los restaurantes chinos de Nueva York. Al cabo de un rato dejó de llamarme Webbie y empezó a llamarme señorita, y luego me llamó sencillamente niña, y cuando fuimos a su diminuta casa, vi que allí había un auténtico árbol de Navidad, discretamente decorado, ya seco. Me llamaba linda y cariño y bonita, me preparaba bebidas muy cargadas y no me preguntaba por qué había ido a Wichita. Su casa estaba desordenada, pero no sucia, era la típica vivienda de soltero, y sobre la repisa de la chimenea había dos fotografías de 18 × 24 cm de muchachas adolescentes. No le pregunté por ellas.

Tiró de la cinta que yo llevaba en el pelo y la acarició con los dedos hasta que esta se soltó y me cayó sobre la cara. Yo le acaricié las sienes, la coronilla. Él no dejaba de sonreír, mostrando un buen puñado de dientes blancos y sanos.

—Estás temblando, pequeña Webbie.

—Hace mucho tiempo que no...

—Es una lástima. Una mujer tan guapa como tú no debería verse obligada a esperar.

—Nadie me obliga a esperar —dije, sin interpretar correctamente sus palabras, y él me cerró los labios con el dedo.

—A lo mejor tú misma te obligas. ¿A qué esperas?

—¿Yo? No sabía que estuviera esperando algo. —Pero nada más decir esto pensé: A que muera mi padre. Aunque no era la verdad; no era más que rabia. Pensé en Wade y en Justin y en Lucy; pensé, pensé, pensé y cerré los ojos.

Supuse que me besaría, pero no ocurrió nada. Tras una larga pausa, pasó suavemente un dedo por mis pestañas.

—¿Dónde estás, dulce Webbie? Vuelve a mí, cariño.

Abrí los ojos.

—¿Qué?

—No cierres los ojos. Nada de lo que vas a ver puede asustarte.

—¿Cómo lo sabes?

Se rió, me puso los dedos en el pecho y desabrochó el botón superior de mi camisa.

—Porque voy a mostrarte a ti misma, tal como eres —dijo, desabrochándome otro botón—. No tienes miedo de ti misma, ¿verdad?

—Por supuesto que sí —dije, y él volvió a reír.

—Bueno, no te preocupes. Esta noche soy tuyo. Esta noche Wallace Anderson está aquí para protegerte de A. William Edward Burger Greeving, si eso es lo que necesitas.

—Te olvidas de Martina.

—También te protegeré de ella. Te protegeré de todo.

Entonces deslizó las manos por debajo de mi camisa y me acarició los hombros, presionando el músculo con unos pulgares fuertes, frotando, con fuerza al principio; luego, suavemente. En un segundo me bajó los tirantes del sujetador y este cayó lo suficiente para dejar al descubierto las puntas de los pezones.

—Nada de preocupaciones esta noche —dijo, volviendo a masajearme los hombros–, nada de problemas; solo Webbie y Wallace, Wallace y Webbie.

Quería besarlo, hacerle callar, acelerar sus movimientos. Quería explicarle que no deseaba ser seducida por un negro, solo follada, quería decirle que no sabía por qué deseaba una cosa así y que tampoco quería saberlo, que lo único que hacía allí era no saber. Pero la presión de sus pulgares me impedía hacer cualquier movimiento. Bajé la vista para mirarme las manos y vi que tenía los puños apretados. Hice un esfuerzo por relajarlos y sentí que la relajación se extendía a mis brazos, a mis hombros, que descendía por todo mi cuerpo; entonces lancé un profundo suspiro, y Wallace dijo:

—Eso es; mucho mejor, ¿verdad?

Lo miré y sonreí, como poniéndolo a prueba, pidiéndole algo, y él me atrajo hacia sí y me abrazó con suavidad.

—Eso es —repitió, frotándome la espalda con sus enormes brazos–. Webbie está con Wallace esta noche. Esta noche Wallace cuidará de Webbie para que ella no tenga que preocuparse por nada.

3.19

COLIN

Desayuno.

En el bar de Cora.

Zumo de uva y café. Huevos no —de verdad–, pero gracias de todos modos.

Había terminado de leer la *Eneida* y pasado —o retrocedido— a la *Ilíada*. Antes de la *Eneida* había leído el *Infierno*. Como verán me interesaban las comunidades cerradas.

No conocía el griego, así que estaba leyendo una traducción.

No había terminado ni el zumo de uva ni la lectura cuando alguien entró en el bar de Cora. Las campanillas de la puerta me sobresaltaron; a la hora a la que yo solía llegar, «el frenesí del desayuno», como lo llamaba Cora, ya había terminado, y solo un par de veces vi a otro cliente entrar mientras yo desayunaba. Además, la puerta del bar era de cristal, y sospechaba que la mayoría de la gente de Galatia se daría la vuelta sin entrar al ver allí una cabeza blanca tan fácilmente reconocible como la mía. De todos modos, siempre me sentaba de espaldas a la puerta, para no participar activamente en el espectáculo.

Como digo, me sobresalté al oír las campanillas, pero no me volví para mirar. Seguí leyendo, aunque por el rabillo del ojo vi que Cora dejaba lo que estaba haciendo detrás de la barra y se quedaba mirando a la puerta.

Fue entonces cuando oí el sonsonete.

—Vaya —dije—, ¡pero si es el malo, malísimo agente Brown!

Cora se echó a reír. Rió con ganas, e incluso después de taparse la boca con la mano la risa siguió derramándose entre sus dedos.

—Buenos días, sheriff —logró decir al fin—. ¿Le preparo una taza de café?

—No, gracias, Cora. Solo estaré un momento.

—¿Y a usted, señora Krebs?

—No, muchas gracias, Cora. Nos iremos enseguida.

Entonces me di la vuelta; me pareció que Rosemary Krebs bien merecía que me volviese, aunque en un primer momento fingí no reparar en ella.

—¿Qué puedo hacer por usted, sheriff?

—¿Cómo dice, señor Nieman? —preguntó el agente Brown, parpadeando.

—Vamos, sheriff. No me diga que está aquí por casualidad. —Posé la mirada un momento en la de Rosemary Krebs y volví a mirar al agente Brown—. Supongo que viene usted para anunciar algo.

El agente Brown parecía a punto de responder cuando, a sus espaldas, se oyó un ruido de pasos, fuertes y apresurados. Una sombra ocupó la puerta, luego la abrió y Grady Oconnor entró precipitadamente en el bar, casi tropezando con Rosemary Krebs. Estaba jadeando y miró alrededor como sorprendido de ver a tanta gente; luego se quitó la gorra con gesto nervioso y la sostuvo entre las manos.

—Discúlpeme, señora —le dijo a Rosemary Krebs—. Buenos días, Cora. Buenos días, sheriff, señor Nieman.

—¿Qué haces aquí a estas horas, Grady Oconnor?

Grady tragó saliva antes de responder.

—A Calvin Brickley se le ha roto un eje del tractor. Se ha enfadado tanto que nos ha dicho a DuWayne y a mí que podíamos irnos a casa para el resto del día.

—¿Y has pensado que podías almorzar un poco antes?

Grady bajó la mirada.

—Es un poco pronto para almorzar, pero no me importaría desayunar otra vez.

—Señor Nieman —dijo el agente Brown—. Tengo mucho que hacer, señor Nieman.

—No faltaba más, sheriff. Continúe, por favor.

El agente Brown me observó con recelo, como para asegurarse de que no estaba burlándome de él. Rosemary Krebs, a su lado, miraba al vacío y lo único que delataba su impaciencia era el modo de taconear. Grady Oconnor seguía mirando al suelo, pero resultaba imposible decir si estaba mirándose los pies o si miraba los de Rosemary Krebs.

—Señor Nieman —repitió el agente Brown—. Si no le importa que hable de sus asuntos en público…

—Por favor, sheriff, hable con toda libertad. No tengo nada que ocultar. Y usted tampoco tiene nada que revelar.

Cora volvió a reír, con menos fuerza, pero aún de manera evidente.

—Se trata de las pruebas, señor Nieman.

Cora dejó de reír bruscamente.

Noté que Grady Oconnor estrujaba la gorra entre las manos.

Rosemary Krebs aceleró el ritmo de su taconeo, y ese fue el único sonido que se oyó en la sala.

—Todo ha salido bien, señor Nieman.

—¿Bien?

—Las muestras que encontramos… Las muestras de sangre y de tejido eran principalmente de Lucy Robinson y de su amigo. El… el semen no se corresponde con el de ninguno de ustedes.

—Quiere usted decir que yo no violé a Lucy Robinson.

—Parece ser que no, señor Nieman.

—Y si podemos fiarnos de las apariencias, sheriff Brown, lo que todos sabemos que es bastante dudoso, pero si esta vez decidimos hacerlo, entonces podemos deducir que tampoco la ataqué o la rapté, sino que fue alguien que llevaba puesta mi ropa.

Grady Oconnor tiró la gorra al suelo; esta aterrizó a pocos centímetros del taconeante pie de Rosemary Krebs, que perdió el ritmo un segundo, pero volvió a cazarlo de inmediato. Parecía que su pie había alcanzado la velocidad de una máquina de coser, y su ritmo *staccato* tiraba de la tela por debajo de su cuerpo y la extendía a sus espaldas; pero su rostro permanecía inescrutable, y, después de mirarlo, Grady Oconnor no hizo el menor amago de recoger su gorra. El agente Brown no me contestó, y al final, Cora dijo:

—Grady, recoge la puñetera gorra de una vez. Eustace, contesta a este hombre. Y, señora Krebs —añadió, en tono cauteloso pero firme—, deje de taconear o tendré que cortarle el pie.

El agente Brown se sonrojó y lanzó una rápida mirada de enfado a Cora. Vi claramente que estaba a punto de anunciar eso de «mi-cargo-es-sheriff», pero antes de que pudiera decir nada Rosemary Krebs dio un último y sonoro pisotón, y se volvió hacia mí.

—Lo que el sheriff intenta decirle, señor Nieman, es que su nombre está fuera de toda sospecha, y tiene usted libertad para marcharse de Galatia.

Grady se inclinó para recoger su gorra a la velocidad de una flecha.

—Lo que le estoy diciendo —dijo el agente Brown— es que puede marcharse de aquí cuando quiera, señor Nieman. Me ocuparé personalmente de mandar a unos cuantos hombres para que lo ayuden a empaquetarlo todo.

—Le agradezco el ofrecimiento, sheriff, pero se da la circunstancia de que aún tengo que resolver algunos asuntos personales, y no tengo intención de marcharme de Galatia por el momento.

Aunque mis palabras iban dirigidas al agente Brown, las pronuncié sin apartar la vista de Rosemary Krebs. Pero fue Cora quien habló a continuación.

—¿Asuntos que resolver? —preguntó.

Aunque no me gustaba darle la espalda al agente Brown —y tampoco a Grady Oconnor o a Rosemary Krebs—, me di la vuelta para mirar a Cora, pues me pareció que no había en sus palabras un tono precisamente amable. Lo cierto es que lo dijo con hostilidad, y vi que me miraba con expresión de asombro.

—Mi... mi libro —dije, un poco aturullado por su reacción.

—Su libro —repitió, intentando reír—. ¿Se refiere usted a ese que está encima de la mesa?

—Me refiero al que estoy escribiendo, Cora. ¿Qué pasa, Cora?

Cora había cogido un trapo y lo retorcía entre las manos. Movió la mandíbula, pero de su boca no salió sonido alguno. Al fin lo soltó:

—Bueno, eso, eso, eso sí que es perverso, señor Nieman. Es «perverso».

—Cora...

—Tú cállate, Eustace; cállate. Y usted —añadió, volviéndose hacia mí—, ¿qué quiere decir, que no piensa marcharse hasta que termine el libro? El mundo es muy grande; váyase a otra parte a terminar su maldito libro.

—Pero, Cora... Es Galatia lo que me inspira.

—Galatia. ¡Y una mierda! Galatia ya no existe. No existe desde que «él» y su jefe aparecieron por aquí. Dice usted que está escribiendo sobre Galatia, pero lo que está escribiendo lo tiene dentro de la cabeza. ¿Por qué no se lleva la cabeza de aquí y escribe en cualquier otra parte?

—Cora, no la entiendo.

—¡No, claro que no! Pues déjeme que se lo explique, señor Nieman. Aquí tenemos un equilibrio muy frágil, señor Nieman; muy,

muy frágil, y usted se lo ha cargado de golpe y porrazo. En cuanto usted llegó todo se fue a la mierda.

—Pero, Cora... El agente Brown acaba de decir que...

—¡Pero Cora... nada! Nunca se me pasó por la cabeza que usted hiciera lo que decían que había hecho, de lo contrario jamás le habría dejado entrar aquí, pero tan segura como que soy negra que esa puta enana blanca que está aquí piensa que quien violó a la pobre Lucy Robinson lo hizo porque usted había venido aquí, y puede que cuando se vaya los problemas desaparezcan. No necesitamos extranjeros en este pueblo, señor Nieman. No nos gustan, no los necesitamos y no los queremos; de manera que lárguese.

Quería ver cómo reaccionaba Rosemary Krebs ante el hecho de que la llamasen puta y enana, pero el trapo que Cora estaba retorciendo se rasgó entonces ruidosamente. Cora se quedó un momento mirando las dos mitades del trapo; luego las tiró cada una en una dirección. En el momento de silencio que siguió a esta acción, Grady tomó la palabra:

—Yo me ocuparé de él, Cora. Si tú quieres.

Grady y Cora intercambiaron una mirada, y entonces, por primera vez desde que llegué a aquel lugar, percibí la palpable división racial que había en Galatia, al ver que los dos negros allí presentes se miraban como si los tres blancos restantes sencillamente no existiéramos.

Cora volvió a hablar en tono más calmado.

—Tú cállate, Grady Oconnor —dijo—. Si hay algo que no soporto es a los fisgones y a los cotillas. Vuelve a tu trabajo.

Grady no se movió, y, un momento después, yo dije, lo más amablemente que pude:

—Cora, seguro que usted no cree que sus problemas desaparecerán porque yo me vaya. Yo no soy la causa, Cora; alguien está utilizándome como catalizador.

Cora se encogió de hombros y su aliento salió entrecortadamente. Parecía agotada por su invectiva, y se dejó caer contra la barra.

—No sé qué significa esa palabra, señor Nieman.

—Catalizador —dijo otra voz. Era la voz de Rosa, que se encontraba en la puerta de la cocina con un barreño lleno de manzanas en las manos; cuando volvió a hablar lo hizo con voz seca y plana, como si recitara de memoria—: Sustancia que puede producir un cambio en el proceso de una reacción química sin consumirse durante la misma.

Cora la miró con expresión horrorizada. Movió frenéticamente las manos en busca de algo a lo que asirse, pero no encontró nada.

—¡Ay, Rosa, mi vida! ¡Ay, Rosa, no sabía que fueras una extraña!
—Y entonces rompió a llorar.

Sin apartar la mirada de los ojos de Cora, Rosa dijo:
—Señor Nieman, señora Krebs, sheriff Brown, señor Oconnor.
—Pronunció con cuidado los nombres de todos, como si los recitara–: Creo que deben marcharse.

Soltó el barreño y se remangó.

—Bueno, Rosa...

—Por favor, sheriff –dijo Rosa, sonriendo un segundo, pero sin darle la espalda a Cora–. No me obligue a recordarle lo que dice la ley.

Entonces se acercó a Cora, sin fijarse para nada en nosotros, y rodeó con sus delgados brazos la ancha espalda de la amiga. Durante un buen rato nadie se movió ni habló; los cuatro que estábamos al otro lado de la barra nos quedamos mirando a las dos mujeres abrazadas detrás, y el espacio quedó inundado por los sollozos de Cora y el olor a comida. Rosemary Krebs se volvió hacia mí y habló en el mismo tono automático que había empleado Rosa.

—Señor Nieman –dijo; luego hizo una pausa y sonrió–. Es un placer saber que seguiremos disfrutando de su compañía. Rosa, Cora, Grady –añadió, sin mirarlos–, buenos días. Eustace –dijo después, aunque sin añadir nada a este nombre. No era necesario; Eustace sabía bien lo que se esperaba de él y, lentamente, como si quisiera evitar que las campanillas sonaran, abrió la puerta. Pero las campanillas sonaron de todos modos.

3.20

DIVINE

Eso es algo que puede pasar. Puedes parar el coche en alguna carretera de por aquí, una de esas carreteras rurales de dos carriles, recta como una flecha y si no tan plana como una tortita sí como una tortilla –una tortilla rellena, con una protuberancia de salchicha o de tomate o de cebolla aquí y allá–, y puedes conducir con el piloto automático, sobre todo de noche, cuando la única distracción es un par de faros enfrente que cambian a cortas y vuelven a largas, puedes reclinar un poco el asiento hacia atrás y conectar el navegador, ya sabéis lo que quiero decir, puedes cascártela en una de estas carreteras y antes de que te des cuenta ya ha pasado una hora y dos y tres, y de pronto descubres que estás en otro estado. En este caso –quiero decir, si sales de Galatia–, el estado podría ser Nebraska o podría no serlo, porque al fin y al cabo no es tan distinto de Kansas, pero se notan pequeños cambios, quiero decir que empiezas a ver señales en la carretera, aunque solo sea eso, y durante un rato, mientras te das la vuelta o decides continuar, te sientes extranjero, viajero, extraño en una tierra extraña, alguien que circula por la carrera que va a y no por la carretera que viene de. Bueno, os diré una cosa. Yo había pensado en eso. Había pensado en lo fácil que sería conducir y conducir y seguir conduciendo, al carajo Colin y al carajo Wade y al carajo el siniestro Justin y todos los demás marcianos de Galatia. Pero Galatia te ata muy corto, y al cabo de treinta minutos en lugar de tres horas, me di la vuelta, vi un área de descanso y me detuve. Porque, claro, yo no soy de esos que se largan a cualquier parte. Y lo que hice fue pararme.

Vale. Bien, un poco de contexto. Colin había tenido una buena bronca en el bar de Cora cuando el agente Brown le dijo que las pruebas de laboratorio habían demostrado su inocencia. Supongo que Colin quería quedarse en el pueblo, pero Cora pensaba que debía largarse enseguida. Da lo mismo; eso es lo que me contó Blaine Getterling, que lo sabía por Grady Oconnor, y Grady estaba allí. Pero cuando Colin llegó a la casa de los Deacon, ya había cambiado de opinión, supongo, y cuando llegué yo, que era bastante tarde porque había estado en el Big M para ver si olfateaba el rastro del Rata, cuando yo aparecí por la finca de los Deacon, Colin había empaquetado todo lo que había en su oficina, quiero decir, todos los papeles que tenía encima de la mesa estaban metidos en cajas y precintados, y las máquinas de escribir también, y todas las cajas estaban amontonadas junto a la puerta.

Las cajas estaban marcadas con etiquetas, cosas como *Versión 1* y *La abducción* y *La cena, tercera parte*, pero a mí me pareció que el mensaje estaba muy claro y era el siguiente: hora de largarse. Me pareció bien, y me puse en plan: Vale, ¿cuándo nos vamos? Y entonces fue cuando saltó toda la mierda, porque Colin dijo, de ese modo que solo Colin Nieman puede decir que no «nos» íbamos a ninguna parte, que «él» volvía a Nueva York y que «él» se llevaba a Justin y que «yo», si era un poco listo, encontraría un lugar donde vivir mejor que Galatia. Y entonces le pregunté que qué pasaba con su novela, y él se puso en plan: No hay tiempo que perder, y yo le dije: Tú le dijiste a Cora y a los demás que no te irías hasta que terminaras la novela, y él dijo: Sí, vale, he cambiado de opinión. Y luego, creo que le di un poco de pena porque se me acercó y empezó a abrazarme y todo el rollo y se puso a decir que estaba a punto de terminar el libro, que podía terminarlo en cualquier otra parte, y que era hora de marcharse. Y entonces yo le dije: Vale, pues que os den por culo a los dos, y esta es más o menos la versión abreviada; en la versión completa Colin me volvió a follar, pero ¿a quién coño le importa eso?

Al señor Colin Nieman desde luego que no; por cierto, Grady me dijo que su apellido significa 'Nadie'. Y también me dijo que Colin es cocainómano y yo le dije que me lo creía por algunas cosas que había leído, y también le dije que a lo mejor Colin sabía más sobre Lucy Robinson de lo que estaba contando, aunque cuando lo dije no quería culpar a Colin de nada, solo lo dije para que Grady tuviese «algo» que contar por ahí, aunque luego, después de ver a Colin, deseé que Grady tuviese «mucho» que contar.

Cuando salí de casa de Colin, primero decidí ir a ver a Wade, pero luego cambié de opinión y decidí ir al Big M, y luego volví a cambiar de opinión y decidí ir al bar de Sloppy Joe, y luego volví a cambiar de opinión y decidí marcharme del pueblo. A ningún sitio en particular; solo marcharme. Al norte, para ser exactos.

Uno de los proyectos de desarrollo urbano que la puta de Rosemary Krebs puso en marcha desde el principio fue una piscina pública. Como pasaba siempre en Galatea, con la biblioteca y la escuela y la comisaría, durante mucho tiempo se vio un puto cartel en un solar vacío que decía: «Futura sede de bla bla bla». En este caso en el cartel ponía: FUTURA SEDE DE LA PISCINA MUNICIPAL DE GALATEA Y PARQUE ACUÁTICO DE OCIO. Y la única razón por la que recuerdo ese rollo palabra por palabra es porque estuvo allí puesto más de diez o doce años, decolorándose y abombándose a medida que pasaba el tiempo, hasta que al fin, una noche, desapareció, junto con los carteles de MINICENTRO COMERCIAL MUNICIPAL DE GALATEA y ZOO MUNICIPAL DE GALATEA. ¿Dónde coño se piensa que está esa puta, en el sur de California o algo así? Pero, bueno, supongo que de todos los estúpidos proyectos con los que soñaba, la piscina era el que la gente más echaba de menos, pues por aquí no abunda el agua y la mayoría no puede permitirse el lujo de tener su propia piscina. El mejor sitio para nadar –donde acabé yo la noche que Colin me dijo que se marchaba– estaba a unos treinta kilómetros del pueblo. A la gente le gustaba porque no era una poza de agua estancada: se encontraba en un recodo del río Bow que formaba un remanso del tamaño de un campo de baloncesto, y unos cuantos álamos de Virginia daban sombra a la poza durante el verano, y con unos buenos brazos uno se podía sujetar de las cuerdas que colgaban de los árboles para saltar al agua.

Había además un sauce enorme y muy antiguo que, según la leyenda, era el padre de todos los sauces del parque de Galatia y, también, según la leyenda, era el sauce del que colgaron a Eric Johnson.

Ya conocéis esa historia.

Pero yo no pensaba en Eric Johnson cuando fui con el coche hasta allí. Pensaba en Lucy Robinson. Supongo que pensaba en ella porque la única vez que me di un revolcón con Lucy Robinson fue precisamente en esa poza, y lo que ocurrió fue más o menos que el Rata me llevó un día a nadar allí y nos encontramos con Howard Goertzen, Darrell Jenkens y Eddie Comedy que estaban a punto de pelearse con Grady Oconnor, DuWayne Hicks y Melvin Cartwrigth, porque nadie tenía claro a quién pertenecían las tierras donde estaba la poza. Lo que sí sabía todo el mundo era que no pertenecía a Rosemary Krebs, y allí se podría haber ahogado la mitad del pueblo sin que nadie se enterase, porque las reglas eran que los blancos y los negros no podían bañarse al mismo tiempo; además, todo el mundo creía que Eddie Comedy había tenido algo que ver en el linchamiento de Eric Johnson, y había que tener en cuenta que a Eddie Comedy lo nombraron jefe del equipo de fútbol del instituto cuando todo el mundo sabía que Melvin Cartwright lanzaba la pelota el doble de lejos que Eddie, y además, Eddie Comedy corría como una niña. Así que podéis imaginaros que los ánimos se caldearon bastante cuando de pronto aparecimos el Rata y yo, y el enfrentamiento chicos blancos/chicos negros dio paso al enfrentamiento chico/maricón, y como el Rata siempre estaba dispuesto a pelearse con quien hiciera falta, pensé que íbamos a salir de allí con el culo bien caliente. Pero lo que pasó fue que antes de que pudiera pasar nada apareció Myra Robinson con un grupo de niñas de carita blanca, Lee Anne Atkins, Shelly Stadler y, por supuesto, nuestra querida señorita Lucy Robinson, y ahí acabó la cosa. Primero porque hay algo en la presencia femenina que tiende a enfriar las ganas de pelea masculinas, ya sabéis lo que quiero decir, sobre todo cuando esa presencia femenina es la de una «madre», aunque solo tenga diez años más que los hombres implicados, y, por otro lado, el más importante, diría yo, el que nos interesa, no había en toda Galatia un solo negro dispuesto a admitir que la jovencita Lucy Robinson tenía un buen par de tetas y mucho menos dispuesto a quedarse allí mientras ella se quedaba en bikini rojo y bajaba con mucho cuidado hasta la poza con unas chanclas de plástico blancas y unas gafas de sol blancas del tamaño de todo Texas al tiempo que decía: Hola, chicos. Es decir, que la cagó por partida doble. Por eso Grady Oconnor y DuWayne Hicks y Melvin Cartwright y hasta yo, sí, yo, le dijimos a Myra que ya habíamos terminado de bañarnos, que ya no nos apetecía seguir bañándonos y que teníamos mucho que hacer; y nos largamos. Tengo que decir que el Rata no se coscó de nada al principio, y Myra, bueno, la verdad es que siempre me ha flipado hasta qué punto algunos, sobre todo si son mujeres, sobre todo si son mujeres blancas, son capaces de hacerse los tontos.

Siempre lo mismo: primero una cosa, luego otra y luego otra. Siempre Eddie Comedy y luego Melvin Cartwright y luego yo y el

Rata, aunque supongo que, al final, al menos por aquí, siempre es Lucy Robinson.

La primera vez que fui a la poza tenía seis años. Mi padre se metió en el agua y mi madre me ayudó a colgarme de la cuerda y me impulsó con fuerza por encima de la poza; yo tenía miedo de caerme y de matarme, y matar a mi madre de paso, si aterrizaba de golpe encima de ella.

La cuerda seguía donde siempre. Parecía tiesa, como se ponen los cables del teléfono en invierno, y brillaba bajo la luna, cubierta de escarcha. Quien la hubiera usado por última vez era un buen vecino, lo que mi madre llamaba una persona considerada, un buen vecino, porque había dejado el extremo de la cuerda enrollado en unas matas, para que resultara más fácil agarrarla.

No sé, me pareció como si estuviera participando en una carrera. En ese preciso instante, Colin y Justin estaban en la casa de los Deacon, embalando para marcharse, y yo en la poza, aunque no era verano y ni siquiera era «ese» año, no tres o cuatro años atrás, sino diez, doce, y parecía como si cuanto más corriera para alcanzar no sé bien qué, más retrocedía en el tiempo.

No era solo que la situación me sobrepasara. Todo me sobrepasaba siempre, qué coño, ya estaba acostumbrado a eso. Pero esta situación no dejaba de complicarse cada vez más, se me escapaba de las manos, y supongo que tuve un breve momento de iluminación en el que vi claro que siempre había sido así, que yo no le importaba una mierda ni a Colin, ni a Wade, ni, ahora que el Rata se había marchado, a nadie de aquel pueblo apestoso que para mí representaba el mundo entero.

Recuerdo que mi padre decía yo te cogeré, y que mi madre decía ya lo cogeré yo si tú no puedes, y recuerdo que, hace exactamente dos años y dos semanas, un día volví del instituto y me encontré la casa vacía; lo único que quedaba en ella era un árbol de Navidad seco y unas cuantas bombillas fundidas en el techo; las que aún funcionaban se las habían llevado.

La superficie de la poza estaba helada; una especie de canal la cruzaba en el centro, donde el río aún fluía, y supuse que en ese momento fluía bajo la capa de hielo. Había hojas y ramas, y un par de latas de cerveza encima del hielo, congeladas, como clavadas en el sitio.

Recuerdo también que una fría mañana de primavera, cuando aún era temprano, fui a la poza y vi que unos brotes verdes empezaban a asomar desde un hoyo convertido en un pequeño iceberg que aún no se había derretido. Entonces no le di especial importancia, y ahora tampoco se la doy, pero lo recuerdo bien.

Una lámina de hielo se desprendió de la cuerda al sujetarla, y pensé en el condón que Colin no se había puesto para follarme.

Algunas ramas crujieron cuando tiré de la cuerda para comprobar si estaba bien sujeta.

Mi padre me lo había explicado así: puedes columpiarte adelante y atrás y no pasa nada, o puedes columpiarte y caer. O puedes meterte en el coche y volver a casa. Le importaba un carajo.

Mi madre me dijo que los escupitajos se congelaban, pero las lágrimas no, porque son saladas, y tenía razón. Eso me lo dijo otra vez, no la primera vez que vine a bañarme en la poza. A mi madre también le importaba un carajo, pero, de todos modos, decía que no soportaba pensar en su niño y ver en lo que se había convertido.

La cuerda estaba atada al sauce.

Para ser sincero, creo que debo decir que cuando me agarré de ella lo primero que pensé es que ojalá tuviera los calzoncillos limpios, pero luego me dije que lo mismo daba, porque el agua estaba sucia y todo quedaría convertido en un bonito y neutro uniforme gris, y me pareció una pena estropear mi abrigo, esa prenda tan bonita que Wade me había regalado las Navidades pasadas, pero debía continuar. La próxima vez ya pensaría en vestirme adecuadamente para la ocasión.

Volví a tirar de la cuerda para asegurarme de que estaba bien sujeta y dije en voz alta: No te andes con rodeos, Divine, y luego me agarré de la cuerda, trepé y salté, y lo único que noté fue un viento gélido en la cara, y quise detenerlo, y lamenté que mi padre no estuviera en el agua y mi madre no estuviera esperándome en tierra firme, y pensé que en ese momento solo tenía dos opciones, o caerme o volver atrás, y me esforcé para que mis últimas palabras fueran buenas, pero no se me ocurrió nada, aunque me pregunté dónde estaría Webbie e incluso llegué a esperar, sorpresa sorpresa, que Lucy Robinson apareciera sana y salva, y luego, en lugar de decir adiós, dije ¡a la mierda!, y me dejé llevar.

3.21

WEBBIE

El segundo día que pasé con Wallace Anderson fuimos a dar un paseo en coche por Wichita y pasamos junto a una biblioteca.

—Para un momento, por favor —le pedí a Wallace, y me pareció que usaba los parachoques de su enorme y viejo Cadillac para despejar un hueco para aparcar entre dos contenedores de basura.

Después de haber pasado varios años en Columbia trabajando a tiempo parcial en una biblioteca, y puesto que también dedicaba dos días a la semana a la biblioteca de Galatia, no necesitaba consultar el catálogo; fui directamente a la sección de criminología y escogí un gran volumen ilustrado sobre el crimen organizado que llevaba por título *Las víctimas y la Mafia*. ¿Qué intentas decirme?, me preguntó Wallace, en ese tono artificial con que hablan quienes no están acostumbrados a visitar las bibliotecas, y di un respingo al oír su voz, porque estaba tan acostumbrada a ir siempre sola a todas partes que se me había olvidado que venía conmigo. Lo miré y sonreí, pero no dije nada; él se alejó de mí para mirar un cartel de un chimpancé con orejas de burro que sostenía un libro al revés, y poco después, supongo que cuando leyó el rótulo del cartel, se echó a reír, se volvió hacia mí y se encogió de hombros. Luego metió las manos en los bolsillos y dijo:

—Sigue, sigue, haz lo que tengas que hacer.

No estoy segura de qué buscaba. La palabra «víctimas» en el título me había llamado la atención, y pasé las páginas, observando a las víctimas, aunque no recuerdo haber pensado en Lucy Robinson mientras miraba aquellas fotografías. Lo que sí recuerdo es una foto de un hombre llamado Salvatore Genovese. Salvatore Genovese, según explicaba el pie de foto, había amasado una fortuna como corredor de apuestas, dirigiendo una operación para no sé qué sindicato de Nueva York, y cuando lo pillaron le cortaron los dedos con la misma herramienta que Coach Carting usaba para abrir las taquillas que aún conservaban la cerradura al final del curso escolar. No sé cómo describir las manos que vi en esa foto, porque no se parecían a nada, ni a la pezuña de un cerdo guisada con verduras, ni al cuerpo de un gato atropellado por un coche, y, desde luego, no se parecían a unas manos. Quienes castigaron a Salvatore Genovese no lo habían matado, pero se jactaban de que, incapaz de soportar el dolor, había saltado por una ventana, traspasando el cristal, desde un sexto piso, y como prueba de su inocencia dijeron que si hubieran tenido intención de tirarlo habrían abierto la ventana. Me quedé un buen rato mirando la foto. Las manos de Salvatore se tornaron borrosas, y por momentos parecían casi normales, pero otras veces se parecían tan poco a unas manos que ni siquiera resultaban amenazantes, aunque siempre volvían violentamente a su estado de mutilación, y, cuando Wallace me quitó el libro de las manos y lo cerró, vi que mis manos estaban hechas un ovillo, más que hechas un ovillo, cerradas, incluso agarrotadas, con los puños fuertemente apretados. Mientras Wallace volvía a dejar el libro en la estantería, me miré las manos e intenté abrirlas, pero no pude. Ya no me respondían, como las manos de la foto, y mientras las miraba recordé una escena del libro de Colin, *La Bestia*, en la que aparecía una anciana que llevaba tanto tiempo con los puños apretados que las uñas se le habían clavado en las palmas de las manos. Entonces recordé que *La Bestia* no era de Colin, sino de Justin, y pensé en la boca de Justin, cerrada como las manos de esa mujer, y como las mías. Vi los labios de Justin sellados e imaginé que sus dientes se clavaban en la carne de las mejillas, y entonces sentí algo parecido a la vergüenza, porque había entrado en la biblioteca pensando en Lucy Robinson y enseguida me había olvidado de ella para pensar en Colin, en Justin, en mí. Wallace me abrazó por detrás; sentí las palmas de sus manos en mis nalgas y el suave tamborileo de sus dedos. Luego dijo:

—No me cuentes nada que no quieras contarme. —Y se quedó allí, abrazándome suavemente, mientras sentía que su respiración entraba por el cuello de mi abrigo abierto y se me metía por la camisa, fresca en comparación con mi espalda sudorosa—. Tómate todo el tiempo que necesites.

Y me pregunté cómo algo que «yo no podía querer» resultaba tan agradable.

Esa noche me desperté con una pesadilla. Soñaba, claro está, con manos mutiladas, pero las manos de mi sueño eran negras: eran mis manos. Al principio me sentí desorientada, y me asusté aún más, pero luego recordé dónde estaba. Reconocí la cómoda de pino con su brillante chapa de poliuretano apagada por el polvo y la luz de la luna; reconocí las ciento doce gorras con distintos rótulos que colgaban de pequeñas perchas en una pared; y reconocí a Wallace. Estaba durmiendo, desnudo. Antes de dormir habíamos tenido una sesión de sexo, nos habíamos duchado y luego él se había puesto unos calzoncillos tipo bóxer; pero yo le metí una pierna entre las suyas y se los quitó, sirviéndose de mi pie para tirarlos al suelo. Wallace me sonrió, chasqueó la lengua y me abrazó con la fuerza de un oso, como si yo hubiera hecho algo prodigioso.

Cuando me desperté, Wallace dormía boca arriba, con el vientre suave y ligeramente ondulado, como la piel de un pudín, y salpicado de vello que parecía chocolate. Respiraba con fuerza, aunque sin llegar a roncar, pero su vientre no parecía moverse con la respiración, como si todo el aire estuviese contenido en las invisibles profundidades de su cuerpo. Tenía una mano entre el pene y el ombligo, y me sorprendió el contraste entre las dos pieles, la piel seca y agrietada de sus manos, con las palmas claras y el dorso ligeramente cubierto de pecas, y la delicadeza casi absurda de su pene suave, que desde donde yo lo miraba y bajo aquella luz parecía el talón del pie de un bebé. Me bastó con mirar a Wallace para recordar su tacto, las manos que me frotaban los hombros como si fueran papel de lija, desprendiendo las impurezas, y el pene, que yo había tenido entre mis manos y dentro de mí, y también contra mis mejillas, aunque Wallace no me había permitido metérmelo en la boca.

Al girar un poco la cabeza le vi la cara, los labios separados y húmedos, las mejillas redondeadas y cubiertas por la barba de un día. Tenía el pelo un poco largo y las pestañas asombrosamente largas y espesas, casi femeninas. Esa noche yo le había estado gastando bromas a cuenta de sus pestañas, y él me dijo entonces que, una vez, su madre le dijo que los únicos rasgos femeninos de Wallace eran sus pestañas y su modestia, y se rió un poco de sí mismo, y bajó la mirada al suelo.

Quedaba en la habitación un ligero olor a sexo. Un olor rancio y penetrante como un guiso al fuego.

Las llaves de mi coche estaban encima de la cómoda. Wallace había doblado mi ropa y la había guardado en un cajón, junto a la suya. Era ordenado, dijo, aunque no demasiado limpio, y cuando le pedí que me explicara la diferencia, escribió mi nombre sobre la capa de polvo que cubría la cómoda.

Ordenado, dijo, pero no limpio.

Escribió W-E-B-B-Y.

La casa entera se estremeció cuando saltó el termostato de la calefacción, pero no me asusté. Ya estaba acostumbrada a ese ruido; la pared temblaba como cuando se cierra una puerta en otra habitación que anuncia la llegada de un vecino ruidoso.

Le había pedido a Wallace que pusiera la calefacción fuerte, para que no necesitáramos mantas ni ropa.

Cogí la mano de Wallace.

Me dije a mí misma que esa no era la razón por la que yo me había ido de Galatia y estaba en Wichita.

No lograba entender qué significaba todo aquello.

Me llevé su mano a la mejilla y dejé que sus nudillos acariciasen mi piel; Wallace murmuró algo en sueños.

No sé si dijo alguna palabra con sentido, pero yo lo entendí de todos modos, y me tranquilicé, me dormí con sus palabras en mis oídos.

—No hace falta que vuelvas —me dijo Wallace—. Puedes quedarte.

Y me quedé una noche más.

3.22

AGENTE BROWN

En cuanto tuvo ocasión le envió un fax al sheriff Peterson, en Bigger Hill, que había investigado la agresión que se produjo en el Big M hacía cosa de tres años. El caso seguía sin resolverse, se dijo el agente Brown, aunque no lo mencionó en la nota que le envió a Petey. Eso habría sido excesivo. Pobre muchacho; el agente Brown no conseguía recordar cómo se llamaba y llegó a pensar que quizá nunca se había sabido su nombre. Daba lo mismo, el muchacho en cuestión estaba rondando por los alrededores del Big M cuando ocurrió todo, y la verdad es, según le dijo Petey al agente Brown, que la víctima, si se puede llamarla así, había sido vista merodeando por el aparcamiento situado detrás del Big M en más de una ocasión, y no hace falta ser detective para entender lo que eso significaba. El caso es que el chico había estado en el mismo cobertizo donde apareció muerto Eddie Comedy en el mes de septiembre —el agente Brown no le preguntaba a Petey en su nota si sabía algo nuevo, pero sí le preguntaba si tenía alguna pista de quién podía haber incendiado el cobertizo semanas antes—, y lo que pasó fue que el chico dobló una esquina, y Petey prefirió no pensar en qué estado se hallaba el pobre muchacho, ja, ja, ja, cuando de pronto se encontró cara a cara con aquel hombre «enorme». Luego dijo que el enorme hombre en cuestión iba comiendo algo de una lata. ¿Con qué lo golpeó el hombre?: al parecer la víctima ni siquiera parpadeó cuando el hombre le asestó el golpe en la frente.

Maíz, según dijeron los forenses, y lo que Petey quería saber era qué clase de hombre anda por ahí con un abrelatas en el bolsillo.

Después el asunto se tornó confuso. El muchacho quedó inconsciente después de recibir el golpe, lo cual fue casi una bendición para él, y se despertó en un hospital al cabo de tres semanas. Al despertarse supo que tenía unas treinta y siete fracturas —el agente Brown pensaba que ese era el número exacto— en los brazos, las piernas y los dedos de las manos y los pies, que se había roto la pelvis y tenía todos los dedos dislocados, sujetos solo por la piel. Un año después de la agresión, el chico seguía impedido y solo era capaz de sostener una cuchara para tomarse la sopa, único alimento que podía ingerir, puesto que había perdido hasta el último diente y las dos fracturas de la mandíbula nunca llegaron a soldarse por completo, y ningún dentista se atrevía a hacer el trabajo protésico necesario para proporcionarle al chico una dentadura en condiciones.

Pero lo más interesante de todo, según le dijo Petey al agente Brown, lo más interesante era que, aparte de los importantes daños sufridos en la mandíbula y, por supuesto, el primer golpe con la lata de maíz, el chico no presentaba otras lesiones en la cabeza ni en el torso, salvo en la pelvis, que quedó fracturada en cuatro puntos distintos, y por eso era muy posible que no pudiera volver a andar, al menos a andar sin dificultad. Pero no había nada que técnicamente, si se puede decir así, representara una amenaza para su vida, aunque habría muerto de no ser porque otros muchachos lo encontraron dos días más tarde. Pese a todo, no podía decirse que le hubieran dado una paliza mortal. Eso, claro está, en el caso de que hubiera llegado a morir, que fue lo que dijo desear en cuanto pudo hacer algo parecido a hablar. Lo que Petey quería decir es que, más o menos, habló. Y dijo que deseaba estar muerto.

El timbre del fax siempre sobresaltaba al agente Brown. No lo usaba lo suficiente para llegar a acostumbrarse a aquel sonido, y la mayoría de las veces quien enviaba el fax era la prima de Nettie, que se llamaba Betty, o Hettie, daba lo mismo, algo que rimaba con Nettie, y como era secretaria en Kansas City usaba el fax de su jefe para enviarle a Nettie recetas, patrones de vestidos y chistes del periódico dominical. Pero esta vez el envío era para él, y era de Petey, y era un retrato robot del agresor del muchacho, según la descripción ofrecida por este. Lo único que Petey había escrito en el papel era: «Ten en cuenta que era de noche y el chico estaba borracho». El agente Brown lo tuvo en cuenta y se quedó un buen rato mirando el fax, luego lo estrujó y lo tiró a la papelera. Nettie le preguntó entonces. Eustace, dijo, ¿era para mí?, y el agente Brown respondió: No, era una de esas pruebas que hace la máquina ella sola, y Nettie volvió a decir: Me gustaría poder desconectarla; ese pitido me vuelve loca, y el agente Brown admitió que a él le pasaba lo mismo, y luego sacó el papel arrugado de la papelera y se lo guardó en el bolsillo, y entonces advirtió que estaba llegando una segunda página, un segundo retrato robot, el del muchacho tal como el policía que lo había dibujado imaginó que podría haber sido antes de perder todos los dientes y de que le rompieran la mandíbula. El agente Brown observó aquel rostro, los labios finos, los dientes saltones, y aunque no entendía cómo el artista lo había adivinado, lo cierto era que, en conjunto, su aspecto recordaba a un hurón, y el artista incluso había llegado al extremo de dibujar un par de espinillas en la frente del chico, y entonces el agente Brown comprendió por qué lo apodaban el Rata. La nota de Petey que acompañaba a este retrato robot pedía ante todo al agente Brown si podía proporcionarle alguna pista sobre la identidad del muchacho, y también decía que este, que según se había figurado el agente Brown aún debía de seguir en el hospital, había conseguido robar un poco de insulina e inyectársela hacía seis meses, que había muerto y que, entre nosotros, decía la nota de Petey, tal vez había sido lo mejor.

El agente Brown también arrancó esa página, se la guardó en el bolsillo con la primera y, mientras lo hacía, se le ocurrió que el hombre le había hecho lo que le había hecho a aquel chico, al Rata, a Lamoine Wiebe —bueno, el agente Brown se lo figuró, aunque ahora eso no servía de nada, y el pobre Carol Wiebe ya había sufrido bastante por su único hijo—, y que le había hecho lo que le había hecho en cuestión de una hora, como máximo, y luego pensó que ya habían pasado dos meses desde la desaparición de Lucy Robinson. El agente Brown se dijo que quemaría las dos páginas del fax en cuanto llegara a casa. Entretanto entonó su más sentido «Perdóname, Señor», pero hizo cuanto pudo por no pensar en qué estado se encontraría Lucy Robinson en ese momento, aunque resultó que eso no tenía la menor importancia, pues no tardaría en descubrirlo con total exactitud.

4

4.01

SAWYER JOHNSON

Mi madre me arrastra para que ande más deprisa, y yo no quiero, casi no puedo respirar, pero ella me arrastra y me lleva cada vez más deprisa. Fuera está oscuro, dice, y yo digo que ya lo sé, y ella me dice que hable en voz baja y que ya debería estar en la cama, pero cuando llegamos a la comisaría, afloja el paso, creo que para dejarme tomar aliento, pero yo levanto la vista y veo que está mirando al edificio, que la ventana está abierta, y oigo voces que gritan, aunque no entiendo lo que dicen, pero las oigo gritar y mi madre vuelve a arrastrarme, más deprisa, ni siquiera tengo aliento para pedirle que vaya un poco más despacio y que no me clave las uñas en la muñeca, y ella me dice que nunca se me ocurra salir de casa solo cuando sea de noche, o terminarás así, dice, terminarás siendo tan solo una voz en una sala.

4.02

HOWARD GOERTZEN

El oscuro montículo parecía una herida en la carretera. Hacía diez años que Lucy Robinson se había detenido en ese mismo cruce, con un vestido sucio y roto, y había gritado pidiendo ayuda por lo que le había hecho ese negro blanco, y ahora solo quedaba el vestido, no el de encaje blanco que llevaba cuando tenía siete años, sino ese otro de terciopelo púrpura que le sentaba tan bien en el baile de Rosemary Krebs, al que asistió acompañada por ese mariquita de Nueva York, y Howard Goertzen se puso unos guantes antes de coger el vestido y tuvo la sensación de que aquello no serviría de nada, pero de todos modos se fue en el coche hasta la comisaría, le entregó el vestido arrugado al agente Brown y se quedó mirando mientras este lo extendía sobre una mesa de aluminio. Había un presagio de muerte en el movimiento del vestido bajo las manos enguantadas del agente Brown, como si la esencia que aquella tela hubiera podido contener se hubiese evaporado, y Howard Goertzen tuvo que tragar saliva para deshacer el nudo que se le estaba formando en la garganta y, cuando al fin pudo hablar de nuevo, lo único que dijo fue «¡Ay, Dios mío!», y cuando el vestido quedó completamente extendido, volvió a decir «¡Ay, Dios mío!», y nada más. El vestido estaba tan hecho jirones que los hilos de la tela parecían formar una red oscura sobre la plateada superficie de la mesa. Estaba deshilachado, hecho trizas, como si se lo hubieran arrancado del cuerpo a latigazos, y parecía descomponerse bajo la capa de barro, sangre y suciedad que lo cubría, y Howard Goertzen le oyó decir al agente Brown «Parece que alguien lo ha metido en una lavadora cargada de cristales rotos», y Howard Goertzen volvió a sentir un nudo en la garganta y volvió a tragar saliva, y luego dijo «Y Lucy... parece como si ese hombre la hubiera metido también en la lavadora». Desde la otra habitación se oía decir a Nettie Ferguson: «Lo que digo es que él dijo que era gay, lo dijo, nada más»; y luego Howard Goertzen dijo: «Pasé por allí con el coche para ver dónde había muerto Charlene. Y allí estaba, justo en el mismo sitio, justo en la esquina de East Adams con la calle Primera. Justo donde ese cabrón la atropelló».

4.03

NETTIE FERGUSON

Era una bolsa de plástico blanca que llevaba escrita la palabra Zabar's en grandes letras mayúsculas de color cobrizo, y no hizo falta que nadie le dijera a nadie de dónde había salido. «Me suena a Nueva York —dijo Eustace nada más verla—. Zay-bar's —dijo, y luego añadió—: Sí, *Jew* York City», y de no ser porque la situación era tan grave y porque Myra Robinson estaba presente, Nettie Ferguson habría soltado una risita por el chiste de Eustace, pero Myra Robinson estaba allí, temblando y sujetando la bolsa por las asas de plástico anudadas, y la bolsa, según había advertido Nettie cuando Myra entró en la comisaría, contenía algo oscuro, blando y aparentemente de poco peso; formaba una especie de pelota en la tripa de Myra Robinson, que la sujetaba con manos temblorosas, y la propia Myra también parecía una enorme pelota ante la gigantesca masa de T. V. Daniels —¡caramba lo que era capaz de comer ese chico!—, que la hacía parecer mucho más pequeña, igual que ella hacía parecer mucho más pequeña a la bolsa, y entre el uno y la otra, Nettie Ferguson apenas veía la bolsa y mucho menos lo que esta contenía. T. V. carraspeó y dijo: «La encontré en su buzón», lo dijo con la voz del chico larguirucho y desgarbado que había sido en otro tiempo, y eso Nettie Ferguson debería saberlo bien, porque lo cuidaba cuando era niño y su Horace aún vivía; por eso, al mirar a T. V. Daniels lo que Nettie Ferguson veía era un niño flaco como un palillo, atrapado bajo un montón de capas de grasa, y a Nettie le pareció triste, le pareció realmente una pena, porque de pequeño le gustaba ver los dibujos animados de *Mickey Mouse* todos los días, y cuando terminaban y sonaba la canción de despedida, el chico estaba tan maravillado que se ponía a bailar delante del televisor, muy despacio, de un modo muy bonito, y Nettie Ferguson era incapaz de imaginar qué aspecto tendría T. V. si ahora sonase la misma canción y se pusiera a bailar. Myra Robinson emitió una especie de chasquido con la lengua al oír las palabras de T. V., y Nettie vio que Eustace le quitaba la bolsa de las manos antes de que se le cayera al suelo. «Vamos, vamos», le decía Eustace para tranquilizarla lo mejor que podía, aunque él mismo admitía que no se le daba muy bien, porque Eustace Brown no sabía consolar. «Vamos, vamos», volvió a decir Eustace —una de las cosas que Nettie Ferguson había aprendido tras años de experiencia en la investigación criminal era la necesidad de precisión en el detalle—. «Vamos, vamos —le decía el sheriff del condado de Cadavera a la desesperada madre de la muchacha desaparecida, a Myra Robinson—. Seguro que no es nada. No pesa nada, no puede ser nada, pero vamos a comprobarlo», y entonces Nettie Ferguson vio que Eustace tiraba de los nudos, que se resistían a sus dedos, y asintió con aprobación cuando Eustace dijo: «Myra, ¿no te habrás encontrado por casualidad con Reginald Packman últimamente?», y Nettie sabía que Eustace intentaba distraer a Myra Robinson para sacarla de su estado de agitación. «Llevo varias semanas buscándolo —continuó Eustace—. No lo encuentro por ningún lado.» Myra Robinson lo miró como si hablase en chino. «¿Qué? —dijo—. ¿Quién?» «Reginald —dijo Eustace, tirando con más fuerza de los nudos— Packman», concluyó, sin haber conseguido desatarlos. Hubo entonces un largo silencio, hasta que T. V. Daniels dijo en voz apenas audible, como con cierta tensión, «Divine». Y Myra Robinson repitió, «¿Divine?» No dejaba de mirar la bolsa que Eustace seguía intentando abrir, como si T. V. le estuviera diciendo que Reginald Packman —¡Divine!— estaba dentro de esa bolsa, mientras Eustace intentaba deshacer el nudo con la llave y Nettie Ferguson pensaba que la bolsa no pesaba nada, y Myra Robinson dijo: «No, no, Divine no», como si ni siquiera existiese, y al cabo de un rato T. V. dijo: «Nadie ha visto a Divine desde hace siglos», y Nettie Ferguson estaba a punto de preguntarle a T. V. cómo estaba tan al tanto de las idas y venidas de Reginald Packman, cuando las asas de la bolsa al fin se soltaron y del interior saltó parte del contenido, derramándose sobre el escritorio de Eustace y formando una especie de nube fina pero casi corpórea. «¿Qué es esto?», dijo Eustace, y T. V. Daniels se tapó la nariz con la mano, como si se tratara de un gas venenoso o algo así, pero Myra Robinson empezó a llorar y a gritar y a toquetear la sustancia, y Nettie Ferguson, que intentaba desenganchar la cadena de sus gafas de los botones de la blusa, tardó un momento en comprender lo que estaba diciendo. «Mi niña –decía Myra Robinson entre sollozos–. Mi niña, mi niña, mi niña. ¡Tu pelo!» Nettie Ferguson sintió de pronto la necesidad de apoyarse en algo y echó mano de la familiar y reconfortante forma del teléfono, que, al sonar inesperadamente, le dio tal susto a la pobre Nettie que esta se desmayó.

4.04

AGENTE BROWN

T. V. Daniels entra con un montón de cartas. «Me pareció extraño –dijo, jadeando– ver todas las banderas rojas levantadas en los buzones. No es normal que todo el pueblo envíe una carta el mismo día.» Siempre que el agente Brown veía a T. V. Daniels tenía que pararse un minuto para asimilar lo gordo que era aquel chico, decir, por ejemplo «setecientos treinta y uno», lo cual no significaba nada, lo cual no era más que el número que le había dado Donnie Miller, el que trabajaba en el silo y había dicho que había pesado a T. V. Daniels igual que pesaba un cargamento de trigo, es decir, pesando el coche de T. V. Daniels con T. V. Daniels dentro, y luego volviendo a pesarlo sin él dentro, pero aquel número en realidad no significaba nada para el agente Brown; lo que sí significaba algo era que Nettie Ferguson se incorporara, quejándose de su artritis a cada paso, hasta abrir la cerradura de la segunda hoja de la doble puerta para que T. V. Daniels pudiera entrar en el edificio, y solo después de asimilarlo el agente Brown fue capaz de coger el montón de fotografías que T. V. le estaba ofreciendo, fotografías que tenían la misma relación con la mano de T. V. Daniels que un sello de correos tiene con las manos de la mayoría de la gente. El agente Brown se puso manos a la obra. Le gritó a Nettie que volviera al teléfono y ojeó las fotografías muy despacio, Polaroids, a juzgar por su aspecto, luego las tiró sobre la mesa y le dijo a T. V.: «Polaroids. De Kodak, para ser más exactos. Lo pone detrás». El agente Brown le espetó a T. V. Daniels: «¿Para qué me molestas con esto? No sirven para nada». T. V. vaciló un momento, luego cogió una de las fotos y dijo: «Mira esta», y el agente Brown entrecerró los ojos y vio que Nettie Ferguson, que no paraba de hacer ruido, intentaba mirar también la foto, por eso el agente Brown se apartó un poco y se puso las gafas, volvió a mirar y dijo: «¿Es una mano?», y T. V. asintió, y el agente Brown dijo: «Lo único que tengo que decir es que quien haya sacado esta foto no sabe enfocar, es lo único que tengo que decir», y entonces T. V. carraspeó y dijo: «Hum, sheriff Brown», lo que fastidió al agente Brown, pues le gustaba que la gente lo llamara primero agente Brown para poder decir que lo llamaran sheriff, pero le gustaba que primero lo llamaran agente Brown. «Sheriff Brown –dijo T. V. Daniels, con voz débil y ahogada–, ¿no ve que la mayoría de las fotos son del mismo color?» Nettie Ferguson pulsó tres teclas en su máquina de escribir. El agente Brown escrutó a T. V. por encima de la montura de concha de sus gafas, que no eran bifocales. «¿Y eso qué significa?» T. V. se pasó las manos por el vientre, cosa que le llevó algún tiempo, y al final dijo: «Creo que son fotografías de un… cuerpo», momento en el que la Royal Electric de Nettie Ferguson produjo ese sonido inconfundible que hace la máquina cuando se encasquillan varias teclas, y el agente Brown se dio una palmada en la frente y dijo: «¡Dios Todopoderoso! ¡La ha descuartizado!». «No, no –dijo T. V. Daniels–. Es lo que parece en las fotos. Pero está entera», y luego se puso a recoger el lío de servilletas sucias y tenedores de plástico y vasos de plástico con varios centímetros de café con leche solidificado en su interior, para extender las fotografías sobre la mesa del agente Brown, y mientras lo hacía decía: «Aquí está la mano, ve… y esta, creo que esta es la muñeca, y este el brazo», y, así, empezó a reunir las piezas una por una, hasta que el agente Brown le sujetó la mano para detenerlo. Nettie Ferguson los estaba mirando, y el agente Brown la miró hasta que ella cogió el teléfono y se lo llevó a la oreja con aire distraído, y entonces le dijo a T. V. con el mejor de sus tonos reprobatorios: «Pareces saber muy bien cómo encajan todas las piezas», y T. V. Daniels interpretó una especie de baile con la mitad superior del cuerpo que el agente Brown no logró identificar en un primer momento con un sencillo encogimiento de hombros, y T. V. dijo: «Están numeradas». Antes de que ninguno de los dos pudiera volver a decir nada, la puerta se abrió y Matthew Edwards, que en el pasado se había quejado de que T. V. no siempre se molestaba en recorrer toda la calle Damar-Palco para llegar hasta su casa (y su buzón), entró con vacilación en la comisaría, sosteniendo en una mano un pequeño rectángulo negro con el borde blanco, se quitó el sombrero para saludar al agente Brown y miró rápidamente a T. V. Daniels, pero antes de que este pudiera decir nada, Matthew Edwards se fijó en la colección de fotografías, con vaga forma de pez, que había sobre la mesa del agente Brown, luego se fijó en la escena que formaban todos ellos y, muy despacio, añadió su propia pieza al rompecabezas que había acabado por convertirse en el cuerpo de Lucy Robinson.

4.05

EL BAR DE CORA, EL CAFÉ DE SUMNERTIME Y EL BILLAR DE SLOPPY JOE

Casi todo el mundo decía lo mismo: no era la primera vez que Myra Robinson vagaba por las calles de Galatia en plena noche, borracha y en un estado que Rosemary Krebs había calificado en cierta ocasión de «desnudez parcial». Por supuesto, normalmente iba cantando y, por supuesto, cuando se encontraba en un estado de desnudez parcial la temperatura no rondaba el punto de congelación, que serían los cero grados Celsius, aunque la mayoría de la gente de por aquí no era capaz de hacer la conversión al sistema métrico decimal, es decir, que tendían a pensar en treinta y dos o treinta y tres grados Farenheit, y, dada la temperatura, a lo que había que añadir una reciente e inesperada tormenta, las calles sin asfaltar de Galatia se habían convertido en una especie de barrizal semicongelado, como uno de esos paquetes de brécol con queso del Gigante Verde que se ha sacado del congelador pero aún no se ha descongelado por completo, y la gente se figuraba que eso tenía algo que ver con el hecho de que Myra Robinson —quien, según Faith Jackson acababa de decirle al reverendo Greeving, no podía en absoluto imaginarse dónde había podido comprar un camisón como el que llevaba puesto, aunque seguro que no lo había comprado por el catálogo de Sears, eso seguro—, Myra Robinson no iba cantando sino lanzando pequeños gritos, lo cual parecía comprensible, dada la temperatura y dadas las circunstancias. Myra Robinson no tenía últimamente razones para cantar. Vagaba por las calles nevadas de Galatea, sollozando, gritando a veces, y siempre lanzando un extraño lamento, «lamento» fue la palabra que usó Matthew Edwards, que se jactaba de tener sangre comanche o chickasaw o algo por el estilo, y cuando Yankee Carting le preguntó a Matthew Edwards cómo coño era ese lamento, este último dijo que como el sonido que emite una india antes de arrojarse a la pira de su valiente esposo, pero antes de que Yankee pudiera preguntar qué era una pira, Matthew Edwards aclaró, al fuego, al fuego funerario. Myra llevaba puesto un abrigo sin abrochar encima del camisón, y apretaba una pequeña caja negra contra su pecho. Luego los vecinos admitieron que les preocupaba que pudiera coger una pulmonía, pero la verdad es que nadie pensó en la helada, porque aquel camisón, con sus pequeños ribetes de falsa piel en el cuello y los puños, con sus encajes y sus lazos –¿has visto qué escote?, le dijo Darrell Jenkens a Sloppy Joe con una mueca burlona–, aquel camisón que Myra Robinson arrastraba por el suelo como un personaje salido de una de esas películas antiguas en blanco y negro, y quién podría haberse imaginado que iba descalza y, bueno, además, comentaba la gente, todo el mundo sabe que no se puede razonar con una persona borracha, lo cual, puestos a ser brutalmente sinceros, es exactamente lo que es Myra Robinson, y con Lucy o sin Lucy, nadie en el condado de Cadavera, que había sido un condado abstemio hasta mediados de la década de los ochenta, sentía demasiada simpatía por una madre separada que tenía problemas con la bebida y llevaba un camisón con un escote que le llegaba hasta el culo. Por eso, nadie acudió en su ayuda hasta que salió del pueblo en dirección a su casa, pasó de largo y continuó en dirección de lo que algunos insisten en seguir llamando la casa de los Deacon y otros llaman la casa de caliza, y solo Wade Painter y Rosemary Krebs llaman la casa de Colin Nieman, nadie la ayudó hasta ese momento, y quien la ayudó fue el nuevo vecino, el hombre cuyo, ¡ejem!, «amigo» había estado presente en la escena del crimen, el hombre cuyo abrigo había sido encontrado allí y cuya bolsa había contenido el pelo de Lucy Robinson y cuya Polaroid o Kodak había sacado todas aquellas fotografías –¿cuántas más pruebas necesitan?, dijo Vera Gatlinger–, el hombre que había comprado la casa, el propio Colin Nieman. Bueno, pues mejor para él, se le oyó decir a T. V. Daniels en el Sumnertime –a T. V., que había dicho que las fotografías se habían tomado con una Kodak– con un tono de voz que parecía absolutamente impropio de él, pero el caso es que cuando Colin Nieman encontró a Myra Robinson, la cinta de la grabadora que Myra llevaba –la grabadora pertenecía a Colin Nieman, ¿no lo sabían?– se había terminado y Myra Robinson se había quedado quieta como un ratón, y cuando Colin Nieman la hizo entrar en su viejo y gigantesco mausoleo, bueno, perdonad, dijo riendo Grady Oconnor en el bar de Cora, en esa «mansión», cuando Colin Nieman la hizo entrar en su casa y vio que iba descalza y que sus pies presentaban un aspecto lamentable, la cogió en brazos, la metió en el coche y se la llevó directamente al hospital de Bigger Hill, ocasión que, como pueden imaginar, Rosemary Krebs aprovechó para decirle al pastor Little que si Galatea tuviera su propio hospital quizá se podría haber hecho algo por los pies de la pobre Myra Robinson. Solo más tarde, cuando Colin volvía del hospital, solo entonces Colin Nieman se acordó de la grabadora, que descansaba sobre el asiento del copiloto, y Nettie Ferguson sabía de buena tinta que Colin Nieman apretó el botón de «eject» y la cinta salió de la grabadora y Colin Nieman la puso en el estéreo del coche, aunque Nettie no recordaba la marca del aparato, pero dijo que estaba segura de que ni siquiera era japonés, era «alemán», y luego hizo una significativa pausa y, sorbiéndose la nariz, dijo que con eso podíamos hacernos una idea de lo que había costado, y dijo también que Colin Nieman rebobinó la cinta hasta el principio en el carísimo estéreo alemán de su carísimo vehículo británico tipo jeep y la escuchó en modo automático, y DuWayne Hicks dijo que el estéreo de su coche, que era un RCA, también tenía modo automático y que era de fabricación estadounidense, norteamericana, que por eso llevaba una A en la marca, RCA, por si no lo sabían, y si recordaban que Colin Nieman había tardado tanto en enterarse de que Myra Robinson andaba vagando por las calles, entonces comprenderían por qué se metió en una zanja con el coche, porque por los altavoces del estéreo no salían más que gritos, no los de una mujer, sino los de una chica, no los de Myra, sino los de Lucy, y en el silencio sepulcral que en el Sumnertime siguió a esta última revelación, Howard Goertzen nos dijo que a él le parecía que ese Colin Nieman seguramente se había metido en una zanja porque ya había demostrado, con-fatales-resultados-para-Charlene, que no era precisamente un buen conductor, es decir, que se le daba más o menos bien avanzar pero no tan bien detenerse, eso era lo único que Howard Goertzen tenía que decir, y luego Elaine Sumner dijo que si les parecía bien prepararía café para todos y les serviría un trozo de tarta de manzana, que ya se olía, porque en su opinión cualquier cuerpo necesitaba un poco de dulce y un poco de estimulante después de escuchar una historia como esa, dijo Elaine Sumner, contoneándose entre las mesas del café, y también dijo que esperaba que la marmota viese su sombra al día siguiente sin más tardanza, porque eso significaría que el invierno estaba a punto de terminar y ella, y no pensaba que fuera la única, pero desde luego, ella, pensaba comprarse de inmediato ropa de colores primaverales, como decía su contable Mary Kay, pues no estaba dispuesta a soportar un día más de aquel invierno, ni uno solo.

4.06

AGENTE BROWN

Myra Robinson empezó a andar de un modo extraño desde el día en que la cinta apareció en el porche de su casa y salió a dar su paseo de medianoche por la nieve fangosa. Los médicos consiguieron salvarle los pies, pero no tenía sensibilidad en ellos; nada, decía, era como si sus piernas terminaran en los tobillos y caminase sobre el aire; se tambaleaba hacia delante y hacia atrás, hacia los lados, y tenía que mover las manos para mantener el equilibrio, pero cuando fue a la comisaría tampoco podía servirse de las manos porque llevaba una caja, y esta traqueteaba cada vez que Myra se echaba hacia delante, y aunque el traqueteo no era especialmente extraño o siniestro, pues todas las cosas pueden traquetear, al agente Brown no se le ocurría qué podía hacer ese ruido dentro de una caja de cartón, y sin razón alguna sintió que se le helaba la sangre. Los médicos le habían puesto a Myra unos zapatos ortopédicos que parecían unas botas, con una armadura de aluminio para sujetar el tobillo que chirriaba y crujía de un modo horrible al andar. Entró en la comisaría, tambaleándose y tropezando, pasó junto a la mesa de Nettie Ferguson, que esta vez fingió no darse cuenta de la llegada de Myra Robinson, y soltó la caja sobre la mesa del agente Brown al tiempo que decía: «¡Ay, Dios mío, ay, Dios mío, ay, Dios mío, ay, Dios mío!», y el agente Brown, que había dejado de comer al oír el traqueteo de la caja y los chirriantes pasos de Myra, dijo: «Vamos, vamos, Myra, cálmate», pero Myra siguió diciendo: «¡Ay, Dios mío, ay, Dios mío, ay, Dios mío, ay, Dios mío!», y al final lanzó un suspiro —Myra detestaba sentarse porque levantarse después siempre era un suplicio— y dijo: «¡Ay, agente Brown, sé que esta vez es algo terrible, terrible, terrible, terrible!». El agente Brown estaba tan petrificado que ni siquiera se acordó de decirle a Myra Robinson que su nombre era Eustace y su cargo sheriff; en lugar de esto, cogió la caja con cautela. No había ninguna señal en ella. Era una caja de cartón marrón, torpemente precintada, del tamaño de una barra de pan. «Por favor —decía Myra, cimbreándose como una espiga azotada por el viento—, por favor, ábrela para que podamos terminar cuanto antes. Ábrela y dime lo que es.» «No hay que precipitarse, Myra —dijo el agente Brown, recobrando un poco la calma—, no queremos más problemas», y al oír esto Myra gritó: «¿Es que piensas que es una bomba, Eustace? No pesa ni medio kilo, ¡por Dios! Pesa menos que un pájaro». «Myra, por favor, cuidado con lo que…», la interrumpió el agente Brown. «¡Abre la puñetera caja de una vez!» «… dices —concluyó el agente Brown, dejando la caja sobre la mesa y estirándose cuan largo era–. Y te agradeceré que me muestres el respeto que mi cargo y mi posición merecen».

Permaneció de pie, balanceándose sin darse cuenta en sincronía con el balanceo de Myra, pero dio un paso atrás cuando esta se inclinó hacia delante, rozó con su mejilla la mejilla del agente Brown y dijo: «¡Escucha, Eustace Rumpford Brown, yo iba al colegio contigo cuando eras un gordo comebollos hijo de un aparcero, que se pasó cuatro años calentando con el culo el banquillo de un equipo de fútbol que ni siquiera tenía once jugadores, y si no abres esa caja ahora mismo, juro por Cristo que me subiré encima de tu mesa, aunque sea volando, y dejaré una cagada tan enorme y olorosa sobre tu preciosa colección de servilletas sucias y tu vajilla de plata que no te librarás del olor en un mes!». En el intervalo que medió entre la «cagada» y la «vajilla de plata» el agente Brown llegó a la conclusión que la dignidad ya no tenía importancia y que no le quedaba más remedio que acceder, de manera que se sacó la navaja del bolsillo, con ganas de clavársela a Myra Robinson en la laringe por haberle llamado calientabancos, porque él era el suplente, y así lo decía en el anuario del colegio; luego le asestó a la caja un navajazo en el centro y arrancó las solapas con tal violencia que el contenido saltó por los aires, rebotó sobre la mesa y cayó al suelo, produciendo un sonido como el que hacen las canicas, y lo primero que le vino a la cabeza al agente Brown fue la alusión de Myra a los pájaros, y se dijo que lo que estaba viendo eran unos huevos pequeños, azules y moteados, y no, como bien sabía, los dedos de Lucy Robinson. «¡Dios bendito!», exclamó, pero Myra Robinson no dijo nada, y Nettie Ferguson, que estaba detrás de ella, preguntó: «¿Qué es, Eustace?», y el agente Brown intentó sacudir la cabeza, pero el movimiento le produjo una arcada y salió corriendo al lavabo, y oyó gritar a Nettie Ferguson, y oyó chirriar los zapatos de Myra al dar varios pasos, y finalmente la oyó caer al suelo, desplomándose como un saco de harina.

4.07

WINDA BOTTOMLY

Ella no quería que nadie lo supiera, pero el caso era que la anciana Winda Bottomly no sabía leer. Aunque no le importaba, nunca le había importado; tenía su televisor en casa, lo único que hacía era ir a la iglesia y por primera vez en su larga, larga vida –un marido, dos hijos, los tres muertos– memorizó todos los salmos que cantaban allí; además, al reverendo Abraham, que era una de las pocas personas que conocían su secreto, siempre le gustaba que un niño o una niña del colegio hiciesen la lectura semanal de las Escrituras, pero había en Galatia más de uno que nunca había aprendido a leer, y no vayan a pensar que este fenómeno era exclusivo de la zona del pueblo situada al este del silo. ¡Ah, y al este del bar de Cora! Winda Bottomly se dirigía al bar de Cora, pero allí no había necesidad de leer: por el olfato reconocías el menú. A pesar de todo, fue Winda Bottomly quien encontró la pintada. Era el primer día de la primavera, y, todos los años, el primer día de primavera Winda visitaba la tumba de su esposo... la de sus hijos, bueno, los hijos habían muerto fuera del pueblo y las autoridades, en un caso un mal marido y en el otro el ejército, no se molestaron en enviar los cuerpos para enterrarlos como es debido, y Winda siempre les decía a sus amigas: «Lo pongo a dormir en invierno y lo despierto en primavera», y ese día se levantó temprano con la intención de ir al cementerio antes de que saliera el sol, porque era un espectáculo digno de verse: el sol derramando su gracia infinita sobre los campos, reptando sobre las puntas de sus largos dedos enrojecidos en el extremo por entre los verdes trigales, hasta alcanzar la brillante cúpula del risco pelado. Y cuando el sol ya estaba alto y Winda había limpiado las hierbas que crecían sobre la sepultura de William y plantado su planta como todos los años, esta vez un lirio blanco, por la paz, cuando hubo terminado de hacer todo esto y emprendió el camino de regreso al pueblo, fue cuando lo vio. Para ella no era más que un garabato sobre la pared blanca del silo de Rosemary Krebs, una maraña de líneas negras pintadas con spray y un par de marcas rojas a los lados, pero, analfabeta o no, Winda Bottomly reconocía una palabra escrita cuando la veía. Enseguida pensó en Webbie Greeving. Tenía que contárselo a ella, pensó Winda, en primer lugar porque Webbie conocía a Winda y en segundo lugar porque Webbie no solo sabía leer sino que te explicaba lo que significaban las palabras, pero nadie le había visto el pelo a Webbie Greeving desde que empezó todo este asunto y, además, pensó Winda Bottomly, la única persona del pueblo que podría estar levantada a esas horas era Cora, por eso fue al bar de Cora, pero quien salió a abrir la puerta fue esa mujer blanca, la señorita Rosetta Stone, según se presentó ella misma, y Winda Bottomly pensó que seguramente era un nombre falso, robado de la Biblia. A Winda no le desagradaba Rosa, no, no llegaba a ese extremo, pero no se fiaba de ella, y cuando Rosa le dijo que Cora estaba durmiendo y que si a Winda le parecía bien ella estaba dispuesta a acompañarla a donde quisiera, Winda la miró con recelo, pero no vio otra solución. Y al final, se marcharon las dos juntas, Winda y Rosa, no exactamente cogidas del brazo, no exactamente como dos buenas amigas, Rosa sin preguntar qué hacía Winda levantada tan temprano y Winda sin preguntar qué hacía Cora en la cama tan tarde, y cuando se encontraron justo enfrente de la pintada que había en el silo, Winda se detuvo y esperó, porque no quería reconocer ante una mujer blanca que no sabía leer, pero Rosa, en lugar de leer las palabras en voz alta, o lo que Winda se imaginara que iba a hacer, Rosetta Stone dejó salir un sonido de su boca que a Winda Bottomly le pareció una blasfemia, luego zarandeó a Winda Bottomly y le gritó: «¿Para qué me ha traído aquí?», y después se marchó corriendo, y hasta tres horas más tarde, cuando Faith Jackson llamó a Winda para preguntarle si se había enterado, Winda Bottomly no supo que lo que había escrito en la pared del silo era una sola palabra: ¡ENCUÉNTRAME!, y Faith Jackson le explicó que las marcas rojas que había a los lados eran los puntos de exclamación.

5

5.01

JUSTIN

Aún estoy aquí.

5.02

DIVINE

El agua estaba fría.

5.03

COLIN

Cuatro semanas y cuatro días después de empezar la última versión de mi novela, es decir, treinta y dos días después de la desaparición de Lucy Robinson, conseguí terminarla. La terminé por la tarde, después de mi pelea matinal con Cora y antes de mi pelea vespertina con Divine; entre ambos sucesos, logré escribir la escena final hasta la última frase, que se me había estado resistiendo durante veinte años, y en cuanto terminé de teclearla, lo empaqueté todo, el manuscrito, las diversas copias mecanografiadas y corregidas con bolígrafo y la versión final, la versión acabada, en varias cajas, y aún seguía empaquetando cuando, horas después, sonó el teléfono y Wade me habló de Divine. Admito que al principio pensé en no hacer caso de su súplica; ¿qué más podía hacer?, ¿acaso no había hecho ya lo suficiente? Pero, finalmente, la razón —iba a decir la compasión, pero en realidad no creo que lo hiciera por compasión— ganó la partida, y dejé mis cajas como estaban para ver si podía ayudar a Divine o a Wade. Estuve fuera menos de una hora —¿qué «podía» hacer, a fin de cuentas?, ¿acaso no había hecho ya lo suficiente?–, pero bastó con ese rato: cuando volví a casa mi manuscrito había desaparecido.

5.04

WEBBIE

Me marché de su lado la mañana de nuestro octavo día juntos. No me resultó difícil separarme de él. Era tan solo un cuerpo grande y oscuro, con los brazos y las piernas extendidos sobre unas sábanas blancas que se habían vuelto amarillas a fuerza de lavados. Roncaba mientras yo me vestía, roncaba mientras yo escribía «Gracias» sobre la capa de polvo que cubría la repisa de la chimenea, junto a las fotografías de dos muchachas sonrientes cuyos nombres seguía sin conocer, roncaba mientras yo abría la puerta y dejaba el periódico encima del sofá. Hasta entonces, todo bien; quiero decir que todo tenía sentido –demasiado sentido–, pero en cuanto salí de su casa, me sentí perdida. Conocía el supermercado de la esquina, conocía el bar donde servían las mejores costillas y el café donde ofrecían la mejor tarta de manzana, y conocía el camino hasta el cine increíblemente largo y estrecho, con una pantalla tan pequeña que si te sentabas en la última fila, donde nos sentábamos nosotros, no parecía mucho más grande que un televisor, pero a pesar de todo me sentí perdida, porque no iba buscando ninguna de estas cosas. Buscaba mi coche. Y tardé casi una hora en encontrarlo, muy nerviosa por si de pronto me encontraba con Wallace por el barrio. No sabía qué le diría si aparecía, no sabía si mis piernas me traicionarían y me conducirían de nuevo hasta su casa. ¿Cómo podía decirle que yo solo quería sentir el tacto de su cara sin afeitar?, ¿cómo podía decirle que después de pasar siete días cocinando y comiendo con él, viendo la televisión, poniendo la lavadora y pasando la mopa, completamente solos, que después de siete días así, yo no lo recordaba a él, sino que recordaba su tacto, el vello arremolinado en su vientre en contacto con mi vientre, sus labios carnosos succionando mi piel? ¿Cómo podía decirle que sentía vergüenza, no de él o de lo que habíamos hecho juntos, sino de mí misma, por pensar en él de ese modo? Finalmente, después de tantos años, había sucumbido: había pensado en él como negro antes que como hombre.

Más tarde, cuando encontré el coche, vi que había una nota sujeta bajo las escobillas del parabrisas: estaba metida dentro de un sobre de plástico, como las multas de tráfico, para protegerlas de la lluvia y la nieve, pero cuando saqué el papel y lo desdoblé vi que solo había escritas seis palabras. La nota decía: «Me llamo Wallace Anderson. Adiós, Webbie».

5.05

JUSTIN

No hay olvido posible. La memoria persiste a pesar de todas las apuestas y todos los esfuerzos. La amnesia es como el color negro: lo borra todo por inclusión. Puesto que no excluye nada, nada puede tener importancia. Y así volví a mis tristes orígenes, a mi falso comienzo: *Ha pasado la medianoche. Es mi cumpleaños.* Si ha pasado la medianoche he logrado vivir veintiún años, y comienzo ahora los veintidós. Durante los últimos cinco años, Colin ha girado a mi alrededor como una luna alrededor de un planeta, y durante lo que parecen años y años antes de Colin, era yo quien giraba alrededor de otro hombre como un planeta alrededor de un sol. Pero ahora afirmo ser un cometa, un cuerpo celeste con su propia trayectoria, que no depende de nadie ni nadie depende de él. Este libro es un telescopio. Mirad a través de él; buscadme: mi ojo resplandeciente, mi halo, mi cola que se arrastra detrás de mí. Podréis ver esa cola años después de mi paso; para entonces, yo tal vez haya implotado, explotado, colisionado con algo hasta desintegrarme, tal vez me haya quedado sin gas o, quién sabe, quizá todavía brille, pero en cualquier caso mi cola me seguirá, se irá desvaneciendo, pero tan gradualmente que nunca sabréis si lo que veis es real o es tan solo una sombra quemada y grabada en vuestros ojos.

5.06

DIVINE

Luego sentí frío. Un frío del carajo. Supongo que el agua no tardó más de un segundo en calarme la ropa. Quiero decir que solté la cuerda, oí crujir el hielo y, aunque sabía que el agua estaría muy fría porque la superficie estaba helada, pasó un buen rato hasta que lo sentí, hasta que sentí el frío o la humedad. Estuve un segundo colgado de la cuerda resbaladiza que se movía como una medusa, y luego, de repente, el frío del agua se me metió en la ropa, no, no se me metió, me perforó la ropa como una taladradora, los brazos y las piernas se me tensaron con un chasquido, me encogí como una pelota y caí de cabeza, hundiéndome como una piedra. Fue como si la mano del diablo saliera del infierno y me arrastrara hasta los abismos. Pero no me asustó, quiero decir, el diablo, ni la idea del infierno. En los tres años que habían pasado desde que perdí al Rata, había perdido también a mis padres y a Wade y acababa de perder a Colin Nieman, incluso había perdido mi nombre de pila y en cierto modo era como si hubiera perdido mi alma. Si Satanás quería un trozo de mi culo tendría que ponerse a la cola, pues no podía darle algo que ya no me pertenecía.

5.07

COLIN

Myra Robinson se encerró en casa desde la noche de febrero que se destrozó los pies. Divine supo por T. V. Daniels que, después de encontrar en el buzón aquella caja que contenía varios trozos de dedos de Lucy, Myra no se había atrevido a recoger el correo; tampoco contestaba al teléfono, y un día, a finales de primavera la llamé y comprendí que lo había desconectado. Esa misma tarde, poco después, pasé con el coche junto a su casa y vi que su coche empezaba a quedar oculto bajo una maraña de yedra, y luego cuando fui al IGA de Vera Gatlinger para pedirle que le sirviera a Myra la compra a domicilio, Vera acabó contándome, después de muchos rodeos, que Myra ya había hecho un trato con Joe Brznski, el propietario de Sloppy Joe, para que todos los lunes le llevaran una botella de Jack Daniel's. Joe, Vera y T. V. eran lo únicos en Galatia que habían tenido ocasión de visitar a Myra —el agente Brown, que no había hecho el menor progreso en la investigación del caso, evitaba pasar por su casa— y todos contaban lo mismo a quien les preguntase: Myra no hacía nada. Absolutamente nada. Se pasaba el día sentada en una extraña mecedora electrónica que le había dado Bea, sus pies sin vida colgados de la armadura ortopédica, y si alguien se atrevía a mencionar el nombre de Lucy, Myra sonreía animadamente y murmuraba algo incomprensible acerca de una tal Angela; aceptaba el whisky o la comida o el correo que le ofrecían, y mientras bebía o comía o leía con expresión ausente, preguntaba a sus benefactores si conocían a su pequeña Angela, a su ángel, a su regalo de Dios.

Bueno. No había logrado encontrar un nuevo título para mi desaparecida novela y estaba poseído por la misma inercia que se había apoderado de Myra. Quien me robó la novela se llevó no solo la versión final, sino también todos los manuscritos, las notas y los apuntes que yo había tomado, dejándome sin el menor rastro físico de lo que había escrito. Durante la semana que siguió al robo ni siquiera fui capaz de salir de la cama —supongo que esto también tenía que ver con lo que le había ocurrido a Divine y con el hecho de que ya no era bien recibido ni en el bar de Cora ni en casa de Wade ni en ninguna otra parte del pueblo—, pero al ver que los siete días de cama solo habían servido para engordar varios kilos en la cintura, me levanté, di mi carrera matinal, me preparé un café y me senté a la mesa, pero no hice nada.

Durante ocho o diez horas al día y durante cinco largos meses en los que el rigor del invierno dio paso a la dulzura de la primavera hasta que llegó el verano, no hice nada. Tampoco es que me pasara todo el día allí sentado. Cuando aún hacía frío encendía un buen fuego en la chimenea; los miles de volúmenes encuadernados en piel y carcomidos que abarrotaban las estanterías cuando nos mudamos a esta casa sirvieron para alimentarlo. Al principio, ojeaba los libros antes de quemarlos para asegurarme de que las páginas estaban realmente deterioradas, pero al cabo de un tiempo empecé a cogerlos indiscriminadamente y a arrojarlos a las llamas con una risa malévola. Las tapas húmedas y las páginas mohosas no ardían fácilmente, y había que esforzarse para mantener vivo el fuego; a veces tenía que alimentar las llamas con unas cuantas hojas frescas, crujientes y secas —y en blanco, admito con dolor— de mi propio papel de escribir.

Luego llegó la primavera, un pequeño romance en abril que no duró más de dos semanas y dio paso casi inmediatamente a los implacables cuarenta grados de un precoz verano en Kansas, y cuando empezó a hacer demasiado calor para encender la chimenea, encontré otros quehaceres para matar el tiempo, inventé otras tareas para mantenerme alejado de mi mesa de trabajo, donde todas las mañanas empezaba el día tecleando las siguientes palabras: *La última línea de esta historia es inevitable,* y todas las tardes terminaba escribiendo *Nunca volví a verlo.* Eso fue todo cuanto escribí, todos los días, durante cinco meses, pues aunque recordaba todas y cada una de las escenas que ocurrían en mi novela con la misma precisión con que las víctimas de un accidente de tráfico recuerdan los momentos inmediatamente anteriores al accidente —sentía la calidez que envolvía el cuerpo del narrador mientras nadaba en la esfera curativa de Otto; sentía, en lo más hondo de mi estómago, su terror al descubrir la pirámide de libros despreciados—, no lograba recordar ni una sola de las palabras que había empleado para describir estas escenas, y me parecía que si no conseguía reproducir con absoluta exactitud mi manuscrito desaparecido, habría... ¿qué? Habría fracasado. No sabía a qué o a quién afectaba mi fracaso, y por eso me quedaba allí sentado, hechizado por aquellas primeras y últimas palabras, perdido en un silencio tan laberíntico como el de Myra y tan ausente como el de Justin, hasta que caía la noche y, al abrigo de la oscuridad, Divine emergía de dondequiera que hubiese estado escondido, en la casa o en los campos, como un fantasma de color cobrizo. Divine. Me envolvía con sus fragantes y flexibles brazos como un recuerdo, me besaba con dulzura la grande, calva e inútil cabeza, me susurraba al oído cariñosas palabras sin sentido con la dulcificada voz de los muertos, y entonces, al menos mientras duraba la noche, me abandonaba a él por completo.

5.08

WEBBIE

Delgada, frágil, sudorosa... La diminuta figura de Rosemary Krebs aparecía apoyada sobre un carro abarrotado de comida. Estaba tan absorta en su batalla que no reparaba en las miradas de las otras tres o cuatro mujeres —yo entre ellas— que había en el supermercado y que la miraban con una sonrisa divertida y ligeramente desdeñosa.

Hacía menos de una hora que había regresado a Galatia. Estaba comprando los ingredientes necesarios para preparar el guiso que mi padre me había pedido la semana anterior.

Rosemary Krebs había cometido el error de ponerse un traje de seda color crema para ir a hacer la compra, y tenía manchas de sudor en las axilas y en la espalda; llevaba, además, una estola de piel colgada del hombro, como una cola de animal. Los zapatos de tacón no eran los más adecuados para el suelo de linóleo del IGA, resbaladizo a causa de la nieve derretida, y a veces patinaba como un espermatozoide de dos colas.

De pronto, pareció tomar conciencia de las miradas y levantó la vista. Al verme, soltó el carro y se enderezó apresuradamente; la barra para sujetar el carro le llegaba a la altura del esternón. Jadeó un poco, pero consiguió hablar con su habitual tono neutro y suave.

—Webbie Greeving —dijo—, buenas tardes.

A veces uno sabe cosas que no sabe que sabe. A veces uno hace cosas sin saber por qué las hace.

—¿Puedo echarle una mano? —me oí decir, y supongo que debí de poner una expresión tan asombrada como la de Rosemary Krebs.
—¿Perdón?
—Parece que está usted peleándose con el carro.
Me había acercado a ella. Olía su perfume y, vagamente, su sudor. Pensé: «Este es el olor que huele el alcalde después de follar». Una parte de mí —no mi mente— recordó a Wallace al pensar en eso, y sentí un ligero estremecimiento.

Rosemary Krebs esperó a que saliera de mi ensoñación con una de sus sonrisas políticas, y entonces dudé muy mucho de que ella y su marido follasen alguna vez.

—Una señora no se pelea, Webbie, aunque a veces tenga... dificultades.

—Sí, claro —dije, y al ver en mi carro de la compra los ingredientes para el guiso de mi padre, añadí—: Si ya ha terminado de comprar quizá... si quiere la ayudo a empujar el carro hasta la caja.

El encogido corazón de Rosemary Krebs latió con fuerza en su diminuto pecho; mi propio corazón parecía latir cada vez más despacio, hasta que al fin ella dijo:

—Muchas gracias, Webbie. Te lo agradezco mucho.

Vera me miró como si tuviera tres ojos y dos narices cuando empujaba el carro de Rosemary Krebs hasta la caja registradora, con ella un paso por delante de mí, como un buen musulmán conduciendo a su esposa. Sin preguntar, empecé a depositar las compras de Rosemary Krebs sobre la cinta transportadora, y Vera, tras un momento de silencio, empezó a teclear los precios.

—Ha comprado muchas cosas, señora Krebs —observé.

—Phyneas y yo tenemos invitados este fin de semana. Una especie de fiesta de Año Nuevo aplazada.

Puse una pieza de brécol sobre la cinta.

—¿Aplazada?

Rosemary Krebs me ofreció una sonrisa casi beatífica:

—Después de lo ocurrido —dijo.

Puse otra pieza de brécol y un manojo de cebollas en la cinta transportadora.

—La verdad, señora Krebs —dije, y para que no quedara lugar a dudas repetí—, la verdad, señora Krebs, usted es la mujer más ocupada que ha habido nunca en este pueblo. Entre los servicios a la comunidad y el fondo para el desarrollo y la atención a su esposo es un milagro que le quede tiempo para dar tantas fiestas.

—Es difícil —admitió Rosemary Krebs, como si se viera obligada.

—Y la comida —dije—. ¡Madre mía!

—Bueno, las mujeres tenemos que desarrollar más recursos que los hombres —dijo, soltando una risita, y vi que no me miraba a mí, sino a Vera, pero Vera no estaba enterándose de nada. Tecleaba en la caja registradora sin dejar de mirarme por encima de las gafas, y yo le devolví la mirada, pero intenté conservar una expresión neutra.

—Vera, ¿cuándo ha subido la carne a cincuenta dólares el kilo?

Rosemary Krebs me miró con gesto alarmado.

—¿Cómo?

Vera dio un respingo y luego escudriñó la larga tira de papel que colgaba de la caja registradora.

—Seguro que se trata de un error al teclear, señora Krebs.

—Creo que cuesta cinco —dije, y mientras Vera anulaba el precio marcado yo le ofrecí a Rosemary Krebs una sonrisa cómplice. Para entonces, ya habíamos descargado el carro, y me dirigí al otro extremo del mostrador.

—¿Quiere bolsas de papel y de plástico, señora Krebs? ¿O solo de papel?

—Solo de papel —dijo Rosemary Krebs, con la voz cargada de autoridad—. Y doble bolsa, claro.

—Por supuesto.

Rosemary Krebs ojeaba perezosamente la programación de la televisión, mirando de vez en cuando el reloj o a las demás mujeres que había en el supermercado mientras yo metía las bolsas de papel en el carro. Vera empezó a cobrarle a Tamara Atkins, la madre de Lee Anne, y Rosemary Krebs y yo nos encontramos frente a frente separadas por el carro de aquella.

—Señora Krebs —dije con vacilación—, disculpe el atrevimiento, pero...

Dejé la frase en suspenso y Rosemary Krebs, en voz tan baja y ansiosa como la del pescador que comprueba si un pez ha picado el anzuelo preguntó:

—¿Sí?

—Bueno, sé que ha estado usted buscando a alguien, ejem, a alguien que trabaje para usted. En su casa, quiero decir.

De nuevo, Rosemary Krebs no se permitió más que una palabra, pero, al temblarle ligeramente la voz, añadió una sílaba extra:

—Si-í.

—Bueno, la verdad es que cuidar de mi padre no me ocupa todo el tiempo y cuando llega la Navidad siempre me doy cuenta de que debería ganarme un dinerillo para mis gastos, como todo el mundo.

Un velo de sospecha cubrió el rostro de Rosemary Krebs.

—Creía que trabajabas en la biblioteca municipal.

—En realidad se trata de un trabajo voluntario —dije, haciendo un gesto con la mano, como para quitar importancia al asunto—. Además, esos libros no van a ninguna parte. Al menos aquí.

Rosemary Krebs guardó silencio un momento; luego, en tono de suave reproche, dijo:

—No deberías subestimar el valor de la palabra escrita, Webbie. Puede cambiar tu vida. —Le sonreí mientras las ruedas y los piñones giraban en su cerebro, hasta que al fin habló más alto que el ruido de la caja registradora—: ¿Me estás pidiendo un empleo, Webbie Greeving?

Vera dejó de teclear y, esta vez, se volvió y nos miró abiertamente. Tamara Atkins, menos descarada, rebuscó un penique en el fondo de su enorme monedero.

—Sí, señora, eso creo.

Rosemary Krebs me miró fijamente, con expresión incrédula, su rostro animado por el recelo y por un placer tan patente que hube de hacer un gran esfuerzo para no mostrar el desprecio que me inspiraba. Luego sacudió la cabeza, como si quisiera aclarar sus ideas.

—¡Dios mío, es tardísimo! Ya estamos casi en el Sabbath. No es momento de hablar de negocios. —Su voz había cambiado bruscamente, recobrando el tono que a buen seguro empleaban sus antepasados para dirigirse a las criadas y a los esclavos—: ¿Por qué no pasas el lunes por mi casa y hablamos de ello con más calma?

—¿Le parece bien a las once, señora Krebs?

—Me parece bien.

Entonces agarró el carro e intentó girarlo, pero este no se movió. Interponiéndome rápidamente entre ella y el carro, la ayudé a maniobrar. Rosemary Krebs se dirigía ya hacia la puerta, y detrás de ella, dije:

—Permítame.

5.09

JUSTIN

Solo un bebé puede guardar silencio en compañía de otras personas, y aun entonces debe soportar el zumbido de palabras, medias palabras y cuartos de palabras que salen de las bocas de los adultos: «ma-ma, ma-ma», «da-da, da-da», «cu-cu, cu-cu», «ca-ca, ca-ca». Pero que dejes de hablar no significa que dejes de pensar. Aunque, a decir verdad, eso es lo que me gustaría y, durante las primeras semanas que siguieron a la agresión, cuando el recuerdo no se me iba de la cabeza y las imágenes, los sonidos y los olores no se me iban de la cabeza, y, sobre todo, las palabras no se me iban de la cabeza –las palabras que mi mente ponía a la escena muda, las palabras que yo dije, como para escribirla en mi memoria–, casi me arrepentí de mi deseo, porque cuando me di cuenta de que no podía tragarme las palabras, quise escupirlas con todas mis fuerzas. Pero sabía que eso no serviría de nada, daría lo mismo. Las palabras no habían salvado a mi madre, no habían detenido a mi padre, no habían preservado mi inocencia ni devuelto la salud a ninguno de mis amigos agonizantes o muertos, y sabía que aunque hubiese sido capaz de hablar en esa carretera helada, de razonar, de gritar o tan solo de suplicar, tampoco habría podido salvar a Lucy. Y no me digan que esa no es la función de las palabras. ¿De qué sirven si no? Se lo diré: si hubiera podido encontrar las palabras adecuadas para arreglar las cosas, las habría dicho. No es que ya no hablara; es que ya no sabía qué decir.

5.10

DIVINE

En cierto modo había dado la impresión de que estaba enamorado de Colin Nieman, o, al menos, de que quería estarlo. Pues no lo estaba. No lo estoy. Quiero decir que, por más que sea como soy, ni estoy ni he estado nunca enamorado de Colin Nieman. Lo que quería entonces, cuando aún deseaba cosas, lo que quería era que él me amara... lo que quería era que él se enamorara de mí. Colin era un montón de cosas; era especialmente guapo, no os podéis imaginar lo guapo que era, guapo e inteligente, y, encima, rico; y a pesar de lo que le dije, era muy bueno en la cama, y durante algún tiempo pensé que Colin era mi pasaporte para salir de Galatia. Pero lo único que nunca fue y nunca podría haber sido es mi amante. Entiendo que alguien se enamore de él, pero yo no me enamoré. No estoy enamorado. Y no lo estaré nunca, porque ese privilegio solo le corresponde al Rata.

El Rata.

Medía un metro sesenta y cinco, y era patizambo y se balanceaba al andar como si fuese un vaquero el doble de alto, y si se imaginaba que alguien lo miraba con aire de burla, entonces atacaba, como una rata, eso me había contado: mano, mano, pie, pie, diente. En dos años jamás lo vi ganar una pelea –ni siquiera estar a punto de ganarla–, pero tampoco lo vi huir nunca. Podía acabar lleno de heridas y cubierto de sangre, apenas capaz de levantarse o de ver de dónde venía el golpe, pero siempre era el otro el que se rendía primero y lo dejaba allí, temblando, gritando con la poca voz que le quedaba: «Sí, eso es, gallina, lárgate antes de que me vuelva loco de verdad». Siempre tenía un ojo morado o sangre seca debajo de la nariz o alguna lesión que parecía como una naranja enterrada bajo su piel, y, además, estaba la cicatriz blanca en el labio superior. Parecía como si tuviera labio leporino, esa cicatriz, pero el Rata llevaba todas y cada una de sus marcas con orgullo. «Le he dado una buena lección –decía, mientras yo lo lavaba y le desinfectaba las heridas–. No volverá a molestarnos.» Nunca me dejaba que le pusiera una venda. «Quiero que vean mis heridas de guerra –decía–. Quiero que todos sepan lo que he hecho por ti.»

Su verdadero nombre era Lamoine Wiebe, pero nadie lo llamaba así. Durante mucho tiempo la gente lo llamó Dwebey, o Dwebe, hasta que alguien dijo que parecía un roedor, una especie de hurón, de rata, y no sé si fue otro quien le puso ese nombre o fue el propio Lamoine quien se lo puso, el caso es que todo el mundo lo llamaba Lamoine el Rata.

El Rata.

Mi héroe.

Yo tenía solo doce años cuando empezó todo, y él dieciséis; pero ya entonces me di cuenta de que el Rata estaba loco de atar. Aunque no por eso dejaba de ser mi héroe, o mi amante.

5.11

COLIN

No le contó a nadie lo que había pasado. Mejor dicho, no se lo contó a Wade ni me lo contó a mí: no nos dijo por qué se marchó de mi casa una tarde, a primeros de enero, con una cazadora marrón y blanca, una camiseta blanca de manga larga, unos pantalones negros muy ceñidos, calcetines blancos y mocasines negros, y apareció de madrugada en casa de Wade, sin cazadora y sin zapatos –además de sin coche– y con la ropa empapada y cubierta de barro. Con el agua, todo rastro de gomina había desaparecido del pelo, que para cuando yo llegué ya estaba seco y flotaba alrededor de su cabeza, revuelto al estilo afro; enmarcaba su rostro como un halo y vibraba con el violento temblor de su cuerpo, sentado en una silla. Wade ya le había quitado la ropa, le había secado con una toalla y le había cubierto con una gruesa manta; la calefacción estaba tan fuerte que al entrar sentí una barrera de calor. Divine tenía la cara sucia; barro incrustado bajo las uñas, y sujetaba con fuerza entre las manos una humeante taza de líquido que, sin embargo, se negaba a beber; también se negaba a hablar o a mirarnos. Tenía los labios y los párpados amoratados, y miraba fijamente a un punto situado fuera de la habitación. Temblaba, tenía convulsiones, se retorcía, como si estuviera agonizando, hasta que le hice soltar la taza que sostenía con los dedos crispados, lo tendí en el sofá y remetí bien la manta por debajo de los almohadones, para hacerle conservar el calor del cuerpo. Wade se retiró a un rincón en cuanto llegué, con expresión de impotencia congelada en el rostro, y no se movió de allí hasta que Divine se quedó dormido; entonces, miré a Wade por encima del cuerpo de Divine —no sería la última vez que lo miraría de ese modo— y dije: «Se pondrá bien». Pero no fue eso lo que dije la segunda vez que interpuse el cuerpo de Divine entre el de Wade y el mío. Cuando volví a casa, como ya he dicho, mi novela había desaparecido.

Divine se pasó una semana en la cama, igual que yo. Su silencio no era tan total como el de Justin, pero se negaba a contarnos lo que había pasado. Específico que no nos lo contó a ninguno de los dos porque sospecho que sí se lo dijo a alguien: la persona a la que le estuvo escribiendo una carta durante los siete días siguientes. Wade dijo que Divine le había robado uno de sus cuadernos de bocetar —esa fue la palabra que empleó Wade, dijo «robado»—; se sentó en la cama, con el cuaderno apoyado en las rodillas, y escribió tan despacio y con tanto cuidado que, según Wade, casi parecía que estaba dibujando en lugar de escribiendo. De vez en cuando arrancaba una página del cuaderno y la arrugaba, y las que iba arrugando las metía en la funda de la almohada y las custodiaba con sumo celo, hasta que una semana después se decidió a salir de la cama. Wade me contó que sostenía en una mano una sola hoja de papel cubierta en letra minúscula; en la otra llevaba la funda de la almohada que contenía sus infructuosos esfuerzos. Metió la hoja en un sobre, lo cerró y no se separó de él ni un segundo; el resto lo metió en un barril y lo quemó en el patio, con funda de almohada incluida. Se dio un baño, se acicaló, se vistió, cogió su carta y el coche de Wade, y se marchó. Apareció con el coche poco después en la casa de caliza, pero ya no llevaba la carta. Entró sin llamar y fue directamente a mi dormitorio, donde, sonriendo con malevolencia, escenificó para mí un pequeño striptease. Empezó en silencio, pero mientras bailaba y se desnudaba comenzó a tararear, a canturrear entre dientes, a cantar y, fue elevando el tono hasta gritar a pleno pulmón cuando al fin quedó comple-

también fue el mejor jugador de futbolín de todo Wichita, y estoy seguro de que ahora, dondequiera que esté, sigue siendo el mejor jugador de futbolín del lugar.

Siempre que podía iba con él a Bigger Hill, a Arcadia. Allí había cientos de máquinas; Arcadia era una sala del tamaño de un campo de baloncesto en la que había todo tipo de juegos estúpidos, como el del topo que asoma la cabeza desde su madriguera y tienes que darle con una especie de bate de plástico, o los futbolines, además de todos los videojuegos imaginables. El oeste de Kansas siempre había sido una zona relativamente atrasada en otros aspectos; las películas tardaban un par de meses en llegar de costa a costa, y no hablemos de la moda; pero en cuestión de videojuegos siempre estaba al día, siempre tenía el último, el mejor. Aunque el Rata pasaba de los videojuegos, una vez le oí decir que eran una «decadencia moderna», y se iba directamente al polvoriento rincón donde había media docena de futbolines, ocupando un espacio que de lo contario estaría vacío, cambiaba una moneda de un dólar y metía los veinticinco céntimos en la máquina. Nunca lo vi gastar más de un dólar, ni siquiera cuando el precio de la partida subió a cincuenta céntimos.

El Rata decía que el secreto está en las caderas.

—El secreto está en el impulso —decía el Rata, y golpeaba la máquina con la pelvis. Se encendían las luces, se oían explosiones. Se oía un grito y me daba cuenta de que era yo quien había gritado.

—Eso es, cariño —decía el Rata—. Anímame. Anima a tu hombre.

A veces, una multitud de curiosos se congregaba alrededor. Alguien pasaba por allí, se fijaba primero en el excéntrico jugador y luego en el marcador, en el número de créditos que había conseguido o en el hecho de que parecía no perder una sola bola. Cuando la máquina cantaba anunciando que había ganado una partida gratis, siempre se acercaba algún curioso, y si nada de esto daba resultado, yo me paseaba por la sala de juegos para hacerle propaganda, en primer lugar porque al Rata lo que le gustaba era jugar con público y en segundo lugar porque el mejor modo de asegurarse de que algún chico pelirrojo y lleno de pecas apostara cinco pavos era que sus amigos estuvieran mirando. El Rata decía que así jugaba mejor, y cuando yo le dije que nunca lo había visto jugar mal, me chupó la barbilla y me llamó bombón, que era como me llamaba a veces. A veces, cuando el público se sumía en ese silencio especial con que los adolescentes muestran su asombro, el Rata se detenía en mitad de la partida. Sujetaba la bola de acero levantando el petaco izquierdo —siempre con el izquierdo, porque yo siempre me colocaba a la derecha de la máquina—, me agarraba del cuello con la mano derecha y me atraía hacia sí para darme un beso, grande o pequeño, con lengua o sin lengua, daba lo mismo, un beso siempre es un beso, y adiós siempre es adiós. «Este es Reggie –decía el Rata a su público–. Reggie me da suerte.» Sin apartar de mí los ojos o la mano derecha, pulsaba el botón del petaco con la izquierda, y empezaban a encenderse luces y a oírse explosiones y la máquina anunciaba otra partida gratis, y el público quedaba en silencio ante esta demostración de chulería. Yo ni siquiera los miraba. No podía apartar la vista del Rata aunque quisiera, y esperaba el momento de silencio que llegaba cuando la máquina se tranquilizaba. Y en ese momento de silencio el Rata siempre decía: «Sin Reggie no podría hacerlo», y aunque sabía que había algo extraño en sus palabras, nunca estaba seguro de qué era lo que me resultaba extraño, aunque ahora creo que lo sé. La verdad es que sí podía. Podía pasarse sin mí. Todos podían.

5.15

COLIN

Esa primera noche se quedó dormido. No digo que estuviera fingiendo, pero me pareció forzado: lo zarandeé un par de veces y no se despertó. Me había abrazado por la cintura, entrelazando las manos, y el aliento que salía de su boca abierta se concentraba en mi abdomen, formando un pequeño charco de agua. Yo estaba despierto, pensando en qué hacer, pero entonces ocurrió algo que me ahorró la necesidad de hacer nada: Justin entró en la habitación. En realidad no entró; se detuvo en la puerta, un figura flaca y silenciosa, empequeñecida por las enormes dimensiones del marco. Cuando reparé en su presencia por primera vez pensé que podía llevar horas allí, inocuo, invisible, sin mirarnos, sin esperar siquiera a que termináramos; sencillamente, allí. «Justin», lo llamé. Pero no contestó. No había nada más que los ronquidos de Divine, el charco que formaba su aliento en mi piel, y al hablar yo me pareció que Divine se sobresaltaba. Lo miré y, cuando volví a mirar a la puerta, Justin ya no estaba. No sé dónde durmió esa noche; el caso es que no había vuelto a dormir conmigo. Las cosas sucedieron así: primero dejó de hablarme, luego dejó de dormir conmigo y, finalmente, empezó a pasar todo el tiempo en casa de Wade. A primeros de mayo encontré una almohada y una manta en el suelo de la cúpula. Digo que lo encontré, aunque en realidad estuve espiando a través de la cerradura, porque Justin siempre dejaba la puerta cerrada con llave. Me tranquilizó saber que pasaba el día en el búnker de hormigón de Wade y que de noche dormía en la ciudadela de la casa de caliza. Quizá me alivió sentir que tenía una preocupación menos. En lugar de preocuparme por Justin, centré mi atención en Divine.

Con ropa o sin ella, Divine era un alma desnuda. Se sentaba a mis pies si no le dejaba sentarse en mi regazo; me seguía a todas partes como un perro fiel. Cuando estaba al alcance de su vista no me quitaba los ojos de encima; ni una revista, ni la televisión, ni una explosión nuclear lograba distraer su atención de mi persona y, cuando nuestras miradas se cruzaban, aunque fuese solo un momento, Divine empezaba a hablar. Vámonos, solía decir casi siempre, vámonos. Y yo siempre le contestaba lo mismo: «No puedo marcharme».

—Eso no son más que sandeces —dijo un día.
—¿Sandeces?
Divine eludió la pregunta.
—Puedes marcharte cuando quieras —dijo—. No hay nada que te retenga aquí.
—Has cambiado —observé—. Antes del accidente nunca habrías usado la palabra «sandeces». Habrías dicho gilipolleces o putas gilipolleces, o puto montón de putas gilipolleces...
—Ya vale —me interrumpió Divine. Se encogió de hombros; esperó; volvió a encogerse de hombros, pero se negó a mirarme—. ¿No podemos irnos?

No le respondí. Me senté ante mi escritorio con las manos sobre la máquina de escribir, abiertas pero inmóviles, como las de un Buda. La hoja de papel de ese día me observaba, coronada como siempre por las siguientes palabras: *La última línea de esta historia es inevitable.* Divine se sentó junto a la máquina de escribir y, con un dedo, sin mirarme, trazó una línea a partir de mi mano derecha, me recorrió el brazo, los hombros, y descendió por el otro brazo hasta la mano izquierda. Su cuerpo seguía la trayectoria de la mano; se apartó del escritorio y empezó a moverse, trazando un lento arco alrededor de mi cuerpo.

—Nadie nos detendrá —dijo, cuando hubo terminado. Se agazapó detrás de mí, apretándome los hombros con los dedos—. Todo el mundo se alegrará de que nos marchemos.
—No puedo irme —repetí, y luego, como si se me ocurriera de repente, añadí—: Hasta que aparezca.

Y entonces me puse a teclear lo que había dicho, pero lo que apareció en el papel fue: *No puedo irme hasta que ella aparezca.*

—Nunca encontrarán nada —dijo Divine—. El agente Brown no es capaz de encontrar ni su propio pompis para limpiárselo.
—«Pompis» —repetí, pero no podía apartar la vista de las palabras que había escrito. Empezaba a comprender algo de lo que no había

sido consciente hasta el momento de escribirlas: que realmente no podía irme hasta que apareciera Lucy. El sentimiento de culpa hizo que se me encogiera el estómago y, por un momento, pensé que iba a vomitar. ¿Cómo era posible que Lucy Robinson hubiera sido desplazada por un montón de cuartillas de papel?

Divine había dejado las manos muertas sobre mis hombros; ni siquiera estaba seguro de que aún siguieran allí, hasta que, tras un largo silencio, sentí que las apartaba de mi cuerpo. Divine surgió de detrás de mí y se colocó a un lado de la mesa; caminó con exagerada lentitud y supe que lo hacía para que yo pudiera fijarme en su trasero. Y admito que lo hice. Le miré el culo. Lo había visto tantas veces que ya no me excitaba. En realidad, creo que nunca me había excitado. No era el culo de Divine lo que yo me estaba follando.

Cuando llegó a donde quería llegar se dio la vuelta y apoyó una cadera en la mesa.

—Me parece que no lo entiendo —dijo tranquilamente. Sonrió al hablar, pero su sonrisa era horrible, como la de un payaso; no tenía nada que ver con la expresión de sus ojos, como su tono de voz tampoco tenía nada que ver con sus palabras. Su expresión y su tono estaban cargados de incertidumbre, de temor incluso (no sabía si de mí o de otra cosa), y lo cierto es que lo único que Divine parecía capaz de hacer con su temor era decir: «Tal vez deberías explicármelo», con una voz tan hueca y vacía como la de una estrella porno que no está pensando ni en los diálogos ni en la escena que viene a continuación, sino en la raya de cocaína que piensa meterse en cuanto haya terminado.

Miré mi máquina de escribir.

La última línea de esta historia es inevitable.

Divine empezó a balancear una pierna adelante y atrás.

No puedo irme hasta que ella aparezca.

—¿Te crees muy sexy, verdad? Te sientas ahí con los pantalones bien ajustados y empiezas a mover la pierna para que te tumbe encima de la mesa y te folle.

Divine aceleró el movimiento de la pierna, pero no dijo nada. Yo seguí gritando; gritando palabras que parecían estar tan lejos de mí como la pierna de Divine parecía estarlo de él.

—Vale, vamos a hacerlo. Date la vuelta y quítate los pantalones. ¿O prefieres que haga como si estuviera violándote? ¿Quieres que te ate con una cuerda y que te meta un calcetín en la boca? —Le agarré la mano y lo atraje hacia mí—. Ven aquí, Divine. —Lo tiré de bruces sobre la mesa y oí que su barbilla chocaba contra la máquina de escribir.

—¡Ay!

—¿Te estoy haciendo daño, Divine? Claro que estoy haciéndote daño. ¿Quieres que te haga daño, verdad? —Entonces le agarré del pelo para obligarlo a mirar el papel que había metido en el carro de la máquina—. Lee. Lee en voz alta.

—¿Qué?

—¡Que leas!

Divine leyó con voz temblorosa:

—«La última línea de esta historia es inev… inevitable.»

—¡Eso no! —Tiré de la página bruscamente y señalé la segunda línea. Estaba tumbado encima de él, con el pene apretado contra su culo—. ¡Esto!

Divine jadeó y empezó a temblar. Intentó hablar, pero solo consiguió emitir una especie de tos ahogada. Se pasó la lengua por los labios y lo intentó de nuevo:

—No… no puedo irme hasta que ella aparezca. —Luego se quedó quieto un momento y, de repente, empezó a llorar muy despacio. Sentía sus sollozos en mis dedos, que aún seguían sujetándole el pelo.

—Muy bien —dije; la rabia abandonó mi voz y mi cuerpo. Le solté el pelo. Se lo acaricié una vez, una sola vez, alisándoselo todo cuanto la brillantina me lo permitía. El cuerpo de Divine temblaba bajo el mío, pero seguía sollozando en silencio, y ninguno de los dos reaccionamos cuando sonó el teléfono.

La última línea de esta historia es inevitable.

El teléfono volvió a sonar.

No puedo irme hasta que ella aparezca.

El teléfono sonó una vez más.

Fue una perversa urgencia la que me hizo incorporarme. Coloqué las manos sobre el teclado y empecé a escribir las palabras con las que siempre terminaba el día. *Nunca volví a…* comencé, pero me detuve, porque no sabía qué pronombre usar. ¿A él? ¿A ella? ¿A ello?

La máquina tecleó. Durante un rato se oyó el zumbido sordo de la cinta del contestador automático, luego, una garganta imposible de identificar en un primer momento carraspeó antes de hablar, y el vozarrón del agente Brown llenó la habitación. «Colin Nieman. Soy el sheriff Brown.» Hubo una pausa. «Creo que hemos encontrado algo, señor Nieman.» Otra larga pausa, esta vez interrumpida por un crujir de papeles. «Nunca volví a verlo», dijo el agente Brown. «Si eso le suena, señor Nieman, supongo que querrá pasarse por la comisaría.»

Volvía a casa horas más tarde. Divine estaba dormido en el sofá. Tenía las mejillas caídas y era evidente que se había alborotado el pelo en un ataque de rabia, porque lo tenía todo revuelto, con el mismo aspecto afro dorado que le había visto esa otra noche en casa de Wade. Yo llevaba bajo el brazo un montón de páginas arrugadas y manchadas de barro; era mi novela y estaba completa; había recuperado la versión definitiva.

Divine no se despertó cuando encendí la luz y tampoco se despertó cuando dejé la novela recuperada encima de la mesa. Como casi todo lo demás —como los trozos del cuerpo de Lucy Robinson—, la novela había aparecido en el buzón de Myra y T. V. Daniels la había encontrado cuando hacía el reparto de la tarde. T. V. dijo que Myra llevaba varios días sin recibir correo, ni siquiera un catálogo, y por supuesto tampoco enviaba nada, de manera que el manuscrito podía llevar allí más de una semana.

La hoja de papel arrugada aún seguía en el carro de la máquina de escribir. *La última línea de esta historia es inevitable, No puedo irme hasta que ella aparezca, Nunca volví a…* y Divine no se despertó cuando saqué el papel del carro y lo dejé sobre la novela. No se despertó cuando empecé a encender la chimenea con unas cuantas hojas de papel en blanco y un viejo volumen sin título que saqué de la estantería, y no se despertó cuando, una por una, tiré al fuego hasta la última página de mi novela. Docenas de frases pasaron rápidamente ante mis ojos antes de desaparecer entre el humo y las llamas. *La última línea de esta historia es inevitable, La mayoría de la gente tiene siete agujeros en la cabeza, Te conté una versión tergiversada, Una persiana de aluminio se abrió de repente, Sucedió en un callejón, Cuando me desperté…* Pero Divine no se despertó. Parecía que no había nada capaz de despertarlo, y, cuando al fin terminé de destruir lo que había creado, me tumbé a su lado en el sofá y me quedé allí, escuchando el crepitar del fuego a mis espaldas y buscando las palabras adecuadas para expresar lo que estaba pensando, pero lo único que me venía a la cabeza era un cliché.

En humo, pensé. Todo se ha convertido en humo.

5.16

WEBBIE

El servilismo dio sus frutos antes de lo que esperaba. Rosemary Krebs era una mujer muy ocupada que, como un hombre de negocios, prefería llevar sus asuntos fuera de casa, y una semana después de que empezara a trabajar para ella me entregó una llave que, según me explicó, solo servía para la puerta trasera, y en lo sucesivo volvió a trabajar en el anexo municipal, que es como ella llamaba al cobertizo que había detrás de la comisaría. La oficina era del alcalde, pero él, cuando no andaba por ahí estrechando manos u ocupándose de las necesidades imaginarias de su pueblo, prefería, como un ama de casa, despachar sus asuntos en casa, donde no resultaba difícil seguirle el rastro, porque siempre se encerraba en su despacho del tercer piso para declamar en voz alta lo que él llamaba su «discurso de campaña», e incluso cuando salía de allí para ir al baño o asaltar el frigorífico, continuaba declamando, recorría la casa dejando tras de sí un reguero de palabras como «trabajando conjuntamente» y «aunando esfuerzos», que revelaban su situación como el pitido de un radar.

La casa de los Krebs —Rosemary Krebs se había referido a ella en alguna ocasión como «la vivienda familiar de Eustace», y a mí me pareció como si hablara de un lavabo público— era un claro ejemplo de la grandeza victoriana, y aunque no era tan antigua como parecía, sí estaba en peor estado de lo que cabía esperar por su edad. Estaba dividida en demasiadas habitaciones, llenas de cortinas y abarrotadas de muebles de un estilo que podríamos calificar de «barroco pionero». Había galones y borlas por todas partes, y las superficies aparecían repletas de tallas que representaban parábolas griegas y cristianas. Las piernas, los brazos y los laterales de las sillas, las mesas y las cómodas aparecían tan profusamente talladas que la acumulación del polvo se convertía en una especie de lección de historia o, más exactamente, de moral: el Señor puede invadir tu cuerpo con absoluta impunidad, como una lengua de fuego o un cisne; si desafías a Dios acabarás en el vientre de la ballena o el mundo se desplomará sobre tu cabeza; si te amas demasiado a ti mismo tu belleza terminará convertida en la frágil y efímera forma de una flor.

Además de su pasión por los adornos y otras peculiaridades sureñas, Rosemary Krebs creía firmemente en la necesidad de exhibir todo lo que pudiera contener un resquicio de historia familiar, de prestigio o, a falta de lo anterior, sencillamente de riqueza. Cristal, plata y figuritas de porcelana: Rosemary Krebs tenía de todo ello en abundancia y se preocupaba de mostrarlo en lugar bien visible, compitiendo su disposición con la compleja y elaborada decoración del conjunto. Y lo que es más, se sabía de memoria la historia de cada objeto: si, estando ella presente, yo cogía una cucharita de plata para abrillantarla, Rosemary Krebs miraba al vacío y decía: «Mi tía Carolinia, la hermana de mi madre, que fue una solterona hasta el día que murió, compró esa cucharilla mucho antes de que papá nos dejara en la ruina». Si yo le respondía con una serie de palabras ordenadas de manera coherente hasta formar una frase —si, dicho de otro modo, yo le hablaba—, Rosemary Krebs guardaba silencio de inmediato, pero si yo continuaba trabajando obsequiosamente, diciendo solo «sí, señora», ella seguía hablando un rato para contarme un notable capítulo de su historia familiar, aunque siempre aderezado con comentarios como «antes de que papá nos dejara en la ruina», insinuando una sordidez que Rosemary Krebs, supongo que en la línea de la gran tradición sureña, prefería considerar como tragedia. En todo caso, yo tomaba nota de todas sus pertenencias, no solo por lo ostentosas y vulgares que eran, sino porque resultaba imposible limpiarlas. Al cabo de una semana de trabajo llegué a respetar a Rosemary Krebs al menos en un sentido: para mantener esa casa tan inmaculada como había estado en otro tiempo y además ser capaz de meter las narices en los asuntos de todo el mundo había que ser una persona con muchos recursos.

Sin embargo, costaba imaginar que en una casa así, donde todo estaba a la vista, pudiera haber algo oculto, pero cuanto más me familiarizaba con la interminable colección de baratijas de Rosemary Krebs más me convencía de que todo aquel exhibicionismo no era más que una elaborada máscara y que el verdadero rostro de la casa de Rosemary Krebs aún permanecía oculto. El sótano y el ático, cuando al fin logré entrar allí, resultaron tan carentes de interés como había imaginado, y no mostraron más que el habitual batiburrillo de vestidos viejos y cuadros de una casa colonial flanqueada por un roble cubierto de musgo. El porche de cuatro columnas, de estilo griego clásico, era sin lugar a dudas el predecesor del que Rosemary Krebs había añadido a la casa de Phyneas Krebs en el momento de tomar posesión de ella; los vestidos, supe más tarde, eran una fuente de pesar para Rosemary Krebs, quien me confió que todas las mujeres de su familia siempre se habían intercambiado la ropa, pero que no había modista capaz de adaptarlos a su pequeña silueta. Además de los cuadros y los vestidos, había cómodas y baúles —las cajas de cartón no tenían la categoría suficiente para albergar los trajes de sus antepasadas— llenos de porcelana, en su mayoría rota, con los trozos envueltos en papel de seda o embalados entre paja. Después de mucho buscar no encontré nada más incriminatorio que un paquete de cartas casi eróticas, muchas de ellas, aderezadas con versos, cruzadas entre la joven Rosemary y su padre con ocasión de sus respectivos cumpleaños; una comprometida correspondencia que concluyó más o menos cuando ella cumplió los diecisiete años.

Fue el alcalde quien finalmente me indicó el camino a seguir. Un día me lo encontré en la biblioteca, y me sorprendió tanto que me quedé sin aliento, no por el hecho de encontrármelo, sino por el volumen que tenía en las manos. Yo suponía que las lecturas de Phyneas Krebs se limitarían a los tres libros que había sobre la mesa de su despacho —*Cómo triunfar en la política local*, *Cómo ser un buen líder* y *Todo lo que necesitaba saber lo aprendí en el parvulario*—, además, y por supuesto, de la inscripción tallada en la cabecera de su cama: «Porque el Señor amaba tanto el mundo». El artesano había tallado las palabras en grande y, al igual que el imán que había en el frigorífico de mi padre, el resto de la cita de Juan 3,16 se había borrado de la cama de los Krebs, como se habían borrado las palabras del libro que sostenía el alcalde. Lo cerró bruscamente, pero tuve tiempo de ver que era un libro hueco; sonrió con expresión benévola mientras se metía una mano en el bolsillo y volvía a dejar el libro en la estantería, junto a los demás. Se quedó un momento sin saber qué hacer, con la sonrisa petrificada en el rostro, y luego dijo:

—Veamos, Webbie. ¿Puedo hacerte una pregunta?

Le sonreí sin apartar la mirada del libro que acababa de dejar en la estantería.

—Por supuesto —dije, una vez que lo hube localizado, y acto seguido añadí—, señor.

—Corrígeme si me equivoco, Webbie. Creo que tienes cierta amistad con el señor Nieman, ¿verdad?

Mi sonrisa se esfumó.

—Yo no diría tanto. No lo conozco bien.

—Bueno, sí, quiero decir, no. No quería decir que lo conocieras bien.

Volví a sonreír.

—De todos modos, me preguntaba si tal vez supieras...

Me acaricié la palma de la mano con las plumas del plumero, como si estuviera impaciente por volver al trabajo.

—¿Sí...? —le interrumpí.

—Bueno, verás... —Titubeó un poco y al fin me espetó—: ¿De verdad era un revolucionario?

La sonrisa se petrificó en mi rostro.

—No lo entiendo, alcalde.

—El caso es que Eustace encontró una copia del manuscrito del señor Nieman el otro día, y lo estuve ojeando en secreto.

—Lo siento, señor, sigo sin entender. ¿Es que el señor Nieman afirma en su novela que es un revolucionario?

—Bueno, eso es precisamente lo que no me ha quedado claro. Todo el mundo dice que ha estado escribiendo sobre Galatea, pero cuando cogí el libro y vi lo que contaba sobre el desierto y el océano... Y también habla de cosas como tatuajes y lentes de contacto y esteroides, en fin, cosas que no he visto que el señor Nieman tenga o use, pero habla de un escritor que en realidad es él mismo y por eso... —Me miró con auténtico terror—. ¿Crees que aquí puede estar pasando realmente una cosa así?

—¿Una cosa así...?

—Quiero decir que pronto habrá elecciones.

Me costó contener la risa antes de hablar, y tuve que mirarle a los zapatos, que se movían con nerviosismo.

—Verá, señor, creo que el señor Nieman ya ha tenido suficiente sin necesidad de... —preferí dejar la frase en suspenso.

—¿Tú crees?

—Eso creo, señor.

—Bien. Me alegro. —Soltó una risita, y me atreví a mirarle a la cara. Luego añadió—: Será mejor que vuelva al trabajo, tengo mucho que hacer. Por cierto, lo estás haciendo muy bien; nunca había visto a Rosemary tan contenta como desde que tú llegaste. —Se despidió entre dientes y salió de la habitación dando tumbos.

—Gracias, señor alcalde —le dije, cuando ya salía—. Que pase una buena tarde.

Cuando un momento después oí que la puerta principal se cerraba, corrí hacia la estantería. El libro que había consultado el alcalde resultó ser un viejo volumen de una enciclopedia, destripado y lleno de dinero. Dejé el libro de inmediato en su sitio; no necesitaba dinero. Había negociado mi sueldo con la única intención de despejar cualquier sospecha que Rosemary Krebs pudiera albergar. Volví a mi tarea. De vez en cuando me reía para mis adentros al acordarme del libro hueco, o de la idea que el alcalde tenía de Colin Nieman como una especie de revolucionario enviado para aumentar la tensión política en Galatia. ¿De qué trataba su libro?, me pregunté. Y nada más hacerme esa pregunta corrí de nuevo hacia la estantería. El libro donde el alcalde guardaba sus ahorros llevaba la inscripción *Dinero*, y de pronto me sorprendí cogiendo otros libros de la biblioteca —era absurdo pensar que el alcalde y su mujer leyeran algo alguna vez, ¿verdad?—, y entonces comprendí que todos aquellos libros, como el resto del mobiliario de la casa, no pertenecían a la familia de Phyneas Krebs sino a la de Rosemary. Después de consultar unos doce libros encontré otro tomo hueco, un ejemplar de *Moby Dick* encuadernado en piel, en cuyo interior había varias horquillas de perlas. Pensé que las perlas, como producto marino, guardaban una relación directa con *Moby Dick*, pero luego caí en la cuenta de que las horquillas, como la colección de bastones de mi padre, eran de marfil, y estaba casi segura de que el marfil, como los corsés ortopédicos del sótano, era en realidad hueso de ballena.

En el curso de las semanas siguientes descubrí que la manía de Rosemary Krebs de exhibirlo todo se complementaba con una manía, igual de intensa, por ocultarlo todo. Y, como en toda obsesión, el acto parecía imponerse sobre el objeto en sí. Igual que T. V. Daniels se comía todo lo que le pusieran delante, Rosemary Krebs escondía todo aquello para lo que encontraba un buen lugar, siempre y cuando fuera capaz de instrumentar un buen sistema de correspondencia entre el objeto y el lugar donde lo escondía. Así, el dinero del alcalde se almacenaba en un volumen en el que ponía «dinero», que, por cierto, seguía estando en su sitio, lo cual me indicó que el alcalde no le había comentado a su mujer nada sobre nuestro encuentro, o que se lo había dicho y ella estaba poniendo a prueba mi honradez. No tardé en descubrir que la función primordial de tanto adorno tallado en los muebles de Rosemary Krebs no era meramente estética, ni siquiera una parábola o, como insinuó Wade, una táctica de distracción; lo que se proponía era ocultar las fuentes y los resortes ocultos que daban acceso a los numerosos compartimientos secretos desperdigados por la casa. Los invitados que saboreaban un té helado en la sala de estar no podían imaginar que sus codos reposaban sobre un muestrario de encaje en el que cada floritura aludía a un vestido, a un velo, a un guante jamás usado; el brazo del sillón oculto bajo el encaje mostraba un relieve de Aracné: primero tejiendo en su telar, luego transformada en araña como castigo por su soberbia. Los invitados a cenar pasaban sus platos sobre un sinnúmero de proyectos, de grandiosas versiones de bibliotecas, centros cívicos y hospitales para el pueblo, e incluso de planos aún más grandiosos para la mansión del alcalde, además de un tribunal del condado, un centro comercial y un Burger King. En cuestión de semanas, una vez que supe con certeza lo que estaba buscando, encontré docenas de objetos ocultos: dedales, pendientes, cartas, un látigo, flores secas, una muñeca de plástico. Buena parte de ellos aparecían cubiertos por una gruesa capa de polvo, que indicaba que nadie los había tocado durante años, y la mayoría, como ya he señalado, parecían inútiles, ocultos no por lo que pudieran significar sino por el mero hecho de ocultarlos. Tras un panel de un armario –en el que aparecía tallado un rollo de pergamino negro– encontré una pluma antigua, con la tinta seca y adherida a la plumilla. Tras el fondo falso de un jarrón de porcelana esmaltada con un dibujo de dragones chinos descubrí un surtido de cajas de cerillas que llevaban los nombres de diversos hoteles europeos. Alguien debería haberle explicado a Rosemary Krebs que los dragones de la mitología china no escupían fuego. En el fondo de un paragüero –un paragüero en Kansas, donde el índice de lluvias anual es inferior a los doscientos milímetros– hallé el mayor de los tesoros: una botella de agua, medio vacía, cerrada y lacrada. La botella llevaba una etiqueta amarillenta, sujeta con un trozo de cuerda, en la que se veían unas palabras escritas con pluma estilográfica, cuya tinta, como la sangre, había perdido su color original, adquiriendo un tono castaño rojizo:

R.–
Precipitaciones, décimo aniversario.
–E.

Creo que, llegado este punto, debo mencionar que «E» era Eminent King, el padre de Rosemary Krebs, aunque cuando encontré el envase no sabía nada más de él.

Y muchas otras cosas: pequeños libros ocultos dentro de otros más grandes, una canica guardada en una lata de té oxidada. Fotografías. Hojas de otoño, con sus colores aún tan vivos que parecían pintadas. El alfil de marfil de un ajedrez antiguo, con el rostro agrietado y ennegrecido por el tiempo, como si fuera un hombre de carne y hueso. Muchas cosas y todas ellas absolutamente inútiles para mí, carentes por completo de sentido; no me proporcionaron ninguna pista, pero aun así seguí indagando, convencida de que entre todo aquel montón de fragmentos y baratijas debía haber un tesoro. Sin embargo, a medida que pasaban los meses empecé a dudar de que realmente hubiera algo de valor, y también a hartarme de aspirar los vapores del agua mezclada con amoníaco y de quemarme las manos con el líquido cáustico con que Rosemary Krebs me obligaba a pulir la plata, y cada vez me molestaba más ver sus pies, diminutos como los de un pájaro, pisoteando el suelo de parqué que yo había barrido y encerado arrodillada mientras musitaba «Sí, señora» y «No, señora», al tiempo que contenía las ganas de asestarle un escobazo, hasta que al fin, inesperadamente, mi perseverancia se vio recompensada. Quizá «perseverancia» no sea la palabra adecuada; quizá deba decir que fue sencillamente la suerte lo que, a falta de otras opciones, me condujo hasta ello, hasta el segundo objeto más importante en mi larga y extraña búsqueda de Lucy Robinson, aunque para entonces ya no estaba en absoluto segura de lo que buscaba. Había aprendido a identificar ciertas cualidades en el modo de esconder las cosas de Rosemary Krebs, sencillamente porque no tenía otra cosa que hacer.

Lo encontré en su dormitorio. Más exactamente en su cama. Un día se me ocurrió que la «o» de la palabra «Dios» que había tallada en la cabecera de la cama tenía una forma sospechosamente oval, como un ojo o un huevo, y me bastó con apretar para acceder a un pequeño compartimiento que albergaba una gruesa Biblia, la cual, en lugar del Éxodo o el Deuteronomio, contenía un pequeño volumen donde se reseñaban la propia ley y el propio éxodo de Rosemary Krebs: su diario. Era un relato extraño, que comenzaba cuando ella tenía diecisiete años y abarcaba, con interrupciones, otros veinticinco años de su vida, hasta poco después del incendio de Kenosha y la fundación de Galatea. Fue este diario, junto con las pequeñas anécdotas que Rosemary Krebs me había relatado ocasionalmente, lo que me permitió reconstruir con coherencia el hilo narrativo de la historia. Era una historia extraña, en sí misma completa, pero que al mismo tiempo y por sí sola no me llevaba a ninguna parte. La imagen que me viene a la cabeza es la de una vía férrea: la historia de Rosemary Krebs discurría por un solo raíl, pero yo sabía que había una segunda vía, aún por descubrir. Lo fui leyendo a saltos, cada vez que cambiaba las sábanas o limpiaba el cuarto de baño del dormitorio principal, y reuní poco a poco las pruebas como hacía en mis tiempos de historiadora, tomando notas que ordenaba y reordenaba a medida que la secuencia de los hechos me iba quedando clara. Y a lo largo de mi investigación, recordé el comentario de Justin sobre la necesidad de que el ser humano descubra su verdadera esencia mediante la confesión escrita. Nada se escribe solo para quien lo escribe, había dicho: siempre va dirigido a un público más amplio. Y, mientras tomaba mis notas, comprendí que eso era tan cierto en mi caso como en el de Rosemary Krebs.

5.17

JUSTIN

Me puso a trabajar. Me enseñó a preparar el bastidor y a tensar el lienzo, a imprimarlo, a pintarlo. No debería decir que me puso a trabajar: me enseñó a pintar. «No soy un director artístico –dijo–. No soy un intelectual. Pinto lo que me apetece.» Los bastidores que construía, que usaba, eran tan temblorosos como las pinceladas con que cubría el lienzo. Wade me proporcionó pintura y pinceles, un caballete y un lugar protegido de la luz del sol, pero luego me dejó a mi aire, y como no sabía qué hacer, intenté imitarlo. Usaba los mismos colores que él, apretaba el pincel y lo arrastraba como él para embadurnar la superficie del lienzo, pero mis cuadros parecían una pared pintada por un epiléptico. Wade nunca criticó lo que yo pintaba, aunque a veces me corregía; me sujetaba la mano para enseñarme a sostener el pincel y decía: «Con suavidad, con suavidad, es un pincel, es un cuadro, no es aguja e hilo».

Un día me distrajo el paso fugaz de una sombra por delante de la ventana. Era un pájaro, pero volaba tan deprisa que no pude reconocer a qué especie pertenecía y, de repente, me vino a la cabeza una imagen de las paredes de la cúpula. En una esquina del lienzo, aún vacía, intenté copiar uno de los pájaros que había en las paredes de la cúpula, una alondra, con el lomo magenta y el vientre lavanda, toda cubierta de motas de color verde fosforescente. Esos eran los colores elegidos por el pintor original, e hice cuanto pude por recrearlos con los colores que Wade había mezclado para mí. Cuando hube terminado recordé que la alondra sostenía en una de sus patas una planta muy parecida a un alga, y decidí añadirla en el último momento. Me separé un poco del lienzo para contemplar mi desigual creación. Me pareció que el pájaro no sería capaz de volar, pero lo era. Entonces me di cuenta de que Wade estaba mirando el cuadro.

—Está muy bien —dijo, en voz muy baja, muy extraña; y, muy a mi pesar, me ruboricé. Wade permaneció un momento sin decir nada, luego cogió un pincel fino de una jarra de barro y lo mojó en una mancha oscura de la paleta. Se acercó hasta mi pájaro y, con breves y rápidos gestos, corrigió ligeramente su forma. Al principio me pareció que solo pretendía que se pareciera más a un pájaro, pero luego comprendí que lo que hacía era transformarlo en «ese» pájaro, el pájaro de la pared de la cúpula. Cuando hubo terminado, retrocedió y dijo—: Bea debió de tomarse muchas molestias para que los murales de esa habitación se conservaran intactos. En un principio no eran muy sólidos —dijo sonriendo; y enseguida añadió—: El yeso de la marca Yankee Carting's TruValue no está hecho exactamente con los mismos materiales que usaban los romanos —observó, sin dejar de mirar el cuadro—. Creo que tenía quince o dieciséis años cuando pinté ese mural. Bea rondaba los setenta y Hank ya había muerto. Fue la primera vez que me pagaron por mi trabajo. Bueno, no es verdad —rectificó—; fue la segunda. —Hizo una pausa y suspiró, pero no me dijo cuándo fue la primera vez que le pagaron por un cuadro—. Bea no se mostró muy concreta. Solo dijo que quería pájaros que volaran hacia las alturas. «Hacia las alturas —dijo—, hacia Henry.» —Guardó silencio de nuevo, pero esta vez cogió otro pincel de la jarra, una brocha plana de un centímetro de ancho. Lo mojó con pintura blanca—. Debe de estar casi borrado. Desdibujado. Desconchado. ¿Está desconchado? —Me miró, pero no me moví—. ¡Ah, se me había olvidado —dijo con una leve sonrisa— que Justin no habla! Justin ni siquiera asiente con la cabeza. ¿Está así de desconchado, Justin? —Me asombró que un solo y enérgico trazo lograra producir un efecto idéntico al yeso desconchado de la habitación de la cúpula—. Se me ocurrió que la alondra (y no era una mala idea para un chico de quince años) que sujetaba un trozo de alga podría ser una versión de la paloma que llevó en el pico la rama de olivo hasta el arca de Noé. Prueba de que fuera, en algún lugar, había agua. —Se echó a reír—. Y además, Bea también tenía el arca.

Cuando dijo esto recordé el hueco en el seto que me permitió ver con claridad el incendio del arca de Noah Deacon, y me entraron ganas de decirle a Wade que, al margen de lo que hubiera sido Bea y lo que hubiera sabido, sin duda estaba al corriente de todo lo que ocurría en el arca varada en su propiedad. Pero no dije nada, y Wade siguió hablando.

—Supongo que ese sueño se estará desmoronando, que estará cayendo al suelo y cubriéndolo de polvo. Cayendo hacia las profundidades. —Mientras hablaba, retocaba sin parar la forma del pájaro, hasta que este desapareció bajo una mancha blanca—. No tardará en esfumarse, ¿verdad? Puede que yo lo sobreviva o puede que no, pero seguro que tú lo sobrevives. —Siguió retocando—. La pared no tardará en quedar otra vez desnuda, con una huella de color aquí y allá, y ¿qué verás entonces, Justin? ¿Verás esto? —Pasó el pincel con energía sobre el lienzo oscurecido y emborronado, y al ver que yo no seguía su trayectoria con la mirada, me volvió la cabeza con una mano que apestaba a pintura—. ¿Qué verás allí, Justin? ¿Te esforzarás por ver al pájaro perdido, o quizá al pájaro real, al que fue necesario sacrificar para pintar el mural? ¿O buscarás lo único que ese pájaro puede enseñarte?

Se detuvo de repente.

—Vamos, Justin; no llores.

Me puse rígido y sorbí con la nariz. No me había dado cuenta de que estaba llorando. Estaba pensando en lo que quedaba de la última novela de Colin, en los restos que había encontrado entre las cenizas de su estudio, y también en una versión anterior de esa misma novela, la que había destruido yo mismo; por eso lloraba. Tras un momento de vacilación, Wade apartó su mano de mi mejilla y luego, muy despacio, con ternura, volvió a posarla en el mismo punto. El olor a pintura era más intenso en él que en mí, y me relajé al sentir el roce de su mano. Wade interpretó mi relajación como una invitación; me abrazó y me estrechó contra su cuerpo. Su abrazo era torpe, era el abrazo de un hombre que sabía envolver, pero no consolar, y su voz resonó clara y casi dolorosamente en mi oído.

—La primera vez que me pagaron por un cuadro yo tenía trece años. Gané un concurso estatal para la restauración del mural de John Brown en el edificio del Capitolio de Topeka. ¿Conoces ese mural, Justin? —Soltó una risita; su aliento, caliente y húmedo, me mojó el oído—. Es un mural muy famoso, muy absurdo, pero muy famoso. John Brown aparece en él con sus pantalones de ante, con el rifle en una mano y la Biblia en la otra, y una mirada firme y orgullosa. No parece en absoluto un libertador, sino un loco, que es lo que a fin de cuentas era. Pero en el momento en que se pintó el retrato no parece nada, porque la pintura del cuadro que se tomó como modelo no estaba bien fijada y se había desescamado con la humedad, como la corteza de un sicomoro. Por alguna razón las autoridades locales pensaron que la restauración del cuadro debía hacerla un ciudadano de Kansas; convocaron un concurso y yo lo gané. El concurso era anónimo, y creo que todo el mundo se quedó un poco sorprendido al descubrir que el ganador solo tenía trece años, pero luego les pareció que eso podría tener un mayor gancho publicitario. Me retrataron con todos los senadores del estado, incluso con el gobernador. No recuerdo su nombre, pero fingí estrechar su mano durante veinte minutos mientras las cámaras disparaban, y luego me subieron a un andamio, como a Miguel Ángel, eso fue lo que pensé entonces, como Miguel Ángel, y me dejaron solo. —Volvió a reír; había ido relajando su abrazo mientras hablaba y empezó a acariciarme distraídamente la espalda con la mano izquierda—. No sé por qué te cuento todo esto —dijo. Y suspiró—: Hice un buen trabajo. No cometí ningún error. Pero solo tenía trece años. Me veía a mí mismo como una especie de joven radical, aunque en realidad era, y sigo siendo, un reaccionario. Lo que quiero decir es que antes de terminar puse mi propio lema en la Biblia de John Brown. Escribí: *John Brown tenía razón*, y al momento lo cubrí de pintura; pero debe seguir estando allí, bajo una buena capa de color marrón y esos falsos jeroglíficos que pretenden representar letras, pero no son más que florituras, trazos, manchas y puntos. *John Brown tenía razón*. Lo consideré mi propia aportación a la historia. ¡Ay, Justin! —exclamó, cambiando de repente el tono de voz, que se tornó más profundo y desesperado—. No termines como yo, por favor; no termines como yo. —Se le hizo un nudo en la garganta y guardó silencio. Pensé que debería decir algo, pero no dije nada y Wade tampoco. Al cabo de un rato, se apartó de mí, cogió una brocha plana y, con hábiles trazos, dibujó de nuevo el pájaro sobre el lienzo, sobre las palabras que había escrito en el cuerpo de John Brown y sobre mí; y no dejó más que una brillante y pulida superficie blanca.

5.18

DIVINE

La primera vez fue en el establo de su padre. Yo tenía doce años y él, dieciséis. Estábamos en un establo vacío, entre un viejo caballo castrado, de color gris, que estaba a punto de dar su último paseo hasta la fábrica de pegamento, y la cerda que nos daría el beicon para el desayuno del año siguiente. Lo conocía desde hacía una semana. Siete días completos.

El Rata dijo: «Te explicaré cómo son las cosas entre nosotros». Me volvió hacia él y me cogió de los hombros. Yo era más alto, le sacaba una cabeza, pero flexioné las rodillas para que no se acomplejara. «Tú eres un maricón, y a mí me gustan los maricones; así son las cosas. La gente como nosotros, la gente que encaja, debe estar junta.»

Ya me habían llamado maricón otras veces, pero era la primera vez que le oía decir a alguien que le gustaban los maricones, y aunque acepté de buen grado esa definición de mí mismo —eso es lo que recuerdo haber pensado entonces–, esperé que me explicara cuál era su papel. No es que no supiera nada sobre el sexo, es que nunca se me había ocurrido que los demás pudieran disfrutar haciéndoselo a sí mismos, en lugar de haciéndomelo a mí, y estaba pensando en algo parecido cuando el Rata se inclinó hacia delante y me besó. El instinto, o algo así, me obligó a flexionar aún más las rodillas, hasta que mi cabeza quedó por debajo de la suya. Estaba tan incómodo que empecé a perder el equilibrio, pero el Rata me sujetó con fuerza... tal vez fuese más alto que él, pero pesaba menos y aún no tenía un solo músculo en el cuerpo. Más tarde, el Rata dijo que esa era una de las cosas que le gustaban de mí, pero ese día apartó sus labios de los míos el tiempo necesario para decir: «Siempre te sujetaré cuando vayas a caerte».

Y entonces me tumbó sobre el heno.

Y así fue. En el establo de su padre, en la cama de su padre, en su coche, sobre una manta en el campo. Nunca lo hicimos en el arca de Noah, supongo que nunca me habría atrevido a ir allí con un blanco, pero también lo hicimos un par de veces en la cueva de las Piedras Ventrales. El agente Brown la había cerrado con candado, pero era bastante fácil desatornillar las bisagras para abrir la puerta y, a juzgar por las latas de comida y los condones usados, además de las otras cosas que el Rata y yo encontramos allí, no éramos ni mucho menos los únicos que lo hacíamos. Una vez lo hicimos en los vestuarios; los demás chicos se habían marchado, pero Coach Carting seguía silbando una estúpida canción en la ducha. «Eh, tú, el del agua —recuerdo que dijo el Rata en esa ocasión–. El Rata quiere beber algo.»

Y por último en mi casa. Mis padres se habían marchado a pasar el día en Hutchinson; mi padre, entre otras muchas tonterías, se había comprado un coche japonés, y Hutch era el lugar más cercano donde había un taller para ponerlo a punto, cosa que, como cabe suponer, había que hacer con cierta regularidad. Mi madre se fue de compras, como hacía siempre, al centro comercial.

El Rata y yo dejamos el colegio definitivamente después de esta primera época. Entramos por la puerta de atrás, por la cocina, y él me tiró directamente sobre el suelo de linóleo. «En todas las habitaciones», me susurró al oído.

Me lo tiré en la cocina. Él me folló por primera vez encima de la mesa del comedor, con la nariz metida en el pimentero. Hicimos el sesenta y nueve en el cuarto de estar, con el televisor encendido, y salimos de mi habitación hechos un asco. En el baño nos aseamos y luego me llevó al dormitorio de mis padres. Le gustaba la idea de cometer una profanación. Estaba desnudo, aún mojado después de la ducha, y se dejó caer de espaldas sobre la cama para luego ponerse en pie de un salto. «Tiene buenos muelles», dijo. El perfil de su cuerpo mojado quedó grabado en la colcha blanca.

El Rata abrió los cajones uno por uno hasta que encontró la ropa interior de mi madre. Mi madre era una mujer menuda, y esa es una de las razones por las que no tuvo más hijos que yo; la otra es que no le gustaba sudar y es casi imposible fabricar un bebé en ninguna de las fases extremas del proceso sin sudar mucho. Yo nunca fui un niño grande y por eso toda su ropa me servía perfectamente, me sentaba muy bien. El Rata rellenó las copas del sujetador con papel higiénico y me vistió de arriba abajo, y allí estaba yo: con tacones altos, medias blancas, liguero, bragas negras (con encaje por delante y un lazo por detrás). El sujetador era picudo y llevaba más de dos centímetros de relleno, cosa que me sorprendió, pues siempre había pensado que el canalillo de mi madre era natural, y la peluca, de ese color que Cora llama miel sucia, es decir, sin colar, olía a polvo. Me pintó los labios de rojo cereza; me miró y dijo: «Mi amor, estás divino».

Y así fue todo.

Yo lo miré en el espejo. Era la primera vez que estábamos delante de un espejo... si hubierais visto alguna vez a Carol Wiebe comprenderíais por qué no había ningún espejo en esa casa. El Rata se puso a besarme por todo el cuerpo, luego lo besé yo o, más bien, lo obligué a que me obligara a besarlo, que fuera desplazando mi cara por todo su cuerpo; sus nalgas temblaron mientras yo se las besaba, le alboroté con las manos el pelo rubio pajizo. Luego seguimos besuqueándonos por delante y vi en el espejo su pálido perfil alrededor de mi cuerpo, como un resplandor, y pequeñas manchas rojas sobre mi piel, allí donde sus besos me habían devuelto el carmín de mis labios.

Señaló al espejo y dijo:

—¿A que nunca habías pensado que a tus padres les gustaba mirarse mientras follaban?

–Eres el primer blanco que entra en esta casa.

–Seguro que se miraban mientras te estaban concibiendo. Seguro que decían: «Vamos a tener el niño negro más guapo del mundo».

–No sé qué les parecería peor, si enterarse de que me estoy acostando en su cama con un chico o de que me estoy acostando con un chico blanco.

–En su cama –dijo el Rata.

–…

–Y ese niño negro va a ser tan guapo, decían, tan guapo, que nadie podrá resistirse a su encanto.

–No creo que mis padres hayan llegado a decirse tantas cosas en toda la vida, pero desde luego tú lo cuentas de maravilla.

–¿Lo cuento de maravilla?

–Todo lo que dices suena a verdad. Y aunque no sea verdad, lo conviertes en verdad.

Mi padre y mi madre no se enteraban de nada. Se imaginaban que yo le ponía a alguna chica la ropa interior de mi madre y me la trajinaba en su cama. Algo así. Mi padre me cogió del pelo y me arrastró hasta su habitación, señalando el perfil de un cuerpo sobre la colcha arrugada. «¿Qué significa esto, señorito?», me gritó. Y lo único que pude hacer fue mirarlo y, después de lo que el Rata y yo habíamos dicho y hecho, ¿cómo podía mentir? Mi madre estaba en la puerta, con los brazos cruzados sobre un pecho que ahora sabía que era falso, mordiéndose el labio y frunciendo el ceño; yo la miré, luego miré a mi padre y dije: «Es el Rata», y ceñí con la mirada la sombra del Rata, que era como la de Peter Pan, porque, dejadme que os diga: no hay nada como la seda barata para conservar una mancha de agua. Mi madre se quedó sin aliento y mi padre se quedó mudo durante dos minutos; luego, muy despacio, empezó a quitarse el cinturón y a bajarme los pantalones; y mi madre dijo: «Vamos, Ronnie, no le pegues», pero mi padre nunca llegó a pegarme. En lugar de pegarme se quedó mirando los mordiscos que yo tenía en el culo y otras pequeñas marcas que el Rata había dejado en mí, y creo que todavía intentó concederme el beneficio de la duda, aunque de ningún modo podía negar la sonrisa que se dibujó en mi cara. Mi padre dejó caer el cinturón al suelo y apenas tuvo tiempo de llegar al cuarto de baño antes de empezar a vomitar; yo ni siquiera tuve el buen juicio de subirme los pantalones y largarme de allí. Me quedé inmóvil, mirando el perfil del Rata sobre la cama, y cuando miré a mi madre comprendí por primera vez el poder del Rata. Mi madre seguía en la misma posición, pero se había encogido un poco. Era como si de pronto hubiese algo más en el mundo, algo que, al instalarse, le arrebatara a ella el espacio.

Poco después de aquel incidente mi padre nos sorprendió un día haciendo manitas; se nos echó encima y le dio tal puñetazo al Rata que oí crujir un hueso. Se quedó un buen rato en el suelo y yo me quedé a su lado, paralizado; mi padre tampoco se movió y empezó a echar saliva por la boca; luego, sin que mi padre o yo nos diéramos cuenta, el Rata se levantó, cogió uno de esos tablones que siempre están a mano cuando los necesitas, y se lo estampó a mi padre en la cabeza con tanta fuerza, que lo dejó seco del golpe. Después volvió a cogerme de la mano y nos marchamos.

Supongo que el Rata ganó al menos una pelea.

Pasamos una semana durmiendo en su coche y, cuando el agente Brown metió al Rata en la cárcel durante otra semana, yo volví a casa. Mi padre me ató las manos a los postes de la cama y me azotó con el cinturón durante noventa y siete minutos seguidos —no dejé de mirar el reloj ni un momento—, hasta que se dislocó un hombro; se pasó dos semanas no solo con una herida en la mejilla casi tan grande como el estado de Kansas, y de forma parecida, sino también con el brazo en cabestrillo. Pero yo no resulté tan herido como os imagináis, porque mi padre no me quitó los pantalones. Al principio lo intentó, pero luego cambió de idea.

5.19

COLIN

Puede que yo deseara que mi novela desapareciera, pero alguien me lo impedía. Dos días después de quemar la primera copia recuperada, apareció la segunda. Era una fotocopia del manuscrito original y fue encontrada en el buzón de Howard Goertzen. Howard no le entregó el manuscrito al agente Brown; me llamó personalmente y, cuando llegué a la granja de cerdos de su padre, encontré mi novela en una caja, manchada de mierda de cerdo, en la que había algo más. Me llevé la caja, la rocié con gasolina y la quemé con su contenido en el foso de obsidiana que rodeaba la casa de caliza; pero a los pocos días apareció otra copia. Estaba metida en una bolsa de plástico, herméticamente cerrada, flotando en la cubeta del molino que había en el parque de Galatia, y fueron ni más ni menos que el reverendo Greeving y sus Damas quienes la encontraron el domingo por la mañana, camino de la iglesia. Una de las Damas me la entregó personalmente; no sé cuál de ellas era, pero se quedó en la puerta de mi casa, parpadeando bajo el sol de la tarde y lanzando breves miradas a derecha e izquierda, como si buscara a las otras dos mujeres que siempre la acompañaban. «El reverendo me ha pedido que le comunique que su lectura de las Escrituras le parece sumamente peculiar», fue todo cuanto me dijo; luego se dio la vuelta y caminó sobre la gravilla en dirección a su coche.

Y así siguieron las cosas: otras seis copias de mi novela aparecieron aquí y allá; nadie más tuvo el valor, o el deseo, de tratar conmigo directamente; todos me la hicieron llegar por intermediación del agente Brown y yo fui recogiendo cada uno de los juegos fotocopiados, en un estado cada vez peor, para quemarlos, a la espera de que aparecieran otros nuevos. En algún momento, mientras veía cómo mi novela se convertía en cenizas por cuarta o quinta vez al cabo de otras tantas semanas, recordé la historia del Ave Fénix, y en lo sucesivo recurrí a la trituradora de documentos para destruir las copias. Podría haber usado unas tijeras, pero había una razón para no hacerlo: la razón por la que tenía una trituradora de documentos. Pero las tiras de papel me recordaban a la primera novela que yo había perdido en mi vida, de manera que, al final, hice un agujero en la obsidiana y las enterré allí, una por una, semana tras semana, hasta que las copias robadas dejaron de aparecer tan inesperadamente como habían aparecido.

No me sorprendió. Suponía que ya se había alcanzado el objetivo: el objetivo era, a mi entender, que todos los habitantes de Galatia supieran lo que yo había escrito sobre ellos y sobre mí mismo. Cuando dejaron de aparecer copias de mi novela, corrían rumores de que yo era un yonqui, un prostituto, un espía, incluso un terrorista, un científico chiflado, un ninfómano y, por supuesto, un ladrón de joyas. La errónea identificación del autor y el personaje era demasiado obvia para ser cómica; y sin embargo, carecía de sentido. Yo estaba allí; existía; los detalles de mi vida y mi personalidad estaban al alcance de cualquiera, pero la gente seguía sintiendo la necesidad de inventar historias extravagantes para explicar mi presencia. Y sucedió que, en cuanto Lucy Robinson desapareció, todo el mundo dejó de hablar de ella. La mayor parte de los días casi parecía que nunca había existido o que había muerto hacía mucho tiempo y todos la habían olvidado, y a medida que su secuestrador nos iba proporcionando nuevas pistas, si no sobre su paradero sí al menos sobre su prolongado sufrimiento, la gente fue dejando de hablar de ella. Y entonces, se me ocurrió que lo que nos estaba pasando a los dos, a Lucy Robinson y a mí, era en cierto modo lo mismo. Nos estaban borrando: a mí con mentiras y a ella con silencio.

5.20

WEBBIE

Papá nos arruinó y lo destruyó todo.

Esta fue la primera frase que la joven Rosemary King escribió en su diario a los diecisiete años, y, como todas las primeras frases, era tan pegadiza como las que Colin escupió en su novela... en su novela desaparecida, debería concretar.

Durante toda una semana lo único que pude saber es que *Papá nos arruinó y lo destruyó todo*, porque nada más abrir el diario oí el inconfundible taconeo de Rosemary Krebs por las escaleras. Esos suelos, viejos, ligeramente alabeados y huecos, eran mi principal aliado: incluso unas pisadas tan livianas como las de Rosemary Krebs resonaban por toda la casa.

Finalmente, pude entrar de nuevo en el dormitorio y acceder al compartimiento secreto de la cabecera de la cama, y supe que el hombre al que Rosemary Krebs había llamado papá se llamaba Justice Eminent King, pero que su familia lo llamaba Juez, sus amigos Emmet, y el periódico local Su Eminencia. Este último es el detalle más significativo. Según la joven Rosemary King: «Mamá siempre dijo que había dos tipos de personas que jamás deben referirse a un caballero sureño por su nombre de pila: un negro que no trabaja en su casa y un periodista... e incluso cuando el negro trabaja en su casa, solo puede usar el nombre de pila del amo con autorización, y solo si antepone al nombre el título de "señor"». Quizá sea gratuito mencionar que bajo la palabra «señor» parecía estar escrita la palabra «amo», pero lo menciono de todos modos, aunque solo sea en aras de la precisión. Sea como fuere, lo que parecía querer decir Rosemary King es que en el caso de que tal cosa llegara a ocurrir la culpa solo podía atribuírsele al propio caballero, pues solo un hombre que ha perdido el respeto de sus semejantes puede ser tratado de ese modo, y, en el caso de Juez King, no hacía falta ser muy perspicaz para descubrir sus vicios: Rosemary los había reseñado en una columna, debidamente numerados, en la segunda página de su diario.

Vicios
1. Juego
2. Alcohol
3. Mujeres de vida disoluta

Bajo el epígrafe «Dudoso» había escrito: *Demasiado perfume* y *Pelo demasiado largo*, y bajo el epígrafe «Cuestionable» había escrito: *Corbatas de lazo*.

No tardé en comprender que «de vida disoluta» era en este caso sinónimo de «negras».

La judicatura de Juez King era hereditaria, igual que su residencia, los Siete Robles –o los Siete Pecados Capitales, como la llamaba el periódico cuando no la llamaba simplemente King's Castle–, a resultas de lo cual el hombre en cuestión pasaba la mayor parte del tiempo perfeccionando el arte de la holganza, jugándose y bebiéndose lo que aún quedaba de la fortuna cosechada por la familia antes de la guerra. Cuando Rosemary King tenía once años, la finca familiar fue sacada a pública subasta, la enorme mansión fue derribada por las excavadoras y sustituida por una plantación de algodón, y el juez, cesado en su cargo, envió a su mujer y a su hija a vivir con una «prima lejana», una solterona llamada tía Syrene, «una mujer cuya visión resultaba aborrecible y su descripción aún más repugnante».

La tía Syrene vivía a una hora de Wichita en dirección oeste, en Hutchinson. «La habían llevado campo a través –escribió Rosemary– como al ganado.» El diario ofrecía un relato esquemático de los años pasados con tía Syrene, pero la casa se describe como «amplia, aunque destartalada», abarrotada de baratijas y «cajas en las que mamá guardaba los tesoros que había podido rescatar de los Siete Robles, desperdigados como el oro entre el limo en la cacerola del minero». Pero lo peor era el hecho de que la casa se hallaba situada en un vecindario que, como la pasión de su padre por la colonia, el pelo demasiado largo y las corbatas de lazo –la imagen es claramente la del coronel Sanders– era «dudoso». «Una mañana –relata Rosemary–, fui a la tienda de la esquina por huevos y limones para mamá, y me encontré con dos mujeres de piel oscura que estaban charlando... ¡¡¡y ni siquiera hablaban en inglés!!!»

La avalancha de pretendientes de tía Syrene solo era comparable a la tendencia de Juez King a cenar fuera de casa. «17 de junio: papá cena fuera; mamá cena en la cama; otra cena a solas con tía S. En un clarísimo esfuerzo por ocultar el hecho de que estaba bebiendo –la semana pasada me sorprendió olfateando su vaso–, tía S. se sirvió la ginebra en la sopa y la removió con mano poco firme. La sopa era de tomate y el vestido de tía Syrene era blanco (¡imagínatelo!). Las manchas contaban su propia historia.» La joven Rosemary no parecía haber perdido aún el amor o la admiración que sentía por su padre, y aunque estas líneas fueron escritas años después de que ese amor hubiera desaparecido, su sombra siempre se dejará sentir en estas palabras. «A fin de cuentas, él era un King, y se había casado con una Hoovier, y el camino de este King fue notorio por lo accidentado y tortuoso, aunque siempre terminaba allanándose, tornándose seguro y conduciendo a donde debía, y yo creía que volvería a llevarnos a todos otra vez a un lugar decente.»

La madre de Rosemary, Hoovier de apellido –Rosemary se refiere a ella en una ocasión como Rubella, aunque me cuesta creer que de verdad se llamara así–, siguió siendo un personaje mudo durante todos estos años; lo único que estaba claro era que Rosemary reservaba para ella todo su desprecio. A la señora King le gustaba desayunar un huevo frito sobre una tostada, una debilidad que le había sido inculcada por su niñera negra. Se «saltaba» el almuerzo, pero siempre merendaba: sándwiches de pepino y berro y té Earl Gray servido en tetera de plata. «Mamá siempre ponía una jarrita de leche en la bandeja de la Caída de Troya, aunque ella tomaba el té solo con limón, y decidía a quién invitaría de nuevo a merendar según si tomaba el té con leche o solo, lo que significaba que normalmente estábamos solas, y nuestra única compañía ocasional, si es que se puede llamar así, era la de Eleanor Vanderbilt, una anciana no tan importante como su nombre podría indicar y que resultó tener problemas para digerir la lactosa. Al parecer, los lácteos le producían flatulencias, pero, desgraciadamente, también se las producía el té, y mamá y yo no tardamos en quedarnos solas.

Pese a estos refinamientos, la señora King era una mujer fracasada. Tía Syrene, por su parte, era sencillamente una mujer arruinada, indigna siquiera de la atención que requiere el desprecio, y Juez King hacía lo único que podía pedírsele a un caballero: «Nunca salía de casa sucio o borracho, y si alguna vez regresaba en semejante estado, se aseguraba de que las mujeres de la familia no lo vieran». El resto de sus defectos carecían de importancia y, además, eran imputables a su esposa: según el código que Rosemary había aprendido de su propia madre, la esposa era la única responsable de limitar las apariciones sociales de su marido, lo que significaba limitar las suyas propias y las de la familia; y la incapacidad de la señora King para hacer tal cosa la convirtió, a ojos de la joven Rosemary, en una mujer fracasada. «Mi madre no fumaba ni bebía, ni siquiera admitía tener hambre en presencia de alguien que no fuera de la familia, y cuando veía un vaso sucio en el salón, incluso después de que nos viéramos obligados a despedir al último de los criados, siempre tocaba la campana. Todos estos esfuerzos por conservar la propia dignidad resultaron vanos, pues no era capaz de conservar la de su esposo y, según me enseñó, el hecho de que una mujer conservara la dignidad a expensas de la de su marido era tan inútil como una vela sin mástil.»

Mientras cerraba el diario para ir a limpiar el cuarto de baño de Rosemary Krebs, detecté un par de palabras –una era «amante», y la otra, «indiscreto»– que despertaron mi interés por saber qué podían significar en el contexto de la familia King. Pero tardé en descubrirlo casi tres semanas: dos días después de leer los pasajes que acabo de referir aparecieron las puntas de los dedos de Lucy Robinson, y durante los diez días siguientes ni Phyneas, ni Rosemary Krebs ni nadie en Galatia pudo hacer gran cosa. Parecía que los granjeros y yo éramos los únicos que seguíamos trabajando normalmente, y casi me vuelvo loca esperando a que Rosemary Krebs volviera a su trabajo. Con quien me enfadé bastante fue con Lucy Robinson. En cierto sentido, estaba resentida con ella por arruinarme el espectáculo, como siempre, como si sus dedos cortados fueran una especie de apoteósica aparición escénica; y a duras penas pude contener la rabia hacia Rosemary Krebs por quedarse merodeando en su propia casa o el entusiasmo cuando al fin volvió a trabajar. Phyneas Krebs también salió de casa esa tarde, y pude leer a mis anchas durante casi una hora.

Había docenas de entradas después de la última que leí, progresivamente más breves y más exasperadas, en las que Rosemary relataba con detalle la rutina diaria en la residencia de los King. La señora King pasaba cada vez más tiempo en la cama; Juez King pasaba cada vez más tiempo lejos de ella; tía Syrene se metía en la primera cama que encontraba; y la joven Rosemary, que acababa de terminar sus estudios en el instituto, vagaba a la deriva entre los tres, servía el té lo mejor que podía e impedía que su tía y su padre terminasen de expoliar las escasas reliquias familiares que aún conservaban. Parecía que la situación podía prolongarse indefinidamente, al menos hasta que Rosemary se casara en mejores circunstancias, hasta que su padre, «eso me parece ahora —escribió años más tarde Rosemary Krebs—, traspasó definitivamente la última barrera: se mostró indiscreto». O tal vez la indiscreta fue su amante. Se presentó en casa de los King a medianoche y llamó a gritos a Eminent King «con groseras expresiones de cariño», pero la primera en despertarse fue Rosemary. «Maldigo el impulso que me llevó hasta la ventana —escribió—, pero, igual que Eva, me dejé tentar por los exóticos gritos que llegaban del jardín de tía Syrene. Como si no me hubiese bastado con oír esa voz para entenderlo todo perfectamente: ni siquiera un blanco del sur era capaz de escupir semejante basura. Pero mis ojos confirmaron el horror. Papá estaba liado con una… —y aquí, en el borrón que sigue al trazo final de la última "a", casi sentí el esfuerzo que hubo de hacer Rosemary King a fin de encontrar fuerzas para escribir la palabra— una negra.» Al final su padre salió al jardín y, tras un encuentro que Rosemary «no soportaba presenciar pero tampoco podía dejar de mirar», echó de allí a la escandalosa mujer. No me sorprendió saber, al mirar la fecha de la entrada, que Rosemary descubriera a la amante de su padre pocos días antes de cumplir diecisiete años, y que este cumpleaños fuera el último en el que intercambiara correspondencia con su padre.

Tras este episodio hay un hueco: en el lomo del diario se observan restos de tres páginas arrancadas, como el muñón de un miembro amputado; la siguiente entrada se escribió seis meses más tarde y revela que, en lugar de retirarle la lealtad a su padre para depositarla en la madre, Rosemary decidió ponerla fuera de la casa. «Él es muy alto, y yo muy bajita», es la primera frase completa que aparece tras las páginas arrancadas, y de inmediato supe que se refería a Phyneas Krebs; digo la primera frase completa porque había también un fragmento en la parte superior de la página que parecía temblar sobre el papel como una cola desprendida del cuerpo de un animal: «Es lo único que puedo hacer». Sobre su futuro marido, Rosemary King escribió lo siguiente: «No me hago ilusiones con respecto a su capacidad. Es tonto de remate. Pero no fuma ni bebe, y si lo hace, tiene el buen juicio de negarlo. Llama rancho a la granja de su padre y, lo más importante de todo, es creyente. Además, no necesitaré cambiar mis iniciales, porque la inicial de su apellido coincide con la del mío. Phyneas cortejó a Rosemary, aunque fue ella quien lo orquestó todo. Luego vino el compromiso. Y, finalmente, la boda, que al parecer fue una parodia de tomo y lomo. Rosemary tuvo que llevar un traje de novia comprado en unos grandes almacenes y, para colmo de males, tía Syrene descubrió el traje nupcial de la familia Hoovier y se lo puso. Según el diario de Rosemary, el padre de Phyneas «solo se lavaba las zonas del cuerpo que no quedaban ocultas por la ropa». La madre de la novia se ciñó la cintura con un cinturón, en lugar de un corsé o una faja, y «parecía un saco de harina tirado sobre un taburete. Por desgracia, y a diferencia de un saco de harina, tenía la facultad de hablar». Juez King lanzó un eructo mientras se pronunciaban los votos, y la señora King se tiró el champán por encima durante la recepción. Fue tía Syrene quien cazó al vuelo el ramo de la novia; se prendió una rosa amarilla en un apolillado agujero del encaje que decoraba el escote de su vestido, y tiró el resto de las flores a la basura.

En lo que, a mi juicio, fue el único acto de sentimentalismo consciente que Rosemary King registra en su diario, la recién casada arrancó un solo pétalo de una de las flores —una rosa amarilla, oscurecida por el tiempo— para guardarlo entre las páginas de su diario; y fue un impulso similar, aunque más hostil, el que me movió a sacar el pétalo y estrujarlo hasta convertirlo en polvo, antes de volver a mi trabajo.

5.21

JUSTIN

Wade quitó el cerrojo despacio, abrió la puerta y me dejó entrar primero. La habitación era pequeña, estaba ensombrecida por las grandes hojas de una viña que trepaba por la fachada de la casa. Al principio me pareció que una fina cortina blanca cubría la ventana, pero luego me di cuenta de que había papeles pegados a los cristales con cinta adhesiva. «Hace mucho tiempo –dijo Wade detrás de mí– esta fue mi habitación.» Al parecer, ahora se había convertido en la de Divine: cientos de retratos de él cubrían el techo y las paredes de la habitación; incluso el suelo. Cuando Wade cerró la puerta vi que también había retratos detrás de ella; los papeles de la ventana eran también retratos, y el sol poniente se filtraba a través del papel y a través de los huecos perfiles del cuerpo de Divine. Había en estos dibujos algo tan repugnantemente pornográfico que me resultaba imposible mirarlos directamente. Incluso en los que no aparecía el rostro de Divine, sino solo una mano o un pie, daba la impresión de que Divine estaba mirándote, y el miembro retratado se ofrecía como un instrumento de placer sexual, aunque resultaba imposible saber si el ofrecimiento procedía de Wade o de Divine.

Miré a Wade y él me devolvió una mirada nerviosa. «Vale –dijo–. No hace falta que te desnudes, aunque es lo habitual.» Se sentó en el suelo y apoyó el cuaderno en las rodillas, afiló los lápices –las virutas, además de sus pies y los míos, ocultaron levemente los dibujos de Divine que cubrían el suelo– y cuando al fin se puso en pie pareció sorprendido de encontrarme en la misma posición. Vaciló un momento, luego se me acercó y me desnudó torpemente. Yo solo llevaba una camisa de manga corta y unos pantalones cortos, de manera que el proceso no fue complicado, y cuando me quedé desnudo, Wade me empujó un poco por el hombro; más que empujarme me sujetó, me guió y me sentó en la franja de luz que entraba por la ventana.

Se quedó un rato mirándome y, para evitar su mirada, miré los dibujos de la pared. Comprendí, a mi pesar, lo que estaba haciendo y lo que se proponía hacer Wade. Antes de que empezase siquiera ese primer dibujo mío, imaginé un nuevo rostro en la habitación, imaginé que mis dibujos la cubrirían en lo sucesivo como hasta entonces la habían cubierto los de Divine. Cuando me senté desnudo en medio de la habitación me pregunté qué parte del cuerpo de Divine quedaría borrada por qué otra parte de mi cuerpo. ¿Mi cuello? ¿Mis muslos? ¿Empezaría Wade por el pene o por la cara? ¿Dibujaría primero todo el cuerpo y luego me desmembraría o me ensamblaría miembro a miembro, trozo a trozo?

—Cruza los brazos, por favor —dijo Wade. Se inclinó sobre mí y, con la misma delicadeza con que una niña coloca a su muñeca encima de la cama, Wade me colocó para dibujarme. Dejé que sus manos me movieran, sentí sus dedos tibios en mis muñecas, en mis mejillas, en mis muslos. Cuando hubo terminado, volvió a sentarse, pero no lo miré. No podía. Pensaba que si lo miraba sus ojos arrancarían palabras de mi boca. Se quedó un momento inmóvil y luego le oí decir—: Divine siempre me miraba. —Luego oí el ruido del lápiz que empezaba a arañar el papel. El sonido me resultaba vagamente familiar, pero tardé un rato en comprender que me recordaba al que hacía Colin cuando escribía con su estilográfica. Me estremecí.

—¿Tienes frío? —No, Wade, no tengo frío. A continuación añadió—: ¡Qué pregunta más tonta! —Y el lápiz volvió a arañar el papel. Cerré los ojos para no ver los de Divine—. No cierres los ojos, por favor —dijo Wade, pero no le hice caso—. ¿Justin? —Seguí sin hacerle caso, y Wade volvió a dibujar. Sentí en mi propia piel el arañazo del lápiz, como si me estuviera tatuando, pero no me moví. Mucho rato después, Wade me zarandeó, y abrí los ojos—. Listo —dijo. Tenía la mano manchada de carboncillo—. ¿Te has quedado dormido? —preguntó, como si no estuviera seguro. Me pasó los pantalones—. No encuentro los calzoncillos. —Por toda respuesta, me puse los pantalones y fijé la vista en el cuaderno. Estaba abierto, pero en blanco, y me sobresalté al ver el vacío. ¿Acaso me había vuelto invisible? —Lo he colgado —dijo Wade. Señaló con la mano hacia las paredes, y las escudriñé rápidamente, pero no conseguí encontrarme. Wade volvió a abrazarme torpemente. Sentí sus huesos sobre mi piel como si fueran lápices, o puntas de pinceles—. Gracias —dijo. Y alejándose de mí añadió—: Es mi vicio secreto. —Mis ojos se posaron en un dibujo de Divine agarrándose el pene erecto. ¿Esperaba Wade que yo hiciera algo parecido?—. Ya ves. Sigo dibujando del natural; a mis años. —Y luego añadió con una risita—: Espero que guardes mi secreto.

5.22

DIVINE

Las cosas cambiaron después de la semana que el Rata pasó en la cárcel. Llevábamos un año juntos: él tenía diecisiete y yo, trece; yo acababa de empezar el instituto y él acababa de dejarlo, y hablaba de largarse de Galatia para siempre. Fue entonces cuando empezó a ir por el Big M.

El Rata no me contó al principio lo que hacía. Un día, al salir del instituto no estaba esperándome, como siempre, y me jodió bastante, porque había tenido unas palabras con ese idiota llamado Merle Potter, y esperaba que el Rata le diera una patada en el culo o me llevara de allí en su coche, pero el Rata no estaba y Merle, que era un tío grande pero fofo, y además era bizco y tenía los ojos muy separados, me arrastró hasta detrás del gimnasio y me dijo que podía elegir entre dos cosas para metérmelas en la boca, una era su puño y la otra era su polla, y yo le dije que vale, que si podía ver primero la polla para saber cuál de las dos cosas era más grande. Y también le dije que esperaba que hubiera aprendido a controlarse un poco con el paso de los años y que si no, más le valía que se buscara una mujer capaz de correrse en treinta segundos, porque yo ni siquiera tenía tiempo para saber cómo reaccionaría ante esto. Lo que quiero decir es que este chico introducía una nueva dimensión en el concepto de «eyaculación precoz».

El caso es que, un poco más tarde, el Rata me encontró donde estábamos siempre: encima del silo. No os lo podéis imaginar. Justo allí, en el centro exacto de todas las cosas, y durante un año entero nadie nos había visto subiendo o bajando, porque el silo de Galatia, perdón de Galatea, tiene una escalera cubierta en lugar de visible sobre la fachada, como la mayoría de los silos, pero lo que quiero decir es que teníamos que aparcar el coche en la calle y cruzar la autopista y todo, y una vez arriba no había donde esconderse. Bueno. Serían cosa de las once, casi medianoche, cuando el Rata apareció en el silo. Venía con una especie de sonrisa de corderito manso; yo había decidido echarle una buena bronca, pero luego nunca podía; se sentó a mi lado, me pasó un brazo por los hombros y me dio un beso tiernísimo en la mejilla; mi rabia se desvaneció al instante. Enseguida supe qué había estado haciendo, porque le olí el aliento; todo el cuerpo le olía a lo mismo, y me dije, vale, mierda, debería enfadarme con él, pero ¿qué he estado haciendo yo, a fin de cuentas?

Tenía un nuevo moratón en el ojo, pero eso era algo tan frecuente en él que ni siquiera le pregunté qué le había pasado.

Entonces el Rata se sacó del bolsillo de los vaqueros un fajo de billetes arrugados, me lo dio y dijo que lo contara; lo conté y había unos ciento diez pavos, más o menos.

Y aunque nadie me había explicado nunca lo que era un chapero, supe perfectamente adónde había ido el Rata y qué había hecho, y le pregunté:

—¿Cuántos eran?
—Solo tres —dijo el Rata.
—No está mal —admití, después de hacer el cálculo mental.
—Hubo más, pero me recompensé con una buena cena.
—¿Más de tres?
—Más billetes. Pero cené en el Big M.
—¿Has estado en el Big M?
—Allí es donde los encontré.
—¿A los tres?
—En el aparcamiento.
—…
—Vamos, cariño —dijo el Rata, con su voz más dulce y especial, y me estrujó con el brazo que rodeaba mis hombros—. ¿Estás llorando? ¿Estás llorando por mí?
Intenté que no me temblara la voz, pero sin mucho éxito.
—Vas a dejarme. Seguirás haciendo esto hasta que consigas el dinero suficiente para largarte y ahuecarás el ala.
—Vamos —volvió a decir el Rata, con una voz dulce y tierna como la carne guisada, y el brazo firme como un tornillo de banco alrededor de mis hombros—. Vamos, vamos, vamos. Vamos, vamos, vamos, vamos, ya, ya, ya —y lo dijo de un modo que parecía una gata a la que se estaban follando en plena noche, y no pude evitar reírme—. ¿Con quién te crees que estás hablando? ¿Eh? Soy el Rata; no soy Merle Potter.
—Ya —dije, pero luego me fijé en su ojo morado—. ¿Fue Merle quien te hizo eso?
—Tendrías que haberlo visto.
La pierna izquierda de Merle Potter era más o menos tan grande como el Rata entero, y todo el mundo sabía que sus padres lo mandaban a clases de taekwondo en Bigger Hill, para mejorar su autoestima, porque era fofo y bizco. El Rata había tenido la suerte de recibir un puñetazo.
—Seguro que estás harto de defenderme —dije.
El Rata volvió al «vamos, vamos, ya, ya, ya», y esta vez me zarandeó con el brazo hasta obligarme a sacudir la cabeza.
—De lo que estoy harto es de esta mierda de pueblo.
—Ves. Te lo dije.
—Y por eso quiero ganar dinero para que nos larguemos de aquí.
—¿Nos?
—¿Te he dado el dinero o no?
Miré el dinero que tenía en la mano.
—¿Me lo estás dando a mí?
—Para que lo guardes. Ya sabes lo… impulsivo que soy.

Sonrió cuando dijo «impulsivo»; apartó la mano de mis hombros y empezó a desabrocharse la hebilla del cinturón.

—Sí, ya lo sé. Eres muy impulsivo.

Estaba quitándose los pantalones, y tuve que tragar saliva. Lo hicimos allí mismo, pero nunca lo hicimos ante los ojos de Dios.

—Y también imprudente —dijo.

—Sí. También eres imprudente.

Se sacó la polla.

—Y loco.

—Y loco.

Y luego echó a andar hacia el borde del silo y yo lo llamé, pero me lanzó una mirada que no entendí, y siguió andando hacia el borde del silo, o, más bien, avanzó dando saltitos, pues llevaba los pantalones a la altura de los tobillos y el culo le colgaba por debajo de la camisa, e incluso en la oscuridad vi unas manchas oscuras en sus prodigiosas nalgas blancas, que tenían toda la pinta de habérselas hecho alguien a puñetazos, pero no le pregunté nada, porque durante un angustioso minuto pensé que iba a tirarse desde allí arriba.

—¡Rata!

Llegó hasta el borde de la plataforma y se detuvo, y debo admitir que suspiré aliviado; luego me eché a reír, al darme cuenta de que estaba meando, estaba regando Galatea, estaba meando la zona del pueblo situada al oeste del silo. Soplaba una ligera brisa que arrastró la meada del Rata hacia un lado, esparciéndola en pequeñas gotitas que brillaron a la luz de la luna, pero fue un poco raro verlo mear, porque como la meada no chocaba contra nada, el agua o el suelo o un árbol, no hacía ruido, no hacía el menor ruido, y siempre había pensado, bueno, no exactamente pensado pero sí imaginado, el ruido que debe de hacer un tío cuando mea. A falta de ese ruido, y como las gotitas de pis brillaban a la luz de la luna, se podía pensar que el Rata estaba derramando cualquier cosa sobre el pueblo, como una poción mágica o polvo de hada, y una parte de mí creyó o quiso creer que el Rata estaba dando el primer paso para sacarnos de allí, que estaba haciendo desaparecer a Galatea, que la estaba borrando del mapa, cosa que, por alguna razón, yo sabía que tendría que pasar si alguna vez llegábamos a marcharnos de verdad.

Cuando terminó se quedó allí un rato sin subirse los pantalones. Luego se llevó las manos a la boca y gritó:

—¡Vete a la mierda, pueblo!

—¡Vete a la mierda! —grité yo, desde donde estaba sentado, porque me daba vértigo ponerme de pie en el borde del silo.

El Rata se dio la vuelta.

Se miró la polla.

—Bueno —dijo, sacudiéndose las últimas gotas de pis—. Ya que está fuera...

Después de ese día el Rata iba al Big M tres o cuatro veces a la semana. Hacer de chapero se convirtió en una especie de droga para él: la primera vez es la mejor y después lo haces por pura necesidad. Creo que nunca volvió a ganar cien dólares en un día, salvo otra vez, pero a veces ganaba cincuenta o sesenta pavos, y no se marchaba del Big M hasta que conseguía por lo menos veinticinco, y la cuenta fue creciendo hasta que, al cabo de unos meses, yo tenía mil dólares en un sobre que guardaba pegado con cinta adhesiva debajo de un cajón; pero el Rata dijo que aún no era suficiente.

—La vida está muy cara —dijo.

Llegó el invierno, y el Rata se puso malo muchas veces de estar allí cogiendo frío, supongo. Además, su padre se había marchado y le había echado de casa, y el Rata se negaba a gastarse el dinero en un motel, me lo daba todo a mí y dormía en el coche; durante el día comía lo que podía robar; una bolsa de patatas fritas o una lata de maíz, de maíz con nata, recuerdo, y decía que se lo tomaba directamente de la lata. Iba al Big M casi todas las noches, tosiendo o sorbiéndose los mocos, pero decía que no importaba, que esos tíos no se fijaban en nada de cintura para arriba. Me lo contaba cuando venía a traerme el dinero, más o menos una vez a la semana. Casi no volvimos a vernos en el silo, porque el Rata decía que hacía demasiado frío allí arriba, pero yo creo que era porque no tenía fuerzas para subir la escalera, y ya no recuerdo cuándo lo hicimos por última vez. Para entonces tenía los ojos hinchados y grandes ojeras, porque se pasaba la noche en vela, y nunca volvió a meterse en peleas en Galatia, porque apenas se le veía por allí, pero seguía apareciendo siempre magullado; al parecer, a esos tíos les gustaba sobre todo pegarle en la cara o en el culo.

Bueno, el caso es que el Rata dijo que la vida estaba muy cara, y yo le dije:

—Pero ¡mira lo que te está costando a ti!

—¡Bah, no te preocupes por mí! Me las arreglo bien.

Y entonces yo ya tenía catorce años y él dieciocho, y el Rata se había encargado de dejar bien claro que yo era el maricón del pueblo, y me daban palizas un día sí y otro no, pero nadie me daba dinero, eso os lo puedo jurar. Y entonces le dije:

—Sí, pero ¿qué pasa conmigo?

Al principio el Rata se quedó un poco cortado, pero luego tomó aliento y dijo:

—¿Qué pasa contigo?

—Nunca tienes tiempo para mí. Como mucho te veo un día a la semana.

Y el Rata se encogió de hombros y se alejó un poco de mí. Conseguí convencerlo para que subiéramos al silo, pero tardamos horas, porque le costaba mucho subir la escalera, y su silueta parecía un perfil oscuro cuando no había estrellas, pero cuando abría la boca para decir algo parecía que escupía estrellas o que se las comía.

Y después de mucho tiempo el Rata dijo:

—Algunos de esos tíos están enfermos. —Y al cabo de un rato aún más largo añadió—: No puedo tocarte. No sé lo que puedo tener.

Y esta vez no pregunté qué podía tener, porque hubo algo en la expresión del Rata que me hizo saber que no era lo mismo, porque... porque... ¿por qué? Porque la diferencia era que yo hacía algo que de verdad me gustaba, aunque no lo hiciera con gente que me gustara, pero al Rata no le gustaba lo que hacía, aunque seguía haciéndolo —lo hacía por mí— y supongo que esa es la diferencia entre un maricón y otro al que le gustan los maricones, lo que, y debo decir que esto no es ninguna sorpresa, seguro que Colin Nieman sabía mejor que nadie.

5.23

COLIN

El primer día del verano Rosemary Krebs llamó por teléfono.

—Señor Nieman —dijo—. ¿Tiene usted un momento para que nos veamos? —Me pidió que pasara por su oficina; le dije que tendría que venir a casa. Se resistió; insistí, pero al final se dio por vencida y dijo—: De acuerdo. Hace muchos años que no entro en la casa de caliza.

No había vuelto a verla desde el mes de enero, en el bar de Cora, y cuando abrí la puerta volvió a asombrarme su estatura. No era más alta que una niña de diez años; su pelo liso era el rasgo más largo de su persona.

Me entregó una bolsa sin decir nada y no tuve necesidad de abrirla para saber qué contenía.

Una vez dentro de la casa, Rosemary Krebs no se molestó en disimular su curiosidad.

—Le apetece ver la casa —dije; y asintió con la cabeza. Sin esperarme, recorrió todas las habitaciones, y en algún momento me di cuenta de que no se fijaba en los cambios que yo había hecho en la casa, sino en la casa en sí, en los detalles de las molduras y el grosor de las paredes. En un extremo del pasillo del segundo piso se detuvo junto a la ventana y observó la finca a través de un hueco estratégicamente abierto en el seto.

—Donald Deacon lo llamaba el hueco de Stonehedge —dijo, tras una larga pausa.

—¿Sí? No lo sabía.

—No. No podía saberlo. Quizá podríamos dar un paseo. Me muero de ganas por ver cómo lleva la finca Kendan Regier.

—Lo hace muy bien —dije.

—Un paseo siempre sienta bien, ¿verdad que sí?

Era evidente que no podía decir que no, de manera que sonreí y dije:

—Cuando guste.

Una vez fuera dijo:

—Las tierras de los Deacon siempre fueron distintas de las demás granjas de los alrededores; en realidad, se parecen más a un rancho que a una granja.

Por un momento casi estuve a punto de jurar que iba a decir una «plantación».

—La mayoría de los granjeros tienen sus propiedades desperdigadas; unos cuantos campos alrededor de la casa y otros desperdigados por el condado. En cierto sentido es un buen sistema. Te impide aislarte, lo cual puede ser un peligro para un granjero.

—Pero sus… «tierras» —dije, e hice otra pausa—… no están exactamente desperdigadas.

Se detuvo y se dio la vuelta para mirarme directamente a los ojos. Su mirada era firme, lo nivelaba todo, y lo digo en sentido literal: parecía que yo me había vuelto tan pequeño como ella. Asintió, se volvió sin decir nada y echó a andar de nuevo.

Seguí el crujido de sus pasos sobre las piedras del patio. Llevaba unos zapatos de tacón bajo, pero caminaba sin la menor vacilación, como si pisara sobre una gruesa alfombra. Una vez hubimos dejado atrás las piedras del patio, las señaló y preguntó:

—¿Piensa dejar esto así?

—De momento, sí. Es muy bonito. A su manera.

Adoptó un tono cortante, casi cáustico para observar:

—Una escultura de Giacometti es muy hermosa. —Me sorprendió oírla decir esto—. A su manera. Pero no me gustaría ponerla en el salón. —Esbozó una leve sonrisa y recuperó su tono normal—. Supongo que las piedras harán que el calor resulte aún más insoportable —dijo, recuperando de nuevo el deje sureño, y señaló con una mano hacia el resplandor de temblorosas líneas que bailaban sobre la negra extensión de piedras.

—Creo que eso es lo que se proponía Bea.
—¿Aumentar el calor?
—Aumentar el espejismo.

Rosemary Krebs me ofreció una media sonrisa y algo más que, de haber salido de una nariz menos refinada que la suya, podría confundirse con un ronquido; luego se dio la vuelta y continuó su camino. Andaba con paso firme y decidido, y la seguí, admirando sus delicados pasos, el modo como sus brazos permanecían pegados al cuerpo, mientras que los míos se movían de un lado a otro para ayudarme a mantener el equilibrio sobre el irregular terreno. En la cima de un monte había un alambre de espino, y Rosemary se volvió y caminó con conocimiento hacia una cancela situada a unos cien metros. Al otro lado de la alambrada el trigo se alzaba un palmo del suelo sobre una tierra ligeramente húmeda y desmenuzada. A poco más de medio kilómetro, un enorme aspersor regaba un campo desde una plataforma en forma de araña. Rosemary Krebs caminó con cuidado entre dos hileras de trigo durante un par de minutos, hasta llegar a la cima de un pequeño risco. Desde el valle no se veía nada más que el cielo; desde aquí resultaban visibles las copas de los árboles de Galatia y la aguja de la iglesia de Abraham Greeving, con los riscos al fondo. En dirección contraria, una nube oscura y pegada a la tierra revelaba los restos de Kenosha. Rosemary Krebs dio una vuelta completa para verlo todo, y algo llamó su atención. Yo estaba detrás de ella, un poco más abajo, y observé su menuda silueta. Parecía alzarse como una torre sobre el paisaje y lo que me vino a la cabeza no fue invención mía, sino de Stevens, en ese poema en el que habla de un jarrón en Tennessee, y me vino a la cabeza la idea de que el jarrón lo dominaba todo.

Rosemary Krebs carraspeó, sacándome de mi ensoñación.
—Seguro que nunca había estado aquí, ¿verdad, señor Nieman?

Miré alrededor como si pudiera distinguir este lugar de cualquier otro en la inmensa pradera, y me encogí de hombros.
—Creo que no.
—Este es el punto más elevado entre el risco pelado y Kenosha. Cuando Kenosha aún existía este era el único sitio desde donde se veían los dos pueblos. Mi padre me llevó a la costa una vez, cuando era pequeña, y años después, la primera vez que vine aquí, pensé que la silueta del silo de Kenosha se parecía a la cresta de una ola en el horizonte.

Miré la nube otra vez. No veía nada parecido a una ola. A una tormenta, quizá sí, aunque pensé que sería una proyección mía. Miré a Rosemary Krebs; ella me miró con expectación, pero no dijo nada. Luego se dio la vuelta y, en voz exageradamente baja, dijo:

—Siempre pensé en darle todo esto a Lucy Robinson.

—¿Cómo iba a darle algo que no le pertenece?

—Como regalo de boda. Solo el dinero, nada que fuera en contra de la voluntad de Bea. Pretendía darle el dinero para que ella lo comprara, y también pretendía dejarle mis tierras. Galatea habría sido de Lucy, señor Nieman. El pueblo entero. Mi sueño se habría hecho realidad con ella. Pero ahora parece que nunca será posible.

El aspersor pareció apagarse por sí solo, y recuerdo que pensé si eso tendría algo que ver conmigo. Puede parecer pura y simple paranoia o puede parecer una reacción lógica tras los sucesos de los últimos ocho meses. Algunos de los hechos ocurridos habían tenido que ver conmigo, y deseé que el aspersor volviera a encenderse, pero no se encendió.

—Señora Krebs —dije. Me detuve y carraspeé con fuerza antes de hablar—: Quiero que sepa que lamento muchísimo todo lo que ha pasado.

—Le creo, señor Nieman. A diferencia de Eustace Brown, no tengo la necesidad de proyectar una falsa culpabilidad sobre alguien solo porque esa persona y yo tengamos diferentes estilos de vida. Hay cosas que debe juzgarlas Dios y hay cosas que deben juzgarlas los hombres, y me parece más prudente dejar los asuntos celestiales en el lugar que les corresponde.

—Se lo agradezco, señora Krebs.

—No me lo agradezca, señor Nieman. No soy su amiga, ni deseo serlo. Pero tampoco le considero un enemigo. Un adversario, quizá. —Y dicho esto se dio la vuelta. Me miró con unos ojos azules que la intensa luz del sol tornaba grises—. No puedo comprar estas tierras, señor Nieman. Pero puedo arrendarlas durante un año, o un siglo, o para siempre. Esto solo depende de usted. Puede marcharse. Puede coger a Justin y marcharse.

—Podría marcharme ahora mismo.

—Pero no quiere, señor Nieman. No ha querido, y debo confesar que no entiendo por qué. Al principio pensé que era por su novela, pero ya la ha recuperado.

Me encogí de hombros.

—¿Por qué no se va, señor Nieman? ¿A qué está esperando?

Con la mayor naturalidad posible, respondí:

—Estoy esperando a Lucy Robinson. No puedo irme hasta que ella no aparezca.

Una torva mirada cruzó fugazmente el rostro de Rosemary Krebs. No era terror, ni miedo, sino una especie de profunda repugnancia; y por primera vez se me ocurrió que algunos preferían que Lucy Robinson no apareciera nunca. Luego, cuando Rosemary Krebs volvió a hablar, comprendí que ella también había leído mi novela antes de devolvérmela.

—Ya —dijo, sin el menor atisbo de simpatía en la voz—. Lo que espera es encontrarse a sí mismo.

5.24

WEBBIE

Rosemary Krebs se mudó a Kenosha el día siguiente de su boda con Phyneas Krebs, llevando consigo todas las pertenencias de los Hoovier y de los King, pero alejándose de su familia definitivamente: ni una sola vez vuelve a hacer referencia a su padre, a su madre o a su tía; ni siquiera menciona cuándo murieron. Incluso podría ser que aún siguieran con vida.

La casa de los Krebs estaba más cerca de Galatia que de Kenosha —«una interesante peculiaridad geográfica que Phyneas olvidó mencionar»—, pero Rosemary Krebs, como el resto de la familia Krebs, hacía sus negocios y sus obras sociales en Kenosha. Kenosha era una población vieja y empobrecida, características estas que conspiraron hasta convertirla, según Rosemary Krebs, «en un lugar más sureño que el propio sur». Todos sus intentos por relacionarse con lo que pasaba por ser la buena sociedad merecieron el más absoluto de los rechazos, principalmente porque, según sus propias palabras, ella solo tenía «dos atributos: educación y el dinero de la familia Krebs, y ambas cosas eran despreciadas en un pueblo que no tenía ni lo uno ni lo otro». Para colmo de males, el diminutivo cariñoso que Phyneas le había puesto en la intimidad había traspasado las paredes del dormitorio conyugal y, aunque nadie la llamaba así a la cara, con frecuencia lo oía pronunciar en voz baja cuando entraba en un sitio público o vocear en la calle a sus espaldas. Los Krebs habían pasado su luna de miel en Maryland; y el diminutivo en cuestión era pastelito de cangrejo. «O cangrejito; a veces me llama su cangrejito, y la verdad es que me entran ganas de tener un caparazón para esconderme dentro, lejos de él y de su malnacido pueblo.»

Pero Rosemary perseveró. Su esfuerzo se vio recompensado por la temprana muerte de su suegro, quien, por medio de Phyneas, le proporcionó el control del rancho, y fue ella quien a los veintiún años tuvo la visión de perforar los primeros pozos petrolíferos, y fue ella quien convenció a Phyneas de que emprendiera los trámites necesarios para abrir el primero y único banco de Kenosha y, años más tarde, una filial en Galatia. Fue ella quien empezó a rehipotecar las granjas que lindaban con el rancho de los Krebs para, años más tarde, apropiarse de ellas y aumentar el patrimonio familiar. Jugueteaba con la idea de poner nombre al rancho, pero, en un raro arranque de humor, escribió: «¿Qué nombre puedo ponerle? ¿Los Siete Algodoneros? ¿Los Siete Olmos Marchitos?». Durante algún tiempo pensó llamarlo Siete Campos, pero finalmente rechazó la idea por demasiado «abstracta». Aún no había cumplido veinticinco años cuando escribió: «Quiero un solo campo, un campo inmenso y ancho como estas llanuras yermas, un campo que se extienda desde un extremo al otro de este feo horizonte. Quiero girar en círculo y no ver nada que no me pertenezca».

Y pasó el tiempo; entre una y otra entrada del diario hay a veces meses de separación; incluso años. «Mi libro de contabilidad es ahora mi diario»: esta es la única frase escrita en 1969. Al parecer, por insignificantes que fueran los recursos de Kenosha, y por más que Rosemary Krebs lograra aumentar los suyos propios, esta pequeña ciudad y sus habitantes aún ejercía el poder de condena o aprobación sobre Rosemary Krebs, quien no parecía conformarse meramente con la aprobación o la aceptación de los lugareños, sino que aspiraba a situarse por encima de este tipo de juicios elementales. La frase más significativa que escribió sobre Kenosha fue la siguiente: «Lo que desprecio es la autonomía de la gente; se mueven como hormigas que carecen de disciplina, de reina». Y entonces ideó un plan, un plan que parece salido más de un cuento de hadas que de una historia real, un plan destinado no solo a eclipsar el pueblo de Kenosha, sino a borrarlo por completo para construir en su lugar un nuevo asentamiento, y al leer estas líneas me vino a la cabeza la bandeja en que le servía a Rosemary Krebs el té todas las tardes. La bandeja contenía la única referencia a la *Ilíada* que yo había encontrado en la casa de los Krebs, y sobre su superficie esmaltada se representaban las murallas de Troya derribadas, cubiertas de cadáveres desperdigados, bajo una espesa nube de humo, y el efecto de la escena resultaba mucho más truculento si tenemos en cuenta que la representación se había realizado con las mismas espirales azules de una bucólica escena de Wedgwood. Aquiles aparece de pie sobre el caballo de Troya, con un pie encima del cuerpo de Paris; en una mano empuña la espada y con la otra sujeta a Helena. La ciudad arde en el fondo de la imagen; entonces oí que una puerta se cerraba en el piso de abajo y solo tuve tiempo de ver la primera frase de la siguiente entrada antes de devolver el diario a su escondite: *Kenosha debe desaparecer.*

5. 25

JUSTIN

—He preparado algo de cenar —dijo Wade una tarde—. Un guiso de primavera, con verduras de temporada. Bueno, la receta es de Cora, pero lo he hecho yo. Vale —admitió, como si yo lo hubiese desafiado—, lo ha preparado ella y yo lo he traído a casa. Podría haberlo hecho yo mismo, pero me dijo que la receta era secreta. —Sonrió tontamente—. Espero que me acompañes.

Wade me alimentaba. Si hubiera hablado habría dicho que el guiso se parecía un poco a los cuadros de Wade y que sabía igual de bien.

Después me dio su piedra ventral.

—Por favor —dijo—; sé lo mucho que significaba para ti. —Me pareció extraño que empleara un tiempo pasado, como si, privado de palabras, yo estuviese también privado de sentimientos.

Wade, consumado seductor. Me besaste con unos labios que sabían a coriandro y a restos de pintura. Pensé: «Mañana dibujarás mi cara. Mañana dibujarás mi polla. Mañana harás un retrato mío de cuerpo entero».

Me acariciaste los párpados con un dedo para cerrarlos. Y dijiste: «Shhh».

Wade, eres un demonio. ¡Quién iba a imaginarse que lloriqueabas como un adolescente! Me acariciaste, conseguiste arrancarme unos mechones de pelo mientras me quitabas la camisa. «¡Qué hermoso eres!», dijiste, como si nunca me hubieses visto desnudo. Me chupaste los pezones como si quisieras sacar leche de ellos; y por alguna razón pensé en Webbie, en la primera vez que cenamos aquí, y en su mano apoyada en el pecho.

Esa noche no ocurrió ningún percance. Te mostraste muy cariñoso, pero la torpeza te evitó caer en un exceso de ternura. No me sorprendió que no te pusieras un condón, pero sí me sorprendió que yo te lo permitiera. Me asombró tu pene, su dureza, aunque al cabo de unas horas me pareció como cualquier otro miembro de tu cuerpo, carne envolviendo el hueso, la dureza su único estado natural. Te observé con atención. Un hombre como tú, en éxtasis, podría haber servido como modelo para retratar a Cristo. Tenías pequeñas manchas de pintura roja en el corazón, de cuando te rascaste sin darte cuenta el día anterior. Cuando se abrieron, tus ojos no me vieron, pero eso no me sorprendió: yo no estaba en esta casa, estaba en la casa de tus padres. Yo no estaba en esta habitación: estaba en tu habitación, aquella en la que habías dormido cuando eras niño. Pero ¿dónde estabas tú, Wade? ¿Dónde te habías perdido? ¿Pretendías llevarme contigo hasta allí? Una parte de mí desea que me lleves, pero sé que no puedo ir. Tú y yo, Wade, y Colin y Divine —¿estarían follando mientras nosotros follábamos?— y Webbie y Rosemary Krebs y Abraham Greeving y Myra Robinson, todos nos parecemos, con levísimas diferencias. Pero tú, Wade, tú estás fuera del círculo, aún más lejos que yo. Te has ido a donde todos anhelamos ir. Te has vuelto loco.

5.26

DIVINE

Una noche entró por la ventana de mi habitación y se pasó allí una hora entera, llorando. No dijo nada; no hizo el menor ruido, pero mientras lloraba se sacó del bolsillo el fajo de billetes más grande que había conseguido hasta el momento. Vi que todos los billetes eran de un dólar, y uno por uno los fue extendiendo y colocando con cuidado en un montón sobre la cama, y no sé por qué pero empecé a contar, entre susurros, para que mis viejos no nos oyeran, empecé a contar, y mientras el Rata lloraba yo contaba, uno, dos, tres, y cuando pasé de los veinticinco o treinta mis ojos se acostumbraron a la oscuridad y fue entonces cuando advertí las marcas que tenía en los brazos; puede que las marcas fueran rojas, aunque no podría asegurarlo porque la luz estaba apagada, y cuando llegué a cincuenta, más o menos, vi que eran quemaduras de cigarro y cuando llegué a cien, me hice una idea de lo que debía de haber pasado, uno, dos, tres, cuatro, cinco, etc., aunque el Rata no podía decir «etcétera», tenía que contar sin parar hasta cien, uno, dos, tres, cuatro, cinco, etcétera.

Después de esa noche el Rata empezó a venir todas las noches a traerme el dinero. Era el único momento que lo veía. A veces dejaba una nota con el dinero; normalmente, las notas decían «Sabes que te quiero», pero una vez el Rata añadió una «Posdata: Lo que me sorprende es que la mayoría de la gente nunca parece sorprenderse».

Mientras tanto, mientras ocurría todo esto, yo seguía yendo al instituto. Tenía catorce años, era un novato, y muy rápido, tanto que parecía casi un defecto genético. Mis padres me dijeron que debía practicar algún deporte, pero cuando llegó la primavera ya había dejado el baloncesto, porque soy bajito, y el fútbol, porque soy pequeño, y lo último que me quedaba era correr, pues espero que no os vayáis a pensar que me proponía jugar al tenis. Me presenté el primer día de entrenamiento y Coach Carting nos agrupó a los novatos por un lado y a los veteranos por otro, y nos dividió en alevines y juveniles, y dijo, lo recuerdo perfectamente: «La única lección que puedo enseñaros en esta vida es que siempre hay alguien que gana y alguien que pierde». Luego disparó al aire, juro que la pistola estaba cargada, y lo siguiente que recuerdo es que fui el primero en cruzar la línea de meta.

El último fue Merle Potter, cosa que entonces no significó nada para mí, pero que ahora sí tiene un significado. Lo que quiero decir es: ¿Por qué no me alejé de él?

Y creo que esto a su vez plantea la pregunta de por qué no me alejé de todos ellos. No solo entonces, sino más adelante. ¿Por qué no huí de aquel hombre con quien me encontré en el arca de Noah, y de Wade y de Colin?

¿Y por qué cuando huí de ellos, por qué solo llegué hasta aquí, por qué me tiré a la poza? Seguro que les tenía miedo, pero creo que tenía aún más miedo de lo que pudiera encontrar en mi huida. Y. Eso. Y. Pero. Y. ¡Qué más da!

En resumen: gané mi primera carrera y Coach Carting me incluyó en el equipo, y cuando gané la primera competición me compré un par de zapatillas de pinchos.

Me las compré con parte del dinero que le guardaba al Rata.

El dinero que pensábamos usar para marcharnos.

En cierto modo, ya no creía para nada en aquel plan. Tenía un montón de dinero escondido debajo del cajón, en tres cajones distintos, porque ya no cabía en uno o en dos, y me parecía que si no éramos capaces de irnos con lo que había allí, ¿qué otra cosa nos permitiría escapar? Y en cierto modo ya no confiaba en él, ya no confiaba en el Rata, era un poco como el Ratoncito Pérez, con la diferencia de que yo no le daba nada y él seguía dejando dinero, cada vez más dinero. Puede que a lo mejor ya no confiara en él, pero sin duda confiaba en su dinero. Lo que intento decir es que creo que me aproveché de él.

—Lo fundamental —dijo el Rata— es el respeto.

Eso fue lo que dijo cuando le enseñé las zapatillas y le conté con qué las había pagado.

Yo no dije nada, porque antes de que él hiciera ese comentario ya sabía que lo que había hecho estaba mal. Le había ofendido.

—Supongo que llegarás muy lejos con estas zapatillas.

Cogió una de las zapatillas. Las quemaduras de las muñecas casi habían desaparecido para entonces; parecía como si hubiera pasado la viruela, o algo así, un mes antes.

La tiró al suelo.

—Muy lejos.

Tiró sobre la zapatilla el dinero que llevaba en el bolsillo.

Y se marchó por la ventana.

No volví a verlo nunca.

Pero entonces pasó algo… quiero decir, en la poza, no en mi habitación. Después de esa noche en mi habitación no pasó nada. Nada de nada. Llevaba toda la vida cayendo, meses, años, siglos, tanto tiempo que, cuando al fin toqué con los pies el fondo de la poza, sentí una auténtica conmoción, y de pronto me encontré allí clavado, hundido hasta los tobillos, en algo que parecía una especie de diarrea congelada, y pensé en mis calcetines; llevaba puestos unos calcetines blancos que no pegaban nada con el resto de mi indumentaria, y pensé «Nunca volverán a quedar limpios».

Pero una cosa más. Mi teoría. Antes de rendirme ante el fantasma. Sobre lo que le pasó al Rata.

Vale. Respira hondo.

Ja, ja.

Vale.

No creo que huyera. No creo que me abandonara. Creo que alguien se lo llevó.

Habíamos vivido demasiadas cosas juntos… lo que quiero decir es que él había pasado demasiado como para tirar la toalla de buenas a primeras. El Rata no es de los que se rajan. Y ni siquiera se llevó el dinero. Pero lo cierto es que no lo sé, porque el dinero siempre pareció ser más mío que suyo.

Una vez, muy al principio, cuando empezó a ir por el Big M, le pregunté si le iba gustando un poco más. Y no es que dijera que no le gustaba, es que ni siquiera quería hablar de ello. No quería contar lo que hacía, y mucho menos admitir que no le gustaba. Se limitó a responder: «Si me gusta ¿qué?», y yo le dije: «Ya sabes», y le puse la mano en el culo, pero él se dio la vuelta y se tumbó boca arriba y se quedó mirando las estrellas, que era lo único que se veía cuando te tumbabas en lo alto del silo, y al cabo de un rato preguntó: «¿Cuánto tenemos?», y yo dije: «Doscientos setenta y seis dólares», o lo que tuviéramos entonces, y el Rata se volvió hacia mí, pero apartando el culo, y dijo: «Ya falta poco», «Ya casi estamos», y recuerdo que yo le pregunté: «¿Ya casi estamos dónde?», y él dijo: «Ya casi nos hemos ido».

Con lo cual supongo que solo falta una cosa.

Me refiero al dinero. Siempre al dinero.

Al dinero que yo guardaba debajo de tres cajones. No volví a tocar un céntimo, ni siquiera lo saqué para contarlo y ver cuánto había. Lo que quiero decir es solo que soy humano, que me equivoco como todo el mundo, pero intento no tropezar dos veces con la misma piedra, y si el Rata volvía en algún momento, yo quería que viera que hasta el último dólar que había ganado como un esclavo seguía estando allí.

Pero ya no está.

Mis padres se lo llevaron.

Se lo llevaron cuando desmontaron la casa en pleno día porque no podían echarme, porque Galatia era un pueblo pequeño y yo nunca estaría lo suficientemente lejos de casa. No sé si al mudarse encontrarían el dinero o no, aunque supongo que no lo encontraron, porque habrían dado alguna señal, porque mi padre y mi madre eran los dos muy glotones, y aunque solo fuera eso, se habrían parado en el bar de Cora para tomar un postre si les hubiera sobrado algo de dinero.

Tenía los pies hundidos en el fango helado.

Lo que más me molestaba de haber perdido el dinero era que el dinero era lo único que me quedaba del Rata, y aunque nunca lo mirara seguía estando allí, donde yo lo imaginaba a todas horas, y con ello pensaba en el Rata, pero después de perder el dinero ya no volví a pensar en él tan a menudo, o del mismo modo.

Pantalones negros, calcetines blancos, zapatos negros, y ese fango helado.

Durante unos meses después de que mis padres se marcharan, los pocos meses que pasaron hasta que conocí a Wade, seguí durmiendo en nuestra casa. Dormía en mi habitación. En la alfombra sobre la que aún se veían las marcas de mi cama, de mi cómoda y de mi silla, y dormía entre los cuatro puntos que señalaban el espacio antes ocupado por la cama, y también iba hasta los cuatro puntos que marcaban el lugar ocupado por la cómoda, y fingía que la abría por la mañana para elegir la ropa, aunque no tenía nada más que lo que llevaba puesto. No es que esto tenga ninguna importancia. Pero necesito contarlo.

Lo que quiero decir es que la caída tuvo su recompensa, y una vez que toqué fondo, lo único que podía hacer era volver a subir, de manera que me impulsé hacia arriba, lo que por supuesto me hizo hundirme más, pero al estirar las manos hacia la superficie estrellada de la poza comprendí que en este caso, en mi caso, daba igual subir que bajar. Comprendí que igual podía morir congelado en un desierto que en el ártico, que podía caer por un agujero de miles de kilómetros sin necesidad de despegar los pies del suelo, y me pareció que si iba a ahogarme, lo mismo podía ahogarme en tierra firme que en el aire.

5.27

COLIN

Rosemary Krebs casi había llegado a convencerme de que decía la verdad cuando hablaba del amor que sentía por esa tierra, pero cometió el error de seguir hablando, y sus palabras acabaron cobrando la falsedad de un discurso político, y entonces empecé a calarla. Caminábamos sin rumbo fijo; yo intentaba volver hacia la casa de caliza, pero lo cierto es que no tenía ni idea de dónde estaba. Traté de orientarme por el sol, pero estaba casi en su cenit, y, además, me di cuenta de que incluso si pudiera servirme de él para determinar la posición de los puntos cardinales, seguiría sin saber hacia dónde debía dirigirme. En algún momento, Rosemary Krebs dijo algo sobre «recursos naturales y arqueológicos», y entonces, como consecuencia de una iluminación repentina que me sacudió como una descarga eléctrica, comprendí dónde tenían escondida a Lucy.

Apenas pude evitar que me temblara la voz cuando hablé:
—¿Rosemary?
—Sí, señor Nieman.
—Disculpe, señora Krebs… pero ¿no estamos cerca de la cueva?
—¿De la cueva?
—La de las Piedras Ventrales.
Se detuvo, con una ambigua expresión en la cara.
—Por favor, señora Krebs. Es muy urgente.
No necesitó mirar alrededor para orientarse. Señaló colina abajo, hacia el oeste.
—Creo que está por allí. Justo detrás del siguiente risco.
Me di la vuelta y eché a andar de inmediato, y enseguida oí sus pasos detrás de mí.
—Señor Nieman —dijo—, ¿puedo preguntarle por qué ese repentino interés por la cueva? Por el modo de preguntarlo supongo que todavía no ha estado allí.
—Estoy segura de que lo entenderá todo cuando le diga que los sucesos de los últimos ocho meses me han hecho desarrollar un sexto sentido.
—…
—¿Ha visto usted las fotos, señora Krebs?
—…
—Las de Lucy. Las que T. V. Daniels encontró en febrero.
—…

—En las fotos Lucy parece tumbada sobre la tierra. El agente Brown pensó que podía estar en un sótano sin terminar de Galatia.
—Bueno, muchas de las casas más antiguas tienen sótanos para guardar la comida y…
—… y una de las cosas que usted le prometió a la gente que se trasladó de Kenosha a Galatea fue un sótano bien construido, con materiales de la mejor calidad para impedir las inundaciones en primavera.
—…
—En todo caso, no han encontrado a Lucy en ningún sótano.
—…
—Según tengo entendido la cueva de las Piedras Ventrales es una cueva artificial. Una excavación, una fosa, un…
—Es un agujero en la tierra, señor Nieman, de unos cuatro metros, por tres y por dos.
—¡Exactamente!
—No crea que yo he estado ahí abajo.
—Eso ya lo sé.
—…
—Señora Krebs, ¿alguien se ha tomado la molestia de registrar la cueva desde que desapareció Lucy?
—Supongo que con «alguien» se refiere usted al sheriff Brown, o quizá, al alcalde.
—Lo que quiero decir es que está aquí. A menos de cuatro kilómetros del pueblo, a menos de dos kilómetros del lugar del secuestro. Está justo…
—… aquí, señor Nieman. Está justo aquí.
Para entonces habíamos llegado a la cima del montículo —del risco, como lo había llamado Rosemary Krebs con mayor precisión— y a nuestros pies, en un valle pedregoso, se encontraba la entrada de la cueva. La repentina visión de un edificio después de varios kilómetros y horas sin ver nada más que hierba y cielo, aunque fuese tan rudimentario como ese minúsculo cono apuntalado con tablones, te obligaba a guardar silencio, y los dos nos detuvimos un momento, limitándonos a mirar. Luego Rosemary Krebs dijo:
—Aproximadamente cada cien años las lluvias de la primavera son tan intensas que el brazo sur del río Solomon se desborda y las aguas anegan la carretera que cruza el extremo occidental de Galatea y llega directamente hasta este pequeño valle. Esto ocurrió por última vez hace más de ciento veinticinco años, y al retirarse las aguas fue cuando se descubrió la entrada de la cueva. Hasta entonces había estado oculta, nadie sabe con seguridad durante cuánto tiempo, probablemente enterrada por el mismo proceso que volvió a sacarla a la luz. Phyneas —continuó, haciendo una pausa para aclararse la voz—, el

alcalde, ordenó levantar esta pequeña construcción hace algunos años, con la intención de preservar la integridad de la estructura original y evitar que los niños cayeran en el agujero.

Había algo forzado también en este discurso, aunque al principio no caí en la cuenta de que solo lo decía porque estaba desconcertada, se encontraba en una especie de punto muerto. No quería bajar a la cueva.

—Usted tiene una llave —dije entonces.

—...

—Quiero decir que la lleva encima.

—Sí —respondió, con un suspiro.

—¡Qué extraña coincidencia! ¿Me la presta?

Rosemary Krebs se metió una mano en el bolsillo del vestido y sacó una sola llave.

—Señor Nieman —dijo, mientras yo echaba a andar sobre el cobertizo—, ¿no sería lógico suponer que si la cueva sigue cerrada es imposible que haya nadie dentro?

—Mire esto.

—...

—Aquí —dije— y aquí, y aquí.

—Son...

—Pisadas. Pisadas muy grandes.

—Eso ya lo veo, señor Nieman. Lo que quiero decir es si son suyas.

—...

—Aunque supongo que no, porque no parecen recientes, y ha dicho usted que nunca había estado aquí.

—Señora Krebs —dije entonces—, la mayoría de los candados llevan inscrito debajo el número de serie. Si escribe usted una carta al fabricante del cerrojo —recorrí con un dedo el objeto plateado que mantenía cerrada la puerta de la cueva— le enviarán una llave nueva.

—Demasiadas molestias para entrar en un cobertizo en mitad de un campo. El hombre que entrara aquí pudo haberlo cortado.

—Le cortó los dedos a Lucy, señora Krebs, porque quería que todo el mundo lo supiera. Pero creo que se proponía mantener en secreto su guarida. Aunque podría haber forzado el cerrojo y sustituirlo por otro.

Introduje la llave en la cerradura y se movió con suavidad; un cuarto de vuelta y el cerrojo se abrió.

—Pero no lo hizo —dijo Rosemary Krebs, aclarándose la voz.

—Pero no lo hizo —repetí—. ¿Se abre este cerrojo con regularidad, señora Krebs?

—Que yo sepa, no se abre desde hace ocho años, a menos que Eustace…

—Se lo pregunto porque se ha abierto con demasiada facilidad, teniendo en cuenta que lleva tanto tiempo a la intemperie.

—…

—Solo lo digo.

Un momento después saqué el cerrojo del pasador. La humedad había hecho que la puerta se hinchara y se pegara al marco y tuve que tirar de ella para abrirla; nada más hacerlo, un olor fétido salió de la cueva.

—¡Dios mío! —exclamé.

—¡Dios bendito! —exclamó Rosemary Krebs al mismo tiempo. Se tapó la nariz con una mano, pero me di cuenta perfectamente de que no se alejó de la cueva.

En cuanto sentí el olor, me invadió una extraña calma. Fuera cual fuese la causa de ese olor, estaba claro que se trataba de algo muerto, y por alguna razón yo estaba casi seguro de que Lucy Robinson seguía con vida.

—Discúlpeme —dije, quitándome la camiseta. Hice una bola con ella y me tapé la nariz.

—Señor Nieman…

Me quité la camiseta de la nariz y dije:

—Voy a echar un vistazo.

—Señor Nieman, no sea insensato. Deberíamos llamar al sheriff Brown.

—Con el debido respeto, señora Krebs, eso sí que sería insensato.

Rosemary Krebs casi sonrió.

—¿Es suya esta linterna?

—…

—Estaba aquí colgada. ¿Quizá se la olvidó al construir el cobertizo?

Rosemary Krebs negó con la cabeza.

Encendí la linterna y un brillante haz de luz se clavó en el cobertizo. Noté que la linterna estaba cubierta por una espesa capa de polvo y también que el polvo se transformaba en barrillo en contacto con mi mano sudorosa.

—Que conste —dije—. Estoy dejando mis huellas dactilares sobre esta linterna en este momento, y no en el pasado.

—Desde luego.

Miré a Rosemary Krebs. Se tapaba la nariz y la boca con una mano, pero sus ojos brillaban con impenetrable expresión.

—Si grito, eche a correr —le dije.

—¿Y si no grita?

—Entonces corra aún más deprisa.

Admito que había algo satisfactorio en el hecho de pronunciar estas palabras, de evocar la historia barata de una película de terror. ¡Crisis! ¡Peligro! ¡Allá vamos!

Dejamos de hablar entonces, y me alegré, porque con cada palabra una bocanada de aquel hedor se adentraba en mi cuerpo, y estaba a punto de vomitar. Conseguí atarme la camisa alrededor de la cabeza formando una especie de capucha y, apuntando con la linterna, me metí en la cueva.

Un pequeño sendero en espiral conducía hacia lo que parecía ser un montón de cantos rodados; en cuestión de segundos dejé atrás la luz del sol y quedé envuelto en la oscuridad, y advertí que muchas de las piedras parecían ligeramente cristalinas y reflejaban la luz de la linterna formando manchas de color que resultaban mareantes, casi hipnóticas. Pero la escasa curiosidad arqueológica que pudiera tener se vio interrumpida cuando el camino concluyó bruscamente. La linterna me mostró un palo nudoso clavado en un agujero en la tierra. El hedor era cada vez más insoportable. La linterna tenía una correa en el extremo lo suficientemente ancha para pasármela por la mano y, colgándola de la muñeca, me agarré al palo y comencé el descenso. En algún momento del pasado —parecía que hubiera sido en otra vida— Justin me contó que Webbie le había dicho que el palo tenía solo tres metros de largo, y me dejé caer con la idea de que si había alguien ahí abajo el factor sorpresa sería mi única ventaja, aunque me resultaba imposible creer que alguien pudiera soportar ese olor sin volverse loco.

Mis pies tocaron tierra blanda. Me separé un paso de la pértiga y mientras tocaba el techo de la cueva con la cabeza y los hombros, mis pies tropezaron con algo metálico; la linterna me mostró una lata vacía, una lata de verduras con la etiqueta carbonizada, y por un momento me distrajo la forma de la lata, pues sus acanaladuras recordaban exactamente a las del neumático de un camión. Se me ocurrió que la etiqueta se había quemado al poner la lata directamente al fuego para calentar la comida, y un momento después el haz de la linterna reveló otra media docena de latas y los restos de una hoguera, todo ello muy cerca del palo. Un poco más lejos había otras latas, también vacías, con las etiquetas quemadas y varios bultos informes, de color marrón, que al principio me parecieron ratas muertas, aunque luego me di cuenta de que eran libros hinchados por la humedad tras haber sido sumergidos en agua, novelas baratas, muchas de las cuales habían servido para alimentar el fuego. Me llamó la atención la disposición de los elementos: las latas, el fuego, los libros empapados y, por supuesto, la propia cueva; me pareció deliberado, deliberadamente simbólico, y no me costó imaginar a aquel hombre, leyendo junto al fuego encendido con las páginas de los libros que consumía y comiéndose la comida que había calentado en las llamas.

A ese hombre. A él. Hablábamos de él casi con familiaridad, como si lo conociéramos.

El haz de la linterna pasó sobre los nichos de la pared de los que me había hablado Justin. Al principio pensé que se habían hundido o estaban parcialmente rellenos, pero luego vi que en cada nicho había una caja, e incluso en la penumbra reconocí que las cajas eran las mismas que Justin y yo habíamos usado para hacer la mudanza. La que se encontraba más cerca llevaba escrita en un lado la palabra «Cobre»; en ella habíamos guardado un cuenco de cobre batido que Justin había comprado cuando estuvimos en El Cairo, un recipiente grabado con falsos jeroglíficos que, según nos dijeron, contenía un hechizo que concedía la inmortalidad a quien preparase cierta poción en él. Uno de los ingredientes para preparar la pócima, lo recuerdo bien, era un litro de sangre humana, y recuerdo que Justin me comunicó entre susurros su asombro por el hecho de que los antiguos egipcios conocieran el sistema métrico decimal.

—¿Señor Nieman? —La voz de Rosemary Krebs sonó débil, aunque audible—. ¿Está bien?

—Estoy bien, señora Krebs. Todo va bien.

La verdad es que no lo creía. Pensé que en aquellas cajas podía haber nuevos trozos del cuerpo de Lucy Robinson, que podía estar muerta, que podía ser la causa del insoportable olor. No fui capaz de abrir las cajas de inmediato y seguí pasando el haz de la linterna por el resto de la cueva —cuatro, por tres, por dos, como me había dicho Rosemary Krebs—; fue entonces cuando lo vi, en una esquina de la cueva: un bulto cubierto con tela.

No se había tomado muchas molestias para camuflar lo que había debajo de la manta, pero, fuera lo que fuese, era demasiado pequeño para ser el cuerpo de Lucy Robinson. Al menos eso esperaba.

Me acerqué hacia el bulto. Puede que estuviera influido por las películas, pero esperaba algo —silbidos de serpientes o ratas, una fosa oculta cavada en la tierra, una trampa de alambre que disparara una flecha mortal— que hiciera aún más peligrosa mi incursión en la guarida del enemigo. Pero solo se oía mi respiración y mis pasos; mi mayor obstáculo eran los afilados bordes de las latas abiertas. En algún punto tropecé con algo medio enterrado en el suelo: un par de botas; mis botas. No tenía la menor duda de que corresponderían a las huellas que había visto fuera y a las de la carretera donde secuestraron a Lucy Robinson. Seguí andando muy despacio, encorvado; enseguida llegué junto al bulto y levanté la manta sujetándola entre el pulgar y el índice. No basta con decir que el hedor se tornó mucho más intenso; inundó, literalmente, hasta el último centímetro cúbico de la cueva. Lo único que introdujo cierto dramatismo en la escena fue una débil rasgadura, que atribuí a la carne en descomposición.

Lo que había debajo de la manta llevaba muerto mucho, mucho tiempo. Una gelatinosa masa de carne colgaba de un esqueleto que en más de un punto dejaba ver los huesos blancos. No tardé en descubrir las pezuñas –¿una ternera?–; luego vi la forma ligeramente chata del morro y comprendí que se trataba de un cerdo. Poco después advertí que tenía rotas las costillas del costado derecho, luego apunté con el foco directamente al cráneo del animal y vi el agujero a la derecha.

Charlene.

Me quedé un rato mirándola, mas no tenía ningún secreto que contarme.

¿Howard Goertzen?

¿El pretendiente de Lucy?

¿Charlene?

Recordé que había sido Howard Goertzen quien encontró el vestido de Lucy, en la esquina de la calle Adams y la Primera.

Recordé también que Howard Goertzen era un hombre bajito, pero gordo, y que con mis botas dejaría hondas huellas en la tierra.

Parecía necesario cubrir de nuevo su cuerpo y volví a manipular con repugnancia la manta rígida y pegajosa. Algo brillante lanzó un destello al levantar la tela. Me detuve; reflexioné. Y decidí cogerlo.

Era un trozo de papel; lo sujeté por los bordes. Era una tarjeta de visita. Mi tarjeta de visita. Vi mi nombre escrito en ella.

Colin Nieman.

Le di la vuelta a la tarjeta.

Sé q e b sc^{a}rás resp est^{a}s aq í.

Era una frase de *La Bestia*, del libro de Justin. El mensaje había sido escrito con mi máquina de escribir, la que dejé de usar después de arrojársela a Justin.

Justin.

Pensé que cualquiera que se hubiese puesto mis botas dejaría huellas en el barro.

Por alguna razón sentí la urgente necesidad no solo de destruir la tarjeta, sino de comérmela, y el pensamiento al fin me deshizo el nudo que desde hacía diez minutos tenía en la garganta. Conseguí darme la vuelta para no ver a Charlene, me abrí camino entre todas las latas de comida vacías y los libros empapados y, muy despacio, con sumo cuidado, me guardé la tarjeta en el bolsillo: mi tarjeta, en mi bolsillo; con el mensaje que estaba seguro que alguien había escrito para mí. Decidí salir a la superficie y volver a mi casa. No a mi casa, sino a la casa, a una casa, una casa que no pertenecía ni a mí ni a Rosemary Krebs sino al desconocido –nadie podría convencerme de que Howard Goertzen tuviera la inteligencia o el valor necesario para cometer semejante fechoría–, el hombre sin nombre que quería arrebatarle la vida no solo a Lucy Robinson sino también, entonces lo comprendí, a todos nosotros.

5.28

WEBBIE

Gene Zwemmer se esforzaba cuanto podía para ser el borracho oficial de Kenosha. El 13 de mayo de 1973, según escribió Rosemary Krebs en su diario, Gene Zwemmer «se presentó a trabajar, en su primer día de trabajo, oliendo como si más que beberse una piscina de alcohol se hubiera bañado en ella». Su fama llegó hasta Galatia, y de vez en cuando se le veía en el bar de Sloppy Joe cuando el alcohol subía de precio en Kenosha. Era un hombre de baja estatura, con la boca continuamente abierta, como una puerta desencajada de sus goznes; también era calvo, pero lucía una barba de casi treinta centímetros, una especie de alfombrilla plana sobre la que se amontonaban los restos de sus últimas comidas. Era una barba de color indefinido, ni castaña, ni rubia, ni pelirroja, descolorida por el sempiterno cigarrillo que, apagado o encendido, siempre colgaba de su labio inferior. Nadie sabía a ciencia cierta si tenía o no tenía casa; si la tenía, nunca volvía a ella para pasar la noche, y el sol de la mañana lo sorprendía casi siempre acurrucado bajo un árbol o un balancín en un porche, tapándose los ojos con la barba para protegerlos de la luz.

Esta fue la persona a quien Rosemary Krebs contrató como chico para todo.

Ella no lo describe en su diario como acabo de hacerlo yo, pero inmediatamente después del incendio de Kenosha varios periódicos del estado publicaron una fotografía de Gene Zwemmer, y entre todos los supervivientes de Kenosha instalados en Galatea, construyeron una leyenda sobre él según la suerte que hubieran tenido, convirtiéndolo en el hombre que había arruinado sus sueños o que les había permitido comenzar una nueva vida, y la almacenaron en su memoria junto a las de Buffalo Bill y Paul Bunyan y Mamá Pata. Pero lo único que Rosemary Krebs escribió sobre Gene Zwemmer fue que «no era del todo humano. Era tan solo apetito, y lo que yo veía en sus ojos me convenció de que tenía derecho a hacer lo que hacía». Esta entrada corresponde al 28 de mayo de 1974, el día que Kenosha fue arrasada por el fuego, y aunque soy de la opinión de que las reconstrucciones no ofrecen más que una historia pobre y poco veraz, sigo siendo incapaz de evitar que mi imaginación se instale en esa mañana e ilumine con su luz todos los rincones que las crónicas existentes dejan en la oscuridad. Pero lo cierto es que esto no es historia, ni siquiera una historia: no es más que una excusa.

Todos los días, durante dos semanas, el termómetro superó los cuarenta grados a mediodía. Ni una nube en el cielo; nada más que el recuerdo de una leve brisa. Sin embargo, la primavera había sido precoz y lluviosa ese año, y casi se había realizado la mitad de la cosecha. Había sido una cosecha rápida y, por esa misma razón, escasa; los precios cayeron y los ánimos estaban por lo general tan caldeados como el tiempo. Gene Zwemmer pensaba que lo que necesitaba el cuerpo en tales circunstancias era una buena bebida tranquilizante, helada pero que quemase el cuerpo como el fuego. Pensaba en el vodka –solo pensaba, porque el bar no abría hasta las tres de la tarde–, pero luego resultó, inesperadamente, que acabaría bebiendo whisky.

Iba en el coche camino del trabajo. Conducía despacio. Lo cierto es que no iba a más de veinte kilómetros por hora, y hasta las viejecitas con gafas para quienes los automóviles seguían siendo una especie de novedad, lo adelantaban en sus polvorientos LTD y Crown Victorias. Pero Gene Zwemmer jamás le había hecho daño a nadie. Era la hora en que los niños salían del colegio, y Gene no era precisamente un hombre de reflejos rápidos. Condujo muy despacio hasta Galatia, hasta la gigantesca casa de muñecas de Rosemary Krebs.

Ella lo esperaba en el porche trasero. A Gene Zwemmer no le importaba demasiado: jamás lo dejó entrar por la puerta principal; siempre le hacía dar la vuelta a la casa. Y tampoco llegó a acostumbrarse a cruzar la puerta: nunca lo dejó entrar en la casa; incluso en pleno invierno salía a recibirlo con uno de sus discretos y elegantes trajes grises para ordenarle las tareas del día.

Pero esa mañana –puede que después del mediodía–, esa tarde, ella lo esperó en el porche trasero y lo saludó con la mano al verlo llegar; él sonrió mientras se dirigía hacia la desvencijada escalera. Apoyó una mano en la barandilla, pero no llegó a subir. A Gene Zwemmer no le gustaban demasiado las escaleras. Prefería la tierra firme. ¿Quién ha visto una sala de billar con escaleras?

Rosemary Krebs estaba de pie en lo alto de la escalera, mirando a Gene desde su privilegiada posición.

—Buenos días, Gene —dijo.
—Buenos días, señora Krebs.
—¿Cómo te encuentras, Gene?
—Muy bien, señora Krebs; gracias por preguntar. —Una pausa; una mirada bizca—. ¿Y usted, señora Krebs?
—Podría estar mejor, Gene; podría estar mejor. ¿Te gustaría pasar un momento?
—¿Pasar?
—A la casa, Gene.
Bueno. Bueno. Bueno.

Gene Zwemmer se agarró a la barandilla y, con mucho cuidado, subió los cuatro escalones. Subir no era tan difícil, a fin de cuentas. Lo malo sería bajar. Ya cruzaría ese puente cuando llegara el momento de hacerlo.

La puerta trasera conducía a la cocina, a través de un cuartucho. En la cocina había los enseres habituales: un fregadero, un fogón, un frigorífico y otros muchos. Montones de copas de cristal colgaban boca abajo de unos soportes como los que se ven en los bares elegantes en la televisión —en Kenosha no había bares elegantes— y los trapos de cocina aparecían pulcramente colocados en sus toalleros. Doce tablas de cortar colgaban de una de las paredes y un enorme cuchillo de carnicero reposaba en un cuchillero sobre la encimera, debajo de las tablas, junto a otros muchos cuchillos, tantos que a Gene le parecieron parte del *atrezzo* de un mago. Lo último que Gene vio, antes de fijarse en la mesa, fueron las diecinueve tazas de té blancas colgadas de otros tantos ganchos en una pared. Había un gancho más, vacío, y Gene se preguntó si la correspondiente taza estaría sucia o si se habría roto.

Luego se fijó en la mesa, y sobre la mesa vio un gran sobre marrón, una caja de puros, una botella de Jack Daniel's y dos vasos, boca abajo. Fue el segundo vaso lo que llamó su atención. ¡Vaya con la señora Krebs! ¡Quién iba a decirlo!

—¿Sabes qué día es hoy, Gene?
—¿Martes?
—Sí, Gene. Es martes. Pero algo más.
—¿Hace calor? —dijo, rascándose una ceja.
—Sí, hace mucho calor, Gene —dijo, acercándose para poner uno de los vasos boca arriba—. Es nuestro aniversario, Gene.
—¿De usted y de Phyn... de usted y del señor Krebs, señora?
—No, Gene. El tuyo y el mío. Un año, Gene. Hace un año que trabajamos juntos.

Lo cierto es que hacía un año y dos semanas, pero Rosemary Krebs tuvo que esperar hasta el momento de la cosecha.

Gene Zwemmer no dijo nada. En su vida había aguantado un año en un trabajo, aunque tampoco lo había intentado. No le parecía especialmente importante, ni siquiera lo bastante como para celebrarlo con una botella de míster Jack Daniel's. Notó que la botella estaba entera.

—Los aniversarios son muy importantes en mi tierra, Gene. En el sur.

—En Georgia, señora. —Gene Zwemmer había oído decir en más de una ocasión que Rosemary Krebs era de Georgia.

—Eso es, Gene. En Georgia. —Fue a coger la botella, pero se detuvo antes de tocarla—. Sírvete tú mismo —dijo, moviendo rápidamente los dedos, como si eso significara algo.

Gene Zwemmer se acercó despacio a la botella, como si esperase recibir un golpe en cualquier momento. Pero no ocurrió nada, y el duro tacto del vaso en su mano lo convenció de que tampoco estaba soñando. Rosemary Krebs no dijo nada mientras Gene abría la botella, y se oyó el crujido del sello de papel al rasgarse cuando Gene giró el tapón. Dejó el tapón sobre la mesa, pero no se sirvió.

—Gene —dijo Rosemary Krebs. Sonrió y luego, tras una larga pausa, puso el otro vaso boca arriba—, he pensado que debíamos señalar esta ocasión.

—¿Cómo dice, señora?

—Con un brindis —dijo Rosemary Krebs—. Por un año de éxito y todos los que vengan.

—Sí, señora.

—¿Tienes la amabilidad de hacer los honores?

—¿Señora?

Rosemary se limitó a señalar los vasos.

—¡Señora!

Gene Zwemmer se precipitó hacia la botella, pero luego sirvió el whisky despacio. Rosemary Krebs no tenía por qué enterarse de que míster Jack Daniel's y él no eran compañeros habituales.

Levantó su vaso y dijo:

—Por Lynchburg.

Rosemary Krebs no levantó el vaso.

—¿Cómo dices?

—Lynchburg, señora —dijo Gene Zwemmer, señalando la botella—. Lynchburg, en Virginia, cuna de Jack Daniel's. En el sur, señora.

Le tembló un poco la mano mientras sostenía el vaso en el aire a la espera de que Rosemary Krebs levantara el suyo.

—¡Sí, claro, Lynchburg!

—Señora. —Gene Zwemmer hizo el gesto del brindis con su vaso—. Por Lynchburg, señora. Por el sur.

Rosemary Krebs volvió a sonreír. Levantó el vaso y lo hizo chocar suavemente contra el de Gene.

—Por Lynchburg —dijo—. Por el sur.

Gene Zwemmer asintió. «¡Adentro!», dijo, o quizá lo pensó, no estaba del todo seguro; y vació el vaso de un trago. Cerró los ojos al sentir el licor en la garganta. Áspero como la miel, dulce como la lija, pensó, y cuando abrió los ojos vio que el vaso de Rosemary Krebs también estaba vacío, y vio también, con esa nítida visión que solo te proporciona el alcohol de buena calidad, que sobre el labio superior de la mujer se formaban siete pequeñas gotitas de sudor. Rosemary tenía los ojos muy abiertos; le temblaban las aletas de la nariz y respiraba con fuerza. Al cabo de un rato, la oyó tragar.

—Bien, bien, bien, señora. Bieeeen.

Rosemary Krebs sonrió sin mostrar los dientes. No dijo nada. Gene Zwemmer volvió a llenar los vasos.

Y los llenó por tercera vez.

Al llegar al cuarto, Rosemary Krebs levantó la mano, pero le animó a que siguiera sin ella; y mientras Gene se servía otra copa, la olía y la saboreaba, se preguntó qué sorpresas le depararía su segundo aniversario, y el tercero y el cuarto y el quinto. Rosemary Krebs movió las manos en el aire, denso como el algodón, para alcanzar la caja de puros. Abrió la tapa como si pesara mucho o como si fuera muy delicada, y observó los tubos de celofán marrón con una extraña sonrisa, antes de decidirse a coger uno.

Lo sujetó por el extremo con la punta de dos dedos.

—Parece… parece… un… chorizo.

—¿Cómo dice, señora?

—Un chorizo, Gene, un largo trozo de mierda…

«No —me dije—. Rosemary Krebs no pudo decir eso.»

Bueno. Yo también había leído la novela de Colin. Nadie en Galatia había escapado de esa plaga.

—Una buena celebración necesita un buen puro —dijo, y un poco confundida por el alcohol se lo puso a Gene Zwemmer en la boca siempre abierta.

—¿Señora?

Rosemary llevaba un encendedor en el bolsillo de la chaqueta, un objeto muy elegante, de vidrio ahumando, en cuyo interior Gene Zwemmer vio flotar una burbuja de aire. Lo encendió y salió una llamarada; lo sostuvo junto al extremo del puro. Le temblaban un poco las manos, y a Gene le costaba acercarse a la llama o leer las letras que había grabadas en el encendedor; pero al final, la punta del cigarro se encendió a veinte centímetros de su cara y logró ver la inscripción.

J.F.K.
—Perdone, señora. ¿No será este el encendedor del difunto presidente?
—¿Cómo?
Rosemary Krebs debió de extrañarse por este comentario tan extemporáneo. Debió de mirar el encendedor un momento y luego, supongo, comprender el error de Gene Zwemmer; finalmente, debió de echarse a reír.
—J.E.K. —explicó—. Justice Eminent King. —Hizo una breve pausa antes de poner el encendedor en la mano de Gene, la que no sostenía el vaso vacío—. Era de mi padre —aclaró—. Pero como ni Phyneas ni yo fumamos... —Apretó con fuerza el encendedor y retiró la mano.
Con sus propias manos, con las dos, le sirvió a Gene un quinto vaso de whisky.
—Señora —dijo Gene Zwemmer. Se sacó el puro de la boca para poder beber, y luego volvió a fumar—. Señora.
Rosemary Krebs tocó el sobre que había encima de la mesa.
—Hoy solo te pediré un pequeño recado, Gene. Si no te importa.
—¿Señora?
—¿Podrías entregarle este sobre a Bruce Hennessy en el silo?
Cuando se marchó llevaba el encendedor en el bolsillo y el puro en la boca; bajo los brazos sujetaba el sobre lleno de informes, la caja llena de puros, y la botella aún a medias con lo mejor de Lynchburg y míster Jack Daniel's.
Rosemary Krebs continuó sentada cuando él se levantó. Presionó las palmas de las manos contra la mesa y su pequeño trasero se elevó acaso un par de centímetros en el asiento, pero volvió a hundirse, y Rosemary no se movió de la silla. Tampoco le deseó que pasara un buen día.
Gene no había contado con los escalones, y la punta del cigarro encendida, ahora a solo doce centímetros de sus ojos, le llenaba la cara de humo, empeorando aún más las cosas. Pero era su aniversario y de ningún modo estaba dispuesto a caer por cuatro miserables peldaños el día de su aniversario. Sin embargo, la incandescente punta del cigarro distorsionaba su perspectiva, y Gene se tambaleó en lo alto de la escalera.
Finalmente, cerró los ojos; cerró los ojos y confió en sus pies; y echó a andar como un niño: uno (y uno), dos (y dos), tres (y tres), cuatro (y cuatro), hasta que llegó al suelo.
Se metió en el coche.
Decidió volver a Kenosha cruzando Galatia. No conducía todos los días con un puro en la boca y una botella de su personal Dios y salvador, míster Jack Daniel's, entre las rodillas.

Las familias negras hacían lo que hacían las familias negras: mecerse en los porches con cortezas de sandía alrededor de los pies mientras los chiquillos corrían descalzos por jardines sin césped y cubiertos de basura, y Gene Zwemmer sonreía a todos ellos, con la punta del cigarro encendida todavía a diez centímetros de su labios.
Pero había un parque bonito.
Cruzó Galatia.
Kenosha surgió en el horizonte tan despacio que parecía elevarse desde un agujero. Lo primero que vio fue el silo, una larga hilera de columnas blancas. La tierra parecía apartarse como un labio que muestra unos dientes resplandecientes.
Sujetaba la botella entre las piernas.
Llevaba el cigarro en la boca.
Agarraba el volante con las dos manos, porque Gene Zwemmer jamás le había hecho daño a nadie.
Terminaron las clases; salieron los niños.
Gene sintió el olor del polvoriento aire que rodeaba el silo. Un aire seco y cargado de partículas que se adherían a la piel, que se metían incluso bajo la ropa, que se colaban por cualquier parte. Se le metía en los ojos y, entre el aire y el humo que salía del extremo del puro, ahora a siete centímetros, a solo siete centímetros de la punta de la nariz, pensó que debía aminorar la marcha.
Se abrió camino hacia las balanzas, junto a cientos de miles de fanegas de trigo, millones y millones de granos, trillones de partículas de polvo de trigo flotando a su alrededor.
Pensó que algo fallaba en aquella escena.
¿Qué era lo que fallaba?
Pensó y, para ayudarse a pensar, suspiró hondo.
La punta del cigarro estaba ya tan cerca de su rostro que sentía el calor en las mejillas cada vez que inhalaba. Abría una especie de tercer ojo, una esfera roja, brillante y vibrante.
Si esto sale bien, lo interpretaré como una señal divina, estaba escribiendo Rosemary Krebs en su diario en ese preciso instante.
Imagino brillar el aire alrededor del rostro de Gene Zwemmer, encenderse, crepitar, chisporrotear como dos trozos de pedernal, como las bengalas que queman los niños el cuatro de julio, Día de la Independencia en el resto del país y Día de los Fundadores aquí, en Galatea.
El diario de Rosemary Krebs era un cuaderno pequeño, pero aún quedaban cien páginas en blanco después de aquella en la que aparecía esta frase. No llegó a llenarlas. Solo escribió una frase más, y luego ocultó su historia –su confesión, habría dicho Justin; y recuerdo que la novela de Colin decía en algún momento que el libro era una con-

fesión— y allí la dejó para siempre. Al parecer bastaba con una señal divina, y no quiso tentar al destino pidiendo una nueva señal.

Lo primero que ardió fue su barba; tres décadas de comida grasienta quedaron reducidas a una viscosa nube negra. El elegante encendedor grabado con las iniciales J.E.K. le explotó en el pecho; la botella de Jack Daniel's le voló los genitales, el depósito de gasolina de la furgoneta le segó las dos piernas... todos ellos daños menores comparados con la bola de fuego que dejaría a Gene Zwemmer convertido en media docena de trozos de carbón.

«El aire abrasa», fue el último pensamiento de Gene Zwemmer. El aire abrasa, el cielo se desploma y todo se convierte en humo. La última frase del diario de Rosemary Krebs decía: *Es la cosa más absurda que he oído en mi vida*; y por primera vez me sentí completamente de acuerdo con ella.

6

6.01

MYRA

Me llamo Myra Robinson, aunque eso no tiene importancia. Lo único que importa es Lucy y que nadie se atreva a decir lo contrario. La encuentren o no; destrozada o intacta: Lucy.

Mi hija.

Lucy.

Ahora cállate y escucha, porque te voy a contar cómo es: cómo es, cómo fue y ocurrió todo.

6.02

WADE

El verano fue tan caluroso como frío había sido el invierno.

Siempre es igual en Kansas, pero no por eso deja de sorprenderte todos los años. En otros estados el otoño es una advertencia y la primavera un feliz preámbulo, pero aquí, en el corazón del país, no disfrutamos de esos lujos. Hace frío hasta que hace calor, y luego hace calor hasta que hace frío. Las dos estaciones ofrecen sus placeres y sus miserias, y aunque la mayoría de la gente piensa que el invierno es peor que el verano, yo diría que los que piensan eso no son de Kansas.

Aquí, el calor mata tanto como el frío.

Aquí, muy pocos tienen acceso a la clemencia del aire acondicionado, y tampoco a una fuente de calor que no sea el aire cargado o una estufa de leña o la grata sensación animal de varios cuerpos amontonados en una misma cama.

Aquí, cada invierno, los habitantes hibernan, y hay en ello cierto placer o al menos cierto alivio. ¿Qué es lo que desea la mayoría de la gente sino dormir?

Pero ese invierno, el invierno que llegaron Colin y Justin y se llevaron a Lucy, fue implacable, y el verdadero secuestrador de Lucy

Robinson consiguió tener a Galatea en jaque con el mero hecho de permanecer en el más absoluto anonimato, pese a que nos recordaba que Lucy Robinson sufría en alguna parte.

El vestido de Lucy.

El pelo de Lucy.

Los gritos de Lucy.

Los dedos de Lucy.

¡Encontradme!

Mientras todo esto ocurría Layton Buzzard cogió a su esposa y a su hijo y se marchó de Galatea. Roman List y su mujer, Stacy, no tardaron en seguirlos.

Sobre la pared blanca de su casa, Roman List pintó con spray las palabras NOS HEMOS IDO, en letras rojas de tres metros de altura.

Al otro lado de la autopista 9, Bruce Cardinal, un hombre soltero, abandonó la casa en la que había vivido su familia desde principios de siglo. Incluso se decía que la anciana Rochelle Getterling, que ya había cumplido los noventa y pasado viuda la mitad de su vida, se marchaba a vivir con su hermana, que también acababa de enviudar, en algún lugar del sur.

Antes de marcharse, Bruce Cardinal cogió un hacha y destrozó la casa por dentro. Hizo astillas hasta el último mueble y la última pared. Inspirándose acaso en Roman List, también dejó una nota: «No es para ti».

Fue un milagro, decía la gente, que no la hubiese quemado.

Nos hemos ido.

No es para ti.

Y cuando la nieve se derritió, había razones para que pareciese que el mundo se había encogido.

Se había encogido realmente.

El calor, cuando llegó, no fue bienvenido, y la mayoría de la gente continuó sumida en su letargo invernal. Pero el sol se regía por sus propias leyes, y los granjeros tuvieron que volver al trabajo porque el sol había regresado, aunque todo lo demás parecía seguir envuelto en el sopor del frío.

A veces, a medida que los días iban templándose, anhelaba el letargo invernal. Pero la urgencia de pintar te quema: el olor de la pintura es caliente; su tacto es líquido y caliente, incluso cuando se seca. Pinté y pinté sin parar.

Pinté mientras Colin escribía y Justin callaba.

Otras personas tenían su vida, pero nosotros teníamos nuestro arte.

Justin, sobre todo, tenía su arte.

6.03

MYRA

Intenta imaginarnos. Intenta imaginar el fuego. Percy Tomkins, que había ido conmigo al colegio, estuvo en esa guerra iraquí y dijo que nunca había visto cosa igual.

El fuego fue como una avalancha de agua. Era una pared el doble de alta que una casa y producía una nube de humo que se extendía hasta más allá de donde alcanzaba la vista, y llovía; os aseguro que caía como una lluvia sobre el pueblo. No creo que ninguno de los que murieron supiera qué le estaba cayendo encima, porque o te largabas de inmediato o quedabas fulminado. No había escapatoria. No había tiempo. Los supervivientes no tienen cicatrices. Los que estaban tan cerca como para preguntarse qué estaba pasando murieron sin conocer la respuesta.

Diecinueve años; mi primer apartamento. Un dúplex con un pequeño jardín detrás y un olmo enfermo de añublo; un aparato de aire acondicionado en la ventana que funcionaba a todas horas para mantener la vivienda fresca.

Yo estaba haciendo galletas.

Si alguien me preguntara cómo es que me dio por hacer galletas a media tarde, un día de mayo, no sabría qué decir. Puede que estuviera haciendo galletas para Stan; no lo sé. Lo que sí sé es esto: hacer galletas me salvó la vida, o, al menos, la vista.

El horno estaba justo enfrente del fregadero y encima de este había una ventana que miraba hacia el silo. El silo se encontraba a más de tres kilómetros, pero no se veía desde la ventana.

La puerta del horno también tenía una ventana, y yo estaba allí agachada, vigilando las galletas. Si alguien hubiera mirado por la ventana que había encima del fregadero habría visto mi trasero, unas cuantas galletas y una preñez más ligera que la de ahora.

Fue mi trasero lo que detuvo el cristal al abrirse bruscamente la ventana.

Primero oí la explosión. Por fortuna, yo no era una chica de reflejos rápidos —esos los desarrollé después de ser madre—, de lo contrario, me habría dado la vuelta y el cristal me habría golpeado en la cara. Lo que hice fue dar un saltito y gritar al sentir la bocanada de aire caliente en la casa. Parecía avanzar despacio, perezosamente, y la sentía hervir alrededor de mi piel como agua caliente. No recuerdo que la ventana estallara. Lo que recuerdo es la extraña sensación de que la ropa y el pelo flotaban en el aire caliente. El aire parecía una mano, una mano capaz de tocarme por todas partes al mismo tiempo.

Supongo que debería haberme asustado, pero al principio no me asusté. En lugar de asustarme pensé: Esto es lo que estaba esperando; y no me refería a Stan.

Sigo sin saber en qué estaba pensando.

6.04

WEBBIE

A veces me pregunto qué pensaría Wallace de mí si me viera con el uniforme de criada. Wallace y el uniforme cubrían igualmente mi cuerpo; los dos parecían conservar su propia identidad, mientras yo me desvanecía bajo ellos. Wallace era un hombre grande y cuando se tumbaba encima de mí yo sentía que su piel cubría hasta el último rincón de mi cuerpo. Y él lo sabía.

—Estás a salvo de todo —me susurraba al oído—; venga lo que venga, primero tiene que pasar por mí. —Y pronunciaba el «mí» de un modo que volvía su cuerpo aún más colosal que las murallas de una antigua ciudadela. Supongo que mi uniforme de criada también ofrecía algún tipo de protección. Una vez que me lo ponía, quedaba envuelta en él; su magia era tan poderosa que el disfraz no desaparecía cuando me lo quitaba. Ya no era Webbie Greeving, una universitaria educada y luchadora; era la criada de Rosemary Krebs.

Pero en cuanto terminé de leer su diario, sentí que mi trabajo en su casa había concluido. Sabía que había encontrado lo que necesitaba encontrar en esa casa, y después de ese momento mi uniforme se limitó a rozar mi piel, como el epíteto de mi padre. Nunca hasta entonces le había oído a mi padre usar el término «negro», ni siquiera para ponerlo en boca de un blanco; ni siquiera en sus sermones, cuando predicaba contra la «moda de la comunicación urbana» —no podéis imaginar hasta qué punto odiaba la música rap—, pronunciaba esa palabra, sino que hablaba del desatino que suponía reivindicar los términos del prejuicio y el odio. Sabía que la rabia de mi padre tenía tanto que ver con Rosemary Krebs como conmigo misma; ella era para él la bestia que engendró al Anticristo, y el hecho de que no tuviera hijos no hacía sino alimentar sus sospechas. La odiaba tanto que la sola mención de su nombre bastaba para desencadenar su furia. Mi padre había sido el principal sacerdote de Galatia durante cuarenta años, responsabilidad esta que había heredado de las cinco generaciones que lo precedieron: una cadena más larga, según me hizo notar en cierta ocasión, que muchas dinastías europeas. Mi padre nunca lo admitirá –bueno, es posible que sí–, pero lo cierto es que se ve a sí mismo como una especie de déspota bueno; su cabeza basta para tomar las decisiones; su mano, para actuar, y aunque esta situación pudiera parecer antidemocrática, era por el bien común y nadie se quejó jamás. Algunos se marcharon –muchos se marcharon–, pero eso era de esperar. La vida rural no era exactamente la moda del futuro. Pero los que se quedaron disfrutaron de las ventajas que ofrece la vida en una pequeña comunidad conservadora y cristiana y, por supuesto, de lo más parecido a la libertad concedida por los blancos que pueda encontrarse en este país.

Rosemary Krebs lo transformó todo y lo hizo contra la voluntad de mi padre y sin consultarlo con él. Cuando, semanas después del incendio de Kenosha, llegaron las cuadrillas de albañiles contratadas por Rosemary Krebs, mi padre, arrebatado por los éxitos del ya lejano movimiento en defensa de los derechos civiles, hizo que el pueblo entero se levantara contra ella. Escribió cartas al gobierno del estado y, al ver que eso no daba resultado, organizó una sentada en las tierras de Rosemary Krebs. Ella ordenó que las excavadoras continuaran trabajando, con gente o sin ella, obligando a mi padre y a su rebaño a dispersarse como ovejas.

De todos mis recuerdos de esa época, el más claro de todos es el de mi padre en continuo movimiento por la casa, en el púlpito, por las calles de Galatia y clamando contra esa «malvada mujer, esa mujer malvada como ella sola». Yo no había llegado a conocerla; no la había visto a menos de un kilómetro de distancia, pero no me daba cuenta de que mi padre tampoco la conocía. La Galatea de Rosemary Krebs había destruido el pueblo de mi padre, pero su negativa a hablar con él lo hirió aún más en su orgullo. Lo trataba como los blancos trataban a los negros en el sur reconstruido –como si no existiera– y su estrategia dio resultado. La furia cegó a mi padre y lo privó de su eficiencia, aunque supongo que Rosemary Krebs habría conseguido sus propósitos de todos modos. Nada de lo que ella hacía era ilegal, al menos nada de lo que hacía en Galatia, y no estoy segura de que tampoco lo que hiciera en Kenosha fuera en contra de la ley. Le compró a un hombre una botella de whisky. Le dio un cigarro puro.

Es la cosa más absurda que he oído en mi vida.

Pasó más de un año desde que comenzó la construcción de Galatea hasta que Rosemary Krebs decidió visitar a mi padre. No sé por qué al fin se decidió a venir, ni tampoco por qué esperó tanto tiempo; puede que hasta entonces no lograse reunir la información que necesitaba. La mayoría de las casas baratas y feas que ella había construido ya estaban habitadas para entonces; otro puñado de gente,

gente que no era rica pero que había cobrado del seguro o tenía capacidad para pedir un crédito, estaba construyéndose casas más agradables. El IGA y el TruValue ya casi estaban a punto, y Silas Brecken, que dirigía el almacén general de Galatia, hablaba de cerrar el negocio para evitar mayores pérdidas. Rosemary Krebs se presentó un sábado, sin avisar; el hecho de que mi padre estuviera en casa esa tarde, a pesar de que los sábados siempre los pasaba fuera, me hizo preguntarme si ella estaría vigilándonos.

La mujer que llamó a la puerta era bastante más menuda que yo. Llevaba un vestido marrón brillante y un collar de perlas de tres vueltas alrededor del cuello. A decir verdad, no podía mirarme desde arriba, pero la expresión de sus ojos no me pasó inadvertida.

—Buenas tardes —dijo—. ¿Está tu padre en casa?

Asentí, mirando con asombro sus diminutas muñecas, sus piernecitas de pájaro, la gran mata de pelo que se alzaba sobre su cabeza como un globo y brillaba con un extraño resplandor azul bajo el intenso sol de la tarde.

—¿Podría hablar con él?

Volví a asentir, pero seguí sin moverme del sitio. La mujer chasqueó la lengua.

—¿Pasa algo?

—¡Pero si es usted tan pequeña como un espantapájaros!

No pretendía ser grosera, pero Rosemary Krebs se ruborizó al instante. Se inclinó hacia mí y me susurró:

—Donde yo nací se castiga a las niñas maleducadas. Ve ahora mismo a buscar a tu padre antes de que le diga lo mala que has sido.

—Lo siento.

—Ve —dijo, con un susurro. Y subí corriendo las escaleras.

Minutos después, bajé agazapada detrás de mi padre. Rosemary Krebs había entrado en la casa y esperaba de pie en la sala de estar. Se fijaba solo en las escaleras, y luego miró a mi padre, como si ninguno de los muebles mereciese su atención.

—Buenas tardes, señor Greeving —oí que decía—. Soy Rosemary Krebs.

—Sé muy bien quién es usted. —Mi padre, con las mangas de la camisa blanca subidas por encima de los codos, miraba la Biblia que aún sostenía en una mano—. La mayoría de la gente me llama reverendo.

—Discúlpeme por interrumpir su estudio, señor Greeving. Me pareció que ya iba siendo hora de que nos conociéramos.

—Me sorprende que no me haya hecho ir a la casa grande —dijo mi padre, bajando otro escalón—. Cuando *massa* viene a los barracones es porque algo pasa.

Rosemary Krebs asintió, mirando a la Biblia de mi padre.

—Siento distraerle de sus estudios, señor Greeving. Intentaré quitarle el menor tiempo posible. —La diminuta mujer que estaba en nuestra sala de estar hablaba como si recitara unos versos que no le interesaban lo más mínimo. Al parecer, la única persona que podía beneficiarse si la creía era mi padre.

—Ya me ha quitado usted demasiado tiempo, señora Krebs. Y ahora, si me disculpa, debo seguir preparando mi sermón.

Pero Rosemary Krebs no se movió.

—Su actitud es muy arrogante, como la de todos los grandes predicadores y líderes de su pueblo, señor Greeving. ¿Puedo preguntarle dónde estudió?

—¿Perdone? —dijo mi padre, soltando ligeramente la Biblia.

—Dónde cursó sus estudios, señor Greeving. Perdón... reverendo. ¿A qué seminario asistió?

Yo no veía la cara de mi padre, pero sus hombros se hundieron un poco. Se quedó un momento callado; luego volvió la cabeza y me descubrió. Parecía consternado.

—Fuera de aquí —dijo.

—¿Papá?

—Vete; vete a casa de Charity Getterling o vete a jugar con Coretta Lewis. Esta señora blanca y yo tenemos que discutir algunos asuntos.

Cuando pasé corriendo junto a ella, Rosemary Krebs me miró y sonrió —no vengativamente, sino con aire triunfal; me pareció mucho más alta que cinco minutos antes— y aunque no sabía lo que podría pasar en mi ausencia, estaba segura de que le diría a mi padre que había sido grosera con ella, y también de que cuando volviera a casa mi padre me amenazaría con lavarme la lengua con jabón si volvía a hablar con esa mujer, y de que me mandaría a la cama sin cenar. Entonces, me pareció que también se estaba castigando a sí mismo, porque él tampoco cenó. Se pasó la noche paseando por el archivo y todo el día siguiente rodeado de miles de papeles con el único propósito de dar a su pueblo la legitimidad que merecía, la legitimidad de la historia. Pero faltaba una hoja de papel en esa colección, y aunque su ausencia pueda parecer trivial comparada con las demás cosas que estaban pasando, compartí el dolor de mi padre, pues yo tenía la misma carencia: a mi padre, como a mí, le faltaba un diploma. Se había otorgado el título de reverendo, como yo me había otorgado el de historiadora, pero ambos habíamos aprendido que no bastaba con eso.

6.05

MYRA

En mi cabeza todo ocurre al mismo tiempo: Kenosha y el incendio y la partida de Eric Johnson y de Stan, y luego Lucy.

El nacimiento de Lucy.

¿Qué puedo decir? Fue un parto rápido. Los dolores duraron como mucho dos horas.

Lo recuerdo de dos maneras. Recuerdo esa terrible presión, como si alguien estuviera llenándome de agua hirviendo, como si me llenaran hasta que estuviera a punto de estallar, hasta que suplicara reventar.

Y recuerdo una luz. Recuerdo estar dentro de esa luz, envuelta en ella como si fuera una manta; una luz suave y cálida que me sostenía y me aglutinaba, como la piel, y mientras me encontré envuelta en esa luz el tiempo desapareció.

Y los dos recuerdos se confunden.

La luz se desplazó rápidamente dentro de mí. Fue entonces, justo entonces, estoy segura, cuando Lucy Robinson se convirtió en la persona que es hoy.

Luego, la presión sacó la luz de dentro de mí. Juro que la luz me salía por los ojos, por la boca y por la nariz, por todos los poros de mi piel, y, por supuesto, por ahí abajo.

Y por eso la llamé Lucy. Habíamos pensado ponerle Mary —mi madre y la madre de Stan, las dos se llamaban Mary—, pero fue Lucy. La luz. Lucy.

Cuando me la entregaron tenía las manitas cerradas en minúsculos puños, gritaba y pataleaba como si al traerla al mundo le hubiéramos causado un gran daño. Recuerdo que quise contarle los dedos de las manos y de los pies, quise asegurarme de que los tenía todos, porque tenía la extraña sensación de que parte de ella había quedado dentro de mí.

Y lo cierto es que me había sacado algo de dentro.

Le estiré los deditos de la mano derecha, uno por uno. Uno dos tres cuatro cinco. Luego los de la izquierda. Uno dos tres cuatro cinco.

Tenía algo en la mano izquierda.

Para entonces la boca de Lucy ya había encontrado mi pezón y el doctor ya había terminado su trabajo y se había marchado a hacer la factura; las enfermeras estaban muy ocupadas. Stan venía desde la sala de espera.

Lucy llevaba una piedrecita en la mano. Una piedra negra, muy pequeña; no mayor que la punta de sus dedos.

Cogí la piedra. Nunca le hablé a nadie de ella. Una parte de mí deseaba tragársela, devolverla a su lugar de origen, pero sabía que volvería a salir, y si no saliera me causaría problemas. De manera que la guardé y cuando volví a casa la puse en el cofre de cedro donde más tarde guardaría el primer rizo de Lucy y el primer diente que se le cayó y la mantita rosa que mi madre empezó a tejer para ella la noche que nació.

Lo último que metí en ese cofre fue un zapato de cuero.

Cuando Stan se marchó, ese cofre fue lo único que se llevó consigo.

6.06

JUSTIN

Puede que hubiera doce caminos distintos para ir desde la casa de caliza hasta la casa de Wade, pero solo dos o tres de estos caminos no pasaban por Galatea. Por alguna razón no quería pasear por el pueblo, pero cada vez que me acercaba me sentía como la niña de esa serie llamada *Siempre hemos vivido en el castillo*, una aristócrata arruinada y obligada a soportar las habladurías de los lugareños. Nadie susurraba cuando pasaba por Galatea; algunos me miraban, pero nadie me señalaba con el dedo. La gente se limita a especular cuando no sabe la verdad, pero en el pueblo todo el mundo sabía la verdad sobre Colin y yo, sobre Colin y Divine, sobre Divine y Wade, y sobre Wade y yo. En ese sentido, creo que iban un paso por delante de los cuatro.

Prefería volver de casa de Wade cuando ya era de noche.

—¡Quédate! —me susurraba siempre; pero yo me levantaba, me vestía y me marchaba. A veces me cruzaba con Divine al salir de la casa. Lo encontraba en una habitación, gruñendo como un caniche cuyos dominios han sido invadidos. A veces me cruzaba con él al llegar a casa. Entonces agachaba la cabeza y se apartaba de mi camino, se escabullía como un gato al que se sorprende merodeando. Pero normalmente nos cruzábamos en el campo; él iba en coche; yo andando: Divine, como yo, prefería no pasar por el pueblo.

La noche produce a veces la ilusión de vulnerabilidad, otras de seguridad. Cuando era niño me aterraba la oscuridad y cuando vivía en la calle evitaba la luz del día como un vampiro. Ahora acepto lo que cada día y cada noche ofrecen. Una noche, un toro solitario me siguió durante más de un kilómetro: los tres cables de un alambre de espino eran lo único que me separaba de esa tonelada de impaciente carne. Otra noche, una lechuza me observó ir y venir desde una valla: se limitó a girar la cabeza ciento ochenta grados y a la luz de la luna parecía completamente blanca y neutral. Los conejos saltaban entre mis pies, contagiándome su propio temor; los perros ladraban y arrastraban las cadenas o se acercaban aullando quedamente para que les acariciara el hocico; el fétido rastro de una mofeta envolvía el aire. A veces se quebraba una rama en alguna de las pequeñas casetas rodeadas de árboles que salpicaban los campos, y entonces me asustaba de veras. Me decía que era un perro o un ciervo y me obligaba a caminar despacio, en línea recta. No corría.

A veces me adelantaba un coche. Si venía desde atrás, yo no hacía nada; si venía de frente, agachaba la cabeza para protegerme de los faros. De vez en cuando los coches aminoraban la marcha para observarme, aunque casi siempre pasaban deprisa. Aquí, la mayoría de la gente duerme cuando llega la noche, los que aún no duermen se disponen a acostarse y nada los disuade de su propósito. Pero una noche unos faros me iluminaron desde atrás; al momento, percibí el ruido del motor y de la gravilla aplastada. El vehículo tardó un rato en alcanzarme, y, sin necesidad de darme la vuelta, comprendí que había aminorado la marcha y que estaba siguiéndome. Mi sombra era tan alargada que se extendía hasta el horizonte; no veía nada más.

Me di la vuelta; los faros eran altos y cuadrados: un camión. Se detuvo. El motor se apagó y cuatro faros lanzaron una ráfaga de luz que dibujó una gran mancha sobre la carretera, derramándose sobre los campos y tiñendo de plata el trigo maduro que se mecía al compás de la brisa. Oí que las puertas se abrían, pero el muro de luz me impedía ver nada. Oí ruido de pasos; había más de una persona. Tres siluetas surgieron de la luz, todas extrañamente delgadas, con largas extremidades y grandes cabezas, como alienígenas, y antes de que hablaran supe quiénes eran.

—¡Vaya, vaya, a quién tenemos aquí! —dijo Darrell Jenkens, arrastrando las palabras.

—Parece que hemos encontrado un gato perdido —le respondió Howard Goertzen.

—Un gato vagabundo —dijo la voz de Grady Oconnor.

—Un gato doméstico, más bien —dijo Darrell Jenkens—. Un minino. Ven, gatito, gatito, gatito. ¿Qué te pasa, minino? ¿Se te comió la lengua el gato?

Las risotadas pastosas de tres bebedores de cerveza rebotaron una contra otra como las bolas de un bombo de lotería, derramando desgracia y misantropía en la noche.

—A mí me parece que es un asesino de cerdos —dijo entonces Howard Goertzen.

—Es un autostopista —dijo Darrell Jenkens.

—Un asesino de cerdos.

—Vamos, Howard, no empieces otra vez con ese rollo —interrumpió, enfadado, Darrell Jenkens.

—¡Darrell! ¡Has dicho mi nombre! Se supone que no ibais a hacerlo.

—Bueno, idiota, ¿quién llama estúpido a quién?

—Pero Char...

—¡Howard! ¡Haird!

Entonces se oyó un golpe sordo, luego hubo un silencio, y después Darrell Jenkens dijo:

—El que mató a tu Charlene fue el otro.

—Son tal para cual... —comenzó Howard Goertzen, pero Darrell Jenkens volvió a cortarle con otro «Howard». Al momento, la voz de Grady Oconnor reanudó la conversación.

—¿Es que esta cosa no sabe que en el estado de Kansas está prohibido hacer autostop? —dijo despacio, y en tono mesurado.

Pensé entonces que tal vez había razones para asustarse. Nunca se habían referido a mí como una «cosa».

—Quizá deberíamos practicar un arresto civil. En beneficio de la gente de bien de Galatea —dijo Darrell Jenkens.

—Por el bien de la gente —añadió Grady Oconnor.

Howard Goertzen farfulló algo inaudible, pero la sensación fue la de una brisa cálida en un día de verano que te deja la piel sudorosa.

—Sí —dijo Darrell Jenkens—, eso parece una buena idea. No hay necesidad de sacar de la cama al agente Brown y molestarle con menudencias. Los hombres adultos son capaces de valerse por sí mismos.

6.07

MYRA

Mi Lucy. Cuatro años. La piel de marfil y el pelo como el ébano, como dice la canción. Tenía siete vestidos blancos, uno para cada día de la semana, todos a cual más bonito. Cuando llegaba el domingo parecía una novia en miniatura. Se sentaba en la iglesia entre Stan y yo, con sus zapatos de cuero apoyados en el suelo, sus guantes blancos, sus calcetines blancos y una flor en el pelo: era la más linda de todas.

Cuando pasaban el cepillo para la colecta, nunca dejaba en él el billete de cinco dólares que le daba Stan; insistía en que lo metiésemos en uno de los sobres que ponían «Donativo».

Solo una mujer del pueblo usaba esos sobres. Y estaban allí por insistencia suya. A los demás les parecía un modo de hacer creer que dabas un montón de dinero cuando lo que dabas en realidad era una miseria. Lo mejor era dar billetes de un dólar y mezclarlos un poco; además, Nettie Ferguson era la encargada de contar el dinero de la colecta todas las semanas para el pastor Little, de manera que no era ningún secreto para nadie lo que Rosemary Krebs ponía en el sobre.

El sobre de Rosemary Krebs siempre estaba en el fondo del cepillo, porque ella siempre se sentaba en el primer banco. Desde donde nos sentábamos nosotros solo le veíamos los hombros y el pelo, grises como el acero e igual de rígidos. Lucy no apartaba los ojos del pelo de Rosemary Krebs durante el sermón. Puede que Dios hiciera milagros en el pasado, pero Rosemary Krebs se llevaba a Lucy al centro comercial todos los fines de semana, y Lucy aprendió a valorar desde muy pequeña lo tangible sobre lo inmaterial, sobre todo cuando esto llevaba un encaje en el cuello.

Siete vestidos blancos, todos a cual más bonito.

No la culpo de nada. Es uno de mis principios: no hay que culpar a los hijos cuando la culpa es de los padres.

Stan y yo la animábamos bastante: «Ve a saludar a la señora Krebs. Seguro que la señora Krebs se pone muy contenta si le llevas estas galletas que acabo de preparar. ¿Por qué no vas a casa de la señora Krebs para ver el catálogo de Sears?». Cuando me di cuenta de que alguien estaba pasándose de la raya, o yo, o Stan, o Rosemary Krebs, o Lucy, ya era demasiado tarde.

Rosemary Krebs decía que era su mentora. Decía que Lucy daba muestras de tener muchas cualidades; ella no tenía hijos y podría ofrecer a Lucy cosas que no estaban al alcance de Stan o de mí.

Para entonces yo ya tenía ganas de decirle que no se acercara a mi hija, pero era Stan quien pagaba las facturas y sabía lo mucho que le debíamos al First National Bank de Rosemary Krebs.

La vida no era fácil para el segundo fontanero de un pueblo como Galatea, pues no había muchos fregaderos o váteres atascados.

Stan aconsejaba cautela.

Cuando me dijo que yo sabía que él había estado hablando con ella —lo único que le importaba a Stan era tomar otra ronda en el bar de Sloppy Joe—, yo le dije que si llegaba a tener la más leve sospecha de que algo raro pasaba en la casa de la plantación le arrancaría a Rosemary Krebs ese panal que llevaba en la cabeza. Pero Lucy estaba contenta, y Dios sabe que el dinero que nos sobraba lo gastábamos en vestidos y juguetes.

La cerveza no es barata cuando se consume una caja al día.

El viejo Henry había muerto por aquel entonces; yo trabajaba para Bea y ella no tenía muy buena salud. Me quitaba mucho tiempo. Stan rara vez tenía trabajo y, como siempre estaba borracho, no era precisamente la persona más indicada para cuidar de una niña. ¿Qué podía decir?

Bueno, supongo que podría haber dicho que no, pero no lo hice.

6.08

JUSTIN

El olor a mierda se volvió más intenso, y enseguida, enseguida comprendí que salía del interior del camión. Aparecieron unas cuantas construcciones de hojalata, un pequeño silo cubierto de tela asfáltica, una granja destartalada con un balancín en el porche colgado de una cadena. Howard Goertzen aparcó el camión junto a un solar vallado. Era la granja de cerdos de su padre. Cuando salimos del vehículo le lancé una mirada a Grady Oconnor. No sé si le transmití algo –no era esa mi intención–, pero me tendió una mano para ayudarme a bajar, y cuando llegué al suelo se dio la vuelta.

Me metieron en uno de los cobertizos de hojalata. Olía a mierda fresca y a mierda vieja al mismo tiempo, y dulce también; el aire era caliente y fétido. Se encendió una luz fría que iluminó los lomos blancos y negros, manchados de barro, de un centenar de cerdos. Los cerdos se agitaron al sentir la luz. Un estrecho pasillo separaba las pocilgas, y lo recorrimos hasta el centro. Darrell Jenkens se inclinó sobre los tablones de la valla, mientras Howard Goertzen y Grady Oconnor se quedaban de pie, a pocos pasos de él. Grady Oconnor se miraba los pies y Darrell Jenkens y Howard Goertzen bebían cerveza.

–¿Es verdad lo que dicen, Howard? –preguntó Darrell Jenkens. Darrell pronunciaba Haird en lugar de Howard.

–¿Qué? –preguntó Howard Goertzen.

–Que un cerdo se lo come casi todo.

–Casi –dijo Howard Goertzen–. Las únicas que se comen lo que no quieren los cerdos son las cabras.

–¿Tienes cabras?

–No.

–Entonces los cerdos tendrán mucho que comer.

–Eso creo.

Hubo un silencio y Howard Goertzen soltó una risita que había estado conteniendo desde que entramos en la pocilga.

–¡Eh, Grady! –dijo.

–¿Sí? –dijo Grady Oconnor, levantando la vista.

—¿De qué estuviste hablando con este maricón ahí fuera?

Grady me miró y luego miró a Howard Goertzen.

—De nada —dijo—. No habla.

—Sí; es verdad. Se me había olvidado. No habla. No dice nada.

—Ni siquiera mueve la cabeza —añadió Grady Oconnor.

—¿Lo has comprobado?

—Pregúntale algo y verás; ni siquiera mueve la cabeza.

—¿Es verdad? —se volvió hacia mí—. ¿Es verdad, nenita? —Lo miré sin decir nada—. ¡Coño, Grady, parece que tienes razón! Ni siquiera mueve la cabeza.

—¡Hay que joderse! —exclamó Darrell Jenkens.

Howard Goertzen soltó una carcajada y dijo:

—¿Creéis que hablaría si yo hiciera esto? —preguntó entonces Howard Goertzen. Estaba detrás de mí y tiró la lata de cerveza contra el suelo de cemento. Me levantó con sus carnosos brazos y me dejó caer sobre la valla de madera. La valla se me clavó en la rabadilla, y me quedé allí sentado, temblando ligeramente, hasta que logré encajar un pie entre los tablones para mantener el equilibrio.

—No —dijo Darrell Jenkens—. No habla. Ha movido la pierna, pero no ha hablado.

—Ya lo ves —dijo Howard Goertzen. Grady Oconnor encendió otro cigarrillo.

—¿Qué os parece esto? —preguntó Howard Goertzen, y me dio un puñetazo en el pecho. Me eché hacia atrás y quedé colgado sobre la pocilga, pero el pie encajado entre los tablones me impidió caer. Los cerdos se removieron debajo de mí.

—Nada —dijo Darrell Jenkens.

—¿Qué tal esto? —preguntó Howard Goertzen. Esta vez me empujó, pero me agarré a la valla y logré incorporarme.

—Se ha agarrado a la valla —observó Howard Goertzen—. No está mal.

—No está mal —admitió Howard Goertzen—. Pero sigue sin hablar. ¿Sabéis lo que pienso?

—¿Qué piensas, Howard?

—Pienso que un hombre que no habla no es un hombre. No es mejor que un cerdo —dijo. Dio una fuerte patada a la valla y los cerdos que estaban más cerca se alejaron de un salto.

—Debería estar con los cerdos —dijo Grady Oconnor, sin apartar la vista de sus pies.

—Parece lo justo —admitió Howard Goertzen—. Nosotros nos los comemos a ellos, ¿por qué no pueden ellos comernos a nosotros? —Me miró fijamente a los ojos—. Tú los matas —dijo; al parecer seguía confundiéndome con Colin—. Ellos te matan a ti. Es justo.

Los cerdos estaban amontonados y casi tenían que montarse unos encima de otros para moverse. Sentí una pezuña áspera en el tobillo. Howard Goertzen volvió a dar una patada a la valla y me empujó casi al mismo tiempo. Me solté de manos, con las rodillas enganchadas en el primer tablón de la valla, y el pie aún encajado entre los tablones. Agité frenéticamente los brazos hasta encontrar el tablón superior, pero no logré incorporarme. Me quedé allí colgado; el vapor del amoníaco era tan intenso que empezaron a llorarme los ojos, y tosí al inhalarlo.

—¿Qué ha sido eso? —dijo Darrell Jenkens—. ¿Ha dicho algo?
—Solo ha tosido. No ha dicho nada —explicó Howard Goertzen.
—No dice nada —dijo Grady Oconnor—. Ni siquiera mueve la cabeza. —Entonces levantó la vista del suelo y, lenta pero intencionadamente, echó a andar hacia mí; entre él y Howard Goertzen me agarraron de la camisa y me levantaron. Tiraban con tanta fuerza que perdí el equilibrio y me incliné hacia él, pero se me soltó el pie que aún tenía encajado en los tablones; él se apartó y caí al suelo. Y me quedé allí tirado. Tenía junto a la cara las botas de Grady Oconnor y Howard Goertzen; Darrell Jenkens estaba detrás de mí. Grady Oconnor llevaba botas de vaquero, de punta afilada, y Howard llevaba botas de faena de color marrón claro, de esas que venden en Sears, esas suecas que están tan de moda entre los clones de Chelsea desde hace años. Nadie pareció reparar en mi sonrisa.

—Ya basta, Howard —dijo Grady Oconnor. Y esta vez pronunció el nombre con dos sílabas. Dijo Howard.

La voz de Howard Goertzen adoptó un tono desagradable que no tenía cuando se dirigía a mí.

—Pero si solo estoy empezando, Grady. —Entonces pensé que Howard odiaba a Grady Oconnor, que lo odiaba de verdad; lo odiaba por algo, y ese algo era probablemente el hecho de que Grady era negro.

Cuando Grady Oconnor le respondió comprendí que el sentimiento era mutuo.

—Le vas a arrancar la mano al pobre chico, y tú acabarás en la cárcel.

—Meterse con un maricón no es un delito —dijo entonces Darrell Jenkens. Le oí apartarse de la valla, oí el sonido de sus pisadas que se acercaban. Una de sus botas me rozó el hombro al pasar por encima de mí, una puntera redondeada, como la de Howard Goertzen, aunque cuando apartó el pie vi que las botas eran negras, no marrones. No sabía si el puntapié había sido intencionado o no; un líquido frío, que según me indicó mi olfato era cerveza, se derramó sobre mi hombro justo después de recibir el puntapié. Darrell Jenkens se detuvo tras esquivar mi cuerpo; se dio la vuelta. Me hundió un pie en las costillas hasta que me puse boca arriba–. Miradlo –dijo–. Es igual que un perro. Es incluso peor que un perro. Un perro al menos sabe cuándo tiene que morder.

Grandes estalactitas de polvo colgaban de las vigas del techo. Se movían ligeramente, como si en algún lugar soplara una leve brisa. En el suelo, donde yo estaba, no soplaba brisa alguna.

Grady Oconnor parecía desconcertado. Me miró suplicando que hablara, que me defendiera, o, al menos, que me levantara.

Darrell Jenkens me dio una patada en la sien. Se tambaleó un poco al levantar el pie del suelo. Y cuando la bota volvió a aterrizar con fuerza, vi la inscripción amarilla escrita en la puntera, justo encima de la suela. «Puntera de acero.»

–¿Qué pasa, Grady? –dijo Darrell Jenkens–. Parece que te gusta este tío.

Howard Goertzen se echó a reír y, al temblarle el cuerpo, la valla sobre la que estaba apoyado se partió. Los cerdos se agitaron en la pocilga.

–¿Te gusta este maricón, Grady? ¡Hay que joderse! ¡Te crees que conoces bien a alguien y luego resulta que le gusta un maricón!

–No me gusta –dijo Grady Oconnor; pero me miró mientras hablaba, rogándome con la mirada que hiciera algo.

El techo de uralita se alzaba como una catedral por encima de las vigas. Las luces de la pocilga colgaban entre las vigas y el techo, y por encima de ellas todo resultaba invisible. Por debajo, la uralita brillaba, parecía casi blanca, pero más arriba daba la impresión de escorarse en la oscuridad. ¿Qué fue lo que dijo Myra en el baile de Rosemary Krebs? En este pueblo todo está cargado de doble sentido. Todo significa algo. Pero Myra no había llegado hasta donde debía llegar. No era que todo significase algo: era que significaba demasiado.

–Si no te gusta, ¿por qué lo miras con esos ojitos? –preguntó Howard Goertzen.

–Ya he dicho que no me gusta –repitió Grady Oconnor. Advertí cierto disgusto en el énfasis que puso al decir «gusta», y supe que mis escasas posibilidades de librarme de la violencia acababan de esfumarse.

–Demuéstralo –le retó Howard Goertzen. Volvió a reír, y la valla se hundió un poco; y los cerdos se agitaron también un poco.

–No pienso demostrar nada –dijo Grady Oconnor–. De momento soy heterosexual; el problema es tuyo.

–Yo no tengo ningún problema –dijo Howard Goertzen–. ¿Tú tienes algún problema, Darrell? –preguntó, pronunciando Darl.

–No tengo ningún problema, Haird.

—Vale —dijo entonces Howard Goertzen—, me parece que el único que tiene problemas es el que está tirado en el suelo de la pocilga de mi padre.

Por encima de las luces, la oscuridad parecía abierta y vacía; tuve la sensación de que podría salir volando. Podría volar hacia ella y ella me salvaría. Me acogería.

—Esto, por ejemplo, es un problema —dijo Darrell Jenkens. Y mientras decía «esto» lanzó la bota hacia delante; y cuando dijo «problema», la bota aterrizó en mi estómago. Me doblé instintivamente, con tanta fuerza que atrapé la bota con el cuerpo. El crujido de mis costillas resonó en toda la pocilga, o al menos eso me pareció, y cuando el sonido se hubo disipado oí la risa de Howard Goertzen:

—¡Joder, Darrell! ¡Eso debe de doler mucho!

6.09

MYRA

Luego tuvieron que sacarme los cristales que se me habían incrustado en el trasero con una especie de tenazas o de fórceps. Fueron necesarias ocho horas y dos médicos, y, pasada la primera hora, el primer médico me inyectó Valium para que me tranquilizara, y todo se tornó nebuloso a partir de ese momento. Lo único que recuerdo con claridad —al menos parece un recuerdo, aunque también parece un sueño, pero al fin y al cabo todo parece un sueño—, es que le pregunté al segundo médico si me quedarían pequeñas cicatrices en el trasero, y el segundo médico dejó las tenazas-fórceps sobre una de esas bandejas metálicas que hay en los hospitales y poniéndome una de sus frías manos, enfundadas en guantes de plástico, en mi candente trasero, me dijo: «No, si yo puedo evitarlo». Luego se echó a reír y añadió: «De todos modos, no creo que nadie se fije mucho después de que haya nacido su primer hijo».

Bueno. Una cosa sí puedo afirmar con total seguridad. No se puede esperar hasta que el pasado sea pasado para darse cuenta de lo importante que es el pasado. Porque cuando ha pasado, pasado está, y si no tomas precauciones para no olvidarlo, seguro que lo olvidas, por más valioso que en su momento te pareciera. Lo único que quedan son trozos, fragmentos, astillas tan pequeñas como las que el médico me estaba sacando de la piel. Trozos y fragmentos que, cuando los unes, no necesariamente reconstruyen lo que se había fragmentado. No sé expresarlo mejor. ¡Escribidlo! Puede que lo diga porque he conocido a Colin y Justin. Pero lo digo. ¡Escribidlo ya!

6.10

WEBBIE

El primer viernes después de completar la historia de Rosemary Krebs, cogí la llave del archivo. Para mí todo estaba en esa llave y en esa cerradura: mi padre jamás había dejado el archivo abierto, aunque desde que tenía cinco años yo podría haber cogido esa llave, que siempre estaba colgada en un tablero de corcho en la cocina, y abrir esa puerta. Pero he tardado casi treinta años en hacerlo. La llave era pequeña y resultaba fría al tacto; no quemaba, como yo había imaginado, aunque la apretaba con tanta fuerza mientras subía las escaleras que me la clavé en la palma de la mano. Entró sin dificultad en la cerradura y giró casi sin ruido. La puerta tampoco hizo ruido; solo la luz emitió un ligero zumbido antes de que se encendiera el fluorescente, un sonido que, sumado al olor a polvo de la habitación, me recordó a un desván, a un lugar donde los objetos abandonados adquieren cierto valor por su misterio; objetos que, cuando los examinas atentamente, resultan ser baratijas. Yo esperaba encontrar solo baratijas.

En cuanto emprendí la búsqueda perdí la noción del tiempo. Transcurridos los primeros minutos dejé de buscar pruebas de algún episodio deshonroso en la historia de Galatia y me dejé cautivar por su pequeña pero bulliciosa comunidad. Durante las horas que pasé en el archivo percibí el amor de mi padre por su pueblo, y su odio feroz por Rosemary Krebs por haberlo destruido: supe por primera vez que había algo que destruir, aunque tanto las fechas de las fotografías como mi propio recuerdo me indicaban que lo que estaba viendo había ocurrido mucho antes de que las excavadoras de Rosemary Krebs irrumpieran en las tierras situadas al oeste de la autopista 9.

El descubrimiento me impresionó mucho. Ni siquiera sabía que yo figuraba en el fichero de la familia Johnson. Había habido un Alessander primero; se había instalado aquí y se había casado con Constance Getterling; tuvieron dos hijas: Blithe, que se marchó del pueblo, y Belinda, que se casó con uno de los hijos de los Deacon; y un hijo, Samuwell, cuya esposa, Cherry Estévez, se marchó con su familia a trabajar la tierra. Samuwell y Cherry eran los padres de Sawyer y Marsha. Sawyer se casó con Cora, por supuesto, y fue padre de otro Sawyer; luego se marchó. Marsha nunca se casó; se prometió a Hally Taylor, que murió en un accidente, cuando conducía borracho (recuerdo vagamente aquella muerte). Todo el mundo había dado por sentado Hally era el padre de Eric, pero según las fechas de las copias notariales del certificado de defunción de Hally y la partida de nacimiento de Eric, habían transcurrido casi once meses entre uno y otro suceso. No me sorprendió: todo el mundo pensaba que Marsha se había vuelto loca de pena y que su locura fue la causa de que Eric naciera como nació. En cualquier caso, Marsha nunca volvió a ser la misma después de la muerte de Hally, y Eric creció más o menos salvaje desde que aprendió a caminar. Y aquí estoy yo, mirando lo que quedó de sus pulgares, envueltos en un pañuelo de encaje blanco con las iniciales R. K., metido a su vez en una bolsita de plástico hermética con una etiqueta escrita por mi padre.

Sobre la bolsa mi padre había escrito: *Pulgares de Eric Johnson*.

Extendí el sucio pañuelo; aún tenía en la mano marchitos fragmentos de hueso y tiras de piel cuando oí que la puerta trasera se cerraba de un portazo. Supongo que habría podido dejarlos donde estaban y cerrar el archivo con llave antes de que mi padre tuviese tiempo de subir, pero no lo hice. La llave y los huesos eran lo mismo; eso lo había entendido de inmediato: reivindicar una cosa implicaba reivindicar la otra. A ojos de mi padre, no habría la menor diferencia.

De manera que me quedé allí sentada. Oí los pasos de mi padre por el piso de abajo y luego el largo y lento gemido de la silla que lo llevaba escaleras arriba. Bajó ruidosamente en el rellano y apareció en la puerta. Me miró un momento, vio lo que había encontrado y se dirigió a un armario que yo aún no había abierto; sacó de él una botella y un vaso. Los llevó con dificultad hasta su escritorio de roble y se sentó en el sillón de cuero. El aire del archivo era tan seco que en cuanto mi padre abrió la botella percibí el olor del alcohol.

—¿Whisky? —dije entonces—. Esta habitación está llena de sorpresas.

—Escocés —aclaró mi padre—. De malta pura. El cuello de la camisa, alto y blanco, le llegaba hasta las mejillas, haciendo que su rostro pareciera tener una sola mandíbula; me recordó a la barba de Lincoln. Bebió un trago de whisky, hizo una mueca y, por un momento, una segunda línea de carne enmarcó su cara.

Extendí la mano que contenía el pañuelo de Rosemary Krebs y los pulgares de Eric Johnson y dije:

—¿Está vivo Eric Johnson?

—No tengo ni idea.

—¿No tienes ni idea? Y esto, ¿qué es?

Volvió a beber y a hacer una mueca:

—Son sus pulgares —dijo, y estaba a punto de exigirle que añadiera algo más cuando continuó—: En uno de esos cajones guardo rizos tuyos y de tu madre; tienen tan poca importancia como esos huesos que tienes en la mano. Pero sé que tu madre está muerta y tú estás viva, no porque esos rizos me ofrezcan ninguna prueba de ello, sino porque a tu madre la enterré yo mismo y a ti te veo todos los días. –Volvió a beber, pero esta vez no hizo ninguna mueca–. No todas las pruebas son concluyentes, hija. Ni siquiera la Biblia bastaría para demostrar la existencia de Dios si no percibiéramos su presencia en nuestras vidas. Y ahora deja eso. Ya has encontrado lo que buscabas.

Miré los pulgares por última vez y los envolví en el pañuelo.

–Me quedo con ellos.

–Como quieras. Lo cierto es que no puedo impedírtelo. –Mi padre encogió el lado derecho del cuerpo, como si quisiera acentuar su enfermedad–. Supongo que se los llevarás al agente Brown.

Asentí.

–Antes de hablar con él debes saber que fue él quien me los dio.

–¿Y esperas que me lo crea?

–Sí –dijo mi padre, dando otro trago.

–Entonces, ¿por qué no has hecho algo?

–¿Algo…?

–Llevárselos al sheriff Peterson de Bigger Hill, o a los que patrullan la autopista; a cualquiera.

Mi padre trazó un arco en el aire con el vaso a medias. El arco parecía abarcar a Galatia, a Galatea, a Bigger Hill, a Kansas, al mundo entero.

–Podrían haber encontrado a Eric Johnson –seguí diciendo–. Podrían haber encontrado a quienes lo lincharon.

–Y eso, ¿de qué habría servido? ¿Para qué traerlo otra vez aquí? ¿Para que siguiera odiando y siendo odiado y atacase a otra chica blanca o a una negra? No creo que encontrarlo le hubiera hecho ningún bien, ni a él ni a Galatia. Y con respecto a quienes lo lincharon, no hace falta que venga nadie de fuera para investigarlo. El populacho puede ocultar su rostro con máscaras, pero no se toma tantas molestias para camuflar sus voces, sus camiones y sus zapatos. Cincuenta y cinco hombres y muchachos ataron a Eric Johnson a ese árbol. Cuarenta y siete blancos y ocho negros. Si hubieras continuado investigando, y no hubieras dejado que tu imaginación quedase bloqueada por un símbolo llamativo aunque inútil, habrías encontrado sus nombres escritos en un papel. Aunque –dijo mi padre, dando otro sorbo de whisky–, la mayoría de esos nombres han pasado a convertirse igualmente en meros símbolos. Solo dos de los que lincharon a Eric Johnson siguen entre nosotros. Los demás se han marchado.

Lo cierto es que solo quedaba uno, pero eso no lo sabría hasta poco después.

–¿El agente Brown? –pregunté, adivinando uno de los nombres.

Mi padre asintió.

—¿Y cómo puedes, tú, un líder de los afroamericanos, vivir con esa carga?

—El delito es suyo, no mío. Y mientras los dos lo sepamos resulta mucho más útil como sheriff que en prisión.

—No puedo creer que estemos teniendo esta conversación. Pareces más un político de ciudad que un cura de pueblo.

—Siempre te has dejado engañar por las apariencias, hija. Galatia es una ciudad. Es tan moderna como Nueva York, Chicago o Los Ángeles, y si este estado de cosas no es de tu agrado la culpa es de tu… jefa. Yo me habría conformado con seguir siendo un anacronismo, el líder espiritual de un rebaño cada vez más pequeño, pero ella arrastró a Galatia hasta el siglo veinte. Nos dio algo que nunca habíamos tenido: conflictos raciales. Nos dio crisis fiscales. Nos dio seguros, proyectos de desarrollo urbano y fondos de inversión. Yo prefería reuniones en la iglesia con ponches con alcohol; pero algunas cosas se perdieron irremediablemente. —Hizo una pausa, volvió a llenar el vaso y bebió—. Tenemos tantas posibilidades de recuperar aquellos tiempos idílicos como las que tiene Eric Johnson, esté vivo o muerto, de recuperar sus pulgares. Pero, como le gusta decir a la señora Krebs, el progreso no puede detenerse.

—¿Y qué lugar ocupa en todo esto el bienestar de Lucy Robinson? —pregunté, cuando mi padre terminó de hablar.

Por primera vez, mi padre pareció sorprendido.

—¿Qué tiene ella que ver con todo esto?

Pese a la advertencia de mi padre, no pude sino blandir el paquete que tenía en la mano.

—¿Te parece una coincidencia que la elegida haya sido ella?

Se quedó un buen rato mirándome, luego se fijó en mi mano, y finalmente, levantó la mirada para encontrar la mía.

—No —dijo en voz baja—. No me lo parece. Creo que el elegido, como tú dices, habría sido cualquiera que acompañase al joven Justin Time —dijo, pronunciando el nombre con una pizca de ironía.

Después de que mi padre hablara, sentí un cambio en la habitación. No estaba segura de si el cambio se produjo en él, en mí o en el ambiente del propio archivo, cerrado durante tanto tiempo y que ahora respiraba libremente por primera vez, pero la figura de mi padre, sentada detrás del escritorio, parecía alejarse mientras yo la miraba, y sentí que también yo retrocedía. Veía ante mí todo lo que había hecho durante los últimos meses, todos mis descubrimientos sin descubrir y esperando ser descubiertos; y comprendí que no servían para nada; para nada en absoluto.

—Dices que había hombres negros. Que algunos negros participaron en el linchamiento de Eric Johnson.

—Ocho.
—¿Tú también…?
Mi padre levantó una mano, y su gesto me alivió sinceramente. Creo que no podría soportar la idea de que se hubiera puesto alguna vez una túnica del Klan.

—Me gustaría decirte que esos hombres hicieron lo que hicieron porque Eric Johnson les había robado, o había molestado a sus hijos, o incluso por lo que le pasó a esa niña. Pero me temo que los movía la misma razón que a los blancos: lincharon a Eric Johnson por el color de su piel, y la culpa de ese sentimiento también la tiene Rosemary Krebs.

La explicación era demasiado sencilla. Yo lo sabía y él también. Al momento, clavó la vista en su escritorio. Se acercó para coger el vaso, vio que estaba vacío y apoyó la mano en el regazo.

—Tú eres su compinche —dije—. Eres su lacayo. Eres su esbirro. —Él me había llamado criada negra cuando le dije que iba a trabajar para Rosemary Krebs, pero lo cierto es que solo era un pobre hombre.

Mi padre se atrevió a sonreír.
—Dilo. Tienes ganas de decirlo.
Me limité a mirarlo.
Se encogió de hombros. Su voz no se alteró cuando dijo:
—La existencia del otro nos obliga a los dos a ser honrados.
—¿Honrados? ¿Y qué es para ti la honradez? A mí me parece que los dos mentís como perros.
—Los perros no mienten. No hablan.
—No se ofuscan.
Mi padre volvió a encogerse de hombros.
—Míralo como quieras: mentira u ofuscación. Yo prefiero considerarme la sombra de esa mujer.

Casi me echo a reír.
—Eso es lo más chocante de todo lo que has dicho esta noche.
—Yo no he elegido este papel. Me limito a interpretarlo por el bien de Galatia.
—¿Y cuál es el bien de Galatia?
—Continuar como siempre, alejada del mundo exterior.
—Vuelvo a preguntártelo —dije, tartamudeando—. ¿Qué lugar ocupa Lucy Robinson en todo esto?

Esta vez mi padre no se estremeció.
—Ella no es responsabilidad mía, hija. Ella no es uno de los míos.

Nos salvó el timbre del teléfono. Mi padre contestó en tono cordial, pero casi de inmediato adoptó una expresión de disgusto y me pasó el auricular.

—Es para ti —dijo—. Al parecer le ha vuelto a pasar algo a tu amiguito.

Cogí el auricular, y le pregunté quién era.

—Howard Goertzen —dijo mi padre, y aunque no era eso lo que yo había preguntado, de pronto supe que él había sido uno de los que participaron en el linchamiento de Eric Johnson.

6.11

MYRA

La primera vez que la oí hablar de Angela no le di demasiada importancia. Creo que Lucy tenía entonces cinco años; estaba jugando con el regalo de cumpleaños que le había hecho Rosemary Krebs: una casa de muñecas tan grande que tuvimos que dejarla fuera de casa. Una casa con torretas, balcones, puentes levadizos, ventanas con barrotes, yeso auténtico en las paredes y su propio foso, que se llenaba de agua con una manguera. Más que una casa de muñecas era un castillo, un palacio para una princesa. Era tan grande que Lucy se podía meter dentro. Uno de los costados de la casa estaba ocupado por una puerta enorme; Lucy entraba por allí y se pasaba el día entero en la casa, con uno de sus vestidos blancos.

Le pidió a Stan que le comprara una sillita, para no mancharse el vestido al sentarse en el suelo; y Stan se apresuró a decir que cada vez que Rosemary Krebs le compraba un regalo a Lucy, el regalo terminaba costándonos dinero. Pero le compró a Lucy una preciosa sillita blanca, decorada con flores azules, y, cuando se la dio, le dijo: «Aquí tienes, princesa. Tu trono».

Sentada en su silla y encerrada en su casita de muñecas, Lucy nos decía:

—Es un castillo encantado. Cuando estoy dentro me vuelvo invisible.

Así es como una niña de cinco años dice: no me molestéis.

Stan y yo fingíamos que no la veíamos cuando estaba en su casita. Lucy, Lucy, ¿dónde estás? Y nos poníamos a buscarla.

Pero el hecho de seguirle el juego tuvo extrañas consecuencias. Por un lado, a nosotros nos resultaba más fácil no hacerle caso, lo cual no es nada natural en los padres. Por otro lado, Lucy empezó a creerse las historias que contaba.

Le dije a Stan que pusiera la casa de muñecas bajo la sombra de las dos catalpas que había detrás de la casa, para que Lucy no pasara tanto calor. Le dije que me imaginaba los titulares: LA BELLA DURMIENTE HA MUERTO: LA PRINCESA DE GALATEA MUERE DE CALOR. No estaría bien.

Aquí los árboles siempre están junto al tendedero.

Lo que quiero decir es que yo no estaba espiándola. Estaba tendiendo la ropa.

—Me llamo Angela —oí decir desde el interior del castillo—. Vivo en la casa más bonita del mundo. Desde fuera parece una casa cualquiera, pero por dentro tiene montones y montones de habitaciones; y en cada habitación hay una sorpresa escondida; y todas las sorpresas son para mí.

Lucy seguía hablando, pero yo ya me había alejado, y no la oía. Estaba tendiendo sábanas, y tenía que moverme de un lado a otro de la cuerda.

En ese momento no me preocupó.

¿Qué niño no se inventa historias?

¿Quién no ha jugado alguna vez a cambiarse el nombre?

Angela.

Cuando iba al instituto, me gustaba que me llamasen María, en vez de Myra; pero la cosa no cuajó.

Recuerdo que soplaba una brisa tan seca y caliente que parecía penetrarte la piel como si te pasaran una bolita de algodón por las piernas sin depilar, y recordé ese otro viento cálido, y mis fantasías de un amante que me tocara por todas partes al mismo tiempo.

Recuerdo que el ligero escozor que sentía en el trasero desde el día del incendio resultaba especialmente intenso ese día.

La brisa me traía retazos de las palabras de Lucy: «... un cofrecito... un espejo mágico... una tiara de plata».

Me pregunté dónde habría aprendido la palabra «tiara» una niña de cinco años.

6.12

JUSTIN

Darrell Jenkens cayó al intentar levantarse.

Howard Goertzen y Grady Oconnor no hicieron nada mientras se levantaba y caía, y comprendí que estaban muy borrachos.

La valla crujió bajo el peso de Howard Goertzen, los cerdos se agitaron y Howard dijo tranquilamente:

—Eh, Darrell, ¿estás bien?

Darrell Jenkens respiraba con fuerza. Me pareció que empezaría a roncar en cualquier momento.

—¡Eh, Grady! —llamó Howard Goertzen.

–¿Sí? –dijo Grady Oconnor.

–Darrell se ha caído, Grady.

–Eso parece –dijo Grady Oconnor.

Howard Goertzen se echó a reír, al compás del crujido de la valla y el bullicio de los cerdos.

–¡Eh, Grady!

–¿Sí?

–¡Darrell se ha caído! ¡Se ha caído!

–Acabas de decírmelo, Howard.

–Quiero decir que se ha caído sobre su propio vómito. –Su risa iba ahora acompañada de hipo, la valla crujía bajo su peso cada vez que hipaba y el nerviosismo de los cerdos iba en aumento. Miré a Howard Goertzen y vi que dejaba caer la lata de cerveza. Supe que había sido un acto deliberado; no un accidente.

–¡Eh, hip, Grady!

–¿Qué pasa, Howard?

–Se me ha caído, hip, la cerveza, Grady.

–¿Y qué, Howard?

Hubo algo en la voz de Grady Oconnor que me obligó a mirarlo. Comprendí que había dicho Haird.

Grady Oconnor tenía una pala en la mano.

–Oye, Grady –dijo Howard, lanzando un fuerte hipido; y pareció hipnotizado por el fino reguero de cerveza que salía de la lata.

Darrell Jenkens empezó a roncar.

–Darrell, hip, está roncando, Grady.

–Haird.

Pensé de dónde habría sacado la pala Grady Oconnor, y luego me pregunté si eso tenía alguna importancia.

–¿Qué quieres, Grady? –Entre la risa, el hipo y la lengua trabada por la cerveza el nombre de Grady Oconnor sonó como si pronunciara una especie de diptongo: Gray.

–Howard –dijo Grady Oconnor avanzando hacia él con la pala en la mano–. Howard, por una vez en tu puta vida de pimpollo blanco, quiero que cierres la puta boca, Howard.

Haird. Haird. Haird. Haird.

Grady Oconnor le clavó a Howard Goertzen el mango de la pala en el estómago. La risa, acompañada del hipo, cobró un brío especial, y entonces Howard Goertzen se unió a Darrell Jenkens y a mí en el club de los vómitos, mientras la valla producía un largo crujido de protesta y los cerdos se ponían a saltar, a gritar y a empujarse.

Grady Oconnor volvió a embestir contra el estómago de Howard Goertzen, y esta vez el único ruido fue el que hicieron la valla y los cerdos. Pero esta vez la valla no crujió: el poste superior se partió bajo el peso del culo de Howard Goertzen. Vi que Howard Goertzen se ponía morado mientras caía de espaldas en la pocilga, que abría y cerraba la boca, pero sin emitir sonido alguno. Parecía masticar el aire, y su cara desapareció en la pocilga.

Los cerdos saltaban como locos, la valla temblaba, y entre los aullidos de los animales me pareció oír una especie de desgarrón.

Ni Howard Goertzen ni Grady Oconnor decían nada. Darrell Jenkens roncaba con más fuerza.

Los gritos de los cerdos cobraron una tonalidad distinta. Más que de pánico eran de ansiedad. Algunos asomaban la cabeza y el lomo por encima de los demás, y me di cuenta de que estaban subidos encima de Howard Goertzen.

Tras una larga pausa, Grady Oconnor se dirigió a la pared de uralita de la pocilga y apoyó la pala muy despacio. Se quedó allí, junto a otra pala y un rastrillo.

Mientras Grady Oconnor volvía hacia mí, que seguía tirado en el suelo, oí por primera vez otro sonido, y mientras este sonido se instalaba entre el ruido de las pisadas de Grady Oconnor, los ronquidos de Darrell Jenkens y los gritos de los cerdos, comprendí que había estado allí todo el tiempo, aunque no lo hubiera oído hasta entonces.

Grady Oconnor no me miró a los ojos cuando se agachó para levantarme. Me cargó sobre su hombro con gran esfuerzo y a punto estuvo de caer en el intento. No decía nada, pero jadeaba y su aliento era muy caliente.

Fuera llovía. Ese otro sonido, comprendí entonces, era la lluvia que chocaba contra el tejado.

—¡Dios mío! —exclamó Grady Oconnor mientras me dejaba en la parte trasera de la camioneta—. ¡Dios mío!

Pero no parecía dirigirse a mí.

6.13

MYRA

Tuve que abrirme camino entre el gentío. La multitud se agolpaba como si estuviera en un sótano presenciando una pelea de gallos. El gatito que Shelly Stadler sostenía en los brazos aullaba desesperadamente, pero Lucy gritaba más. Cuando al fin pude llegar hasta ella, vi que tenía los ojos cerrados y los puños apretados como cuando nació. Su vestido blanco estaba hecho un asco, y le faltaba un zapato.

Tenía la boca abierta y de ella salía un prolongado grito. De vez en cuando se detenía, suspiraba, tomaba aliento y volvía a gritar. La cogí en brazos. Cerró la boca como si fuera una trampilla, y se agarró a mí con fuerza, sin dejar de temblar.

Sentí que todo el mundo me miraba, esperando mis preguntas.
¿Qué había pasado?
Esperé hasta que Lucy se calmó un poco. Le acaricié el pelo, la espalda y los brazos.
Al fin habló:
—Me ha tocado.
Se me heló la sangre. No pregunté dónde. No pregunté cómo. Pero recuerdo que pensé que la niña que tenía en brazos podía no ser mi hija.
—¿Quién te ha tocado, cariño?
Tardó mucho en contestar. Seguí acariciándole el pelo, la espalda y los brazos. Como si pudiera convertirla de nuevo en Lucy.
Lucy se removió. Volvió primero la cabeza y luego todo el cuerpo. Y habló en voz alta.
Le habló a la multitud.
—El negro blanco —dijo.

6.14

CORA

Seis de la mañana. Grady Oconnor llama a mi puerta. Tuvo que llamar dos veces y con fuerza hasta que logré oírlo entre el tamborileo de la lluvia y el sopor del sueño que aún no me había abandonado por completo. No me había terminado mi primera taza de café, y eso significaba que «oír» era para mí un concepto extraño, por no hablar de lo difícil que me resultaba abrir la puerta; Rosa estaba arriba, duchándose. Debo decir que cuando al fin oí que alguien llamaba a esa hora, me dio un vuelco el corazón; subí la persiana muy despacio y tuve que mirar dos veces a Grady Oconnor mientras pensaba: Rosa ha vuelto a hacerlo. Anoche volvió a cerrar las persianas.

Grady entró ladeado, y cerré la puerta tras él sin darme cuenta de lo que hacía; lo primero que noté fue que Grady llevaba la gorra en la mano y que tenía la ropa seca y el pelo húmedo, lo que a esa hora, con solo media taza de café y con la que estaba cayendo, me resultó incomprensible. Grady agachaba tanto la cabeza que parecía capaz de tocarse los pies con ella, y vi que llevaba puestos sus mejores pantalones y una camisa de manga larga con botones perlados que desaparecían bajo el valle que su brillante cinturón formaba a la altura de la barriga. Lo que quiero decir es que no iba vestido para trabajar en el campo. De eso no cabía duda.

—¿Qué pasa, Grady? Parece que vas a la iglesia.

—No, señora —dijo; y me bastó con cómo pronunció esas dos palabras para recuperar el aliento.

Cuando dejó de temblarme el pecho dije:

—¿Por qué no pasas y te sientas? Es un poco temprano para desayunar, pero si quieres puedo prepararte un par de huevos fritos.

—No tengo hambre, señora.

—En primer lugar, deja de llamarme señora. Y más vale que me cuentes lo que pasa.

Grady parecía que iba a romper la gorra de tantos tirones que le daba.

—Kendall Hendricks me ha pedido que vaya hasta Wichita por piezas de repuesto para esa máquina nueva. Ya le dije que no comprara máquinas de la marca International Harvester; no son de buena calidad y es muy difícil encontrar recambios. —De pronto soltó la gorra—. He pensado aprovechar el viaje. Tengo un amigo que vive en Wichita. —Y muy despacio añadió—: No volveré por lo menos hasta mañana. Puede que no vuelva hasta el domingo.

Le serví una taza de café mientras hablaba. Le temblaban tanto las manos que la taza tintineaba sobre el platito como si estuviera encima de una lavadora en pleno centrifugado. Como no podía hacer nada para evitar que le temblasen las manos, puse una servilleta entre la taza y el plato para amortiguar el ruido, y cuando el café quedó en silencio le pregunté:

—¿Necesitas que me ocupe de alguna cosa mientras estás fuera, Grady?

Entonces me miró con ojos brillantes y asustados.

—Cora, tienes que decirle a ese hombre que se vaya del pueblo. Que se vaya. No me importa Rosemary Krebs, ni el agente Brown ni Lucy Robinson. Dile que se vaya. —Siguió mirándome un buen rato después de hablar, luego apartó bruscamente la cabeza y volvió a clavar la vista en su café.

Bebí un poco de café. Rosa ponía a veces un chorrito de sirope de chocolate en el fondo de la taza, solo un poquito, pero no lo removía, para que se fuera mezclando poco a poco. Eso significaba que yo no notaba el sabor hasta que estaba a punto de terminar la taza, y para entonces ella ya se había metido en la ducha. Entonces caí en la cuenta: Grady acababa de ducharse. Por eso tenía el pelo húmedo y la ropa seca, aunque estuviera lloviendo. Eso era lo raro. Grady Oconnor siempre se duchaba por la noche, porque su madre, Starling, trabajaba como auxiliar de clínica en el hospital de Bigger Hill y empezaba su turno a las siete de la mañana, y su padre, George, siempre se duchaba justo después que ella, antes de salir al campo, y apenas había agua caliente para dos duchas en esa casa, y como en un pueblo pequeño todo el mundo lo sabe todo sobre todo el mundo, yo sabía que Grady Oconnor siempre se duchaba antes de acostarse, y volví a sentir miedo.

Entonces sentí el sabor de la moca, una sensación densa y dulce en mi lengua, mezclada con el café, más fluido y amargo; y cuando el último resquicio de dulzura hubo desaparecido, dije:

—¿Qué ha pasado, Grady? —Y terminé de un trago la taza de café que Rosa me había preparado.

—No ha pasado nada —dijo, como suspirando—. Todavía no. Pero va a pasar. Algo se va a romper; algo va a estallar. —Pero no dijo «estallar» en voz alta, como cabría esperar. Lo dijo en voz baja.

—Grady…

—La semana pasada estuve trabajando con DuWayne Hicks, ayudándolo a desplazar el ganado. Ya sabe usted que Jim, el padre de DuWayne, tiene un perro, un cruce de pastor con las orejas caídas y las patas traseras un poco torcidas. Pues resulta que el bicho ayer se puso de muy mal genio, cogió a un ternero y empezó a mordisquearlo; nada serio, nada que no se pudiera arreglar con una patada ya sabe usted dónde. Pero DuWayne le pegó un tiro y lo dejó tirado en la cuneta, y cuando volvimos a la casa le contó a su padre que el perro se había metido debajo de las ruedas de ese hombre que tiene un jeep tan grande.

—¿Adónde quieres ir a parar, Gra…?

—Le pegó un tiro, Cora. Le pegó un tiro a bocajarro.

Había manchas marrones en el fondo de la taza, manchas marrones oscuras de café y manchas marrones claras, casi brillantes, de moca caramelizada. Casi brillantes, pero no del todo.

Grady miró la gorra que tenía entre las manos, luego echó la silla hacia atrás y se levantó.

—Tengo que irme. El viaje hasta Wichita es largo.

—El domingo —le dije.

—A última hora —dijo él.

—No olvides el paraguas.

—¿Cómo dice?

—Cuando entraste tenías la ropa seca. Tenías la ropa seca y el pelo mojado; por eso supongo que has dejado el paraguas fuera.

—¡Ah! —dijo Grady—. Sí, señora.

No me molesté en corregirle, tampoco le contradije cuando se sacó un billete de dólar del bolsillo y lo dejó sobre la barra, ni lo detuve cuando se dirigió a la puerta, la abrió y salió. En cuanto se hubo marchado llené el fregadero de agua jabonosa para lavar las dos tazas, y cuando terminé de lavarlas cogí el carrito lleno de frascos de sal, pimienta y tabasco y los fui repartiendo por las mesas para el desayuno.

6.15

MYRA

–Me llamo Angela.
Yo estaba acostando a Lucy.
–Vivo en la casa más bonita del mundo, con mi madre, que es una princesa encantada. Mi padre es un ogro que solo sale del bosque por la noche. Tiene siete brazos, siete piernas y siete ojos, y es tan feo que mi madre tuvo que convertirlo en una vela. Lo encendió, y mi padre ardió; y ahora ya no lo vemos nunca.
Se quedó dormida con una sonrisa en los labios y el puño izquierdo apretado.

6.16

DIVINE

Fui yo quien lo encontró. Eran alrededor de las cinco de la mañana, esa hora en que la luna y el sol están al mismo tiempo en el cielo. Yo me estaba levantando, aún entumecido, y recorrí sigilosamente la casa pensando en que Justin estaría soñando despierto en su buhardilla cuando salí y me lo encontré tumbado debajo del seto.
Al principio me pareció que estaba dormido.
–Vaya, vaya –dije en voz alta–. Parece que la señorita se suelta la melena de vez en cuando.
Pero luego me acerqué un poco más y vi que tenía una herida en la mejilla. Tenía un ojo morado, que empezaba a hincharse, y supuse que le habrían dado la paliza hacía como mucho dos horas.
–¡Qué coño…!
La voz sonó detrás de mí. Me di la vuelta y vi a Colin. ¿Cómo describirlo? Por un momento me sentí feliz como nunca me había sentido desde que se marchó el Rata, porque me pareció que Colin me había seguido, pero enseguida echó a correr por el jardín con sus

pantalones cortos, descalzo y clavándose en los pies las piedras afiladas y húmedas, y mientras me daba un empujón tan fuerte que me tiraba al suelo, me di cuenta de que había estado esperando a que yo me marchara para levantarse.

Luego se acercó a Justin. Se arrodilló a su lado, le cogió la cabeza entre las manos, le acarició el pelo y se puso a gritar: Malditos cabrones, y siguió gritando a pesar de que Justin se despertó y parecía que sus heridas no eran graves. Al final, Colin se volvió hacia mí y me dijo a gritos:

—¡No te quedes ahí parado, idiota! ¡Ve por el coche!

6.17

MYRA

Desde que se me congelaron los pies solo podía estar sentada. Y me senté. Estar sentada era casi lo único que hacía. Alguna vez me levantaba, como cuando encontré esa caja que el agente Brown pensó que contenía huevos de cuco. Pero me pasaba casi todo el tiempo sentada.

Esmalte de uñas azul. Ya le dije que no iba bien con el color de su vestido, pero no me hizo caso. No pienso hacerme responsable de ciertas cosas.

No es que no pudiera andar. Podía. Podía avanzar tambaleándome y perdiendo el equilibrio, pero no soportaba la sensación de caminar, el hormigueo que empezaba justo debajo de las rodillas y se convertía en esta especie de extraña nada justo encima de los pies. Era como si no tuviera pies, y al andar sentía que no tocaba el suelo, y la sensación me resultaba insoportable. Algunos querían volar e inventaban aviones, cohetes espaciales y ciencia ficción, pero a mí siempre me había bastado con mirar al horizonte. Yo siempre había vivido pegada a la tierra. Creía que si uno se alejaba mucho acabaría cayendo por el borde de la Tierra, pero desde que me quedé sin pies tenía la sensación de caer en todo momento, cada vez que me levantaba y daba un paso.

Por eso decidí quedarme sentada. Sentada y meciéndome. Casi siempre pensaba en mi Lucy, pero a veces pensaba en Rosemary Krebs, y al igual que me pasaba con Lucy, la imaginaba en el pasado, cuando tenía unos diecisiete años, le atribuía la edad de Lucy, le alisaba las arrugas y le teñía el pelo de negro; le inyectaba un poco de carne en las tetas y en las caderas, y me encontraba con Rosemary Krebs cuando tenía diecisiete años, pequeña como una ninfa, siempre con un vestido blanco como el que más tarde le compraría a Lucy, y, por alguna razón, cuando pensaba en Rosemary de joven, siempre pensaba en su embarazo. Sí, en mi imaginación Rosemary Krebs tenía un bebé y, supongo, un amante; tenía las mejillas sudorosas y arreboladas, las sábanas manchadas de sangre, y no paraba de suspirar, jadear y llorar. Y siempre, en mi imaginación, le quitaba a su hija. Yo era la madre de ese bebé, la madre que decía: «No estoy de acuerdo, señorita», y enviaba al bebé al mundo como si fuera una carta sin destinatario ni remitente, como Moisés en su cesto de juncos, flotando río abajo.

Las cosas me resultaban así más fáciles. De ese modo casi podía perdonarla por haberme quitado a Lucy. Porque me la había quitado: incluso la niña cuya imagen yo conservaba en mi recuerdo, la alegre niñita que sabía cantar «Swanee River» a los cinco años, esa niña era más de Rosemary Krebs que mía. Rosemary Krebs la alejó de mí con vestidos, caramelos y grandes promesas. La llevó hasta la colina más alta que había entre Galatea y Kenosha y le dijo: «Todo lo que ves será tuyo». Alimentó la codicia que anidaba en el alma de Lucy como en todas las almas, en las vuestras, en la mía y en la de toda niña de once, doce, trece años, sin padre y con una madre que bebía y solo podía ofrecerle una pequeña cuenta de ahorros que, como mucho, daría para enviarla dos años a estudiar en una universidad pública, lo cual, según me dijeron en cierta ocasión, bastaba para enseñarte lo que no sabes, lo que no tienes y nunca tendrás. Rosemary Krebs alimentó la codicia de Lucy hasta que esta creció en su interior y acabó devorándola; y a veces, mientras me mecía y me mecía, solo podía pensar en uno de esos extraños tomates o calabazas o pepinos que se ven en la feria de Hutchinson, vegetales mutantes que alcanzan el tamaño de una casa, siempre acompañados de su cultivador que luce una sonrisa de orgullo y un lazo azul, aunque nadie se los coma, aunque nadie los use para preparar quinientos litros de salsa de espaguetis, o una tarta de calabaza del tamaño de una rueda de tren, o una simple ensalada, preparada en una piscina y servida con un par de remos.

6.18

COLIN

Divine estaba enfurruñado en un rincón de la sala de espera. Sentí remordimientos por haberle gritado, pero antes de que pudiera disculparme, Webbie y Wade entraron precipitadamente en el hospital.

—Solo tiene unas cuantas heridas y una costilla rota —dije.
—¿Quién ha sido? —preguntó Webbie.
Me encogí de hombros.
—¿Ha sido…?
—No —interrumpí.
—¿Cómo lo sabes? —preguntó Wade. Parecía preocupado. También parecía agresivo.
—Lo sé —dije. Y luego añadí—: Después de seis años, lo sé.
—¿Está despierto? —preguntó Webbie—. Quiero verlo.
—¿Qué quieres ver? ¿Sus heridas? ¡Deja que descanse!
—Solo quiero que sepa que estamos aquí. Por si necesita algo.
—¿Qué puede necesitar? ¡Está en un hospital!
—Mira, Colin —empezó a decir Wade; pero Webbie lo interrumpió.
—Déjalo. No digas nada —dijo Webbie, poniendo una mano en el hombro de Wade y empujándolo hacia la puerta. Wade se quedó un rato inmóvil, mirándome fijamente, desafiándome. Estaba a punto de aceptar el desafío cuando noté que tenía manchas de pintura no solo en la ropa que llevaba sino en la piel, y recordé que Justin tenía la misma pintura en la piel y en la ropa. Entonces me alejé de Wade, me acerqué rápidamente a Divine y apoyé una mano en su hombro.

Wade volvió a decir:
—¿Eres consciente de lo que estás haciendo?
Me di la vuelta, sin apartar la mano del hombro de Divine, y miré a Wade. Estaba de pie en el pasillo de la sala de espera. Webbie estaba detrás de él. Wade parecía dispuesto a jugar con una baraja trucada, a hacer una revelación, a herirme.

Definitivamente quería herirme.

Sentí la calidez del hombro de Divine, su blandura. Empecé a masajearlo.

—¿Que si sé lo que estoy haciendo aquí?
—En Galatea —dijo Wade.
—En Galatia.
—¿Sabes cómo encontraste este sitio?
—Lo encontré porque Yonah me habló de él. Me dijo que era interesante.
—Yonah no te envió aquí porque Galatea sea interesante.
—¿Acaso no es interesante?
—Galatia —dijo Divine, en voz baja. Noté que se le había tensado el hombro y que estaba más caliente.
—Yonah te mandó aquí para saber qué estaba haciendo yo.
—¿Qué estabas haciendo…?
—Yonah te mandó aquí para saber si yo estaba pintando.

—¿Y estás pintando? —pregunté, con una sonrisa.

—Es muy posible —dijo Wade, en tono de frustración— que si Yonah te mandó aquí es porque ni siquiera le caes bien.

—¡Ah! De manera que no le caigo bien.

—¿No le caías bien?

—No le caía bien.

—Wade —intervino Webbie.

—Me estás haciendo daño —dijo Divine.

Aparté mi mano de su hombro.

—A Yonah le gustaba Justin —dijo Wade.

Volví a apretar el hombro de Divine.

—Yonah pensó que a ti te gustaría Justin.

—Y me gusta.

—Yonah estaba en lo cierto —dije, volviendo a sonreír.

Webbie empujó a Wade hacia la sala de espera. Me miró y luego miró a Wade. Después miró un momento a Divine y volvió a mirarme.

—¿Habéis terminado ya? ¿Habéis terminado definitivamente?

Llegado este punto, Divine se echó a reír.

—Webbie está enfadada —dijo.

Webbie empezó a decir algo, pero Divine la interrumpió.

—Webbie está celosa.

—¿Que Webbie está celosa? —dijo Wade.

Divine me estrujó la mano con la que yo le estaba estrujando el hombro. Me clavó las uñas.

—Porque nadie se pelea por ella. Por eso está celosa. Porque está sola.

Hubo un silencio después de que hablara Divine, un silencio terrible, insoportable, y yo dije:

—A Yonah le gustaba Justin. Decía que le gustaba porque no tenía nada que temer de él.

6.19

MYRA

Las palabras de Lucy causaron un gran revuelo. Era de esperar. El aire estaba cargado de polvo, y la gente empezó a darse empujones, como si alguno de ellos pudiera ser Eric Johnson.

Pero Lucy, que seguía en mis brazos, no se movió. Tenía el cuerpo rígido, la mirada fija. Seguí su mirada con la mía.

Lucy estaba mirando a Stan.

La gente pedía armas, cuchillos y cuerdas; se urgían unos a otros a arreglar las cosas. Pero Stan estaba igual de quieto que Lucy, mirándola.

Se acercó a mí y me tocó.

El negro blanco.

Stan parpadeó y vio que yo lo estaba mirando; volvió a parpadear y se marchó con los demás.

6.20

THELMA GOERTZEN

Un disparo quebró el aire de la mañana, luego cantó el gallo y después sonó otro disparo. Tenía las salchichas en el fuego, pero lo apagué, salí corriendo y oí otro disparo. El jardín estaba embarrado y lleno de charcos, el gallo volvió a cantar; los cerdos berreaban en la pocilga; hubo otro disparo. Lyle estaba en la pocilga y habían muerto cinco cerdos; otro disparo, seis cerdos muertos y una vibración que casi me tira al suelo y los berridos de los cerdos y el polvo y la escopeta semiautomática del 22 con veintiún cargadores y los dos cargadores de repuesto en el bolsillo de Lyle y otro disparo y siete cerdos y la vibración y sangre saliendo por las orejas de Lyle y el jardín y el barro y los charcos y el teléfono sonando en la cocina y Nettie Ferguson y el agente Brown y otro disparo y los charcos y el barro y el jardín y otro disparo y demasiados cerdos muertos como para seguir llevando la cuenta y varios montones de una sustancia marrón y viscosa en el suelo de cemento y latas de cerveza y otro disparo y la sustancia marrón resultaron ser vómitos y solo había dos latas de cerveza y había demasiados cerdos muertos como para seguir llevando la cuenta y los aullidos y otro disparo y la vibración y la sangre que salía por las orejas de Lyle y Howard que no aparecía y entonces vi las botas de Howard en la pocilga y a los cerdos muertos y otro disparo y los aullidos y otro disparo y los aullidos y otro disparo y la vibración que me tiró al suelo y la sangre en las mejillas de Lyle recién afeitadas y en el cuello de la camisa y otro disparo y las botas de Howard en la pocilga y otro disparo y algo que mantenía unidas las botas de Howard. Hubo otro disparo. Y allí estaban las botas de Howard, las botas de Howard, las botas de Howard, con los cordones atados hasta el tobillo y algo que las mantenía unidas y otro disparo y la vibración y la silenciosa caída de un cargador al suelo y el silencioso crujido de otro cargador al entrar en la escopeta y otro disparo y las botas de Howard y la sangre de Lyle y algo caliente en mi cuello y la escena y el humo y el latigazo de otro disparo y otro disparo y otro disparo y los cerdos muertos y los cerdos vivos y la sangre de Lyle y las botas de Howard y otro disparo y el vómito y las latas de cerveza y otro disparo y ya no quedaban cerdos vivos y no se oía nada y Lyle en ningún momento se volvió para mirarme y las botas de Howard y la escopeta de Lyle y la boca de Lyle y la escopeta de Lyle y luego otro disparo.

6.21

MYRA

Al día siguiente de nacer Lucy una enfermera entró en mi habitación y dijo que quería pedirme disculpas. Dijo que tenían que cambiar las luces del laboratorio y la sala de partos, y que estaban en plena faena cuando yo llegué. Dijo que yo estaba a punto a las once y media y no habían tenido tiempo de volver a colgar las pantallas.
Dijo que las luces eran de esas espirales fluorescentes.
Dijo que debí de quemarme los ojos mirando esa luz.

6.22

WADE

La imagen de la sala de espera, con sus grandes fotografías de praderas, sus padres fuertes, sus madres sonrientes, sus niños sanos, todos ellos exageradamente destacados por la luz de los fluorescentes, que zumbaban y parpadeaban, me había dejado exhausto. Gracias a Dios que Webbie estaba allí; de lo contrario, creo que Colin y yo nos habríamos pegado. Pero luego, cuando nos marchamos, me sentí extraño, nervioso, casi eufórico, y al momento volví a sentirme agotado, cuando al fin me bajó la adrenalina. Por primera vez en muchos meses no pude pintar; volví a casa lo antes posible y me metí en la cama, y allí me pasé todo el día.
Al día siguiente volví a pintar. No tenía otra cosa que hacer: no podía llamar a Justin para saber cómo estaba; tampoco podía ir a verlo. Ni podía llamar a Webbie. Cuando volvíamos a casa ella se había referido a Colin como «ese puto maricón calvo de Nueva York», y los

dos nos echamos a reír; luego me preguntó en voz baja por qué no estaba buscando a Lucy Robinson, pero creo que no le habría gustado mi respuesta. Y continuamos el viaje en silencio. Estaba de nuevo en mi estudio.

Me temblaba tanto la mano que empecé a pensar si tal vez podría encontrar el modo de transferir el temblor al lienzo, pero antes de resolver el dilema oí que el suelo crujía detrás de mí. Me di la vuelta. Era Justin.

Llevaba una camiseta y unos pantalones cortos. Siempre vestía igual en verano, pero su piel desnuda aparecía cubierta de heridas azules, moradas y negras que resultaban casi obscenamente hermosas. Quise abrazarlo, pero temí hacerle daño. Balbuceé un saludo y lo seguí a la que hasta entonces había sido la habitación de Divine. Justin esperó a que yo abriera la puerta, luego se quitó la camiseta y los pantalones, echó a andar —me di cuenta entonces de que estaba descalzo y no tenía heridas en los pies, pero de todos modos estaban negros después de andar cinco kilómetros por caminos embarrados— hacia el centro de la habitación y se sentó con cuidado en el suelo. Sus extremidades resultaban tan nítidas como líneas trazadas a lápiz; no tenía sentido dibujarlas. Pero se quedó allí sentado, esperando, y por primera vez no cerró los ojos.

6.23

MYRA

El médico que vino de Bigger Hill no ejercía normalmente como pediatra. Me pidió que saliera de la habitación mientras exploraba a Lucy, pero me negué.

Yo misma le quité a Lucy el zapato, los leotardos y las bragas.

No se movió mientras el médico le levantaba el vestido, le abría las piernas y la volvía a uno y otro lado.

Llevaba una linterna como un bolígrafo.

La sujetaba con la boca, porque tenía las dos manos ocupadas.

Por primera vez miré la línea que mi hija tenía entre las piernas como miraba la mía: como un objeto que despertaba el interés de los hombres. Supongo que pensé que aún era demasiado pequeña para ser una mujer, demasiado pequeña para ser siquiera una muchacha. Pensé que no era más que una niña, pero ahora lo comprendo: los niños aprenden a ser niños, mientras que las niñas nacen siendo niñas.

Tenía el zapato de Lucy en la mano y lo estaba limpiando con la punta de mi camisa.

El médico fue rápido y un poco seco, y luego me pareció que era preferible a que se hubiese mostrado amable pero lento.

Cuando terminó la exploración se sacó la linterna de la boca. Se pasó la lengua por los labios para limpiarse un hilillo de baba y dijo que no había indicios de penetración reciente.

Me preguntó si era necesario explorarla por el otro lado. Tardé un rato en comprender qué quería decir —tardé un rato en asimilar la palabra «reciente»— y luego negué con la cabeza.

Con mi autorización, le dio una pastilla a Lucy para que durmiera bien.

En ningún momento preguntó dónde estaba mi marido.

Mi marido estaba colgando a Eric Johnson de un árbol.

6.24

WEBBIE

Lo vi bajar por la calle. Caminaba despacio, con un ligero balanceo, y a primera vista me pareció que estaba desnudo. Llevaba la camisa en la mano y sus pantalones cortos, de color caqui, estaban tan sucios como bronceada su piel. Aún tenía un moratón en forma de medialuna alrededor del ojo y una ligera hinchazón en la base de la caja torácica, y aunque me dolía ver estas señales, pensé que si no las tuviera yo habría huido de él, pues a medida que se acercaba me pareció la persona más inviolable que había visto en mi vida; más que una persona parecía una piel andante, una única y sólida extensión sin entrada ni salida. Era por la boca, claro, porque siempre tenía la boca cerrada.

Pero en lugar de huir lo cogí del brazo y eché a andar a su lado.

—Te he estado buscando —dije—. Me gustaría enseñarte algo, si no te importa. —Sentí que se le tensaban ligeramente los músculos del brazo, pero no ofreció resistencia. Aunque eso no significaba nada: nunca se resistía—. Estás muy moreno —dije, para que se relajara un poco. Le acaricié el hombro—. Te sienta muy bien. —Caminábamos despacio; nos dirigíamos al pueblo, a Galatia: a la verdadera Galatia, la Galatia de mi padre—. De pequeña me gustaba mucho tomar el sol. Tenía que irme lejos de casa porque al reverendo no le parecía bien que las chicas se pusieran en traje de baño; pero siempre terminaba como un tizón. —Guardé silencio. Cada vez que callaba esperaba que él dijera algo. Sabía que no hablaría, pero me parecía absurdo que solo hablara uno de los dos. ¡Habíamos tenido conversaciones tan maravillosas!

La pausa se prolongó demasiado y no supe cómo reanudar la conversación. Conversación: reí para mis adentros, pero no dije nada; entramos en Galatia en silencio. El peso y el calor del brazo de Justin en el mío me hacían tomar conciencia no solo de él, sino del pueblo que me rodeaba. Su habitual letargo había ido en aumento, hasta convertirse en algo subyacente, reprimido. No había coches en las calles; ni un alma. Nadie podaba el césped o tendía la colada, y aunque las vacaciones de verano habían empezado hacía casi un mes, no veía niños jugando, ni tampoco los oía por ninguna parte; faltaban pocas semanas para la fiesta del Día de los Fundadores, pero, por el momento, no se habían hecho ningún tipo de preparativos, no se habían decorado las calles, no había pancartas que pidieran donativos, comida o bebida. Había cuatro o cinco nuevas casas vacías, y este vacío parecía haber inclinado la balanza en contra de Galatia. Los carteles inmobiliarios, fantasiosos hasta lo absurdo, se mecían en la cálida brisa de la tarde. Los carteles decían SE VENDE, pero sus grietas indicaban: Nos hemos ido.

En el parque hacía más fresco y respiré con alivio. El aire cargado de abandono aún no había penetrado allí: la hierba crecía tan densa y verde como siempre bajo los sauces y la tierra húmeda se me pegaba a las suelas de los zapatos. Justin se soltó de mi brazo y se alejó unos metros. Tenía una expresión de asombro, pero también una ligera sonrisa en los labios mientras caminaba junto a la hilera de sauces. Extendió los brazos y las ramas los rozaron ligeramente. Chapoteaba al andar entre el barro. Se le soltó la camisa que llevaba colgada de la cinturilla de los pantalones y cayó al suelo, pero Justin pareció no darse cuenta.

—Justin —le dije, y se dio la vuelta bruscamente. Tenía los ojos clavados en los míos; los brazos aún extendidos. La boca seguía cerrada. Me disponía a señalar hacia su camisa, pero me detuve al ver su boca. Y entonces, no sé por qué, un arrebato de maldad me impulsó a decir—: Siempre he detestado este parque. Solo venía aquí cuando el reverendo me lo ordenaba, cuando iba a castigarme. —De pronto guardé silencio y aparté la mirada de los ojos de Justin. Seguí hablando, sin apartar la vista de sus pies—. Pero cuando volví para cuidar de él todo cambió; sabía que no volvería a castigarme. Ahora, me encanta venir aquí. Vengo siempre que puedo. Me parece aún más bonito por ser un lugar conquistado, indultado.

Volví a mirarlo. Había bajado ligeramente los brazos, no por cansancio, sino como el anciano que empieza a encogerse con la edad.

—Justin. Está vivo. Eric Johnson está vivo. ¿Sabes quién es Eric Johnson, Justin? Lo sabes, te he hablado de él. Myra te habló de él. Está vivo, Justin; no murió en ese árbol. —Rebusqué en mis bolsillos y dije—: Mira, Justin; estos son sus pulgares.

Oí mis propias palabras y casi me echo a reír por lo absurdas que me resultaron. *Estos son sus pulgares.*

Un rayo de sol se abrió camino implacablemente entre las hojas del sauce. Se reflejó sobre la bolsa que sostenía en la mano extendida y el resplandor ocultó su contenido. Parecía una bolsa llena de droga.

Mientras yo hablaba, Justin fue bajando los brazos; primero despacio, luego más deprisa. Cuando terminé de contárselo sus brazos golpearon suavemente, inaudiblemente, contra sus costados. Agachó un poco la cabeza y arqueó la espalda. El bulto de las costillas se hinchó como si estuviera a punto de estallar. Sin mirarme, se dio la vuelta y echó a andar.

—Justin, perdóname, por favor.

Salpicaba tal cantidad de barro al andar que iba formando charcos a cada paso que daba; parecía que caminaba sobre el agua.

—Justin, por favor; no sé por qué te lo he dicho. Por favor, no volveré a hablar de ello.

Justin se detuvo bajo el sol. Vi que tenía una herida en el muslo que no había visto hasta entonces. Parecía más una marca amorosa que el resultado de una agresión. Entonces me acordé de Wallace y dejé caer el brazo que tenía extendido.

—Justin —lo intenté por última vez—. Necesitaba hablar con alguien. No es necesario que me contestes. Solo quiero hablar con alguien —dije, pero ya estaba demasiado lejos para oírme.

Me quedé mirándolo hasta que dobló una esquina. Cuando hubo desaparecido, su camisa tirada en el suelo llamó mi atención; me guardé la bolsa en el bolsillo y recogí la camisa. La miré medio ausente y la llevé al pozo para lavarla.

El pilón estaba ennegrecido y cubierto de musgo, pero olía a agua limpia y fresca, y sumergí la camisa en ella. Me distrajo un destello. Al principio, me pareció un pez de colores, pero luego comprendí que se trataba de un objeto muy pequeño, una ampolla de cristal, y lo saqué del agua. La camisa se extendió y se posó en el fondo del pilón. La ampolla aún contenía parte de un líquido rosado.

El último chico con el que salí en la universidad se llamaba Karl Louis. Era blanco, no negro, y era un chico muy estudioso, no un atleta; tenía el vientre suave y pálido, cubierto por un vello duro, y unas manos grandes que manejaban mi cuerpo con la misma diligencia con que pasaban las páginas de los libros. Me acariciaba el pelo, me quitaba la ropa, me acariciaba, primero la cara, luego el cuello, luego los pechos, el vientre y la vagina: con Karl siempre una cosa llevaba a la otra, y cuando sus manos al fin llegaban a su destino, me separaba los muslos y me penetraba. El condón o el diafragma no entraban en sus planes; y la píldora me sentaba mal; supongo que fue inevitable que un mes no me viniera la regla, y al mes siguiente tampoco. Tal vez si esto hubiera ocurrido mientras Karl aún estaba en la universidad las cosas habrían sido distintas. Pero él, igual que yo, había terminado sus exámenes orales y se había marchado a estudiar dos años a Edimburgo, donde esperaba redactar su tesis doctoral sobre un oscuro poeta escocés. Debería recordar el nombre del poeta, pero no lo recuerdo.

La pauta no había cambiado en diez años: en Galatia había una mujer embarazada. Reí para mis adentros; me olvidé de la camisa de Justin. Volví a casa con la ampolla en la mano, y cuando metí la mano en el bolsillo para buscar las llaves, rocé la bolsa de plástico que contenía los pulgares de Eric Johnson y comprendí quién iba a tener un bebé.

6.25

MYRA

Los hombres intentaron apagar el fuego con cubos de agua, sacos de arena y largas mangueras desde las casas situadas en las afueras del pueblo; pero las mujeres y los niños parecían saber que la guerra terminó tan inesperadamente como empezó.

Kenosha había desaparecido.

La vimos arder: una larga hilera de madres, hijas, hermanas y nietas que discurría al oeste del pueblo.

El poco viento que soplaba iba en dirección este.

Por primera vez en la vida comprendí la expresión «convertido en humo». La vida de las gentes —sus casas, sus coches, su ropa, sus muebles, sus geranios, sus ahorros y media docena de almas— flotaba en el aire lanzando cenizas grises y formando una nube tan fina que apenas parecía peligrosa.

Media docena de perros correteaban entre las piernas de la gente, ladrando y aullando. Por alguna razón, el fuego los había vuelto locos, y uno por uno corrieron hacia los campos. Creo que nunca volvieron.

Excepto uno.

Un perro de piel canela, que se había quemado hasta volverse casi negro; este perro siguió merodeando por las afueras del pueblo. Se mantuvo a medio camino entre la gente y los edificios en llamas.

Recuerdo que algunos niños lo llamaban. «Ven, Boner. Ven, Boner», suplicaban. Pero en ese momento solo se me ocurrió pensar: «¡Qué nombre tan horrible para un perro!».

El perro aullaba y gruñía, apartaba la vista del fuego para mirar a los niños, y volvía a mirar el fuego. Estaba tumbado y se levantó. Babeaba como si tuviera la rabia.

«Ven, Boner», lo llamaban los niños.

El intenso calor del fuego se dejaba sentir a varios cientos de metros de distancia.

El perro vomitó y se comió su propio vómito. Miró a los niños, les ladró; su ladrido parecía más una invitación que una advertencia.

Y luego echó a correr hacia el fuego.

Los niños gritaron y una niña salió corriendo detrás de él. Una mujer agarró a la niña de la coleta y la tiró al suelo.

Cuando vi que la mujer sujetaba a su hija, sentí una oleada de calor por todo el cuerpo, una ráfaga de aire caliente que me retenía como un amante —como una madre, comprendí—, y, ahora, cuando pienso en Lucy, siento la mano de esa mujer sujetando el pelo de la hija.

Recuerdo que cuando Stan volvió, más tarde, me miró de arriba abajo y me preguntó si estaba bien; yo dije que todo lo bien que podía estar, dadas las circunstancias. Y él dijo: ¿Dado que lo hemos perdido todo? Y mientras le respondía que no teníamos nada que perder, al menos por el momento, pensé en la mano de esa madre agarrando a su hija por el pelo. Realmente no, dije. Todavía no.

6.26

WADE

Cuando estaba dormido, Justin perdía la rigidez. Convulsionaba, temblaba, no paraba de dar vueltas, consumido por las pesadillas que parecían atravesarle todo el cuerpo. Pero si lo tocaba, inmovilizaba esa parte del cuerpo que entraba en contacto con mi mano: si le ponía una mano en el brazo, el brazo se tranquilizaba; si la ponía en la cabeza, la cabeza dejaba de moverse. Pero el resto de su cuerpo seguía en el mismo estado de agitación. Era como una serpiente atropellada por un coche, con la cabeza aplastada contra el asfalto, que sacudía furiosamente la cola. Parecía que no hubiera conexión entre las distintas partes de su cuerpo, como si en sueños se desmembrara. A veces quería saber qué era lo que turbaba su sueño, pero casi prefería no saberlo, por temor a que invadiese también el mío.

Mis sueños estaban llenos de invasores. Mis sueños estaban llenos de mí mismo y de un hombre llamado Yonah Schimmel. Mis sueños estaban llenos de gente que ya no existía.

El concepto de tiempo nunca había significado demasiado para mí, ni siquiera en circunstancias óptimas, y ahora las circunstancias eran todo lo contrario. ¿Por qué no deslizarse hacia el pasado o hacia el futuro? ¿Por qué no instalarse en un pasado que nunca existió? ¿Por qué no? Porque no podía.

La memoria es como un río; recordar es como nadar. Para algunos es como flotar. Para Myra Robinson era como flotar; una deriva interminable que reemplazaba a la necesidad de un suelo más firme, más sólido. Para otros –para Justin– era como ahogarse, hundirse hacia profundidades tan inmensas que todo se volvía agua, y al ser todo agua, todo se convertía en nada. Mas para la mayoría de nosotros, para mí y para Divine y para Webbie Greeving, era simplemente como nadar, una tarea más o menos difícil, según las aptitudes y los condicionamientos de cada uno. A mí siempre me ha resultado difícil nadar, y solo me aventuro en aguas tranquilas. Baste con decir que esas aguas, las de ese río, el río en el que acechaban mis recuerdos de Yonah Schimmel, no eran en absoluto tranquilas, y aunque quería seguir nadando solo llegaba hasta donde empezaba a sentir la fuerza de la corriente, que me invitaba a flotar, a ahogarme. Quería sentirla, pero no entregarme a ella: no quería ahogarme ni flotar; ni siquiera quería nadar. Supongo que se podría decir que solo quería evadirme.

No es que pretenda ocultar nada, ni siquiera a mí mismo. De hecho, no hay nada que ocultar. Dicho de otro modo, no hay nada que decir. Una vez, hace veinticinco años, pasé dos años acostándome con alguien que también se había acostado con Justin, teniendo extraños sueños en los que aparecían sus extremidades retorcidas y yo las sosegaba con mis manos nerviosas.

En una versión de nuestro encuentro, Yonah dijo que yo había entrado en su galería: había entrado en busca de un amante, dijo, y había salido con un marchante. Pero lo cierto es que nunca salí de allí.

En otra versión de nuestro encuentro, Yonah me obligaba a ponerme a cuatro patas para representar una pequeña escena pornográfica, bien abierto por delante y por detrás para recibir lo que quisieran meterme, desesperado, dijo, suplicando que me llenaran. Pero en esa versión del encuentro, Yonah no mencionó, ni siquiera pareció darse cuenta, que era él quien me llenaba.

En mi versión favorita de nuestro encuentro, Yonah decía que iba andando junto a mi estudio una noche de verano y me veía pintando por las ventanas abiertas, y daba un paso atrás y me veía pintando bajo una luz artificial y...

Llegado a este punto del relato, se distraía, y nunca llegué a saber qué hacía, y nunca supe cómo nos encontramos. De todos modos, jamás he pintado de noche.

La primera noche que Justin durmió conmigo, me senté en la cama y me quedé mirándolo mientras dormía. Me senté, lo miré y sosegué con mis manos sus extremidades retorcidas, como había hecho con Yonah, y en algún momento me descubrí trazando dibujos imaginarios con un dedo sobre su cuerpo, pero jamás he pintado de noche.

Lo único que le importaba a Yonah era el encuentro, no lo que pasaba después, no cómo terminaba. Nunca le oí contar historias sobre nuestra separación, nunca le oí hablar de esa desastrosa mañana después de que yo intentara follármelo. Que yo sepa, jamás ha dicho nada.

Yo mismo he construido estas historias. Con el paso de los años he ido tejiendo muchas versiones diferentes de los mismos hechos y, como Colin Nieman, he registrado algunas de estas versiones. Pero tal y como están las cosas ahora, una versión prevalece sobre todas las demás.

Nos hemos ido.
No es para ti.

6.27

MYRA

Me llamo Angela. Vivo en la casa más bonita del mundo con mi madre, que es una princesa encantada y me ha regalado un caballito mágico: Azul. Azul tiene los cascos de color turquesa y los ojos del color de la llama incandescente; su cuerpo es del color del mar y su crin y su cola son del color del cielo. Lo monto sin silla ni riendas, confiando en la firmeza de su grupa entre mis piernas y de su cuello entre mis brazos, y en mi madre, que jamás me regalaría nada que pudiera hacerme daño. Una mañana me desperté y vi que el sol entraba por la ventana, se reflejaba en las cuatro paredes de mi habitación, y pensé: ¡Qué hermoso día para montar a caballo! Y me puse mi vestido blanco de los miércoles y fui al dormitorio de Azul. Azul ya estaba despierto, esperándome; me subí a su lomo de un salto y salimos por la ventana. Azul corría y corría sin parar, y sus crines me nublaban la vista como si fueran nubes. Oía traquetear sus cascos como un tren que viaja a gran velocidad, los oía chapotear como ranas en una charca, tintinear como el cristal al romperse, y cabalgamos por bosques y ríos y montañas, hasta que Azul empezó a correr tan deprisa que no veía más que sus crines en mis ojos; entonces cerré los ojos y me concentré en el movimiento del cuerpo de mi caballito, y cuando abrí los ojos todo estaba oscuro, muy oscuro, y me asusté mucho. Pero Azul era un regalo de mi madre, y me dijo que no tuviera miedo. Sentí que su cuerpo se movía bajo el mío, que se daba la vuelta para decirme que él me llevaría a casa, y cuando dejó de hablar, me di cuenta de que no hacía ruido con los cascos, y al mirar hacia abajo vi que volábamos por encima de las estrellas, pero Azul me dijo que era un lago sobre el que se reflejaba el cielo. Empecé a tener frío en la oscuridad, pero Azul me envolvió con sus crines como si fueran una manta, y corrió y corrió a través de la noche hasta que llegamos a un bosque de árboles tan altos y con los troncos tan negros, que hasta sus sombras eran sólidas y había que esquivarlas, pero las crines de Azul me protegían el cuerpo, y aunque se retorcía y giraba bruscamente para sortear los árboles y sus sombras, avanzaba con la quietud del agua de un estanque en un día sin viento, y se me pasó el miedo, aunque estaba muy nerviosa. Vi un resplandor a lo lejos y pensé que eran los ojos de Azul que iluminaban nuestro camino, pero al asomar la cabeza vi que eran las luces de nuestra casa, y entonces salimos del bosque y volvimos a entrar por la ventana del dormitorio de Azul, aterrizando sobre su blando lecho de paja. Froté a Azul de arriba abajo con un trapo fuerte para secarle el sudor de la cabeza y los flancos; desenredé los nudos de su cola y lo besé entre los ojos. Volví corriendo a la cama. El sol entraba a raudales por las ventanas, y acababa de meterme bajo las mantas cuando se abrió la puerta de la habitación y mi madre entró sonriendo; me besó y yo le cogí una mano para que me acariciara el pelo. Cayó un mechón de pelo y vi que estaba trenzado con una hebra azul, y las dos nos quedamos mirándola y nos reímos, y mientras mi madre transformaba esa hebra en un lazo para mí, me preguntó: ¿Piensas pasarte todo el día en la cama?

6.28

WEBBIE

Rosemary Krebs me había dicho que la llave que me había dado solo servía para la puerta trasera, pero también abría la puerta principal.

Nunca la había probado; pero cuando fui a su casa para devolverle el pañuelo en el que se habían envuelto los pulgares de Eric Johnson, entré por la puerta principal, porque había decidido dejar mi trabajo. Al principio pensaba llamar, pero un impulso me hizo sacar la llave del bolsillo para abrir la puerta; y resultó que abría.

Rosemary Krebs me esperaba al otro lado. Miró de arriba abajo mi ropa de calle y dijo:

—Estás despedida.

Le tiré el uniforme a los pies.

—Soy yo la que se marcha —dije. Y le entregué el pañuelo que había servido para envolver los pulgares de Eric Johnson. Ahora estaba vacío, sucio y ligeramente acartonado—. Creo que esto es suyo.

Rosemary Krebs no miró el pañuelo.

—Algún día, señorita Greeving, comprenderás que el verdadero privilegio de la posesión reside en rechazar lo que en justicia te corresponde.

Entonces retrocedió y yo me dispuse a entrar, pero me cerró la puerta en las narices.

6.29

MYRA

Cuando Stan volvió a casa esa noche tenía la ropa empapada de sudor y apestaba como un hombre que se hubiera pasado el día follando con otra mujer. Le dije que se me subía el estómago a la boca, pero lo cierto es que mi corazón, que sí estaba en la boca, no lo habría permitido.

Me senté a la mesa frente al reluciente zapato de Lucy.

Stan entró y cerró la puerta. Respiraba con agitación. Al fin dijo:

—¿Ha perdido también un zapato?

—Ha perdido un zapato.

—Supongo que no tiene importancia. Rosemary Krebs le comprará otro par.

—No será necesario.

—Bueno, nosotros también podemos comprarle zapatos a nuestra hija.

Negué con la cabeza y dije:

—Este es el zapato perdido.

Stan no dijo nada.

—El otro lo lleva puesto.

Stan seguía sin decir nada.

—Se empeñó en acostarse con él. Con un vestido limpio y su único zapato negro.

—No entiendo —dijo Stan.

—Quería acostarse con el zapato puesto.

—Pero si lo había perdido…

—Este es el zapato perdido.

—No entien…

—Este es el zapato perdido. Lo encontré en el cesto de la ropa sucia.

—Myra —dijo Stan—, ¿qué intentas decir?

—Lo que estoy diciendo es que nadie lo encontró en la calle. Nadie lo encontró en Galatia. Estaba en el cesto de la ropa sucia, envuelto en una toalla.

—Tú…

—Estuve lavando su vestido.

—Estuviste lavando su vestido.

—Y encontré el zapato.

Hubo una larga pausa.

—Sigo sin entender.

—No, Stan, supongo que no lo entiendes. Supongo que el paradero del zapato supuestamente perdido por tu hija no significa nada para ti, y tampoco el hecho de que apestes; te aseguro que me das asco.

—Myra…

—No soy capaz de decirlo, Stan. No soy capaz de pronunciar esas palabras.

—Myra, no te entiendo.

—No digas que no me entiendes. No quieres entender.

—No, no te entien…

—No quieres entenderme. Creo que yo ya he entendido demasiadas cosas. —Me levanté y estrujé el zapato de Lucy—. Y creo que tú entiendes mucho más que yo. —Por primera vez me atreví a mirarlo a los ojos—. Porque supongo que si no me entendieras me habrías roto la mandíbula. Supongo que eso es lo que haría un hombre decente en tu situación.

—¿Es eso lo que quieres, Myra? ¿Una pelea? ¿Quieres que te rompa la mandíbula?

—Sí, Stan, eso es lo que quiero. Quiero que me saques la verdad a golpes.

Me quedé allí, sujetando el zapato de Lucy. Stan no se movió; seguía sudando, apestando. Al fin dijo:

—Me voy a la cama.

Se dio una ducha antes de acostarse y se puso una camiseta y unos calzoncillos antes de subírseme encima.

Esta es la prueba definitiva; ¿qué más pruebas pueden pedirse?
Le di la espalda. Apreté el zapato de Lucy contra mi pecho.
Angela.
Empezaba a entender la necesidad de una Angela.
A medianoche sonó el teléfono. Recuerdo que al oírlo pensé: Esto es lo que estaba esperando. Stan atendió la llamada en la otra habitación; luego se vistió y salió de casa.
Fue entonces cuando terminaron lo que habían empezado.
Fue entonces cuando mataron al chico.

6.30

COLIN

Me sentía perdido. Estaba atrapado en las murallas de una ciudad perdida, de una Troya, de una Pompeya, de una Babilonia... y entonces, un grito atravesó la noche. Otra vez. Era ininteligible. Puede que ni siquiera fuese una palabra, pero venía de encima de mí, iba dirigida a mí, en cualquier lengua; solo podía ser mi nombre. Salté de la cama, sorprendido de ver mi cuerpo desnudo bajo mi cabeza; Divine murmuró detrás de mí con voz soñolienta: «¿Cariño?». La puerta de la cúpula estaba cerrada y tuve que aporrearla. «¡Justin!», grité con todas mis fuerzas, pero solo encontré silencio. Dejé entonces de aporrear la puerta con la mano y empecé a golpearla con la cabeza, y al sentir la áspera madera contra mi coronilla, vi las huellas de barro en las escaleras, pisadas enormes, del tamaño y la forma de remos o de hélices, solo una hilera de pisadas que conducía escaleras abajo, y volví a aporrear la puerta, pero la puerta solo me devolvía el sonido de mi propia voz.

6.31

MYRA

A la mañana siguiente, cuando fui a la habitación de Lucy y dije: «Lucy, cariño, es hora de levantarse», ella estiró los brazos y las piernas como si fuera una princesita, sonrió dulcemente y dijo: «Me llamo Angela». Perdí los nervios, la saqué de la cama agarrándola del pelo y le arranqué el zapato y el vestido blanco arrugado, la llevé a empujones hasta el cuarto de baño y le lavé la boca con jabón. Luego le dije: «¡Si vuelvo a oírte hablar de Angela...!». Después quemé los siete vestidos blancos en el patio, y también el zapato, y dije: «De ahora en adelante yo me encargaré de la ropa de Lucy. Y del nombre de Lucy. Por el bien de Lucy». Luego metí el zapato que había encontrado en el cesto de la ropa sucia en el cofre de cedro, junto a la piedra que traía en la mano cuando vino al mundo, su primer rizo de pelo, el primer diente que se le cayó y la mantita rosa que mi madre empezó a tejer la noche que nació Lucy.

Eso fue lo único que Stan se llevó cuando se marchó un año después.

Una piedra.

Un diente.

Una manta.

Y un zapato negro.

Dejó el rizo del fondo del cofre. Como mucha gente de pelo castaño, Lucy había nacido rubia y se había ido oscureciendo poco a poco. Supongo que a Stan le pareció que no valía la pena llevárselo.

Y a Lucy tampoco. A Lucy también la abandonó. Sawyer Johnson se marchó a la vez que Stan, dejando a Cora sola con el bebé, como Stan nos había dejado solas a Lucy y a mí. Un día, mientras paseaba con Lucy, me encontré con Cora Johnson que iba paseando con su hijo, y ninguna de las dos se detuvo, ni dijo nada, ni siquiera hizo un gesto de saludo con la mano.

Ya digo que es la prueba definitiva. ¿Qué más pruebas hacen falta?

A mi modo de ver, solo dos personas pudieron poner ese zapato en el cesto de la ropa sucia: Lucy o Stan. Decidme cuál de las dos cosas es peor.

Además, Lucy nunca preguntó adónde se había ido Stan. Y yo tampoco.

Porque aquí en Galatea nadie hace preguntas. Porque todas estas preguntas, «¿Dónde? ¿Quién? ¿Qué?», siempre acababan conduciendo a la misma pregunta: «¿Por qué?». Y por aquí nadie se atreve siquiera a saber la respuesta. Nadie quiere saberla.

A veces es preferible no saber si tienes razón. Al menos así no sabes que no la tienes. Colin dijo que todos los escritores cuentan su historia en el espacio que hay entre estas dos frases, y yo dije: Vale, sí, lo entiendo, pero ahora creo que esa no es la verdad. Ahora creo que no tiene sentido decir mentiras, a menos que de veras creas lo que estás diciendo. Y yo lo creo todo.

7

7.01

T. V. DANIELS

Era uno de esos viernes por la noche en los que el esfuerzo de quitarse la ropa y el vago temor premonitorio del trabajo necesario para volver a ponérsela a la mañana siguiente le resultaba inabordable, por eso se tendió completamente vestido sobre la pila de cinco colchones aplastados que usaba a modo de cama y se quedó dormido. Por la mañana se comió las primeras lonchas de beicon directamente de la sartén, sin esperar a que estuvieran bien tostadas; lo había hecho tantas veces que le bastaba con sacudir una sola vez el tenedor para escurrir la grasa del beicon antes de metérselo en la boca. Cuando se terminó el beicon, cascó una docena de huevos en la sartén y los removió hasta que cobraron la consistencia y el color del café con leche —el color por los dos centímetros de grasa de beicon acumulada en la sartén—, y se los comió sin molestarse en servirlos en un plato. Los últimos restos de huevo eran filamentos crujientes, como telarañas carbonizadas, y aunque chirriaban entre sus dientes, no lograba partirlos, de manera que los acompañó con medio litro de leche.

No tomaba café porque le sentaba mal al estómago.

Después de comer fue al cuarto de baño, se abrió la camisa y los pantalones, sin quitárselos del todo, se aplicó en los sobacos y los genitales un desodorante y volvió a ponerse la ropa. Se afeitó al tacto —había quitado todos los espejos de la casa después de que muriera su madre, la primavera pasada—, se peinó el pelo hacia atrás y se puso a hacer gárgaras. Se sirvió medio vaso de Listerine y se enjuagó la boca contando muy despacio hasta cien; luego se tragó el Listerine. El colutorio le produjo un cálido cosquilleo en las puntas de los dedos de las manos y los pies, lo que hizo que el esfuerzo de atarse el cordón del zapato izquierdo resultara casi surrealista —no se había quitado los zapatos la noche anterior, pero se le había desatado el izquierdo— y tuvo que arquearse con enorme dificultad para atarse el puto zapato; luego cogió el coche y recorrió las dos manzanas que separaban su casa de la oficina de correos, para comenzar el reparto de la mañana.

No trataba de manera distinta el correo que enviaba del que recibía; no lo clasificaba para entregarlo antes o después; lo iba metiendo en una caja mientras hacía la ruta, por eso no descubrió que el retrovisor lateral de Divine estaba en su buzón hasta la hora de comer.

Antes de abrir el buzón ya sabía que había algo dentro, porque la bandera roja estaba subida y no había sacado el correo esa mañana. Trataba su correo igual que el de todo el mundo y cuando tenía que enviar una carta la metía en el buzón y levantaba la bandera roja para acordarse de recogerlo durante su ronda matinal.

Supo que era el retrovisor de Divine porque siempre veía el coche cuando se encontraba con Divine a la salida del bar de Sloppy Joe, y aunque había pasado un año recordaba cómo era el espejo y que al coche de Divine le faltaba un retrovisor lateral.

En ningún momento se le ocurrió que Divine hubiera metido el espejo en su buzón.

Dejó el espejo sobre el asiento del pasajero, con el cristal hacia arriba, y durante el resto del día el espejo reflejó la luz del sol, produciendo una sombra que fue desplazándose lentamente por la carrocería del vehículo de reparto. No había nada extraño en este reflejo —era sólido, con un perfil uniforme y ovalado–, y hasta el final del día, cuando cogió el espejo para llevárselo a casa, no se fijó en él. Entonces vio tres cosas. En primer lugar vio que el espejo estaba roto, luego vio que su cara era demasiado grande y el espejo no la abarcaba por completo, por último vio, con una nitidez casi antinatural, cuatro huellas perfectamente definidas, y tras mirar largamente su perfil dividido, diseccionado y borroso, limpió el espejo, frotándolo contra su barriga y entró en su casa tambaleándose. Normalmente, los sábados por la noche cerraba todas las cortinas, se quitaba la ropa, la lavaba y se lavaba él también; normalmente, se quedaba desnudo hasta el lunes por la mañana, comía en la cama, sujetando el plato en la depresión que se formaba allí donde su esternón se unía con el pecho cuando estaba tumbado, pero esa noche no se desnudó porque no pensaba pasar el día siguiente en casa. Pensaba salir. Se dijo que debería renunciar a ese placer de todos modos, porque el día siguiente era el Día de los Fundadores, aunque lo cierto es que no había previsto asistir a la fiesta, pues ya no le gustaba comer en público.

Como los demás habitantes del pueblo, pensaba que había que hacer algo. Pero hasta que logró ver el trozo de su cara que no veía en el retrovisor roto del coche de Divine no se dio cuenta de que era él quien tenía que hacerlo.

7.02

WADE

Domingo por la mañana
Siete de la mañana.
Día de los Fundadores.

Esa mañana, como todas las mañanas, salí de la casa que yo había construido y entré en la casa que construyeron mis padres. Había en el aire un acre olor a humo, un sabroso aunque invisible rastro que hizo que se me hiciera la boca agua. El olor a cerdo a la parrilla avanzaba hacia mi casa desde una distancia aproximada de tres kilómetros. O quizá fuera mi imaginación, cosa tan probable como cualquier otra, dado que el humo habría tenido que luchar contra el viento para llegar hasta aquí.

El camino que llevaba desde la puerta trasera de mi casa hasta la puerta principal de la casa de mis padres era tan recto y estrecho como los que predicaban el pastor Little o el Reverendo Abraham; parecía una senda de ganado, una angosta depresión pelada de apenas treinta centímetros de ancho, y yo tardaba unos sesenta segundos en recorrerlo todos los días, normalmente una vez en cada dirección. Con el paso de los años ese paseo se convirtió en una especie de trance, un modo de vaciar mi cabeza de todos los pensamientos que me distraían para que durante el resto del día nada interrumpiera la conexión que se establecía entre mi ojo y mi mano.

Mientras andaba, miraba al suelo, las formas que había en él, las espirales de rocío, la hélice que formaba el rastro de una serpiente y los destellos de los minúsculos guijarros de cuarcita que reflejaban la luz del sol entre los tenues rastros de mis propias pisadas de días anteriores.

Esto fue lo último que pasó por mi cabeza antes de extender la mano para abrir la puerta de mi estudio; luego agarré el pomo, abrí la puerta y, estaba a punto de entrar allí, de salir del mundo, de ponerme a pintar, cuando me distrajo un destello de luz sobre la barandilla del porche.

7.03

DIVINE

Esa mañana me desperté en la cama de Colin. Para entonces todo me resultaba familiar: las paredes de cal blancas y cubiertas de polvo, los óleos que colgaban de ellas, grandes objetos oscuros repletos de santos y mártires con un halo brillante alrededor de la cabeza y enmarcados en molduras doradas. Conocía los cuatro postes de la cama, de más de dos metros de alto, gruesos como la pierna de un futbolista e igual de musculosos, supongo que debería decir tallados, aunque puede que nudosos sea la palabra más adecuada. Esos postes parecían trabajados a cuchillo por Katharine Hepburn, con las manos temblorosas y los ojos vendados, y la verdad es que me daban escalofríos. Había una marca circular alrededor de cada poste justo a la altura del colchón, y no hace falta ser detective o un pervertido consumado para saber qué aspecto tiene una cuerda quemada. Colin me dijo que esa cama tenía ciento cincuenta años y que empezó sus días en una plantación de café de Guatemala, así que era posible que las cuerdas quemadas estuvieran allí mucho antes de que Colin tomara posesión de ella, incluso antes de que él naciera, pero preferí no preguntárselo. Pensé que ciertas cosas era preferible no saberlas.

Pensé que muchas cosas era preferible no saberlas.

La verdad es que también podría haberse tratado de una plantación de plátanos, si es que la diferencia tiene alguna importancia.

El caso es que me levanté esa mañana.

Nada menos que el Día de los Fundadores. El Día de la Independencia en el resto del país, el cuatro de julio, pero el Día de los Fundadores en Galatea, Kansas, república de Rosemary Krebs.

Para entonces, ya lo conocía todo, como he dicho; nada me resultaba nuevo. Era como si a la hora de respirar pudieras elegir entre un gas venenoso o un perfume de rosas.

Colin estaba dormido. Era un misterio para mí por qué su despertador mental no funcionaba los domingos, cuando los demás días de la semana a las seis tenía los ojos abiertos. Pero eran más de las ocho, los pantalones vaqueros seguían colgados de la ventana abierta y el amplio pecho de Colin subía y bajaba de acuerdo con la tranquila pauta de la respiración durante el sueño. Las sábanas eran de seda blanca y aparecían enrolladas en las piernas de Colin, destacándolas como, no sé qué, como moldes de escayola o condones, pues producían la impresión de algo duro y blando al mismo tiempo, y por un momento, debo admitirlo, me dolió reconocer todo lo que yo no era y lo que Colin Nieman sí era. Uno de sus pies asomaba por el borde de la cama; las líneas de los huesos en los dedos eran tan limpias, rectas y fuertes como los dientes de un rastrillo recién comprado, y no soportaba mirarle a la cara. Dicen que Dios rompe el molde después de crear a algunas personas, pero en el caso de Colin creo que fue él mismo quien rompió el molde, que lo reventó a patadas y puñetazos para venir a este mundo y luego se sacudió tran-

quilamente de encima el polvo de su madre y le robó el corazón a todos los que admiraron su sonrisa de serpiente.
   Púas. Los afilados dientes del rastrillo se llaman púas.
   Salí entonces de la cama y me vestí en el pasillo para no despertar a Colin. Las paredes de la casa de caliza parecían no llegar nunca a su destino: daba la impresión de que siempre había un cuartito justo antes del que buscabas, vestíbulos, recovecos y antecámaras, y esa mañana las recorrí todas hasta que al fin salí al exterior y cogí el coche.
   El coche no arrancaba.
   Estaba completamente muerto y tan caliente que podías freír un huevo —o achicharrarte los muslos— en esos putos asientos de vinilo.
   Volví a girar la llave. El coche solo emitía una especie de balido, como una oveja recién degollada y medio muerta. Vi que la aguja de la gasolina estaba muy baja y fue entonces cuando empecé a preocuparme porque habría jurado que llené el depósito la noche anterior. Pero las cosas se habían vuelto tan confusas que tampoco podría asegurar si había sido la noche anterior o la anterior a la anterior o el mes pasado. O a lo mejor me había quedado sin gasolina la noche anterior. ¿Quién sabe? Aunque casi podría jurar que había llenado el depósito la noche anterior.
   No tenía sentido quedarse allí para morir de calor y decidí salir del coche, pero tampoco fuera hacía más fresco: esas piedras negras y brillantes, sobre las que aún se apreciaban las líneas de las púas del rastrillo que habían pasado el día anterior, eran una auténtica parrilla, y enseguida volví a la casa para pensar con calma qué hacer. Casi no tuve que tomar ninguna decisión porque nada más entrar tropecé con Colin. Cruzaba el vestíbulo en dirección a su despacho, vestido solo con unos pantalones cortos. Sostenía una taza de café en una mano y el pequeño cuaderno de notas que guardaba en su mesilla de noche en la otra, y llevaba en la boca una de sus estilográficas, como si fuera un puro.
   Nada más verlo pensé que había estado esperando a que yo me marchara para levantarse y ponerse a escribir, y cuando me miró supe que estaba en lo cierto.
   Luego torció la boca sin soltar la pluma para esbozar una grande y pícara sonrisa, soltó el café y el cuaderno, se sacó la pluma de la boca y le dio un toque con el dedo como si estuviera tirando la ceniza de un cigarro auténtico.
   —Mi pequeño pollito —dijo—. ¿Tan pronto estás de vuelta?
   —El coche no arranca.
   Se me echó encima y me dio un abrazo demasiado fuerte para ser real.
   —Lo que para ti es mala suerte, para mí es buena.

Me eché hacia atrás, pero sin alejarme demasiado. Sin quedar fuera del alcance de sus brazos.

—Tengo cosas que hacer.
—¿Cosas?
—Rollos.
—¿Rollos?
—Solo he venido por un vaso de agua antes de volver andando a ca… a casa de Wade.

Colin me miró de arriba abajo. Estaba claro que sopesaba sus opciones, que pensaba en el modo más rápido de deshacerse de mí sin parecer grosero.

Me pareció que los pensamientos de Colin giraban como un torbellino tras sus ojos y se me ocurrió que me apreciaba lo suficiente como para sentirse culpable por el hecho de herirme. Supongo que eso era algo. Era más que nada. No era el premio gordo, pero al menos era un premio menor.

Atlantic City era uno de los lugares a los que yo quería que Colin me llevara. Atlantic City y Las Vegas, y ese país llamado Monarchy, donde vive la princesa Grace. Donde vivía.

Entonces Colin eructó o hipó; no hizo ruido, pero el olor a gases estomacales mezclado con café inundó mis fosas nasales.

Había que reconocer que preparaba un café muy bueno.

Suspiró y dijo:
—Te llevaré.
—Gracias. Puedo ir andando.
—No quiero que vayas andando. Hay demasiados tramos desiertos en el camino hasta casa de Wade.
—Hoy no habrá caminos desiertos. Es el Día de los Fundadores. Todo el mundo se echará a la calle.
—Razón de más para que te lleve.
—Y a Justin le dejas que vaya andando.
—Justin va andando porque quiere ir andando. Yo no le permito ni le prohíbo nada.

Se dio la vuelta antes de que pudiera contestarle, corrió hacia las escaleras y subió a su habitación. Supongo que podría haberme largado, pero ¿de qué me habría servido? Solo había un camino para ir a casa de Wade, solo había un camino directo a cualquier parte, y Colin me habría alcanzado enseguida. Al cabo de un minuto volvió con unos pantalones cortos, una camiseta y sus zapatillas de correr. Se había puesto protector solar en la cabeza y le brillaba la calva, y mientras caminábamos hacia el coche sobre las piedras crujientes, no pude aguantarme las ganas de frotarle para que el aceite le penetrara bien en la piel. El caso es que al hacerlo tuve la sensación de que él lo estaba esperando.

—Ahora sé por qué nunca te bronceas.

Un pitido cortó el aire cuando Colin desconectó la alarma electrónica del coche.

—Si sigues conmigo llegarás a conocer todos mis secretos.

No me reí cuando dijo eso, aunque creo que debería haberlo hecho.

Recordé que el nombre de las piedras negras y brillantes que rodeaban la casa de caliza era obsidiana y que el nombre del país donde vivía la princesa Grace era Mónaco, y creo que la cama de Colin había salido de una plantación de café de Guatemala. Aunque nada de eso importaba.

—Sí —dije, al entrar en el coche—, seguro que acabaré sabiéndolo todo.

7.04

WEBBIE

Lo estuve mirando durante el servicio. Vi que observaba a mi padre, el honorable reverendo Abraham Greeving, cuyo sermón arreciaba como una tormenta el domingo más próximo al Día de los Fundadores. Era el único servicio del año al que me esforzaba por asistir, porque me gustaba ver a mi padre tan encendido, aunque ese año tenía previsto saltármelo, pues, dadas las circunstancias, sabía que no habría nada divertido en el juicio y la condena emitidos desde el púlpito de Galatia. Pero esa mañana, después de dejar a mi padre con Faith, Hope y Charity, me sentí sola en casa. Me dolía el hombro y, para hacerme compañía, pensé en el archivo, en los pulgares de Eric Johnson y en la prueba de embarazo de Lucy Robinson; sobre la repisa de la chimenea yacía la mitad de la piedra ventral partida en dos que Justin había acariciado hacía ya mucho tiempo. Esa piedra —y los pulgares y la prueba de embarazo y el archivo y los diez altos escalones de piedra del porche de nuestra casa— me parecían símbolos de la vida en Galatia, símbolos cargados de significado y al mismo tiempo totalmente desprovistos de sentido, de capacidad para influir en las cosas, para producir cambios, y estando allí, en la casa de mi padre, al sentir el humo que entraba por las ventanas, no me costó convencerme de que yo era una pieza más, igual de irrelevante, en esa interminable lista. Por eso fui a la iglesia. Por eso o por la barbacoa que habría después. Me mezclé con el resto de la gente que asistió al servicio esa mañana, ahora lo sé, para oír cómo mi padre expresaba con palabras la impotencia que todos sentíamos. No creo que nadie esperase que sus palabras cambiaran las cosas, pero había al menos cierta camaradería –compañerismo es la palabra que habrían empleado otros feligreses–, compañerismo y canciones bonitas.

No se movió del asiento durante el servicio; estaba casi rígido, con la espalda ligeramente arqueada, los brazos caídos y una estudiada expresión de atención en el rostro –las cejas ligeramente levantadas, los labios ligeramente separados–, y, después de mirarlo un buen rato, reconocí que era la misma expresión que yo había cultivado durante los largos años de la infancia, cuando iba a la iglesia dos veces a la semana: era la cara que a mi padre le hacía creer que yo prestaba atención.

Pero ese día no intenté fingir. Puede que fuese a la iglesia con la intención de escuchar el sermón, pero en cuanto vi a Wallace me olvidé por completo de mi padre, y al cabo de un rato me olvidé también de Wallace. Me dio por imaginarlo la mañana que lo dejé. ¿Qué sabía yo de él, salvo cómo se comportaba en la cama y que cada vez que tenía hambre, fuese de día o de noche, respondía a este impulso preparando un par de huevos con beicon? Nada más. Pero sabía de todos modos que no era de esos hombres que andan por la casa desnudos cuando están solos. Las cortinas siempre estaban abiertas de par en par; había vecinos y algún familiar podría presentarse en cualquier momento; al menos había una foto de dos niñas en la repisa de la chimenea. Como mínimo se pondría unos calzoncillos, una camiseta y unos calcetines. En la cocina, café, desayuno. Mientras el beicon se tostaba en la sartén, saldría a recoger el periódico de la puerta. Una vez fuera, incluso en invierno, se rascaría la tripa y se subiría los calzoncillos al ojear los titulares, luego, sintiendo de repente el frío, entraría rápidamente y cascaría un par de huevos para acompañar el beicon. En menos de cinco años sería hipertenso y tendría que medicarse. Yo le prepararía una tostada de trigo integral por la mañana y él se quejaría de que el sucedáneo de la mantequilla repugnaría incluso a los cerdos, y hablando de cerdos, ¡cuánto daría por una loncha de beicon…!

Sonreí entonces tan abiertamente que Faith Jackson asintió como encantada. Pensaba que yo había reencontrado a Dios, que había vuelto al rebaño. Le devolví la sonrisa diciéndome para mis adentros: Estoy imaginándome el tacto de los labios y de la lengua de mi marido entre mis piernas, ávido por encontrar algo que pueda sustituir a una dieta alta en colesterol.

Pero mi sonrisa se desvaneció bruscamente. ¿Qué coño estoy haciendo?, me dije. ¿Wallace… mi marido? Era más bien un número, mi hombre negro, mi caballero andante en un reluciente Coupe De

Ville con los bajos oxidados. Entonces caí en la cuenta de que estaba enfadada con él, furiosa porque había sido él y no yo quien había tenido el valor de escenificar la historia, de arriesgarse por mí. Yo me había quedado cómodamente sentada, esperando. Había jugado a ser detective y lo único que había conseguido era ser la criada de Rosemary Krebs, y finalmente era mi padre quien nos unía.

7.05

CORA

Fue Rosa la primera que dijo que pasaba algo.
No creo que a nadie le sorprendiera, pero fue la primera que lo dijo en voz alta.
Vino conmigo a escuchar el discurso del alcalde.
—Rosa, no hace falta que vengas si no quieres.
—Prefiero no quedarme sola en casa.
—Sawyer...
—Siií. Yo voy a emborracharme —dijo Sawyer.
—Cuidado con lo que dices —le contesté, pero Sawyer ya había salido corriendo por la puerta, con el inhalador colgado del cuello.
—Rosa —le dije—, tú no te encuentras bien, no te gusta la gente, debes quedarte en casa. Quédate en la cama oyendo música. Prepárate un té con menta; eso te entonará.
—Venga, Cora —dijo Rosa, y su voz sonó muy lejana. Ella estaba sentada a una de las mesas y yo estaba detrás de la barra, terminando mi guiso de verano—. Cora —dijo Rosa, con la voz cargada de distancia—, ¿por qué tienes tanta paciencia conmigo? Te saco de quicio, pero tú siempre me tratas con dulzura y amabilidad. No te merezco.
Removía el guiso con tanta fuerza que derramé un poco de salsa y esta se pegó al quemador.
—Cállate. No digas tonterías.
—Cora, presiento que va a ocurrir algo malo. ¿No lo sientes en el aire? Es como humo, Cora; el aire huele a humo.
—A lo que huele es a barbacoa.
—¡Cora!
—A las parrillas de las barbacoas. ¡Dios mío! ¡Estás a la que salta!
Se me acercó y me puso la palma de la mano en la base de la espalda. La abracé con el brazo izquierdo y nos mecimos suavemente mientras yo aprovechaba la suma de nuestros pesos para remover el enorme caldero con el guiso.

—Tú no te muevas de aquí y yo cuidaré de ti.
—De acuerdo. No me moveré de aquí.
Pero no la creí. Y tuve que repetírmelo.
—Tú no te muevas de aquí. No dejes nunca a Cora, Rosa; y Cora no te dejará nunca.

7.06

DIVINE

—Puede que esté en el estudio —dije—. Lo digo por si quieres saludarlo.
—Supongo que debería, ya que estoy aquí. Fuimos al estudio por el sendero que usaba Wade. El interior del estudio estaba en calma como una iglesia.
—¿Wade?
Subí las escaleras.
—¿Wade?
Entonces lo vi saliendo de mi habitación… de la habitación que había empapelado con dibujos míos. Cuando me acerqué, cerró la puerta y la cerró con llave.
—Hola —dije.
Wade hizo tintinear nerviosamente las llaves antes de guardárselas en el bolsillo.
—Hola, Divine —respondió.
Entonces supe que algo pasaba.
—Hace mucho tiempo que no entro ahí.
—Sí, hace mucho tiempo.
—Supongo que deberíamos hacer una sesión un día de estos.
—Sí —repitió. Y nos quedamos un rato callados.
—Colin está abajo —dije al fin—. Mi coche no arrancaba.
A Wade se le iluminaron los ojos.
—¿Tu coche? —preguntó; y empezó a bajar las escaleras.
—¿Qué pasa con mi coche?
—¿Es tuyo esto? —preguntó, saludando a Colin con la mano cuando pasamos junto a él.
Se dio la vuelta. Tenía en la mano un objeto pequeño, brillante y plateado. Tardé un rato en reconocer que era mi retrovisor; luego no sé qué me pasó, pero por espacio de dos segundos me convertí en un niño de cinco años.
—¡Recórcholis!

—¿Es tu retrovisor? —preguntó Colin.

—Cc... creo que sí.

—Déjame adivinarlo —le dijo Colin a Wade—. Lo has encontrado en el buzón.

—Es domingo —dijo Wade—. Los domingos no hay correo.

—¿Acabas de encontrarlo?

—Hace media hora —dijo Wade. Se me acercó y me puso el espejo en la mano—. Estaba en la barandilla del porche.

El espejo estaba partido por la mitad y el borde dentado del soporte roto estaba oxidado. Me resultó rígido y frío, pero apenas pesaba; como un gatito muerto.

—¿Divine? —dijo Wade, apoyándome una mano en el hombro—. ¿Te encuentras bien, Divine?

Le aparté la mano.

—Necesito una copa —dije, y lo aparté de un empujón; aparté a Colin, que también intentó ponerme una mano en el hombro, y aparté el aire denso y cargado del estudio de Wade para salir al aire denso y polvoriento del exterior; lo aparté todo para abrirme camino hacia la casa. Wade y Colin me siguieron. Oí que hablaban, pero no entendí lo que decían. Los oí reír un par de veces.

Se rieron los dos, pero no al mismo tiempo.

Una vez dentro, me abrasé la garganta con tres dedos de Jack. Colin y Wade entraron sin decir nada y se apostaron cada uno en un extremo de la habitación.

—Divine —dijo Colin, mientras yo me servía otra copa—, ni siquiera son las once de la mañana. ¿Qué pasa?

—¿Que qué pasa? ¿Es que no lo pillas?

—Divine —dijo Wade. Yo hice un gesto con la mano y sentí que el whisky empezaba a hacer su mágico efecto—. Es evidente que no «lo pilla», de lo contrario no preguntaría. —Me asqueó el modo como dijo «lo pilla», como si yo hablara en otro idioma o en una jerga insultante. Pero me limité a mirar el whisky y dije—: Ahora viene por mí. —Al decirlo en voz alta me pareció ridículo, y me bebí otro trago de whisky.

—¿Qué? —dijo Wade—. ¿Quién...? —pero Colin lo interrumpió.

—No seas absurdo. ¿Por qué piensas eso?

Volví la cabeza hacia él.

—¿Quién si no se dedica a hacer estas cosas? ¿Quién va dejando por ahí trozos, qué sé yo, de tu pasado, o algo así?

—Divine, lo que dices no tiene el menor sentido.

Volví la cabeza hacia Wade.

—¡Tiene mucho sentido! ¡El vestido de Lucy, el pelo de Lucy, los gritos de Lucy, los dedos de Lucy...!

Había ido enumerando con los dedos, pero al acordarme de los dedos me detuve y cerré el puño instintivamente.

Al cabo de un minuto logré continuar:

—La bolsa de la compra de Colin. La grabadora de Colin. Las cajas de Colin. Y ahora ese espejo. Mi espejo.

—Divine —dijo Colin.

Me giré.

—Divine —dijo Wade.

Volví a girarme.

—Divine, ¿de verdad piensas que quien raptó a Lucy ha dejado tu espejo en el porche?

Miré el espejo que aún tenía en la mano... una prueba más de que no podía ir a ninguna parte, a menos que alguien lo trasladara.

—¿Quién si no podía saber que el espejo era mío?

—Divine —dijo Colin; me di la vuelta—. ¿Cómo sabía él que el espejo era tuyo?

—Porque lo sabe todo, ¿o no? Parece que lo sabe todo.

—Divine —dijo Wade.

Me giré.

—Divine —dijo Colin. Y volví a girarme. Esta vez la amplia y blanca extensión del pecho de Colin colmó mi visión, que se había desenfocado un poco a consecuencia del whisky y de los giros. Me abrazó, supongo que con la intención de consolarme, pero a mí me resultó extraño porque no le veía los brazos. Solo sentía que me rodeaban, que me apretaban cada vez más—. Divine, sea quien sea, es un hombre. Estamos hablando de un hombre, no de un ser omnisciente.

—No sé lo que significa omnisciente.

Colin suspiró y dijo:

—Que no es Dios.

—O Santa Claus —añadió Wade detrás de mí.

Colin me acarició la espalda.

—No puede saberlo todo.

Por un momento me relajé en brazos de Colin, pero entonces se me cayó el espejo de la mano y aterrizó en el suelo con gran estrépito. Los tres dimos un salto, y aquello bastó para que volviera a ponerme tenso. Me aparté de Colin.

—¿Qué importancia tiene? Tú lo perdiste y él lo encontró. Lo encontró y te lo ha devuelto, para avisarme de que me sigue vigilando.

—La verdad —dijo Wade— es que, sea quien sea, me lo ha devuelto a mí.

Entonces miré a Wade, pero Wade estaba mirando a Colin. Me volví hacia Colin, que respondía a la mirada de Wade con otra mirada. Wade se acercó entonces al bar y sirvió dos copas.

—Me gustaría acusarte de incoherencia, como hace Wade —dijo Colin—. Pero todo esto tiene demasiado sentido.

Y entonces les conté cómo perdí el espejo el otoño pasado, al salir del Big M, cómo lo arranqué al salir a toda prisa de ese granero donde encontré a Eddie Comedy. Les hablé de ese tío de aspecto agitanado con el que me lo hice aquella noche, el que yo llamaba Vlad el Empalador, el que olía a patatas fritas con sal y vinagre pero no sabía nada del Rata, y luego les hablé del Rata, de las noches que pasamos juntos en el silo. Les hablé de los rastrojos de trigo que crujían bajo mis pies y de la colcha de satén arrugada por el peso del Rata, incluso les conté cómo me tiré a la poza y que la poza me devolvió a la superficie de nuevo, y luego, no sé por qué, supongo que por el whisky —necesité varias copas para contarles la historia completa—, todo empezó a confundirse, la noche que me tiré a la poza y la noche que estuve en el Big M y todas esas noches en el silo, pero lo único que no les dije fue lo que pasó en el arca de Noah. Puede que fuera el momento perfecto para contarlo, para contárselo a alguien finalmente, pero no dejaba de ver la frente de Colin con las palabras «Papel superior» grabadas en ella, y por eso no dije nada.

Cuando terminé de hablar, Colin me miró tan fijamente que tuve que bajar la vista.

—¿Has oído? —oí que decía, supongo que a Wade, y por su voz me di cuenta de que estaba tan borracho como yo—. Ni un puto... ni una mierda de... ni un...

—Polvo —dijo Wade—. Ni un mísero polvo. —Hubo algo en el tono de Wade que me hizo levantar la vista justo a tiempo de ver cómo le decía a Colin—: Parece que al final Divine ha decidido ser el niño que nunca fue. —Y vació el vaso de un trago, para volver a llenarlo de inmediato.

Para entonces debía de ser mediodía. No había sombras en la habitación y el whisky había empezado a brillar en los vasos, como una pecera de color ámbar, y cuando ya empezaba a pensar que estaba completamente acabado, acabado de verdad, Colin dijo algo así como: No había vuelto a estar tan borracho desde la última vez que vi a Yonah Schimmel.

Y Wade dijo: No había vuelto a estar tan borracho desde la última vez que follé con Yonah Schimmel.

Y entonces Colin hizo una especie de chasquido con la lengua y Wade se puso a murmurar para sus adentros, Yonah, y Jonah y John.

Y Colin susurró: Justin.

Y Wade susurró: Justin.

Y entonces supe por qué Wade no me había dejado entrar en mi habitación del estudio.

Y pensé: ¿Justin? ¿Quién estaba allí entre los dos? Yo. Pero ¿en quién pensaban ellos? En ese maldito Justin.

Wade entonces se dio la vuelta y se dirigió a la pared de la sala de estar, y tuvo que esquivar el retrovisor que seguía en el suelo, donde se había caído; al llegar a la pared se sacó un trozo de algo negro del bolsillo de los pantalones, supongo que era carbón porque parecía el mismo material que usaba para dibujarme, y, con el vaso de whisky en una mano y el carbón en la otra, trazó una, dos, tres, cuatro líneas negras sobre la pared blanca, de arriba abajo, todas de la misma longitud, y con un gesto lento y fácil, que pareció prolongarse por muchos años y muchos kilómetros, dibujó una diagonal que unía las demás líneas, se volvió hacia Colin, hacia mí y hacia Justin, que estaba más presente que todos los demás, y dijo: «Esos somos nosotros». Y lo éramos, juro por Dios que lo éramos; éramos nosotros y eso era todo cuanto éramos.

Me di la vuelta para mirar a Wade y oí que Colin dejaba el vaso en el suelo detrás de mí y decía: «Divine, ven aquí». Wade se había dado la vuelta y no me miraba; supongo que miraba a Colin, y luego, muy, muy despacio, volvió a guardarse el trozo de carbón en el bolsillo de los pantalones y dejó la mano ahí dentro.

7.07

WEBBIE

Me encontré con él en el aparcamiento, después del servicio. Respondí inconscientemente con la cabeza al saludo de veinte cabezas, veinte rostros, veinte bocas que no decían ni «Buenos días» ni «Buenas tardes» —no había relojes en la iglesia, pero mi padre siempre terminaba justo antes o después del mediodía–, sino «Bienvenida al rebaño, señorita Webbie», y yo pensaba: No soy una oveja, idiotas, mientras me dirigía al único coche del aparcamiento que no pertenecía a nadie del pueblo; y esperé. Lo vi acercarse, rastreando con la mirada el aparcamiento, la calle, el parque, buscándome. Cuando estuvo a unos tres metros de mí, dije:

—Hola.

Sujetaba con las dos manos una hoja de papel rosa, el programa de actos para la semana siguiente. Tembló todo él al oír mi voz y el papel se rasgó entre sus manos. Se rompió, y Wallace se quedó mirándolo, luego se echó a reír y al fin me miró y dijo:

—Señorita Webbie, ¡qué casualidad encontrarla aquí!

—¡Qué casualidad encontrarlo aquí, señor Wallace!
Se encogió de hombros.
—Supongo que no puedo fingir que pasaba por aquí casualmente. Aunque lo cierto es que ha llegado hasta Wichita la noticia de que el reverendo Abraham Greeving es un poderoso testigo del Señor.
—¿Eso fue antes o después de conocerme?
—¿Quieres decir si he estado haciendo preguntas por ahí?
Me encogí de hombros.
—Quiero decir lo que digo —respondí, y Wallace se rió.
—He estado haciendo preguntas.
Nos miramos un momento y nos echamos a reír al mismo tiempo, y al fijarme en los extraños movimientos de sus manos, como si estuviera haciendo trucos de magia, caí en la cuenta de que las mías hacían los mismos movimientos, y supe que nuestras manos recordaban la forma del cuerpo que habían acariciado, y cuando dejamos de moverlas, nuestros pies, que también guardaban el recuerdo de nuestra intimidad, nos habían acercado unos cuantos pasos.
—Es mi padre —dije.
Asintió.
—Greeving no es un apellido corriente. —Se rió un poco—. Cuando era pequeño, los chicos contaban historias sobre la hija del pastor Littlejohn. Decían que estaba loca. Decían que los hijos de los curas siempre estaban locos.
—¿Y yo estaba... yo estoy loca, Wallace?
Miró los dos trozos de papel que tenía en la mano. Los arrugó despacio y se guardó cada uno en un bolsillo. Las bolas de papel resultaban ligeramente visibles bajo el poliéster gris.
—Esos pantalones son horribles —observé.
—Mamá siempre decía que a algunos hombres se les juzga por su ropa de domingo y a otros por la del sábado por la noche.
—Quedan otros seis días hasta el sábado.
—Si cuentas hacia atrás solo queda uno. Menos de uno.
—Quedan seis.
—Bueno, en esos días Dios tuvo tiempo de hacer el mundo.
—¿Tú crees en todo eso? —pregunté, señalando con la mano hacia la iglesia, hacia la congregación desperdigada, hacia mi padre.
—A mi modo de ver, un poco de fe no le hace mal a nadie.
—Y esperanza —dije yo— y caridad.
Sonrió amablemente y asintió.
—Y esperanza y caridad.
Entonces me di la vuelta y miré su coche, cubierto por el polvo de más de doscientos kilómetros, aunque debajo se veía brillar la chapa limpia y encerada, y supe que lo había lavado para mí.

Hablándole al coche dije:

—Yo no te haré feliz. No te preparé el beicon por las mañanas y te obligaré a comprar unos pantalones nuevos para ir a la iglesia, aunque no te acompañe, y me quejaré de que solo lees el periódico.

—*The Eagle and Beacon's* no es un mal periódico. Y puedo prepararme el desayuno yo solo.

Seguí sin apartar la vista del coche. Era verdad que tenía los bajos oxidados.

—Un Cadillac —dije al fin.

—Mi padre decía que un buen coche debe tener un buen asiento trasero para hacer niños, y luego para llevarlos cuando hayan nacido.

—¿Es que tus padres siempre hablaban con aforismos?

—¿Y tu padre siempre cita la Biblia?

—¡Pues sí! —dije, casi gritando.

Respondió tranquilamente.

—Sí. —Se encogió de hombros—. Casi siempre. —Sonrió—. Mi abuela decía que una palabra bien dicha es como un regalo.

—¿También leía los apócrifos tu abuela?

—Solo si estaban en la Biblia.

—¿De verdad crees que puedes presentarte aquí, encontrarme y llevarme en tu asiento trasero?

Volvió a mirarse las manos, pero ya no tenía ningún papel, y se las guardó en los bolsillos.

—Me ha costado unos cuantos viajes, pero lo he conseguido. Al fin te he encontrado.

—¿Unos cuantos viajes?

—Siete —dijo, levantando la vista.

—¿Has venido hasta aquí siete veces?

—Es un viaje agradable —dijo, y señalando a su coche añadió—: La mejor suspensión que se ha hecho nunca en Detroit. Es como ir en una barca de remos.

—¿Siete veces?

—Aunque parezca extraño, cada vez resulta más fácil. Algunas cosas son así.

—¿Algunas cosas?

—Algunas cosas van volviéndose cada vez más fáciles, en lugar de más difíciles.

—¿Mamá? ¿O papá?

—Ninguno de los dos. Wallace.

—Siete veces —repetí en voz baja, casi entre susurros, y luego añadí—: Por mí.

—Mil quinientos kilómetros en cada sentido. Por ti. —Entonces se atragantó y dijo—: Es todo lo que tengo. Esto es lo que te ofrezco.

7.08

CORA

Al principio se sintió a gusto en la fiesta, se quedó en la mesa, sirviendo a la gente con una sonrisa y poniendo una ración extra a quienes lo pedían. Pero al cabo de una hora empezó a distraerse, no se daba cuenta si alguien le hablaba y le daba pan de maíz aunque hubiera dicho que no quería, luego no atinaba a meter el cazo en el cuenco y la segunda vez que derramó el guiso por todas partes, le quité el cazo de la mano, la llevé hasta una silla y le dije: «Siéntate». Se sentó. Y le dije: «Quédate aquí». Y se quedó. Al cabo de un rato le llevé una limonada; dio un respingo cuando le puse una mano en el hombro, y tuvo que sujetar el vaso con las dos manos.

—Rosa, dime qué pasa.

Me miró con una sonrisa triste.

—No puedo decírtelo. No puedo decírtelo.

—Si sigues diciendo tonterías te llevaré a casa ahora mismo —dije, pero Rosa soltó una risita tonta. Bajó el vaso sin darse cuenta de que se había vertido toda la limonada por encima y luego, señalando hacia la tribuna que el alcalde había ordenado instalar en un extremo del aparcamiento de Vera dijo:

—Cora, hay un hombre dentro de esa tribuna.

7.09

T. V. DANIELS

Más tarde la gente dijo que quizá no pudo hacer otra cosa, pero de todos modos...

7.10

AGENTE BROWN

Myra Robinson no estaba presente, pero tenía una buena excusa. Rosemary Krebs tampoco había asistido, aunque podía ir y venir cuando le viniera en gana y había dicho que se pasaría a eso de las cuatro, para escuchar el discurso. Darrell Jenkens y Dave Helman estuvieron todo el día entrando y saliendo desde que instalaron la tribuna, cargando comida y cerveza. Dave dijo que Darrell lo ayudó a arreglar el Mustang del 68 que llevaba tres años desguazado en el patio de su casa, pero más valía que Dios protegiera al que se sentara al volante de un coche reparado por esos dos. Dijo que le ponía enfermo, que beber le parecía, en general, una costumbre propia de degenerados, y que por mucho Día de los Fundadores, seguía siendo Sabbath. Dijo que al menos esperaba que ninguno de los allí presentes pensara volver a casa en coche, que no tenía más que decir. No podía culpar al pastor Little o al reverendo Greeving por no dar señales de vida: seguro que esa mañana se habían encontrado la iglesia medio vacía a la hora de pronunciar su sermón. El agente Brown tuvo que admitir que nunca se había fijado en cómo eran más de trescientas personas cuando se reunían. Shelly Stadler —que ya era una chica guapa y bien desarrollada, tuvo que taparse la mano con la boca en dos ocasiones para disimular un eructo— le dijo que había vendido trescientas diecisiete entradas, que solo se admitía una por persona y, suponiendo que la gente fuera honrada, eso significaba que todos los habitantes de Galatea estaban en la fiesta. Colin Nieman no estaba, y tampoco su amigo Justin. Wade Painter no había aparecido, aunque eso no era ninguna sorpresa, y el agente Brown se alegró igualmente de que Reggie Packman no anduviera mariconeando por allí. Webbie Greeving tampoco había asistido. Al parecer la pandilla se había propuesto boicotear la reunión, y él se alegraba mucho. Eso le facilitaba bastante el trabajo. Mucha gente preguntaba por el alcalde, y el agente Brown sonreía y decía que el alcalde llegaría en cualquier momento, en cualquier momento. Entonces se dio cuenta de que tampoco estaba T. V. Daniels, pues aunque T. V. no fuese precisamente el alma de la fiesta —el agente Brown rió para sus adentros ante la idea de que T. V. pudiera ser el alma de alguna fiesta— jamás faltaba a una comida, sobre todo si era gratis. El agente Brown pensó que no tardaría en llegar.

7.11

DIVINE

Después solo quedaron trozos y fragmentos sueltos, y creedme si os digo que no estoy empleando mis propias palabras: parecían restos de un rompecabezas perdido durante mucho tiempo, y aunque algunos podrían pensar que el rompecabezas era gigantesco, las piezas sueltas bastaban para revelar todo lo necesario sobre la imagen completa.

En primer lugar estaban Wade y Colin, borrachos como cubas y tirados cada uno en un sofá, y yo entre ellos, sintiendo la presión de las baldosas frías en la barbilla, en el pecho, en el vientre, en las rodillas y en los empeines mientras una brisa fría me acariciaba el culo y la boca.

Estaba mi retrovisor y la pequeña mancha de luz en forma de huevo que proyectaba sobre una pared, y las cinco líneas que Wade había trazado en la otra.

Había un vaso al lado y cuatro dedos largos y mojados de whisky que avanzaban por el suelo hacia mí, y el dibujo que Wade haría un día con esos dedos, y la historia que escribiría Colin, pero yo ya sabía que en ese dibujo, que en esa historia, no habría ningún Divine.

El whisky tenía un significado, y los dedos y el suelo y la sombra que dejarían detrás, pero yo no significaba nada.

Supongo que no podía culpar a nadie más que a mí. Les había enseñado, de verdad, que eso era lo único que quería, que era lo único que podía consolarme. ¿Quién iba a pensar que acabarían creyéndome?

Yo era el niño que llamaba al lobo, que llamaba a la bestia que acechaba en la oscuridad.

Trozos y fragmentos: un montón de ropa, donde rebusqué hasta encontrar la mía, y un dolor de cabeza que me partía en dos el cráneo y me nublaba la vista; y, sobre todo, la necesidad de correr, correr y correr, de alejarme para siempre de ese puto agujero.

Pero ya había intentado salir corriendo una vez, y no había salido bien, por eso esta vez me fui andando, andando muy despacio por un camino de gravilla que me abrasaba los pies a través de las suelas de los zapatos. Fui andando hasta el pueblo.

7.12

T. V. DANIELS

Con toda honestidad, Darrell Jenkens era casi la última persona a la que T. V. Daniels hubiera querido llevar en coche a alguna parte, en cualquier circunstancia, y ese día Darrell había hecho cosas que daban literalmente sentido al apelativo de borracho de mierda, pero lo cierto es que Darrell no solo sabía conducir una carretilla elevadora sino que además estaba deseándolo.

T. V. Daniels no había bebido ese día, quiero decir alcohol, porque sí había tomado su habitual trago de Listerine a primera hora de la mañana. Darrell y Dave Helman se habían turnado para llevarle platos de comida, raciones de bebé, según T. V., pero no se daban suficiente prisa, no lo hacían al gusto de T. V. A veces hay que sacrificarse por una causa noble.

Por la mañana, antes de que Darrell y Dave se marcharan para instalar la tribuna del alcalde, T. V. estuvo examinando el montón de palas que Dave guardaba en el cobertizo. El examen consistió en pisarlas hasta que, tras el sexto intento, encontró una que no crujía bajo su peso.

Darrell había traído el sillón de mimbre del cuarto de estar de T. V., pero el sillón se balanceó al colocarlo sobre la paleta de la elevadora, que estaba alabeada; Dave sacó entonces unos clavos gruesos como lápices y casi igual de largos, y a pesar de lo borracho que estaba, los clavó con certeros martillazos para asegurar la silla a la paleta, e incluso torció las cabezas que sobresalían un poco, para mayor seguridad.

De vez en cuando soltaba una risita, Dave Helman, y a medida que avanzaba el día la risita se fue transformando en hipo, luego en ronquidos, hasta que se quedó tirado boca abajo en un rincón del cobertizo, con la cabeza vuelta hacia un lado y su culito de niña reblandecido por la cerveza asomando de tal modo que Darrell Jenkens lamentó no tener a mano una picana y una cámara. Junto al roncante cuerpo de Dave había un montón de vasos, botellas y latas de cerveza vacíos, con los que en el transcurso del día Dave había dibujado su nombre.

Se había quedado en DAVE H.

T. V. miró a Dave desde el sillón, frunció el ceño, ajustó perezosamente la correa de su bolsa de cartero y sonrió. Darrell Jenkens volvió a entrar en el cobertizo con un último plato de comida para T. V., quien se la comió mientras Darrell se sentaba y lo miraba, fumando despacio un cigarrillo muy largo y bebiendo de vez en cuando un trago de cerveza. Cuando T. V. hubo terminado, Darrell siguió mirándolo fijamente, hasta que T. V. dijo: «¿Quieres algo?». Y Darrell bajó la vista, aunque no a tiempo de ocultar una mueca, y a T. V. le pareció oír que Darrell decía entre dientes: «¿Qué coño?». T. V. le preguntó a Darrell: «Dijiste a las cuatro, ¿verdad?» Y Darrell dijo: «Ya te he dicho que puso el despertador delante de Dave y de mí». Y T. V. dijo: «Vale, vale».

T. V. volvió a comprobar su bolsa de correo, como si su contenido pudiera escapar inesperadamente. Darrell y T. V. se quedaron allí sentados unos minutos, hasta que Darrell suspiró, se levantó y empezó a recoger los platos que T. V. había dejado desperdigados. Los amontonó y, sin mirar una sola vez a T. V. o a Dave Helman, usó los platos para dibujar el nombre de T. V. en el suelo del cobertizo.

TERRENCE VINCENT DANIELS, escribió, y con los platos que le sobraron añadió ESTUVO AQUÍ. T. V. no le dijo que su primer nombre se escribía con una sola «r».

7.13

DIVINE

Una vez en el pueblo, me abrí camino entre el gentío reunido bajo una carpa en el aparcamiento del IGA Algunos se acercaban a la tribuna situada en el extremo norte, y pensé que parecían un ejército de hormigas que se disponía a transportar un palo. Fui a comer algo. Más bien, a beber algo, pero también había comida.

—Hola, Percy Schuyler —le dije a Percy Schuyler.

El padre de Percy Schuyler tiene un silo de veinte metros de alto con una escalera lateral y una puerta arriba, y una vez, cuando yo tenía unos catorce años, Percy me llevó allí, abrió la puerta y ¡toma!, el silo estaba lleno hasta los topes, y Percy y yo nos metimos allí dentro y él dio un nuevo significado al término «plantó su semilla». Luego me pasé dos días cagando trigo.

—¡Vaya, pero si es Quincy Cross y su mujercita Cheryl!

En el bar de Sloppy Joe a Cheryl todo el mundo la llamaba «Campo a través» porque se había enrollado con todos los hombres del condado de Cadavera con los que yo no me había enrollado y supongo que con la mitad de los otros con los que yo sí me había enrollado. Quincy me miró, agarró a su mujer y se fue lo más lejos que pudo, ofreciéndome entretanto una bonita vista de su gran culo de negro, sobre el cual se dejaban sentir los efectos de las comidas de Cheryl.

Luego me encontré con Richie Riose, y puedo afirmar tres cosas: una, que su verdadero nombre es Ricardo; dos, que igual que Dionne Warwicke le había añadido una «e» a su apellido; y tres, que es un diamante en bruto, como todos los espaldas mojadas con los que yo había tenido relación. Richie tuvo la amabilidad de llenarme el vaso, pero no me dijo nada; yo tampoco le dije nada, me limité a sonreír y me di la vuelta.

Tropecé entonces con Sam Hall, a quien todo el mundo sigue llamando por el apodo que yo le puse, Sam el Carnicero, aunque debo añadir que yo nací después de que empezara a emitirse la serie *La tribu de los Brady*. Os diré que Sam hace lo que buenamente puede con lo que tiene —creo que a eso se le llama «compensación»–, pero lo cierto es que salió del vientre de su madre antes de tiempo.

–Perdón –le dije a Sam–, estaba buscando la carne. –Y seguí mi camino.

En la mesa de la carne quedé emparedado entre Titus y Ulysses Foster; lo cierto es que yo ya había estado «allí» y debo decir que tardé dos meses en recuperarme, por eso me olvidé del perrito caliente que pensaba tomarme y me escabullí lo antes posible. Algunos se preguntan por qué dos hombres fuertes y atractivos como ellos no están casados, pero Titus y Ulysses siempre responden que están esperando encontrar a un par de gemelas como ellos, y lo único que puedo decir es que más valdría que fueran siamesas, porque Titus y Ulysses seguían durmiendo en la misma cama la última vez que los vi.

En una esquina de la carpa vi a Rosa Stone, sentada en una silla, sola. Se acunaba formando círculos, como si quisiera atornillarse al suelo, y mientras la miraba Victor Bradfield se le acercó y le dijo algo, pero ella ni siquiera levantó la vista.

–¡Eh, Victor! –le llamé. Se volvió para ver quién lo llamaba, me vio y se marchó sin comprobar qué le pasaba a Rosa. Victor Bradfield había sido mi última conquista en el pueblo antes de Wade…

Entonces alguien gritó y alguien respondió con otro grito, y antes de que entendiera lo que estaba pasando todo el mundo gritaba y corría hacia la tribuna, y a mí me pareció excesivo el entusiasmo que mostraban por ver al alcalde. Distinguí entre la multitud a Xavier Leroi. Nadie sabía por qué sus padres le habían puesto ese nombre, pero ahí estaba, por cierto que no tenía muy buen aspecto y se sujetaba el costado mientras corría.

Me quedé quieto un par de minutos mirándolos correr, y luego oí que alguien tarareaba. Me di la vuelta y vi al agente Brown, tarareando esa maldita canción como si no se supiera otra.

Vio que lo miraba. Me esforcé por sonreír y me acerqué a él. El agente Brown no dejó de tararear, pero noté una especie de castañeteo y comprendí que estaba tarareando con los dientes cerrados.

Llegué hasta él y esperé a que dejara de emitir ese estúpido sonido.

–¿Quieres decirme algo, Reggie?

–Sí –dije–. En primer lugar, me llamo Divine. Y en segundo… –Me detuve. Sonreí. Casi le pongo la mano en la polla para comprobar si la tenía dura, pero no lo hice–… Y en segundo, Leroy Brown era negro.

Luego me marché para ver qué era lo que emocionaba tanto a todo el mundo.

7.14

ROSEMARY KREBS

Día de los Fundadores.

Que conste que la idea fue de mi marido, no mía. Me parecía prematuro pensar que ya había algo fundado.

El lino azul marino era la indumentaria perfecta para una fiesta así: el lino reduce la transpiración y el azul marino la oculta en caso de que llegue a producirse. Algunas mujeres se quejan de que los trajes de lino se arrugan en cuanto te sientas, pero como decía mi madre, eso es porque no saben estar de pie.

Había logrado aceptar seis brebajes diferentes sin beberme ninguno. Luego me senté en una silla en la primera fila de la carpa, con un vaso de limonada.

Eran casi las cuatro, y Phyneas dijo que llegaría a las cuatro. O que aparecería.

—Buenas tardes, señora Krebs —dijo Portland Oregon Smith—. Betty me ha pedido que le pregunte cuándo llegará el alcalde. La gente empieza a impacientarse.

—Buenas tardes, Porter. Un día espléndido para una fiesta, ¿verdad?

—Sí, señora.

—¿Cómo está Betty?

—Está bien, señora.

—¿Y Porter junior?

—Estamos todos bien, señora.

—Me alegro. —Miré el reloj—. Creo que el alcalde debe de estar a punto de llegar.

—Bien —dijo Porter—. Se lo diré al…

—¿A quién?

—Perdón, señora Krebs. Mire eso.

Porter no acabó la frase, y yo me levanté despacio.

Miré mi vaso para asegurarme de que no me lo habían cambiado por algún brebaje espumoso y alucinógeno, pues aunque había visto que por la ventana de mi estudio entraba el humo de un incendio que tenía lugar a veinte kilómetros de allí, por primera vez en la vida no di crédito a lo que veían mis ojos.

El vaso era de plástico y aparentemente solo tenía limonada.

Levanté la vista de nuevo.

T. V. Daniels se sumaba a la fiesta.

Llevaba puesto su uniforme de cartero y la bolsa del correo colgada del hombro.

Las caderas le sobresalían de la silla en la que se sentó, que en realidad era una silla de confidente.

La silla se elevó unos tres metros del suelo, colgada de los ganchos de una máquina elevadora. Darrell Jenkens manejaba la elevadora, que avanzaba a trompicones por el peso de T. V. Daniels. Una sonrisa, como una cuña de queso de bola, se dibujó en el rostro de Darrell Jenkens, pero T. V. Daniels no alteró su expresión de dignidad pese a que tenía manchas de salsa barbacoa por toda la boca y pese a que las vibraciones de la pala hacían que la cara le temblase como un flan.

Alguien gritó y alguien respondió con otro grito, y la multitud corrió hacia la tribuna y la elevadora.

La elevadora dio una sacudida.

Volví a mirar mi limonada. Había desaparecido. Pensé que a lo mejor estaba alucinando, pero bajé la vista y vi que el vaso se había caído al suelo y que me había mojado los zapatos.

Llevaba unos zapatos de ante rojos; pensé que si me marchaba enseguida podría limpiarlos y cepillarlos.

Miré de nuevo a T. V. Debo reconocerlo: su sincronía era perfecta.

El dicho «Quien no malgasta, no padece» me pareció especialmente acertado a la vista de su imponente masa, y me fui a casa para salvar mis zapatos.

7.15

DIVINE

T. V. Daniels entró en escena como un personaje salido de la peor pesadilla.

Más bien entró en la tribuna.

Luego los que estaban más cerca de la tribuna dijeron que habían oído un timbre dentro, como el de un despertador viejo, y a las cuatro en punto, una trampilla se abrió en el suelo de la tribuna y la cabeza del alcalde asomó al momento. Supongo que si te paras a pensarlo era lo que tenía que pasar, pero aun así la gente se quedó sin habla, aunque no estaba del todo claro si por el alcalde o por T. V. El alcalde tenía la cara roja como un tomate y el pelo y el cuello de la camisa pegado a la piel por el sudor, pero lucía una sonrisa como fijada con cinta adhesiva, y logró estirar un brazo, bien para saludar a sus admiradores, bien para alcanzar el micrófono que llevaba el día entero cociéndose sobre la tribuna, cuando la pala de la elevadora, la pala que transportaba los trescientos ochenta kilos de T. V. Daniels chocó contra la puerta de la trampilla, que se cerró de golpe sobre la cabeza del alcalde, que quedó atontado por el impacto. Volvió los ojos al cielo y la cabeza se agitó como un globo en un día de viento. Luego se hundió de nuevo bajo la tribuna, moviendo el brazo como la cola de una rata, hasta que se cerró la puerta.

Alguien que estaba a mi lado se rió, y una voz de madre ordenó silencio.

La elevadora resollaba como una mula obligada a trabajar en un día de verano mientras recorría los últimos metros con T. V. encima; después, no sé si Darrell Jenkens apagó la máquina o si esta se murió a consecuencia del esfuerzo, pero lo cierto es que el motor dejó de funcionar y el aire se inundó de voces y luego todo el mundo guardó silencio, pues ¿qué se podía decir?

T. V. no se levantó.

Tampoco sería exacto decir que se inclinó sobre el micrófono. Tengo en la cabeza una imagen, una especie de radiografía del esqueleto de T. V. enterrado bajo kilos y kilos de grasa, y cuando inclinó el esqueleto como todo el mundo, el resto de la masa se desplazó o, mejor dicho, se derritió, y le oír decir claramente a Blaine Getterling: Se va a romper, se va a romper, se va a romper. Pero no estaba seguro de si se refería a la silla donde estaba sentado T. V. o a la tribuna.

T. V. volvió a sentarse derecho, jadeando tras el esfuerzo de recoger el micrófono; luego encendió el micro y lo primero que se oyó fue una especie de gemido, y después la agitada respiración de T. V. amplificada por cien.

Creo que T. V. estaba esperando a que todo el mundo guardara silencio, aunque lo cierto es que nadie estaba hablando. Todos se habían quedado mudos.

T. V. esperaba.

Al fin habló:

—Tengo en mi poder —dijo, dando una palmada a algo que sobre su cuerpo parecía un monedero colgado de una cuerda— varias cartas. —Comprendí que se trataba de la bolsa del correo—. O documentos, si lo preferís, documentos —dijo, hizo una pausa, sonrió nerviosamente y continuó—: Documentos de interés para algunos de los que viven en este pueblo —explicó; y luego, sin ninguna razón, me miró y terminó diciendo—: Para hombres presentes en esta reunión.

Entonces se me heló la sangre y quise salir corriendo, pero algo me detuvo, como el pájaro petrificado por la mirada de la serpiente.

—Estos documentos —dijo T. V.—, estas cartas, van dirigidas a un tal Rata, cuyo verdadero nombre es Lamoine Wiebe, a distintos lugares del país, y llevan como remite un apartado de correos que según he podido saber está registrado a nombre de nuestro querido Reginald Packman.

Bueno, eso era mentira, porque el apartado de correos iba a mi nombre: Divine.

Hubo un murmullo entre la multitud, un murmullo mucho más aterrador de lo normal porque cuando miré a los demás a la cara vi que nadie estaba emitiendo sonido alguno.

—¡Maldito cabrón! —grité entonces—. ¡Puta bola de sebo! ¡Me has robado mis cartas!

En cuanto abrí la boca, la gente que me rodeaba retrocedió unos pasos, lo cual tuvo dos efectos inmediatos: por un lado me dejaron más espacio para respirar, y por otro formaron un compacto círculo de cuerpos a mi alrededor, y supe entonces que ya no podría salir corriendo.

Supongo que podría haber negado que las cartas fueran mías, pero aunque se me hubiera ocurrido tal cosa, no habría sabido cómo hacerlo. Nunca he negado nada.

T. V. había dejado de decir gilipolleces. Cuando volví a mirarlo estaba rebuscando en su bolsa de correo, y sacó un montón de cartas que dejó desperdigadas sobre su regazo. Metió la mano en la bolsa tres veces más, hasta que quedó cubierto de sobres arrugados.

Hubo una especie de zumbido mientras el montón de cartas crecía y crecía, y debo admitir que incluso yo estaba asombrado. No sabía que hubiera estado tan ocupado en los últimos años.

—Cada uno de estos documentos —decía T. V.—, todos y cada uno de ellos llevan el sello «Devuelto al remitente». —Entonces me miró—. Yo hice mi trabajo. Yo hice mi trabajo.

Parecía necesario responderle, y grité:

—Y yo también, gilipollas.

T. V. no me prestó atención. Cogió una de las cartas del montón.

—El mal —dijo, y su voz pareció perderse en la distancia, tanto que tuve la inconfundible impresión de que había ensayado esta parte del discurso—... el mal está dentro de este sobre. El mal está en cada uno de nosotros. El mal está entre nosotros. Pero el mal —dijo, abriendo el sobre por el extremo— puede detenerse y evitarse y erradicarse...

—Oye tú —gritó alguien—, no se puede abrir el correo de otro. Eso no está bien. No es legal.

Tuve la extraña sensación de que no sabía quién había hablado. No reconocí la voz.

T. V. pareció un poco cohibido.

—El mal —dijo, intentando recuperar el tono que había empleado antes, aunque sin conseguirlo— debe ser nombrado.

–Nada de eso –gritó otra voz–. Eso es asunto solo de Lamoine Wiebe y Reginald Packman.

T. V. tragó saliva. Tenía la nuez del tamaño de una manzana, y era un espectáculo digno de verse.

–La verdad –dijo, con una voz que había perdido toda su fuerza, mientras blandía el sobre que tenía en la mano–. ¿La verdad os hará libres?

Hubo entonces una especie de abucheo general y por un momento pensé que la gente iba a ponerse de mi parte. Entonces alguien dijo:

–Lo que hay que hacer, lo único que hay que hacer es devolverle el correo a su propietario. A Reggie Packman.

Lo que estaba pasando era muy raro. Estaba yo, y estaba T. V. y estaban todos los demás, y todos los demás eran, no sé, como una sola persona; no como una persona, sino como una cosa. Una voz. Un deseo.

Una turba, pensé entonces. Una turba.

–¡Devuélveselas! –gritó la turba–. ¡Son suyas!

La turba empezó a avanzar, arremolinándose alrededor de la tribuna, arrollándome a su paso. Aún conservaba un pequeño espacio a mi alrededor, y vi que T.V parecía preocupado. La multitud levantó las manos, empujó la tribuna, que empezó a moverse adelante y atrás, y T. V. dijo: Vale, vale. Y empezó a tirar las cartas al aire. Las cartas resplandecieron como chispas bajo el sol mientras la gente seguía gritando «¡Devuélveselas!», «¡Son suyas!», pero entre los gritos oí otra voz, una voz débil que gritaba «¡Socorro! ¡Sacadme de aquí!», y al principio pensé que era mi propia voz, pero luego comprendí que era la del alcalde, que gritaba desde el interior de la tribuna.

Entonces una carta, hecha una pelota, me dio en la cara.

Parecía que pesaba cinco kilos y casi me deja seco.

Otra carta me dio en el pecho y me tambaleé hacia atrás, después de quedarme sin aliento.

Otra carta chocó contra mi espalda, y estoy casi seguro de que aún había una mano sujetándola y me preparé para recibir la avalancha de cartas y de manos que me esperaba, y esta vez las manos no ocultaron sus intenciones de darme puñetazos. Empecé a recibir golpes en la cara y en el estómago, rebotando de puño en puño, y se me ocurrió que debía esforzarme por seguir de pie. Pensé que mientras siguiera en pie no me pasaría nada.

También se me ocurrió que si decía algo la gente reaccionaría. Recordarían quién era yo: una persona, uno de ellos, un chico nacido y criado en Galatia. Pero no pude decir nada, y aunque hubiera podido, lo único que se me ocurría decir era «Soy Divine», pero me estaban demostrando de manera concluyente que eso no era verdad.

Un tobillo se enganchó con el mío y caí al suelo.

Lo extraño es que no perdí el conocimiento. Tuve una visión de los ojos del alcalde girando y de su cabeza balanceándose adelante y atrás, y pensé que eso era lo que iba a pasarme a mí, pero no. En cuanto caí al suelo la multitud se cerró sobre mí como el agua y tuve la clara sensación de que estaba ahogándome, de que estaba siendo arrastrado por olas que en realidad eran patadas y puñetazos, pero en ningún momento cerré los ojos ni dejé de oír ruidos, muchos ruidos, aunque todo parecía transcurrir bajo el agua, cada sonido era más o menos igual que el anterior, voces, puñetazos, los golpes y las rasgaduras de la carpa que se vino abajo a mis espaldas, el crepitar del fuego que empezaba a prender, y luego quedé sumergido, me ahogaba, el aire era denso y caliente y parecía empujarme hacia abajo, y, como hacen los ahogados, me di por vencido, me relajé y esperé a que ocurriera lo que tuviera que ocurrir.

Después la multitud desapareció.

Parpadeé.

Se habían ido.

Volví a parpadear. Me di la vuelta y miré alrededor.

Un extremo de la carpa, el que estaba más próximo a las barbacoas, se había venido abajo o lo habían tirado, y de allí era de donde venía el humo. La verdad es que no había demasiado humo y apenas había llamas, pero el humo salía del nailon de la carpa y no hay nada que apeste más que el nailon quemado. La carpa se fundía en gotitas de fuego aceitoso que caían sobre las mesas preparadas para la fiesta, sobre los platos de papel, las servilletas de papel y los manteles de papel, que también empezaron a arder, pero no tan deprisa como cabría imaginar, más bien como si el fuego le estuviera dando a alguien la oportunidad de apagarlo, y era evidente lo que pasaría si nadie lo apagaba.

Entonces oí una voz.

–¡Eh! ¿Hay alguien ahí? ¿Reggie? ¿Reggie? ¿Estás ahí?

Era T. V. Me levanté despacio. No sentía dolor –no había vuelto a sentir nada desde que me alcanzaron las primeras cartas–, y vi a T. V. subido a la tribuna, sentado en su silla de confidente, mirando al fuego.

–¿Reggie?

Del interior de la tribuna no salía ningún ruido.

Di un paso para comprobar si todo estaba en orden. Seguía sintiéndome como si estuviera debajo del agua. Mis brazos y mis piernas se movían mucho más despacio de lo normal, como si tropezaran con algún obstáculo. Di otro paso, y otro, y otro más. Seguía sin sentir dolor.

Entonces T. V. me vio.

—Reggie. Reggie, tienes que ayudarme. Reggie, Darrell se ha ido, ¿puedes poner en marcha la elevadora?

No le contesté. Ni siquiera se me pasó por la cabeza contestarle. No le odiaba, ni nada por el estilo. No sentía nada, ni hacia él, ni hacia mí mismo, ni hacia la multitud que se había esfumado. Solo andaba, paso a paso, y esperaba el momento en que volvería a hundirme o a romperme en pedazos o a desaparecer.

—¿Reggie? ¿Reg... Divine? Divine, por favor. Yo no pretendía que pasara nada de esto.

Y no sé por qué, lo creí. Creí que no pretendía que pasara nada de eso. Nadie pretende nada en Galatia. Pero de todos modos, seguí andando. Un paso, otro. Me alejé. Vi las llamas en la hierba seca del jardín de Vera Gatlinger, que estaba cerca de su IGA. Vi el rastro que había dejado la multitud al alejarse de mí, y me di la vuelta, fue la única vez que me di la vuelta en todo el día, y me marché en dirección contraria.

—¿Divine?

Caminé en línea recta. Paso a paso.

El sol se iba. Desaparece, me dije; el sol no se va, desaparece.

Paso a paso.

Galatea era un pueblo pequeño y no tardé en salir de allí. Estaba en Galatia y estaba fuera.

Me dirigía hacia el este.

Paso a paso.

No me llamo Reginald Packman. No sabía que la gente me odiara tanto. De hecho, no creo que me odien.

No me llamo Divine, y la gente tampoco me odia.

Podría llamarme Eric Johnson. Todo el mundo odiaba a Eric Johnson. Puede que no tenga nombre. Puede que eso sea lo que la gente no soporte.

Tengo muchos nombres y los odio todos.

Paso a paso. Paso a paso.

7.16

ERIC JOHNSON

26 de junio de 1984

Me llamo Eric Johnson y vivo en el país de la fantasía.

Mi mamá dice que llevaba mucho tiempo sin limpiar la casa antes de que yo entrara en su vida, y por una vez no me cuesta creerla. El aire está tan cargado de motas de polvo que parecen dibujadas a lápiz y flotan de habitación en habitación, millones y millones de copos plateados del tamaño de una moneda que rebotan al chocar unos con otros y relucen bajo la luz de la mañana, y la mañana se convierte aquí en una hora muy especial, en una hora mágica, que diría mi mamá, y aunque no creo en la magia sí creo en mi mamá, o al menos la comprendo, lo que viene a ser lo mismo. Mi mamá lo llama polvo de hada, dice que por eso no lo barre. Intenté explicarle que el noventa y cinco por ciento del polvo que hay en la casa es en realidad piel humana, pero dijo que daba lo mismo. A veces me pregunto si lo que intentaba decir era que éramos hadas, pero supongo que es mejor no preguntárselo, al menos a ella. El caso es que el polvo cambia las cosas. Afecta a la vista, al sonido y al tacto. Mi mano parece estar a un kilómetro de mí, las líneas del libro que estoy leyendo tiemblan más que la superficie del lago Webster en un día de viento. El polvo se posa sobre todas las cosas: superficies, sábanas, comida, incluso en los pomos de las puertas si no se abren cada cinco minutos, y cuando se posa sobre mi piel, apenas lo noto, aunque está ahí, mil veces más ligero que las pisadas de una mosca –iba a decir de un hada, pero prefiero no alejarme del mundo real, pues por una vez el mundo real me gusta–, y mientras leo y sudo a chorros por los brazos y las piernas y la tripa, el polvo se desprende formando finos chorretes marrones y pinta mi cuerpo de rayas, como si fuera una cebra. Ir hasta el baño o la cocina es como flotar. Allí abajo, en algún lugar, está el suelo: pequeñas nubes en forma de champiñones saltan a cada paso que doy, tragándose mis pies y amortiguando el ruido que de lo contrario harían, y si giro la cabeza veo cómo el polvo se esparce por el espacio vacío que acabo de dejar atrás. Mi mamá dice que el que mantiene los ojos y el corazón abiertos puede ver la magia, y si eso es verdad lo que ocurre en nuestra casa un sábado por la mañana es mágico. En el suelo, delante de cada habitación, hay un cuadrado de luz teñido de rojo, azul o amarillo, porque la luz se filtra por las viejas toallas de baño con que mi madre cubrió las ventanas en lugar de poner cortinas. Sabemos que a veces han aparecido palabras escritas sobre el polvo en una cómoda o en una mesa, palabras como «A un tonto no le agrada comprender, pero eso es algo que su corazón puede descubrir por sí solo», y cosas así, pero dejadme aplacar vuestras sospechas diciendo que mi madre puede firmar un cheque, aunque solo después de que Vera Gatlinger en el IGA o Yankee Carting en el TruValue se lo pidan. A veces la tele funciona bien y otras veces no funciona. A veces oigo música de piano que viene del ático, y es bonita, pero otras veces oigo un redoble de tambores en el sótano, y no es bonito. No. No lo es. Mi madre solo compra alcohol, pero el congelador siempre está lleno de comida. Aquí es más fácil que al abrir el grifo salga un chorro de aire seco o de óxido dorado en lugar de agua. Mi mamá me dijo que una vez lo abrió y salió una serpiente roja, dorada y verde... pero también me dijo que una vez dio un mordisco a una manzana y se encontró con la moneda de oro que ahora lleva colgada del cuello, y también me dijo que yo no tenía papá, que ella me creó mezclando el polvo de una astilla de hueso que encontró en su piedra ventral con un cuarto de ron portorriqueño y bebiéndoselo a medianoche a la luz de la luna llena. Mi mamá jura que la astilla salió de una enorme ballena que vivió y murió hace un millón de años y que por eso he salido como he salido.

Que por eso salí blanco.

7.17

COLIN

La única razón por la que en un relato alguien se queda dormido después del sexo es para que el otro se pueda marchar. Los amantes no se quedan dormidos después del sexo –puede que las parejas que llevan muchos años casadas sí se queden dormidas, pero los amantes no–, y yo jamás me he permitido usar este recurso en mis novelas, pues siempre me ha parecido una pieza mal montada en la maquinaria de la trama. Pero después de compartir a Divine con Wade –o tal vez debería decir después de que Wade y yo nos repartiéramos a Divine–, Wade y yo nos quedamos dormidos, y cuando me desperté comprendí que había una motivación legítima para delimitar la zona, además de todo lo que habíamos bebido.

El hecho de quedarme dormido tan pronto hizo que el sexo pareciese un sueño, puede que una pesadilla, en todo caso algo irreal, por lo cual no hacía falta explicarlo sino interpretarlo. Pues no podría decir por qué hice lo que hice, aunque de inmediato comprendí lo que significaba.

Divine se había marchado. Aunque no había nada que indicara que hubiera hecho algo más que salir de la casa, sentí cierto vacío, una especie de oquedad, como si al marcharse se hubiera llevado consigo no solo su cuerpo, sino parte de la esencia que normalmente dejaba tras de sí. Y yo también me fui. Quería encontrarlo, no para detenerlo, porque creo que tiene razón al huir de nosotros, sino para garantizarle un viaje seguro. Intenté salir de la habitación sin hacer ruido, pero la voz de Wade me detuvo.

—Colin Nieman —dijo.

Me paré en seco y me di la vuelta. Wade estaba tumbado en la cama, apoyado sobre un codo, con la camisa gris abierta a la altura del torso flaco, como unas cortinas separadas. El maldito Divine parecía haber limpiado el aire que había entre nosotros, y fuimos directos al grano.

—Me gustaría hacerte algunas preguntas sobre tu novela.

Lo miré. No accedí a su petición, pero tampoco la rechacé.

—Me gustaría saber —dijo— de dónde sacaste los nombres de Martin y John.

—¿Martin y John? —Me quedé un rato mirándolo, pensando si Justin le habría contado algo que no me hubiera contado a mí, y al final me encogí de hombros. ¿Acaso importaba?—. Los saqué de un sueño. De un sueño de Justin. Son nombres que él pronunciaba en sueños.

Wade asintió con la cabeza; sonrió ligeramente, como si yo acabara de confirmar algo que él ya sospechaba, y dijo:

—A veces me pregunto si no seremos todos un sueño de Justin.

Hubo algo en ese comentario que me irritó sobremanera... no exactamente sus palabras, sino la absoluta falta de emoción con que las pronunció, y de pronto empecé a gritar:

—¿Te crees que entiendes a Justin, verdad?

Wade no me miró.

—Creo que me entiendo a mí mismo, cosa que tú no puedes decir de ti.

—¿Sigues culpándome de lo ocurrido, verdad? Eres como Cora o como Webbie. Crees que he destruido un delicado equilibrio con mi llegada aquí y que toda Galatia debe pagar por mis pecados.

Wade no respondió, pero muy despacio, deliberadamente, cerró los ojos.

—Y Justin. Sobre todo Justin tiene que pagar. Eso es lo que crees.

La voz de Wade llegó desde detrás de sus ojos cerrados, como si se concentrara, como si se esforzara por recordar un discurso aprendido hacía mucho tiempo.

—Creo que lo ha pasado muy mal —dijo, y me pregunté si se refería a Justin o a sí mismo.

Mis palabras, cuando al fin hablé, parecieron estar tan lejos de mí como lo estaban las de Wade de él, parecían ensayadas, recitadas, debo admitirlo, y sentí algo que últimamente sentía con frecuencia: que todos nos limitábamos a interpretar un guión escrito por otro.

—Ese es tu Justin —dije—. No mudo sino enmudecido, no silencioso sino silenciado. Escúchame, Wade. Se ha retratado entre las cuatro paredes en las que vive, y eres tú quien le conserva la pintura fresca, animándolo a seguir interpretando este pequeño melodrama. Sientes compasión de él, te parece una víctima. Pero eres tú, Wade, y yo, y Lucy Robinson los que somos víctimas de Justin.

Al oír el nombre de Lucy a Wade le temblaron los párpados, pero no abrió los ojos y tampoco habló.

—Ojo por ojo, me dijo Justin en una ocasión. Diente por diente y libro por libro. Sí, libro por libro. Dijo que yo le había robado *La Bestia*, que la había publicado, que la había hecho real. Pero no creas que él me lo permitió así como así. *La Bestia* y *El país de la fantasía*. Yo le robé su libro y él me robó el mío. Pero yo le dije que él seguía teniendo *La Bestia*, que estaba ahí, en la biblioteca. Y él me dijo que yo seguía teniendo *El país de la fantasía*, y entonces volcó un saco que tenía en la mano, un saco que no era importante hasta que lo vació. ¿Y sabes lo que había dentro? ¿Sabes lo que cayó al suelo? Pues mi libro, por supuesto. Hasta la última palabra de mi libro. Sí; hasta la última palabra. Justin había destrozado mi manuscrito con unas tijeras, quince años de trabajo, lo había desmembrado palabra por palabra, página por página, año por año. Y entonces me dijo: «Aquí lo tienes; es todo tuyo. Hasta la última palabra».

Wade abrió los ojos de pronto y pude ver en ellos una imagen de sus propios cuadros, hechos jirones a manos de Justin y volando por sus queridas praderas. En voz muy baja, casi con un susurro, preguntó:

—¿Qué hiciste?

—¿Que qué hice? Reírme de él. Le dije que si se pensaba que por cortar una historia en pedazos podía destruirla. Cogí un puñado de palabras y le dije: «Antes esto era una historia; ahora son muchas». Le arrojé mis palabras y tuve la satisfacción de ver que mi historia caía como la nieve sucia sobre la casa, tan leve que hasta la más leve brisa la hacía arremolinarse formando torbellinos, y al mismo tiempo se extendía por todas partes, como una red formada por cien veces más espacio abierto que materiales sólidos, aunque sus escasas cuerdas bastaban para atrapar todo lo que caía en ella. Y tú te crees que es indefenso. Te está devorando y ni siquiera te das cuenta.

Wade guardó silencio un buen rato, luego se cerró la camisa y volví a pensar en unas cortinas que se cerraban, en un telón que ocultaba el escenario.

—Dime una cosa —dijo entonces—. Cuando tú y yo recordemos este día, ¿quién crees que tendrá la responsabilidad final? ¿Tú por haberlo empezado o yo por haberte seguido el juego?

—Creo que los dos lucharemos ferozmente por ese premio hasta el final.

Wade cerró los ojos y se los cubrió con una mano.

—Todo es ya feroz. Lo único que deseo es que termine cuanto antes.

7.18

T. V. DANIELS

La carpa ardió despacio. Ese mismo día Darrell Jenkens le había contado a T. V. que Yankee Carting siempre le daba un buen manguerazo antes de la fiesta, para limpiarla, refrescarla y protegerla del fuego. Ardía despacio, pero ardía irremediablemente.

El humo ascendía en penachos negros y densos como la nata montada. Olía a pelo de perro, y cuando una columna de humo cubría la tribuna, a T. V. le lloraban los ojos, se atragantaba y se tapaba la nariz con su bolsa de correo vacía.

Divine se había marchado, la multitud se había marchado, Darrell Jenkens también se había marchado y hacía un buen rato que el alcalde había dejado de hacer ruido.

T. V. aún no se había levantado, pues temía que una de las planchas de la pala elevadora se partiera bajo su peso y lo lanzara sobre la tribuna, que a él le parecía muy estrecha. De modo que se quedó sentado, intentando no mirar el fuego.

En algún momento vio el micrófono, aplastado entre su cadera y el costado de la silla, lo tocó y le dio unos toques para comprobar si funcionaba.

Un zumbido hueco salió por los altavoces.

—¿Hola? ¿Hay alguien ahí?

Esperó un momento y luego, como no oía nada, soltó el micrófono.

Se atragantó cuando una nueva ola de humo inundó la tribuna.

Pero seguía sin levantarse. Se echó hacia delante muy despacio, lo más despacio que pudo, hasta que las patas delanteras de la silla se doblaron; T. V. se encogió sobre su estómago antes de oír un crujido y caer al suelo, cuatro metros abajo. Rebotó una, dos, tres veces, y se quedó inmóvil.

7.19

COLIN

Lo cierto es que vi el humo, pero no le di importancia. Todo el mundo llevaba una semana hablando de la barbacoa y yo había visto el tamaño de las parrillas: tenían la profundidad y la anchura suficiente para producir una columna de humo tan grande como la que estaba viendo o, tan pequeña, porque la fina cinta negra que ascendía en espiral desde el centro del pueblo parecía inofensiva, un simple remolino en lugar de un tornado.

Pero en cuanto hube entrado en el pueblo supe que algo pasaba. No fue una intuición: un escenario de destrucción cortaba el paso en la calle Monroe. Había vallas y buzones derribados, setos pisoteados, un coche aparcado con los cristales rotos. Mientras avanzaba despacio con el coche, comprendí que una turba había arrasado la calle, dejando un rastro polvoriento como el de una serpiente gigantesca, y entonces vi el aparcamiento del IGA, la tribuna, la elevadora y la carpa derribada y en llamas. Doblé la esquina y aceleré un poco, pero el sonido de la gravilla que levantaban las ruedas me obligó a reducir la marcha. No era un héroe; no iba a rescatar a nadie. Solo quería ver qué había pasado.

La tribuna estaba ligeramente ladeada. Algo, aunque no parecía ser la elevadora, puesto que la tribuna se encontraba fuera de su alcance, había intentado volcarla. Sobre ella había restos de algo —¿una silla?— hecho pedazos, como si le hubiera caído encima un yunque, igual que en los dibujos animados de los sábados por la mañana. Un lecho de latas, botellas de cerveza y vasos de plástico cubría el aparcamiento, y una ráfaga de aire desperdigaba los manteles de papel como gigantescos copos de nieve. La carpa ardía despacio, produciendo un humo tóxico. El olor a carne asada se mezclaba con el olor a petróleo ardiendo, y al sentir que me lloraban los ojos y la boca se me llenaba de agua, no supe si era por el mal olor, por el bueno o por la mezcla de ambos. Me quedé mirando el incendio o los pequeños focos de fuego, mucho rato. Pensé en coger una manguera de la casa más próxima, o en llamar a los bomberos. ¿Llamaba alguien a los bomberos en Galatia? ¿Era así como se respondía aquí a una emergencia? No estaba seguro y, en todo caso, el asunto era discutible, porque yo tampoco hice nada al ver el fuego, sino que me quedé sentado en el coche observando cómo ardía. Si es que en algún momento pensé en el fuego, fue con el vago deseo de que las llamas escaparan a todo control, de que arrasaran el pueblo entero, porque yo pensaba marcharme, y si el pueblo ardía no tendría la sensación de huir, sino de irme por necesidad, sin más remedio.

Algo llamó mi atención. Una cabeza con el pelo gris asomaba por detrás de uno de los olmos medio muertos que flanqueaban la calle Jefferson, una figura con la cara gris que se escondió nada más verme. El impulso de huir me abandonó tan deprisa como me había invadido; salí del coche de un salto y corrí hacia el árbol. La basura acumulada sobre la pradera crujía bajo mis pies, y la figura agazapada detrás del árbol salió corriendo al oír el ruido.

—¡Rosa! ¡Espera, Rosa! ¡Soy Colin, Colin Nieman!

Pensé entonces que no había razón alguna para que se detuviera al oír mi nombre; y no se detuvo, siguió corriendo mientras el bolso rojo que llevaba colgado del hombro rebotaba sobre su cadera. Entonces pensé que era la primera vez que alguien huía al verme, que alguien tenía miedo de mí. Justin nunca había huido por miedo —por disgusto tal vez, pero nunca por miedo—, y la idea de que alguien pudiera huir de mí aterrorizado me hizo aflojar un poco la marcha. De todos modos, no tuve que esforzarme demasiado para alcanzar a Rosa. Le puse una mano en el hombro y se detuvo, de lo que me alegré, pues no era mi intención tirarla al suelo. La habría perseguido durante kilómetros antes de hacer una cosa así.

No estoy seguro de si Rosa ya estaba hablando antes de que nos detuviéramos o si empezó a hablar cuando sintió el tacto de mi mano.

—¡Tiene que marcharse! —dijo, con la voz entrecortada—. Tiene que marcharse. Usted, yo, todo el mundo. ¡Tiene que marcharse de aquí!

—Tranquilízate, Rosa. Toma aliento.

Rosa movía los ojos como enloquecida; miraba a todas partes, pero no me miraba a mí.

—No hay tiempo. No queda ni un segundo. Hay que marcharse de aquí antes de que sea demasiado tarde.

La sujeté entonces de los hombros y la obligué a volverse hacia mí. No me gustaba tener que recurrir a la fuerza, pero no se me ocurrió otra cosa. La miré fijamente hasta que logré que me mirara, y mantuve la mirada hasta que se tranquilizó un poco.

—No pienso irme a ninguna parte. Y tú tampoco. Todavía no. Respira hondo, tranquilízate y cuéntame qué ha pasado.

Rosa me miraba como si estuviera embrujada, pero enseguida comprendí que mis posibilidades de abandonar el pueblo eran tan escasas como las suyas. Se tensó un momento, al roce de mis manos; luego se desinfló con un largo suspiro y cayó al suelo.

—Todo es inútil —dijo, susurrando, o suspirando—. Todo es inútil.

Me arrodillé junto a ella.

—¿Qué es lo que no sirve de nada, Rosa?

Me miró. Una lágrima asomó en sus ojos, formando una línea sucia al resbalar por la cara cubierta de polvo. Sus lágrimas parecían falsas, artificiales, como las que un payaso se pinta en la cara, o como las rayas verticales que dividen en dos el rostro de las marionetas. Me acarició la mejilla con la mano húmeda.

—Usted me cae bien, señor Nieman. Siempre me ha caído bien. Todos los demás piensan que es usted un arrogante, un cabrón sin escrúpulos, pero Cora y yo siempre supimos que usted no era mala persona. Solo está fuera de lugar.

—Rosa...

—Solo está preocupado. Agobiado. —Me apretaba con tanta fuerza la mejilla, que me pareció que iba a cortármela. Luego dijo—: Yo sé muy bien lo que es estar agobiado.

—Por favor, Rosa...

Dejó caer la mano y bajó la vista al suelo.

—Usted piensa que la culpa fue suya, señor Nieman, pero no lo fue.

—¿De qué hablas, Rosa?

—Piensa que fue usted quien rompió el equilibrio, como dijo Cora. El de Galatia. Pero no fue usted. Fui yo.

—Rosa, me parece que no te entiendo.

—El equilibrio, señor Nieman. Todo lugar tiene su propio equilibrio. Bien y mal, vida y muerte, Dios y Satanás, señor Nieman, que inclinan la balanza a un lado o a otro. Usted cree que fue usted quien rompió el equilibrio, pero fui yo.

—Vamos, vamos, Rosa. ¿Por qué tiene que ser culpa de alguien más que de la persona que ha hecho todo esto?

Rosa me miró como si fuera un niño.

—Once años, señor Nieman. Él ha tenido once largos años para vengarse.

—¿Once años?

—Hace cinco años que llegué a Galatia. Puede preguntarle a cualquiera. Todo el mundo le dirá que entonces empezaron a pasar cosas extrañas. Empezaron a desaparecer cosas. Lámparas, pasta de dientes, baterías de los coches. Cosas sin importancia, no la clase de cosas que se llevaría un ladrón. Era más bien como que alguien hacía la compra a costa de los demás.

Entonces comprendí lo que decía:

—Estás hablando de Eric Johnson.

—Empezó despacio, señor Nieman. Empezó por cosas sin importancia. Como la bola de nieve que cae desde la cumbre de una montaña. Pero ha ido creciendo y ganando velocidad desde que yo llegué. Usted —dijo, riendo un poco—, usted ha llegado para ver el fin.

—Escúchame, Rosa. Eric Johnson está muerto. A Eric Johnson lo lincharon y lo mataron. Lo mataron, Rosa, ¿lo entiendes?

Rosa pareció confundida.

—¿Lo mataron?

—Sí, Rosa. Lo mataron.

De repente sonrió dulce, inocentemente.

—Él no es de los que mueren así como así.

—Sí, Rosa. Está muerto.

Luego, con un susurro, en voz tan baja que tuve que acercar el oído a su boca, dijo:

—Entonces, ¿dónde está?

—Muerto, Rosa. Está muerto.

Y de pronto empezó a gritar.

—¿Dónde está su cuerpo? Nadie está muerto hasta que no se encuentra el cadáver. ¡Para estar muerto hay que demostrarlo!

Después dio un salto y habría echado a correr si no se lo hubiera impedido. Se dejó caer sobre mí y empezó a murmurar:

—Todo es culpa mía. Mía; solo mía. La culpa es solo mía.

—Rosa, por favor, créeme. Tú no has hecho nada. —Tuve una sensación extraña al decir eso. Creía en mis palabras antes de pronunciarlas, pero al oírlas me parecieron falsas. No sé por qué (seguía sin entender de qué hablaba Rosa), pero por alguna razón sabía que no estaba diciendo la verdad.

—Cuando vine aquí traje el mundo conmigo. Traje el mundo a Galatia.

—Por esa regla de tres yo soy tan culpable como tú. ¿Acaso yo no llegué aquí con mi dinero, mi cultura y mi Justin? Yo también he traído cosas; más cosas que tú.

Sentí que Rosa se estremecía entre mis brazos, y al principio no caí en la cuenta de que estaba riéndose.

—¡Ay, señor Nieman! Es usted como un niño tonto. —Se incorporó sin levantarse y me miró—. Siempre intentando apoderarse de todo, siempre intentando apropiarse de todo. Sí —dijo, y se quedó callada un buen rato—, usted ha traído cosas. Puede que lo haya traído todo. Pero yo lo traje a usted.

—¿Qué quieres decir, Rosa?

Sus lágrimas brillaban intensamente, y tuve tiempo de pensar que estaba loca de remate antes de que ella hablase de nuevo, con una voz cargada de tristeza y arrepentimiento.

—Primero vino la madre y luego el hijo.

Sus palabras me impresionaron, y tuve que contener las ganas de retroceder, asustado.

Rosa se quitó el bolso rojo que llevaba colgado del hombro y se lo puso sobre el regazo.

—Llegué hasta aquí caminando. Me marché para huir de todo y refugiarme aquí, para huir de todas las personas que habían formado parte de mi vida. Mi cuerpo ha amado a hombres y a mujeres y ha parido hijos e hijas, y a todos los he visto crecer y envejecer y morir. Esto me ha pasado cientos de veces, miles de veces, señor Nieman. No se imagina la historia que dejé atrás para venir aquí. Huí de todo. Lo dejé todo. Todo. Caminé miles de kilómetros, desnuda como el Todopoderoso me había creado, y no supe que era él quien me enviaba aquí hasta que recibí la señal.

Abrió el bolso. Dentro del bolso había una piedra ventral, entera, del tamaño de un melón pequeño. Intenté tocarla instintivamente, pero Rosa cerró el bolso.

—Es mía —dijo; y al decirlo parecía una madre regañando a un niño—. Esta era mi señal. La dejaron para mí en mitad de la carretera. La encontré entre los restos de una matanza, pero estaba intacta, prístina, sin abrir, y en su interior contiene un mundo propio donde resplandece el glorioso sol de Dios. Entonce supe adónde debía ir.

Echó un vistazo por encima de mi hombro. Me volví para ver qué miraba y vi la cresta del risco pelado, cegadoramente blanco bajo la luz de la tarde.

Miré a Rosa.

—Matanza. ¿Has dicho matanza? ¿De qué matanza hablas? ¿Dónde?

Rosa parpadeó muy despacio.

—¿Dónde?

—¿Dónde ocurrió la matanza, Rosa? ¿Dónde encontraste la piedra?

Rosa se aferró al bolso.

—Es mía —dijo; y esta vez parecía el niño, en lugar de la madre—. Es mi señal.

—Ya sé que es tuya, Rosa. No pretendo quitártela. Solo quiero saber dónde la encontraste.

—¿Dónde? —Rosa parecía confundida—. Pues en el lugar de donde vengo. Donde nací. Donde nació Galatia. Y usted también; usted también nació allí.

La sacudí, muy a mi pesar.

—¿Dónde, Rosa? ¿Dónde nací yo?

Rosa tembló y se encogió sobre el bolso. Entonces tuve una visión: imaginé que Rosa desaparecía dentro de la piedra ventral como un genio en el interior de su lámpara. Pero en ese momento ella levantó la vista mientras una radiante sonrisa le iluminaba el rostro y el brillo de la locura resplandecía en sus ojos.

—Pues en Kenosha, por supuesto.
—¿En Kenosha?
—Por supuesto. ¿Dónde si no?

7.20

ERIC JOHNSON

Hoy cumplo trece años, pero eso no tiene importancia. En cuanto aprendí a gatear supe —o al menos sentí, y sentir a veces equivale a saber—, comprendí que el tiempo no tenía importancia para mí: habría un tiempo en el que estaría vivo y otro tiempo en el que no lo estaría, pero en cualquier caso siempre estaría solo y siempre sufriría, y eso no cambiaría si me cagaba en el pañal que mamá me cambiaría después o si cagaba en el váter que iba a dar a un pozo séptico y tenía que llamar a Stan Robinson para que lo desatascase. Claro que cuando aprendí a gatear aún no conocía esas palabras. Y lo cierto es que tampoco las había aprendido a los trece años, pero os lo cuento de todos modos. Os cuento que no hay paz posible en Galatia... perdón, en Galatea. No hay paz posible para alguien que tenga mi aspecto, lo mismo da que sea joven o que sea viejo, y tampoco importa cómo se llame o dónde viva. No soy negro, pero estoy seguro de que tampoco soy blanco: lo que soy es feo, y podría marcharme de Galatia, pero estoy seguro de que seguiría siendo feo en cualquier parte. Mi madre también decía que hay magia que viene de fuera y magia que viene de dentro, y si aunque no sé si tengo poderes mágicos, sí sé que puedo hacer que cualquiera huya despavorido nada más verme.

Tío Sawyer y tía Cora vienen a mediodía para celebrar mi cumpleaños. Solo están ellos, además de mamá y yo, que aún dormíamos cuando llamaron a la puerta. Es verdad que se habían pasado toda la semana prometiendo que vendrían, pero yo no me lo creí hasta que oí el coche, por eso tengo que darme prisa y salir de la cama y vestirme sin despertar a mamá. Al abrir la puerta, una ráfaga de polvo de hada de mamá inunda el vestíbulo, y el tío Sawyer y la tía Cora tosen y apartan el aire con las manos, y se esfuerzan por fingir que no pasa nada, pero yo veo que el tío Sawyer lleva una caja envuelta en un papel plateado y que pone mucho cuidado en no volcarla, y veo que la tía Cora lleva un molde de tarta cubierto de papel de aluminio, y tengo que aguantarme las ganas de abalanzarme sobre la tarta y el regalo, pero sigo sujetando la puerta y no me muevo hasta que el polvo se posa, y entonces el tío Sawyer y la tía Cora empiezan a cantarme «Cumpleaños feliz», pero ninguno de los dos dice mi nombre. Tal vez debería explicar que mi madre me llamó Eric por su padre, y a todo el mundo le pareció una falta de respeto, teniendo en cuenta que mamá me trajo al mundo sin haber contraído el vínculo sagrado del matrimonio y todo eso, pero mi madre decía que tenía sus razones, por eso la mayoría de la gente no me llama de ningún modo, menos el tío Sawyer, que me llama hermano.

El tío Sawyer y la tía Cora son casi la gente más guapa que he visto en mi vida; y están muy enamorados. Ahora que es verano tienen la piel tan oscura como la cama de nogal de su dormitorio, y la tía Cora tiene además un tono rojizo que ella dice que es por su herencia cherokee, que también se le nota en los ojos, en las mejillas y en los labios, e incluso cuando los dos me desean feliz cumpleaños, veo que ponen toda su atención en el otro, aunque a mí no me molesta, porque ellos son así. El tío Sawyer se tambalea un poco y hasta yo me doy cuenta de que finge estar borracho para poder rozar con su brazo el brazo de tía Cora. Él lleva un mono limpio, aunque descolorido, y ella un vestido de verano sin mangas de color azul cielo, con florecitas blancas, y cuando el tío Sawyer le roza el brazo, la tía Cora suelta una risita y le da un manotazo en el brazo y dice: «Ponte derecho, tonto; cualquiera podría pensar que estás borracho un sábado a mediodía». Y luego le da un codazo en las costillas. «Marsha está durmiendo –digo–. Salió muy temprano al bar de Sloppy Joe y volvió con una botella en el bolso; me dijo que era Coca-Cola, y yo le dije que más valía que me dijera que era 7-Up porque al menos tenía el mismo color que el líquido de su botella, que supongo que era ginebra. De todos modos, los refrescos tienen burbujas, pero la ginebra no.» El tío Sawyer y la tía Cora no pierden la sonrisa, y yo digo: «Se ha bebido la botella entera». El tío Sawyer carraspea y dice: «Bueno, vale. Cora, cariño, ¿por qué no preparas al chico para la fiesta mientras yo intento despertar a mi hermana?». Le entrega mi regalo a Cora con gran ceremonia y me señala con un dedo al tiempo que dice: «No sacudas la caja, porque se romperá lo que hay dentro». Luego se marcha hacia el dormitorio. La tía Cora lleva la tarta y la caja con el regalo a la cocina y los deja en la mesa; se levanta una nube de polvo que le hace toser de nuevo. «¡Hijo mío, no entiendo cómo podéis respirar aquí dentro!» y, con gran asombro por mi parte, arranca las toallas que cubren las ventanas y las abre todas de par en par. «Esta casa necesita aire fresco», dice, y cada vez que se inclina para abrir una ventana se le transparenta el culo bajo el fino vestido de algodón, y cuando empuja la ventana por arriba, las tetas le asoman ligeramente por el escote, como si fueran unidades independientes solo sujetas al cuerpo por el sujetador. «En mi vida he visto tanto polvo –dijo–. Es como vivir en un sueño.»

Cuando el tío Sawyer sale del dormitorio con mi madre, la tía Cora y yo estamos sentados en la sala de estar. La tía Cora está viendo un programa de la tele donde unas veces salen mujeres jugando al golf y otras hombres jugando a los bolos, y yo finjo leer mi libro de Tarzán aunque en realidad contemplo el viento de Kansas que sopla dentro de nuestra casa. Lo observo por la sencilla razón de que «puedo», pues algo que normalmente es invisible resulta por una vez visible: fuera de la casa el día es limpio, claro y caluroso, un día como otro cualquiera, pero dentro el polvo hace visibles las corrientes de aire, como el agua que corre por el río Solomon. Es como si una corriente de agua inundara nuestra casa, como si fuéramos peces, y como la mayoría de los peces que yo he visto siempre están en peceras, tengo la extraña sensación de que alguien está observándome, aunque siempre tengo esa sensación, y tal vez es porque las ventanas están abiertas por primera vez, sin nada que las cubra, y si alguien quiere, puede ver lo que pasa dentro.

«No puedo perderme el cumpleaños de mi hijo», dice mi madre mientras el tío Sawyer la ayuda a entrar en la habitación. Ha logrado ponerse un vestido para cubrir su desnudez, pero su cuerpo tiembla bajo la tela. «¿Qué tonterías me estás contando, Sawyer Johnson? ¡Como si yo pudiera perderme el cumpleaños de mi único hijo! ¡Vamos, hombre! –Y luego grita–: ¡Eric, cariño, ve y tráeme una aspirina del botiquín. Tengo un dolor de cabeza del tamaño del pueblo entero y me vendría muy bien una aspirina.» Voy por la aspirina y se la doy a mi madre, con un vaso de ese líquido que guarda en la petaca del botiquín, que es lo que en realidad desea tomar, y mi madre coge el vaso con una sonrisa y un guiño. «Tráeme también un poco de agua. ¡Qué buen chico eres!» Siento en mi pelo su mano áspera y torpe que se retira de inmediato, mientras que la mano que sujeta el vaso para llevárselo a la boca es suave, firme y lenta, y mi madre se bebe el líquido –creo que es vodka, vodka barato, pésimo, caliente–, a sorbos lentos, fingiendo que es agua. Cuando termina emite un sonido, como si se quedara sin aliento, pero intenta disimularlo cerrando los labios y lanzando un suspiro de satisfacción, aunque el tío Sawyer tiene una expresión tan severa, frunce el ceño con tanta fuerza que se le llena la cara de arrugas, desde los ojos hasta la barbilla partida. «¿Qué pasa?», dice mamá, fingiendo inocencia, pero el tío Sawyer no dice nada, no habla, sino que le quita a mi madre el vaso de las manos y me dice: «Hermano, será mejor que tu madre beba un poco más de agua. Se ha bebido el vaso entero pero se ha olvidado de tomarse la aspirina». Mi madre mira las dos pastillas que tiene en la mano, intentando sonreír; la tía Cora, sentada en el sofá, mira con mucho interés la televisión, pero al ver que todos guardamos silencio vuelve la cabeza hacia nosotros, mira de nuevo la tele y dice: «¡Semipleno! ¿Cómo que semipleno? ¡Si los ha tirado todos!». El tío Sawyer me agarra del hombro cuando voy al cuarto de baño y me empuja hacia la cocina. «Quiero oír cómo corre el agua del grifo –dice detrás de mí, y luego, tras una pausa en la que yo sé que él estaba pensando lo mismo que yo (que es muy fácil llenar un vaso de alcohol mientras corre el agua del grifo), añade–: Pero que no corra demasiado.»

7.21

CORA

En algún momento, en medio de la confusión, perdí de vista a Rosa.

Me gustaría decir que no sé qué le pasó a la gente, además de que había bebido mucha cerveza y había tomado demasiado sol, pero sería mentira.

Ese hombre que estaba encima de la tribuna, T. V. Daniels, había comido en mi restaurante más de una vez. Todos lo habíamos alimentado y ahora veíamos lo que habíamos criado.

Y al mismo tiempo, nadie sabía qué decían esas cartas. ¡Ay, Reggie! Ya le dije en cierta ocasión que era bobo si se pensaba que unas cartas podían salvarlo. Hoy día hace falta un vídeo para llamar la atención de la gente, o, al menos, unas fotos en color. Pero también le dije que ya que lo hacía se molestara en hacerlo bien. Hazte a la idea de que son fotos, le dije; haz copias de ellas, pero conserva los negativos. Pero Reggie se limitó a decir: «Yo soy el negativo», y no me hizo caso.

Bueno. En cuanto vi aparecer a T. V., agarré a Sawyer del brazo y no volví a soltarlo, y cuando me quedó claro que la situación iba a descontrolarse me puse a buscar a Rosa por todas partes. Como no la veía, pensé que se habría ido a casa y hacia allí me marché con Sawyer, tan deprisa como sus jadeantes pulmones nos lo permitían.

Incluso antes de subir la escalera del porche supe que algo pasaba. La puerta estaba abierta y batía a merced del viento.

Fue Rosa quien la cerró cuando salimos de casa. La cerró y echó la llave. Por si acaso, dijo, como decía siempre. Por si acaso.

La puerta estaba abierta pero las persianas estaban cerradas, y cuando salimos las dejamos abiertas.

Ni siquiera la llamé cuando entramos. Senté al pobre y aturdido Sawyer en una silla y corrí al dormitorio.

La piedra ventral había desaparecido.

Rosa la había tenido escondida durante cinco años para que yo no la viera, y yo había fingido no saber nada. Ahora había desaparecido.

Me sorprendía que no me sorprendiera. Pero no me sorprendió.

Y me entristecía que no me entristeciera. Pero tampoco me entristeció.

Ambas cosas llegarían más tarde, lo sabía, pero en ese momento solo pensé en ese pequeño rincón del escritorio de Rosa: vacío, con unas cuantas migas cubiertas de polvo, que podrían ser los restos de un trozo de pan rancio.

Bajé las escaleras para volver con Sawyer.

—Mamá —dijo Sawyer.

—¿Qué quieres, cariño? ¿Te encuentras bien?

—Mamá —dijo Sawyer—. Mira.

Miré a Sawyer, vi que señalaba hacia arriba, y sin necesidad de mirar supe lo que quería enseñarme, pero miré de todos modos.

Mi retrato había desaparecido.

Los dos Sawyer seguían allí, pero yo no estaba. El taburete de la cocina estaba detrás de la barra, justo debajo de los retratos, y conservaba las huellas de dos pies. En la pared también quedaba una marca donde antes estaba el cuadro.

Entonces me sorprendí, y también me entristecí; me dejé caer sobre una silla, apoyé la cabeza encima de una mesa y me puse a gritar, porque Rosa me había dejado, a pesar de que me quería, se había llevado la piedra para decirme que no pensaba volver, pero también se había llevado mi retrato para decirme que no era de mí de quien huía, sino de Galatia y de ese algo que Rosa llevaba dentro, de lo que la había traído hasta aquí y ahora la obligaba a marcharse, y lloré y lloré, porque Rosa era mi segunda oportunidad y nadie tiene una tercera. Sawyer se acercó, me puso una mano en la espalda y susurró ¿Mamá?, pero seguí llorando, aunque contuve las ganas de apartar su mano. ¡Ay, Sawyer!, si pudiera culparte te culparía, y si pudiera liberarte también te liberaría, de mí, de Rosa, de tu padre y de Galatia, pero todos nos hemos ido, y lo que ves no son más que espectros de lo que un día fuimos, y tú, Sawyer, estás tan atrapado como todos nosotros, y quizá, tal vez, si tenemos suerte y tienes suerte, la ciudad que tú construyas será una ciudad hermosa, y todos podremos al fin volver a casa.

7.22

COLIN

Primero fui a casa.

Le pregunté a Rosa si podía hacer algo por ella, si quería que la llevara a algún sitio, pero dijo que no, que no necesitaba nada, y cuando le puse una mano en el hombro con la intención de llevarla al Range Rover, se escabulló como un ratón a la vista de un gato y salió corriendo en dirección contraria, huyendo del coche, de mí, de Galatia. Y esta vez dejé que se fuera.

De camino pasé junto a la casa de Myra. Pasé por el lugar donde Lucy fue secuestrada el invierno pasado, pero intenté no pensar en ello. Me fijé en la morera y, por primera vez, vi una cinta amarilla que alguien, probablemente Myra, había atado al tronco del árbol; la cinta estaba deshilachada y desvaída y apenas resultaba visible entre la densa capa de hojas y moras rojas y negras y el brillante follaje de una yedra trepadora, y me asombró no haber reparado antes en ella. La casa de Myra se encontraba a menos de cien metros del árbol —me di cuenta entonces de lo cerca de casa que había estado Lucy— y Myra estaba en el porche agarrada a una de las columnas que soportaban el peso del tejado. Miraba fijamente hacia el pueblo. Eché un vistazo por el retrovisor lateral y vi la columna de humo que ascendía en espiral desde el centro de Galatia, luego miré a Myra y vi que se balanceaba ligeramente sobre sus pies tullidos, como la columna de humo a mis espaldas, como una cobra o un remolino o una brizna de hierba. Myra se balanceaba como un animal o un objeto inanimado, y tuve que resistir el impulso de detenerme y saludarla, o de detenerme y dispararle como había disparado a Charlene.

Cuando llegué a casa, las lascas de obsidiana negra salpicaron la fachada de caliza amarilla al detener el coche. Subí directamente a la cúpula de Justin. Empecé a llamarlo mientras subía las escaleras, no porque pensara que pudiera responderme, ni siquiera salir a mi encuentro, sino porque no quería irrumpir inesperadamente y asustarlo. Quería que supiera que era yo.

Lo vi de pie en el centro de la cúpula cuando llegué al final de la escalera de piedra. Había abierto la puerta al oírme llegar; me detuve un momento en el rellano, porque no deseaba violar un espacio que para él era sagrado y al mismo tiempo porque no sabía bien cómo actuar.

—Justin —dije. Y me detuve. Quería saber cuál era su verdadero nombre, usarlo siquiera una vez.

Justin tenía los pies juntos y se balanceaba ligeramente sobre los talones. La ventana situada tras de él miraba hacia Kenosha. La ciudad no se veía, pero yo sabía que estaba allí.

Y entonces tomé una decisión.

—John —dije, y avancé un paso—. Lucy —dije, y guardé silencio—. Creo que Lucy está en Kenosha.

No me atrevería a jurarlo, pero me pareció que Justin se estremeció un poco al oír el nombre de Lucy y al oír el nombre de John. La luz de la ventana me daba directamente en los ojos. Justin volvió a temblar ligeramente.

—Me voy a buscarla —dije—. Solo quería que lo supieras.

Esta vez estoy seguro de que Justin no se movió.

—Escucha, la encuentre o no, en cuanto vuelva nos marcharemos de aquí. Se acabó, ¿lo entiendes? Se acabó. Nos vamos a casa.

Se quedó mirándome.

Vi que tenía los puños apretados. Me pregunté si era un acto consciente o espontáneo.

—Deberías ir haciendo las maletas —añadí rápidamente—, porque en cuanto vuelva nos marcharemos. ¡Joder! Siento mucho que las cosas hayan terminado así. Yo... adiós Justin. Volveré lo antes posible.

7.23

NETTIE FERGUSON

—Cierra esa puñetera puerta —le dijo el agente Brown a Nettie Ferguson—, y por el amor de Dios deja en paz el teléfono. Siéntate y, por una vez en la vida, cierra la boca.

Nettie Ferguson miró un momento al agente Brown con expresión ausente; luego hizo lo que se le pedía.

—¿Se han ido? —preguntó el agente Brown un momento después.

Nettie Ferguson no respondió.

—Mando central a Nettie. Nettie, te estoy hablando. ¿Se han ido?

Nettie Ferguson sollozó:

—Me has dicho que cierre la boca.

—Ahora te estoy diciendo que hables.

—Lo que iba a decir es que este día me recuerda a ese otro en Kenosha. ¡Dios mío! ¡Han pasado ya más de veinte años...!

—¡Nettie! ¿Se han ido?

—Se han ido —dijo Nettie. Se quedó un rato en silencio y luego se aventuró a decir—: ¿Hacia el norte?

—A casa de Rosemary Krebs.
—Hacia el norte.
El agente Brown hizo una pausa, luego cogió el teléfono y se lo apoyó en las rodillas.
—Supongo que debería llamar a la señora Krebs.
Nettie Ferguson alzó la voz ligeramente.
—Dijo que no se la molestara bajo ningún concepto.
—No creo que pretenda celebrar una fiesta.
—Creo que dijo que el sol le había dado dolor de cabeza y que por nada del mundo debíamos turbar su paz y su descanso.
—Sí —dijo el agente Brown—. Seguro que dijo eso.
—...
—¿Dices que iban hacia el norte?
—Al norte —dijo Nettie Ferguson, señalando con el brazo.
—Pueden ir a cualquier parte.
El agente Brown cogió el teléfono y volvió a dejarlo encima de la mesa. Nada más apoyarlo, el teléfono lanzó un breve pitido que vibró en el silencio de la habitación.
Nettie Ferguson sorbió con la nariz. Al ver que el agente Brown no reaccionaba, dijo:
—¿Alergias?
El agente Brown tamborileaba con los dedos sobre la mesa, mirando al vacío.
Nettie Ferguson volvió a sorber con la nariz, luego se la limpió con un nudillo hinchado.
—El tejado lleva toda la semana cubierto de polen.
El agente Brown seguía tamborileando con los dedos.
—A mí me gusta el Clor-Trimeton, pero en el IGA de Vera no les quedaba, así que tuve que comprar ese Sudafed Plus para la fiebre del heno, que no es igual de bueno. Al menos para mí. —Volvió a sorber con fuerza, pero como el agente Brown seguía sin reaccionar, Nettie Ferguson dijo:
—Nunca pensé que presenciaría este día.
El agente Brown seguía tamborileando con los dedos.
—Verás —dijo Nettie Ferguson—, fue más o menos por la misma época del año, ¿verdad? Sí, claro. Quiero decir que el Día de los Fundadores aquí se celebra uno o dos meses después del día del incendio. No recuerdo la fecha exacta; ni siquiera estoy segura de si fue en mayo o en junio. Lo que sí recuerdo es que hacía un calor de mil demonios. Un calor de mil demonios, te lo aseguro. A veces me parecía que iba a arderme el pelo, y ya sabes que fue un milagro que no muriese más gente. Si no recuerdo mal, tú no estabas allí; creo recordar que Rosemary Krebs te había enviado a un recado en Bigger Hill ese día y,

¿qué estaba diciendo?, ¡ah, sí!, yo se lo comenté a ella, porque nos encontramos en las afueras del pueblo, me incliné, claro está, no hace falta que lo diga, y le dije: Es un milagro que no haya muerto más gente. Para entonces ya se sabía que la mayoría de la gente se había salvado, gracias a Dios. ¿Y sabes lo que me contestó? ¿Lo sabes? ¡Cómo ibas a saberlo! Tú no estabas allí, y aunque hubieras estado estarías con los hombres, apagando el fuego, por eso te lo cuento. Rosemary Krebs dijo: He observado que los que moran en esta parte del mundo son por lo general lacónicos. Te juro que esas fueron exactamente sus palabras: Que los que moran en esta parte del mundo son por lo general lacónicos, dijo. Y luego dijo que cuando alguien enciende fuego debajo de su... perdona pero ella fue la primera que lo dijo... debajo de su culo, no tiene más remedio que salir corriendo. ¿Te das cuenta? ¿Has oído en tu vida una cosa igual? ¿Cómo es posible que cuando uno emplea un lenguaje soez sea el otro quien le haga sentirse grosero? De todos modos, eso me dio que pensar. Lo que quiero decir es que me asombró. Me pregunté si éramos gente tranquila o si en realidad éramos un puñado de entrometidos pero no lo admitíamos. Quiero decir que cuando ocurre algo como lo que ha ocurrido hoy, o como lo que ocurrió aquel día, a uno le da que pensar.

Nettie Ferguson se detuvo para tomar aliento.

El agente Brown seguía tamborileando con los dedos.

—¿Eustace?

El agente Brown seguía tamborileando con los dedos.

—¿Eustace?

El agente Brown seguía mirando al vacío y, cuando al fin abrió la boca, a Nettie Ferguson casi le da un ataque.

—¿Decías algo, Nettie?

7.24

ERIC JOHNSON

Ahora estamos en un campo de piedra amarilla.

El campo se encuentra fuera del pueblo.

Algo alejado.

Otra cosa que me prometieron el tío Sawyer y la tía Rosa fue que podríamos celebrar mi cumpleaños en el centro del pueblo, con los sauces, el molino y el estanque de peces de colores, y esa tierra que siempre está húmeda y esponjosa, cubierta de hierba verde, pero mientras el tío Sawyer nos lleva a todos al coche me dice: «Hoy habrá mucha gente allí. Cora me ha dicho que el reverendo Abraham tiene una reunión con las Damas de la iglesia y algunos de los ancianos». Cuando le señalo que el parque está completamente vacío el tío Sawyer se limita a sacudir la cabeza. «Empieza a la una. Me lo ha dicho Cora.» No digo nada, aunque ya es la una y cuarto. La tía Cora lleva la tarta sobre el regazo y mira por la ventanilla tan fijamente mientras pasamos por la zona nueva del pueblo que cualquiera pensaría que en la vida había visto gente blanca. Creo que no me sentiría tan decepcionado si el tío Sawyer y la tía Cora no hubieran seguido adelante y no hubieran roto la primera promesa que me han hecho, la promesa de la fiesta, pero así son las cosas: en cuanto depositas la menor confianza en alguien, estás expuesto a su traición.

Me siento en el asiento trasero y veo que mi madre revuelve en la cesta de la merienda que ocupa el espacio entre nosotros. «¿Qué lleváis en esta enorme cesta?», dice mi madre, apartando sándwiches envueltos y recipientes de plástico, hasta que encuentra lo que busca: una pequeña bolsa marrón que contiene la forma ligeramente convexa de una botella de licor achatada. Mi madre me mira, me hace un guiño, palpa la botella y vuelve a dejarla en la cesta, saciada momentáneamente con el vaso que acaba de beberse y la promesa de seguir bebiendo. Cierra la cesta, se acomoda en el asiento y dice: «¡Tiene una pinta espléndida, Coretta! Parece que nos has preparado una comida de primera».

El tío Sawyer llama «el interior» al lugar donde estamos en ese momento. Me refiero a ese campo, no a Kansas, ni a Galatia. En realidad el campo forma parte de las tierras de los Deacon y creo que ahora pertenece a la anciana Bea, pero está bastante alejado, en mitad de la nada. La cueva de las Piedras Ventrales se encuentra varios kilómetros más cerca del pueblo; incluso el arca de Noah está más cerca; casi estamos en territorio de Kenosha o de lo que antiguamente era Kenosha. Los campos no son cultivables en esta zona. El terreno es irregular y está salpicado de depósitos de caliza, donde se abrieron las canteras para construir la casa de caliza. Toda la piedra útil se extrajo hace mucho tiempo; la zona es ahora un caos de fragmentos que te cortan los tobillos si no te andas con cuidado, si no prestas atención, las aristas de la piedra te destrozan los tobillos, y hay también una especie de fosos cuadrados, muy profundos, que se hunden en la tierra, algunos llenos de agua, como pozas sin fondo, y otros completamente secos, y no me preguntéis por qué, pues no lo sé, aunque lo cierto es que por aquí nunca se ven animales más grandes que una serpiente de cascabel, aparte de mi tío Sawyer, a quien siempre le ha gustado mucho este sitio. Alguna vez le he oído hablar a la amiga de Cora, a Webbie Greeving, a la hija del reverendo Abraham, la que ahora está en la universidad, de «belleza dura», para referirse al atractivo que las Grandes Llanuras podían tener para la gente que decidió establecerse aquí. Siempre me ha gustado la señorita Webbie. Creo que se refería exactamente a la cantera de caliza abandonada: a mí me recuerda mucho a la superficie de la luna, con la diferencia de que aquí hace mucho más calor, y la visión de esa larga hilera de humo y ceniza sobre el horizonte me da escalofríos. Yo prefería sentarme a la sombra de un árbol y acompañar los sándwiches de pollo asado que ha preparado Cora con un poco de agua fresca del pozo del parque. Pero supongo que el tío Sawyer no quiere que lo molesten. Supongo que piensa que de este modo las cosas son más fáciles para mí, o tal vez para él.

Hay ensalada de patata además de sándwiches de pollo, y rebanadas de melón sin pepitas, y me parece que tardamos una eternidad en comer la tarta. Antes de tomarla, la tía Cora saca una cajita de velas, y me resulta muy raro, porque hace mucho viento; pero ella clava las trece velas en la tarta y una de más, para seguir creciendo, y las enciende con un mechero que se saca como por arte de magia de otro bolsillo, y las velas prenden y arden al viento, como minúsculas bolitas de luz bajo el brillante y enorme sol. Me pregunto por qué se consumen con tanta facilidad: son velas de broma, de esas que no se apagan y si por casualidad se apagan vuelven a encenderse ellas solas. Soplo una vez, con mucha fuerza, y todas se apagan, algunas incluso se doblan sobre el baño de azúcar que cubre la tarta, pero al momento vuelven a encenderse produciendo un ligero chispazo, y parpadean a causa del viento y sueltan pequeñas bolitas de cera rosa, azul y amarilla sobre mi tarta de cumpleaños. Miro a la tía Cora, al tío Sawyer. Los dos sonríen maliciosamente y les brilla la frente porque han ayudado a mi madre a pulirse una botella de aguardiente. Miro a mi madre. Sostiene un vaso con las dos manos, justo por encima de su colgante de oro y justo por debajo de la nariz. Tiene los ojos cerrados, las aletas de la nariz abiertas y temblorosas y el pecho le sube y le baja con fuerza al respirar. Vuelvo a mirar al tío Sawyer y a la tía Cora, y luego, una por una, quito todas las velas de la tarta y las tiro sobre las rocas. Después agarro la tarta con las dos manos y arranco más o menos la mitad, y mientras me alejo de los mayores, hundo la cara entre las manos y me meto en la boca un enorme pedazo de tarta. La tarta es de chocolate. La tía Cora quería prepararme comida de ángel, pero mi madre se rió y dijo que yo no era un ángel y que debía preparar comida de diablo; mi madre no sabía que yo estaba en la habitación de al lado, o tal vez sí lo sabía, y el caso es que dijo: Hazle al chico algo que sea lo más negro posible, pues sea cual sea su color por fuera, por dentro es tan negro como el mismísimo diablo.

7.25

COLIN

Me fui andando.

Por distintas razones. Por un lado quería dejar el coche en casa. Para Justin. Por si acaso.

Por otro lado había visto los fragmentos de Lucy que su secuestrador nos había enviado: su vestido, su pelo, las fotografías de su cuerpo magullado, las puntas de sus dedos... No tenía prisa por ver lo que quedaba de ella.

Y era un hermoso día.

El sol teñía de anaranjado el cielo sin nubes; la tierra cubierta de rastrojos era su espejo.

En realidad fui corriendo. Bueno, haciendo *jogging*. Puede que la palabra más adecuada sea «trotando». Me concentré en el movimiento, para no pensar en nada ni en nadie más. No volaba, ni me arrastraba, ni me deslizaba, ni nadaba. Pensaba que un hombre solo tenía unas cuantas posibilidades para recorrer su camino.

En un momento dado me detuve. Fue en la colina desde la que, según me había dicho Rosemary Krebs, se podía ver al mismo tiempo la aguja de la iglesia de Abraham Greeving y el silo de Kenosha, como la cresta de una ola. Me detuve cuando llegué a la cima de esa colina porque a lo lejos vi la nube gris que indicaba la situación de Kenosha y su fuego distante. A pocos cientos de metros vislumbré la pequeña fortaleza que rodeaba la cueva, asomando sobre la tierra como la afilada punta de un lápiz; un par de kilómetros más allá se encontraban las cenizas del arca de Noah Deacon, y puede que a otros seis kilómetros estuviera Kenosha. A dos kilómetros detrás de mí —no me di la vuelta para mirar, por miedo a que hubiera desaparecido— se alzaba la casa de caliza, y detrás de ella Galatia, y detrás de todo ello se elevaba el risco pelado, pero tampoco me volví para mirar si el fuego se había extinguido o si se había propagado sin control, si la pálida cresta del risco aparecía cubierta de rastrojos grises y escupía niños entre las llamas.

Eché a andar, a trotar, a correr, y al fin llegué.

Un círculo irregular señalaba la antigua frontera del fuego como la línea de la marea, y la hierba que crecía en el interior del círculo era más densa y verde que la de fuera, pero todo lo demás estaba en ruinas. El asfalto que antiguamente se extendía formando una limpia retícula, se había derretido y endurecido formando caprichosos remolinos y charcos, y los cimientos de las casas, de ladrillo, hormigón y piedra, asomaban como esqueletos desde antiguos pozos de alquitrán. La escena resultaba a un tiempo prehistórica y postapocalíptica, y tuve que esforzarme por recordar que Kenosha se había incendiado hacía solo un cuarto de siglo y que la naturaleza no había hecho sino empezar a borrar todo rastro de la ciudad. Corrientes de polvo y plantas rodadoras se amontonaban en el costado oeste de algo que sobresalía más de treinta centímetros del suelo, y era fácil adivinar que la tierra acabaría sepultando a la ciudad por completo, tal como había sepultado a otras muchas ciudades a lo largo de la historia.

La búsqueda no fue difícil. En realidad solo había un lugar donde que buscar, y este se hallaba entre el laberinto de paredes de ladrillo marrón que señalaban el lugar antiguamente ocupado por el centro de la ciudad. Un banco, me había dicho Myra, un supermercado y la escuela. Al acercarme vi que las paredes eran cáscaras huecas: los restos de las estructuras que en su día albergaron quedaron reducidos, tras el paso de las excavadoras, a un único montón que se alzaba en el extremo de lo que antiguamente debió de ser la escuela. La suciedad se había acumulado sobre la pila de cascotes, y entre ellos crecían hierbajos, hiedra y árboles raquíticos y retorcidos, pero el montículo resultaba en conjunto tan frágil y al mismo tiempo tan inexpugnable que no era fácil decir si eran las raíces de las plantas las que lo mantenían en su sitio o si era la basura acumulada la que había atrapado a las plantas entre sus huecos. El montículo llamó mi atención y, a medida que me acercaba, me pareció que emergía de la tierra como una langosta que se despierta tras su período de hibernación. Pero en realidad no se parecía a eso.

¿A qué se parecía?

Se parecía a una piedra ventral. A una piedra ventral partida por la mitad y aplanada; o a una piedra ventral intacta y medio enterrada, y si hasta entonces no había sabido que había llegado a donde quería llegar, lo supe en cuanto pensé en la piedra y supe también por qué me equivoqué al suponer que Lucy estaba escondida en la cueva de las Piedras Ventrales. Lucy no estaba en la cueva de las Piedras Ventrales. Lucy estaba dentro de una piedra.

Me acerqué al montículo y lo rodeé despacio. Al principio me pareció sólido, pero enseguida advertí media docena de agujeros parcialmente camuflados. La sombra que proyectaba el tablero carbonizado de una canasta de baloncesto era en realidad el vacío espacio de un túnel; una de las puertas de un coche daba acceso a otro hueco, mientras que la otra se adentraba en un agujero oscuro; un enorme montón de telas descoloridas cubría otra entrada, y así sucesivamente. La hierba estaba pisoteada en cada uno de los accesos, y en una zona pelada, junto a la boca de una alcantarilla de acero galvanizado, encontré huellas de pisadas y reconocí aquellos pies, su tamaño y la húmeda marca que dejaron en la tierra junto a la escalera que conducía hasta la cúpula.

La alcantarilla era grande, de aproximadamente un metro de diámetro; me puse a cuatro patas y entré reptando en el sofocante túnel. Durante unos segundos la luz que entraba a mis espaldas proyectó mi sombra por delante, pero la oscuridad no tardó en envolverlo todo, y di varias veces con la cabeza contra las irregulares paredes de la alcantarilla. Poco después salí del túnel; el aire era más fresco y supe que había llegado hasta un espacio abierto. Una leve brisa me erizó el vello de los brazos, las piernas y el pecho. Me levanté despacio, cubriéndome la cabeza con una mano para protegerla de un obstáculo en realidad inexistente. La brisa me acarició la piel pegajosa. Continué caminando con los brazos extendidos hacia delante, las palmas vueltas hacia arriba, y empecé a percibir ocasionalmente un lejano resplandor. La fortaleza no era tan inexpugnable a fin de cuentas, me dije. No era una fortaleza, ni siquiera una piedra ventral: no era más que un montón de mierda antigua. Poco a poco recuperé la visión; el negro se fue aclarando y en las zonas más oscuras surgieron formas y sombras. Avanzaba despacio, con dificultad. Pisaba sobre algo que crujía y rechinaba, y supe que era inútil intentar avanzar con sigilo. Incluso se me ocurrió gritar, pero algo me lo impidió. Bastaba con el ruido de mis pasos.

Era imposible decir cuánto tiempo llevaba andando o cuánta distancia había recorrido. Tenía la sensación de que habían pasado horas y había recorrido muchos kilómetros. Estaba convencido de encontrarme atrapado en una especie de laberinto que daba vueltas y vueltas alrededor del montículo, pero no sabía si avanzaba en espiral, adentrándome cada vez más, o si simplemente rodeaba su perímetro. El camino se bifurcaba tantas veces que ya había perdido la cuenta; la primera vez giré a la izquierda, porque me pareció que esa sería la vía para acceder a las profundidades, y en cada nueva bifurcación volví a girar a la izquierda. El aire parecía más caliente, pero quizá era una sensación producida por el ejercicio. Sin embargo, acabé comprendiendo que no había posibilidad de regresar, pues no tenía ni idea de cuál era el camino de regreso, y seguí andando, paso a paso, paso a paso.

Y de pronto supe que había llegado.

Las irregulares paredes del túnel comenzaron a alejarse de las puntas de mis dedos, y una vez más sentí que el espacio se ensanchaba alrededor. No me había dado cuenta de que mi propio aliento resonaba en mis oídos hasta que el eco se extinguió; tampoco había notado que la tenue diferencia entre forma y sombra también había desaparecido hacía tiempo y lo cierto es que no veía nada. Di un paso más y sentí que algo ligero y duro rebotaba al chocar contra mi pie, produciendo un sonido hueco y metálico. Por alguna razón supe de inmediato que lo que acababa de oír era el ruido de una lata vacía al chocar contra otra.

Me detuve.

Me di la vuelta despacio, buscando un mínimo resplandor, pero no vi nada.

Entonces percibí un olor pestilente. Comprendí que llevaba oliéndolo un buen rato, pero fue entonces cuando invadió por completo mi olfato, y sentí náuseas. Olía a mierda, a pis, a podredumbre y a carne no solo sucia, sino en descomposición, un olor que solo había sentido en los suburbios de algunas ciudades de la India y en las chabolas de cartón de Tompkins Square Park, pero, en el espacio cerrado del montículo, el olor no solo resultaba repugnante y nauseabundo, sino verdaderamente terrorífico, y más que de vomitar tuve ganas de salir corriendo. Pero estaba perdido en la oscuridad, y la idea de ir adelante o atrás, a derecha o izquierda parecía inútil además de absurda, de manera que me quedé muy quieto, sintiendo arcadas, y antes de que pudiera tomar una decisión, una bombilla se encendió inesperadamente. Tuve tiempo de ver las abombadas paredes de una cueva, un suelo irregular cubierto de algo que instintivamente reconocí como el reverso negro y mullido de una moqueta, una silla desvencijada, un montón de almohadas y sábanas mugrientas y otro bulto que al principio no logré identificar: era Lucy. Me sentí como si caminara sobre la cuerda floja, poniendo un pie justo delante del otro y con los brazos extendidos para guardar el equilibrio, pero no llegué a ver la bombilla ni quien la había encendido, pero entonces algo me golpeó en la cabeza y pensé en Jewel, en Jewel y en el hombre al que yo había llamado John, y la estancia desapareció de nuevo, y yo con ella.

7.26

WADE

Después de que Colin se marchara volví a invocar el bendito sueño. Casi podría decir que fue el sueño quien me invocó a mí, o que ambos nos invocamos mutuamente. Podría describirlo con diversas y pintorescas expresiones, pero la única verdad es que después de que Colin y yo nos hubiéramos intercambiado esas breves palabras, volví a cerrar los ojos y no los abrí hasta que me convencí de que se había marchado. Cuando al fin estuve seguro, abrí los ojos, y allí estaba yo: Wade Painter, el mayor imbécil que haya pisado jamás la tierra, en un pueblo de imbéciles. Colin se había marchado, claro está, y Divine, pero tardé un rato en darme cuenta de que el retrovisor de Divine también había desaparecido; me esforcé por hallar en mi resacosa y cargada cabeza el recuerdo de haberlo visto la primera vez que abrí los ojos, pero no recordé nada, y eso me pareció la mayor pérdida del día. Ese objeto pequeño e inocuo al que yo deseaba culpar de la confusión del día se había esfumado, y entonces no quedó más que la confusión, desnuda, sin adornos ni paliativos, y decidí que el único culpable era yo. Podría decirse que Colin tenía alguna responsabilidad en lo ocurrido, o incluso Divine, pero al final —o tal vez debería decir, al principio— una sola persona le había hablado a Colin de la casa de caliza, y esa persona era yo. La verdad es que quise que Colin se instalase en el pueblo porque me cayó mal nada más conocerlo, y pensé que si algo podía derrotarlo sería este pueblo, y estaba en lo cierto, pero no fui capaz de predecir la encarnizada batalla que estallaría antes de la caída de Colin. Y quise que se viniera aquí y que trajera a Justin.

Me levanté. Del sofá, quiero decir. Me levanté y me marché. Dejé la casa revuelta, el whisky tirado por el suelo y todo lo demás. ¡Por qué andarse con remilgos!: no limpié el whisky ni la mierda que había en el suelo y busqué mis zapatos, pero no pude encontrarlos; salí de la habitación y cerré la puerta. Entonces me pareció, como me parece ahora, que aunque hubiera intentado limpiar y adecentar la casa habría tenido que pasarme la vida frotando, así que cerré la puerta, como ya he dicho, y me fui descalzo hasta mi estudio.

¿A qué otro sitio podía ir? No tenía hambre, no estaba cansado, y aún había buena luz.

En el suelo del vestíbulo de la puerta trasera encontré un paquete de tabaco de Divine, con una caja de cerillas sujeta bajo el envoltorio de celofán; lo cogí y me lo guardé en un bolsillo de los pantalones.

Una vez en el estudio vagué de puerta en puerta, de habitación en habitación, de suelo en suelo, pero mis ojos no veían los cuadros inacabados y a la espera de que yo los terminase; en lugar de eso, veía los fantasmas de mesas, sillas, camas, toallas de baño, cazuelas, sartenes, platos y alfombras, y me reí al pensar que en algún momento yo les había arrebatado aquella casa a mis padres, a mi familia y a mi pasado.

Al final, inevitablemente, llegué hasta la puerta de la habitación de Justin. Sentí el paquete de cigarrillos de Divine, frío y resbaladizo en mi mano, mientras rebuscaba en el bolsillo la llave de aquella puerta, luego entré, me encontré en el dormitorio de mi infancia y tiré al suelo los cigarrillos, la llave y un par de monedas; me quedé un buen rato mirando el desorden hasta que la habitación fue reafirmando su presencia gradualmente, y todas las demás cosas, todos los demás pensamientos, fueron desalojados de mi mente.

De todos los retratos de Divine ya solo se veía uno. Un apunte, un boceto de su cara sonriente con los ojos muy grandes. Todos los demás habían quedado sepultados bajo fragmentos del cuerpo de Justin.

Un cuaderno y un carboncillo parecían esperarme en el suelo.

Miré alrededor buscando algo que dibujar. Supongo que buscaba a Justin, o a Divine, o a mí mismo, pero ninguno de nosotros estaba allí. Ninguno de nosotros resultaba visible; ninguno de nosotros seguía en la habitación, y lo único que veía eran líneas negras sobre el papel blanco y las cosas que se me habían caído del bolsillo: una llave, un paquete de tabaco, un par de monedas, y una voz que debía de ser la de Yonah —o acaso la de Justin— susurrando: *Nos hemos ido. No es para ti.*

Tenía el cuaderno en una mano y el lápiz en la otra; me senté en el centro de la habitación y, como Justin, cerré los ojos.

Una de las cosas que aprendes cuando dibujas del natural es que la imagen no sale de la mano sino del ojo, por eso la mano debe seguir al ojo, y no al revés; y lo primero que aprendes cuando asistes a un buen curso de dibujo del natural es a dibujar un objeto, normalmente tu propia mano, sin mirar el dibujo. El resultado, indefectiblemente, es un caos, un mapa de líneas confusas, pero por alguna razón que nunca he llegado a entender del todo, la lección es la mentira que demuestra la verdad de la superioridad del ojo; jamás lo he olvidado, he repetido muchas veces el mismo ejercicio a lo largo de mi vida y en un cajón del piso de abajo guardo los restos de docenas de garabatos; lo único que puedo decir al respecto es que todos son iguales.

Una vez a Yonah le ofrecieron varios miles de dólares por esos apuntes.

Ya había recibido el cheque, y lo sorprendí envolviendo los dibujos; y como no estaba seguro de si romper el cheque o romper los bocetos, decidí romper las dos cosas.

Tenía los ojos cerrados.

En aquella habitación no me dibujaba a mí mismo, sino que dibujaba a Justin, y como Justin no estaba, yo cerraba los ojos.

Mi primer impulso fue manchar el papel de negro por completo, porque eso era lo único que veía cuando intentaba evocar la imagen de Justin; luego pensé que debía dejar el papel en blanco, porque luego el vacío sustituyó a la negrura y parecía aproximarse mucho más a Justin que la negrura, pero al final el recuerdo de lo que yo creía que era su rostro volvió a mi mente, y empecé a dibujar.

No sé cuánto tiempo estuve dibujando, pero cuando abrí los ojos la habitación estaba a oscuras. La llave, el paquete de tabaco y las monedas que había tirado al suelo emitían un débil resplandor, pero la forma de lo que había dibujado me resultaba invisible.

La luz llegaba de lejos, de Galatea, que estaba ardiendo; y yo necesitaba más luz.

Lo dije en voz alta. Necesito más luz, dije, y la voz que pronunció estas palabras era la misma que antes había dicho: *Nos hemos ido. No es para ti.*

Me agaché para coger los cigarrillos y la caja de cerillas metida en el paquete.

Encendí una cerilla.

Me quedé un rato mirando el dibujo que había hecho, y todo cuanto puedo decir, todo cuanto deseo decir es esto:

Parecía mi mano.

Luego lancé la cerilla sobre el cuaderno.

La cerilla chisporroteó antes de apagarse; luego, después de mirar a las llamas en el horizonte, encendí otra cerilla y esta vez la acerqué hasta el borde del papel y la sostuve allí hasta que una llama empezó a lamerlo como la lengua de un perro lame un charco de leche derramada en el suelo; luego dejé el papel en llamas en el suelo sobre el único dibujo que quedaba de Divine y me marché de allí, salí de la casa.

De la casa de mis padres.

El viento soplaba de oeste a este, y, aún descalzo, me dirigí hacia el oeste por el campo cubierto de rastrojos; no me volví para mirar si lo había conseguido o no, pues para entonces ya había perdido la medida del éxito o del fracaso. El aire olía a polvo, y el polvo, debo decirlo, no huele igual que el humo, pero a mí me olía a humo.

7.27

AGENTE BROWN

Sonó el teléfono.

Nettie Ferguson hizo ademán de responder, pero el agente Brown le aconsejó no hacerlo, indicando con un gesto que si lo hacía le cortaría el pescuezo.

El agente Brown dejó que sonara siete veces antes de responder. Al tercer timbre, Nettie Ferguson tuvo que sentarse encima de las manos para no coger el auricular, y al séptimo, empezó a temblar definitivamente.

Entonces el agente Brown descolgó el teléfono.

—Sheriff Brown.

La voz que llegaba del otro extremo de la línea sonó ligeramente bronca. El agente Brown pensó al instante que quien llamaba intentaba disimular su verdadera voz, aunque lo cierto es que parecía como si quien hablaba sencillamente acabara de despertarse.

—Lucy Robinson está en Kenosha —fue cuanto dijo la voz, y la línea se cortó.

7.28

ERIC JOHNSON

Pero, como ya he dicho, es imposible escapar. Encuentro una poza pequeña, de unos tres metros de profundidad; un fino charco en forma de triángulo cubre el ángulo inferior de su base inclinada y una nube de mosquitos pulula sobre la espumosa superficie del agua; descendiendo, agarrándome a los agujeros practicados con taladros y cinceles. Pero no puedo huir. Abajo hay una sombra. Abajo la temperatura desciende diez grados y los mosquitos se apartan del agua y empiezan a revolotear alrededor de mis brazos y mis piernas, como un millar de lunas diminutas, y sobre un pequeño saliente, no mayor que mi pulgar, se acumula la tierra suficiente para que arraigue un brote de trigo, mientras desde abajo me llegan las voces de mi madre y del tío Sawyer y de la tía Cora. Un curioso truco acústico transporta sus voces hasta donde estoy yo, como si hubiera descolgado un teléfono supletorio mientras ellos hablan. «Marsha —dice la tía Cora—, no pensarás dejarle que se quede ahí abajo, ¿verdad? Podría pasarle algo.» «El chico es grande y gordo, pero no es torpe —dice mi madre—, grande, gordo y blanco, pero trepa a los árboles como un mono.» Y la tía Cora dice: «¿Cómo puedes habar así de tu propio hijo…?». «Bah, cállate —le interrumpe mi madre—. Es mi hijo, y de nada sirve engañarse pensando que es distinto de lo que es.» «De lo que parece —dice la tía Cora—, no de lo que es.» «Da lo mismo», dice mi madre. Hay entonces un breve silencio antes de que el tío Sawyer hable: «¿Qué tal van las cosas en la fábrica?». Y mi madre dice: «Pero ¡en qué mundo vives!, hace tres semanas que no trabajo allí. Me han despedido. —Y tras una pausa añade—: Ha habido recortes». Todo eso es mentira, por supuesto, y todo el mundo lo sabe —la única verdad es que mi madre ha ido a trabajar borracha demasiadas veces–, pero el tío Sawyer y la tía Cora se limitan a decir: «Es una pena» y «Seguro que te readmitirán enseguida». «Bueno –dice mi madre, y casi la oigo sorber la nariz–, dame un poco más de esa bebida. ¿Cómo dices que se llama?» «Peppermint», dice el tío Sawyer, y mi madre repite el nombre y luego se echa a reír y dice: «Dame un poco más de peppermint».

Me hace gracia oír hablar a mi madre y al tío Sawyer sin verlos. Otra historia familiar: el verdadero nombre del tío Sawyer es Marshal para mi madre, que se llama Marsha, y según la leyenda él es el hermano gemelo de mi madre. Digo según la leyenda porque al verlos nadie lo sospecharía, quiero decir que son hermanos. El tío Sawyer no es gran cosa; no es que sea bajito, pero su cuerpo solo ocupa el espacio que necesita, y tiene la piel tan tensa que no es que se pueda decir que el tío Sawyer esté delgado sino que resulta imposible imaginar que pueda engordar. Una vez, después de haber estado sembrando con Kendall Hendricks toda la noche –Kendall es muy supersticioso sobre el momento de sembrar–, yo pasé por su casa muy temprano y me encontré al tío Sawyer dormido como un tronco. Fue en abril, creo, o en mayo, pero hacía bastante calor, y el tío Sawyer estaba durmiendo encima de las sábanas. La tía Cora había ido al IGA a comprar sirope de arce para hacerme tortitas, y el tío Sawyer solo llevaba puestos unos calzoncillos. Hay una cosa en la que el tío Sawyer sí se parece a mi madre: en el color de la piel, oscura como la madera de nogal de la cama en la que duerme con la tía Cora y... bueno, yo no tenía más de cuatro o cinco años, pero no pude aguantar las ganas de tocar esa hermosa piel marrón que tenían el tío Sawyer y mi madre y mi abuelito, que aún vivía con todos nosotros. Sentí la imperiosa necesidad de demostrarme a mí mismo que esa piel era real, que no era pintada, que no era una broma que me gastaban continuamente por no ser como ellos, por eso me acerqué a la cama de puntillas y apoyé la palma de la mano en la espalda del tío Sawyer. Hacía calor y él tenía la espalda cubierta por una fina capa de sudor y, entonces, ¡ajá!, pensé, está pintada, pero al quitar la mano vi que seguía igual, quiero decir mi mano, seguía siendo blanca, y la espalda del tío Sawyer también seguía igual, oscura como el chocolate; lo único que sentí fue el sudor de su piel, pero luego noté que el sudor se había secado donde yo le había puesto la mano y en su lugar había una zona de piel aún más oscura, con la forma de mi mano, y entonces volví a ponerla exactamente en el mismo sitio y luego puse la otra. Puse las manos sobre la cálida y resbaladiza piel de su espalda, y al principio las dejé quietas, pero luego empecé a frotar muy despacio, empecé a mover las manos arriba y abajo por la espalda del tío Sawyer y, como ya he dicho, tenía la piel tan tersa que me parecía como si estuviera pasando las manos por la tapicería de vinilo de su nuevo sofá; moví las manos arriba y abajo hasta que el sudor se secó y la piel del tío Sawyer pareció tornarse cada vez más oscura, más negra y brillante, y, al final, ya no me recordaba a la madera de nogal o al chocolate, sino a los pozos de alquitrán que había visto en algún libro, y mientras seguía moviendo las manos, imaginé que se hundían en el alquitrán de la piel del tío Sawyer, que se adentraban en su cuerpo y me arrastraban tras ellas, que me hundiría bajo su piel y saldría tan oscuro como él, igual de real, convertido en un hombre negro. Pero lo que pasó fue que el tío Sawyer —que tenía la cara vuelta hacia el otro lado y apoyada en la almohada— lanzó un pequeño suspiro que me desconcertó, y no supe si debía dejar de acariciarlo o si debía seguir, pero el tío Sawyer emitió otro sonido, un sonido como el que haces cuando pruebas el primer bocado de una tarta y compruebas que aún está tibia, recién hecha, y llena de sabores a crema y a azúcar moreno y a coco, y entonces la espalda del tío Sawyer se arqueó bajo mis manos, haciéndolas rozar la cinturilla del calzoncillo, incluso deslizarse un poco por debajo, y eso debería haberme convencido de su solidez, haberme demostrado la futilidad de mi empresa, pero seguí frotando y suplicando que me dejara penetrar en su secreto, hasta que la puerta se abrió y volvió a cerrarse en la habitación contigua, y al momento la voz de tía Cora me llamó: «¿Eric? Traigo el sirope para tus tortitas», y el tío Sawyer y yo nos quedamos helados: él se quedó tumbado, con la cara vuelta hacia otro lado, sin respirar, y yo me quedé en el sitio, con las manos apoyadas en sus riñones, y luego, deprisa pero sin hacer ruido, me di la vuelta para marcharme de allí, como si quisiera borrar lo que acababa de hacer, como si quisiera que pareciese que nunca hubiera ocurrido, y salí sigilosamente del dormitorio andando de espaldas, recorrí el pasillo andando de espaldas e incluso abrí la puerta del cuarto de baño con el culo; luego tiré de la cadena y salí justo cuando la tía Cora estaba sacando las tortitas del horno, donde las había conservado calientes mientras iba al supermercado, y los dos nos sentamos a desayunar, pero el tío Sawyer no se levantó hasta pasado el mediodía, aunque para entonces yo ya estaba en mi casa.

Pero estaba hablando de la voz del tío Sawyer. Quería decir que es idéntica a la de mi madre. Hace mucho tiempo yo estaba empeñado en lo siguiente: que la voz del tío Sawyer —Marshal de nacimiento; el mote, según me contó mi madre, se lo pusieron «porque siempre estaba jugando con la madera», y a ella le hacía mucha gracia— es idéntica a la de mi madre, lo que refuerza la idea de que realmente son gemelos, aunque mi madre sea un desastre y el tío Sawyer un hombre estupendo. No sé bien cómo expresarlo, aunque lo que quiero decir es esperanza; tengo la esperanza de que si él ha logrado ser una persona tan distinta de su hermana gemela —y también de su padre, que era un completo desastre; su madre había muerto mucho antes de que yo naciera— puede que yo también pueda cambiar, puede que un día me pase lo mismo que al patito feo que se convirtió en un hermoso cisne, y así no tendrán que alquitranarme, ni emplumarme, ni pintarme con el polvillo de hada de mi madre, porque el cambio se producirá dentro de mí.

Termino la tarta mientras los mosquitos me acribillan los brazos y las piernas. Luego salgo del agujero, me froto los ojos y el vientre y digo: «No me encuentro muy bien. Quiero irme a casa». Y el tío Sawyer dice: «Parece que alguien ha comido demasiada tarta». Y la tía Cora dice: «Ven aquí, deja que te lave la cara. Parece que te has metido en un charco de barro». Luego suelta una risita tonta, una risita de borracha, y después se tapa la boca con la mano y no dice nada más; en el silencio, mi madre lanza un lento y sonoro eructo. «Bueno, ¿es que no piensas abrir tu regalo?», me pregunta. Se me ha olvidado por completo, y al ver sus caras expectantes me siento obligado a adoptar un aire despectivo y a frotarme con las manos la cara sucia de tarta. Miro a la tía Cora, pongo la voz más burlona y desdeñosa que puedo y digo: «Ha sido tu tarta. Me ha sentado mal. Estaba mala». Luego me vuelvo hacia el tío Sawyer, clavo mis ojos en él y digo: «¡Guárdate esa mierda! No la quiero».

Nunca llegué a saber lo que había en la caja.

Cuando el tío Sawyer nos deja en casa, alguien ha escrito estas palabras sobre el polvo que cubre el televisor. *¿Cómo quedó tan solitaria la ciudad que estaba llena de gente?*

Mi madre se pasa el resto del día clavando otra vez las toallas en los marcos de las ventanas. Cuando termina ya es de noche y se mete en la cama.

Luego el piano empieza a sonar en el piso de arriba, y los tambores lo responden desde el sótano. Apago la tele, pero antes de irme a la cama vuelvo a leer: *¿Cómo quedó tan solitaria la ciudad que estaba llena de gente?*

No es ningún milagro que las tuberías se atasquen en el sótano o que los ratones correteen sobre las teclas de un viejo piano abandonado en el segundo piso de nuestra casa, pero no me preguntéis cómo ha llegado el piano hasta allí. Y por lo que respecta a las palabras escritas sobre el televisor, tengo que admitir que no pudo escribirlas nadie a quien yo conociera.

En el dormitorio, con las toallas clavadas en las ventanas y la puerta bien cerrada, hay tanto polvo y tanta oscuridad como siempre, y en la cama de al lado está el cuerpo de mi madre; cuando ha bebido mucho y está desnuda, me parece que su cuerpo es algo que le pertenece pero que no es realmente ella. Está sudando y roncando, estirada sobre la cama, y le sale un olor extraño por la boca y por el coño. Entonces, igual que hice un día con el tío Sawyer, empiezo a acariciar a mi madre, a frotar esa piel negra que bajo esta luz o esta ausencia de luz no muestra cambio alguno, pero sigo frotando con la esperanza de descubrir qué es lo que se oculta bajo tanta negrura, qué es lo que significa, y luego empiezo a frotarme a mí también, mis manos describen círculos cada vez más pequeños, y se me van cansando los brazos, hasta que al final giran solo sobre el centro de nuestros cuerpos, y allí sigo frotando, sigo apretando, sigo suplicando encontrar a mi madre en algún lugar, bajo mi piel, y si eso no puede ser, al menos encontrarme a mí mismo en algún lugar, dentro de mi madre.

Mañana Lucy Robinson me señalará con el dedo y gritará.

Mañana las afiladas llamas de las antorchas me quemarán los pies mientras permanezco colgado de los pulgares, pero me concentraré en el borboteo del agua del río Solomon y no sentiré el fuego, no sentiré el dolor en los pulgares mientras intento apartar a puntapiés las antorchas que me abrasan. Me concentraré en el sonido del río, y en su olor, el fresco olor del agua, y después, cuando se me haya roto el pulgar derecho, y luego el izquierdo, sentiré que el agua me envuelve al zambullirme en ella y la sentiré también dentro de mí, la sentiré correr por esos dos nuevos agujeros de mi cuerpo.

7.29

COLIN

Una bombilla colgaba del techo, sujeta a un grasiento cordón amarillo; de ella procedía la luz. La pantalla había sido arrancada y la luz de la bombilla desnuda era tan intensa que solo podía mirarla por el rabillo del ojo. El espacio iluminado por la bombilla no era ni habitación ni cueva; me pareció que un caprichoso vacío ocupaba el espacio donde antes había habido algo sólido, y resultaba imposible decir si el agujero se había hecho cuando las excavadoras amontonaron allí la basura o si había sido excavado con posterioridad. Todo lo que había en el suelo, las paredes y el techo de la habitación estaba quemado, roto y amontonado de tal manera que resultaba irreconocible. Las puntas de acero fundido de lo que podría haber sido un taburete de bar atravesaban parte de una pared; una hilera de tachuelas sobresalía del techo como las púas rotas de un gigantesco peine; vi los miembros de media docena de personas, estoy seguro; los restos carbonizados de varios maniquíes, pero no pude ver nada más. Todo lo demás era negro como la tinta y resultaba indistinguible, salvo yo, y Lucy Robinson, y el hombre que nos tenía prisioneros.

No soy capaz de describir a Lucy Robinson. No diré más que esto: aún no estaba muerta, aunque las únicas personas que yo había visto con el aspecto que ella presentaba eran los enfermos de sida de los hospitales de Nueva York, lo que equivale a decir que no parecía que Lucy pudiera seguir con vida por mucho tiempo.

Tampoco soy capaz de llamar Eric Johnson al hombre que nos retenía. Bueno, sabía que era él —¿quién si no podía tener esa piel, y esas manos, y quién podía tener tantas razones para odiar?–, pero la figura que se movía por la habitación no parecía humana. Sé que esto es un tópico, una expresión manida, pero no puedo decir otra cosa.

Eric Johnson me había atado las manos a una especie de poste que salía del suelo, y parece que estuvo allí hasta que abrí los ojos, porque en cuanto los abrí, agarró a Lucy por un tobillo con los cuatro dedos de una de sus manos y arrastró su cuerpo desnudo hasta situarlo en mi campo de visión. Solo la mostró un momento; luego, al ver que yo no apartaba los ojos de ella, cogió de un hueco de la pared algo que parecía un viejo mantel de plástico y cubrió con él el cuerpo de Lucy. Una de sus manos —o de lo que quedaba de ellas— asomaba bajo el mantel, y Eric le dio un puntapié para ocultarla. Lucy quedó convertida en un bulto que brotaba falsamente bajo flores derretidas como los relojes de Dalí, y el levísimo suspiro que salía de sus pulmones no parecía respiración, sino un objeto roto, algo que se ha quedado sin cuerda. Lucy no emitió el menor sonido en ningún momento, y nuestro raptor tampoco.

Eric me miró. Se puso en cuclillas, y de vez en cuando me daba un golpe en la cabeza con sus manos tullidas. Cuando acercó las manos a mis ojos, vi por primera vez las largas cicatrices que se extendían por sus antebrazos hasta la altura de los codos, en el lugar donde le habían arrancado la piel a tiras, y la pequeña esquirla ósea que asomaba en la mano izquierda, donde debería estar su pulgar; en la mano derecha tenía un hueco enrojecido y arrugado, tallado en la piel como una boca o un ano. La esquirla se movía nerviosamente, y me obligaba a mirarla, como si fuera el péndulo de un hipnotizador. Mientras la miraba me pareció que el hueso chocaba contra algo, aunque no sabía contra qué, y que la carne sonaba como cuando se desgarra un trapo húmedo.

Me golpeó la cara con esas manos, con esos brazos, con ese cuerpo; a veces me abofeteaba y luego retrocedía como para darme un puñetazo, pero se daba la vuelta y dirigía sus golpes contra el cuerpo de Lucy Robinson, que parecía absorber el impacto como una almohada de plumas.

Noté, sin embargo, que nunca le pegaba en el vientre. Le pegaba en las piernas y en los brazos, en la cabeza, y cuando alguna parte de su cuerpo asomaba bajo el mantel al recibir el golpe, la ocultaba enseguida de un puntapié.

Al cabo de un rato empezó a llorar. Sus pálidas mejillas cobraron cierta tonalidad, una especie de hinchazón venosa que parecía emerger de su piel como las colinas de una cuenca fluvial, y las lágrimas fluyeron en abundancia. Después empezó a sollozar y a lanzar tremendos gemidos mezclados con escupitajos. Eran los primeros sonidos humanos que emitía en mi presencia y parecían aumentar su histrionismo: sollozó, con el cuerpo tembloroso, se tiró al suelo a cuatro patas, la cabeza colgada, la boca abierta, escupiendo primero saliva, luego coágulos de sangre, hasta que los músculos del abdomen se le tensaron y, con una convulsión, expulsó un vómito sanguinolento. Recogió parte del líquido con las manos, lo miró un momento, se dio la vuelta y me miró; yo empecé a revolverme, intentando huir, pero no pude, y aquella repugnante sustancia me salpicó en la cara. Su olor y su sabor me provocaron arcadas, pero no llegué a vomitar, y el ataque cesó tras unas cuantas convulsiones. El líquido apestoso y caliente empezó a enfriarse en mis mejillas y en mi pecho; me sorprendió que su tibieza me resultara casi agradable y recordé que la criatura que estaba ante mí era un hombre, apenas un muchacho, poco mayor que Justin o Divine. Entonces, sin hacer un esfuerzo consciente, hablé. Pretendía escupir el vómito que me había entrado en la boca, pero lo que escupí fue su nombre y el mío.

—¿Eric Johnson? —dije con un susurro—. Soy Colin Nieman.

La buena educación se demuestra con buenas maneras, decía siempre mi madre, y muy a mi pesar me reí un poco.

Entonces se volvió loco, me dio doce patadas y doce puñetazos, hasta que cayó al suelo, lanzando un grito. El sonido fue ininteligible; no estoy seguro de si pronunció alguna palabra, pero enseguida se tranquilizó, y esta vez logré entender lo que dijo.

—Eric Johnson ya no existe —dijo—. Mi nombre es Nadie Nunca. Lo que yo fui quedó enterrado hace tanto tiempo que ya no existe, por eso me tomo mi venganza en secreto y sin miedo a las represalias, y dejo que otros reciban los latigazos destinados a mi espalda, a mi espalda y a quienquiera que ellos pensaran que yo era entonces.

Lo miré un momento y dije:

—Tu nombre es Eric Johnson. Naciste en Galatia hace veintidós años, de una mujer llamada Marsha P. Johnson y de un padre desconocido; y pese a las mutilaciones y las injusticias que han caído sobre ti, sigues siendo Eric Johnson.

—¡Soy Nadie Nunca!

—Eres Eric Johnson y hace once años te colgaron de los pulgares por abusar de una niña llamada Lucy Robinson, que está aquí con nosotros.

—¡Soy Nadie Nunca y jamás le puse la mano encima, jamás!

—No —dije—. No fuiste tú. Fue su padre. Fue el padre de Lucy. Stan Robinson merecía el castigo que te impusieron a ti.

Me miró con los ojos muy abiertos y los labios separados; luego giró en círculo, le dio una patada a Lucy en la cabeza y gritó:

—¡Esta cosa no tiene nombre, y por tanto no tiene padre!

—Deja que me vaya —le dije—. Deja que Lucy se vaya. No tiene sentido seguir prolongando esta situación. Deja que nos marchemos. —Suspiré. No creía en lo que estaba diciendo, pero las palabras fluían de mí con la urgencia del salmón que remonta el río para desovar y morir—. Libérate también tú, Eric.

Entonces arremetió contra mí, saltando sobre el cuerpo de Lucy; me agarró de la garganta y empezó a golpearme la cabeza contra el poste al que me había atado.

—Te lo estoy contando —me gritó—. Esta historia es mía, no tuya; no eres tú, Nieman.

Continuó sacudiéndome hasta que mi garganta escapó de su torpe mano, y cuando recuperé el aliento dije:

—En realidad no te crees lo que estás diciendo.

—¡Estoy contando la historia!

—La historia te está contando a ti.

Pero continuó como si yo no hubiera hablado.

—Yo no hice nada, ¿lo entiendes? Me castigaron por algo que no hice; me castigaron pero me dejaron con vida para que mi cuerpo mutilado sirviera de advertencia a quien se atreviera a transgredir las normas. Por eso yo también castigo a los inocentes, por eso los dejo con vida. Yo también extraeré la verdad de las mentiras. Por eso Lucy. Porque es Lucy y siempre será Lucy, por los siglos de los siglos, Lucy.

Entonces retrocedió de un salto y tiró de la tela que cubría el cuerpo de Lucy.

Cerré los ojos para no ver nada, porque quería decir algo y no sabía si sería capaz de hablar después de ver a Lucy.

—No te dejaron vivo —dije, desde el vacío de mis ojos cerrados—. Volvieron para matarte.

—Me dejaron caer como la fruta podrida. Me dejaron allí para que me pudriera.

—No te dejaron. Tú escapaste antes de que pudieran matarte. Te escapaste —dije. Y entonces abrí los ojos y añadí—: Y ni siquiera lo sabes.

Entonces vi a Lucy. Me quedé con la boca abierta, pero lo único que salió de ella fue mi aliento, tan destrozado como su cuerpo.

Mi silencio pareció servir para que Eric recuperara el aplomo, y nuevas palabras salieron de sus labios:

—Mira a tu esposa —dijo—. Mira a la mujer que se atrevió a mirar atrás y quedó convertida en una estatua de sal. Pero yo he vuelto a reconstruir su carne para ti, Nieman, he preparado este matrimonio para ti. Por la mañana, la madre verá la sangre en las sábanas colgadas de la ventana, y sabrá que su hija se ha mantenido pura hasta el momento en que tú la atacaste, y en lo sucesivo seréis conocidos como hombre, y mujer, e hijo.

—Eric —dije—. Eric, Eric, Eric.

No era mi intención enfurecerlo. Ni siquiera era mi intención hablar. Pero las palabras se me escaparon sin poder evitarlo, y Eric dio un salto y volvió a patear a Lucy en la cabeza, y la cabeza produjo un chasquido, y el vientre hinchado de Lucy siguió subiendo y bajando, pero por lo demás Lucy no se movió.

—Eric —dije—. Tú no hiciste nada malo.

—En eso te equivocas, Nieman, nacido hace cuarenta y cuatro años de Ellen Powys y Charles, y casado con una mujer llamada Susan, aunque ahora tiene un amante llamado John y una fortuna valorada en diecisiete millones de dólares.

—Justin —dije—. Él se llama Justin.

—El nombre de Nieman aparece en dos libros, de los cuales solo uno fue escrito por Nieman, y el pecado de Eric Johnson es el mismo pecado, un pecado más original que el del mestizaje. Porque el pecado de Eric Johnson es el de haber nacido o, quizá, el de no haber nacido. El de no haber nacido negro y no haber sido tú.

—No te entiendo.

—Pues entonces no lo entenderás nunca, porque mi papel en esta historia ha concluido. Me voy. Pronto toda Galatia estará aquí, y entonces también tu papel habrá concluido.

—¿Toda Galatia?

—Un misterio, Nieman. Otro misterio. Al final todo son vaguedades en lugar de claridad, se cosechan más preguntas de las respuestas que se sembraron.

—Pero una cosa está clara. Te llamas Eric Johnson.

—Me llamo Nadie Nunca.

—Te llamas Eric Johnson.
—Me llamo Colin Nieman.
—Soy yo quien se llama Colin Nieman.
—Tú te llamas Eric Johnson.
Y dicho esto, desapareció.

7.30

CORA

Había fuego detrás de mí y fuego delante de mí: el fuego del sol poniente iluminaba el horizonte al oeste. Sawyer me preguntó mil veces: «¿Adónde vamos, mamá? ¿Adónde vamos, mamá?». Pero tuvo que preguntármelo mil y una antes de que yo pudiera responderle. «Nos vamos –dije–. Nos vamos muy lejos. Vamos a liberarnos de esta tierra. Al fin vamos a ser libres.»

7.31

ROSEMARY KREBS

Era una noche calurosa y me había sentado en el porche con un vaso de té helado. Esa fue casualmente la primera jarra de té helado que me preparé desde que Webbie Greeving dejó de trabajar para mí, y estaba pensando que en cierto sentido era un alivio haberme librado de ella, porque hacía un té pésimo. Supongo que lo hacía a propósito –como suelen hacer los criados–, aunque es probable que no tuviera el menor talento culinario. En todo caso, una jarra marrón de lo que mi madre llamaba siempre agua negra parecía tener poca importancia frente al hecho de quedarme sin alguien que me limpiara la casa, y me preguntaba si podría aprovechar el jaleo de la noche para procurarme una nueva criada, preferiblemente una que supiera cocinar además de limpiar.

En realidad casi esperaba encontrar a Coretta Johnson entre la multitud que ahora se abría camino entre mis lilos, aunque lo dudaba. Coretta Johnson siempre se comportaba con educación. Pero un pueblo del tamaño de Galatea no necesita dos restaurantes, sobre todo si en los dos sirven el mismo tipo de cocina, y una madre sola no tiene muchas opciones.

Veía un fuego en el horizonte, pero ¿qué importancia podía tener eso, después del incendio de Kenosha? Además, no había sido yo quien lo había provocado.

Esperé bebiendo un poco de té.

La multitud inundó el jardín como el agua que entra en una botella, rodeando lentamente la casa. Sus voces resultaban a un tiempo claras e indistinguibles: lo que intentaban decirme era que habían venido porque se sentían ofendidos, pero, lo supieran o no, en realidad estaban allí para recibir órdenes. Lo supe por el cuidado que ponían para no pisotear mis lilos.

Todos apestaban a alcohol, y me alegré de no haberme puesto azúcar en el té por una vez y tomarlo solo con zumo de limón. Sostuve el vaso bajo mi barbilla, aspirando el aroma dulce y limpio y esperé hasta que llegaron los más rezagados.

Al final vi que la multitud se arremolinaba, no faltaba nadie más. Todos los habitantes de Galatea estaban delante de mí, detrás de mí, alrededor; apenas cabían entre los lilos —si hubiese llegado una sola persona más, se me habrían echado todos encima—, y mientras esperaba a ver quién sería el pobre diablo que se atrevería a hablar en primer lugar, me permití esbozar una sonrisa de orgullo protegida por el vaso de té. La multitud era un logro nada desdeñable, valía más que una fortuna, un cuadro, un niño. Tenía ante mí trescientos niños, trescientos cuadros, trescientas fortunas. Hablo de potencial humano, no de cualidades reales. Hablo de la peculiar alquimia de una masa de cuerpos reunidos según un plan más grande que cualquiera de ellos por separado, y la visión de aquellos rostros, no solo de los negros, sino también de los blancos y de esos otros que no eran ni del todo claros ni del todo oscuros, la visión de todos aquellos rostros me hizo envidiar por un momento la sencillez de las plantaciones de mis antepasados. Bien. Entonces tenían la ley de su parte, y a la iglesia, y trescientos cincuenta años de historia y de sentido común, y si alguien dijera que mis métodos no siempre eran amables, me vería obligada a dar una respuesta poco convincente: lo importante es el contexto.

Los tiempos han cambiado.

Hace tiempo, en este país bastaba con castigar a los miembros más fuertes y más débiles de la oposición para poner a las masas en su sitio. Ahora había que tolerar a los más fuertes, mimar a los más débiles y castigar a todos los demás. Me parecía que los viejos métodos eran más sencillos para todos los implicados, pero de nada sirve ponerse nostálgico.

Una voz gritó desde el centro de la multitud.

—¡Rosemary Krebs!

Al principio no logré identificarla, y dejé el vaso de té sobre la barandilla del porche. Lo único que sabía es que era un hombre.
—Buenas noches —dije.
—No queremos hipocresía, señora Krebs.
El que hablaba era blanco.
—Por supuesto —dije—. Por supuesto.
—Queremos justicia.
Sheldon Stadler.
—Queremos que nos devuelva nuestro pueblo.
Sheldon Stadler debía tres letras de la hipoteca que había contraído sobre su casa. Llevaba dos meses de retraso en el pago de la deuda del embargo sobre la granja de Wilma, y yo sabía además que Wilma Stadler, que era quien hacía los pasteles para el café de Elaine Sumner y el Art Penny's Café de Bigger Hill, ganaba mucho más dinero a la semana que Sheldon.
Elaine Sumner tampoco había pagado la hipoteca el mes pasado. Era la tercera letra impagada en dos años.
—Si no nos lo da por las buenas, lo tomaremos...
—Sheldon Stadler —dije, y calló de inmediato—. Lucy Robinson —dije, y entonces todos se pusieron a hablar al mismo tiempo. Pero no levanté la voz. Sabía que los que estaban más cerca me oirían sin dificultad y correrían la voz—. Lucy Robinson está en Kenosha —dije—. Y también Colin Nieman.
Luego volví a coger el vaso de té.
Las palabras se extendieron como las ondas sobre el agua tras lanzar una piedra en un estanque. Al cabo de un rato, todo el mundo guardó silencio. La luz de las antorchas proyectaba sombras temblorosas sobre sus rostros y el lejano fuego parecía una mera línea naranja dibujada entre el negro plano de la tierra y el plano azul oscuro del cielo.
Aparté el vaso sin beber.
—A mí también me gustaría ver que se hace justicia.
La multitud salió del jardín con menos orden del que había entrado.
Advertí que Alma Kiehler partía varias ramas que se le habían enredado en el pelo.
Alma Kiehler había trabajado algún tiempo en el café de Coretta Johnson, antes de que Rosa Stone llegara al pueblo.
No podía asegurarlo en la oscuridad, pero me pareció que Alma Kiehler era más o menos de la talla de Webbie Greeving.

7.32

COLIN

Cuando abrí los ojos, Eric se había marchado.

Sentí un dolor nuevo en la cabeza. Supongo que me habría golpeado. Me llevé una mano a la cabeza y vi que me había desatado antes de marcharse.

Pensé en marcharme yo también. Había dejado la luz encendida y veía las bocas de una media docena de túneles, pero la luz no iluminaba más allá de treinta centímetros y no confiaba en que ninguno de ellos condujera a alguna parte, a menos que uno los conociera lo suficiente como para recorrerlos a ciegas, y si bien había logrado llegar hasta allí sin dificultad, estaba seguro de que salir no me resultaría tan fácil.

Y allí estaba Lucy.

Lucy Robinson.

Lucy parecía algo que primero hubieran construido y luego destrozado. Parecía un decorado roto. En los fragmentos que aún quedaban, podía apreciarse lo que antaño había sido, pero ya no era como había sido, ni volvería a serlo nunca.

Sé que no hago bien al expresarme con una metáfora, pero cuando intento acercarme a su cuerpo descubro que solo puedo hacerlo poco a poco, como Nadie Nunca.

Lo que antes habían sido las manos de Lucy no eran ahora más que muñones ennegrecidos. Las habían sumergido en algo que parecía alquitrán caliente, y supongo que Eric lo hizo no solo para hacerle daño a Lucy, sino para cauterizar las heridas, para cortar la hemorragia y evitar el riesgo de infección, para mantenerla con vida.

También presentaba quemaduras en la piel del abdomen y aunque sospechaba, teniendo en cuenta la naturaleza de Nadie, que lo que había ahí era una palabra, acaso un nombre, o posiblemente solo un dibujo, fuera lo que fuese, lo cierto era que la hinchazón del útero de Lucy lo había vuelto irreconocible.

Una costra marrón rodeaba su boca. Me esforcé por relacionarla de la manera menos repugnante posible con las latas de comida para perros vacías que se amontonaban en el suelo.

Caí entonces en la cuenta de que también había libros, cientos de libros empapados y mugrientos, apilados como para hacer una hoguera con ellos, más que para ser leídos, pero por lo que Eric había dicho, por el modo como se había expresado y había representado su papel, supe que los había leído todos, y por alguna razón la imagen de Eric manipulando aquellos libros con las mismas manos con las que había torturado a Lucy Robinson me produjo más repugnancia que lo que le había hecho a la propia Lucy.

Y había un televisor. No lo había visto antes; no sé si es que no estaba, si estaba tapado o si sencillamente me había pasado por alto; tampoco recordaba haber visto los libros. Era un televisor viejo y un cable colgaba alrededor de sus patas antes de desaparecer en las sombras de la pared, mientras la antena llegaba hasta el techo. Para asegurarme, repté despacio hasta el aparato, dando un rodeo para evitar el cuerpo de Lucy, y lo encendí. La pantalla zumbó y cobró vida, y una imagen en blanco y negro de un mapa del tiempo realizado por ordenador ocupó el monitor. No había sonido y vi al sonriente meteorólogo que ofrecía el pronóstico para el día siguiente.

Cielos despejados.
Máxima: 45°.
Mínima: 30°.
Vientos: E/SE, 16-40 km/h.
Posibilidad de precipitaciones: 0.

7.33

JUSTIN

Me dejó el coche. Me dejó muchas otras cosas, especialmente su dinero, y los últimos restos carbonizados de su amor, y el peculiar olor que siempre dejaba tras de sí después del sexo, pero sobre todo me dejó solo y me dejó el coche.

Una vez, cuando era niño, no tan pequeño como para necesitar el cuidado de mis padres, pero sí lo suficiente como para seguir acariciando uno de los principales sueños infantiles –deseaba volar más que nada en el mundo–, fui a la feria que habían instalado en el pueblo donde vivíamos, y con el dinero que me dieron mis padres para montar en la noria y en la montaña rusa y entrar en la casa de la risa, me compré todos los globos de helio que encontré en la feria y me los llevé, de uno en uno, de dos en dos y en pequeños montones hasta un hueco que había entre dos tenderetes, los até a dos postes de hormigón ligero y los dejé allí. No se me ocurrió hasta años más tarde que los postes de hormigón pesaban menos que yo, de lo contrario habría abandonado mi empresa de inmediato; el caso es que después de registrar la feria de punta a punta logré reunir unos cien globos –y quedarme sin dinero–, luego me escondí en aquel hueco y empecé a unir los globos con un rollo de cuerda para cometas que había comprado. Recuerdo que hacía viento, un viento racheado que azotaba el estrecho hueco y hacía que las cuerdas de los globos se enredasen y que los globos me diesen en la cara, pero perseveré, y al fin conseguí unir todos los globos hasta formar una especie de óvalo que entonces me pareció un ramillete de uvas multicolores, pero que ahora me recuerda a una fotografía microscópica de los alveolos pulmonares; luego, con mucho cuidado, solté los globos de los postes y me los até a la cintura y a los tobillos. Los globos me oprimían con fuerza las extremidades, el corazón me latía de emoción, y en la mente me formaba la imagen de las cúpulas de los tenderetes vistos desde arriba, los rostros asombrados de los que montaban en la noria cuando yo los saludaba, el azul profundo de un mar que estaba mucho más lejos de lo que yo pensaba, y cuando terminé de atar a mi cuerpo el último cabo me solté del cable al que había estado agarrado hasta ese momento y, al sentir que los globos arremetían contra el cielo, salté con ellos, salté al aire...

Y casi al momento volví a caer. Digo casi. Hubo algo, un instante, una ligera elevación, una sensación —puede que solo fuera una sensación—, antes de aterrizar de bruces contra el suelo y antes de que una ráfaga de viento arrancase uno de los manojos de globos que llevaba atados a la cintura. Las cuerdas me cortaron la piel al soltarse, y cuando dejé de mirar mi mano ensangrentada para mirar al cielo, los globos ya no se veían, habían salido volando por encima de algún tenderete.

Colin me dejó así, sin más, como una mentira en la que yo ya no creía. Me dejó con un sentido tanto de las limitaciones como de los méritos de mi propia humanidad, pero como aún necesitaba una ficción a la que aferrarme, salí en busca de otra. Antes de que pudiera marcharme la aldaba de la puerta resonó en la casa.

Era Myra Robinson.

No tuve tiempo de saludarla. Me agarró de la mano. Al principio me pareció que estaba temblando, pero luego sentí un objeto pequeño y duro contra mi palma. Cuando Myra retiró la mano, vi un pequeño guijarro negro. No estaba seguro, pero me pareció un trozo de obsidiana del foso que rodeaba la casa de caliza.

—Esto es lo único que dijo Lucy —me dijo Myra—. Puede que un día te ayude a recuperar el habla. —Luego me besó en la frente y, acto seguido, tambaleándose exageradamente sobre sus pies tullidos, se metió en el coche y se marchó.

De modo que me llevé el dinero de Colin, y el coche, y también me llevé un trozo del mural que Wade había pintado en la cúpula, el pájaro multicolor que volaba hacia el cielo en busca del marido perdido y de una mujer llamada Beatrice, y me llevé también la piedra que me dio Myra, pero dejé la piedra ventral, como había hecho Beatrice, y creo que aún sigue allí, esperando a quien llegue a continuación.

7.34

WEBBIE

Dos horas después de salir de Galatia el sol alcanzó al fin la línea del horizonte y su resplandor pareció extenderse como un incendio sobre la pradera. El cielo se mostraba veteado de púrpura y naranja, de negro y de rosa, y de un oscuro azul cerúleo, y mientras catalogaba mentalmente estos colores, de pronto sentí que echaría de menos a Wade más que a nadie, más que a Cora, a Divine, incluso a Justin o a mi padre. Echaría de menos su olor y el modo como sus ojos parecían retener la huella del último cuadro en el que había trabajado, y también echaría de menos el escalofrío que me produjeron sus manos la única vez que le dejé que me acariciara los pechos e intentó meterse mi pezón en la boca. Eso también lo echaría de menos. Entonces miré a Wallace y me pregunté si alguna vez vería en sus manos algo menos sólido que un volante, un taladro, un tenedor; Wallace me miró y la luz del crepúsculo resaltó las pecas de sus mejillas, haciéndolas brillar. Tenía una expresión irónica, como si nuestra melodramática huida lo incomodase un poco, y creo que me sonrió para infundirme confianza más que otra cosa. Apartó una mano del volante para tocarme un momento el muslo, luego volvió a centrarse en la conducción, pero en la reciente curva de la palma de su mano entreví un recuerdo, un eco de una forma que jamás había visto en las manos de Wade, ni en las de nadie, y era la forma de mi pierna, mi propia forma.

7.35

COLIN

Al oír el estrépito de pisadas que se acercaban supe que no era Nadie Nunca quien volvía. Él conocía bien esos caminos y sabía pisar sin hacer ruido.

Apagué el televisor y esperé. Pensé en apagar la luz, pero no sabía cómo.

Lo primero que vi fue una mano que sujetaba una pistola, luego un brazo cubierto por una manga marrón, un pecho decorado con una insignia y el sucio sombrero blanco del agente Brown.

Me vio y luego vio a Lucy Robinson, y se quedó un rato mirándola como si estuviera embrujado, con la boca ligeramente abierta, la mirada fija y brillante, y antes de que se me pasara por la cabeza la idea de detenerlo, apretó el gatillo. La cabeza de Lucy, trasquilada y cubierta de cicatrices, se partió en dos, y mientras el disparo aún resonaba en mis oídos, oí por última vez su aliento entrecortado; cuando los ecos del disparo se extinguieron solo quedó silencio.

El agente Brown dirigió su arma hacia mí. Me apuntó a la cabeza, pero su mirada, ligeramente desenfocada, se dirigía a otra parte; evitaba mirarme a los ojos, como si al hacerlo yo pudiera sacarlo de su trance y atraparlo en el mío.

—Voy a decirle la verdad con toda franqueza —dijo.

No respondí.

—La verdad es que no creo que tenga usted nada que ver en todo esto. Nada que ver con ella.

Hizo un gesto con la mano libre, pero no miró a Lucy.

—Pero eso no importa —dijo, y se detuvo un momento. Luego tomó aliento. Yo veía cómo las palabras cobraban forma en su cabeza, palabras que había tomado prestadas de alguna otra historia, palabras que más tarde repetiría como un loro ante cualquiera que le preguntase—. Voy a disparar. Sí. Voy a matarlo. Y por si acaso también voy a pegarme un tiro, quizá en el brazo, o en la pierna. Luego le contaré a todo el mundo que usted era el culpable, que la mató a ella, que intentó matarme a mí y que luego se mató.

Calló de nuevo, pero yo seguía sin decir nada.

—Bueno —dijo—. La verdad es que no espero que nadie me crea. No. Pero eso tampoco importa. Porque hoy he aprendido algo importante, y lo que he aprendido es esto: la gente, al menos la gente de aquí, y me atrevo a afirmar que la gente de Galatea no es muy distinta del resto, no quiere saber la verdad. Lo único que quiere es una explicación, y que las cosas tengan un final.

Parecía haber terminado. Me miró, miró la pistola que tenía en la mano, sujetó con la mano libre la temblorosa mano con la que empuñaba el arma y volvió a mirarme.

Miré al agente Brown y a la oscura pistola que me apuntaba, el cañón brillante por el reflejo de la luz, e intenté con todas mis fuerzas entender lo que el agente Brown acababa de decir, pero me distraje mirando a Lucy, su cuerpo al fin apaciguado, y esa imagen borró todas las palabras que él había pronunciado. Incluso me pregunté si el agente Brown no habría hecho a fin de cuentas lo correcto.

No me estremecí al oír el disparo, pero cuando el agente Brown soltó el arma y cayó de bruces al suelo, debo admitir que me sorprendió mucho; tomé aliento y comprobé si me había herido, luego miré alrededor de la cueva y me pareció un buen final que el rostro que finalmente emergió de la oscuridad de uno de los túneles fuese el de Abraham Greeving, seguido a escasa distancia por los alarmados rostros de dos de sus Damas, Faith y Hope, o Hope y Charity, o Faith y Charity; y los tres entraron trotando.

Abraham Greeving se apoyaba en las dos mujeres, pero en cuanto pisaron suelo firme se soltó, le entregó el arma a una de ellas y se sujetó sobre el bastón que llevaba colgado del brazo.

—No voy a preguntarle cómo ha llegado hasta aquí.

—Con mucha dificultad —dijo Abraham Greeving— y con la ayuda de Dios.

La mujer que se había hecho cargo del arma la dejó caer en su bolso como si fuera un pañuelo sucio, y la otra cubrió el cuerpo de Lucy con el mantel.

—No le preguntaré cómo ha sabido que debía venir aquí.

—Por Nettie Ferguson —dijo. Sacó un pañuelo del bolsillo y se enjugó la frente—. Alguien llamó a la comisaría —dijo—; Nettie esperó hasta que Eustace se hubo marchado y luego hizo lo que hace siempre. —Volvió a guardarse el pañuelo en el bolsillo—. Supongo que ya se habrá enterado todo el mundo. Supongo que el pueblo entero estará en camino.

—Y no le preguntaré por qué lo ha matado.

—Lo he matado —dijo el reverendo— porque era mi turno.

—Ni siquiera le preguntaré por qué no me ha matado.

El reverendo sacudió entonces la cabeza, sonrió y dijo:

—El pecador se asombra al ver que no ha sido castigado por sus pecados.

Las Damas asintieron, pero gracias a Dios no dijeron nada.

El reverendo me miró.

—No le he disparado —dijo—, porque usted nunca me ha hecho nada.

—No quiero parecer ingenuo —dije—, pero no lo entiendo.

—Eustace Brown —dijo Abraham Greeving—. Howard Goertzen. Eddie Comedy. Odell Painter. Stanley Robinson. —Fue contando con los dedos a medida que pronunciaba los nombres y, por alguna razón, aquel gesto me pareció el acontecimiento más macabro de todo el día, dada la proximidad de las manos de Lucy Robinson, de las manos de Eric Johnson y de las marchitas manos del propio reverendo.

—Esos son los cinco hombres que mataron a Eric Johnson, y a mí me ha tocado la tarea de recordarles sus propias acciones.

—Pero Eric Johnson no está muerto.

—En eso se equivoca usted —dijo Abraham Greeving—. Eric Johnson está definitivamente muerto. Más muerto que Eustace, o que Lucy Robinson, o que usted, o que yo.

Sacudí la cabeza.

—Sigo sin comprender.

El reverendo sonrió irónicamente.

—Son cosas de Dios. Es imposible que lo comprenda.

Intenté hablar de nuevo, pero él levantó su mano marchita.

—El pueblo entero está en camino, y me llevará su tiempo abrirme paso por estos túneles. —Me miró—. Le dejaré aquí, porque, como ya he dicho, usted nunca me ha hecho nada.

—¿Y la gente del pueblo?

El reverendo guardó silencio antes de decir:

—Espero, señor Nieman, que usted les cuente una historia, y si esa historia es lo suficientemente buena, entonces no tendrá de qué preocuparse. En todo caso, nunca es demasiado tarde para pedir ayuda al Señor.

Empezó a darse la vuelta para marcharse —la maniobra le resultaba muy difícil—, y yo dije:

—Por favor, me gustaría hacerle una pregunta.

El reverendo se detuvo.

—Me gustaría saber si ha esperado.

—¿Si he esperado?

—Hasta que mató a Lucy..

El rostro del reverendo se ensombreció un instante. Frunció el ceño, pero su expresión volvió a relajarse y me bendijo con su última y más cálida sonrisa.

—Es cierto —dijo—. Es usted un hombre de palabras.

7.36

Me llamo Angela.

Un día mi madre estaba jugando con sus primas las hadas junto al arroyo que surcaba los campos en el lugar donde vivíamos. Habían construido unas barcas doblando hojas en forma de corazón sobre piedrecitas que servían de lastre, y lanzaban sus embarcaciones corriente abajo. El hada cuya barquita ganara la carrera, según me contó mi madre, sería la primera en contraer matrimonio, y ese día fue la barca de mi madre la que navegó más rápido y llegó más lejos. Mi madre la seguía corriendo por la orilla, tan alegre y risueña por el avance de su embarcación que no se dio cuenta de lo mucho que se alejaba de sus compañeras. Se detuvo cuando su hoja encalló en la raíz de un árbol que crecía en el agua y, quitándose los zapatos, se recogió las faldas con una mano y se metió en el frío arroyo para rescatar su barca. De pronto oyó una voz que llegaba desde las alturas. «¿Quién eres y qué haces aquí?» Mi madre levantó la vista y advirtió entonces que se había adentrado en el bosque que bordeaba los campos. Miró a su alrededor, pero no vio a nadie; solo veía los altos troncos de los árboles y el distante caleidoscopio que formaban las hojas y el cielo. «¿Quién eres?», inquirió otra voz. «¿Qué estás haciendo aquí?», preguntó una tercera; y esta vez, al oír las palabras, mi madre notó que las ramas y las hojas de un árbol, las del árbol que había detenido la barca con sus raíces, temblaban ligeramente, y luego vio que el tronco se inclinaba y que lo que ella había tomado por un simple montón de nudos de madera eran en realidad bocas y ojos: muchas bocas y muchos, muchos ojos. «¡Dime cómo te llamas!», ordenó una voz. Mi madre se asustó tanto que soltó su falda y esta se hundió en el agua, pero por lo demás se quedó donde estaba, mirando los parpadeantes ojos del árbol. «Me llamo Angela», dijo al fin, porque mi madre y yo nos llamamos igual, y mi abuela también se llamaba Angela, y mi hija se llamará Angela. «¿Por qué has entrado en mi bosque?», preguntó otra boca; a lo cual mi madre respondió: «Lo siento mucho; no me di cuenta. Iba siguiendo a mi barca». «¿Qué barca?», preguntó una voz; y otra dijo: «Yo no veo ninguna barca». Mi madre advirtió entonces que ojos y boca eran lo mismo en aquel árbol. «Esta barca», dijo mi madre, mostrando la piedrecita cubierta con una hoja. El árbol se inclinó un poco más; bizqueó los ojos y torció las bocas; torció los ojos y bizqueó las bocas, y luego, uno de aquellos orificios emitió un «¡Bah!», y otro dijo: «Yo solo veo una hoja». El árbol agitó entonces sus extremidades y una lluvia de hojas de cinco dedos cayó sobre mi madre, agarrándola del pelo y de la ropa. «Y a mí, ¿de qué me sirven las hojas?» «No es solo una hoja —dijo mi madre—. Es una hoja con una piedrecita dentro», y desdobló la hoja para mostrar la piedra. «¿Una piedra? —dijo una boca—. ¿Qué tipo de piedra es esta?» «Una roca —dijo mi madre—. Pequeña, compacta y dura; no se puede romper.» «Una piedra. —Parpadeó otro ojo—. Jamás he oído hablar de una cosa así. Sé lo que es la tierra y el agua, el sol y el aire, el tronco y las ramas y las hojas.» «Y los pájaros», añadió otra boca. «Sí, los pájaros que se posan y luego se marchan volando. Pero… ¿una piedra?» Entonces mi madre supo lo que debía hacer. Se llevó la piedra a los labios y la besó. «Hummm —suspiró—, es deliciosa.» «¿El qué? ¿La piedra?» Mi madre volvió a besarla. «¡Qué bien sabe!», exclamó. «¿Bien?» «¿Bien?» «¿Bien?», repitieron todos los orificios; y mi madre no supo si lo que expulsaban era saliva o lágrimas. «Vamos, danos eso tan bueno. Dánoslo ahora mismo.» Mi madre sonrió, besó la piedra por tercera vez para completar el hechizo y la lanzó al orificio más cercano. El árbol era tan voraz que ni siquiera masticó; se tragó la piedra entera y al momento empezaron a sonarle las tripas con gran estruendo. «¿Bien?» «¿Bien?» «¿Bien?», preguntaban las demás bocas, mientras la boca que se había tragado la piedra reía y bromeaba y tosía. Se convirtió en un ojo, pero solo vertía lágrimas. Luego volvió a ser una boca, y escupió, pero en lugar de la piedra lo que salió fue el tierno brote verde de una enredadera, un fino tallo que parecía rizarse interminablemente, formando una espiral. La planta creció, se hizo más fuerte, y de ella brotaron hojas en forma de corazón y tiernos zarcillos que también crecían y se fortalecían, enredándose sobre el tronco del árbol, sobre las ramas y las hojas, cegando todos sus ojos y amordazando todas sus bocas, creciendo y creciendo hasta que el árbol se puso a temblar, atrapado entre los numerosos brazos de la enredadera. Finalmente, algunos de los brazos de la enredadera se desprendieron del árbol. Descendieron reptando hasta mi madre, sosteniendo un paquetito envuelto entre sus hojas, y lo depositaron dulcemente en sus brazos. Mi madre apartó las hojas, y allí estaba yo. Recuerdo que mi madre se quedó un buen rato mirándome, asombrada, mientras yo la miraba. Luego me besó en la frente. Uno, dos, tres, cuatro, cinco, contó los dedos de mi mano izquierda. Uno, dos, tres, cuatro, cinco, contó los de mi mano derecha; y allí, dentro del puño apretado, estaba la piedrecita que ella le había metido a mi padre en la boca, pulida, brillante, oscura y húmeda, como mis ojos. «Angela —dijo mi madre al ver la piedra—. Te llamas Angela.» «Algunos nacemos distintos y otros nacemos iguales», dijo. «Angela —dijo—. Tú no has salido de mí sino que has entrado en mí.» Entonces me quitó la piedra de la mano y se la metió en la boca. «En mí», dijo, tragándosela. «Un hechizo es la más sencilla de las artes mágicas —dijo—, y ahora me perteneces.» El agua fluía roja, espesa y tibia alrededor de sus faldas. Luego, muy despacio, muy despacio, muy despacio, perdió su color y reveló un lecho de miles y miles de piedrecitas, todas a la espera de ser tragadas, todas desesperadas por nacer.

Esta obra, publicada por
MONDADORI,
se terminó de imprimir en los talleres
de Artes Gráficas Huertas, S.A., de Madrid,
el día 15 de febrero
de 2001